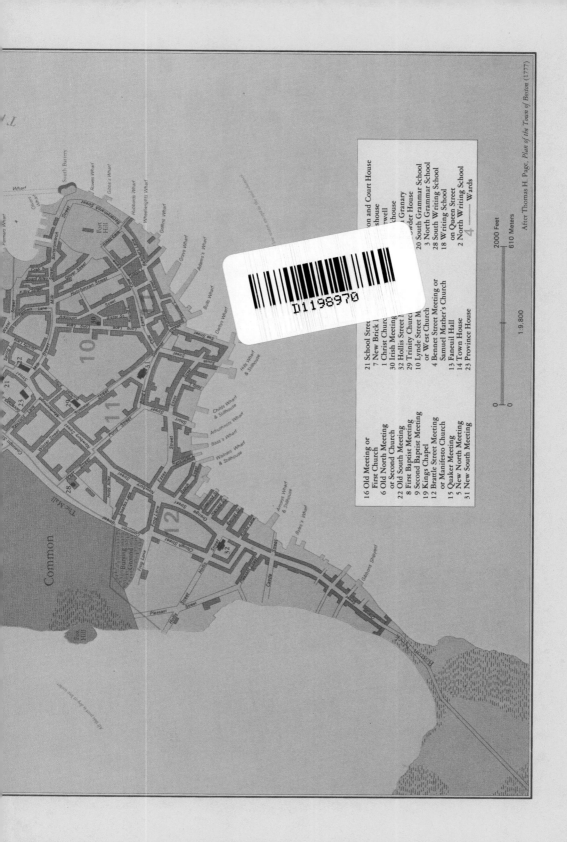

After Thomas H. Page, *Plan of the Town of Boston* (1777)

Crowd Action
in Revolutionary
Massachusetts
1765-1780

This is a volume in

STUDIES IN SOCIAL DISCONTINUITY

A complete list of titles in this series appears at the end of this volume.

Crowd Action in Revolutionary Massachusetts
1765-1780

Dirk Hoerder

Academic Press

NEW YORK   SAN FRANCISCO   LONDON

A Subsidiary of Harcourt Brace Jovanovich, Publishers

ACADEMIC PRESS, INC.
111 Fifth Avenue, New York, New York 10003

United Kingdom Edition published by
ACADEMIC PRESS, INC. (LONDON) LTD.
24/28 Oval Road, London NW1

Library of Congress Cataloging in Publication Data

Hoerder, Dirk.
    Crowd action in Revolutionary Massachusetts, 1765–1780.

    (Studies in social discontinuity)
    Includes bibliographical references.
    1.   Massachusetts—Politics and government—Revolution,
1775–1783.   2.   Crowds.   3.   Riots—Massachusetts.
4.   Massachusetts—Social conditions.   I.   Title.
II.   Series.
E263.M4H65   301.18'2'09744   77-4073
ISBN 0–12–351650–1

To my friends

Contents

Preface

Political, social, and economic direct action by people from the lower classes of society has long been labeled "mob" action. This study explores riots and "frolics" and demonstrations and crowd rituals in Massachusetts from the Stamp Act period to the Constitutionalist movement, without relying on the outdated "mob concept." Within the framework established by recent studies on French and English crowds, revolutionary direct action and its development from the colonial tradition is described and analyzed. Such action in redress of grievances was regarded as legitimate provided that certain preconditions were met. An attempt has been made to demonstrate what ideological concepts were behind these activities and how they related to changing circumstances.

In the 1760s internal and external factors combined to bring about changes in frequency, intensity, and patterns of crowd action. The British efforts to obtain revenues from the colonies met with opposition while at the same time internal colonial societal conditions had changed toward more rigidity and increased stratification. Thus problems that customarily could bring about crowd action became more frequent. The experience gained in the opposition to British revenue collectors was applied to colonial officials. They, too, met with increasing opposition, when violating traditional norms.

This became evident for the first time during the Stamp Act riots. Accordingly, care has been taken to present all relevant details. The extrainstitutional interaction changed relationships between established political leadership and crowds. New patterns of action on the part of the rioters and statements from political leaders have been used to provide an understanding of this process, which accelerated after 1774 when the political changes forced both sides to redefine their position and interests. Increased militancy among mechanics and farmers, its causes and results in terms of political awareness, participation in decision making, and direct action have been traced and examined. But the study does not attempt to prove an "increased militancy hypothesis." The evidence for Boston, to name one example, points to decreasing militancy among mechanics after the nonimportation period. The complex developments as evident from the sources demand a complex explanation. To achieve this, a "from the bottom up" approach has been used. Limited to direct action and the political, social, and economic elements and processes in which it was embedded in colonial Massachusetts, this approach does not give a complete picture of everyday life among the lower classes. But it yields better results and gives a broader perspective than a "from the top down" approach.

The Massachusetts people provide a wealth of insights which I have tried to understand and describe. There was the man who, seeing British warships cause trouble in Boston harbor, suggested to a town meeting to put His Majesty's ships under Massachusetts command when in Massachusetts harbors. In a bold stroke this man cut through the problems that beset the empire. With a single stroke of his sword, Alexander, "the great" cut the Gordian knot. He, the king, is remembered, but who has heard of the Bostonian? Many historians have combed the innermost recesses of Cotton Mather's mind, spending endless hours collecting sermons of New England divines. But who has pondered the remark of a rioter, who, turning to a newspaperman on the scene, said that he was doing God service? Thomas Hobbes's conservative political philosophy is well known. But who knows the political theory of Silas Burbank of Scarborough, Maine, holding it unlawful and immoral to thrive and wield political power by exploiting others? Are historians partisan to the emperor, the divines, the political philosopher? To me those styled "inarticulate" by the deaf are as real personalities as the great men. Am I partisan to their side? Their capacity to reason and to act has certainly impressed me, and I prefer their quest for an equitable social order to the stale, unimaginative pursuit of stability of a Count Metternich whose reactionary policies ended the age of revolution in Europe begun in America by people in Boston, Scarborough, and in many other places. Have I been too assertive about their ideology and action? Edmund Morgan once cautioned me not to make my findings sound like truths coming straight from the horse's mouth. I have tried to follow his advice without sacrificing the argument. For this I take responsibility.

Acknowledgments

While working on the manuscript for this book I have incurred many debts. John R. Howe, Jr. was always willing to discuss research problems and findings. I am very appreciative of Bernard Bailyn's support at the Warren Center. Most encouraging in the later stages of writing and research was Alfred F. Young whose incisive comments and high standards were a constant challenge. In the highly competitive academia, it was gratifying to find support and encouragement rather than hard-nosed competition. I am deeply indebted to George Rudé whose seminal work on the French Revolution influenced my thinking at a point when, as a student, I had just realized that the average person had generally been left out of history by its chroniclers and interpreters.

My brief exploration of the Italian revolutionary tradition has been aided by Walter Wallace, a student of Alfred Young, and Gisela Bock. John Bohstedt pointed out similarities to English crowd action. As to the American scene I have benefitted from research papers by Edward Countryman and John Kern as well as by Michael Feldberg and Theodore Hammett on the 1830s. Paul Faler and Thomas Dublin were partners of several discussions on the role of the mechanics. They generously shared findings of their research and results of their approaches with me before they were published. Andreas Burckhardt and Hans-Christoph Schröder vigorously critized shortcomings of the first draft. I am grateful for a review in the *American Historical Review*. Research and writing were made possible by a grant-in-aid from the Deutscher Akademischer Austauschdienst in 1969 and by a Charles Warren Fellowship, 1974–1975.

It has been reported that President Andrew Jackson had little respect for people who could think of only one way of spelling a word. Reading eighteenth century sources and not writing in my native language, I think I could have scored some respect from him. For getting my spelling back to the rigors of Webster, praise is due to Joan Regensburger and Ruth Wethekam who typed the manuscript and to Grace Holloway for diligent copyediting. None of these were easy tasks, as all three can assure you. I am grateful to all of them.

The following acknowledgments are for use of the endpapers.

Front endpaper: Reprinted by permission of Princeton University Press from the *Atlas of Early American History: The Revolutionary Era, 1760–1790,* edited by Lester J. Cappon, copyright (©) 1976 by Princeton University Press. Published for The Newberry Library and The Institute of Early American History and Culture.

Back endpaper: Reprinted with permission of Harvard University Press and Richard D. Brown; based on a map of New England showing the Province of Massachusetts Bay composed for Carrington Bowles and printed in London, 1772; redrawn and adjusted for this book at the John F. Kennedy-Institut, West Berlin, by Hans-Joachim Kämmer.

Bibliographic Note

The footnotes contain extensive references to old-fashioned town histories and new essays on social conditions. As to sources, the papers of revolutionary leaders are well known, either published or in manuscript collections. Since crowds and the common people with whom we deal here could neither afford private archives or libraries with annotated copies of important books nor take time off from the daily work routine to write diaries there is little to list.

Almost every collection of sources, personal and public, printed or manuscript, that exists for this period of Massachusetts history has been checked for references to crowd action. Of more than usual value were the, of course, severely biased reports of crown officials and papers of crowd targets. The transcripts of depositions and letters made by the anti-crowd historian Frederick L. Gay, now in the Massachusetts Historical Society, contain much material on the years 1768 and 1769, but are limited to riot targets or hostile observers. Of unusual value are the few court records about crowd action that have survived and the petitions of towns or even of rioters in the Massachusetts Archives, deposited in the Massachusetts State Archives. The town petitions may not seem relevant at first glance, but since riots often occurred after petitions or other institutional remedies failed, they are of extraordinary importance. They show social, political, and economic conflict, the attempts to find solutions, and the societal and ideological framework. They were written by people who had to solve problems, not to expound Whig ideology or to demonstrate consensus. They reflect a reality, material and ideological, that was complex, and the attempts of all people to grapple with that complex reality.

List of abbreviations used in footnotes for journals, newspapers, depositories, and manuscript collections.

AAS	American Antiquarian Society, Worcester, Massachusetts
AASP	*American Antiquarian Society Proceedings*
AHR	*American Historical Review*
BCH	Boston City Hall, Boston, Massachusetts
BEP	*Boston Evening Post*
BG	*Boston Gazette*
BNL	*Boston Newsletter*
BPB	*Boston Postboy*
BPL	Boston Public Library, Boston, Massachusetts
BTR	*Boston Town Records,* in *Reports of Record Commissioners of the City of Boston,* 39 volumes (Boston, 1886, and later).
CSMP	*Colonial Society of Massachusetts Publications*
EIHC	*Essex Institute Historical Collections*
Essex Institute	Essex Institute, Salem, Massachusetts
Evans	Charles Evans (compiler), *A Chronological Dictionary of All Books, Pamphlets and Periodical Publications Printed in the United States of America from the Genesis of Printing in 1639 Down to and Including the Year 1820,* 14 volumes (New York, 1903–1955; short title: *American Bibliography*). (Eighteenth century publications listed in Evans or *Mass. Brds.* are listed by their number in the bibliography.)
Forbes Library	Forbes Library, Northampton, Massachusetts
HBS	Harvard University Business School, Baker Library, Cambridge, Massachusetts
HHL	Harvard University, Houghton Library, Cambridge, Massachusetts
JAH	*Journal of American History*
LC	Library of Congress, Washington, D.C.
Mass. Brds.	Worthington C. Ford (compiler), *Broadsides, Ballads etc. Printed in Massachusetts 1639–1800,* (checklist) (Boston, 1922) [volume 75 of *MHSC*]
MA	Massachusetts Archives, 242 volumes., MSA
MSA	Massachusetts State Archives, State House, Boston, Massachusetts
MF	microfilm
MHS	Massachusetts Historical Society, Boston, Massachusetts
MHSC	*Massachusetts Historical Society Collections*
MHSP	*Massachusetts Historical Society Proceedings*
MVHR	*Mississippi Valley Historical Review*
NEHGR	*New England Historical and Genealogical Register*
NEHGS	New England Historical and Genealogical Society, Boston, Massachusetts
NEQ	*New England Quarterly*
NYPL	New York Public Library, New York, New York
PRO	Public Record Office, London
SCCH	Suffolk County [Massachusetts] Court House, Boston, Massachusetts
SCF	Suffolk [County, Massachusetts] Court Files, manuscript collections, SCCH
WMQ	*William and Mary Quarterly*

Introduction

Studies of crowd action and of the popular ideology that motivated it have to deal with an unusual number of problems. Some of these I want to discuss briefly before proceeding to describe and analyze crowd action in Massachusetts during the struggle of the 13 colonies for independence. The first question, of course, is, What is a crowd? It should come as no surprise to social scientists that scholars cannot agree on a clear definition and on a theory of crowd action that encompasses more than just a few instances—that historians differ from sociologists, sociologists from political scientists, and all from psychologists.

CONCEPTS OF CROWD BEHAVIOR

The field, unfortunately, is burdened with traditions that obscure the character of crowd action rather than clarify it. Of these, three main trends can be discerned. The first dates from the progenitor of the field, Gustave Le Bon (1895). To him, crowds display mental unity—that is, dogmatism, intolerance, irresponsibility, and a feeling of reckless and irresistible power. Second, the crowd members lose their individual psychology while showing such emotional behavior as impulsive, fickle, intense, and extreme reactions. (In Le Bon's words, crowds are of a feminine nature!) Closely related is Le Bon's third main line of argument, the irrational character of crowds. They are credulous; their ideas are simple, sometimes contradictory. Taken together, these characteristics result in a view of crowds as transforming rational individuals into brutes agitated by mental contagion and demagogic leaders.[1]

Another interpretation of mass action arose in response to the one-party regimes in Europe, Stalinism and, more especially, fascism in Germany and Italy. It seems very questionable whether communism and fascism can be lumped together in that way, but that is not our point here. Rather, we want to take a look at the mass movement itself. Such mass actions were under the strict control of centralized, powerful, and all-pervasive parties. Under fascism, masses did not act on their own;

[1]Gustave Le Bon, *Psychologie des foules* (1895), trans. *The Crowd* (London, 1903).

1

they marched behind leaders. Pogroms against Jews and other minorities were initiated, organized, and monitored by the party. Thus, totalitarian organization and paramilitary storm troopers were equated with crowds and rioters.

The third approach, starting from the assumption that the main variable of mass action is violence, can be termed the violence school of thought. It grew out of the student movement and the ghetto rebellions of the sixties. It is often more interested in riot control than in understanding riots, more concerned with merely a single part of the action, violence, than with the causes and the patterns of thought that provoked these rebellions. In its worst form this school produced instant apologetics for politicians, whose responsibility for the conditions prompting a riot or rebellion was obvious but who needed ''explanations'' for public relations purposes.

This brief survey of three interpretations of crowd behavior is necessary for understanding many of the underlying concepts of recent crowd studies. They are still popular among scholars as well as public officials and silent majorities. An outline of the *Principles of Sociology* dating from 1946 states that ''acting on the basis of impulse, the crowd is fickle, suggestible, and irresponsible.''[2] Such reasoning assumes that the masses are apolitical and passive, at best capable of a *jacquerie*. R. W. Brown attempted in 1954 to systematize ''mass phenomena.'' ''Crowds'' is made the generic term for such widely varying behavior as lynchings, panics, and recreational or information-seeking audiences.[3] The only common denominator of these events is that masses of people are present. Smelser's *Theory of Collective Behavior* of 1963 explicitly acknowledges its heritage from the dark ages of the study of political and social militancy, Gustave Le Bon's *The Crowd*.[4] According to Smelser, ''In all civilizations men have thrown themselves into episodes of dramatic behavior, such as the craze, the riot, and the revolution.'' Their cognitive faculties are reduced to ''generalized beliefs.''[5] Couch and Canetti stress factors of emotion and irrationality, suggestion and contagion.[6] Blumer's work of 1946 has lost some of its influence since Turner and Killian published their *Collective Behavior*. But the basic ideas remain the same. Crowds ''respond uncritically to suggestions,'' are in ''moods,'' do not follow rational arguments.[7] To repeat Blumer's metaphor, crowds are like stampeding cattle. Even the 1968 edition of the prestigious *Encyclopedia of Social Sciences* repeats such prescientific statements. ''Direct action, essentially undemocratic because it denies the opponent the chance to discuss the issue, is often resorted to when legitimate political action fails. In extreme situations the movement will culminate in a violent revolution.''[8]

[2]Herbert Blumer, ''Collective Behavior,'' *New Outline of the Principles of Sociology,* ed. A. M. Lee (New York, 1946), p. 180.

[3]R. W. Brown, ''Mass Phenomena,'' *Handbook of Social Psychology,* ed. G. Lindzey, vol. 2 (Cambridge, Mass., 1954), pp. 833–876.

[4]Smelser, *Theory of Collective Behavior* (Glencoe, Ill., 1963), p. 80. For a critique of Smelser, see Elliott Currie and Jerome H. Skolnick, ''A Critical Note on Conceptions of Collective Behavior,'' *Annals Am. Acad. Pol. Soc. Sci.* 391:34–45 (Sept. 1970).

[5]Neil J. Smelser, *Theory of Collective Behavior,* pp. 8, 20.

[6]Carl J. Couch, ''Collective Behavior: An Examination of Some Stereotypes,'' *Social Problems* 15:310–322 (1968); Elias Canetti, *Crowds and Power* (New York, 1966).

[7]Ralph H. Turner and L. M. Killian, *Collective Behavior* (Englewood Cliffs, N.J., 1957; text ed., 1972).

[8]Rudolf Heberle, ''Social Movements: Types and Functions,'' *Encyclopedia of Social Sciences,* ed. D. L. Sills, vol. 14 (New York, 1968). p. 442.

Although unrecognized by its author, the article in the *Encyclopedia* does contain the issue at which critical questioning has to start: Why does legitimate political action fail? The entire field of scholarly research into collective behavior is studded with unasked questions, unsolved problems, implicit prejudices, underlying but untested assumptions. Even if questions are asked, they often aim in the wrong direction. A particularly striking example is an incident during the 1913 strike against the Calumet and Hecla Mining Company, in Michigan. The miners, receiving about a dollar a day, struck after company officials had announced a 400 percent dividend for the stockholders. A Christmas party was organized for the children of the striking miners. To disturb the fun, a deputy sheriff yelled, ''Fire!'' The children panicked, rushing toward the narrow exit, and 73 were smothered to death in the scramble for safety. There was no fire. Crowd historians and sociologists inquire into the allegedly irrational behavior of the crowd during the panic. None questions the sanity of the deputy.[9]

Though each of the approaches described has a limited usefulness, none of them is of any general value. Le Bon can explain panics, in which the crowd members do not know one another, do not know the amount of danger, do not know how best to escape. The explanatory validity of the party leadership thesis is limited to fascist societies and, even then only if related to social structure, a declining and threatened middle class, and authoritarian personality. The violence school, with few exceptions, does not deal with governmental violence—with force or repression—and thus considers such a tiny fraction of a social problem that from a scholarly viewpoint it might almost be assumed to be negligible.[10]

The breakthrough in the study of popular direct action, incidentally giving an important impetus to the study of history from the bottom up, was George Rudé's 1959 study of the crowd in the French Revolution. Through his work and that of E. J. Hobsbawm and E. P. Thompson, a conceptual framework for studying crowds is developing that is well grounded in theory and substantiated by empirical studies, and the body of scholarly work on European crowds by other authors is growing quickly. In fact, with the introduction of assembly-line principles into crowd study by Charles Tilly at the University of Michigan Center for Research on Social Organization, data are becoming so abundant that quantitative methods can be applied to them. That represents quite a change from having, like an archeologist, only a few fragments with which to reconstruct a whole.

The basic concern of most of these works is with what Rudé has termed the preindustrial crowd.[11] Its tenets are that crowd behavior is rational and goal-di-

[9]Elizabeth Gurley Flynn, *The Rebel Girl: An Autobiography* (1955; rev. ed., New York, 1973), pp. 187–188; Richard O. Boyer and Herbert M. Morais, *Labor's Untold Story* (1955; reprint ed., New York 1973), pp. 188–189.

[10]Exceptions are the ''Skolnick Report,'' Jerome H. Skolnick, *The Politics of Protest*. Report submitted to the National Commission on the Causes and Prevention of Violence (New York, 1969). Robert Blauner, ''Whitewash over Watts,'' *Transaction* 3:3–9 (March–April 1966); Robert M. Fogelson, ''Violence as Protest,'' *Urban Riots: Violence and Social Change*, ed. R. H. Connery (New York, 1968), pp. 25–41. That there is no lack of appropriate theories for analyzing crowd action has been demonstrated by Richard A. Berk in his study of a 1972 student demonstration; see ''A Gaming Approach to Crowd Behavior,'' *Am. Soc. Rev.* 39:355–373 (June 1974). Berk uses a combination of game theory and decision theory.

[11]George Rudé, *The Crowd in the French Revolution* (Oxford, 1959); E. J. Hobsbawm, *Primitive Rebels: Studies in Archaic Forms of Social Movement in the 19th and 20th Centuries* (New York, 1965); E. P. Thompson, *The Making of*

rected, that it is guided by a set of traditional norms about social relations and positions of groups within the social structure—that rioters are self-conscious and act according to concepts coming down by oral tradition rather than straight from the magistrates' law books. Much of the oral tradition had once been on the law books or in the Bible but had been expunged by those in power. Riots are spontaneous in the sense that neither outside agitators nor police *agents provocateurs* nor influential men of the local community manipulate it. Of course, they may do so, but leadership is not a prerequisite for crowd action, though crowds may have spokesmen. In addition, crowd action, as opposed to repressive force, need not be violent. Symbolic action or the mere presence of large numbers of people is frequently sufficient to achieve the desired goal. Other means are mock trials, processions, and nonviolent ritualistic imitations of legal punishments. In this study, crowds will be defined as groups of persons with common traditions intentionally acting together outside existing channels to achieve one or more specifically defined goals. Crowds are a "quasi-institution"[12] interlocking with a whole system of institutional and informal activities and therefore will not be artificially separated and dissected.

Daniel Chirot and Charles Ragin have attempted to synthesize the conceptual framework that several historians and sociologists used to explain different peasant rebellions. Hobsbawm, Tilly, Wolf,[13] and Moore[14] stress "the survival of peasant traditionalism following the intrusion of capitalist market forces."[15] Commercialization of traditional subsistence farming or agricultural production for only limited areas subjects the agrarian communities' value system and social structures to a variety of strains. In the historical processes studied by these authors, collective social action for redress of grievances has followed the pattern of peasant rebellion. When, for whatever reason, such constructive forms of protests and direct action are not available or are not sanctioned by the community, reaction to changes may take very different directions. Boyer and Nissenbaum have shown, in their excellent study of the witchcraft episode in Massachusetts, that the accusers came from a geographical and social section of Salem Village that remained bound to subsistence farming, while those allegedly seized by the devil came from a section of the township that because of a road and access to the port of Salem slowly turned toward commercial activities. This reaction may be called a negative form of protest

the English Working Class (New York, 1963), and "The Moral Economy of the English Crowd in the Eighteenth Century," *Past and Present* 50:76–136 (Feb. 1971); Charles Tilly, *The Vendée* (New York, 1967); Charles Tilly and James Rule, *Measuring Political Upheaval* (Princeton, N.J., 1964). All of these authors have published further studies dealing with crowd action and strikes. For works on Great Britain by other scholars, see John H. Bohstedt, "Riots in England, 1790–1810, with Special Reference to Devonshire" (Ph.D. diss., Harvard Univ., 1972), pp. 449–457. For reasons of space, it is impossible to list other works dealing with European crowds, comparative studies, and treatises on crowd action in ancient and medieval history.

[12]E. J. Hobsbawm, "From Social History to the History of Society," *Daedalus* 100:20–45 (1971).

[13]Eric Wolf, *Peasant Wars in the Twentieth Century* (New York, 1969).

[14]Barrington Moore, Jr., *Social Origins of Dictatorship and Democracy: Lord and Peasant in the Making of the Modern World* (Cambridge, Mass., 1967).

[15]Daniel Chirot and Charles Ragin, "The Market, Tradition and Peasant Rebellion: The Case of Romania in 1907," *Am. Soc. Rev.* 40:429 (Aug. 1975).

that used established authorities, church and state, to repress or even annihilate the modernizing forces in the community.[16]

Chirot and Ragin reject a different explanatory model, Stinchcombe's thesis "that among all types of land tenure systems in which there exist markets for agricultural produce, those systems characterized by family-sized tenancy will prove most volatile."[17] While the first model probably explains the rural mobilization in the New England states with predominantly family-size holdings, Stinchcombe's model seems to apply to rural crowd action in the tenancy areas of New York and perhaps in other colonies with quitrent systems.[18]

The plausibility of these models notwithstanding, they cannot be uncritically applied to the American Revolution. Crowd action in 1765 began in the urbanized areas. Only 10 years later, at the time of the Coercive Acts against Massachusetts and the subsequent Declaration and War of Independence, rural militancy often surpassed that of the more urbanized seaboard areas. At present a complex model explaining all of the American Revolution does not exist and will not be constructed in this study. The hypotheses advanced so far to interpret the revolutionary process in the British colonies on the American mainland remain basically political, whether "imperial," "constitutional," or "ideological." Carl Becker's important statement that the revolution was a dual struggle, not only for home rule but also for who should rule at home, has become a commonplace among historians rejecting the consensus interpretation of American history or predominantly political interpretations. But it is a commonplace and not a theory. Taking a societal approach to the revolutionary developments in Massachusetts and using generalizing concepts of the previously mentioned students of European crowd action, this study is intended as a contribution to the explanatory model that seems to be slowly emerging from the heavy output of specialized work on colonial society in the eighteenth century, from comparable studies on similar historical processes in other, particularly European societies, and from comparative studies of social movements, rebellions, and revolutions.[19]

[16]Paul Boyer and Stephen Nissenbaum, *Salem Possessed: The Social Origins of Witchcraft* (Cambridge, Mass., 1974).

[17]Arthur L. Stinchcombe, "Agricultural Enterprise and Rural Class Relations," *Am. J. Soc.* 67:165–176 (1961); Chirot and Ragin, "Peasant Rebellion," p. 429.

[18]Cf. the studies of New York society in general as well as of tenant uprisings and urban rioting by Bonomi, Countryman, Friedman, Lynd, Mark, and Young. See note 19 for titles.

[19]Contributions to a societal view of the American Revolution are the township studies, especially those concerned with the concept of corporate communities (e.g., Bumsted, Hoerder, Lockridge and Kreider, and Zuckerman); the land distribution studies (e.g., R. D. Brown, Land, Lemon and Nash, and Lockridge); tenancy studies (e.g., Lynd, Berthoff and Murrin); studies of urban lower classes and of mobility (e.g., Henretta, Kulikoff, Lemisch, Main, Morris, Ryerson, Nash, and Young); analyses of crowd action (e.g., Alexander, Countryman, Hoerder, Kern, Maier, and Young); the studies by Merrill Jensen's students (e.g. Becker, Egnal, Ernst, Hoffman); and the studies of ideology, imperial concepts (Bailyn, Bumsted, and Maier) of institutions (Greene, Main) and of the political economy of revolution (Egnal and Ernst).

John K. Alexander, "The Fort Wilson Incident of 1779. A Case Study of the Revolutionary Crowd," *WMQ* 3.31:589–612 (1974); Bernard Bailyn, *The Ideological Origins of the American Revolution* (Cambridge, Mass., 1967); Robert A. Becker, "The Politics of Taxation in America, 1763–1783" (Ph.D. diss., University of Wisconsin, 1971), and "Revolution and Reform: An Interpretation of Southern Taxation, 1763 to 1783," *WMQ* 3.32:417–442 (1975); Rowland Berthoff and John M. Murrin, "Feudalism, Communalism, and the Yeoman Freeholder: The American Revolution Considered as a Social Accident," in *Essays on the American Revolution*, eds. S. G. Kurtz and

NOTES ON TERMINOLOGY AND METHODS

While the term "crowd" is replacing the term "mob," with its negative connotations, it should be kept in mind that crowds were not as respectable as historians' accounts sometimes make them appear. Rudé's image of purposefully acting French rioters could easily be adopted to the needs of the ideological interpretation of the American Revolution. Differences between middle-class Whig authors and politicians and lower-class rioters almost vanished. Jesse Lemisch's description of sailors and Robert Patterson's carefully drawn distinction between the concepts of leaders like Samuel Adams and those of farmers from the western counties have done something to remedy this situation. But much remains to be explored. The present study attempts to look at the role of the little people, their concepts and expectations. It neither emphasizes the importance of Whig ideology as much as Bernard Bailyn thinks justified nor stresses constitutional and political concerns to the extent Jack P. Greene has done. Rather, it takes up the argument, cautiously and sympathetically advanced by Edmund S. Morgan, that the social, economic, and political interests of colonial groups were of great importance for decisions and actions during the revolutionary process and, for that matter, at any time. Staughton Lynd and Alfred F. Young have stressed this aspect. Merrill Jensen has emphasized the role of the people. Without imitating any one of them, this study is influenced by all of them and by other scholars focusing on socioeconomic conditions and on the little people.

There is still much imprecise use of the term "people." People are the sovereign constituents of society, according to modern constitutional thinking in the West. But

J. H. Hutson (Chapel Hill, N.C., 1973), pp. 256–288; Patricia U. Bonomi, *A Factious People: Politics and Society in Colonial New York* (New York, 1971); Richard D. Brown, "The Confiscation and Disposition of Loyalists' Estates in Suffolk County, Massachusetts," *WMQ* 3.21:534–550 (1964); J. M. Bumsted, "Religion, Finance, and Democracy in Massachusetts: The Town of Norton as a Case Study," *JAH* 57:817–831 (1970-71), and "'Things in the Womb of Time': Ideas of American Independence, 1633–1763," *WMQ* 3.31:533–564 (1974); Edward Countryman, "Legislative Government in Revolutionary New York, 1777–1788," (Ph.D. diss., Cornell University, 1971), and "The Problem of the Early American Crowd," *J. Am. Studies (GB)* 7:77–90 (1973), and "'Out of the Bounds of the Law': Northern Land Rioters in the Eighteenth Century," in *The American Revolution*, ed. A. F. Young (DeKalb, Ill., 1976), pp. 37–69; Marc Egnal and Joseph A. Ernst, "An Economic Interpretation of the American Revolution," *WMQ* 3.29:1–32 (1972); Joseph A. Ernst, *Money and Politics in America, 1755–1775: A Study in the Currency Act of 1764 and the Political Economy of Revolution* (Chapel Hill, N.C., 1973); E. James Ferguson, *The Power of the Purse: A History of American Public Finance, 1776–1790* (Chapel Hill, N.C., 1968); Bernard Friedman, "The Shaping of the Radical Consciousness in Provincial New York," *JAH* 56:781–801 (1969–70); Jack P. Greene, *The Quest for Power: The Lower Houses of Assembly in the Southern Royal Colonies, 1689–1776* (Chapel Hill, N.C., 1963), and "The Social Origins of the American Revolution: An Evaluation and an Interpretation," *Pol. Sci. Q.* 88:1–22 (1973); James Henretta, "Economic Development and Social Structure in Colonial Boston," *WMQ* 3.22:75–92 (1965), and *The Evolution of American Society, 1700–1815. An Interdisciplinary Analysis* (Lexington, Mass., 1973); Dirk Hoerder, *Society and Government 1760–1780: The Power Structure in Massachusetts Townships* (Berlin, 1972); Ronald Hoffman, *A Spirit of Dissension; Economics, Politics, and the Revolution in Maryland* (Baltimore, 1973); Robert F. Jones, "William Duer and the Business of Government in the Era of the American Revolution," *WMQ* 3.32:393–416 (1975); John Kern, "The Politics of Violence: Colonial American Rebellions, Protests and Riots, 1676–1747," (Ph.D. diss., University of Wisconsin, 1976); Allan Kulikoff, "The Progress of Inequality in Revolutionary Boston," *WMQ* 3.28:378–412 (1971); Aubrey C. Land, "Economic Base and Social Structure: The Northeastern Chesapeake in the Eighteenth Century," *J. Econ. Hist.* 25:639–654 (1965); Jesse Lemisch, "Jack Tar in the Streets: Merchant Seamen in the Politics of Revolutionary America," *WMQ* 3.25:371–407 (1968); James T. Lemon and Gary B. Nash, "The Distribution of Wealth in Eighteenth-Century America. A Century of Change in Chester County, Pennsylvania, in everyday usage the term has a different meaning. It can mean those forming a nation (population) or a town (inhabitants). It may denote enfranchised persons (voters) or anybody indiscriminately (folk). Most important, however, are meanings 3 and 4 listed in the *Oxford English Dictionary.* "(3) Persons in relation to a superior, or to someone to whom they belong." Subjects, servants, parishioners, workers, crews, members of the household, slaves, and so forth fall into this category. The connotation of subordinate rank may be extended from the level of individuals or groups to the whole society. "(4) The common people, the commonality; the mass of the community as distinguished from the nobility and ruling or official classes." If the lower status is to be made explicit, "populace" is substituted for "people." This meaning, the equivalent of the Latin *plebs* (as opposed to *populus*), was most often used by eighteenth-century colonials.[20] Witness John Adams, who noted concerning the establishment of a new constitution, "But we had a people of more intelligence, curiosity, and enterprise, who must be all consulted, and we must realize the theories of the wisest writers, and invite the people to erect the whole building with their own hands, upon the broadest foundation." Obviously, Adams considered himself and his colleagues above the people. They were the ones who condescended to invite the common people. The quote is, in fact, from Adams's autobiography, written two decades or more after the event. During the debates about the Massachusetts Constitution from 1776 to 1780, he had argued:

> There is one Thing . . . that must be attempted and most Sacredly observed, or We are all undone. There must be a Decency, and Respect, and Veneration introduced for Persons in Authority, of every Rank, or We are undone. In a popular Government, this is the only Way of supporting order.

1693–1802," *J. Soc. Hist.* 2:1–24 (1968–1969); Kenneth A. Lockridge and Alan Kreider, "The Evolution of Massachusetts Town Government, 1640 to 1740," *WMQ* 3.23:549–574 (1966); Kenneth A. Lockridge, "Land, Population and the Evolution of New England Society, 1630–1790," *Past and Present* 39:62–80 (April 1968), and "Social Change and the Meaning of the American Revolution," *J. Soc. Hist.* 6:403–439 (1972–1973); Staughton Lynd, "Who Should Rule at Home? Dutchess County, New York, in the American Revolution," *WMQ* 3.18:330–359 (1961), and "The Tenant Rising at Livingston Manor, May 1777," *N.Y. Hist. Soc. Q.* 48:163–177 (1964); Staughton Lynd and Alfred F. Young, "After Carl Becker: The Mechanics and New York City Politics, 1774–1801," *Labor History* 5:215–276 (1964); Pauline R. Maier, "Popular Uprisings and Civil Authority in Eighteenth-Century America," *WMQ* 3.27:3–35 (1970), and *From Resistance to Revolution: Colonial Radicals and the Development of American Opposition to Britain, 1765–1776* (New York, 1972); Jackson T. Main, *The Social Structure of Revolutionary America* (Princeton, N.J., 1965), and *The Upper House in Revolutionary America, 1763–1788* (Madison, Wis., 1967); Irving Mark, *Agrarian Conflict in Colonial New York, 1711–1775* (1940; reprint ed., New York, 1965); Richard B. Morris, "Class Struggle and the American Revolution," *WMQ* 3.19:3–29 (1962); Gary B. Nash, "Urban Wealth and Poverty in Pre-Revolutionary America," *J. Interdisc. History* 6:545–584 (1975–1976); Stephen E. Patterson, *Political Parties in Revolutionary Massachusetts* (Madison, Wis., 1973); R. A. Ryerson, "Political Mobilization and the American Revolution: The Resistance Movement in Philadelphia, 1765–1776," *WMQ* 3.31:565–588 (1974); Alfred F. Young, "The 'Bailyn' Thesis and the Problem of 'Popular' Ideology. A Comment," (Paper prepared for the annual convention of the Organization of American Historians, Denver, 1974), and editor, *The American Revolution. Explorations in the History of American Radicalism* (DeKalb, Ill., 1976), and *From Ritual to Rebellion* (forthcoming); Michael W. Zuckerman: "The Social Context of Democracy in Massachusetts," *WMQ* 3.25:523–544 (1968), and *Peaceable Kingdoms: New England Towns in the Eighteenth Century* (New York 1970).
[20]See contemporary diaries and letters, such as those of Ezra Stiles, John Rowe, John Adams, and John Hancock. This seemingly obvious fact has been overlooked by R. E. Brown in his *Middle-Class Democracy and the Revolution in Massachusetts, 1691–1780* (Ithaca, N.Y., 1955), a book more notable for reflecting the consensus interpretation of American history than for a judicious use of sources. On "populace," see *BG,* 12 Aug. 1765.

As for consulting the people, "it is a Pity" that the constitution will have to be submitted to them; "it will divide and distract them."[21]

In agrarian communities, however, such notions of class were not always accepted. While John Adams labored on an elaborate constitution with checks and balances, property qualification, and indirect election, the people of Westminster, Worcester County, considered Adams and the like not one iota better than themselves: "The oftener power Returnes into the hands of the people the better. . . . Where can the power be Layed So Safe as in the hands of the people? . . . or Who has the Boldness—Without Blushing? to Say that the people are Not Suitable to putt in their own officers." Without blushing, the delegates to the Massachusetts constitutional convention juggled the votes of the people in a manner that disregarded all amendments suggested by the people, so that John Adams's constitution was accepted.

The "We the People" of the small corporations and towns was applied in the national Constitution to the inhabitants of 13 different states—never submitted directly to these people. The use of "we" constituted an attempt to cloud existing differences between the states and between various economic and social groups, to suggest a national unity and a social and political equality together with a direct democracy that in fact did not exist.

The conservative concept of those days was aptly summarized by Peter Oliver, chief justice of Massachusetts: "As for the People in general, they were like the Mobility of all Countries, perfect Machines, wound up by any Hand who might first take the Winch." Thomas Paine, besides Jefferson the most democratic thinker of his time, wrote:

> We ought to reflect, that there are three different ways, by which an independency may hereafter be effected; and that one of those three, will, one day or other be the fate of America, viz. By the legal voice of the people in Congress; by a military power, or by a mob.

The representatives, the "legal voice of the people," are thus opposed to the enfranchised people themselves acting directly (the "mob").

John Adams, who wanted the lower house to be "an exact portrait . . . of the people at large," remarks a few lines further on that it would be "apt to make hasty results and absurd judgements; all which errors ought to be corrected, and inconveniences guarded against by some controlling power." By this he meant a second house consisting of men qualified by property ownership and not elected by the people at large but by the upper economic groups of the social pyramid. When political power was at stake, the concept of one people was abandoned for a dualistic notion of popular and aristocratic sections of society, the famous mixed government, with the leaders members of the "natural aristocracy." The fundamentally false concept contained in the abstract notion of "the people"—that is, the

[21]John Adams, "Autobiography," in *The Works of John Adams,* ed. Charles F. Adams, 10 vols. (Boston, 1850–1856), 3:16; *Warren–Adams Letters: Being Chiefly a Correspondence among John Adams, Samuel Adams, and James Warren,* 2 vols. (MHSC vols. 72, 73; Boston, 1917, 1925), 1:234, 322.

substitution of a conceptual, idealistic singular for an actual plurality—was upheld by the substitution of the derogatory term "mob" whenever the incongruity of concept and reality became obvious. The later confession of Tocqueville that he was a democrat by intellect but remained an aristocrat by heart is applicable to the vast majority of colonial leaders, though both terms have to be taken with a grain of salt in considering colonial society.[22]

In terms of political participation and legal definition, "the people"—that is, free, white, adult males—were freeholders and inhabitants. They voted and decided in the town meeting, provided they met the property qualifications. Town meetings and corporate geographical units were the only sphere in which the people could act politically. Neither as individuals (citizens) nor in other units (interest groups) could they exert political influence. The concept of a citizen as an independent, conscious, active, and equal individual in a community had not yet been developed. Only in the seventies did the term begin to make a cautious appearance in the theoretical literature. The notion that the people consist of a large, perhaps infinite number of groups with divergent interests was contrary to the idea of corporate unity or even uniformity. A few conscious formulations of this principle exist, however, again from the early seventies onward.[23]

A further differentiation of terminology is reached when "the people" acted spontaneously. Usually treated by hierarchically minded officials and leaders with benevolent paternalism, they were contemptuously called "mob," "rabble of the lowest sort," and "banditti" when going beyond their chartered or traditional rights. Political sympathies determined the intensity of the condemnation; people rioting were a "hellish crew" (Thomas Hutchinson) for Loyalists and crown officials, the "lowest class" (John Adams) for Whigs. In such circumstances, little was left of "free-born British subjects" and "virtuous patriots" united by a general consensus. Only a few contemporaries spoke of an "incensed populace" or of "justly enraged multitudes."

Of course, political opportuneness also contributed to the nature of the judgments pronounced on riots. Mere demonstrations fitting into the Whig policy were even celebrated. Some violence was condescendingly forgiven: "It was indeed a very improper way of acting, but may not the agonies of minds not quite so polished as your own be in some measure excused?" Large-scale property destruction was called "outrageous" and its perpetrators prosecuted when it was motivated by social tensions, but it was lauded in lyrical terms when it was egged on by Whig leaders. "This [the tea riot] is the most magnificent movement of all. There is a

---

[22]Westminster opinion, MA 160:17–19, MSA; Samuel E. Morison, "The Struggle over the Adoption of the Constitution of Massachusetts, 1780," *MHSP* 50:353–412 (1916–1917); Peter Oliver, *Peter Oliver's Origin and Progress of the American Rebellion: A Tory View*, ed. Douglass Adair and John A. Schutz (Stanford, Calif., 1961), p. 65; Thomas Paine, *The Complete Writings of Thomas Paine*, ed. Philip S. Foner, 2 vols. (New York, 1945), 1:45, John Adams, *Works*, 4:205–206. Cf. 6:418–419 and Samuel Adams's comments on this view, *ibid.*, 6:420ff. Joseph Dorfman, in "The Regal Republic of John Adams," *Pol. Sci. Q.* 59:230 (1944), noted, "Adams, like any respectable colonial of his generation, thought of 'people' in two rather distinct senses—the spiritual and the civil."

[23]Oscar Handlin and Mary F. Handlin, eds., *The Popular Sources of Political Authority: Documents on the Massachusetts Constitution of 1780* (Cambridge, Mass., 1966), pp. 154, 163, 364, 437, 571ff. The concept of interest groups came into its own only during the constitutional debates; cf. especially James Madison's *Federalist Paper* no. 10.

dignity, a majesty, a sublimity, in this last effort of the patriots, that I greatly admire.''[24] Similarly, the utterances of crown officials oscillate between condemnation and justification. When they had to explain to the British government why they submitted to popular demands, the mob was all-powerful; if they could not call the crowd violent but had nevertheless given in, it was because of the justified wishes of the "Landholders of this County." Governor Bernard, thundering against mobs in his private letters, cautiously mentioned in. public "a great Number of People unlawfully and riotously assembled."[25]

The social stratification in the colonies, already implied in the term "people," cannot be simply skirted by talking about "the colonists" or by lumping everyone together and coming up with a middle-class democracy, a consensus, or, to oversimplify a recent thesis, peaceable kingdoms. In talking about stratification, I will classify society into three groups, as colonials did: lower classes, middling interest, and better sort. These terms, used by contemporaries in newspapers and private correspondence, are important. A "sort" is merely a classificatory term. An "interest," on the other hand, has a clear economic connotation. Members of this group did not strive for the public good, nor did they define themselves as very different from society at large; they merely had an "interest" of their own. This group, to turn to our specific case, certainly existed in Boston but is difficult for historians to trace. In the forties and fifties, and later in the eighties, the middling interest appeared as a distinct social group in contemporary writings. In the sixties and seventies, the revolutionary period, this part of society was almost inarticulate. The Boston caucus system integrated master craftsmen, shopkeepers, and small merchants into a political system that saw no election contests, no openly expressed interests. The third term denotes a separation from the whole. To this group, the lower classes, belonged the sailors and laborers, the apprentices and journeymen mechanics. But, and this is the problem of most studies dealing with the social history of this period, other groups are much less easily classified. Master artisans? They were often lower class if they were self-employed. They could have been middle class if they were employers or incipient artisan—entrepreneurs. Shopkeepers? According to most definitions, they were considered lower middle class. But their social standing and their economic problems were very similar to those of master artisans. Merchant–captains were usually middle class, but their operating capital was often so small that one disaster, a shipwreck, could throw them back into the lower classes. Large shopkeepers, middling merchants, some of the professional men, captains, and merchant–captains would form the middling interest. Wealthy merchants, lawyers, and officials from the justice of the peace upward would belong to the better sort.

Of course, many individuals were not permanently locked into one class. There was some upward mobility and, as Henretta has shown, more downward mobility in terms of percentage of total population. Furthermore, an explicit and coherent class

---

[24]John Dickinson, *Political Writings*, vol. 1 (Wilmington, Del., 1801), p. 128. John Adams, *Works*, 2:323. See Elisha P. Douglass, *Rebels and Democrats: The Struggle for Equal Political Rights and Majority Rule during the American Revolution* (Chapel Hill, N.C., 1955), p. 18.

[25]Oliver to Dartmouth, 3 Sept. 1774, *CSMP* 32:485; *BG,* 5 Sept. 1774; *BEP,* 2 Sept. 1765.

ideology seems to have been missing. Lemisch has detected class consciousness among sailors, and Egnal and Ernst have outlined the emergence of the merchants as a separate and self-conscious group. For mechanics in Boston, such analysis is extremely difficult. Alfred F. Young's meticulous study of the transfer of English popular ideology to Boston mechanics has greatly improved on all existing studies of crowds and ideology. But even when occupations are known, we usually have no indication whether a certain artisan was a journeyman, self-employed, or a small-scale employer. Wherever possible, I have tried to differentiate beyond the three-strata model according to profession or property ownership.[26]

A further terminological difficulty centers around the word "grievances." It has been suggested—I think by Jesse Lemisch—that the term "conflicts" be used instead. A grievance is something that by minor remedial action can be alleviated or redressed (abolished). A conflict is something basic that requires structural changes. I have decided to use the term "grievances" because in my understanding a social conflict—and that is the kind of conflict we are talking about here—also requires an awareness that the particular problem at issue requires basic changes. I will argue that such a consciousness existed in only rudimentary form among Boston's lower classes and among Massachusetts farmers. That, economically, the conflict was there has been shown beyond doubt by Henretta and Kulikoff (as well as by other scholars for other towns). But, at least for the historian, it rarely surfaced in articulate form. From my reading of the sources, I will also argue that this is not merely a shortcoming of the available sources but is one aspect of contemporary social stratification and social relations.

The attitudes of Whig leaders toward the people and toward violence have been used to classify them as moderate or radical. The latter classification cannot be regarded as evidence for a position tending toward popular control of government or toward social revolution. Very few of the Whig leaders advocated basic social changes. The meaning can only apply to more or less strong advocacy of independence and the means to achieve it. (This might include a temporary emphasis on the rights of the people and the necessity of their action.) Radical opinions about political and socioeconomic equality were, however, to be found in rudimentary form at the grass-roots level of the colonial population.[27]

Two further notes on the usage of the term "radical" have to be inserted to encompass the wide variety of meanings injected into the term by historians. Cecelia Kenyon has argued in a stimulating essay that the real radicals were those who forged the economic system of the new nation.[28] Hamilton's fiscal policies

[26]James Henretta, "Economic Development," *WMQ* 3.22:75–92 (1965); Allan Kulikoff, "The Progress of Inequality," *WMQ* 3.28:378–412 (1971); Jesse Lemisch, "The American Revolution from the Bottom Up," *Towards a New Past: Dissenting Essays in American History,* ed. Barton J. Bernstein (New York, 1968), pp. 3–45, and "What Made Our Revolution?" (Review of Bernard Bailyn's *The Origins of American Politics*), *New Republic,* 25 May 1968; Marc Egnal and Joseph A. Ernst, "An Economic Interpretation," *WMQ* 3.29:1–32 (1972); Alfred F. Young, *From Ritual to Rebellion* (forthcoming).

[27]Douglass, *Rebels and Democrats;* Oscar Handlin and Mary F. Handlin, "Radicals and Conservatives in Massachusetts after Independence," *NEQ* 17:343–355 (1944).

[28]Cecelia M. Kenyon, "Republicanism and Radicalism in the American Revolution: An Old-Fashioned Interpretation," *WMQ* 3.19:159–182 (1962).

were indeed a radical departure from previous approaches, but they were intended to achieve conservative aims. "They give stability to Government," reported financier and Superintendent of Finances Robert Morris to Congress, "by combining together the interests of moneyed men for its support."[29] It seems a rather formalistic use of the term "radical" applied in this sense. Probably, these economic policies were also already in the "womb of time."[30]

Another variant of the radicalism theme is Bailyn's suggestion that to abolish slavery during the revolutionary period would have been "fanaticism." Gary B. Nash, in a review of the essay and in an exchange with Bailyn, bluntly and justifiably states:

> It is equally arguable that those who shoved aside the human rights enunciated during the Revolution in order to achieve political modernization were fanatically in pursuit of centralized government and the supremacy of private property, and that opposing this false national security were truly moderate men who wished to pursue national government *without* abandoning the revolutionary credo of human freedom and dignity.[31]

Finally, the term "radicalism" loses any meaning when used as follows: "Whig radicalism was nearer to that of John than of Samuel Adams; it was the radicalism of the conscientious lawyer, not of the social leveller, the Gironde not the Mountain."[32]

The discussion about the structure of Massachusetts society, its economy, and its political framework has been hampered by attempts to label it democracy, a term frequently having a twentieth-century connotation. Contemporary conservatives condemned "anarchical democracy" (Governor Bernard) or "democratic despotism" (Daniel Leonard). R. N. Lokken in a penetrating study summarized the contemporary argument:

> The colonists conceived of two kinds of democracy—one, an unmixed or simple democracy; the other, a mixed constitution in which democracy was represented by one of the branches of government. The ideal unmixed democracy was that of Periclean Athens, in which all the male adult members of the *demos* participated in the *ecclesia*. The mixed constitution was a combination of the three known forms of government—monarchy, aristocracy, and democracy.[33]

[29]Quoted in E. James Ferguson, "The Nationalists of 1781–1783 and the Economic Interpretation of the Constitution," *JAH* 56:247 (1969–1970).

[30]See Dirk Hoerder, "Vom korporativen zum liberalen Eigentumsbegriff: Ein Element der amerikanischen Revolution," *Geschichte und Gesellschaft,* special issue no. 2, pp. 76–100 (Göttingen, Fall 1976).

[31]Bernard Bailyn, "The Central Themes of the American Revolution: An Interpretation," in *Essays on the American Revolution,* ed. S. G. Kurtz and J. H. Hutson (Chapel Hill, N. C., 1973), p. 29; cf. *WMQ* 3.31:311–314 (1974); 3.32:182–185 (1975).

[32]Lee N. Newcomer, "Yankee Rebels of Inland Massachusetts," *WMQ* 3.9:164 (1952).

[33]Roy N. Lokken, "The Concept of Democracy in Colonial Political Thought," *WMQ* 3.16:570–571 (1959). See also Jack R. Pole, "Historians and the Problem of Early American Democracy," *AHR* 67:626–646 (1962); Richard Buel, Jr., "Democracy and the American Revolution: A Frame of Reference," *WMQ* 3.21:165–190 (1964); R. R. Palmer, "Notes on the Use of the Word 'Democracy,' 1789–1799," *Pol. Sci. Q.* 68:203–226 (1953).

To determine the degree of participation of all sectors of the society in all its transactions, it is necessary to look into the distribution of property, into the egalitarian or hierarchical aspects of the social system, and into the participatory or excluding features of political life.[34]

Neither the elitist belief that only the upper classes matter in history nor a deep-seated but vague faith in "the people," the virtuous "common man," or "the workers" is adequate. Neither autonomous individuals acting against the background of a countless population nor essentially noble masses existed. The activities of "the people," the relations between rulers and ruled, and the traditional belief in a leader–mass hierarchy have hardly been subjected to sufficient scrutiny. It is perhaps symptomatic that the very name for the period after 1760, "the revolutionary era," is extremely imprecise. Who makes a revolution? People, crowds, mobs? Ringleaders, enlightened leaders, heroes? Few historians have attempted to conceptualize the term to make it applicable to similar situations in different countries at different times, to give it an analytical value applicable to a historical (and modern) phenomenon rather than a merely descriptive function for one particular event in American history. The statement that the American Revolution "was the most conservative of revolutions and, therefore, the most constructive" (Newcomer) is obviously based on a double non sequitur. If the years 1763 to 1783 saw merely a struggle for independence, the term "revolution" is not warranted unless independence implied important changes in the social and political structure of the colonies. If, however, this period was one of social upheaval centered on the question of who should rule at home, it probably was a revolution, or an attempt at one.

In colonial New England, people were politically and socially more equal and had more economic opportunities than in most countries in the Old World. This comparative aspect, however, has been used and misused for integrative ideological purposes, necessary to obfuscate social and economic differences and consequently any concept the people of the "lower sort" might have of themselves in relation to other groups. The Berkshire Constitutionalists considered the comparison of the rights of American people to oppression suffered by those of other nations as intentionally misleading. "To measure the freedom, the rights and previleges of the American Empire by those enjoyed by other Nations would be folly."[35] The American situation has not been measured against a coherent theory that can be used to develop alternative policies of political participation by the people—for example, Robert Dahl's *Preface to Democratic Theory.* Nor has it been tested against an empirically derived system of social classification, which might have been used as a yardstick until quantitative methods began to intrude into historical "interpretation."

The emphasis on popular action creates a methodological difficulty: how to avoid treating the many as faceless masses or as unrelated individuals. During the "revolutionary period," Massachusetts had nearly 300,000 inhabitants. The population of

---

[34]See the later section in this chapter entitled "The Societal Framework."
[35]Handlin and Handlin, eds., *Popular Sources,* p. 377.

Boston varied between 15,000 and 18,000. Treating these people only statistically denies their individuality from the outset. Each and every one of them participated in the shaping of the course that Massachusetts steered in those years. These people were not mere ciphers commanded by a few, nor were they pawns moved by history. None could achieve great changes on his own; there were no autonomous individuals above social bounds and norms. Instead, the contradictory actions of thousands and hundreds of thousands of individual social beings added up to trends, were history.

I have tried to describe the actions of some extensively without uplifting them so as to overshadow the others whose similar actions were not merely the background for but an element of the described participants' actions. For those who had more influence than others in a specific situation or in the long run, I have emphasized their position and their connections rather than depicting them as supermen. Towering figures like Sam Adams, James Otis, and King Hancock—to name only a few—could not have acted on their own. None of the three was more virtuous than those who threw stones or beat officials. Samuel Adams tried to maintain the unity of leaders and followers by a rhetorical device: He commenced his own sentences with "The people think...." But he condemned the "vulgar prejudices," "mobbish" doings, and similar activities of those for whom he sought to speak. Hancock tried to induce magistrates to break their oath (1768) and actually induced people to take risks in opposing the British while he himself cooperated with the latter for private gain (1768). Whig official Otis abused British officials but condemned those of the population as "scum" who criticized the Whig magistrates.

Methods to reach the lower rungs of society include the use of tax lists, court records, official documents, and any other contemporary sources available, such as newspapers, private papers, letters, and diaries.[36] I have purposely refrained from selecting as sources "important" newspapers or personal papers of "representative" individuals. It has been made abundantly clear by the Handlins' publication of the "popular sources" for the Massachusetts constitutional debates that a selection of a few well-known individuals or official documents would mean following one's own class bias or an outdated theory of history. Of course, even "popular" documents were written by men elected to committees by town meetings for this purpose, and they frequently were members of the towns' upper socioeconomic strata. Thus, again the very bottom level of society remains inaccessible to the historian. But by using these sources, we do get closer to this class.

One step further in this direction is the laborious task of examining court records for the names of rioters and then locating them in the tax lists. For many riots it is possible to identify some participants, but most rioters remain unknown. Therefore, it is impossible to analyze the social background of Massachusetts rioters and their political beliefs as exactly as Rudé was able to do for the French Revolution by using the police records. An important source for the opinion of the economically disadvantaged social groups is their petitions to the General Court. Here those who

---

[36]On reading and understanding eighteenth-century sources, see Bernard Knollenberg, *Origin of the American Revolution: 1759–1766* (New York, 1960), pp. 256–258.

did not leave diaries and volumes of correspondence expressed their opinion about economic conditions and their causes and suggested methods to improve them.

I have attempted to show the changing patterns and motives of rioting, the connections and differences between different kinds of direct political action, and to discuss the degree of spontaneity of the masses and of premeditated or on-the-spot leadership. In this respect, the years after 1774 pose additional difficulties: The Whig leaders, now in power, suppressed news of riots that were again deemed licentious and rebellious—in short, dangerous to their position. The relations between riots and the established institutions and officialdom are explained by the changes that they effected on the political scene. Also, more needs to be known about how political theories were received by or formed in those sections of the population whose activities—that is, participation in town meetings and riots—were confined to the local level.[37]

Stressing the importance of crowd activities has been called by Richard Frothingham a "semi-Tory view," tending to "overlook the remarkable adherence to social order that is seen through ten years of exciting controversy." R. E. Brown has called the emphasis on social differences and the resulting tensions a "neoprogressive" view of history. Both classifications unduly simplify the position taken in this study, which, the imperfect records notwithstanding, is an attempt to analyze the political participation of the lower-income groups in revolutionary Massachusetts and its social and economic background. I have rejected a personalistic approach as well as the oversimplification of a rigid system of classes. Instead, I use social and economic groups as categories that, on the one hand, are sufficiently adaptable to prevent historical evidence from being hammered into an inflexible system and, on the other hand, are barriers to the deification of individuals and to the viewpoint that the population is just one big herd of faceless beings.

HISTORIOGRAPHY AND RESEARCH IN PROGRESS

The study of crowd action in the American mainland colonies has evolved through several stages. Early historians of "mobs" contrasted the "noble array of as pure, unselfish, and self-devoting patriots as the world has ever seen" with "mobsters," "this element [that] was in every aspect as harmful and detrimental as it was unlawful and immoral."[38] Of significance, on the other hand, were the works of the progressive historians, such as Becker and Beard. Their emphasis on social and economic questions and on the differences of interest within the colonial population made it possible to view the American Revolution as more than merely a colonial struggle for independence and to focus on internal dissentions. But to them the elites created the crowd, molded it, and led it, though sometimes in a sort of

---

[37]Alfred F. Young, "The 'Bailyn' Thesis and the Problem of 'Popular' Ideology."

[38]Andrew P. Peabody, "Boston Mobs before the Revolution," *Atlantic Monthly* 62:322 (1888); Walter K. Watkins, "Tarring and Feathering in Boston, 1770," *Old-Time New England* 20:30–43 (1929); R. S. Longley, "Mob Activities in Revolutionary Massachusetts," *NEQ* 6:98–130 (1933). Cf. Carl L. Becker's trenchant commentary on the attitudes of middle-class contemporaries toward the "mob element": "Growth of Revolutionary Parties and Methods in New York Province, 1765–1774," *AHR* 7:63 (1901).

Frankensteinian turn the infuriated masses became uncontrollable. This line of argument finally interpreted the broadsides and pamphlets of the leading Sons of Liberty as mere propaganda, designed to agitate the minds of fellow colonials and to arouse the rabble to do what mere writing could not. Arthur M. Schlesinger's detailed account of the role of the merchants mentions crowd action, but it contrasts "mobs" and their "vandalism" with the "sober" thought of the merchants who were occasionally "swept by the surge of popular feeling into measures of which their best judgment disapproved."[39]

Historians from the left have stressed the economic and social stratification of colonial society. Jack Hardy refuted the idea that the "revolutionaries were . . . wild mobs." The "humble and underprivileged masses" fought for freedom, "organized in trained, orderly, and highly disciplined bodies." They found themselves "caught in the countless oppressions and constrictions of class society and sought some measure of release and the opening of opportunities for themselves and their families." Later Herbert Aptheker and, because of his different topic, to a more limited degree William A. Williams took a similar but more sophisticated position.[40]

Among more recent studies, Gipson's monumental work on the British Empire and Sibley and Shipton's equally monumental work on Harvard graduates represent a viewpoint hostile to crowd action and popular participation.[41] Carl Bridenbaugh, on the other hand, documents that crowd action was a component of everyday colonial life. Participants were not "a mere 'rabble' " but came from or acted with the approval of the middle class to redress what they considered grievances and hardships or to voice their disapproval of persons or policies. The interest of the small property owners, agrarian as well as artisan, in an equalization of political influence and of economic opportunities and resulting action has been described by Elisha P. Douglass. In his pilot study he adduces thorough evidence of class conflicts and of the existence of a minority whose socioeconomic position resulted in political theories and opinions far ahead of those of the Whig leadership.[42]

Several monographs on the Sons of Liberty are also concerned with the involvement of the lower classes in politics. Richard Walsh, dealing with the situation in Charleston, South Carolina, points out that while the mechanic's position in society was humble, he himself was not always humble. Riots were a means to improve his social situation but could not achieve a profound change in economic conditions.

[39]Arthur M. Schlesinger, Sr., *The Colonial Merchants and the American Revolution, 1763–1773* (1918; reprint ed., New York, 1957), p. 289.

[40]L. M. Hacker, "The First American Revolution," *Columbia Univ. Q.* 37:259–295 (1935), and "The American Revolution: Economic Aspects," *Marxist Q.* 1:46–67 (1937); Jack Hardy, *The First American Revolution* (New York, 1937); Herbert Aptheker, *The American Revolution, 1763–1783 . . . An Interpretation* (New York, 1960); William A. Williams, *Contours of American History* (Cleveland, 1961).

[41]Lawrence H. Gipson, *The British Empire before the American Revolution*, vols. 10, 11 (New York, 1961, 1965); John L. Sibley and Clifford K. Shipton, *Biographical Sketches of Those Who Attended Harvard College*, esp. vols. 13–16 for 1751–1767 (Cambridge, Mass., 1965–1972).

[42]Carl Bridenbaugh, *Cities in the Wilderness: The First Century of Urban Life in America, 1625–1742*, 2nd ed. (New York, 1955), and *Cities in Revolt: Urban Life in America, 1743–1776* (New York, 1955); Douglass, *Rebels and Democrats;* Stephen E. Patterson, *Political Parties in Revolutionary Massachusetts* (Madison, Wis., 1973).

Philadelphia mechanics, according to Charles S. Olton, effected a major transformation of their roles in social, economic and political life. Substituting a tightly knit
and powerful inter-trade organization for the craft guilds they selfconsciously
voiced their interests and became a major political factor. In New York, artisans,
sailors, and laborers had a great political potential. But as they did not succeed in
voicing a reform program representing their interests, they did not become an
independent factor in New York politics. Instead—so runs the argument of Roger
Champagne—they remained instruments in the hands of those leaders who appeared
to be responsive to popular demands. This view has been challenged by Staughton
Lynd and Alfred Young, who have been able to detect clear concepts of purpose and
class consciousness together with action determined by these factors among the
mechanics of New York and the tenants in agrarian counties of the state.[43] Pauline
Maier's study of the Sons of Liberty shows them to be "respectable members of
their communities and included professional men, merchants, even local officials."
But this is the result of her interest in the uses made of "the 'Real Whig' tradition of
seventeenth- and eighteenth-century England" during the American Revolution and
the consequent neglect of the lower classes.[44] The question of what ideology
motivated those below the respectable members of colonial society remains unan-
swered and, in fact, cannot be answered from the sources used by scholars adhering
to the so-called Bailyn thesis.

Arthur M. Schlesinger, Sr., who, in his study of colonial merchants, had already
pointed to the role of crowd action, squarely stated in 1955, "Mass violence played
a dominant role at every significant turning point of the events leading up to the War
for Independence."[45] Many historians still reject this point of view, but numerous
monographs and articles have substantiated this thesis. Schlesinger explicitly considered crowd action as limited to political intentions related to the movement for
independence. Particularly the studies of Edmund Morgan on the Stamp Act period
and of Benjamin Labaree on the tea duty disturbances have added to our knowledge
about the character of this kind of crowd action and have emphasized its internal
repercussions.[46] Other studies—Hiller B. Zobel's account of the Boston Massacre is
the most outstanding example—have contributed nothing except to perpetuate
clichés about unlawful mobs. Zobel's law-and-order account distorts evidence and
pictures the British as acting "to uphold the law, hence behaving honorably, while
their opponents acted against the law, and thus unacceptably. This position naturally
rules out the validity of any revolutionary effort since all revolutions contest given
legal orders." Scholars as different in viewpoint and method as Jesse Lemisch and

[43]Richard Walsh, *Charleston's Sons of Liberty: A Study of the Artisans, 1763–1789* (Columbia, S.C., 1959); Roger J.
   Champagne, "The Sons of Liberty and the Aristocracy in New York Politics, 1765–1790" (Ph.D. diss., Univ. of
   Wisconsin, 1960); Lynd and Young, "The Mechanics and New York City Politics, 1774–1801"; Lynd, "The Tenant
   Rising at Livingston Manor"; Charles S. Olton, *Artisans for Independence: Philadelphia Mechanics and the American Revolution* (Syracuse, N.Y., 1975).
[44]Maier, *From Resistance to Revolution,* p. 297.
[45]Arthur M. Schlesinger, Sr., "Political Mobs in the American Revolution, 1765–1776," *Am. Phil. Soc. Proc.* 99:244
   (1955).
[46]Edmund S. Morgan and Helen M. Morgan, *The Stamp Act Crisis. Prologue to Revolution* (Chapel Hill, N.C., 1953);
   Benjamin Woods Labaree, *The Boston Tea Party* (New York, 1964).

Pauline Maier share this evaluation of Zobel's work.[47] The study of the crowds of the American Revolution has generally been hampered by the scholars' reliance on contemporary accounts, written mainly by supporters of the British administration or by conservative Whig leaders. Sources close to the crowds and (quantifiable) economic data to determine the rioters' social position have long been neglected.

Lloyd I. Rudolph and William A. Smith both compared European and colonial "mobs" and agree that they were essentially different in economic motivation and forms and degree of violence used. Rudolph and Smith stress the impact of the crowds on the political scene as early voices for political participation in decision making but emphasize at the same time that they stopped short of revolutionary demands in the colonies. Both are valuable studies, but both tend to put too much weight on the uniqueness of the American experience and on the economic well-being of the "mobsters." Bernard Bailyn also stressed the differences between the moderate goal-directed American crowds and violent disorders in Europe.[48]

Gordon Wood, in 1966, took to task those historians who, like Rudolph, Smith, and Bailyn, had stressed the ferocity of European crowds and the restrained character of American crowds.[49] Wood suggested that the differences did not exist. The European crowds were not more violent or even bloodthirsty. Violence was not exerted by the masses but by the governments. In America, where no army or police existed, the crowds escaped the blame for the outrages of the law-and-order forces. Wood based his reassessment on Rudé's influential work.

Pauline Maier elaborated on this thesis. She realized that crowds had other than political aims—for example, food distribution or enforcement of social norms—and that they acted throughout the colonial period, not merely during the struggle against the British after 1765.[50] But by stressing the norm enforcement for individuals, crowd action is turned into authority-supporting behavior. This no doubt explains many crowd objectives, but there remain large unexplored areas, particularly those to which the progressive historians had pointed, the conflict-of-interest situations between different groups of society. In this study I have attempted to include these social and economic dissensions that led to direct action and to explore their bearing on the anti-British crowd action.

One step further in the direction of giving an adequate picture of crowd behavior and the underlying concepts has been taken by Jesse Lemisch and others. His attempt to write "history from the bottom up" not only accepts mass violence as one component of colonial life and institutions. He places Jack Tar as an individual

---

[47]Hiller B. Zobel, *The Boston Massacre* (New York, 1970); reviews by Jesse Lemisch, "Radical Plot in Boston (1770): A Study in the Use of Evidence," *Harvard Law Review* 84:485–504 (1970–1971) and Pauline Maier, "Revolutionary Violence and the Relevance of History," *J. Interdisc. Hist.* 2:119–134 (1971–1972), esp. p. 120–121.

[48]Lloyd I. Rudolph, "The Eighteenth Century Mob in America and Europe," *Am. Q.* 11:447–469 (1959); William A. Smith, "Anglo-Colonial Society and the Mob, 1740–1775" (Ph.D. diss., Claremont Graduate School and Univ. Center, 1965); Bernard Bailyn, *Pamphlets of the American Revolution*, vol. 1 (Cambridge, Mass., 1965), pp. 581–585.

[49]Gordon S. Wood, "A Note on Mobs in the American Revolution," *WMQ* 3.23:635–642 (1966), and "The People Out-of-Doors," *The Creation of the American Republic, 1776–1787* (Chapel Hill, N.C., 1969), pp. 319–328.

[50]Pauline R. Maier, "Popular Uprisings," and "The Charleston Mob and the Evolution of Popular Politics in Revolutionary South Carolina, 1765–1784," *Persp. Am. Hist.* 4:173–198 (1970).

in the context of this class within society and describes his grievances, concepts, and actions in relation to his political rights, his social status, and his economic position. Joel Shufro has traced the connections between impressment riots and the colonial economic situation.[51]

A number of scholars are presently studying lower-class political, social, and economic activities during the revolutionary era and the ideology behind them. John Kern has investigated the Boston market riots of the 1730s. In his work as well as in my own dissertation, in accord with one trend of current historiography, popularized versions of Whig theory found in rioters' statements have been used to explain the crowd action. These adaptations of Whig theory, in my opinion, were directly opposite in their meaning to the social tenets of Whig leaders and pamphleteers, studied by Bailyn and his students. Walter Wallace, a student of Alfred Young, is working on the question of why and how a lower-class crowd leader of Boston's riots against the Stamp Act was compared by contemporaries in Massachusetts as well as in London to Thomas Aniello, leader of the Naples uprising of 1647, during which fishermen, shopkeepers, and workers attempted to overthrow the local aristocracy. It seems that from this only briefly successful movement derived a whole oral and written tradition of the power of the lower classes. Edward Countryman, in "The Northern Rural Crowd in the Eighteenth Century: A Comparative View," has thrown much light on the mobilization and motivations of colonial crowds. The most ambitious study has been undertaken by Alfred Young. He is able to document the Puritan–Protestant ways of thinking of Boston rioters, and perhaps colonial crowds in general. His explanatory model, including popular recreations, ritualized criticism of rulers, and the influence of Cromwellian Protestantism, helps to illuminate parts of crowd action not explainable by the "inverted" Whig theory mentioned earlier. These new findings have been taken into consideration in this study. But I have concentrated on the processes of crowd action and its societal setting in the colonies rather than on the transfer of elements of class consciousness from England to America.[52]

The limits set for this study, 1765 and 1780, place serious restraints on the scope of the subject. The year 1765 saw the passage of and resistance to the Stamp Act. But before that, a long tradition of crowd action had been in existence. In the next chapter I trace the background and traditions that shaped crowd action before the new imperial policies demanded opposition that drew on this experience. For the next decade, up to the Declaration of Independence, levels of anti-British crowd activity were very high. The frequency of crowd action declined after Lexington and Concord, when first the militia and then the army took over. It seemed wrong, however, to end the study at this point, because it might have reinforced the myth

---

[51]E.g., Lynd, Young; Jesse Lemisch, "Jack Tar in the Streets," and "What Made Our Revolution?"; Joel Shufro. "The Impressment of Seamen and the Economic Decline of Boston, 1740 to 1760" (M.A. thesis, Univ. of Chicago, 1968).

[52]John Kern, "The Politics of Violence" Chap. V, A; Walter Wallace, " 'Massaniello of Naples' and the Image of the Anti-Stamp Act Mobs in Boston" (Seminar paper, Northern Illinois Univ., Jan. 1973). Edward Countryman, "Northern Land Rioters," and "The Early American Crowd"; A. F. Young, "Pope's Day, Tar and Feathers, and 'Cornet Joyce, jun.'," forthcoming as *From Ritual to Rebellion.*

that after the expulsion of the British a happy people lived in unity and harmony. Instead, crowd action continued against Tories, against profiteering from the shortages of provisions, and against Whig governmental institutions. Together with town meetings and county conventions, crowd activity culminated in the years before the Constitution of 1780 was declared accepted after the delegates had used rather dubious methods to count the people's votes. After 1780, in my opinion, crowd action and governmental repression of it changed. There still was rioting against limited grievances. These and larger actions, the western uprisings named by leadership-oriented people and historians after "instigators" (Ely's in 1782 and Shays' in 1786), were now considered rebellions against established government and were quelled militarily. Dangerous amounts of such "combustibles" existed in every state, in General Washington's opinion, ready to ignite. This view, of course, takes crowd actions to be licentious antigovernment outbursts that have to be quelled rather than relating crowds to social processes and social change. To see the post-1780 rioting in Massachusetts *merely* as a continuance of the prerevolutionary tradition would so limit the perspective, in my opinion, as to blur the issue. These actions must be dealt with in a national perspective that includes the Whiskey Rebellion and the Fries Rebellion and the host of other riots and rebellions that took place all over the new nation.

But Massachusetts' developments alone also furnish ample subjects (and, it is to be hoped, material) for studies of crowd action in the next decades. By 1781 the *Massachusetts Spy* ran an article about wealth in the Roman Empire, telling its readers that Romans who had gotten rich had to explain how to the public. By 1783 there was an article about a rebellion of British war veterans. They had once been called pillars of the state, but after victory had been obtained, nobody cared about them—certainly not the government. Motto: "Applicable to the present time." On the other hand, some newspaper writers declared not only riots but even the peaceable county conventions, generally approved of during the height of resistance to British rule, as being illegal and in opposition to republican principles of government. Thus, 1780 was not an end. It merely marked the conclusion of some of the developments discussed here but, in fact, gave rise to new reasons for and forms of crowd action under the changed political and institutional circumstances.

THE SOCIETAL FRAMEWORK

The tradition of crowd action developed in a sociopolitical framework that can best be described as combining participatory and hierarchical elements. The latter included some aristocratic aspects, a basic patriarchal orientation and an oligarchic system. The participatory element has often mistakenly been called democratic. While governmental institutions on the provincial level were developed at least in part under the influence of the theory of mixed government, local institutions can best be analyzed by using the concept of community power as a frame of reference.[53] Within it, two schools of interpretation have to be distinguished, the stratifi-

[53]Thomas J. Anton, "Power, Pluralism, and Local Communities," *Adm. Sci. Q.* 7:425–457 (1962–1963); Nelson W.

cation approach and the pluralist approach. A comparative study of five Massachusetts towns[54] and the recent crop of studies on the social structure of New England
towns[55] suggest that the stratification approach has more explanatory validity than
the pluralist approach, though in periods of change of power elites the pluralist
approach may be useful.[56] To consider the colonial period the first of five stages of
urban history, or rather of the multidisciplinary urban studies, as Blake McKelvey
has done,[57] may be misleading and would lend weight to the criticism that the
application of the community power concept to prerevolutionary history is merely
another futile attempt to force social conditions of the past into modern categories.

In the colonial period only a tiny fraction of the population lived in towns of 4000
or more inhabitants. In fact, only seaboard towns lend themselves to interpretation
within the concepts developed by urban studies. It is suggested that the models and
approaches mainly from urban studies developed for later periods of American
history be combined into a theory that has explanatory value for what I want to call
"township history." A New England township not only included the "village" or
"town," where the inhabitants had their homes and barns, but also the land surrounding it. As a whole it was a "corporation."

The meaning of the term "corporation," legally, structurally, and ideologically,
was that each member had an obligation to the whole but was also entitled to a share
of the benefits. The rights of the members were not distributed equally, however.
All the members had the right to the help of the community in case of disaster or
poverty, and all had the right—indeed, were expected—to send their children to
school. But only a restricted number of white male inhabitants could participate, in
different degrees, in the conduct of the political affairs of the town. In practice, a
much smaller number usually exerted the actual power—that is, made important
decisions, guided policies, supervised the morals and labor of the others. These
leaders had only very limited institutional means to enforce their decisions, but they
expected and received deference to their position and their conduct of affairs. They,
in turn, were expected to make their decisions within the framework set not only by
the laws but also by community norms and traditions. The participatory effect of the
annual elections was limited by sociopolitical devices to secure reelection of
decision-making officials as well as to retain broad property holding as the basis of
political decisions. Crowd action occurred when traditions and institutions were not
sufficient to achieve consensus on specific issues.

Recent township studies suggest that the founding generation of each town, and
of its settlement and property-holding patterns, did achieve a high degree of cohesiveness, which began to decline only when new generations came of age and when

---

Polsby, *Community Power and Political Theory* (New Haven, Conn., 1963); Floyd Hunter, *Community Power Structure: A Study of Decision Makers* (Chapel Hill, N.C., 1953); Philip M. Hauser and Leo Schnore, eds., *The Study of Urbanization* (New York, 1965); Thomas R. Dye, "Community Power Studies," *Pol. Sci. Annual* 2:35–70 (1969).
[54]Dirk Hoerder, *Society and Government.*
[55]See Chapter 1, note 7.
[56]For example, when—according to Lockridge—the first generation of settlers loses its dominance over community affairs.
[57]Blake McKelvey, "American Urban History Today," *AHR* 57:919–929 (1951–1952).

distribution of property, offices, settlement clusters, and religious communities changed. This change in socioeconomic conditions brought about a change in political practices. There were often temporary shifts of power from selectmen to the town meeting and new election patterns to ensure broader representation among the top officials. Toward the middle of the eighteenth century, political structures again tended to become more rigid and exclusive.

The socioeconomic changes were not accompanied by ideological changes. The corporate ideal remained powerful. Divisions of towns were undertaken to create new small units in which cohesiveness might again be the guiding principle of social structure and action. Petitions, legislation, and crowd action were used to prevent individuals or groups from leaving the corporate fold or from furthering separate interests. While to most twentieth-century historians the differentiation that took place in eighteenth-century New England seems natural, given population factors and economic development and their own hindsight, it was by no means natural to contemporaries. Many strove mightily to preserve the old ways. Incredible numbers of petitions testify to these efforts, as does much of the legislation passed by the General Court in response to the petitions. Among the revolutionary leaders, Samuel Adams was probably the epitome of those who followed corporate ideals and saw the struggle with Great Britain as a struggle to preserve a way of life.[58]

Crucial to the stemming of the transformation of society was the role of property; and crucial to our understanding of it, given recent scholarly emphasis, is eighteenth-century socioeconomic ideology.[59] Property in corporate societies did not confer absolute rights—nor could it be taken away arbitrarily. It entailed a social function, a social responsibility. This philosophy was expressed at one end of the spectrum by the thinking and practice about poverty. Since poor people unable to support themselves became a charge of the community, infringing on every other tax-paying community member's property, poverty was to be avoided. One way to do so was the warning-out system, which excluded persons who might have become a charge of the community and which, at least in the early decades, was also used to prevent ruinous competition in the economic sphere. If only one carpenter could make a living in a particular town, there was no point in admitting a second, because instead of having two self-supporting carpenters the town would have two poor men to support. But the town also made sure that the sole carpenter could not charge monopoly prices by fixing his rates in the town meeting.

At the upper end of the economic scale, tradition and law provided institutional mechanisms and social restraints that were intended to prevent people from becoming so rich that they could exploit others and thus make more poor people charges of the public. Such legal and moral restraints did not work, of course. The best-known example is the everlasting haggling over fee tables for magistrates. Less known but equally important was the morality governing price setting. The merchant, the farmer, or anyone else in commerce was not to "overreach" himself and, if caught

---

[58]Patterson, *Political Parties*, pp. 32 *passim*, esp. 202–203.

[59]Crawford B. Mcpherson, *The Political Theory of Possessive Individualism: Hobbes to Locke* (Oxford, 1949); Bernard Bailyn, *The Ideological Origins of the American Revolution* (Cambridge, Mass., 1965); Young, "The 'Bailyn' Thesis."

doing so, was to make "restitution" to those who had been cheated.[60] Ideologically there was little or no difference between robbery on the one hand and overcharging for merchandise on the other. In practice, of course, theft was punished, while high and unwarranted prices were reluctantly accepted. Exhortations by magistrates and ministers against greed in business and politics were the rule in the seventeenth and early eighteenth centuries, but even they then began to decline. At the same time, particularly along the coast and along rivers that made transportation easy, more commercial attitudes developed, and a more liberalist notion of property and its use came about. Merchants felt hampered by the corporate concept of property and its restrictions on the individual's free use of his property. And while once the agrarian producers had been the basis of the economic system, the notion slowly grew that commerce was the main means of wealth and was necessary for a flourishing community.

So far, we have been concerned with the economic aspects of ideology. Recent historiography has mainly concentrated on its political and constitutional aspects, thereby disregarding the concept of ideology as a whole. Here we understand ideology as a set of beliefs explaining and guiding man's social, political, and economic life, as dependent on material conditions, but also as influencing them. The relationship between societal conditions and ideology is thus a two-way one. Little needs to be said about the constitutional aspects of ideology, since the concepts have been extensively dealt with, though much work is left to be done to show whether and how Whig and Commonwealthmen concepts filtered down to the lower classes. In analyzing the crowds, we certainly do not find rioters with the mentality of Whig pamphleteers.

The second component of ideology, the tradition of common law and equity, has received much less attention, though rioters wanting not a leveling but more equitable social conditions talked about it. The third component is the Protestant–Puritan tradition, with its notions of just dealing, yet deference to the earthly successful, and humility in the powerful. Covetousness, ambition, pride, and ostentation were sins, as was licentiousness. With increasing social and economic differentiation, the possibilities for sinning certainly increased more for the wealthy than for the lower sort, whose "licentiousness," if it existed at all, did not get them anywhere.

Thus, much work remains to be done on the interrelationship of social conditions and ideology. Many of the questions raised and statements made in the preceding brief discussion are barely touched upon in the subsequent chapters of this work. I freely admit that, while doing research for this study, for a long time I considered a law entitled "An act to prevent damage being done unto Billingsgate in the town of Eastham, by cattle and horse-kind, and sheep feeding on the beach and islands adjoining thereto" as having no bearing on the questions I was asking. It then turned out that the process leading to such an act involved innumerable discussions in town, often recorded in petitions to the General Court, between different economic

---

[60]Josiah H. Benton, *Warning Out in New England, 1656–1817* (Boston, 1911). No comparable works on overcharging exist; it is still best to go back to contempoary pamphlets. But see Bernard Bailyn, "The *Apologia* of Robert Keayne," *WMQ* 3.7:568–587 (1950); Edgar A. J. Johnson, "Economic Ideas of John Winthrop," *NEQ* 3:235–250 (1930), and *American Economic Thought in the Seventeenth Century* (London, 1932).

interests, each trying to further its economic advance or to protect its economic standing without hurting other groups. If these negotiations and resulting petitions had no result, rioting was justified. In other words, what is needed are studies similar to Pauline Maier's but dealing with the township level of societal, not just political, ideology and using as sources not pamphlets—except those about the currency and other economic controversies—but petitions, legal papers, and sermons dealing with "just" economic relations and their translation into political action. Only when this has been done will we be able to speak about an ideological interpretation of the colonial period and the Revolution.

The basic participatory institution in the political system of colonial Massachusetts was the town meeting. Enfranchised voters were adult white males meeting the property qualification—that is, a minimum ratable estate of £20 (£40 for the election of representatives). These "freeholders" and/or "inhabitants" were the basic elements of the political system.[61] The legal definitions, however, were merely the formal aspects of the process of admission to town meetings. Application of the laws varied from town to town and from year to year, as did money values, valuation of property, and so on.

During the conflicts with Great Britain, special meetings had to be called to broaden support. In Marlborough white males under 21 years of age met separately. In Boston the so-called Body-meetings extended the voting right to those white adult males not qualified by law. In the decade after 1765, the importance of town meetings greatly increased because the inhabitants began to vote on provincial affairs and on the relations with Great Britain. The frequent proroguing of the General Court also resulted in a shift toward greater importance of these local meetings.

Among the voters three groups may be distinguished: those qualified according to current interpretation of the law, those who did not meet these requirements, and a third group in between these two who customarily could attend because they were known and established inhabitants but whose legal qualifications were doubtful. The admission to town meetings was thus usually handled pragmatically rather than legalistically to prevent cleavages in the community according to property lines or other divisions. Conservative officials and wealthy inhabitants repeatedly complained that town meetings were mainly attended by the "lowest Order," but these were in fact excluded from participation by laws and usage. Additionally, the right to vote, to participate, cannot be equated with actual opportunities. Meetings were held on weekdays, and journeymen laborers, even if owning sufficient property, would have to get permission from their masters to attend. Shopkeepers and others, dependent on their daily earnings, could probably not afford to lose a day's business either. That this was a serious problem is shown by the recommendation of a town meeting in Boston concerning the Constitution of 1780. Attendance was so meager that it was suggested that the meeting adjourn and reconvene at a time when all

---

[61]J. R. Pole, *Political Representation in England and the Origins of the American Republic* (London, 1966), pp. 47ff.; John F. Sly, *Town Government in Massachusetts (1620–1930)* (Cambridge, Mass., 1930). Particularly illuminating to historians are documents about contested elections.

shops and workshops would be closed. In consequence, attendance jumped more than fourfold and was 78 percent higher than the average attendance from 1760 to 1780.

The meetings were called, as the law demanded, by the selectmen upon their own motion or upon a petition by at least 10 inhabitants. In the debates every qualified person had a right to speak and to vote. A moderator, usually a wealthy and influential member of the community, directed the business. The meetings afforded great opportunities for politicking. Admittance of latecomers could be manipulated, and debtors and laborers could be taken as a "crew" of voters by their creditors or employers, as John Adams related.

At the two meetings for election of officials, the March meeting for town officers and the May meeting for representatives, the candidates had to obtain at least 50 percent of the votes cast. Voting was by show of hands, open ballot, or diverse other contrivances, such as colored balls. Candidates had to have some popularity or great influence. Being on good terms with local tavern keepers was said to be helpful.

Each town's inhabitants had to fill about two dozen different offices, for which, in the seventies, Boston needed more than 150 men annually. These officials may be classified into four groups according to their influence and status. The first group held the most influential offices; they were the policy-making officials (selectmen and so forth). Group 2 included two sorts of officials, those who followed Group 1 in influence (surveyors of highways, town clerk) and those with less influence but high social prestige (wardens and fire wardens). The main task of the officials in Group 3 was to put into effect specific laws, bylaws, and orders of officials and to supervise certain trades and products. These functions can be classified as auxiliary. Group 4 comprised minor town officials.[62]

A comparison of office holding over a 20-year period (1760–1780) in five Massachusetts towns of different sizes, ages, and socioeconomic structures rendered the following picture. Formally, the laws required no qualifications for office holding except for jurors and representatives. But an analysis of the magistrates' properties shows that with increasing wealth the importance and numbers of offices grew. This increase in wealth and offices was dependent on the size of the town. The smaller the town, the more equal the distribution of wealth was among all families.[63] In agricultural communities nearly everybody owned land, livestock, and a dwelling place. In the mercantile coastal towns, with their manufacturing enterprises, the economic differences were larger because the division of labor was developed further and because some inhabitants used capital and the labor of other people to make a profit. Others, the small property holders and the propertyless, whether shopkeepers, artisans, or laborers, lived on limited incomes and wages. They just sold their labor, which required no investment but rendered no large profits. This economic organization determined the principal traits of the social structure: They

---

[62]The following outline is based on Hoerder, *Society and Government*. A "warden" was an official surveying certain things, e.g. fire-engines, in a ward, that is an administrative unit within a town, or if the town was sufficiently small in the whole town.

[63]"Wealth," as determined from property valuation and tax lists, excluded household necessities and, to a certain degree, workers' tools.

were (1) a fact of the socioeconomic organization of a community (interdependence) and (2) a state of mind of the inhabitants (dependence). A systematic explanation of the political system must center on the electorate, the system of offices, and the officials.

In the minds of the electorate, the smaller the town, the closer the inhabitants were to economic equality and the stronger was their confidence in officials—and the more suspicious they were of power elites. From this it follows that (a) the periods of continuous service by the same man in the same office were shorter[64] and that (b) the average total time in various offices was also shorter. (c) The yearly elections did not lead to a regular high turnover of officials in larger towns. In fact, wholesale reelection was frequent. Boston officials of Groups 1 and 2 were usually reelected until they asked to be excused from serving. Elections were merely a means of getting unpopular officials out of office in special cases, but even this effect was curbed by the customary deference toward men of the "better sort." (d) The only data pointing to strong apprehensions about the partiality of wealthy officials in the larger seaboard towns appear in the case of the assessors, who rated the townsmen's property for taxation. The inhabitants elected men from the middle segment of the economic scale. Other officials of similar influence were in general considerably more wealthy.

Concerning the system of offices, the larger the town, the more offices there were and the more important were the functions of the higher officials. (a) The large amount of business to be handled led to growing specialization and an increase in the number of officials. (b) New problems were created by the size and structure of the town and necessitated additional offices. Separate overseers of the poor were elected not because the selectmen had no time to deal with this problem but because the town's social structure made poverty possible. (c) To facilitate the continuous functioning of the administration, devices were developed to ensure continuity. (d) The growing size of the "executive" necessitated coordination by the selectmen. (e) Consequently, the inhabitants assembled in the town meeting no longer dealt directly with the particular officials but with the coordinators. (f) Thus, the coordinators ranked above the others, who in turn developed notions of rank. Such attitudes led to the manipulation of office holding, to the barring of qualified men from higher offices, and to the promotion of those who had the "necessary" standing.

The first generalization about the attitudes of officials is that the smaller the town, the less developed were notions of rank. The aspect of duty to the community/electorate prevailed over the notion of power and prestige for the individual officeholder. Accordingly (a) officials in policy-making offices also held less influential offices and (b) no offices were regarded as especially "honorable." Second, the occupational differentiation in larger towns led to a differentiation in patterns of thinking and of concepts about community structures according to social position. The most wealthy merchants and most knowledgeable lawyers held the most

---

[64]This rule does not apply to new settlements. Cf. Lockridge and Kreider, "Evolution of Massachusetts Town Government."

important offices. Small-scale traders and artisans held small offices. They were never elected to higher ones. Third, the officials themselves developed patterns for assuring their reelection by diminishing their dependence on the general electorate (family ties, connections, dependents, caucuses; Hancock's *panem* and sometimes even *circenses*).

The most important device to ensure continuity as well as power was plural office holding. A comparison of towns of different sizes shows that office holding was most diversified in the smallest town. The stability of office holding grew with the importance of the office. From 1760 to 1780, approximately 3500 offices in Boston were held by about 750 men. Of the total number of offices, nearly one-third were held by one-sixth of the officials, averaging slightly more than nine years of office each. These were men belonging to Group 1. The average time of service declined to three and a half years for Group 2, with one-sixth of the offices. The average duration of serving in one specific office (disregarding plural office holding) was for all towns highest in Group 1, lowest in Group 4. It grew according to the size of the town. When membership on committees and juries is considered, the same social stratification is found. The higher the rank of office, the larger the number of committees the officeholder sat on and the more important the committees. The minor officials, being the least wealthy, held the fewest seats. Even jury members were chosen according to their status in the community.

After 1776 the rule that the more important the man, the more important the jury, committee, or office he was elected to, still applied. But the Revolution provided an opportunity for some men who had not belonged to the power elite to get into major offices.

Aside from official institutions, political power was wielded by more or less formally organized groups of inhabitants. The most important unofficial institution that exerted strong influence on politics in Boston was the caucus system, supplemented by clubs of Bostonian and provincial politicians. Evidence of similar organizations in other towns is scarce. During the seventies Whigs and Tories met in formal groups or at informal gatherings to consolidate their interests in the town meeting.

The origins of the Boston caucus organization are obscure, but by the middle of the eighteenth century several distinct bodies existed and acted as powerful political instruments. Procedures resembled those of the town meeting: A clerk and a moderator were chosen, and then political measures of consequence were discussed and candidates for important offices named. In the town meeting the members voted en bloc and distributed voting slips prepared in advance to nonaligned voters.[65]

The Northend Caucus consisted of small merchants and independent artisans, often just above the minimum property requirement for voting. Many of them held no town office but were important figures in the unofficial power structure of the town. The caucuses did not extend the franchise to men with little or no property. Rather, the caucuses were organizations to counterbalance the influence of the

[65]G. B. Warden, "The Caucus and Democracy in Colonial Boston," *NEQ* 43:19–45 (1970), revised in Alan Day and Katherine Day, "Another Look at the Boston 'Caucus,'" *J. Am. Studies (GB)* 5:19–45 (1971).

merchants at the top of the economic scale. Their purpose was to prevent any open contest and dissension in the town meeting, a factor necessary to protect the influential magistrates and caucus candidates from criticism and opponents and to protect corporate unity in a town of growing differentiation accompanied by a particularization of interests. The middling interest, close to mechanics and laborers, derived some influence from the caucus voting system and could exert influence downward or relay grievances upward.

In other port towns, artisans, sailors, and laborers were the target of numerous pamphlets. In New York and Philadelphia, Jack Bowlings and Tom Hatchways from the ship *Defiance* called upon their colleagues to vote for certain candidates. "Mr. Axe," "Mr. Hammer," and the "Leatheraprons" agreed. In Boston hardly any pamphlets or election handbills were published from 1760 to 1780.

Boston laborers and sailors never organized formally. The traders occasionally acted as a group, but they did not institutionalize their cooperation. The middling interest had been submerged by the caucuses. Only some merchant seamen still met regularly. The only active and effective organization of an economic group was the Merchants' Club, and it lost some of its political influence during the seventies, when it split into Whig and Tory factions.

Other political clubs in Boston were the Monday Night Club, where town and province officials of the higher echelons met to exchange information and to concert policies. The Long Room Club, of which James Otis, Samuel Adams, and probably John Hancock were members, met in the building of the printers of the *Boston Gazette*. Many of its members came from the circle of the merchant–captains. Among other political clubs were the Loyal Nine, whose members organized the Stamp Act riots.

Many more institutions, militia companies, fire clubs, engine companies, masonic lodges, and congregational (or other) parishes influenced the political scene, without, however, achieving a dominant importance. In the militia the lower-ranking officers were elected by the men, the more important ones appointed by the governor. The masonic lodges reflected the social system: different lodges for different economic strata. The democratic component of such groups went no further than election of the chairman by all members. Once elected, the officers were not content with respect for their abilities but demanded deference. Turnover among them was low, and many of them had connections with the official town hierarchy or were members of it.

In provincial government, the representatives for the legislature, the General Court, were elected annually. Their patterns of office holding were similar to those of high-ranking town officials, and they came from the same socioeconomic level. The representatives served for many years and frequently held local offices at the same time. In towns more than a few miles away from Boston, only those inhabitants were eligible who could afford to be absent from their farms or businesses for several months each year.

Voting patterns in the election of representatives show a remarkable stability. In Boston newly elected representatives received from 55 to 75 percent of the total votes cast, while reelected representatives normally received 95 to 100 percent. In the first five decades of the century, the numbers of reelection votes hardly ever reached similar heights. The stability of the pattern grew until 1776. In the subsequent years, turnover was higher, percentages of votes cast for incumbents somewhat lower. Once representatives were elected, voters could still influence them by instructions. Analysis shows that constitutents grew more conscious of this right after 1774, when tensions between voters and magistrates grew. "It is our inalienable right to tell you our sentiments," the inhabitants of Barre, Berkshire County told their representative in 1783. "We expect you will hold yourself bound at all times to attend to and observe them."[66]

All towns received a printed copy of the *House Journals,* but with the exception of the rare roll-call votes there was no indication of how a representative had voted. Accordingly, there was little possibility of checking faithfulness to the town's instructions, and the representatives sometimes intentionally disregarded them. Furthermore, though passed by a town-meeting vote, the instructions were drawn up by a committee from the "better sort." There was widespread apprehension that the representatives might prefer their own interest to that of their constituents. They indeed raised their own renumeration, restricted public attendance at their deliberations, and developed an extraordinary skill in distributing lucrative offices among themselves.

The reelection of representatives, and especially of councillors, was so common that the British governors distributed offices to representatives and councillors to make them dependent. Once a representative had accepted such an office, any vote against the governor's politics or politicking was considered base ingratitude. That the governor's or the empire's interests might conflict with those of a representative's local constituents was not yet part of political thought.[67]

In the General Court a hierarchy developed among its members, as Robert M. Zemsky has demonstrated.[68] The preparatory work necessary for the laws, resolutions, and votes of the House of Representatives was done in committees. One-eighth of the members accumulated 51 percent of the committee assignments, and another eighth held a further 25 percent, so that three-quarters of the members had to share the remaining places (24 percent). Using these figures, Zemsky divided the representatives into leaders, subleaders, and backbenchers. To achieve stability and continuity, requirements for effective decision and policy making, a group of experts was necessary. This did not preclude popular participation if the representatives could be controlled. The questions are therefore whether Massachusetts representatives were promoted to influential positions because of organizational skills,

---

[66]Waste sheets to tally votes, Misc. Unbound Papers, BCH, and newspaper reports on total votes; Barre Town Records, 26 March 1783, quoted in Lee Nathaniel Newcomer, *The Embattled Farmers: A Massachusetts Countryside in the American Revolution* (New York, 1953), p. 96; cf. Franklin P. Rice, ed., "Worcester Town Records," *Worcester Soc. Antiq. Coll.,* vol. 2 and later (1881 and later), 4:264.

[67]For patronage politics, cf. John J. Waters and John A. Schutz, "Patterns of Massachusetts Colonial Politics: The Writs of Assistance and the Rivalry between the Otis and Hutchinson Families," *WMQ* 3.24:543–567 (1967).

[68]The following summary is based on R. M. Zemsky's excellent essay "Power, Influence, and Status: Leadership Patterns in the Massachusetts Assembly, 1740–1755," *WMQ* 3.26:502–520 (1969).

expertise, experience, or other abilities and whether all sectors of the population had equal access to these positions provided they had sufficient ability. The answer to both questions is negative. Leadership positions were obtained by "inherited social prestige, judicial office, and a connection with the province's merchant community." Members from the eastern seaports, the Connecticut Valley "River Gods," Harvard-educated men, and sons of prestigious families formed the most influential group of representatives. The aristocratic aspect of this setup was, however, somewhat counterbalanced, since the "upper-class leadership" was neither a monolithic interest group nor an absolute reference group for the backbenchers. But because of their family connections and educational background, these men were able to formulate political alternatives and to manage the legislative processes. Zemsky concludes "that the House leader enjoyed personal power and influence because he alone possessed sufficient opportunity and expertise to translate general goals into specific policy choices. While he could not persuade the backbencher to abandon prior policy commitments, the leader could subtly bend such commitments to his own interests."[69] The interests were those of "Families of Distinction, Education and Substance."[70]

Economic opportunities decreased toward the middle of the eighteenth century. Unsettled lands had become scarce, and westward expansion was impossible because New Yorkers could not be driven off their lands as Indians were. As a result, even those who had the capital to move to a western county and to start a farm were faced with rising land prices and the decreasing quality of the land obtainable. Still, the inhabitants of many agrarian towns accepted their "honest poverty" (Lenox, Berkshire County)[71] because they thought it to be a basis for advancement and a limited degree of personal independence, both of which were reason enough to participate in politics.

In longer-settled regions, especially where subsistence farming had given way to the cultivation of marketable crops, large sections of the community enjoyed economic security. But these were only the areas close to the populous coastal towns. Many of them had been settled for several decades, and the distribution of property had become increasingly unequal. The quality of a man's land and its nearness to the center of a settlement, the size of his family, and the length of time his family had lived in a particular township influenced his economic standing. The financial resources to employ others, a renumerative ("lucrative" was the contemporary designation) office, trade, and connections further enhanced the accumulation of property.

In larger towns, especially in the mercantile centers along the seaboard, a different kind of property further increased the gap between the wealthy and those

---

[69]*Ibid.*, p. 519.

[70]Samuel Fisk, *The Character of the Candidate for Civil Government* (Boston, 1731), p. 40, quoted in Zemsky, "Power, Influence and Status," p. 520.

[71]Handlin and Handlin, eds., *Popular Sources*, p. 254. On poverty and land shortage, see, e.g., the petitions in consequence of the tax law of 1777–1778 and the memorials concerning the incorporation of the town of Hancock; A. C. Goodell *et al.*, eds., *Acts and Resolves, Public and Private, of the Province of the Massachusetts Bay*, 21 vols. (Boston, 1869–1922), 5:656ff., 831ff.

living at the subsistence level. The great merchants had large investments in stocks and ships. Their capital gave them considerable influence over small shopkeepers and artisans. These were extremely dependent on their daily business or work; any recession jeopardized their living standard and their economic position. This became abundantly clear during the nonimportation periods and during the closing of the port of Boston in 1774, when artisans faced the constant threat of poverty. Even under normal conditions the number of poor people in Boston had increased from 14 percent of the total tax-paying population in 1689 to 29 percent in 1771.[72]

The large difference in property holding had important consequences for economic opportunities. In a suit about a land claim, the claimant argued that, "The said Proprietors being Rich Numerous & having large connections," the suit should be moved to a different county. In the home county any jury would be partial, which would have a "direct Tendency to Enable the longest Purse and not the Justest cause to prevail."[73]

Those groups operating with capital were more flexible. They could speculate in land, and they received interest and profit from their investments. The shopkeepers, frequently dependent on credits, and the artisans, laborers, and sailors, dependent on regular employment, had only few opportunities. This lack of economic opportunities created more discontent than its cause, the actual amount of wealth of the richer members of the community. It was agreed that everybody had a right to property as a basis for his personal liberty and therefore lived in a free society. The implicit assumption was that a large part of a community held fairly equal shares of property. This concept, held but hardly defended by the middling interest, had been abandoned by the wealthy because of their "ambition" and "lust for power."[74]

The social system has been praised for its egalitarian aspects. However, the authors of such remarks were either European visitors used to the much greater differences in their own societies or members of the colonial upper classes (at the beginning of the conflict with Great Britain, mainly Tories, later mainly Whigs). Such authors were contradicted by a large section of lower-income groups and wage earners who expressed their thoughts about equal rights, equal opportunities, and equal status eloquently and sometimes vociferously in many of the towns' returns on the constitution.

The town meeting was the most democratic component of the contemporary political system, but of the whole of colonial society (including Negro slaves), the free, white, male adults constituted less than 25 percent. Of these, 45 to 98 percent,

[72]Henretta, "Economic Development," p. 85; Benjamin W. Labaree, "Newburyport, Massachusetts, during the American Revolution, 1764–1790" (Ph.D. diss., Harvard Univ., 1957). The confiscation of the property of exiled Loyalists did not broaden the distribution of property; see R. D. Brown, "Loyalists' Estates."

[73]Cf. contemporary sermons and pamphlets on economic problems. Memorial of Nathaniel Donnell, 6 June 1764, MA 6:334.

[74]*BTR* 16:229; "The Answer of the Auctioneers," *Acts and Resolves*, 5:360–362; *To the Freeholders of the Town of Boston* (Boston, 1760), p. 3; Vincent Centinel [pseud.], *Massachusetts in Agony* (Boston, 1750); Cornelius Agrippa [pseud.], *Appendix to Massachusetts in Agony* (Boston, 1751). Samuel Adams once realized the basic importance of property and the concurrent dangers; *The Writings of Samuel Adams*, ed. Harry A. Cushing, 4 vols. (New York, 1904–1908), 3:83–84.

depending on the economic structure of the town, were enfranchised by the laws.[75] Futhermore, the percentage of persons disenfranchised because of their poverty, up to 55 percent of the white male adults in the coastal towns, was highest where the settlement was densest. Only in western counties, where a mere fraction of the population lived, were more than 85 percent of the white male adults legally enfranchised.

Opposed to the democratic institutional pattern were hierarchical ones— patriarchal, aristocratic, oligarchic. Elements of these were evident in eighteenth-century Massachusetts society. Its basic unit, the family, revolved around the paterfamilias.[76] In the larger social units—the parishes, the wards, and the townships— the patriarchal system was represented by the ministers, the overseers, and the teachers. These, in turn, reinforced the patriarchal structure of the family. The democratic form—election of the overseers in the town meeting, selection of the ministers by the parishes, and selection of the teachers by a committee of the town—was offset by the deference due to these people.[77] The possibility that they formed or belonged to a separate class or interest group within the social body remained subconscious among the electorate–subjects. Only rarely did they voice the idea.

Poverty was a visible sign that an individual did not belong to the elect. In the contemporary view, poor people were responsible for their lot and should not presume to be better than they were; to the successful, they were convenient examples of the results of idleness, profaneness, and lewdness. There was no place in contemporary thought for the concept that the ''natural'' place and condition of the poor were merely the result of societal and environmental forces.

It may be argued that the education given to the children of the poor contradicts this assessment. However, the educational aspect was embedded in a system designed to inculcate social conformity. The children of the poor were ''bound out'' to masters coming from better-situated sections of the community. For their work the indentures granted the children board and education. They learned deference to their master and to his family. They were taught to look up to their master's social position and to believe that by hard labor they could achieve a similar or at least a modestly secure position. Thus, they were integrated into the system, and their labor could be used by their social and economic superiors. The possibilities for an accumulation of social discontent were reduced if not eliminated.

The element of supervision is also apparent in the functioning of many other officials. Tithingmen, wardens, and constables performed such duties, as did the jurors and especially the selectmen. These officials were elected annually in the

---

[75]R. E. Brown, *Middle-Class Democracy;* lower estimates are given in Edward A. McKinley, *The Suffrage Franchise in the Thirteen English Colonies in America* (Philadelphia, 1903), pp. 355ff., and in Chilton Williamson, *American Suffrage from Property to Democracy* (Princeton, N.J., 1960), pp. 33–36.

[76]John Demos, ''Notes on Life in Plymouth Colony,'' *WMQ* 3.22:264–286 (1965); Philip J. Greven, Jr., ''Family Structure in Seventeenth-Century Andover, Massachusetts,'' *WMQ,* 3.23:234–256 (1966).

[77]The concept of deference, first developed by the English political thinker Walter Bagehot, has been applied to colonial society by J. R. Pole, ''Historians and the Problem of Early American Democracy,'' *AHR* 67:645–646 (1962). Less useful is John B. Kirby, ''Early American Politics—The Search for Ideology: An Historiographical Analysis and Critique of the Concept of 'Deference,' '' *J. Politics* 32:808–838 (1970).

town meeting. But upon a closer look, this again proves to be a democratic formalism: Power was in fact concentrated in the hands of a few men who were regularly reelected and who expected to be reelected. Access to the higher offices, by law open to all, was in social reality limited to the more wealthy members of the community; the Massachusetts townships were in fact ruled by an oligarchy, which in itself was hierarchically organized too.

Several qualifications are necessary, however, to make this statement more precise. The incidence of men with grammar-school or college education among the leadership is much higher than among the population in general. Thus, one might be led to speak of a meritocracy. Such an argument, however, begs the fundamental issue that these men, again coming from the financially better-off sections of society, had distinct (though not express) interests of their own. The leisure that—as contemporary upper-class members argued—was necessary to improve one's capabilities and knowledge to the level where one was able to manage the affairs of the community or the state was based on the work of others, who precisely because of their work had no time for education.

A second argument against the term "oligarchy" is that offices became partially hereditary and that the term "aristocracy" should therefore be substituted. Several propositions support this point of view. In the eighteenth century the view that offices were the property of the officeholder was still a common notion. In newly founded towns the offices were often held for decades by one family, and in the west of Massachusetts especially, the judicial offices were concentrated to a high degree in a few leading families. In a sense some offices became semihereditary. Wealth, education, and power were centralized in some families for long periods of time.[78] But competition among the influential families and by newcomers, together with social mores, which did not allow for the existence of "nobles" (that is, an "unnatural aristocracy"), prevented the emergence of a class of hereditary magistrates. The designation of the system as oligarchic is therefore more appropriate.

While the importance of such signs of material and immaterial prestige is difficult for historians to assess, they had sufficient meaning for contemporaries to list Harvard and Yale students according to the rank of their families and to make seating arrangements in the meeting house depend on the social rank of the parish members. The Superior Court of Judicature handed down a decision in 1767 stating that a warrant against "a Gentleman" omitting this designation was not valid. Differences, especially economic ones, were expected to continue. Even in a time when the economic opportunities were greater than after the middle of the eighteenth century, trade and commerce were considered in Boston—sometimes called the cradle of liberty—as a means "for the advancing and enobling of the Rich [and] for the support of the Poor." The author of this maxim called himself Amicus Reipublicae.[79]

---

[78]Cf. the "titles" King Hancock and "River Gods." John Adams and the authors of the "Essex Result" (Handlin and Handlin, eds., *Popular Sources*, p. 335) used the term "natural aristocracy." On hereditary features, see John Adams, *Defence of the Constitution of the Government of the United States,* 3 vols. (Philadelphia, 1797), 1:110–111. Exiled Loyalists expected compensation not only for their property but also for the loss of offices.

[79]Samuel M. Quincy, ed., *Reports of Cases Argued and Adjudged in the Superior Court of Judicature of . . . Massachu-*

To sum up, we will return to the concept of corporation.[80] Settlements, districts, or plantations were incorporated into townships by act of the legislature. The corporations were closed societies; newcomers had to be admitted to membership by the selectmen. The latter could and did refuse residence to strangers who might become a charge on the town or who endangered the economic advance and social position of the established members. The corporation as a whole had rights—that is, representation in the provincial legislature, the making of bylaws for its own affairs, and the election of its own officers—and it had duties—for example, the payment of taxes for the support of local and provincial government, the local school, and the local minister. When differences arose within a corporation or between different townships, the provincial legislature could be called upon to act as arbiter. This was an important device for maintaining or reestablishing unity in the corporate structure of the towns.

The internal structure of the corporation was rigid: Each member had duties and was responsible for the well-being of the whole corporation. The members also had rights, but the rights were not equal. Only a restricted number of them could participate, in different degrees, in the conduct of the political affairs of the town. Conventionally, a much smaller number exerted the actual power, made the decisions, and supervised the morals and labor of their neighbors—in short, led the others.

These leaders had few institutional means to enforce their decisions, but those who were led had only rudimentary concepts of a political implementation of the theory of equality (at least according to what historians know about them). The maintenance of the corporate structure of the towns necessitated compromises and intense discussion (or politicking) so that most votes could be unanimous or at least carried by large majorities. A small majority, scoffed at by opponents as "a trifling majority," was frequently not accepted as binding by the minority. Divisions within the community were dangerous to its functioning. In the words of the legislators, such partisan politics "may tend to the utter subversion of peace and good order."[81]

The members of a corporation were united by a common interest: the economic

setts Bay, 1761–1772, by Josiah Quincy, Junior (Boston, 1865), pp. 237–238; Lovell to Boston Selectmen, *CSMP* 6:74; Adams to Gerry, 18 June 1775, in James T. Austin, *The Life of Elbridge Gerry with Contemporary Letters, to the Close of the American Revolution,* 2 vols. (Boston, 1828, 1829), 1:89; Amicus Reipublicae, *Trade and Commerce Inculcated* [(Boston), 1731], p. 3; Robert J. Dinkin, "Seating the Meeting House in Early Massachusetts," *NEQ* 43:450–464 (1970); Jules Zanger, "Crime and Punishment in Early Massachusetts," *WMQ* 3.22:471–477 (1965); Samuel E. Morison, "Precedence at Harvard College in the Seventeenth Century," *AASP* 42:371–431 (1932).

[80]William Blackstone, *Commentaries on the Laws of England,* 4 vols. (Philadelphia, 1771), 1:467ff., for legal definitions. The concept of corporate structure has been applied to Massachusetts townships by Michael W. Zuckerman in "Social Context of Democracy," and in *Peaceable Kingdoms.* Zuckerman correctly maintains that no pluralism ever became legitimate in Massachusetts towns before the Revolution. But this does not mean that no differences, separate interests, or contentions existed. Zuckerman contradicts himself when he obscurely describes the corporate structure as "a democracy despite itself, a democracy without democrats" but continues that the (presumably) wide franchise "was premised on stringently controlled access to eligibility" and that "voting was not designed to contribute to a decision among meaningful alternatives" ("Social Context," pp. 527, 535, 539). Cf. David G. Allen, "The Zuckerman Thesis and the Process of Legal Rationalization in Provincial Massachusetts," *WMQ* 3.29:442–468 (1972).

[81]Peter Force, ed., *American Archives: Consisting of a Collection of Authentick Records, State Papers, Debates and Letters,* 9 vols. (Washington, D.C., 1837–1853), 4.2:1055.

advancement of each family. This common goal was to be attained, however, not by common exertions but by the work of each individual (family) for himself—by the accumulation of private property. A nearly exclusively agrarian society with free or cheap land for all could not anticipate the fundamental antagonism between the system of social organization and the basic economic principle. This antagonism determined a priori the answer to the question of whether private interests or public interest should be the guideline for the conduct of the members of the corporation. The former (a plurality) were acceptable only if they coincided with the latter (one common interest). When an individual seemed to act counter to the public interest, his action was explained not by his social and economic position but by individual lack of virtue and by innate shortcomings of human beings. As a result, the principal differences between private property and common social goals continued to exist throughout colonial history and in the new Constitution.

As the corporations grew, their structure was influenced by a number of factors. Economic and consequently social diversification labeled people as proprietors, settlers, or squatters; as farmers or merchants; as artisans, mechanics, sailors, or laborers. With religious contention came the division of communities into different parishes and wards. Geographical factors, the settlement of outlying sections of the township, poor lands (difficult to till, yielding poor crops), and regions without easy access to the local market, added to these changes. Stratification increased, differences came out into the open, and consensus or an acceptance of the officials' or the majority's rulings could no longer always be achieved. Supervision of all by all and especially by the officials became more difficult or even impossible.

As a result, the corporation became more open. Proprietors were no longer set apart from the settlers, and the admission of strangers was more difficult to control. Religious controversies among the Puritans increased tolerance and broke up homogeneous communities.[82] By the middle of the eighteenth century, however, this trend toward a more open society was offset by increasing rigidity in the social stratification and by the fact that no more land was available for settlement. Thus, economic opportunities became more limited, and the gap widened between expectations, societally encouraged goals, and actual opportunities for achievement.

The corporate aspects of the community seem to have been the most important ones. But as they were often based on tradition or convention, they are sometimes

---

[82]On the limitations of homogeneity in early Massachusetts towns, see Darrett B. Rutman, "The Mirror of Puritan Authority," in *Selected Essays: Law and Authority in Colonial America*, ed. George A. Billias (Barre, Mass., 1965), pp. 146–167. Rutman states that the people in Massachusetts and probably in other colonies "were not acting within the concept of authority and cohesive, ordered society which modern historians have so carefully delineated and pronounced to be characteristic of Puritanism" (p. 160). He accuses New England's intellectuals, the "better sort," of clinging to an outdated ideal of social organization, in the preservation of which they had a personal interest. Clifford K. Shipton's essay "The Locus of Authority in Colonial Massachusetts," in the same volume, pp. 136–148, is an example of the kind of historiography that Rutman criticizes. Shipton concludes, "Massachusetts in her first century and a half was an ideal proving ground for the principles on which our democratic way of life rests. . . . The critical moment of the American Revolution came in the first decade of settlement, when the individual settlers took into their own hands and managed through democratic town and church machinery, all of the matters of property, civil government, and religion which could be handled at that level" (pp. 147–148).

difficult to define.[83] Here we shall deal with the question of what happened when consensus within or among corporations could not be achieved, when tensions and rifts in the community could not be solved by debates and votes, when they could not be blamed on scapegoats. In such cases, society had a specific remedy: direct action, or riots. These became a decisive instrument against what was felt to be British imposition and oppression. Because the riots implemented the corporate concept in the colonial period, they were a means of translating ideological controversies with Great Britain into political, economic, and social action. The rioters transposed the contentions from the level of the abstract theory, from the realm of the wealthy, leisured, and educated, to practical actions. In this process their interests became part of the action and began to be felt and to be articulated. As riots were patterned by tradition and by the newly propagated concepts of rights and resistance, by way of feedback they shaped contemporary political theory.

The main integrative factor, the deferential social pattern, was by definition tradition-oriented and thus an obstacle to political renewal. The Whig leadership was successful in convincing an active part of the people that British policies (or politics) hurt the interests and liberties of the colonial population in general. This development was possible because of the legal and political role of ''the people'' as freeholders. It was deflected to internal problems because ''the people'' were not a homogeneous whole but a conglomerate of diverse interest groups. Probably the ''Tories'' came mainly from the passive, politically disinterested part of the population.

---

[83]The diversification and growth of Massachusetts society diminished the relative homogeneity but at the same time increased its rigidity. It may be hypothesized that this development was a subconscious reason for the war against Great Britain. Resistance to an external enemy is always accompanied by increased internal conformity and cohesion. Additionally, internal problems could be projected onto or traced back to an outside power and its representatives on the spot.

PART I

Colonial Traditions
and New Imperial Policy

"Vox populi est vox dei," the voice of the people is the voice of God, was a Boston slogan used during the crowd action against the Stamp Act in 1765. This bold assertion, however, did not always receive unqualified support. Especially those who considered themselves above the people had reservations. A royal governor of Massachusetts once explained that rioters act "constitutionally" under certain conditions, but at another time he damned them as a "hellish crew." The colonial "cradle of liberty," the Boston town meeting, voted its "utter detestation" of one riot and celebrated another. James Otis opposed "private" riots; other Bostonians participated in them and considered them to be in the public interest. It seems, then, that the plain slogan simplified a rather complex state of affairs. The first part of this study traces the origins and traditions of the "voice of the people," mainly as expressed in direct action, and assesses its place in eighteenth-century Massachusetts society.

Crowd actions will not be treated as isolated outbursts or spasmodic reactions that the adherents of "order" could not control. I will show that riots were at one end of a continuum of social protests that began at the other extreme with discontent and criticism. Before direct action was considered justifiable, other channels of redress had to have been tried, such as town meetings, parish meetings, petitions, and judicial action. The one exception was a situation in which immediate action was necessary to prevent irremediable changes of circumstances.

Once the traditions have been outlined, I will describe and analyze their adaptation to the imperial context during the exigencies of the Stamp Act period. Confident about their hold over the crowd, the opposition leadership in Boston, the merchants and politicians alike, decided to use symbolic crowd action to intimidate the local stamp distributors, and they did so with specific expectations about its usefulness and its limits. I will argue that despite these assumptions there were already signs of social conflict as a motivating force behind some of the rioters' actions, even on the first day of the demonstrations in Boston. This may sound like a hypothesis coming straight from the much-maligned progressive school of historians. But putting a label on an argument does not affect its validity. To me, at least, contemporary documents besides those dealing with the stamp tax issue point to internal conflicts.

On the day of the first crowd action against the Stamp Act, 14 August 1765, and in the following two weeks, a kind of *rudimentary* feeling of class began to surface. (It may have surfaced earlier, but in these days it became particularly visible for historians.) It reached a height of expression in the famous crowd action against Lieutenant Governor Hutchinson on the night of 26 August 1765 and was ruthlessly repressed afterward, never to reach similar heights again during the period under consideration here.

While armed units of "gentlemen volunteers" patrolled Boston to reestablish what, from their point of view, was order, the resistance to the Stamp Act continued. Town meetings and crowds, lawyers' arguments and constitutional thought, were combined in Massachusetts to render the act ineffectual without stopping all those government and business transactions that required stamps. In a number of country towns too, latent social tensions came out into the open. Debtors were fearful that no bail bonds would be available, that no deeds to sell land could be obtained—in short, that no redress could be had from imprisonment for debt. In other instances, townsmen began to consider who would be most likely to become the local stamp distributor and thereby draw a handsome salary while all others had to pay the additional tax. Not surprisingly, the latter usually became suspicious of the influential or the wealthy and already disliked townsmen. That this way of thinking was not far-fetched can be easily demonstrated by pointing out that the British ministry had come up with exactly the same ideas. Influential and wealthy colonists were to be made stamp distributors in order to diminish opposition to the act among the colonials, and possibly also to deprive oppositional forces of their customary leadership. This thinking was certainly not far off the mark, as the scramble of wealthy colonists for the lucrative offices testified.

As a result of the extensive crowd action and its implications, the colonial leadership reversed itself and disavowed direct action. When in the fall of 1767 the news of the Townshend duties arrived, ideology was logically developed one step further, to include opposition to external taxation. But actual resistance, according to the leadership, should not take the form of escalated crowd action. Instead, nonconsumption agreements were to involve the whole population, nonimportation policies the merchants. Active involvement of the latter was important, as many Whig politicians thought, because commerce was necessary, but any excess of it would introduce luxury and corruption and thus endanger the corporate structure of the communities. Many Whigs found it debatable whether anything like a "mercantile virtue" could exist at all or whether all business was permeated by a "mercenary" spirit.

Whether this policy of "No Mobs—No Confusion—No Tumults" was successful and whether the crowd did indeed vanish from the scene will be the subject of Part II.

The Crowd in Colonial Massachusetts—An Institution

1

In April 1689, Boston crowds placed the royal governor of the Dominion of New England, Sir Edmund Andros, under arrest.[1] Three-quarters of a century later, Boston crowds forced stamp distributors appointed by the British government to resign, as did crowds throughout the colonies. From the vantage point of the chronicler of imperial relations or of the student of political institutions, hardly any crowd action is noticeable in the intervening years, except perhaps for a riot against a British admiral, Sir Charles Knowles, in 1747. To conclude that direct action was merely an erratic and spasmodic reaction to extreme political stimuli would be premature. A bird's-eye view does not reveal the variety and frequency of local direct action in response to the numerous local grievances and conflicts. Rioting in 1765 and after, protesting and obstructing imperial policies, was based on this tradition, which partly continued English customs and partly arose in response to colonial problems. Interpretations of revolutionary violence that do not take into account these roots in colonial history and social structure are apt to distort its significance and to misunderstand its character.

The following summary of crowd action in Massachusetts from the rebellion against Governor Andros to the end of the period of "salutary neglect" is based on some 50 episodes, several of them involving more than one riot. This number represents a mere fraction of the total amount of direct action that did occur. Contemporary accounts often merely noted that certain kinds of riots "have of late been very frequent" or had been common in earlier periods of Massachusetts history.[2] Notwithstanding the limited number of events for which records exist, the sources furnish ample evidence of patterns of action, of traditional concepts and norms governing them, and of changes in these patterns brought about by changing

[1]Michael G. Hall, Lawrence H. Leder, and Michael G. Kammen, eds., *The Glorious Revolution in America: Documents on the Colonial Crisis of 1689* (Chapel Hill, N.C., 1964), pp. 9ff.; Thomas Hutchinson, *The History of the Colony and Province of Massachusetts Bay,* ed. Lawrence Shaw Mayo, 3 vols. (Cambridge, Mass., 1936), 1:297–351.

[2]Adjusted for size of population, the incidence of crowd action in Massachusetts is comparable to that in England. John H. Bohstedt, "Riots in England, 1790–1810, with Special Reference to Devonshire" (Ph.D. diss., Harvard Univ., 1972), p. 1. For other North American colonies, see Pauline R. Maier, "Popular Uprisings and Civil Authority in Eighteenth-Century America," *WMQ* 3.27:3–35 (1970); Richard M. Brown, "Violence and the American Revolution," in *Essays on the American Revolution,* ed. S. G. Kurtz and J. H. Hutson (Chapel Hill, N.C., 1973), pp. 81–120; Dirk Hoerder, comp., *Violence in the United States: Riots, Strikes, Protest, and Suppression—A Bibliography* (Berlin, 1973), pp. 20–31.

circumstances and needs. Compared to the records on which George Rudé based his study of French revolutionary crowds, most documentation for crowd action in America and the concepts that motivated it is of a more circumstantial nature, similar rather to the materials that E. P. Thompson used to reconstruct the moral economy of the eighteenth-century English crowd.[3] There are three kinds of data from which inferences about the rioters' concepts of society and its functioning can be drawn. Riots were usually preceded by petitions to the appropriate authorities and institutions, in which concepts about the "proper" state of affairs, whether political, social, or economic, were made explicit. Second, the very repetitiveness of certain specific and clearly circumscribed patterns of action, or rather reaction to well-defined contingencies, suggests underlying patterns of thought. In addition, sermons, pamphlets, and arguments in court provide valuable material on general patterns of thinking about protest and its causes.

The two basic forms of crowd action in colonial Massachusetts were norm enforcement in areas of conduct for which widespread community consensus existed and conflict resolution when group interests prevented consensual or amicable solutions within the regular institutional processes. Such disputes arose about questions of political authority, of economic interests, and—infrequently—of social structures. They will be considered in this sequence. Their relationship to other forms of popular action will be outlined at the beginning.

SOME ELEMENTS OF CROWD ACTION IN COLONIAL SOCIETY

In colonial Massachusetts, patterns of group action evolved from work habits and celebrations, from religious and political customs; militia duty and law enforcement also provided experience. Such self-directed cooperation required common values and traditions. Similarly, goal-oriented crowd action depends to a large degree on established social relationships.[4] In colonial communities, living quarters, recreational facilities, and place of work had not yet been divided into separate spheres and different geographic localities. Thus, a community was identical with the inhabitants of a township or a section of it. In 1776, 94 percent of the Massachusetts townships had a population of fewer than 3000 inhabitants, averaging slightly below 1000. Twelve seaboard towns had between 3000 and 5000 inhabitants; Boston alone numbered more, approximately 15,000.[5] The different size of the "metropolis," as contemporaries called Boston, accounts for the scale of variance in political behavior and community action as compared to the inland towns. The differences of

---

[3]George Rudé, *The Crowd in the French Revolution* (Oxford, 1959); E. P. Thompson, "The Moral Economy of the English Crowd in the Eighteenth Century," *Past and Present* 50:76–136 (Feb. 1971).

[4]On the question of community, the literature on group dynamics is preferable to that on violence and "mobs." Cf. "Groups," and especially "Group Formation," *Encyclopedia of Social Sciences*, 8:259–293, ed. D. L. Sills (New York, 1968).

[5]Stella Helen Sutherland, comp., *Population Distribution in Colonial America* (New York, 1936), pp. 16–20; Evarts B. Greene and Virginia D. Harrington, *American Population before the Federal Census of 1790* (New York, 1932), pp. 21–30.

economic and social structure between mercantile centers and agrarian towns explain different patterns of action. In the larger units, direct action by crowds was not hampered by anonymity and lack of community, since subcommunities formed— for example, parishes or the Northend and Southend in Boston.

Of foremost importance for the expression of community sentiments was the political organization of townships and province. Town meetings provided the basic institutional framework, where local problems were dealt with, magistrates elected, and representatives to the General Court instructed. But only free, white, male adults, about one-quarter of the population, were enfranchised, provided they owned a certain minimum amount of property. Varying with the economic structure of a town, 45 to 98 percent of them met the property qualification. In addition, social customs, as well as settlement and work patterns, influenced attendance.[6] The franchise was most restricted among the mercantile and maritime populations of the densely settled coastal towns. Most sailors, laborers, journeymen mechanics, tradesmen, and small, self-employed artisans could not vote. In the town meetings a moderator from the top social group of the town and the most prominent magistrates dominated the proceedings. The patriarchal position of the male voters provided the link between the town meeting and nonenfranchised sections of the community. This increase of hierarchical elements meant decreasing possibilities for political independence and broadly based political activities, though other social institutions and customs provided opportunities to exchange political opinions, develop social links, and practice self-organization.[7] The militia, for instance, comprised all white

[6]Chilton Williamson, *American Suffrage from Property to Democracy* (Princeton, N.J., 1960), pp. 33–36; Edward A. McKinley, *The Suffrage Franchise in the Thirteen English Colonies in America* (Philadelphia, 1903), pp. 355–357; R. E. Brown, *Middle-Class Democracy and the Revolution in Massachusetts, 1691–1780* (Ithaca, N.Y., 1955). Cf. reviews by John Cary, "Statistical Method and the Brown Thesis on Colonial Democracy," with a rebuttal by R. E. Brown, *WMQ* 3.20:251–276 (1963), and Robert Taylor, "Review of Robert Brown, *Middle-Class Democracy in Massachusetts*," *MVHR* 43:111–113 (1956); James A. Thorpe, "Colonial Suffrage in Massachusetts: An Essay Review," *EIHC* 106:169–181 (1970).

[7]Anne Bush MacLear, *Early New England Towns: A Comparative Study of Their Development* (London, 1908); John F. Sly, *Town Government in Massachusetts, 1620–1930* (Cambridge, Mass., 1930); David Syrett, "Town-Meeting Politics in Massachusetts, 1776–1786," *WMQ* 3.21:352–366 (1964); Kenneth A. Lockridge and Alan Kreider, "The Evolution of Massachusetts Town Government, 1640 to 1740," *WMQ* 3.23:549–574 (1966); John J. Waters and John A. Schutz, "Patterns of Massachusetts Colonial Politics: The Writs of Assistance and the Rivalry between the Otis and Hutchinson Families," *WMQ* 3.24:543–567 (1967); Kenneth A. Lockridge, "Land, Population and the Evolution of New England Society, 1630–1790," *Past and Present* 39:62–80 (April 1968); Charles E. Clark, *The Eastern Frontier: The Settlement of Northern New England, 1610–1763* (New York, 1970); Michael W. Zuckerman, "The Social Context of Democracy in Massachusetts," *WMQ* 3.25:523–544 (1968), and *Peaceable Kingdoms: New England Towns in the Eighteenth Century* (New York, 1970); Robert M. Zemsky, "Power, Influence, and Status: Leadership Patterns in the Massachusetts Assembly, 1740–1755," *WMQ* 3.26:502–520 (1969), and *Merchants, Farmers, and River Gods: An Essay on Eighteenth Century American Politics* (Boston, 1971); Van Hall Beck, *Politics without Parties: Massachusetts, 1780–1791* (Pittsburgh, 1972); Dirk Hoerder, *Society and Government, 1760–1780: The Power Structure in Massachusetts Townships* (Berlin, 1972); Stephen E. Patterson, *Political Parties in Revolutionary Massachusetts* (Madison, Wis., 1973); John J. Waters, "From Democracy to Demography: Recent Historiography on the New England Town," in *Perspectives on Early American History: Essays in Honor of Richard B. Morris*, ed. Alden T. Vaughan *et al.* (New York, 1973), pp. 222–249; John M. Murrin, "Review Essay [on early New England town histories]," *History and Theory* 11:227–275 (1972). Studies on individual towns: Sumner Chilton Powell, *Puritan Village: The Formation of a New England Town* (Watertown, Sudbury, Marlborough) (Middletown, Conn., 1963); James Henretta, "Economic Development and Social Structure in Colonial Boston," *WMQ* 3.22:75–92 (1965); Philip J. Greven, Jr., "Family Structure in Seventeenth-Century Andover, Massachusetts," *WMQ* 3.23:234–256

males between the ages of 16 and 50. The companies chose their own captains and lieutenants. Only the higher echelons of the officers were appointed by the governor as commander in chief. This arrangement was based on the notions that each man is capable of judging the performance of the others and is interested in having qualified and respected officers and that men fight best when they understand aims and movements of battles. But here, as in political affairs, deference led to high reelection rates for officers.[8] The consequences of these organizational principles in the establishment of the militia were important for crowd action as well as for crowd control. No magistrate could order the militia to quell a riot if its goals had broad community support. Militiamen refused to act or were active already as rioters. Militia drummers occasionally turned out on their own initiative to help collect a crowd. During the anti-British crowd action of the revolutionary period, militia units were to play an important role, acting as self-organized groups when their officers were Loyalist in sympathies.[9]

In religious matters the inhabitants also had a considerable measure of self-

---

(1966); Kenneth A. Lockridge, "Population of Dedham, Massachusetts, 1636–1736," *Econ. Hist. Rev.* 2.19:313–344 (1966); John J. Waters, "Hingham, Massachusetts, 1631–1661: An East Anglican Oligarchy in the New World," *J. Soc. Hist.* 1:351–370 (1967–1968); Donald W. Koch, "Income Distribution and Political Structure in Seventeenth-Century Salem, Massachusetts," *EIHC* 105:50–69 (1969); Philip J. Greven, Jr., *Four Generations: Population, Land, and Family in Colonial Andover, Massachusetts* (Ithaca, N.Y., 1970); Kenneth A. Lockridge, *A New England Town, the First Hundred Years: Dedham, Massachusetts, 1636–1736* (New York, 1970); Edward M. Cook, Jr., "Social Behavior and Changing Values in Dedham, Massachusetts, 1770 to 1775," *WMQ* 3.27:546–580 (1970); J. M. Bumsted, "Religion, Finance, and Democracy in Massachusetts: The Town of Norton as a Case Study," *JAH* 57:817–831 (1970–1971); Allan Kulikoff, "The Progress of Inequality in Revolutionary Boston," *WMQ* 3.28:378–412 (1971). Connecticut and Rhode Island: Richard L. Bushman, *From Puritan to Yankee: Character and the Social Order in Connecticut, 1690–1765* (Cambridge, Mass., 1967). See also John Demos, "Notes on Life in Plymouth Colony," *WMQ* 3.22:264–286 (1965) and "Families in Colonial Bristol, Rhode Island: An Exercise in Historical Demography," *WMQ* 25:40–57 (1968); Charles S. Grant, *Democracy in the Connecticut Frontier Town of Kent* (New York, 1961); Linda A. Bissell, "From One Generation to Another: Mobility in Seventeenth-Century Winsor, Connecticut," *WMQ* 3.31:79–110 (1974); William F. Willingham: "Deference Democracy and Town Government in Windham, Connecticut, 1775 to 1786," *WMQ* 3.30:401–422 (1973).

[8]For aspects of office-holding concepts, particularly due submission to magistrates and offices as freeholds of those elected, but also on the dangers of officeholders' ambitions, see the election sermons before the Massachusetts General Court: Lindsay Swift, "The Massachusetts Election Sermons," *CSMP* 1:388–451 (1892–1894); A. W. Plumstead, ed., *The Wall and the Garden: Selected Massachusetts Election Sermons, 1670–1775* (Minneapolis, 1968). The notion that offices were freeholds was also expressed by the exiled Loyalists, who demanded compensation for lost offices before the claims commission in London. Whigs in the colonies and, later, states expected reelection as their due. On office-holding and reelection patterns, see Hoerder, *Society and Government*, pp. 23–59, and other township studies listed in note 7.

[9]Louis Morton, "The Origins of American Military Policy," *Military Affairs* 22:75–82 (1957); John W. Shy, "A New Look at Colonial Militia," *WMQ* 3.20:175–185 (1963), and "The American Revolution: The Military Conflict Considered as a Revolutionary War," in *Essays on the American Revolution*, ed. S. G. Kurtz and J. H. Hutson (Chapel Hill, N.C., 1973), pp. 121–156. Massachusetts: A. C. Goodell *et al.*, eds., *Acts and Resolves, Public and Private, of the Province of the Massachusetts Bay*, 21 vols. (Boston, 1869–1922), 2:40–41, 5:445–454. The notion of popularity of officers was one reason for commissioning officers during the Revolutionary War; they had to enlist a sufficient number of men to form a company to serve under them. On the importance of well-informed men, see Timothy Pickering's manual on military duty, *An Easy Plan of Discipline for a Militia* (Salem, Mass., 1775), p. 10 (main section), Evans 14404. On the role of the militia during civil disturbances, see the discussion of the impressment riot in Boston, 1747, and the Stamp Act riots, 1765. Edward Countryman, "The Northern Rural Crowd in the Eighteenth Century: A Comparative View," in *The American Revolution: Explorations in the History of Radicalism*, ed. Alfred F. Young, (De Kalb, Ill., 1976), pp. 37–69. In New Jersey, 1746, a militia officer called upon his men to quell the land riots. A crowd leader called in the same men, and they decided to act as a crowd.

determination. Parish members elected deacons and voted on the choice of a minister. The distribution of pews was decided by an elected committee. But again, social deference imposed limitations on the participatory features. The seating arrangements in the meeting house depended on social rank. Only in commercialized Boston were pews sold to the highest bidders. The minister, once settled, belonged to the circle of dignitaries and expected submission, which, however, was not always easy to obtain, since the townsmen had to decide on his salary whenever the original agreement, because of rising prices and so on, became unsatisfactory.[10]

In addition to the political, military, and religious institutions, daily work habits and conditions were an important component in the formation of behavioral processes that made self-organized crowd action possible. Any task that surpassed the capacity of the basic economic unit, the family or the small artisanal workshop, had to be accomplished by voluntary cooperation. This included raising the frame of a house or barn, building or repairing a meeting house or town hall, harvesting a crop, launching a ship, or extinguishing a fire. A foreman or a master artisan might coordinate the work, but since working processes had hardly begun to be compartmentalized by specialization, most participants were capable of self-direction and self-organization. Some cooperative ventures were fixed by season and tradition, such as husking Indian corn in the fall. Others were decided upon by those concerned, such as raising a meeting house. Private ventures, such as building a new barn, were started by the interested person or family, who then asked neighbors for help. Once the task was finished, a social gathering, a "frolic," ended the day. Spontaneous mutual aid was also practiced, as when people, sometimes numbering more than 1000, gathered to search for a child lost in the woods. They organized themselves into search parties and combed the neighborhood for days if necessary.[11]

A third kind of training ground for self-organized direct action was the quasi-crowd activity strengthening community bonds, public celebrations and law enforcement. Punitive power had not yet been delegated entirely from the community at large to specialized agencies (police forces, prisons).[12] Involvement in the act of punishing seemed also desirable because of its supposedly deterrent effect on partic-

[10]Jacob C. Meyer, *Church and State in Massachusetts from 1740 to 1833: A Chapter in the Development of Individual Freedom* (Cleveland, 1930); Ola Elizabeth Winslow, *Meeting House Hill, 1630–1783* (New York, 1952); Edwin Scott Gaustad, *The Great Awakening in New England* (New York, 1953); John C. Miller, "Religion, Finance, and Democracy," *NEQ* 6:29–58 (1933); Bumsted, "Religion, Finance, and Democracy in Massachusetts," pp. 817–831; Bushman, *From Puritan to Yankee*, Pt. 4; Robert J. Dinkin, "Seating the Meeting House in Early Massachusetts," *NEQ* 43:450–464 (1970).

[11]Work parties: Nathaniel Ames, "Diary of Dr. Nathaniel Ames," ed. Sarah Breck Baker, *Dedham Hist. Reg.*, vols. 1–14 (1890–1903), 1:147, 2:97, 98; William Thomas, "Memoranda Entered by William Thomas, Father of Robert B. Thomas, Author of the *Farmer's Almanac*," ed. J. H. Fitts, *EIHC* 14:263 (1877); Ballantine's Journal, 1 April 1761, Judd MSS., Rev. Matters, p. 150, Forbes Library; Cotton Mather, *Advice from the Watch Tower* (Boston, 1713), Evans 1616. Search parties: *BEP*, 6 Oct. 1766 (1500 persons active); Ames, "Diary," 3:22; Ballantine's Journal, 31 May 1767, Judd MSS., Rev. Matters, p. 146, Forbes Library.

[12]On the process of delegation of police powers, see Roger Lane, *Policing the City: Boston, 1822–1885* (New York, 1971); Michael Feldberg, "The Philadelphia Riots of 1844: A Social History" (Ph.D. diss., Univ. of Rochester, 1970), and "The Crowd in Philadelphia History: A Comparative Perspective" (Paper prepared for the American Historical Association Convention, 1971), p. 14. The lower classes protected themselves by rioting; the middle class lobbied for a police force. Cf. also John C. Weicher, "The Allocation of Police Protection by Income Class," *Urban Studies* 8:207–220 (1971).

ipants and spectators. A part of the prosecution was effected by magistrates—that is, justices of the peace, sheriffs, and constables. The justices were aided and controlled by juries, the sheriffs supported by the "hue and cry" and the posse comitatus. As to constables, most towns had only one or two; Boston, with 12 officers, had one per 1250 inhabitants. Thus, magistrates were dependent on public support, including supportive direct action. Such support, as well as collective punishment, demanded a high degree of social and cultural homogeneity and a sense of equitable justice unless it was to become merely vigilante-type terrorism.[13]

Elaborate patterns of involvement of the public had developed. Jury indictments charged the accused with having acted "in evil example" to others. In the process of punishment, the accused could ritualistically reaffirm their adherence to community standards. Participation ranged from passive attendance to active support, from public confession to social ostracism. Thousands watched the hanging of capital offenders. Hundreds pelted and abused petty criminals at whipping posts or at the stocks. Poems and "dying speeches," sold at the scene, drew lessons from the criminal's fate for the edification and moral improvement of the spectators. Such public action did not conflict with patterns of deference, since persons of middling or higher rank were fined rather than punished corporally and, in addition, often had their fines remitted.[14]

One step further toward active participation was social ostracism and boycott, used exclusively in the early period of the colony. Direct action in support of executive authorities found its most straightforward realization in the posse comitatus. Originally the king's prerogative, the call on the people to assist lawful authority was crowd action institutionalized by law. Though all combinations of subjects were deemed dangerous, the statutory restraints and the guidance and command by officials were considered sufficient safeguards against unauthorized activity. Thus, the crowd as posse acted legally but by definition could not act spontaneously.[15]

Public involvement in law and norm enforcement underwent considerable change after the first century of colonial settlement, when the meeting-house hill was no

[13]Maier, "Popular Uprisings," pp. 18–22; George R. T. Hewes, *Traits of the Tea Party: Being a Memoir of George R. T. Hewes,* ed. Benjamin B. Thatcher (New York, 1835), p. 208, for a "hue and cry" in Boston, 1774. In later decades, vigilantism as pregovernmental law enforcement in newly settled areas followed this tradition of crowd action for the purposes of law enforcement. This kind of action is not to be confounded with the bigoted norm enforcement and confinement of blacks, workers, and outsiders to socially inferior positions by violence and lynchings. Richard M. Brown, "The American Vigilante Tradition," *Violence in America,* ed. H. D. Graham and T. R. Gurr (New York, 1969), pp. 154–226, and "Legal and Behavioral Perspectives on American Vigilantism," *Persp. Am. Hist.* 5:59–146 (1971).

[14]On connections between social rank and type of punishment, see Jules Zanger, "Crime and Punishment in Early Massachusetts," *WMQ* 3.22:471–477 (1965). Peltings: *BEP,* 17 Dec. 1750; *BG,* 13 May 1765, 22 Feb. 1768. Executions: *Essex Gaz.,* 21 Jan. 1772. Exhortatory broadsides: *Mass. Brds.,* 1003, 1004, 1008, 1077, 1078, 1268, 1269, 1335, 1349 *passim.*

[15]See William Blackstone, *Commentaries on the Laws of England,* 4 vols. (Philadelphia, 1771), for: posse, 1:343–344, 4:122, 142–143, 146–147, 433; hue and cry, 4:290–291; "tumultuous petitioning," limiting signatures on petitions to 20 names, delegations to 10 persons, 4:147; treason, 4:74–93. *An Abridgement of Burn's Justice of the Peace and Parish Officers* (Boston, 1773), pp. 310–318; Samuel M. Quincy, ed., *Reports of Cases Argued and Adjudged in the Superior Court of Judicature of . . . Massachusetts Bay, 1761–1772, by Josiah Quincy, Junior* (Boston, 1865), pp. 176, 177, 221, 261.

longer the social and spiritual center of the small communities in which the inhabitants controlled one another's daily lives and morals. The increase in population and the resulting changes in occupational and settlement patterns, together with religious, economic, and social diversification, brought about a gradual decline of homogeneity and of the effectiveness of public punishments. Some, such as public confessions, became almost obsolete. Juries refused to bring indictments for offenses now condoned by a changed public opinion. Stocks and whipping posts were destroyed at night.

But public involvement received new significance in the revolutionary period, when patterns of crowd action were derived from it and when the political struggles brought about attempts to revive public confession and social ostracism. Pelting and abuse were used against crown officials. Broadsides similar to the "dying speeches" were printed during nonimportation times, when effigies of importers were hanged. Boycotts and ostracism of crown supporters and officials, designed to bring them back into the fold, brought about emigration and expulsion of the Loyalists instead.[16]

Just as presence at public punishments was intended to leave a negative impression on the spectators, suggesting and effecting dissociation from the misdeed, public celebrations, mainly political, were intended to impress the minds of the participants favorably about state and society, whether the event celebrated was national, provincial, or local. Festivities to reaffirm loyalty to the ruling dynasty and to the empire were accession, coronation, and birthday anniversaries of the reigning monarchs, their spouses, and their designated successors, as well as victories of the British armies.[17] An event of provincial significance, but practically limited to Boston, was the annual election of the council.[18] Local matters of importance were militia training days, the installment of ministers, and commencement at Harvard.[19] The standard components of such festivities were special sermons and orations; military musters; sumptuous dinners; and illumination of houses by candles and of streets and hills by bonfires. To stress events of importance, fast and thanksgiving days could also be appointed. It is obvious that this tradition could be used for partisan ends once the corporate cohesiveness of the towns declined. The crowds of participants, in Boston often 3000 strong, contained a strong potential for direct action, and they were a receptive audience for political sermons: "Stand fast there-

---

[16]For attempts to revive punishment by public exposure of the offenders, see *BTR* 16:217; suggestion to read names of deficient taxpayers in public, 1767, *ibid.* 18:213; committee recommendation to Bostonians not to buy from vendors disregarding the market regulations, 1775, *ibid.* 18:265.

[17]Examples are the Prince of Wales's birthday, *BG*, 19 Aug. 1765 and victories, *BEP*, 13 Oct. 1760. Unsuccessful campaigns, on the other hand, could evoke derision and abuse from crowds against returning officers, as happened after the abortive siege of Port Royal, 1707. John Winthrop to Fitz-John Winthrop [July 1707], *MHSC* 6.3:387–390 (1889).

[18]Council election: John Rowe, *Letters and Diary of John Rowe, Boston Merchant, 1759–1762, 1764–1779*, ed. Anne Rowe Cunningham (Boston, 1903; reprint ed., 1969), 30 May 1770, p. 203.

[19]*Resolve of His Majesty's Council Relating to the Disorders on the Days of Ordination of the Ministers: With Proceedings of the Convention of Ministers Thereon* (Boston, 1759). Disorders in religious meetings also occurred in protest a variety of small innovations, such as new pews or choir singing. Cotton Mather, *Diary, 1681–1724, and Papers, MHSC* 4.8, 7.7, 7.8 (1868, 1911, 1912), 2:693, 797; Ballantine's Journal, 16 Feb. 1763, 30 March, 3 May 1767, 17 Jan. 1768, Judd MSS., Rev. Matters, pp. 146–147, 151, Forbes Library.

fore in the Liberty wherewith Christ hath made us free, and be not entangled again with the yoke of Bondage."[20] In the seaboard towns the "gentlemen" frequently drank their toasts inside the town hall; large numbers of the "people" celebrated outside.

The effusions of loyalty on coronation day, 1762, were somewhat marred when stones were thrown through the windows of the council chamber while "his Excellency with the Council, and other Gentlemen of Distinction were assembled." A similar incident occurred in Marblehead. The rioters were charged with having acted "in Contempt of Government and in defiance of Executive Officers." Such disorders, often associated with the celebrations, frequently centered around the town hall and may have sprung from a resentment that town leaders celebrated in the exclusive atmosphere of the selectmen's or council chamber while many had to stay outside and probably could hardly afford to drink to anybody's health. Crowds also sometimes opposed what they considered high-handed conduct of officers or magistrates during the celebrations.[21]

The feasting occasioned considerable expense, and only well-to-do persons could attend on the more elaborate occasions. On election day, when the new provincial council took office, the freshmen legislators were expected to treat their senior colleagues. They had to be broken in, and the custom was accordingly called "Shoeing Colts." At the commencement, the display of wealth reached such proportions that regulations were passed to control it.[22]

In addition to those at these officially sponsored events, contemporaries throughout the eighteenth century reported "Disturbances . . . on various occasions, both political and Ecclesiastical." Occasionally a few windowpanes were broken in an overflow of excitement and exuberance. The safety of windows was more imperiled when groups of men and boys assembled simply to let off steam. It has often been assumed that such "disorders" were most likely to occur in the densely populated seaboard towns. But although people in the country lived dispersed over wide areas, they were as ready as Bostonians to stop by, to watch or to participate, to applaud or to oppose, whatever the situation might demand. Little inducement was needed for a "frolic" or a celebration. A wedding, the installment of a minister, the tearing down of an old meeting house—all caused "a great concourse" and reinforced patterns of collective behavior.[23]

To prevent such disorders, the legislature passed acts, and ministers' councils and town meetings passed resolutions. Their effect seems to have been limited. "An act to prevent disorders," passed by the General Court at the beginning of the century,

[20]John W. Thornton, *The Pulpit of the American Revolution: or, The Political Sermons of the Period of 1776* (Boston, 1860), p. ix; Swift, "The Massachusetts Election Sermons," pp. 419, 421; Plumstead, ed., *The Wall and the Garden,* pp. 10–15.

[21]*BTR* 19:214; Council Records, 15:181 MSA; SCF 83317 SCCH; Rowe, *Letters and Diary,* 11 Sept. 1764, p. 61; *BNL,* 5 Nov. 1741.

[22]Rowe, *Letters and Diary,* 29 May 1765, p. 98.

[23]Mather to Winthrop, 9 March 1720, *MHSC* 4.8:438 (1858); Mather, *Diary,* 4 April 1721, *MHSC* 7.8:611 (1912); *BTR* 19:198–199, 25:45; *Acts and Resolves,* 3:500–501, 509, 1749–1750, Ch. 24; MA 88:171–174; *BEP,* 13 July 1761; *BNL,* 4 Nov. 1773.

was ostensibly directed against Indians and slaves, but court records and diaries leave the definite impression that most of the "disturbers of the peace" were whites. Then, as today, blacks often had to take the blame for rioting, while white rioters often got off scot-free. The Boston watch, established in 1761, "forasmuch as considerable numbers of dissolute persons have sometimes riotously met," in fact had to come to the aid of Negroes attacked by whites, ranking from sailors to gentlemen.[24] Disorderly violence cannot be explained by the rudeness of a violence-prone "rabble" or "poorer sort" of people. Court records show that affrays and brawls were common among all classes of society. Only the descriptive terms varied: Lower-class people "beat" and "clubbed"; higher-ranking men "fought duels" or "dealt out canings." Paul Revere was fined for assault; a commissioner of His Majesty's Customs and the secretary of the province of Massachusetts Bay thrashed each other in the town hall; customs official Hallowell beat up an abusive British admiral.[25]

Participatory institutions, cooperative work patterns, collective action to punish offenders, public celebrations, and brawls and affrays help to illuminate some elements of crowd action, but, taken by themselves, they do not explain it. A particular reason for a crowd action may be only a catalyst; any one goal may become just one step in a sequence leading to a particular crowd action. A town-meeting debate about the breaking of community norms could, if the offender remained recalcitrant, induce those assembled to enforce the norms directly. Public punishment could bring about a rescue riot if the public did not agree with the verdict. Dissatisfaction about prices in the market could lead to riotous action by other sellers feeling undersold or by buyers enraged about the high prices. In each case, laws and customs prescribed redress short of direct action: petitions, judicial action, selectmen's ordinances, as well as more informal solutions. However, such devices to redress grievances were limited to issues on which widespread consensus existed, which did not involve basic conflicts of interest. A growing population and social as well as economic diversification resulted in increasing numbers of conflicts. One possibility for ending divisions within a community was a permanent separation of conflicting sections into new parishes or towns. Another was emigration to the west as long as there were unsettled lands, legislative or proprietorial consent, and means for defraying the cost of the move. If neither of these alternatives was feasible, or when existing institutions proved inadequate under changed circumstances and were unresponsive to petitioning, the aggrieved parties resorted to direct action.

[24]*Acts and Resolves,* 1:535–536, 1703–1704, Ch. 11, 3:305–306, 1746–1747, Ch. 11, 4:462, 1761–1762, Ch. 5, 5:301–303, 1773–1774, Ch. 12. *BEP,* 20 July 1761.

[25]Cf. the minute books, records, and plea books of the courts and lawyers. Evarts B. Greene, "The Code of Honor in Colonial and Revolutionary Times, with Special Reference to New England," *CSMP* 26:367–388 (1924–1926). *Acts and Resolves,* 2:516–517, 1728–1729, Ch. 15. Colin Loftin and Alan Lizotte, "Violence and Social Structure: Structural Support for Violence among Privileged Groups" (Paper presented at the American Sociological Association Convention, Montreal, Aug. 1774). Rowe, *Letters and Diary,* 24 Dec. 1764, 23 Feb. 1765, 15 July 1769, pp. 71, 77, 189; John Boyle, "Boyle's Journal of Occurrences in Boston, 1759–1778," *NEHGR* 84:142–171, 248–272, 357–382 (1930), 85:5–28, 117–133 (1931), 16 Sept. 1762, 84:159.

ENFORCEMENT OF COMMUNITY NORMS

Among the different kinds of direct action, riots enforcing community norms had the longest tradition. The norms required a common value system and a relatively cohesive corporate community. Laws regulating the admission of new inhabitants, as well as those for warning out strangers, were based on the concept of corporate responsibility, in which any newcomer, poor or not, might become a charge on the public. The poor, outsiders in an economic sense, did not have to be coerced by riots to submit to the laws and to accept their lowly position. Even in Boston, where in the late colonial period the propertyless amounted to 29 percent of the population traditional norms kept them from "uppity."[26]

On the other hand, men from an above-average economic section could evade laws, resist the lawful authorities, and generally act contrary to the feelings and interests of the community. In a tradition-directed society with a weak executive and judiciary, their conduct of business was frequently out of the reach of legal sanctions. But by forsaking the value system of the community, that amount of room granted to each individual by the implicit consensus of the community, the transgressor lost its protection. The community reacted, as a whole or in part, by rioting. Extralegal crowd action was a generally accepted means of forcing these people to conform to community laws, customs, and interests. Without such actions, the corporate system of social organization would have been doomed. Accordingly, the participants in such riots were protected against prosecution or retaliation by sympathizing officials and by the jury system, which often made rioters still at large judges over those who had been caught. In addition to using economic power to the detriment of the community, commonly accepted norms could be violated by breaking religious customs or moral standards and by acting against the beliefs or prejudices concerning illness, inoculation, or death.

Religious minorities—Baptists, Quakers, Anglicans—were considered outsiders throughout the colonial and provincial period (and later as well). Roger Williams and his followers had been banished in 1635, Anne Hutchinson and other antinomians in 1638. The death penalty had been added to the law against Quakers in 1658. Any new doctrine threatened the status quo, the harmony, in a community. It also endangered the position of the religious and political leadership. When, later, these laws were liberalized, and when, especially after the Great Awakening, religious homogeneity decreased, the established inhabitants, who on other issues did not countenance violence, frequently participated in violent action against dissenters. But they preferred to use their power and position as magistrates to "administer" illegal harassment and violence such as unlawful taxation or imprisonment to religious outsiders in hopes of forcing them to leave or to submit. Official punishment of dissenters varied according to their social position. A Harvard president was merely admonished. Others were fined. Those too poor to pay a fine were whipped, men and women. "There is no doubt," said McLoughlin in his study of New

---

[26]Josiah H. Benton, *Warning Out in New England, 1656–1817* (Boston, 1911); Henretta, "Economic Development," p. 85.

England dissent, "that the social persecution by their neighbors and fellow church members was at least as potent a force in their suppression as the punishments meted out by the courts." Probably to justify their own harsh reaction against religious dissenters, and to rally support among the people, the establishment accused Baptists of breaking moral norms too, by spreading slanderous stories about women being baptized naked.[27]

Some evidence suggests that social issues were involved in the harassment of Separates. The lower a man's or a family's status on the social ladder, the larger the likelihood of becoming Separates. Said one of them to Jonathan Edwards, "I won't worship a wig!"[28] Several Bristol towns with a heavily Baptist population revolted in 1744 against the taxation of the Congregational parishes imposed by the General Court. In a rescue riot, hundreds of men freed an imprisoned local tax collector.[29] In some towns, riots intensified in the seventies when Baptists proved reluctant to renounce allegiance to the crown, which to some degree had protected them against the impositions of the provincial religious and political establishment. Since the question of Toryism was relatively peripheral while the problem of nonconformity to the town's majority continued to be the central issue at stake, one of the incidents will be used as an example of direct action against religious minorities.[30]

Inhabitants of the town Pepperell, Middlesex County, opened the mail of local Baptists. When a Baptist itinerant in March 1778 announced his coming, the information was first communicated to a town meeting. Then the top magistrates asked whether the preacher, a mere "fox-hunter's son," should be permitted to come to town. Not all townsmen were ready to accept such social slurs. Someone mentioned that the same derogatory attitude had once prevailed toward the carpenter's son. A first sermon was allowed to go on undisturbed, but during a second meeting a crowd, among them some town leaders, assembled. These "friends to freedom and unitedness," as they called themselves, ordered a passing stranger to enter the private home and break up the meeting. Another crowd, headed by militia officers and Whig leaders, prevented a baptism at a river on private land belonging to a Baptist, calling one of the Baptists a Tory. The rioters then held a mock baptism for drunken men and dogs, interrupted further meetings, and whipped individual Baptists.[31]

This riot was typical of violence against outsiders and minorities. Town officials, whose leadership in religious matters and whose demands for unlawful taxes in support of the Congregational minister had been rejected by the Baptists, were active in the crowd. The rioters did not relinquish their claim to act for the commu-

---

[27]William G. McLoughlin, *New England Dissent, 1630–1833: The Baptists and the Separation of Church and State,* 2 vols. (Cambridge, Mass., 1971), 1:15–22, 550. On the Rogerenes, see John R. Bolles and Anna B. Williams, *The Rogerenes* (Boston, 1904), pp. 168, 185, 233, 236, 249, 257–258, 290–291, 293.

[28]McLoughlin, *New England Dissent,* 1:333, 354–355, 403–405. Cf. Paul Boyer and Stephen Nissenbaum, *Salem Possessed: The Social Origins of Witchcraft* (Cambridge, Mass., 1974).

[29]See notes 62 and 63.

[30]Other incidents occurred in Warwick (Ha.), 1774; Hingham (Su.), 1782; Lancaster (Wo.); Ashby (Mi.). McLoughlin, *New England Dissent,* 1:549–550, 598, 640–642.

[31]Isaac Backus, "Government and Liberty Described; and Ecclesiastical Tyranny Exposed" (Boston, 1778), in *Isaac Backus on Church, State, and Calvinism: Pamphlets, 1754–1789,* ed. W. G. McLoughlin (Cambridge, Mass., 1968), pp. 345–365, esp. 361–364.

nity; "freedom and unitedness" to them seemed to be one and the same. To provide for the possibility that unity within the community could be reestablished, part of the disruptive violence was ordered to be done by a stranger. If no reunification resulted from the direct action, the stranger would at least be more difficult to prosecute. Given the interest of the town leadership in preserving its position, it is no surprise that, after 1765, Whig Sons of Liberty, middle-class oriented in New England and including many town officials, headed crowds persecuting the Rogerenes and Shakers.[32]

Riots to enforce moral codes were aimed at either the individual offenders or centers of offense, bawdy houses. Throughout the century riotous crowds punished adulterers in, for example, Boston in 1705, Dedham in 1758, Northampton in 1761, Attleborough in 1764, and Salem in 1771. A Boston newspaper complained in the mid-sixties that these riots "of late have become very frequent" and demanded that the rioters be punished. In the second half of the sixties, such riots were also reported in Connecticut, Rhode Island, and New York. It is possible that social and economic changes were accompanied by a relaxation of moral standards. An alternative explanation is that increased anxieties resulting from the changes in society brought about a stricter enforcement of moral norms, which could be more easily controlled than, for example, economic changes. Surviving data do not permit an in-depth analysis of the social position of rioters and their victims, which would be necessary to confirm the tentative explanations for the increase in antiadulterer riots.[33]

The rioters forced the offender to ride on a wooden rail with sharp edges. This method, called Skimmington, was based on an English custom of ridiculing marital quarrels, exposing adulterers, male and female, to the contempt of the community, and punishing unchaste widows and at the same time restoring them to the legal enjoyment of their deceased husband's estate.[34] While its application to sexual offenders can be explained, because the treatment afflicted the sexual organs, it is not clear why the same method of riding the "wooden horse" was used as a disciplinary punishment in the militia and the revolutionary army as well as by crowds against Tories.[35]

---

[32]*Conn. Gaz.*, 5 April 1766; Bolles and Williams, *The Rogerenes*, p. 293; Marguerite F. Melcher, *The Shaker Adventure* (Princeton, N.J., 1941), pp. 24–34; Henry S. Nourse, *History of the Town of Harvard, Massachusetts, 1732–1893* (Harvard, Mass., 1894), pp. 259–267.

[33]Lawson: Samuel Sewall, *Diary of Samuel Sewall, 1674–1729*, 3 vols. (*MHSC* 5.5–5.7; Boston, 1878–1882), Feb.–March 1705, 2:124–126; remittance of fines, Misc. Bound Papers, vol. 7 (1703–1713), 26 Sept. 1705, MHS. Dedham, 1758: Superior Court of Judicature, Records, 1758, ff. 424–425, SCCH. Northampton: Ballantine, Journal, 21 Sept. 1761, Judd MSS., Rev. Matters, p. 150, Forbes Library. Attleborough: *BPB*, 29 Oct., 5 Nov. 1764; *BEP*, 29 Oct., 5 Nov. 1764. Salem: *Essex Gaz.*, 23 April 1771. Rhode Island: *Newport Mercury*, 12 Nov. 1764; *N.Y. Gaz.*, 11 July 1765. Elizabethtown, N.J., 1752–1753: James E. Cutler, *Lynch-Law: An Investigation into the History of Lynching in the United States* (New York, 1905), pp. 46–47.

[34]Skimmington: Note in *WMQ* 3.23:478 (1966); Samuel A. Drake, *A Book of New England Legends and Folk Lore in Prose and Poetry* (Boston, 1883; rev. ed., 1910), pp. 227–233, "Skipper Ireson's Ride." Edward P. Thompson, "'Rough Music': Le Charivari Anglais," *Annales* 27:285–312 (1972); Natalie Zemon Davis, "The Reasons of Misrule: Youth Groups and Charivaris in Sixteenth Century France," *Past and Present* 50:41–75 (1971). For later American usage, see Alva Davis and Raven McDavid, "'Shivaree': An Example of Cultural Diffusion," *American Speech* 24:249–255 (1949), and other articles, *ibid.*, 8:22–26 (1933), 15:109–110 (1940).

[35]Militia and army: Samuel A. Green, ed. "Louisburg Journals," *MHSP* 2.11:437, 441, 442 (1896–1897) (including

In the thirties, the time of religious revival, "a new Sort of Reformers, vulgarly called, The Mob," as a Boston newspaper put it, made public disorderly houses their target. A number of economically motivated riots happened in the same period. George Whitefield, the evangelist, had just concluded a tour of New England, and in Boston economic distress was again high in 1771, when "the mob Routed the Whores" at a house known by the name of Whitehall—an interesting comment on Bostonians' attitudes toward the seat of the British ministry. The year before, a similar riot had taken place in Newburyport. In Newport, Rhode Island, four "notable misses" were tarred and feathered, a treatment hardly ever inflicted on women. While the coincidence of moral and economic rioting in Boston is striking, no direct connections can be traced from the data available. The increase of bawdy houses during the years when British troops were quartered in Boston was to become a constant source of irritation to the sober inhabitants, and more than one riot happened when Bostonians waylaid drunken army officers leaving them.[36]

Firm beliefs about illness and death, when offended by the behavior of individuals, prompted crowd action commonly known as smallpox, inoculation, or doctors riots. Dissection of corpses, necessary for the advancement of knowledge and for practicing surgery, was repugnant in contemporary public opinion. Throughout the eighteenth century and well into the nineteenth, physicians doing so were targets of crowd action. The best-known riot probably is the 1788 New York doctors riot, which kept the town in an uproar for days. A Worcester, Massachusetts, apothecary, Elijah Dix, was harassed by a crowd in 1771, when, as permitted by law, he prepared the skeleton of a recently executed criminal for preservation for scientific purposes.[37] As for the dreaded smallpox, inoculation against it was for a long time considered the equivalent of deliberately spreading it. The latter was a criminal offense; the former was sometimes punished by crowds. The Reverend Cotton Mather, in 1721, had a "Granado" thrown through his window for merely advocating inoculation. During the 1764 epidemic, when Boston's selectmen decided to open a hospital, people from the neighborhood, among them the county's chief law enforcement officer, Sheriff Greenleaf, feared infection. They formally complained to the selectmen, and, having been turned down, they informally threatened to riot. Intervention by the governor and the provincial council was necessary to induce the sheriff to abstain from lawless but community-sanctioned violence. In Marblehead, crowd action against unauthorized inoculation occurred in 1774 and 1777, the former action lasting intermittently for months. Reportedly, the security regulations

---

one instance of riotous opposition to the punishment); Rowe, *Letters and Diary,* 11 Sept. 1764, p. 61; Caleb Haskell, *Caleb Haskell's Diary, May 5, 1775–May 30, 1776: A Revolutionary Soldier's Record before Boston and with Arnold's Quebec Expedition,* ed. Lothrop Withington (Newburyport, Mass., 1881), 29 June, 9 Aug. 1775, pp. 7, 9. Tories: Peter Oliver, *Peter Oliver's Origin and Progress of the American Rebellion: A Tory View,* ed. Douglass Adair and John A. Schutz (Stanford, Calif., 1961), p. 155.

[36]*BG,* 25 March 1734; *BEP,* 14 March, 4 July 1737, 26 June 1738; Rowe, *Letters and Diary,* 24 July 1771, p. 218; *Mass. Spy,* 25 July 1771. Nearly six decades later, in 1827, crowds still followed the same pursuit in Boston. Newport: Dwight Foster to Nabby Foster, 22 July 1774, Dwight Foster Papers, 1757–1790, MHS. Newburyport: Superior Court of Judicature, Minute Books, vol. 93 (Essex), p. 10 (1770), SCCH.

[37]Linda G. De Pauw, *The Eleventh Pillar: New York State and the Federal Constitution* (Ithaca, N.Y., 1966), pp. 149–151. Worcester: *BG,* 25 Feb. 1771; SCF 152513.

voted by a full town meeting had been disregarded by the hospital's doctors and proprietors.[38]

The riots against religious minorities, moral offenders, doctors, and inoculation hospitals and their proprietors, in addition to the primary cause, overstepping of limits set by community norms, were frequently motivated by other grievances as well. Analyzing the Norfolk, Virginia, smallpox riots, Pauline Maier has stressed that one function of many riots was support of authorities when the latter could not enforce the law, because of the offenders' social position and connections, or support of the law when authorities refused to or neglected to enforce it.[39] This was the case in the 1705 Boston riot. The offender, Roger Lawson, not only imprudently insulted the townsmen's feelings but was also involved in shady business transactions as an associate of the governor and of another merchant. The trio traded with the enemy during the French and Indian War. The sheriff was unwilling to take the required legal action against so influential a person. Threats of crowd action caused the General Court to intervene in 1706. Public morality was at issue. As one historian concisely put it: "Despite commercialism and liberal religious practices, Puritan traditions were still strong enough in Boston to provoke public anger against the Governor's pride, Lawson's lust and the merchants' greed."[40]

The attitudes of town leaders toward direct action against outsiders were ambivalent at best. They supported norms and laws via established institutions. They feared spontaneous action because it endangered their position. But dissenting groups, newcomers, and new doctrines threatened their status even more, and they became willing to turn to what in modern Pentagonese would be termed a protective reaction strike; they would become aggressive. Perceived threats were countered less on the basis of their actual potential or measurable effects than on the basis of the threatened group's perception. When laws, institutions, and norms failed or seemed insufficient to protect their group interests, the local leadership used norm-enforcing community riots for their own separate interests. Thus, the Worcester apothecary, Dix, harassed for dissection of a corpse, was a newcomer in town and according to his testimony was closely watched by established men. At least one of them wanted to monopolize profits; the town's settled and till then only apothecary was one of the more active men in the crowd.[41] The sudden indifference of "gentlemen of property

[38]Mather, *Diary,* 18 July, 14 Nov. 1721, *MHSC* 7.8:632, 657–658; Anonymous, *A Letter from One in the Country, to His Friend in the City; in Relation to the Distresses Occasioned by . . . Inoculation* (Boston, 1721), Evans 2229; *BNL,* 20 Nov. 1721. In 1764 a Bostonian protested the calling of a town meeting to consider preventive measures on grounds that the smallpox was a punishment sent by God. *BTR* 20:91–94; *BG,* 2 April 1764; *BEP,* 30 April, 2 July 1764. For other incidents and the impact of smallpox on everyday life, prices, and politics, see Franklin P. Rice, ed., "Worcester Town Records," *Worcester Soc. Antiq. Coll.,* vol. 2 and later (1881 and later), 4:218, 319–321 (1774); William T. Davis, ed., *Records of the Town of Plymouth, 1636–1783,* 3 vols. (Plymouth, Mass., 1903), 3:319, 321, 322, 342, 344 (1776–1778); George A. Billias, "Pox and Politics in Marblehead, 1773–74," *EIHC* 92:43–58 (1956); George F. Dow, ed., *The Holyoke Diaries, 1709–1856* (Salem, Mass., 1911), pp. 27–28 (1764); James Warren to John Adams, 17 July 1776, *Warren–Adams Letters: Being Chiefly a Correspondence among John Adams, Samuel Adams, and James Warren,* 2 vols. (Boston, 1917, 1925), 1:261.

[39]Maier, "Popular Uprisings," pp. 6–7; Patrick Henderson, "Smallpox and Patriotism: The Norfolk Riots, 1768–1769," *Va. Mag. Hist. Biog.* 73:413–424 (1965).

[40]G. B. Warden, *Boston, 1689–1776* (Boston, 1970), pp. 63–64; Sewall, *Diary,* 2:123–126; fines remitted, 26 Sept. 1705, Misc. Bound Papers, vol. 7 (1703–1713), MHS; *Acts and Resolves,* 6:63–68.

[41]*BG,* 25 Feb. 1771; Dix's testimony, SCF 152513, SCCH. The opposition to religious groups was partly motivated by

and standing" to their own law-and-order principles has recently received attention from several historians focusing on the 1830s and 1840s. Theodore M. Hammett has plausibly advanced the thesis that when the perceived threat to established interests reached a threshold level, the prevailing ideology, with its stress on order, temporarily lost its restraining effect. Then interest overrode ideology.[42]

Smallpox epidemics and inoculation drives were exacerbated by resulting economic problems. Farmers did not dare to come to town with their supplies, so prices rose, and provisions became scarce. Some inhabitants could pay for inoculation, while others could not. The danger of infection for the latter was increased, however, because the safety measures against the spread of the disease were somewhat rudimentary even in well-regulated inoculation hospitals with conscientious doctors. The poorer sort knew this all too well. Newspapers explained to the farmers that there was no danger of infection, and doctors felt compelled to offer to inoculate the town's poor inhabitants free of charge. Legislators investigating the Marblehead smallpox and inoculation riots of 1774 uncovered strong tensions between poorer and better classes.[43]

In addition to violation of religious norms, moral norms, and prejudices concerning inoculation, illness, and death, economic norm breaking by individuals to the detriment of the community brought about counteraction in its own right. When the damage to the economic interests of the poorer and middling inhabitants was directly felt, surpassed a certain threshold level, and was traceable to one or more of the wealthy members of the community, the alignment of the community against the norm-breaking wealthy appeared openly. During the second intercolonial war, 1702–1713, the wealthy Boston merchant Andrew Belcher, as commissary general, supplied the British troops. In Boston grain prices climbed steeply. A drought and a disastrous fire in Boston aggravated the hardship. In April 1710, hungry Bostonians demanded more grain for the town. Belcher continued to load his ships for exportation. There were higher profits to be made elsewhere. A crowd prevented this kind of profiteering from badly needed supplies by cutting the rudder of a ship laden with grain and ready to sail.

Only *after* this direct action did the selectmen of Boston, friendly to mercantile interests, petition the General Court to put a stop to the exportation of grain because "of the uneasieness of the Inhabitts of this Town with respect to the Scarcity of Provisions." The council granted the petition, excepting, however, in a move to save faces, the grain already on the ship. A few days after the riot, the Superior Court convened the grand jurors, since they were responsible for indicting rioters. In view of this, several jurors desired to be dismissed. The attorney general objected to others on the ground that they too favored the riot. A judge, wanting to uphold the

---

economic interests. Roger Williams criticized the Puritans' harsh treatment of the Indians and the disregard for their rights; Anne Hutchinson repudiated the doctrine of works; the Shakers opposed private property.

[42]Theodore M. Hammett, "Two Mobs of Jacksonian Boston: Ideology and Interest," *JAH* 62:845–868 (1975–1976); Leonard L. Richards, in *Gentlemen of Property Standing: Anti-Abolition Mobs in Jacksonian America* (London, 1970), persuasively argues that antiabolition violence increased parallel to the threat it posed or was perceived to pose not only to the racial but, more important, to the social supremacy of the "gentlemen of property and standing."

[43]See Boston newspapers, 1764; report to the General Court, 1774, MA 87:384–385.

law without causing further riotous opposition, thought it would be "most convenient to proceed with a few [rioters] and not seek to inflame the Reckoning by multiplying Articles." Belcher's insistence on judicial prosecution reminded other observers of the medieval Inquisition. The jury brought in an *ignoramus*.

The argument pitted a large number of people adhering to the old concept of common weal in a corporate society against some whose business interests were better served by sanctity of their own private wealth and by economic laissez faire. Those opposing the exportation of grain in times of need argued for just prices for producer, merchant, and consumer, as measured by the cost and work input of the first two plus a profit assuring them reasonable well-being and as measured by the consumer's ability to pay considering the level of wages or other income. To opponents of this ideology and this type of socioeconomic organization, direct action in support of it was "evil" and "seditious," to be suppressed promptly and severely by the magistrates. They argued for free markets. There was grain to be had, and it should be bought at the prices demanded by the sellers. Since wages had not risen, as was admitted by the free-market advocates, people would have to consume less—a euphemism for going hungry. They also argued that wages would be sufficient, provided the wage earners abstained from enjoying a number of simple amenities of life and saved their money, to pay high prices for provisions whenever the sellers demanded them.[44]

Three years later, in 1713, with grain prices still unusually high, selectmen and a town meeting again asked Belcher to refrain from shipping off corn. Again he defied the community and thus provoked a riot, in which 200 or more rioters broke open his warehouses and distributed the stores. The General Court, which had not taken any precautionary measures earlier, now began to act. To stop direct action by the lower sort, it was deemed justified to regulate the business activities of the better sort. The importance of the corporate public good, which had not been protected in time, was thus reestablished. Exportation of grain and its use for distilling were prohibited to stop prices from becoming even more "extravagant." The council, upon receiving "information of a tumultuous and riotous assembly of the inferior sort of people," ordered distribution of grain stores to inhabitants and bakers at fixed prices, thus acknowledging the justification and the necessity of the riot. The insolence of the "inferior sort" was merely active support for the resolution of the town meeting and the selectmen against one member of the community who preferred his private interest to the common welfare. The "inferior sort" opposed the power of wealth by the power of numbers, the possibility of "violent" hunger by violent distribution of supplies.[45] Tumults about grain prices are recorded again for

[44]Depositions by John Sutherland and John Roberts, Misc. Bound Papers, vol. 7 (1703–1713), MHS; *BTR* 11:106 (1710); Council Records, 5:221–225, MSA; Sewall, *Diary,* 2 May 1710, 2:280–281; Carl Bridenbaugh, *Cities in the Wilderness: The First Century of Urban Life in America, 1625–1742,* 2nd ed. (New York, 1955), p. 196. Just price and calling: John Cotton, "The Just Price," in *Settlements to Society,* ed. Jack P. Greene (New York, 1966), pp. 108–111, and "Christian Calling," in *The Puritans: A Sourcebook of Their Writings,* ed. Perry Miller and Thomas Johnson (New York, 1963), pp. 319–327; John Winthrop, "A Model of Christian Charity," *Winthrop Papers,* 5 vols. *(MHSC;* reprint ed., Boston, 1929–1947), 2:282–295; "The Puritan Economic Ethic," *The Colonial Merchant: Sources and Readings,* ed. Stuart Bruchey (New York, 1966), pp. 91–116.
[45]Sewall, *Diary,* 2:280–281, 317, 384–385; *BTR* 8:99, 101, 104, 11:194–197; Council Records, 6:37, MSA. Note that

July 1729, and apprehensions in 1741.[46] But by then a significant shift had occurred. The economic stagnation of the thirties had been accompanied by a crumbling of the old values.

Riots still defended the interests of a unified community against extortionate individuals who placed themselves outside the traditional norms. But the riots also pitted interest groups against each other in market riots, currency riots, and others.[47] Already in the first two decades ministers preaching about just prices and fair dealing had felt it necessary to defend their right and duty to give advice on business matters. Later they either abstained from it or were openly opposed in pamphlets.[48]

Opposition to individual profiteering surged once again during the last decade before 1776, when British troops had to be supplied, and thereafter when American troops had to be supplied. Trading with the enemy had sparked crowd action in 1706,[49] and supplies to the British or colonial troops had been granted only reluctantly when the local communities feared shortages for themselves. In the seventies, diary entries and town-meeting debates, regional conventions, and local riots dealt with this issue, and their records show that what was at stake was still the theory of just prices versus private profits and of the well-being and corporate conduct of the community and its affairs versus individual getting ahead to the detriment of others.[50]

DEFIANCE OF POLITICAL AUTHORITIES AND MAGISTRATES

The rioting in support of community norms often, but by no means always, supported magistrates and the law or protected the public good against encroachments by separate private interests.[51] When members of the town elite used their offices to further their private interests, when they enforced laws contrary to public opinion, or when they passed laws or regulations disregarding the interests or

---

the contemporary meaning of "violent" was "extreme." Cf. Warden, *Boston*, pp. 65–66, 128.

[46]Council Records, 6:38, MSA. In July 1729, crowds rioted to "prevent ye landing of Irish, and to hinder the merchants from sending away ye corn as they attempted." Bridenbaugh, *Cities in the Wilderness*, p. 383. In 1741 a merchant thought it necessary to dispel apprehensions by advertising that he had neither exported grain nor bought up large quantities to prevent its going to the land bank or to raise prices. *BEP*, 18 May 1741.

[47]See notes 79–85.

[48]E.g. [Cotton Mather], *Lex Mercatoria: Or the Just Rules of Commerce Declared* (Boston, 1705), Evans 1215; Benjamin Wadsworth, *Fraud and Injustice Detected and Condemned* (Boston, 1712), Evans 1590; Joseph Sewall, *A Caveat against Covetousness* (Boston, 1718), Evans 1997; Peter Thacher, *The Fear of God Restraining Men from Unmercifulness and Iniquity in Commerce* (Boston, 1720), Evans 2188. Basic to most of the sermons on commercial dealings was I Cor. 10:24: "Let no man seek his own, but every man another's wealth." It was an integral part of what in this study is called the corporate ideology. S. E. Morison, "A Generation of Expansion and Inflation in Massachusetts History, 1713–1741," *CSMP* 19:271–272 (1916–1917).

[49]George M. Waller, *Samuel Vetch, Colonial Enterpriser* (Chapel Hill, N.C., 1960), pp. 58–65, 83–99, 198–199; cf. *Acts and Resolves*, 6:62–68; Thomas Hutchinson, *Diary and Letters of His Excellency Thomas Hutchinson*, ed. Peter Orlando Hutchinson, 2 vols. (London, 1883, 1886), 1:52–53 (1745). In one instance the majority of the inhabitants of a town traded with the enemy and rioted against an official who tried to stop the trade. *Acts and Resolves*, 19:245–246 (1776); MA 138:293–294.

[50]See Chapter 14.

[51]Maier, "Popular Uprisings," p. 4.

opinions of substantial sections of the people of the province, they themselves became the targets of riots. By violating their trust, popular interests, and popular ideological concepts, they also ended the inviolability of their persons, property, and position. To redress the wrong, the aggrieved parties frequently resorted to violence against the persons of magistrates as representatives of unpopular institutions, laws, or decisions. In this respect the riots differed from crowd action motivated by economic conflict with private community members, which, whenever feasible, was directed against material conditions and objects but did not harm persons.

Criticism of authorities, including all elected officials, was frequent, but only a small part of it was expressed in rioting. The vast majority of cases of direct action involved only individual officials; only rarely was it directed against the provincial legislature. On three counts, impressment, customs duties, and property rights over mast pines, the opposition was directed against imperial authorities. In these instances colonial officials frequently sympathized with the riot or actually supported it.

A conflict between the economic interests of officials and the interests of the town caused a riot in Boston in 1731. A petition for a new street had been rejected by the selectmen in a report signed by Selectman Jonathan Loring. A special town committee found "a Difficulty" in negotiating with the property owners and advised that the justices of the peace and the "disinterested" selectmen lay out the street. Certainly not disinterested was Selectman Loring, owner of the real estate in question. He proved obstinate, and his barn, which obstructed the passage, was torn down by a crowd one night. In the next year he failed to get the necessary votes for reelection. His offense was not so much that he opposed the public interest as that he used his official position to do so.[52]

Attempts to hinder magistrates in the execution of their duty usually involved no more than a dozen persons. Particularly liable to meet with opposition were sheriffs and their deputies, constables and watchmen, tax collectors, clerks of the market, and tithingmen or wardens who enforced the proper observation of Lord's Day. A Boston warden arresting several men for trespassing found himself surrounded by 150 persons "with an intent and design to intimidate and discourage the Wardens . . . and prevent their faithfully discharging the Duty of their said Office." Eight of the rioters, coming from diverse social groups—three merchants, one gentleman, one mariner, one brazier, and two infants—were indicted, and three of them were found guilty. Men from specific trades were normally involved in combinations and riots against the clerks of the market or against the respective surveyors of their business when these confiscated their wares because of poor quality or underweight.[53] Watchmen, who had to enforce policies and ordinances of the

[52]*BTR* 12:21, 23, 24, 25, 27, 29, 13:250–251; Council Records, 7:380, MSA; Petition of Jonathan Loring and Jonathan Jackson to Governor and Council, Sept. 1732, Curwen Family Papers, 3:97, AAS.

[53]Anti-justice of the peace: Boston, 1748, *BNL,* 20 Oct. 1748, *Mass. Brds.* 886; Machias, Nov. 1770, Council Records, 16:516, 568–569, 584–585, MSA, Hutchinson to Longfellow, 17 Dec. 1770, Letterbooks, MA 27:79. Anti-clerks of the market: Boston, July 1762, *BTR* 19:204. Anti-warden: Boston, July 1764, Superior Court of Judicature, Records, 1764, ff. 125–127, SCCH; SCF 100382; Rowe, *Letters and Diary,* Sept. 1764, p. 62. Anti-selectmen: Boston, Aug.

higher officials, were attacked instead of the latter. Court records show that among those who opposed the watch were men from all social ranks. Once a Boston "gentleman" beat up a watchman who had attempted to stop him from abusing a free Negro. Militiamen feeling abused by officers riotously vented their anger, and so did soldiers against unjust punishments or Harvard students against oppressive conduct of tutors.[54]

Rescue riots carried the opposition to authorities somewhat further. The rioters attempted to nullify actions of authorities by rescuing prisoners either directly from the hands of the arresting officials or later from prison. This relatively frequent type of riot, often executed by only a few close relatives or friends of the prisoner, was not punishable when the rescued person was later found to be innocent or when the arrest warrant was considered to be of doubtful authority.[55] In contrast to the usually limited character of these riots, the following two examples show that the defiance of authorities could happen on a larger scale. They also illustrate the self-assurance found among the rioters.

On a training day a Boston militiaman "behaved saucily to his Captain" and was sentenced "to Ride the Wooden Horse." The crowd of spectators disagreed ("got foul"), broke the wooden horse, freed the man, and covered his escape. Among the rescuers was one William Wheeler, member of a fire crew, whom the selectmen dismissed for his "misconduct," thereby ending his exemption from militia duty. However, the fire crew took a different view of the matter and expressed it. As a consequence of that, the crew's captain was dismissed for "disrespect" toward the selectmen. The whole crew then petitioned the selectmen to reinstate their captain and demanded "the privilege" to choose captains and fill vacancies without the meddling of the authorities. When the slectmen remained adamant, the whole crew resigned.[56]

Imprisoned debtors were sometimes rescued, especially when their fellow townsmen thought the debt or the methods used by the creditor unjust. A man from Woburn, Middlesex, having reportedly declared that he intended to keep a debtor imprisoned for life, was visited by about 75 men from the neighboring towns who broke his windows and then ordered him to accompany them to the gaol in Cambridge, seven miles away. There he had to sign a statement permitting the release of

---

1764, twice, *BTR* 20:98, 101. Anti-gaol keeper: Dec. 1736 (threat only), *BNL,* 10 March 1737. Anti-tax collector: 1750, MA 105:373–374. Rescue riots: Newbury, Sept. 1725, *BNL,* 9 Sept. 1725, *Mass. Brds.* 519; Boston, 1749, Proclamation, *ibid.,* 401; Boston, 1758, Superior Court of Judicature, Records, 1758, ff. 553–554, SCCH; Uxbridge, 1765, *ibid.,* 1765, f. 274; Falmouth, 1768, *Mass. Gaz.,* 4 Aug. 1768, *Mass. Brds.* 1450; Falmouth, 7 Nov. 1772, Thomas Smith and Samuel Deane, *Journals of the Rev. Thomas Smith, and the Rev. Samuel Deane, Pastors of the First Church in Portland,* ed. William Willis (Portland, Me., 1849), p. 332; Cambridge, 31 March 1774, *BNL,* 7 April 1774, *Mass. Spy,* 7 April 1774.

[54]*BTR* 20:100–101; Superior Court of Judicature, Records, 1764, f. 127; SCF 100388. Soldiers: John Winthrop to Fitz-John Winthrop, July 1707, *MHSC* 6.3:387–390 (1889); John Barnard, "Autobiography of John Barnard," *MHSC* 3.5:196 (1836); "Louisburg Journals," quoted in John Murrin, "Anglicizing an American Colony: The Transformation of Provincial Massachusetts" (Ph.D. diss., Yale Univ., 1966), pp. 121–169. Harvard: William C. Lane, "The Rebellion of 1766 in Harvard College," *CSMP* 10:33–59 (1904–1906).

[55]Quincy, ed., *Reports,* pp. 91–93, *Rex* v. *Gay.* Cf. court records throughout the century.

[56]Rowe, *Letters and Diary,* 11 Sept. 1764, p. 61; *BTR* 19:78–81 (exemption), 20:114 (dismissal), 120 (petition); Arthur W. Brayley, *A Complete History of the Boston Fire Department . . . [1630–1888]* (Boston, 1889).

the debtor. The creditor, who by law had to pay the prison expenses, was also ordered to give "the Cash [that] he had a short Time before deposited in the Hands of the Gaoler [to the released man], to bear his Expenses Home, as the Man belonged to a neighboring Town." The contemporary account concludes: "The Affair being thus settled three Cheers were given, and the Parties returned from whence they came."[57]

These riots were a check on established local authorities and their interpretation of the laws.[58] They were a common occurrence in the other colonies too.[59] While most were directed against individual officers ranking not higher than county sheriff, a few were aimed at the governor or the General Court, the summit of provincial authority. Up to the sixties no direct attacks on Massachusetts governors were reported. But the coach house and carriage of Lieutenant Governor Dumner were destroyed in 1725, and after the impressment in 1747, Governor Shirley was threatened by a crowd.[60] The General Court became the target of crowd action over three economic issues, the land bank, taxation, and currency.

The General Court's rejection of the Land Bank proposals, in 1739, caused discontent among its supporters all over the province. They threatened to force the governor and the council to approve land bank bills as currency by a march on Boston planned for 19 May 1741. Individuals were threatened with violence when they refused to accept the bills. Lack of organization and coordination among the rioters prevented the mass action, which according to rumors was to involve more than 20,000 men. Then the prospective rioters by their voting power returned a pro-land bank majority to the House of Representatives. But the governor, subservient to the so-called hard money interests in Great Britain and Massachusetts, dissolved the assembly. Hard money was constantly drained to pay mercantile debts in Britain. The resulting currency shortage depressed land values, led to payment of wages in scrip, and exacerbated debtor–creditor tensions. Debtors willing to pay could not obtain currency. Boston mechanics combined to end payment in scrip. Many merchants saw the inequity of the system and joined in the promotion of a paper currency based on real estate as security. The counterargument was that paper money depreciated and thereby put creditors and men on fixed salaries at a disadvantage. Based on sound principles, paper currency did not necessarily depreciate, but the hard money interests backed by the political authorities won the struggle.[61]

---

[57]*BNL*, 7 April 1774; *Mass. Spy*, 7 April 1774. In Portland, Me., in 1768, an attempt was made to rescue a debtor because people thought the debt was unjust. Smith and Deane, *Journals*, p. 214.

[58]Blackstone, *Commentaries*, 1:212.

[59]E.g., two incidents involving an unusually large number of people in Rhode Island (April 1774) and Pennsylvania (May 1775), in which the militia was called out. In Rhode Island 600 or more men from several country towns assembled and marched on Providence to rescue a convicted prisoner. Dwight Foster to Nabby Foster, 17 May 1774, Dwight Foster Papers, MHS; Christopher Marshall, *Extracts from the Diary of Christopher Marshall, Kept in Philadelphia and Lancaster, during the American Revolution, 1774–1781*, ed. William Duane (Albany, N.Y., 1877; reprint ed., 1969), p. 27.

[60]Bridenbaugh, *Cities in the Wilderness*, p. 383; *New Eng. Courant*, 24 July 1725; William Shirley to Lords of Trade, 1 Dec. 1747, *Correspondence of William Shirley, Governor of Massachusetts and Military Commander in America, 1731–1760*, ed. Charles H. Lincoln, 2 vols. (New York, 1912), 1:412–419.

[61]Depositions, MA 102:159–167; Council Records, 10:513–516, MSA; Hutchinson, *Diary and Letters*, 1:51, and

In 1744, large-scale antitax riots erupted in Bristol County. When the governor and the assembly attempted to enforce their authority, several towns seceded. The tax collector of the town of Swanzey, arrested for refusing to execute the tax laws, was immediately rescued from jail by hundreds of townsmen and inhabitants of neighboring townships. The militia was ordered out, and after the rioters surrendered they were indicted in a special session of the Superior Court.[62] Ninety-two men came from Swanzey, the others from four adjoining towns (Freetown, Tiverton, Barrington, and Dighton). Their occupations or statuses were listed as gentlemen (6), yeomen (71), mechanics (22),[63] mariners (3), and laborers (2), a cross-section of the communities. Tax riots also occurred in Berkshire in 1777–1779.[64]

A few years later, in 1749, during another currency controversy, a crowd of paper money supporters from agricultural towns actually marched into Boston to put pressure on the General Court. Among the representatives, however, the hard money faction under the leadership of Thomas Hutchinson prevailed and additionally adopted an act for the suppression of riots. Bostonians refused to reelect Hutchinson as representative but elected him tax collector in angry irony. When his house caught fire accidentally, there was some talk of letting it burn down. The council felt obliged to offer him a military guard.[65]

In the fifties the excise controversy pitted seaboard communities against inland farmers, poor or little people against the more wealthy ones, and brought about new potential for crowd action. This issue, however, was settled after a lively pamphlet war.[66] Other colonies, too, were beset by social and economic dissentions as well as violence, proprietary troubles, outright rebellion, large-scale land or tenants' riots, and "regulator" movements, which pitted different social and economic levels against each other and against established authorities.[67]

In almost all of the rioting against central colonial authorities, economic tensions were at the bottom of the disputes. But no simple pattern of class conflict or of seaboard versus frontier emerged. Mercantile and agrarian interests opposed each

---

History, 2:298–304; *Mass. Brds.* 744, 755. For the relevant documents, see A. M. Davis, comp., "Calendar of the Papers and Records Relating to the Land Bank of 1740, in the Massachusetts Archives and Suffolk Court Files," *CSMP* 4:1–121, 122–200 (1910), and "The Merchants' Notes of 1733," *MHSP* 2.17:184–208 (1903); cf. George A. Billias, *The Massachusetts Land Bankers of 1740* (Orono, Me., 1959); Theodore Thayer, "The Land Bank System in the American Colonies," *J. Econ. Hist.* 13:145–159 (1953); E. James Ferguson, "Currency Finance: An Interpretation of Colonial Monetary Practices," *WMQ* 3.10:153–180 (1953); Susan L. Grigg, "Currency Arguments in Massachusetts, 1714–1741: A Study in the Growth of a Popular Political Appeal" (M.A. thesis, Univ. of Wisconsin, 1970); William D. Metz, "Politics and Finance in Massachusetts" (Ph.D. diss., Univ. of Wisconsin, 1945).

[62]*Journals of the House of Representatives*, 1744–1745, pp. 81, 154, 163; McLoughlin, *New England Dissent*, 1:129–148; Superior Court of Judicature, Records, 1740–1745, April 1745, ff. 179–181, SCCH; *Acts and Resolves*, 13:419, 14:30; Council Records, 11:229–230, MSA; *Mass. Brds.* 794.

[63]The mechanics were shipwrights (7), blacksmiths (3), joiners (3), cordwainers (2), wheelwright (1), glazier (1), housewright (1), currier (1), miller (1), cooper (1), clothier (1).

[64]*Acts and Resolves*, 5:828, in the towns of Lee and Stockbridge.

[65]*BTR* 14:167; *Indep. Advertiser*, 18 Sept., 25 Sept. 1749; *BEP*, 25 Sept. 1749; Hutchinson, *History*, 3:6–7, and *Diary and Letters*, 1:49–50, 53–54; "incendiary" letters, *Acts and Resolves*, 3:479, Ch. 7, 1749–1750, notes, pp. 504–505. Andrew M. Davis, *Colonial Currency Reprints, 1682–1751*, 4 vols. (Boston, 1911).

[66]Paul S. Boyer, "Borrowed Rhetoric: The Massachusetts Excise Controversy of 1754," *WMQ* 3.21:328–351 (1964).

[67]See appendices to Brown, "Violence and the American Revolution," pp. 117–120, and, for rebellions, pp. 83–87 in the same volume. These lists of colonial and revolutionary riots are based on sporadic research only.

other on some issues. Sections of both combined on other problems to oppose the middling interest, subsistence farmers, or some merchants. This shows that within the system of deference and corporate cohesiveness there was a great potential for conflict and that by the 1730s the conflict involved general questions of authority and interest, not merely outsiders who had to be brought back into the fold.

In addition to this opposition to local or provincial authorities, three areas of regulation established by an external authority, Great Britain, led repeatedly to riotous resistance. Impressment and the customs duties were resented by sailors and merchants.[68] The white pine laws were a constant source of discord between farmers and crown officials.[69] All three alienated colonials from the British crown and set precedents for a general defiance of its authority.

In 1741, several British warships, lying in the Boston harbor, lost 50 men by desertion, and the commander, Captain Scott, applied for an impressment warrant, which was granted. The British began to impress, and sailors responded by rioting. The press gangs mistreated seamen and others and threatened to carry on the kidnapping at the meeting-house doors on Lord's Day. Several hundred inhabitants, some armed, in turn threatened to carry out immediate punishment at Captain Scott's door. The list of grievances arising from impressment was imposing to the inhabitants. Business stagnated because laborers and tradesmen did not dare to be seen on the streets. Prices for firewood and provisions rose because the suppliers did not dare to come to town. Trade declined because ships did not venture into the harbor.[70] A press gang in 1745 killed two Boston men. No riot ensued, but two years later, during another antiimpressment riot, the participants named as one of their grievances the fact that those who had been convicted of the killing had not been punished. In 1746, Bostonians voted that the grants of impressment warrants were "arbitrary and illegal proceedings of the Governour and Council" and petitioned the General Court to stop this practice, several late warrants having caused "great and insupportable Grievances." They added that

> the Injury is still heightened by the Behaviour of the Officers, who with their Lawless Rabble, like ruffians entered the Houses of some of the Inhabitants in the night to their great Terror and acted Tragical Scenes, which was closed in the inhumane murder of two brave men, who had been employed in the hottest Service during the [Louisburg] Expedition. . . .

[68]Dora M. Clark, "The Impressment of Seamen in the American Colonies," in *Essays in Colonial History Presented to Charles McLean Andrews by His Students* (New Haven, Conn., 1931), pp. 198–224; James F. Zimmerman, *Impressment of American Seamen* (New York, 1925); Neil R. Stout, *The Royal Navy in America, 1760–1775* (Annapolis, Md., 1973); Jesse Lemisch, "Jack Tar in the Streets: Merchant Seamen in the Politics of Revolutionary America," *WMQ* 3.25:371–407 (1968). See p. 381, note 44, of Lemisch's paper for further literature on impressment.

[69]Robert G. Albion, *Forests and Sea Power* (Cambridge, Mass., 1926); Joseph J. Malone, *Pine Trees and Politics: The Naval Stores and Forest Policy in Colonial New England, 1691–1775* (Seattle, 1964). For the impact of the early anti-British regulations riots on the revolutionary period, see Bernard Knollenberg, *Origin of the American Revolution: 1759–1766* (New York, 1960), pp. 127–130.

[70]Joel Shufro, "The Impressment of Seamen and the Economic Decline of Boston, 1740 to 1760" (M.A. thesis, Univ. of Chicago, 1968); Council Records, 10:519–522; *BNL*, 4 June, 11 June 1741; report, June 1741, Robert Treat Paine Papers, vol. n.d.–1755, MHS.

This procedure was deemed a breach of the Magna Charta, the province charter, and an act of Parliament.[71]

On the morning of 17 November 1747, a press gang came ashore in Boston and took 46 men from vessels in the harbor. Reportedly upon the orders of Admiral Knowles, whole crews with the exception of the captains were taken, and outward-bound vessels were raided for men.[72] Sailors were enraged because of the violence of their persons. Merchants protested because they had advanced wages to some of the impressed men. Inhabitants were infuriated because prices were rising again. The press gang had hardly finished its job when—in the words of a leading inhabitant—"a Mob, or rather body of Men arose, I believe with no other Motive, than barely to rescue if possible their Captivated Fr[ien]ds." The crowd proceeded deliberately to places where navy officers had taken lodgings to seize them as hostages. Messages to Roxbury brought about the same results there. A sheriff who interposed was put in the stocks and exhibited to public resentment. He had used "Rigour instead of Mildness," a procedure against oppressed people that had been condemned in Parliament in 1737. Governor Shirley and two councillors addressed the crowd, which listened for a while. Then, instead of following the suggestion to disperse, the rioters, sailors and artisans, began to interrogate the three officials about the impressment warrants. Dissatisfied with the answers, the rioters threw some stones through the townhouse windows, where the General Court was in emergency session. The crowd then went to the shipyards to burn a 20-gun ship that was being built there for the British navy, but settled on a barge supposedly belonging to one of the king's ships. A plan to burn it in front of the governor's mansion was discarded because of the danger to the wooden houses. It was burned on the common. While the town's militia defied an order of the governor to muster and to reestablish order, the crowd threw a line of watches around the town to prevent any navy officers from escaping during the night. The riot was subsequently blamed on "Foreign Seamen, Servants, Negroes" by the same town officials who arrested 11 rioters—6 sailors, 3 laborers, 1 bookkeeper, and 1 housewright—all liable to be impressed, none a black man, none a servant, none a minor.[73]

In the next decade there was hardly any impressment. Only at the height of the revolutionary struggles in 1768 did new disorders occur and become part of the general pattern of resistance. But in country towns the British navy's demands for mast pines caused riots. By law, trees of a certain minimum size standing on lands not granted to private persons before a certain fixed date were reserved for the navy.

---

[71]*BNL,* 28 Nov. 1745; proclamation, *Mass. Brds.* 827; Superior Court of Judicature, Records, 1746, f. 267, SCCH. *BTR* 14:77, 84–87, 17:115.

[72]This procedure was unlawful, because it endangered the safety of the ship that had to sail with a reduced crew.

[73]Samuel P. Savage to ——, 21 Nov. 1747, Samuel P. Savage Papers, MHS; letters from Gov. Shirley, *Correspondence,* 1:406–423; *BNL,* 27 Nov. 1747; "Philopatriae," *BG,* 17 Nov. 1747; *Mass. Brds.* 865; Superior Court of Judicature, Records, 1747, ff. 87–88, SCCH; orders for a military watch, 17 Nov., 19 Nov. 1747, Wendell Family Papers, 1691–1846, MHS; petition to selectmen, 20 Nov. 1747, Colburn Collection, 12 vols., 1:201, MHS, *CSMP* 3:215 (1869); *BTR* 14:127–131; committee report about the "lawless Invaders of our Libertys," in Misc. Unbound Papers, BCH; *BEP,* 14 Dec., 21 Dec. 1747; *BG,* 4 Jan. 1748; *BNL,* 17 Dec., 31 Dec. 1747, 7 Jan. 1748; *BPB,* 14 Dec. 1747; John Noble, "Notes on the Libel Suit of Knowles v. Douglass," *CSMP* 3.213–240 (1869); John A. Schutz, *William Shirley, King's Governor of Massachusetts* (Chapel Hill, N.C., 1961), pp. 127–132; George A. Wood, *William Shirley, Governor of Massachusetts, 1741–1756: A History,* vol. 1 (New York, 1920), pp. 384–388.

Loggers, farmers, and landowners were well aware of the pines' economic value for shipbuilding and disregarded the acts wherever possible. In 1763, 1366 unlawfully cut logs were seized in April, 598 from May to June, and 6389 from July to September. A surveyor of the King's Woods, John Bridger, had complained in 1707 that trees were constantly cut down, and so did his successor Surveyor John Wentworth in 1769: "these People . . . have thus, trespassed in open avowed defiance and contempt of the Law, publicly declaring they have done it, will persist, and that no Officer shall come among them."

When officials attempted to prevent evasion of the acts, the loggers accused the officials of racketeering (1718), complained that enforcement meant "a breach on our Estates and properties," and retaliated by rioting. Surveyor Bridger had to ask for a guard of 6 or 8 men to protect him while doing his duty. Surveyor Dunbar, in 1734, sent 10 men up the Connecticut River to seize and carry off illegally cut logs. The men were chased out of town by farmers and loggers, and their means of transportation was destroyed. The local justices of the peace, in breach of the laws, refused to support the surveyor. In another instance a justice refused to read a proclamation by the governor against cutting of logs, explaining, "the Governor did not understand the affair: if he had, he would not have put out such a proclamation." Israel Williams, commander of the Hampshire militia regiment and a staunch supporter of the crown during the Revolution, did read the proclamation but refused to issue a warrant to impress men for the king's service as loggers.[74]

In the third area of regulation, the trade laws, including the customs duties, most opposition was bribery or evasion by smuggling. Only five anticustoms riots were reported for the years from 1692 to 1763, not counting assaults by individuals on customs officers or harassment by colonial officials—for example, an attack on a customs informer by an official in South Carolina in 1701. In the first years after the beginning of the strict enforcement of the trade laws, crowd action increased considerably; two riots occurred in 1764, three in 1765, five in 1766. A fourth area of potential friction, the presence of British troops in the colonies, triggered only a relatively small amount of crowd action.[75]

[74]Hutchinson, *History*, 2:167–170, 186–191; Jeremy Belknap, *The History of New Hampshire*, 3 vols. (Philadelphia, 1784–1792), 3:73; editorial note to "Admiralty—White Pine Acts Jurisdiction," in John Adams, *Legal Papers of John Adams*, ed. L. K. Wroth and H. B. Zobel, 3 vols. (Cambridge, Mass., 1965) 2:247–259. 1718: MA 1:73–79, 80, 465–467. 1734: *BNL*, 9 May 1734; *New Eng. Weekly*, 29 April 1734; Charles H. Bell, *History of the Town of Exeter, New Hampshire* (Exeter, N.H., 1888), pp. 72–75. 1743: "An Act for Preventing the Destruction of White-Pine Trees . . . ," *Acts and Resolves*, 3:116–117, 1743–1744, Ch. 14. 1763–1765: *BNL*, 14 July 1763; Samuel Willis and Matthew Talcott to Jared Ingersoll, 9 April 1764, "A Selection from the Correspondence and Miscellaneous Papers of Jared Ingersoll," ed. F. B. Dexter, *New Haven Colony Hist. Soc. Papers*, 9:266–268 (1918); Eleazer Burt and Elijah Lyman to Governor Bernard, spring 1764, MA 56:421–422, extract printed in Josiah G. Holland, *History of Western Massachusetts . . . ,* 2 vols. (Springfield, Mass., 1855), 1:182–183; "A Mob in Hadley on account of logs," Josiah Pierce, "Almanac, 1765," quoted in Alice M. Walker, *Historic Hadley* (New York, 1906), p. 62. 1769: Instructions to Governor Bernard, no. 39, 18 March 1769, Instructions to the Governors, p. 2108, MHS; *Surveyor General* v. *Logs, Kennebec Company, Claimant,* case 5, John Adams, *Legal Papers*, 2:265–274; Wentworth to Loring, 10 April 1769, *ibid.*, pp. 262–263.

[75]1693: Boston (MA 61:390, 412, 453–459, 463, 477–479). 1719: Newport, R.I. 1724: Hartford County, Conn. 1735: Boston (*BNL*, 1 Jan. 1736). 1757: Portsmouth, N.H. (Maier, "Popular Uprisings," p. 10). 1764: Newport, R.I., *Rhoda* rescue, *St. John* shelled. 1765: Boston, Newport, R.I., Dighton, Mass. 1766: Boston, Falmouth, Newbury, Mass., New Haven, Conn., and Norfolk, Va. Troops: Alan Rogers, Empire and Liberty: American Resistance to British Authority, 1755–1763 (Berkeley, Cal. 1974), p. 37–48 passim; *Acts and Resolves*, 3:504–505.

The king's claim to the mast pines was always taken to be a trespass upon private property. It certainly did conflict with local economic interests. The king's claim to forced service of sailors on warships was always considered by those liable to be impressed as a trespass on their individual rights. It sometimes did conflict with merchants' interests and inflicted considerable hardship on entire communities. The customs regulations, which were easily evaded, caused wide resentment, but before 1764 they sparked relatively little violent opposition. The grievances caused by these regulations and the experience in anti-British crowd action contributed considerably to the willingness of those affected by them to accept, in later years, the claims of colonial Whigs that the British government was harmful to the colonies but could be opposed successfully, if necessary, by rioting.

SEPARATE ECONOMIC INTERESTS AND DIRECT ACTION

Originally in the small agrarian communities with fairly widespread property holding there was little economic friction that led to alignment along lines of wealth. Discontent about the quality of one's land as compared to the land of others was expressed along family lines more than between social groups.[76] With growing diversification and the resulting concomitant stratification the cleavages were no longer between families or the community and one individual but between different groups of the community. Descendants of the original settlers, those who lived far away from the town center, complained about their land's poor quality, about lack of access to roads and thus to markets, and about the distance of the meeting house. Any changes such as rerouting of roads or relocation of the meeting house meant dislocation or at least economic decline for other community members. Such problems frequently could not be solved by compromises in the town meeting. Innumerable petitions to the General Court demanding more equitable land usage, a change of town lines, and separations were the result. They were grounded in the notion that acquisition and use of private property as well as of common resources meant and demanded social responsibility for and from the owner or user. The corporate concept of private property was still widespread and, as popular republican ideology, survived well into the nineteenth century.

The first economic dissensions to appear in the colonial communities centered around ministers' salaries, religious taxes, and the location of the meeting house. Contrary to conflicts with Separates or other denominations, these were not relationships with outsiders but conflicts within the Congregational churches. In newly founded towns the parishioners clustered together geographically, socially, and economically. The later growth and spread of the population made attendance at public worship—and, by the way, at town meetings—rather difficult for the outlying residents. Some would attend church in neighboring communities, because the distance was shorter, or attempt to hire a minister of their own. Thus began a usually extended haggle over the distribution of church rates with the older settlers. Divi-

[76]See, e.g., Boyer and Nissenbaum, *Salem Possessed;* Lockridge, "Land, Population and New England Society," pp. 62–80.

sion of the community into two parishes, by legalizing and formalizing the partition, would put an end to internal haggling while at the same time increasing costs; two ministers and two meeting houses had to be supported.

Economic conflict also came out into the open when the old meeting house decayed and had to be replaced. The question was whether to rebuild on the same spot or at a place more convenient to outlying inhabitants. Since real estate values were highest in the old center, where shops, taverns, and the town hall were concentrated, the decision had important economic consequences. Relocation meant decreasing property values in the old center and increasing them in the new.[77] Compromises were difficult to achieve under these circumstances, and crowd action attempted to prevent decisions from being executed when not all groups had been accommodated.

A few examples will be used to illustrate some of the patterns of direct action in such cases. In Newbury a controversy about the meeting house began in 1685. Nearly three decades later, with still no compromise in sight, one of the groups tried to precipitate matters by riotously tearing down the old building. An attempt by one part of the inhabitants to rebuild on the old spot was stopped by the General Court upon a petition of the other groups. In 1736 several Charlestown inhabitants petitioned to be excluded from supporting the minister. The town meeting dismissed the petition. Ten days later a nightly watch had to be stationed at the house of the Reverend Hull Abbot because it had been attacked twice by groups of dissatisfied men. A 10-year controversy in South Hadley (1751–1761) included several riots preventing the erection of a new meeting house in a new location. Either the prepared beams were carried off, or the carpenters and villagers found the chosen ground occupied by a rival group on the day that had been fixed for raising the new frame.

The opposition of established settlers to relocation has been described by an inhabitant of Needham during that town's controversy:

> There had been much conversation, and some warm dispute, with respect to pulling down the old and building a new house. But there appeared but little probability that it could ever be effected in an orderly way, *as some of the wealthiest people among us* were zealous for patching up the old house and making it answer for years to come, as it had for many years before.

In October 1773 the old building was intentionally set on fire, a case of individual direct action. This solved the question of repairing or rebuilding, but the inhabitants could not agree on a new site. Finally "a small majority" voted for the old location. The corporate concept, with its emphasis on accommodation for all interests, was violated by this kind of decision making, and the other inhabitants accordingly complained of cruel oppression by a "trifling" majority and planned a riot to stop their opponents from raising the building in the old location.[78]

[77]Bushman, *From Puritan to Yankee*, pp. 54 *passim*.
[78]Newbury: Joshua Coffin, *A Sketch of the History of Newbury, Newburyport, and West Newbury, from 1635 to 1845* (Boston, 1845), pp. 176, 185. Charlestown: Richard Frothingham, Jr., *The History of Charlestown, Massachusetts*

In the second quarter of the eighteenth century, other kinds of economic conflict between groups emerged, rending communities into factions. The resulting direct action pitted interest groups against each other. In Boston the conflict centered around the question of whether to centralize the sale of provisions in market halls. In the country towns, farmers with lands along rivers opposed the erection of milldams; inhabitants depending on fishing for their own diet opposed others who wanted to commercialize this trade; farmers and fishers disagreed on the use of beaches. A whole series of institutional steps for redress had to be taken before any group would consider resorting to crowd action, and petitions to the General Court give a vivid picture of townships divided by interest groups, yet clinging to the concept of a just solution that would not damage any interest. The resulting legislative action shows that notions of equity still prevailed among all sections of society and that economic liberalism, though increasingly practiced, was not yet officially sanctioned. When negotiations did not bring about a compromise, the aggrieved group or groups—majority or minority—used direct action to defend the status quo. This means that the rioters prevented others from infringing on their rights to the detriment of their economic welfare. Whenever possible, the violence was directed against objects—fences, buildings, milldams—hardly ever against their owners.

The question of building a market to exclude shop and door-to-door trade agitated Boston for decades. Those "Projecting Gentlemen" who favored regulation were charged with covetousness, with wanting to lord it over the little people "and also in part to live upon them." The issue was one of "Great Men" versus "their Poorer Neighbours [who] stand up for equal Privileges with them." Substantial interests were involved, and during the debates in 1733–1735, town-meeting attendance was unusually high. The selectmen resorted to the unusual procedure of ordering the town clerk to be present with the assessors' valuation list "in Order to determine any Disputes which may happen to arise, respecting the Qualifications of Persons offering their votes."[79] At one meeting the inhabitants had to file in with their votes while the assessors sat at the door. Thus, the poorer people were excluded. The legality of this procedure was questioned in a petition signed by more than 100 men. The vote to build a market, said the petitioners, "was obtained (as we are firmly persuaded) not according to Law; Sundry freeholders and others, Legally qualified,

---

(Boston, 1845), p. 255. South Hadley: SCF 82330, 82388, 83198, 83297; *Acts and Resolves*, 4:1011–1013, 1768, Ch. 2, notes pp. 1033–1035; Sylvester Judd, *History of Hadley, Including the Early History of Hatfield, Smith Hadley, Amherst and Granby, Massachusetts* (1863; Springfield, Mass., 1905), pp. 391–392; cf. *ibid.*, pp. 389–390. Needham: *Acts and Resolves*, 5:866–871; George K. Clarke, *History of Needham, Massachusetts, 1711–1911* (Cambridge, Mass., 1912), pp. 197, 202. For other disorders, see J. M. Bumsted, "A Caution to Erring Christians: Ecclesiastical Disorders on Cape Cod, 1717 to 1738," *WMQ* 3.28:427 (1971) (Billingsgate, Mass., 1727); Cook, "Social Behavior and Changing Values in Dedham," p. 563; *BNL*, 14 Feb. 1760; *Mass. Brds*. 1199.
[79] John Kern, "The Politics of Violence: Colonial American Rebellions, Protests and Riots 1676–1747" (Ph.D. diss., Univ. of Wisconsin, 1976), Chap. V, A; Warden, *Boston*, pp. 74–79, 102 *passim*, 115–124; *Dialogue between a Boston Man and a Country Man* (Boston, 1714), Evans 39588; cf. Albert Matthews and Worthington C. Ford, "Protests against the Incorporation of Boston," *CSMP* 10:345–356 (1904–1906); *Mass. Brds*. 451, 456, 620, 621, 681, 683; *BNL*, 7 March, 2 May 1720, 17 May 1733, 1 April, 21 April 1737; Benjamin Colman, *Some Reasons and Arguments* (Boston, 1719), Evans 2049; *Some Considerations against Setting Up of a Market* (Boston, 1733), Evans 40029, 40030; *BTR* 12:46–48, 48–49, 65, 69–74, 98, 161, 170–172, 15:20, 30. Andrew McF. Davis, "The Merchants' Notes of 1733," *MHSP* 2.17:184–208 (1903).

being at sd. meeting by some unusual Methods, deprived of the Liberty of voting; who in the Decisions of Matters of the greatest Importance had never before been denied that Priviledge." Indeed, similar steps were never taken when matters of less direct economic impact were on the agenda. Those outvoted legally or illegally resorted to direct action.[80]

In 1735, several stalls on Dock Market Square were destroyed.[81] In 1737, prices for provisions, especially meat, were high, "not because there is a Scarcity . . . but, as we are informed, by the Management of the Drovers and Butchers, who, ('tis affirmed) have agreed to keep up the Price of Beef . . ." Arrogant behavior of the butchers was resented as "an Insult" and fights between them and other townsmen erupted. About midnight of March 24, a great number of persons pulled down the Middle Market and several adjoining shops and "Sawed Assunder Several of the Posts of the North Market."[82]

Efforts to discover the rioters were answered by an anonymous letter ordering the sheriff to desist immediately unless he wanted a civil war with a bloody ending. Five hundred men had founded a Solemn League and Covenant[83] in support of the rioters and 700 more were ready to join. A second letter ordered the commander of the militia to see to it that plans to raise the country regiments and to build private markets did not materialize, or they would cause him "and the whole Authority to Repent any such Proceeding." The letter continued, "I Now in the behalf of my self and others who assembled as a Mob assure you, That we have done what we think proper; and are of the Opinion you had as goods be still and silent, and let your Drums and Guns, for we had no Design to do the Town any Damage, but a great deal of Good."[84] One inhabitant noted,

> a great and new affliction . . . [and] shameful and vile Disorder at Boston; murmuring ag[ains]t, ye Governmt. & ye rich People among us, as if they could (by any means within their Power, besides prayer) have prevented ye Rise of Provisions . . . & none of ye Rioters or Mutineers have been yet discovered, or if suspected seem to regard it, their favourers being so many.[85]

Numerous other inhabitants did not feel that high prices were God-given, especially since the farmers sold the same provisions for much less. Accordingly, each fall, during harvest time, large numbers of Bostonians left the town on Sundays to buy directly from the farmers. Merchants' and shopkeepers' interests were affected, and magistrates began to act. They explained that "the Publick worship of God" was more important than expeditions to the country. To stop what they called

[80]*BTR* 12:258–259; Misc. Unbound Papers, 1740, BCH.

[81]*BTR* 13:270 (1735).

[82]*BEP*, 21 March 1737; *BNL*, 1 April, 29 April 1737; Council Records, 10:99–100, MSA; Governor Jonathan Belcher to the Duke of Newcastle, 14 April, 1 June 1737, State Papers, 11:4–10, Gay Transcripts, MHS.

[83]A Solemn League and Covenant had been adopted in England on 25 September 1643 pledging Parliament and the nation to a "real reformation." The idea was taken up again later during the struggles for independence. For the influence of British crowd action on Boston crowds, see Kern, "Politics of Violence," Chap. V, A.

[84]Quoted in *BEP*, 18 April 1737, Governor Belcher's proclamation.

[85]Benjamin Colman to Samuel Holden, 8 May 1737, Colman Papers, 2 vols., vol. 2, MHS.

"loose vain Persons negroes etc.," they stationed guards on the Neck, the connection between the peninsula on which the town was built and the adjoining countryside. The guards, not surprisingly, met with abuse. Another magistrate, the chief justice of the province, now stepped up the official campaign in support of Boston merchants. He included the traffic to the countryside in his charge to the grand jury. The jurors, who probably were among those charged with disturbing the public peace, ridiculed the fact that economic interests were disguised in religious rhetoric: The disorderly persons brought to Boston "corn, Apples, and other fruits of the Earth, to the great disturbance of the publick peace and Scandal of our Christian profession." They then turned the charge onto the coach-owning judges:

> at the same time [we] cannot but observe to your Honours the great disturbance occasioned to the several assemblies for publick worship in the Town of Boston by Coaches and Chaises passing and repassing near those places in the time of Service, which disorder as it has been often complained of by good Men of all denominations So we would humbly hope your Honours will in your wisdom Endeavour to point out such Methods as for the future shall effectually prevent; all which is humbly submitted.

Remarked the clerk of the court, "This Court are well satisfied, no doubt, with the Grand Jurors' Zeal."

Owners of coaches and chaises were the well-to-do, who either profited from the high prices of the provisions or could use their carriage to send out servants and family members to buy from the farmers during the week when those going on Sunday had to work for their living. In 1742 the townsmen demanded a bylaw to stop "the great Inconveniences and Disorders" resulting from use of coaches on Lord's Day. The wealthy selectmen only regulated their speed. When in 1750 the townsmen demanded a bylaw to stop Negroes and servants from buying provisions, the committee of leading inhabitants never brought in a report. Coaches, symbols of wealth and of the means to increase it, had been the target of crowd action earlier and remained so throughout the struggle for independence.[86]

Mutually exclusive occupational interests also led to rioting. Millers, dependent on water power, dammed rivers. Farmers, whose low-lying lands were flooded, and fishermen took to direct action. They destroyed milldams and, sometimes, the mills too, to prevent reerection of the dams. These riots were frequent in the forties. Later, most of these differences were solved by petitions to the General Court.[87]

Gloucester people opposed the exclusive rights of the original settlers to the clams along the Essex River. Stating that fishing was free by law and by usage, they began to dig clams, always proceeding in groups to make sure that they could deal with

[86]*BTR* 13:223 (1732), 15:2 (1736); *ibid.*, 14:11, 174, 324, 17:268–269; declaration of the jurors, 8 Aug. 1738, Superior Court of Judicature, Records, 1738, f. 169, SCCH. The foreman of the jury was Middlecott Cooke, son of the popular leader Elisha Cooke, Jr.

[87]Milldams: "Novanglus V," John Adams, *The Works of John Adams,* ed. Charles F. Adams, 10 vols. (Boston, 1850–1856), 4:77; milldam riot near Milton, SCF 86309; petition concerning milldam, 1730, MA 105:126–130; acts concerning the flooding of meadows and the passage of fish, *Acts and Resolves,* 3:133–134, 1743–1744, 263–264, 1745–1746.

forceful opposition.[88] Riots similar to the enclosure riots in Great Britain occurred about conflicting land titles when differences arose between proprietors and inhabitants, between settlers and squatters, between owners of good lands and owners of poor lands. If the person against whose property the riot was directed was so obnoxious to the rioters or to the whole community that they were unwilling to tolerate his presence in the town, his house would be pulled down. These methods were also adapted to partisan politics during the revolutionary period: Lands belonging to Tories were laid waste.[89]

Border riots were a special kind of land riot. They had their origin in unsettled boundary lines betwen colonies, which led to overlapping grants from different authorities.[90] In 1755–1756 the rioting on the Massachusetts–New York boundary approached warlike dimensions. New York land speculators and manorial lords used established authorities: sheriffs, justices, and even British troops. Spontaneous action by Massachusetts settlers received support from magistrates. Once a sheriff even raised a posse to repel British troops. The rioting, always directed toward the achievement of a specific aim, involved frequent and thorough destruction of property because one of the contending claimants had to be driven off the land. The rioters were yeomen, sometimes disguised as Indians. The size of the crowd depended on the situation; 20 or 40 came to pull down individual houses, and 50 or more assembled when some resistance was expected. Upwards of 100 or 200, often led by militia officers, opposed New York authorities and freed imprisoned rioters.

Tensions between New York manorial lords and their tenants contributed to the violence. General Gage, commander of the British troops in the American colonies, reported these economic origins: "I find many of the lower Class in this and other Provinces who defend them [the rioters], by saying they have been ill treated by their Landlords, and complain of the steps taken by the Government here to Suppress them." In 1768, after a temporary lull, rioting broke out again, and in 1780, disturbances occurred in the New Hampshire grants.[91]

Rhode Island, Connecticut, and New Hampshire had patterns of rioting similar to those of Massachusetts. Societal riots enforcing community norms, their frequency, and their status as accepted means of redress show that a certain homogeneity did exist in eighteenth-century New England towns. Sometimes they were used by town

---

[88]*Patch* v. *Herrick*, case 32, in John Adams, *Legal Papers*, 2:4–9.

[89]Boston, 1739–1740: Dilapidated fort on Fort Hill pulled down to make room for a bowling alley. *BTR* 12:247–248, 257, 14:5, 15:171. Maine, 1753: *Mass. Brds.* 968. Newcastle, Lincoln County, Me., 1762: Superior Court of Judicature, Minute Books, 1758–1764, vol. 13, no. 76, June 1762, case 31, SCCH; SCF 81909, 82268. Woolwich, Lincoln County, Me., Dec. 1768: *BEP*, 26 Dec. 1768; Council Records, 16:384–385, MSA; Boston, 1767: *BTR* 18:13 *passim*; *Emmons* v. *Brewer*, case 33, in John Adams, *Legal Papers*, 2:9–15. Cambridge, 1770: Superior Court of Judicature, Minute Books, April 1770, vol. 15, no. 88, SCCH. Countryman, "The Northern Rural Crowd."

[90]Hoerder, comp., *Violence in the United States*, pp. 26–27.

[91]1766: *BG*, 14 July, 18 Aug. 1766; *BNL*, 10 July, 14 Aug. 1766; Council Records, 16:21, 203–205, MSA; Thomas Gage, *The Correspondence of General Thomas Gage*, ed. Clarence E. Carter, 2 vols. (New Haven, Conn., 1931, 1933), 1:89–91, 99–100; 102–104, 2:362–363. 1768: *BEP*, 26 Dec. 1768; Council Records, 16:384–385; SCF 88541. New Hampshire grants: petition of Charles Phelps, 2 June 1780, MA 186:225. Oscar Handlin, "The Eastern Frontier of New York," *N.Y. Hist.* 18:50–75 (1937); Franklin L. Pope, "The Western Boundary of Massachusetts . . . ," *Berkshire Hist. and Scientific Soc. Pub.*, 1886, p.49; Irving Mark, *Agrarian Conflicts in Colonial New York, 1711–1775* (New York, 1946); Patricia U. Bonomi, *A Factious People: Politics and Society in Colonial New York*

leaders to strengthen their own position. But if necessary these authorities met with riotous opposition too. Obviously the homogeneity had definite limitations. Later, increasing diversification caused riotous enforcement of economic interests of one group. It would be all too easy, however, to condemn as hypocritical rioters' statements that they were acting for the public good or to accept official derision of dissolute Bostonians' walking many miles into the country to get provisions at lower prices. The last 50 years before the revolutionary decade saw numerous changes in the distribution of wealth and power in Massachusetts society. The gap between rich and poor increased considerably. There was probably little economic tension in a newly settled community, where all inhabitants were landowners. There might be serious problems 50 or 100 years later, when fathers could no longer provide land for their sons because every acre was already in use.[92] Stony lands that had to be taken into cultivation and the resulting low standards of living increased social tensions.[93] Such changes were obvious to a man living on the outskirts of a Massachusetts township who had to walk miles each Lord's Day with his wife and children to reach the meeting house. But the obvious was not necessarily part of the ideology. Many problems could still be solved by dividing the township into two, three, or four parishes, by rotating the location of the town meeting, by sending off young men to unsettled areas in New Hampshire. The laborious struggles in many a town meeting not to vote down a minority, to achieve a consensus, show that the ideal of a common interest, *the* public interest, was still important. Only when no compromise could be found, when the economic standing of some geographical sections, of some occupational groups, or of some social classes was endangered by the action of others, by what was derisively called a "bare" or "trifling" majority, did the farmers defend themselves by rioting. Riots supported the old notion of economic opportunities for all.

Slowly, very slowly, it dawned on some that defensive rioting was not sufficient. To prevent the wealthy from oppressing the poorer sort, inhabitants of country towns petitioned the General Court to restrict the economic freedom of the wealthy. Such limitations were in fact beneficial for all. Within the corporate system and ideology, it was as unjust to deprive the lower classes of their precarious economic independence, their means of living, as it was unjust to burden the public unnecessarily with the support of impoverished community members. Along the seaboard the situation was worse. Among the 15,000 Bostonians the selectmen in 1753 counted 1153 widows, 7 percent of the population.[94] In 1771, 29 percent of the ratable taxpayers had no property at all. Among the lower classes a feeling about social class developed and articulated itself in occasional instances of protest and riot, in crowd action against social rank.

(New York, 1971); Staughton Lynd, "Who Should Rule at Home? Dutchess County, New York, in the American Revolution," *WMQ* 3.18:330–359 (1961), and "The Tenant Rising at Livingston Manor, May 1777," *N.Y. Hist. Soc. Q.* 48:163–177 (1964).

[92]See, e.g., Lockridge and Kreider, "Evolution of Massachusetts Town Government," pp. 549–574.

[93]E.g., town of Hancock, *Acts and Resolves,* 5:656–660.

[94]Petition of Kittery, *ibid.,* pp. 184–185; cf. Chapter 9, note 9. Carl Bridenbaugh, *Cities in Revolt: Urban Life in America, 1743–1776* (New York, 1955), pp. 5, 124. Warden's *Boston* deals thoroughly with the economic development of the town.

SOCIAL RANK: GRIEVANCE OR CONFLICT

As far as we know from the meager sources, the question of social rank, unrelated to specific economic conflicts of interest, was raised in crowd action only in the larger seaboard towns, especially in Boston. Two annual celebrations gave rise to rioting directed at rank or its symbols. One was reserved to the upper classes, commencement at Harvard; the other, Pope's Day, had devolved upon the lower classes. One was celebrated in the exclusiveness of suburban Cambridge, in shaded yards and a scholarly atmosphere, the other in the bustling noisy streets of Boston's crowded quarters.

Commencement, for those who could afford to send their sons to Harvard, was an occasion for inviting friends and acquaintances to sumptuous dinners, especially when their scion had graduated. This was not merely an entertainment; it was an introduction of aspiring graduates to society, to business connections, whether mercantile or professional. But when the portly gentlemen and their families returned to Boston, the poorer classes awaited them at the Boston side of the ferry. At the landing in the Northend, Boston's low-income section, passing was "unsafe." Crowds vented their anger against this assembly of rich and powerful families, intentionally displaying their wealth in dress, coaches, chaises, and personal servants. The assemblage was extravagant to a degree that not only crowds but even authorities were concerned. Regulations were an attempt to limit or suppress such an exorbitant display of position and power. Just as these regulations dealt with the display, not with the sources of rank, the crowds were sufficiently integrated into social stratification to attack the symptoms rather than the causes, into the ideology of deference to let off the mighty and to manhandle their lowly human property instead. Servants and slaves of the wealthy were knocked down in lieu of their masters. In 1754, constables had little success in containing the crowd. The "rabble" numbered 200 in 1755 and behaved worse than ever in the opinion of their social superiors, who demanded better protection from law enforcement officers in the future.[95]

In addition to the servants, some of the women among the Cambridge feasters became targets, mainly of "indecent" verbal abuse, though some were "most indecently handled" by the rioters. The question of why they were selected is difficult to answer. Their position in colonial society was, of course, weaker than that of men. Whether display of jewelry, expensive silk clothing, and the like played a role we do not know. Natalie Z. Davis has explained aspects of religious riots in sixteenth-century France as purification or desecration. Protestant noblewomen led from a conventicle to prison were called *putains* (whores) by Catholic crowds. There were no religious undertones in the account we have of the 1755 commencement affair, but a broadside of 1740 had criticized the reveling at the college as a "Pagan Party," where "incarnate Devils dance," where "Sons of Vice" debauched in

---

[95]*BG,* 14 July 1755; *BNL,* 14 July 1763; Rowe, *Letters and Diary,* pp. 86, 103, 170, 218, 230–231; Josiah Quincy, *The History of Harvard University,* 2 vols. (Boston, 1860), 2:91–95; Samuel E. Morison, *Harvard College in the Seventeenth Century* (Cambridge, Mass., 1936), pp. 465–470.

"lawless games." There was also a connotative association between ostentatious display of luxury and unjust wealth and income on the one hand and "women of easy virtue" on the other. The women abused on commencement day came from notable families. "Notable misses" was a euphemism for prostitutes. Middle-class and upper-class women begrudged their maids and nurses the high wages. Were employed women among the crowd, comparing their earnings to the wealth of their employers? Did commencement disorders contain an element or role reversal, similar to "Negro Election Day" or the "Lords of Misrule?" From the evidence available, none of these questions can be answered with certainty. One hypothesis, that of a virtuous people versus an elite rioting in luxury, is supported by evidence from a contemporary print: "Vast Numbers" of spectators witnessed the lawless and un-Christian display of wealth at commencement, and each and every one of them knew that this was the present and the future provincial elite in politics, law, and religion, an elite that had consciously and successfully endeavored to increase and rigidify notions of rank, so that by 1750 all students were ranked exclusively according to the social prestige of their parents.[96]

The awareness of the rioters that their opponents considered themselves superior and their challenge to this stratification are evidenced by the frequent statements that they were as good as their higher-placed opponents or prosecutors. Such self-assertiveness was often twisted into "insolence" or even "licentiousness" in reports by better-placed observers to whom any behavior different from the standard they set for themselves and others was disorderly. Articulate spokesmen in a crowd became "insolent fellows" because they dared pose questions to their social superiors. But most societies even have specific customs permitting reversal of social roles, so that those who usually belong to the inarticulate and lowly can for a day or two assume the role of the articulate rulers. Ritualization and characterization as a "game" channel the societally explosive forces behind such activities into the sphere of "recreation" and frolic.[97]

In Massachusetts this reversal of roles took place on Pope's Day, originating in the Gunpowder and Popish Plots. The day was intended to encourage "an Abhorrence of Popery and Forming a Spirit of Loyalty," and its activities have usually been reported to consist merely of a procession carrying the effigies of a Pope, a pretender, and sometimes a person called Nancy Dawson, which were finally committed to a bonfire. A more detailed investigation of the customs reveals that

[96]Natalie Zemon Davis, "The Rites of Violence: Religious Riot in Sixteenth-Century France," *Past and Present* 59:59, 79 (May 1972). Providence: Dwight Foster to Nabby Foster, 22 July 1774, Dwight Foster Papers, 1757–1790, MHS; *A Satyrical Description of Commencement* (Boston, 1740?), Evans 40209; "Rebeckah Housewife" and "Hannah Prudence," in *BG*, 21 Jan. 1765. On "Lords of the Misrule," see Robert Malcolmson, *Popular Recreations in English Society, 1700–1850* (Cambridge, 1973), pp. 28, 165–166 *passim;* Alfred F. Young, "Pope's Day, Tar and Feathers, and 'Cornet Joyce, jun.': From Ritual to Rebellion in Boston, 1745–1775" (Paper prepared for the Anglo-American Labor Historians' Conference, Rutgers Univ., April 1973), pp. II 18–19 (forthcoming). Negro Election Day: Nathaniel B. Shurtleff, "Negro Election Day," *MHSP* 13:45–46 (1873–1874); Rowe, *Letters and Diary,* 11 Sept. 1764, p. 61; *Mass. Spy,* 29 Sept. 1770; Samuel E. Morison, "Precedence at Harvard College in the Seventeenth Century," *AASP* 42:374–380, 412–417 (1932).

[97]E.g., Shirley to Lords of Trade, 1 Dec. 1747, *Correspondence,* 1:413, about one of the impressment rioters; Hutchinson, *History,* 3:88, about the Stamp Act rioters.

contributions were collected from those in the community who could afford it. For once, lower-class people could collect money and in the process enter the houses of the wealthier ones, enact little plays, and, to "the great annoyance" of their hosts, behave as though they were masters of the house.[98]

Boston's Pope's Day constituency came from the Northend and the Southend, the town's low-income sections, where artisans of the shipbuilding and outfitting trades predominated. The Northend was the oldest section in town, and in the forties the people in the newer and expanding Southend became jealous of the former's predominance. The developing rivalry expressed itself in separate Pope's Day parades and in town-meeting politics. But both sections were of one mind when it came to rejecting magistrates' interference in Pope's Day activities.[99]

The Pope's Day crowds had a tradition and lore that stemmed from English practices and expressed a rudimentary class consciousness: "a tradition of patriotic anti-Stuart Protestantism, the Puritan's seventeenth-century heritage"; a popularized ritual, already politicized in England, including effigies, pageantry, mummery ("street theater"), bonfires, and effigy burning; and a practice of reversal of social roles, collection of contributions by posing as haughty "better sort." The annual celebration provided experience in self-organization for the lower classes, a training ground for direct action and violence, and an occasion for expression of "ill-defined feelings of class and defiance of authorities." On this day, interference by officials, who belonged to a different social class, was fought off by the crowd, consisting mainly of mechanics and apprentices. It was on this tradition that Boston's leadership drew when it needed manpower for the symbolic mass action against the Stamp Act, or rather it drew on those visible parts of the tradition that it knew and accepted. It neglected to inspect the lore and its implications for social relations between crowds and leaders, between rioters and riot targets of the better sort.[100]

On other festive occasions the separation of elite and people brought about articulation of discontent about the exclusiveness of the "gentlemen of distinction" celebrating inside the town hall.[101] The Boston gentlemen also formed separate military companies, exempted from militia duty, which filled their ranks by co-optation and took on a somewhat aristocratic bearing. The Cadet Company, geared

[98]Young, "Pope's Day," pp. II 18–19, notes 84–88. On role reversal; *Acts and Resolves,* 3:664; James Freeman, Notebook, 1745–1765, MHS; for celebrations in Gloucester, see Samuel Chandler, Diaries, 1761–1764, 1769–1772, 5 Nov. 1764, Essex Institute, Salem, Mass. Salem: Henfield Diary, 5 Nov. 1767, quoted in Joseph B. Felt, *The Annals of Salem from Its First Settlement* (Salem, Mass., 1827) p. 470. See also Chapter 2, notes 30–35. See *Encyclopedia Britannica* for the Gunpowder Plot by Robert Catesby and Guy Fawkes in 1605 and the Popish Plot more than 70 years later by Titus Oakes. Figuratively, "popery" meant "Assumption or acceptance of authority like that of the pope" (*Oxford English Dictionary*). It was used in this meaning in the Berkshire County Statement, 17 November 1778: "When Men form the social Compact, for the Majority to consent to be governed by the Minority is down right popery in politicks, as submission to him who claims Infallibility, and of being the only Judge of Right and rong is popery in Religion." Oscar Handlin and Mary F. Handlin, eds., *The Popular Sources of Political Authority: Documents on the Massachusetts Constitution of 1780* (Cambridge, Mass., 1966), p. 375.

[99]*Acts and Resolves,* 3:647–648, 1752–1753, Ch. 18, note p. 664; SCF 82310.

[100]Rowe, *Letters and Diary,* 5 Nov. 1764, pp. 64–68. I am grateful to Alfred F. Young for permission to quote and paraphrase his conclusions from his paper "Pope's Day," p. II 20; forthcoming as *From Ritual to Rebellion.*

[101]Council Records, 15:181, MSA; SCF 83317.

to ceremonial duties for the governor, was open to master craftsmen and seems to have become controversial only during the anti-British struggles, when the question arose whether it should do duty in honor of disliked placemen. The Ancient and Honorable Artillery Company, once a volunteer force to protect Boston, had become superfluous. But it still mustered on Artillery Election Day to name its officers. Crowds mustered too, among them, in 1765, a man calling himself Veritas, who watched the Ancient and Honorable feasters finish off "a quarter of beef, six hams of bacon, five quarters of lamb, two dozen of ducks, six dozen of dunghill fowls; besides partridges, plumb-puddings, custards, cheese, a quarter-cask of wine, two barrels of punch, etc. etc. etc." "So much pomp, not to say ostentatious appearance," said Veritas, was "diametrically opposite to the public interest." That ministers in their special sermons called the members of the company "guardians of the people, and only bulwark of the country" was simply "ridiculous." If they wanted to, the men might open a private shooting club for their diversion instead of posing as a public institution and even drawing government subsidies.

Veritas was by no means a social radical. Artillery Election Day should also cease to be a popular holiday, occasioning according to his calculations a loss of income of £600.[102] Similar arguments about profitable use of resources were a distinct part of colonial concern about changes in the sixties and seventies. Their meaning for the relationship between different sections of the community and more specifically between crowds and merchants as well as political leadership is obvious. Personal and cultural relations began to be replaced by financial and commercial considerations. The social primacy of the corporate system was challenged by the primacy of economic effect, mutual obligations were replaced by everybody's obligation to maximize the "gross national (here, local) product," and equitable distribution and participation were sacrificed to liberalistic getting ahead. Such changes had been in the making for many decades; witness the endless currency debates, the changes in economic rioting, the ever recurring emphasis on local manufactures, the increasing conceptualization of social differences as something negative, threatening the community structures. They were to come into their own only with the stress on manufacturing, and even later—the protective tariff system in the early national period. But they were a potent force in the revolutionary struggles for an American economy and an American ideology.[103]

Display of wealth, as on commencement and Artillery Election Day, and the economic and social stratification that lay at its root led to "murmuring" among the people, as Samuel Adams would have put it. For 50 years, coaches, chaises, and

---

[102]Veritas, *BEP*, 22 April, 6 May 1765, answered by "N.G." in the supposedly radical *BG*, 29 April 1765; Anna Green Winslow, *Diary of Anna Green Winslow: A Boston School Girl of 1771*, ed. Alice Morse Earle (Boston, 1894), 1 June 1772, p. 66; *BEP*, 14 June 1773; John Andrews, "Letters of John Andrews, Esq., Boston 1772–1776," ed. Winthrop Sargent, *MHSP* 8:373 (1864–1865), 4 Oct. 1774. Andrews called the members of the company "pompions."

[103]The economic side of thought and action has been much neglected in post-World War II consensus scholarship, as has been repeatedly pointed out in this study. It is still necessary to go back to the contemporary pamphlets on the currency, market, bank, and excise issues. See the bibliography in Miller and Johnson, eds., *The Puritans*, pp. 792–798, notes in Marc Egnal and Joseph A. Ernst, "An Economic Interpretation of the American Revolution," *WMQ* 3.29:1–32 (1972), and notes in Dirk Hoerder, "Vom korporativen zum liberalen Eigentumsbegriff: Ein Element der amerikanischen Revolution," *Geschichte und Gesellschaft*, special issue, no. 2, pp. 76–100 (Göttingen 1976).

carriages, which only the wealthy could afford, were attacked in lieu of their owners when these had offended the community. Such incidents were recorded for 1727 and 1738. They happened during the revolutionary period (1765, 1768, and 1770) and later (1785), as well as in other colonies. Hostility was extended to the riding horses of wealthy Tories in the countryside after 1774. Windowpanes were selected as targets not merely because they were easy to break but because they were expensive imports.[104] In Boston, well-stocked wine cellars, silver plate, and expensive furniture caused concern among rioters who entered the houses of wealthy crown officials. It did not escape their attention that Whig officials and merchants could afford similar luxuries. The furniture in the mansion of Nicholas Boylston, a wealthy Boston merchant, was alone worth £1000 sterling—200 times as much as the average total real estate holdings of a Pope's Day rioter. There were moral implications. Wealth led to pride and arrogance; its ostentatious display was sinful. There were religious implications. Coaches could be used for fashionable visits or outings on Lord's Day, when humble praying would have been appropriate. And there were economic implications. Sending servants out to buy cheap food in the countryside reduced the necessity for farmers to bring their produce to town for sale, thus decreasing competition. The wealth of some thus worked to the detriment of others and was resented accordingly.[105]

Testimony about the existence of and awareness about the problems created by wealth comes from the innumerable sermons exhorting Massachusetts people to lead a frugal life without ambition and ostentation, covetousness and pride. Petitions about the immediate concerns of daily life show a similar concern. Thus, one Nathaniel Donnell, suing the wealthy proprietors of the town in which he lived, demanded that the trial be moved to a different county in order to find an impartial jury. The sheriff for Suffolk County did not serve a court summons on Boston's representative and wealthy merchant, John Hancock, because of his "unwillingness to be further importunate with a *Gentleman of his great superiority.*"

People also resented high judicial fees and the arrogant behavior of judge and lawyers. Both prospered in times of economic hardship, when cases to recover debts were numerous, for they had a monopoly on the understanding of the technicalities of the law. The case of a sailor versus a shipowner may serve as an example. The captain of a ship seized by a privateer left the mate as hostage to the pirates. When the shipowner refused to pay ransom, the mate, "in a sick and destitute condition," remained in prison for six years. Finally his friends raised £213.10 by subscription—four to eight years' total wages. Lawyers and courts argued about jurisdiction, shipowners' rights, and whether appeal was admissible in cases involving sums of less than £300. The sailor lost his case, in addition to his health, money, time, and costs. To him, law and justice must have appeared to be tools of wealthy shipowners.[106]

---

[104]To this must be added the attempts to tax coaches, 1755, 1768, 1773.

[105]For coaches, see the Declaration of the Grand Inquest, 1738, Superior Court of Judicature, Records, 1738, f. 169, SCCH. For John Adams's description of Boylston's house, John Adams, *Diary and Autobiography of John Adams,* ed. L. H. Butterfield, 3 vols. (Cambridge, Mass., 1961), 16 Jan. 1766, 1:294.

[106]Memorial of Nathaniel Donnell, 6 June 1764, MA 6.334 o-r; Greenleaf to Murray, 4 May 1770, in John Adams, *Legal Papers,* 1:217–218; Gerald W. Gawalt, "Sources of Anti-Lawyer Sentiment in Massachusetts, 1740–1840,"

Not only did the judicial procedures suffer from the partiality to high rank. Even greater dangers to the rights and standing of common people arose from the use of political institutions for the exclusive benefit of men of the better sort. Townsmen all over the colony repeatedly made this danger the theme of their instructions to their representatives. In 1753, 600 Boston voters angrily complained that legislative land grants "Serve Some Perticuler Persons and give Others an Oppertunity to Inritch them Selves by Indirect means." They demanded equal distribution to the corporate communities.

In 1764 the demand was made that representatives accepting "Posts of Profit from the Crown or the Governor" should vacate their seats "till their Constituents shall have the Opportunity of Re-Electing them if they please—or of returning others in their room." At the same time a high official congratulated a beneficiary of such political patronage, adding that he would now be able "to look down with a Smile of Contempt on Town Meetings."[107]

Later debates over the Constitution showed how widespread were suspicions about men corrupted by power and prestige. Deference, inculcated over a century and a half, could sometimes give way to opposition based on an ideology emanating from three different strains of thought, the Protestant–Puritan tradition (virtue versus corruption in all men), the rudimentary concepts about the dangers inherent in high rank (honest poverty versus treacherous grandeur), and the Whig–Commonwealthmen warnings about the consequences of unchecked power.

Experience in self-government, a relative economic independence of large sections of the agrarian population, and the three components of ideology explain the emergence of popular concepts about government. The notions of a stake in society and of deference placed restrictions on both self-government and the expression of criticism. From the beginning of the settlement, the legislators had attempted to strengthen social deference and social distinction. But until the revolutionary period the same legislature also attempted to maintain a relative economic equality of opportunities in keeping with the concept of corporate cohesiveness and public good. The ideal state would be a community with neither poor people who could become a charge of the public nor rich people who could overcharge the public.

While liberalistic use of property slowly eroded the corporate social responsibilities, the habit of deference stayed and had an impact even on rioting. Violence increased with decreasing social rank of the target. Crowds acting against members of the better sort merely turned against outward signs of their position. By attacking coaches, rioters desecrated symbols of rank and wealth. The actual social and

---

Am. J. Legal Hist. 14:283–300 (1970); Zanger, "Crime and Punishment in Early Massachusetts," pp. 471–477. Thus, when Chief Justice and Loyalist Peter Oliver complained about crowds that "Brick bat Law is very partial" (*American Rebellion*, p. 69), only his class bias prevented him from seeing that the same was true for statute law. *Scollay* v. *Dunn, Dunn* v. *Scollay*, Quincy, ed., *Reports*, pp. 74–83, 187–188.

[107]*BTR* 12:42–44, 16:120; Sewall to Thomas Robie, 25 May 1770, Robie-Sewall Papers, 1611–1789, MHS. Samuel Paine's claim for compensation as refugee Loyalist stated about judicial offices: "The appointments were during good behaviour but always continued for Life." B. F. Stevens, Transcripts of American Loyalist Claims, vols. 13 and 14: Massachusetts Loyalist Claims, NYPL, MF in MHS, 13:231; cf. Oliver to ———, 7 May 1767, printed in Israel Mauduit, *A Short View of the History of the Colony of Massachusetts Bay* (London, 1769), pp. 31–36.

economic standing of the owners was hardly impaired. Only enclosure riots in the countryside were directed against the actual basis of economic position.

John Hancock, proudly displaying his wealth, appeased the townsmen by frequent gifts, thus creating the impression that he remained down to earth and that he used his private wealth for public purposes.[108] The prerequisites for tension due to social rank and economic position were present, resentment against wealth and its display was latent among inhabitants of middling property or less, but an explicit commitment to leveling principles or even a program of social reform was lacking. In Boston, class consciousness existed perhaps subconsciously, surfacing only when other reasons caused social contentions; compared to New York or Philadelphia, Boston seemed a niche of social harmony. Election contests and the intense partisanship over economic issues—currency, banks, town–country relationships, markets, excise—that from the overthrow of Governor Andros to the 1750s agitated the community seemed a thing of the past. Such controversies were solved or smothered in the broad range of clubs, particularly the Merchants' Club and the caucuses. Under the far-reaching influence and skillful management of Samuel Adams and of those who shared with him the ideology of corporate economics and politics, Boston seemed closer to corporate cohesiveness in its political life than many a smaller community with fewer social differences and less economic diversification. Lower-class protest correlates positively with middle-class reform activity, as other studies have shown, and the latter was absent from Boston politics. That this artificial equilibrium was rather precarious was shown by the expression of lower-class interests during the Stamp Act period, August to December 1765, and by the "mercenary" spirit of the merchants during the nonimportation period, 1768 to 1770. That the quest for the corporate ideal had become anachronistic was evidenced when merchants in Boston and developments in the whole province by-passed its advocates in the late seventies.[109]

Social stratification was apparent almost everywhere—for example, when meeting-house pews were assigned or, as in Boston, sold, and when Harvard students were no longer ranked according to achievement, as in the early decades of the college, but according to the social standing of their parents. Leading town officials expected reelection and, in Boston, won reelection majorities of up to 100 percent of the votes cast, 90 percent or more being the rule. Lucrative appointive offices, in keeping with seventeenth- and eighteenth-century traditions, were con-

[108]Richard D. Brown, in *Revolutionary Politics in Massachusetts. The Boston Committee of Correspondence and the Towns, 1772–1774* (Cambridge, Mass., 1970), pp. 119–120, points out the inward-directed suspicions about men in power in the towns' responses to the publication of Hutchinson's letters to the home government in 1773. Cf. Patterson, *Political Parties*, pp. 165–166 *passim*. On Hancock, see *BTR* 18:51; *BG*, 24 Feb., 18 May 1772, 26 Sept. 1774; William Pynchon, *The Diary of William Pynchon of Salem*, ed. F. E. Oliver (Boston, 1890), 25 June 1778, p. 54.

[109]Alan Day and Katherine Day, "Another Look at the Boston 'Caucus,'" *J. Am. Studies (GB)* 5:19–45 (1971); Roger J. Champagne, "Liberty Boys and Mechanics of New York City, 1764–1774," *Labor History* 8:115–135 (1967); Staughton Lynd and Alfred F. Young, "After Carl Becker: The Mechanics and New York City Politics, 1774–1801," *Labor History* 5:215–276 (1964); Charles S. Olton, *Artisans for Independence: Philadelphia Mechanics and the American Revolution* (Syracuse, N.Y. 1975); Richard Walsh, *Charleston's Sons of Liberty: A Study of the Artisans, 1763–1789* (Columbia, S.C., 1959). Patterson, *Political Parties*, p. 251.

sidered the property of the officeholder to a degree that they almost became hereditary. Titles, the outward badges of office and position, still retained their meaning by
the middle of the eighteenth century. A study of all ranks of town officials reveals
that the higher the rank of an officeholder, the more titles—esquire, gentleman,
deacon, colonel—he had. Legal usage confirms these findings. Legal documents
omitting a title were invalid, as is shown by a case brought by someone designated
merely as yeoman, though his commission made him "a *Gentleman* by office."
The court was less particular when an artisan attempted to have a writ abated
because he had been called a blacksmith. Anybody could be a blacksmith, a
gunsmith, and so forth, but his particular calling was that of nailor. The judges did
not abate the writ but were sufficiently well informed about craft consciousness that
some of them argued that the writ was not abated merely because the nailor had "at
certain Times done some Articles of Blacksmith's Work."[110]

While rank and deference remained the all-pervading principles of social relations, courts, in session after session, acted against "licentiousness" from below,
and crowds on rare occasions opposed it when the better sort was getting uppity, as
on commencement. Only the struggles against wealthy placemen and powerful
officials after 1765 brought about a decline of deference. The new awareness was
expressed in debates about a new political system after 1774, in crowd action during
"tours of education" against Tories, and occasionally in expulsion of those who
arrogated for themselves the top position in the community.

LEGALITY AND LEGITIMACY OF CROWD ACTION

Several times in the course of the history of the province, attempts were made to
curb crowd action by legislative action. A 1703 law was directed mainly against
disorders of any kind. In 1721 Governor Shute's complaints about "levelling ten-
dencies" and his rejection of two popular Boston representatives, Elisha Cooke and
John Clarke, as Speakers of the House of Representatives led to considerable
political ferment. The governor demanded a riot act, but Boston's representatives
successfully opposed it. Occasionally measures against Pope's Day crowds were
taken, because these celebrations had been found "to encourage . . . opposition to
all government and order." As a result, a law tightened the definition of rioters to
(1) three persons, any or all of them armed with sticks or other weapons, or disguised or with painted faces, carrying posters, or exacting money; (2) three unarmed persons assembled between sunset and sunrise; and (3) any persons concerned in lighting a bonfire within 50 yards of any house. Any such people could be
arrested and punished without reading them a proclamation to disperse. Masters
were to be held responsible for their servants. Chief Justice Hutchinson explained
after the Pope's Day riot of 1764 that rioting implies "an Intent to commit some

[110]Dinkin, "Seating the Meeting House," pp. 450–464; Morison, "Precedence at Harvard College," pp. 371–431, and "Ye Mastery of Ye Ages Solved, or How Placing Worked at Colonial Harvard and Yale," *Harvard Alumni Bull.* vol. 57 (1954); Hoerder, *Society and Government,* pp. 41 *passim;* Quincy, ed., *Reports,* pp. 8–9, 237–238; Norman H. Dawes, "Titles as Symbols of Prestige in Seventeenth Century New England," *WMQ* 3.6:69–83 (1949).

unlawful Act.'' If rioters "take not one Step they ought to be punished for this Intent [as unlawful assembly]; if they move forward, it is a Rout; if they commit any one Act, it is a Riot.'' The law remained on the books throughout the revolutionary period. This was not the case with an act passed against politically motivated riots.[111]

After the "currency riots" of 1750, the General Court thought it expedient to pass a new riot act, to suppress crowd action expressing political opposition. Its main provisions were that assemblies of 12 or more persons, armed with clubs or other weapons, or 50 or more unarmed persons could be dispersed by any civil magistrate if they were unlawfully gathered. If the rioters did not leave within one hour's time, they were to be arrested, if necessary with the help of a posse recruited from other inhabitants. Officers were to be "held guiltless" if any rioter resisting arrest was killed. The punishments were severe: forfeiture of a part or the whole of their estates, whipping, or imprisonment for one year with quarterly whippings at the pillory. Rescue riots, on the other hand, were punishable only after the principal was obtained. Should the rescued prisoner, upon trial, be acquitted of the accusations leveled against him, the previous rescue was justified and nonpunishable.[112]

The combination of subjects to redress public grievances, however, could also be viewed in a different way. "Levying War against the King is High Treason; as where People set about redressing public Wrongs." Even combinations of more than 10 persons to present a petition were punishable. Influential colonial lawyers and politicians extended the limitations on redressing public wrongs even further. Josiah Quincy reported Hutchinson as saying, "Yet, for Persons under Pretence of Rectifying publick Wrongs, to invade private Rights is highly criminal." But on this issue there was anything but unanimity. Colonists in 1764 quoted a speech in Parliament of the year 1737:

> The People seldom or never assemble in any riotous or tumultuous Manner, unless when they are oppressed, or at least imagine they are oppressed. If the People should be mistaken, and imagine they are oppressed, when they are not, it is the Duty of the *Magistrate* to endeavour first to correct their Mistake by fair Means and just Reasoning; in common Humanity he is obliged to take this Method, before he has Recourse to such Methods as may bring *Death* and *Destruction* upon a great Number of his Fellow-Countrymen; and this Method will generally prevail, where they have not met with any real Oppression: But when this happens to be the Case, it cannot be expected that they will give Ear to their Oppressor; nor can the severest Laws, nor the most rigorous Execution of those Laws, always prevent the People's becoming tumultuous:—You may short them—You may hang them—But till the Oppression is removed or alleviated, they will never be quiet, till

[111]Warden, *Boston*, p. 98; *Acts and Resolves*, 1:535–536, 1703, 2:24–25, 1715–1716, 3:647–648, 1752–1753, 4:634, 1762; *BTR* 8:154–155; Council Records, 14:467, MSA; instructions to the grand jury, March 1765, Quincy, ed., *Reports*, pp. 113–114; Hutchinson, *History*, 2:166, 174–178.

[112]*Acts and Resolves*, 3:544–546, 1750–1751, Ch. 17; *The County and Town Officer, or an Abridgement of the Laws of the Province of the Massachusetts-Bay*, by a gentleman (Boston, 1768), pp. 37, 43, Evans 10967; Blackstone, *Commentaries*, 4:131.

the greatest Part of them are destroyed. The only effectual Method to suppress Tumults will be, to enquire into the Causes, and to take such Measures as may be proper for removing those Causes: For in the *Body Political,* as in the *Body Natural,* while the Cause remains, it is impossible to remove the Distemper.

Royal governors and Whig lawyers both accepted this reasoning. Said Thomas Hutchinson in 1768, "Mobs a sort of them at least are constitutional." "If Popular Commotions can be justifyed," noted John Adams somewhat more cautiously, "in Opposition to Attacks upon the Constitution, it can be only when Fundamentals are invaded, nor then unless for absolute Necessity and with great Caution."[113] Blackstone, considering divisions between "society at large and any magistrates," noted that they must "be decided by the voice of society itself: there is not upon earth any other tribunal to resort to." These principles help to illuminate crowd action and other forms of the struggle for independence as well as rioting within colonial society.[114]

In everyday language the use of the term "riot" varied considerably from its use in legal practice. "Riot" generally stood for any "wanton, loose, or wasteful living; debauchery, dissipation, extravagance." The basic implication is that something is done in an unrestrained manner. This is the key to understanding eighteenth-century rioting. Riots were an extraordinary means to get redress from extraordinary conduct of individuals or groups. Overstepping of bounds set by social norms justified casting aside traditional restraints on violent counteraction. Those who "lived in riot," "overcharged" the public, "rioted on the spoils of the people," or "rioted in luxury and power"—that is, displayed their wealth and power extravagantly—provoked riotous, violent punishment or opposition. In Great Britain unrestrained profit making or display of luxury had once been punishable offenses similar to the unlawful use of violence. Because of such offenders' standing in society and because of the judges' social position, such laws were difficult to enforce and, with one minor exception, had been repealed at the beginning of the seventeenth century. But their intent was kept alive in popular lore, and crowd reaction against the symbols of wealth continued throughout the colonial period.[115]

---

[113]*The Conduct of the Paxton Men* (Philadelphia, 1764), reprinted in John R. Dunbar, ed., *The Paxton Papers* (The Hague, 1957), pp. 278–279; Hutchinson to Grant, 27 July 1768, Letterbooks, MA 26:317; John Adams to Abigail Adams, 7 July 1774, *Adams Family Correspondence,* ed. L. H. Butterfield, 2 vols. (Cambridge, Mass., 1963), 1:131; Quincy, ed., *Reports,* pp. 219–221, 246–250.

[114]Blackstone, *Commentaries,* 1:212; Gerald Stourzh, "William Blackstone: Teacher of Revolution," *Jahrbuch für Amerikastudien* 15:184–200 (1970). Cf. J. H. Plumb, *The Origins of Political Stability in England, 1675–1725* (Boston, 1967); Max Beloff, *Public Order and Popular Disturbances, 1660–1714* (Oxford, 1938); T. A. Critchley, *The Conquest of Violence: Order and Liberty in Britain* (London, 1970). The issue came up during the debates over the Declaration of Independence, noting the consent of the governed as a prerequisite for government and the right to abolish unjust governments. It should be noted that the inscription on the Jefferson Memorial in Washington, D.C., omits the words "consent of the governed" [Frank W. Fetter, "The Revision of the Declaration of Independence in 1941," *WMQ* 3.31:133–138 (1974)]; and that the Pennsylvania Bicentennial Commission reversed its decision to mount a campaign for citizens' pledges to the Declaration, arguing, "it's a pretty revolutionary document. There may be a lot of people unwilling to sign it" [*The Progressive* 38(12):13 (Dec. 1974), quoting the commission].

[115]*Oxford English Dictionary; BTR* 14:58–60, draft instructions to the representatives, 25 Sept. 1744; Blackstone, *Commentaries,* 4:158–60 (usury, forestalling, regrating, engrossing, monopolizing), 169–170 (idleness, luxury). Ezra Stiles once spoke explicitly of an "extravagant" mob. *Extracts from Itineraries and Other Miscellanies of Ezra*

Punishments inflicted or destruction done by rioters resembled patterns established by law—forfeiture of goods or estates to prevent the offender from repeating his misdeed or destruction of the means of the offense in a monarchy. The penalty for high treason was "to be out of the King's protection"; in Massachusetts the traitors left the protection of the community. According to law and custom, they were to be "drawn to the gallows, and not [to] be carried or walk; though usually a sledge or hurdle is allowed, to preserve the offender from the torment of being dragged on the ground or pavement." Crowds replaced the sledge by a cart and forced their victims to sit under the gallows with a rope around their necks. The similarity of the punishments for offenses against the sovereign monarch and the people may suggest that a rudimentary concept of the people's sovereignty existed and that certainly a concept of equality before the law existed. As to the alleged severity or even brutality of some crowd actions, official usage was frequently more brutal. Tarring and feathering, condemned as a beastly practice of a mean rabble, had been introduced by Richard I as retribution for mere theft in the navy. In contemporary armies corporal punishment was infinitely more merciless and cruel. It is by now a commonplace that crowd action never caused as much suffering and as many casualties as did the repressive action of government, military, and later private police and thug forces.[116]

An evaluation of crowd violence has to consider the possibility of its having mythological aspects.[117] Infliction of violence was originally intended to purify, not punish. The common origin of ducking offenders in harbors or rivers, keelhauling, and religious baptism is the idea of a symbolic purification. In contemporary armies these redemptive components of punishments had been replaced by brutality and terror. The infliction of 1000 lashes meant beating the offender to a pulp and terrifying others rather than purification. Fumigation, used in colonial Massachusetts against smallpox and against Tories, was supposed to have cleansing effects or even inspiring ones (oracles). Noises and fires were designed to exorcise evil spirits. Public exhibition of offenders, usually explained by its deterrent effects, had a parallel in the belief that evil spirits, once brought out into the open, lose their powers. Some rites and punishments had sexual undertones.[118]

The complex nature of the mythological aspects becomes manifest in the implica-

Stiles, 1755–1794, with a Selection from His Correspondence, ed. Franklin B. Dexter (New Haven, Conn., 1916), p. 509.

[116]Blackstone, *Commentaries*, 4:92, 117, 374–381.

[117]James G. Frazer, *The Golden Bough*, 13 vols. (London, 1922); H. B. Alexander, *North American Mythology* (Boston, 1916); F. G. Child, ed., *The English and Scottish Popular Ballads*, 5 vols. (New York, 1956); *Journal of American Folklore* (Boston, 1888 and later); G. L. Kittredge, *Witchcraft in Old and New England* (Cambridge, Mass., 1929); S. Thompson, *Motif-Index of Folk-Literature*, 6 vols. (Helsinki, 1932); John Brand, *Observations on Popular Antiquities* (Newcastle-upon-Tyne, 1777), rev. ed. by Henry Ellis, 2 vols. (London, 1813); Henry Bourne, *Antiquitates Vulgares; or the Antiquities of the Common People* (Newcastle, 1725); Malcolmson, *Popular Recreations*.

[118]For "riding Skimmington," see note 34. The lawful punishment of "drawing" meant that the offender, after having been hanged, had his genitals cut off and his intestines extracted and burned. This punishment, though it sounds medieval, was meted out to the leader of the 1766 tenant rising in New York. See Staughton Lynd, *Anti-Federalism in Dutchess County, New York: A Study of Democracy and Class Conflict in the Revolutionary Era* (Chicago, 1962), pp. 37–38.

tions of tarring and feathering offenders. Tar was known for its curative effects, but its black color also symbolizes evil. The aspect of disguise as protection against demons was also transferable to the social sphere. Disguise makes the victim unrecognizable as a community member; it even dehumanizes him for inhuman punishment or for (rough) resuscitation. On the individual level a disguise may show the victim's uncertainty about his own identity and the necessity of community help to rediscover the real, conforming personality. This custom was also called macaroni making. In Britain a macaroni was a person so influenced by foreign (often Italian) fashion that he slavishly imitated it, often to a ridiculous degree. He sneered at others, though a living joke himself. He was a medley, not quite knowing where he belonged, a fop. He also spent lavishly and, in Walpole's expression, like the East India Company "begot poverty." Was it necessary to tell customs informers and Tories by tarring and feathering them that they had become macaronis, had lost their roots in the community and impoverished it?[119]

This reference to mythological elements in crowd action should not obliterate recognition of similar aspects in other kinds of action and customs, such as the adoration of "liberty trees." The connotations of trees are immortality, growing life, generative powers. Disguises to transform a character or to cast off social norms are still common features of carnivals. An educated colonist spoke of "exorcizing the evil spirit behind the [British] throne," and many revolutionary songs contained mythological elements.[120]

The meaning of rioting as excessive extravagance implied criteria for its application. Common and well-known social norms were a prerequisite for determining excess. When the conduct of individuals or groups exceeded the accepted limits, when legal sanctions were inapplicable or ineffectual, when magistrates themselves committed the extravagances or refused to prosecute those committed by others, when the societal status quo was immediately endangered, crowd action could redress grievances and repel encroachments. It was in its nature defensive. Preventive action came into use only in the seventies against Loyalists. Rioters, always acting deliberately to achieve specific aims, sometimes made use of procedural forms developed for conventions or courts. Inhabitants, having decided on a policy in the town meeting, might then proceed to enforce it directly and immediately. Their actions were spontaneous, but leaders could accentuate issues or emerge on the spur of the moment.[121] In order to decrease the stress on the community,

---

[119]See relevant section of works cited in note 117. For curative uses of tar, see also *An Abstract from Dr. Berkley's Treatise on Tar-Water, with Some Reflexions Thereon, Adapted to Diseases Frequent in America,* by a Friend to the Country (New York, 1745), Evans 5539. Macaroni: M. Dorothy George, *Hogarth to Cruickshank: Social Change in Graphic Satire* (New York, 1967), pp. 37, 38, 39, 44, 59–61, 118; M. D. George *et al.,* eds., *Catalogue of Prints and Drawings in the British Museum,* Division I: "Political and Personal Satires," 11 vols. (London, 1870–1954), esp. vol. 4, no. 4520, quoting Horace Walpole to Sir H. Mann, 9 April 1772.

[120]Frank Moore, ed., *Songs and Ballads of the American Revolution* (Pt. Washington, N.Y., 1855), pp. 1–17, 55–58, 60, 84, 114, 128, 132, 169; B. Waterhouse, *An Essay on Junius and His Letters . . .* (Boston, 1831), p. 65.

[121]For contemporary articulation of the still fashionable ringleader view: Governor Jonathan Belcher, object of repeated crowd action, called Elisha Cooke "his mobility" [Belcher to Waldron, 4 March 1734, *MHSC* 6.7:22–24 (1894)]. Governor Bernard, witnessing the growth of crowd action against the British, spoke of a "trained mob" (Bernard to Conner, 4 July, 1768, Adm. Off., Sec. Dept., In-Letters no. 483, PRO).

strangers were sometimes asked to confront offenders. For the same reason, strangers were also frequently used as scapegoats after a riot had taken place. In short, a comprehensive tradition with consciously as well as unconsciously practiced elements guided crowd action.

Crowd activity was undertaken for the common good, the public interest, "common" meaning a fairly large section of the whole community, not simply a majority. A minority, when outvoted by a "small" or "trifling" majority, felt justified in rioting if the majority used its power, political or economic, to enforce its policy instead of attempting to achieve a compromise or agreeing to retain the status quo. A vote that injured part of the community was not in the common interest, meant "oppression"—that is, extravagant use of an institution designed to serve the whole community.

"Private" or "petty mobs" were opposed, since they did not articulate community sentiments. Many a crowd voted, after accomplishing its business, to discourage private use of direct action. This difference was not always clear to the better sort. Private interests were evident when the enforcement of community norms provided a screen for some of the better sort to strengthen their own position. Similarly, thieves sometimes used the occasion to enrich themselves. While the private interest of the better sort was evident throughout the century, thieves seem to have appeared in crowds only in the sixties and later. The lack of understanding for popular concepts of the public interest was evidenced by John Adams. He said about a riot against a wealthy merchant:

> I am engaged in a famous Cause: The Cause of King, of Scarborough vs. a Mob, that broke into his House. . . . The Terror, and Distress, the Distraction and Horror of this Family cannot be described by Words or painted upon Canvass. It is enough to move a Statue, to melt an Heart of Stone, to read the Story. A Mind susceptible of the Feelings of Humanity . . . must burn with Resentment and Indignation, at such outragious Injuries. These private Mobs, I do and will detest.

Adams's feelings were somewhat one-sided. Social bias prevented him from being equally "susceptible of the Feelings of Humanity" vis-à-vis the suffering of those who felt oppressed by the merchant and who decided "to punish his Body (because . . . he had been a bad Man, destroyed the poor and taken away Peoples Estates)." One participant explained that he "will ruin us all, if he goes on at this rate; if something or other is not done with him, if he is not humbled, it is not worth while for any of us to live here; and he is hard hearted to the widow and orphan." Adams, it seems, spoke for one interest group only.[122]

This claim of acting for the public good was more difficult to maintain when the uniformity, homogeneity, and coherence of the towns were declining. In fact, rival interpretations of the public good appeared openly. The legislature, claiming to represent the whole of the inhabitants, faced crowd action claiming to defend the people's interests against the particular interests of the representatives or against a

---

[122]John Adams, *Legal Papers*, 1:122, 124, 134; *Adams Family Correspondence*, 1:131.

section of the community that had gained preponderant influence in the General Court.

Colonial officials, even if principally averse to crowd action, acknowledged its goal-oriented character. Jonathan Judd thought that some rioters acted "like mad people, tho well for a Mob." Lieutenant Governor and Chief Justice Thomas Hutchinson mused about a Stamp Act crowd whether "such a public regular assembly can be called a mob." Riots were recognized as part of the contemporary social and political institutions, their commonly accepted guidelines as part of the political tradition.[123]

[123]Jonathan Judd, Diary, 2 Feb. 1775, quoted in James R. Trumbull, *History of Northampton, Massachusetts, from Its Settlement in 1654*, 2 vols. (1898; Northampton, Mass., 1902), 2:373; Hutchinson to Benjamin Franklin, 18 Nov. 1765, Letterbooks, MA 26:175.

Stamp Act Crowds and Social Stratification in Boston

2

AMERICAN COLONIES, NEW IMPERIAL POLICIES, AND BOSTON'S REACTION

In the Treaty of Paris, which ended the last of the intercolonial wars in 1763, France ceded to Britain all its territories east of the Mississippi and Canada. Financial exigencies and a number of problems common to the 13 existing colonies and Nova Scotia induced the ministry in London to formulate new policies in which the American possessions were to be treated as a whole and to be integrated more closely into the structure of the empire. This ended the so-called policy of salutary neglect. Specific provisions of the new policy alienated large sections of the colonial population. In predominantly Congregational New England, the establishment of Catholic Quebec, one of three new colonies, was resented. The permanent stationing of a British army of 10,000 men, prompted by the acquisition of large territories with a hostile population, by the danger of Indian attacks, and by suspicions about the loyalty of the original colonies, caused an outcry against the dangers arising to a free society from standing armies. The line dividing the British American and Indian settlements and territories along the ridge of the Appalachian range produced hostility among settlers and land speculators. The strict enforcement of trade regulations alienated the already restive merchants even more. The provisions curtailing the issue of colonial currencies severely hampered trade, decreased property values, and made payments of debts more difficult—in short, compounded the perennial monetary problems of the colonies even further. The scarcity of money had agitated Massachusetts people since the beginning of the century, and those of other colonies as well.

The mapping of the new imperial policy coincided with a development in the American mainland territories that has been called the Anglicization of the colonial societies. This process engendered a transformation of originally extremely heterogeneous settlements with widely divergent social, political, and religious ideologies and aims into sociocultural units whose institutions and economic life had moved closer to the British example, thereby achieving more similarity than ever before. An intermediate high point had been reached in the Albany Congress and Plan of Union in 1754. This meant that the imperial administration in London began to direct controversial policies to all colonies at the same time, just when the colonies became capable of mounting united resistance. In addition, the demands for higher or new duties and taxes came when the colonies were experiencing a severe postwar depression.[1]

In 1764 the British chancellor of the exchequer, George Grenville, submitted to Parliament the American Revenue Act (''Sugar Act''), the proceeds of which were to be used ''for defraying the expenses of defending, protecting, and securing'' His Majesty's dominions in America. The act and corollary measures included the following provisions. The Molasses Act of 1733, which had been unenforceable and was due to expire, was continued. The duty, lowered from 6d. to 3d. per gallon, was still considered prohibitive by colonial merchants.[2] Duties on a number of important colonial imports and exports were increased substantially. Direct trade with Continental European countries was further restricted, and the whole apparatus for collecting the duties was made more efficient. Customs officials could no longer act via local deputies, who could easily be bribed, but had to reside in the colonies. Bonds and certificates (''cockets'') were multiplied. Prosecution of all violations of the acts was to be undertaken in the admiralty courts, which operated without juries. Navy officers were deputized as customs agents. They, as well as the customs officials, received a reward for any condemned seizure but could not be held liable for damages when the seizure proved to have been unjustified or illegal. A new Vice Admiralty Court with jurisdiction over all colonies was established in Halifax, Nova Scotia, far away from the main trade centers and shipping routes. Finally, a clause, not implemented at once, called for an additional revenue measure, a stamp tax.[3]

In June, when the Revenue Act was published in the colonies, consternation reigned. The colonies protested immediately against the ''Black Act.'' Grenville's attempt to balance the British budget was plausible to Parliament but not to colonial legislatures. The balance of trade between most colonies and the mother country

---

[1]Charles H. McIlwain, *The American Revolution: A Constitutional Interpretation* (New York, 1923); Lawrence H. Gipson, *The Coming of the Revolution, 1763–1775* (New York, 1954); Richard L. Merritt, *Symbols of American Community, 1735–1775* (New Haven, Conn., 1966); John M. Murrin, ''Anglicizing an American Colony: The Transformation of Provincial Massachusetts'' (Ph.D. diss., Harvard Univ., 1968). Two summaries of the results of and problems raised by the recent social history studies are Kenneth A. Lockridge, ''Social Change and the Meaning of the American Revolution,'' *J. Soc. Hist.* 6:403–439 (1973), and Jack P. Greene, ''The Social Origins of the American Revolution: An Evaluation and an Interpretation,'' *Pol. Sci. Q.* 88:1–22 (1973). Jackson Turner Main, *The Social Structure of Revolutionary America* (Princeton, N.J., 1965); Merrill Jensen, *The Founding of a Nation: A History of the American Revolution, 1763–1776* (New York, 1968); Stanley N. Katz, ed., *Colonial America: Essays in Politics and Social Development* (Boston, 1971). An attempt to synthesize the results of the research of the last decade is James A. Henretta's brief volume *The Evolution of American Society, 1700–1815: An Interdisciplinary Analysis* (Lexington, Mass., 1973). Joseph A. Ernst, ''The Currency Act Repeal Movement: A Study of Imperial Politics and Revolutionary Crisis, 1764–1767,'' *WMQ* 3.25:177–211 (1968); John J. Waters and John A. Schutz, ''Patterns of Massachusetts Colonial Politics: The Writs of Assistance and the Rivalry between the Otis and Hutchinson Families,'' *WMQ* 3.24:543–567 (1967).

[2]Later the duty was lowered to 1d. As a result, the annual revenue produced by it increased substantially.

[3]Jack P. Greene and Richard M. Jellison, ''The Currency Act of 1764 in Imperial Colonial Relations, 1764–1776,'' *WMQ* 3.28:485–518 (1971); Joseph A. Ernst, *Money and Politics in America, 1755–1775: A Study in the Currency Act of 1764 and the Political Economy of Revolution* (Chapel Hill, N.C., 1973). Revenue act and colonial remonstrances: Edmund S. Morgan, ed., *Prologue to Revolution: Sources and Documents on the Stamp Act Crisis, 1764–1766* (Chapel Hill, N.C., 1959), pp. 4–26.

contained large deficits; the molasses trade and distilling industry had to make up most of the difference. The mercantile community was in an uproar. Boston merchants had combined earlier to oppose the writs of assistance for customs officials (1761). They had founded a kind of chamber of commerce in the early sixties, "The Society for Encouraging Trade and Commerce within the Province of the Massachusetts Bay." The more than 150 members lobbied against the multiplicity of forms, bonds, and other certificates, against the great number of customs officials and their fees, and against duties and taxes in general as well as the methods of collecting them.[4]

Opposition began to take shape in August 1764, with an "Agreement to suppress extravagance and promote frugality," signed by about 50 men, mainly merchants, among them members of both branches of the legislature. Its main intent was to end the expensive British imports of fashionable clothing. A supportive but separate move was made by the "respectable tradesmen"—that is, artisans of Boston—and, in a bid for the new market, some shopkeepers advertised their goods as local products.[5] To broaden participation, several campaigns for nonconsumption and an increase in local manufacture were initiated.[6] Spinning bees for women, temporarily very common, were a shrewd token rather than a permanent achievement. While spinning, the ladies heard lectures on liberty, felt that they were participating in saving their country, and, by donating the results of their labors to the poor, could show their Christian charity. Thus, they could continue to wear elaborate British dresses while the poor, under the care of stern overseers, were clothed in homespun, as befitted their lowly place. The better sort limited their homespun apparel to demonstrative purposes—Harvard commencement gowns and the like.[7]

Social tensions were articulated. A frugal life, lectured "Rebeckah Housewife" and "Hannah Prudence," befitted maids and nurses. Their complaints and gossip about meager wages and frugal tipping should be stopped, and their food and dresses should be more austere. Maids were getting uppity daring to wear more extravagant dresses than their mistresses. Work should be harder, demanded Hannah Prudence; "Do we not see those of our own Sex, that we *necessarily* employ, *robbing us* of a great deal *of their labour . . .* ?"[8]

For a few months, newspaper items about frugality (by "Rusticoat") and about local industry abounded. This may suggest that a people on the brink of being corrupted by extravagant British imports renounced this dangerous temptation in

[4]Edmund S. Morgan and Helen M. Morgan, *The Stamp Act Crisis: Prologue to Revolution* (Chapel Hill, N.C., 1953), pp. 27–28. Regulations of the Merchants' Society: Charles M. Andrews, "The Boston Merchants and the Non-Importation Movement," *CSMP* 19:161–163 (1916–1917). Arthur M. Schlesinger, Sr., *The Colonial Merchants and the American Revolution, 1763–1776* (New York, 1918); John Rowe, *Letters and Diary of John Rowe, Boston Merchant, 1759–1762, 1764–1779*, ed. Anne Rowe Cunningham (Boston, 1903; reprint ed., 1969), p. 64; Thomas Cushing to Jasper Mauduit, Jan. 1764, *MHSC* 74:145 (1918).

[5]*BG*, 13 Aug., 24 Sept., 1 Oct. 1764; *BEP*, 24 Sept. 1764.

[6]*BG*, 13 Aug., 24 Sept., 1 Oct. 1764; *BEP*, 24 Sept. 1764; shoe manufacture, *CSMP* 19:195n (1916–1917).

[7]Andrew Burnaby, *Burnaby's Travels through North America*, ed. Rufus R. Wilson (New York, 1904), p. 135; Peter Oliver, *Peter Oliver's Origin and Progress of the American Rebellion: A Tory View*, ed. Douglass Adair and John A. Schutz (Stanford, Calif., 1961), pp. 63–64.

[8]*BG*, 21 Jan. 1765 (emphasis added).

happy unison and returned to a virtuous life while at the same time improving their balance of trade. Interest in these measures declined very soon, however, though it reappeared whenever the political or economic situation demanded it. Although the pressure created by the negative trade balance as well as demands for profitable use of capital and entrepreneurial talent should not be underestimated, at this stage of development Lieutenant Governor Hutchinson's estimate that reduction of imports was not achieved seems correct. Rather, the measures "served to unite the people in an unfavourable opinion of parliament, as being biassed by the immediate interest of the kingdom, separate and distinct from the interest of the colonies."[9]

Concerning the proposed stamp tax, the right of Parliament to tax the colonies had been a matter of debate since accounts of Grenville's speech of 9 March 1764 had been received in America. Most of the colonies were willing to contribute to the war expenses provided the taxes were levied by their own assemblies, and the people of Massachusetts had paid a stamp tax for colonial usage in 1755. Therefore, a letter of instructions to the colony's agent in London, Jasper Mauduit, was deemed sufficient. Copies of it, accompanied by a request for similar action, were sent to the other colonies. This was the minimum to be done.[10]

When more news from Great Britain had arrived, a special session of the General Court was called for the express purpose of debating provincial tax measures in order to prevent the imposition of a stamp tax by Parliament. Oxenbridge Thacher, representative for Boston and member of a committee to correspond with the other colonies, produced the draft of a petition to the king and Parliament. It was accepted by the House but not in council. The House version pointed to the "rights" of the colony, but upon the suggestion of the lieutenant governor, the councillors substituted "privileges." Finally, "liberties" was accepted as a compromise, setting off an acrimonious public debate.[11] Other colonies, in their petitions, declared outright that Parliament had no authority to impose taxes.

The petitions remained unsuccessful. On 27 May 1765, John Boyle, a Boston printer, dryly noted in his diary: "Capt. Jacobson arrived here from London, has bro't over the Act of Parliament for levying certain Stamp-Duties in the British Colonies, which Act is to take Place the first Day of November next."[12] At least officially, Bostonians took little notice. The town's economic situation was precari-

[9]*BEP*, 21 Jan. 1765; Thomas Hutchinson, *The History of the Colony and Province of Massachusetts Bay*, ed. Lawrence Shaw Mayo, 3 vols. (Cambridge, Mass., 1936), 3:84; cf. Hutchinson to Pownall, 8 March 1766, Letterbooks, MA 26:207–214.

[10]A. C. Goodell *et al.*, eds., *Acts and Resolves, Public and Private, of the Province of the Massachusetts Bay*, 21 vols. (Boston, 1869–1922), 3:793–796, 1754–1755, Ch. 18, 3:867, 1755–1756, Ch. 8. The same method of taxation was used again in Massachusetts in the first years after independence had been won. *Ibid.*, 1784, Ch. 75, pp. 186–192. Mack Thompson, "Massachusetts and New York Stamp Acts," *WMQ* 3.26:253–258 (1969). *BTR* 16:120–122. Hutchinson (*History*, 3:80) asserted that the House instructions to the agent were based on James Otis's pamphlet *The Rights of the British Colonies Asserted and Proved* (Boston, 1764). "Massachusetts Stamp Act 1755," *NEHGR* 14:267–270 (1860).

[11]Bernard to Jackson, 16 Aug. 1764, Sparks MSS., 4.3:248–249, HHL; Hutchinson, *History*, 3:81–83; *BG*, 20 Jan. 1766; *Journals of the House of Representatives*, 1764, pp. 97–98, 102, 108–109, 111–112, 115, 129, 132–133.

[12]John Boyle, "Boyle's Journal of Occurrences in Boston, 1759–1778," 27 May 1765, *NEHGR* 84:168 (1930); cf. *BG*, 20 May 1765. Edmund S. Morgan, "The Postponement of the Stamp Act," *WMQ* 3.7:353–392 (1950); Morgan and Morgan, *Stamp Act Crisis*, Ch. 5; extracts of the act in Morgan, ed., *Prologue to Revolution*, pp. 35–43.

ous because of the "Great Fire" of 1760 and the smallpox epidemic of 1764. The postwar depression culminated in the bankruptcy of a large-scale war contractor, which brought about a large number of secondary bankruptcies. Town meetings were concerned with local issues—taxes, short weight, private profit, and a law to prohibit erection of wooden buildings, which would decrease fire hazards but put house ownership beyond the means of those who could not afford brick.[13]

Opposition to the Stamp Act began to rally in June, when the Virginia Resolves in their expanded form became known. Referring to the "spirited Resolves," the *Gazette* published a biting attack on Hutchinson's "Cursed Prudence," which had demanded "that the word *Rights* must not be once named among us!" While in the House of Burgesses only four of Patrick Henry's resolves had been adopted, the newspapers enlarged their number to seven, giving them a much sharper ring than intended by the burgesses. During the debate on the resolves, resistance to the act had been mentioned, but a resolve to that effect had been rejected. Official sanction for resistance was given only in Rhode Island, where the assembly ordered government officials to proceed after 1 November as though the act had not been passed and indemnified all officials in advance for doing so.[14]

The Massachusetts General Court sent a letter to the other colonies, no longer advocating separate petitions but demanding a united remonstrance. Delegates from all the colonies were invited to meet in New York. But the date set for the congress, 7 October, precluded any effective action before the act would be in force. Though Massachusetts had taken the lead in calling the congress, its delegates were among the moderates. Two of them had been chosen because of backstage efforts by the governor. The third, James Otis, until then one of the boldest to assert colonial rights, did not choose to stick his neck out. In fact, he supported parliamentary authority and declared publicly that the Virginia Resolves were treason. The Stamp Act Congress played no role in stimulating resistance, but it did serve a function in uniting the colonies. No passive resistance in the form of stringent nonconsumption agreements or large-scale nonimportation was debated.[15]

The unwillingness to advocate or even to debate resistance in the legislatures and among the leadership can be explained by examining the established procedures

[13]*BTR* 16:144, 147–149; James Otis to George Johnstone *et al.*, 25 Jan. 1765, *MHSP* 43:204–207 (1909); Bernard to Board of Trade, 8 April 1765, Sparks MSS., 4.3:203–204, HHL.

[14]For a detailed account of the passing of the resolves, see Morgan and Morgan, *Stamp Act Crisis,* Ch. 7. The Morgans suggest that the additional resolves printed in the newspapers probably came from Patrick Henry's original draft but had not been accepted in the House of Burgesses. The resolves, in several different forms, as well as those of other colonies, are reprinted in Morgan, ed., *Prologue to Revolution,* pp. 46–62. Also see *BG,* 8 July 1765; John R. Bartlett, ed., *Records of the Colony of Rhode Island and Providence Plantations, in New England,* 10 vols. (Providence, R.I., 1856–1865), 6:451–452.

[15]Resolves and petitions of the Stamp Act Congress in Morgan, ed., *Prologue to Revolution,* pp. 62–69; Bernard to Board of Trade, 8 July 1765, Sparks MSS., 43.4:28, HHL. *Journals of the House of Representatives,* 1765–1766, pp. 110, 163–164. On Otis, see Morgan and Morgan, *Stamp Act Crisis,* pp. 104–105; Ellen E. Brennan, "James Otis: Recreant and Patriot," *NEQ* 12:691–725 (1939). Contemporary accounts are Hutchinson, *History,* 3:85–86; "Jemmibullero," *BEP,* 13 May 1765; *BG,* 13 May 1765. See also William Tudor, *The Life of James Otis of Massachusetts: Containing Also Notices of Some Contemporary Characters and Events from the Year 1760 to 1775* (Boston, 1823), Chs. 14–16; John J. Waters, *The Otis Family in Provincial and Revolutionary Massachusetts* (Chapel Hill, N.C., 1968), pp. 155–156.

that, according to contemporary thought, were open to the colonies for opposing the Stamp Act. The lawful way to obtain redress was to send a humble petition to the king in England and to wait for him to signify his pleasure. This, however, did not stay the execution of the act in the meantime. Colonial legislatures, by definition, could not void an act of the British Parliament, nor could any other legally established institution of the colonies. Thus, humble petitioning was not just one lawful way; rather, for political institutions, it was the only lawful way. There was no alternative except open rebellion, or so contemporary thought had it. As yet, there was no concept of an escalation of protest from petitions over passive resistance to more direct measures, and then going on to rebellion only if none of the previous steps brought about the results desired.

The issues raised during the Stamp Act debates, however, prompted cautious attempts to conceptualize means of redress short of rebellion. At the beginning it was merely debated whether the charters and liberties of the colonies were rights or privileges. On the basis that they were constitutional rights, a new doctrine began to emerge within the concept of constitutionalism, the notion that legislative or executive acts could be ''unconstitutional''—a new word even, at that time. In the next decade these new concepts were to become part of a chain of argument, at first, and of institutionalized devices, later, to bridge the gap between submission and rebellion. For the solution of the immediate problems caused by the Stamp Act, they matured too late.[16] Thus, in 1765 the traditional political concepts, the established institutions, and consequently the established leadership were found wanting. Who, then, acted to transform the opposing resolves into action? Who ''enacted'' the thought?[17] The leadership had to turn to the crowd, to those who had little or no direct access to institutional channels for obtaining redress from specific grievances. Direct action was their means when cumbersome legal processes seemed too slow, or the lawyers', clerks', and justices' fees too high; when institutional remedies had been exhausted or when no redress was to be expected from justices or representatives. There was no relief to be expected from Parliament, an institution that had refused even to consider the colonial petitions.

''EVERY PERSON IS AFFECTED BY THE STAMP ACT''

At the end of July, the *Boston Gazette* advertised:

> The *Stamp Act* to be Sold by Edes and Gill. As every Person is, almost, more or less affected by the Stamp Act, it is absolutely necessary that all should become

---

[16]The development of constitutional and political thinking has been the theme of Bernard Bailyn's works. See also Pauline R. Maier, *From Resistance to Revolution: Colonial Radicals and the Development of American Opposition to Britain, 1765–1776* (New York, 1972). Cf. the papers and comments given at the Organization of American Historians' Convention, Denver, April 1974, on the Bailyn thesis and the problem of ''popular'' ideology. The lack of a theory of resistance before the revolutionary crisis has been outlined by Gerald Stourzh, *Vom Widerstandsrecht zur Verfassungsgerichtsbarkeit* (Graz, 1974).

[17]Note that the term ''enact,'' as used in the context of politics, includes a hierarchical component. Legislatures ''enact'' bills, but citizens cannot ''enact'' political concepts.

acquainted with it, in order to avoid the many Forfeitures they might otherwise be liable to, for a Want of a proper Knowledge thereof.

In Marblehead, 22 couples married on a single Sunday to avoid the stamp duty for their marriage licenses. In Boston, members of a fire club resolved that "if the stamp office should be on Fire (and no other Buildings be in Danger) they would not assist in extinguishing it."

Newspapers, almanacs, deeds, warrants, indentures, leases, bills of sale, bonds, and customs forms all had to bear the stamp tax. To colonials, whose perennial complaints were high fees and cumbersome legal processes, the additional expense seemed a general concern. In the instructions of the town of Braintree to their representative, the economic threat to everybody was clearly spelled out:

> We have called this a burthensome Tax because the duties are so numerous and so high and the embarrassments to Business in this infant, sparcely settled Country so great that it would be totally impossible for the people to subsist under it. . . .
> [C]onsidering the present scarcity of money . . . the execution of that act for a short space of time would dreign the Country of Cash, strip multitudes of the poorer people of all their property and Reduce them to absolute beggary.

More than 40 other towns subscribed to this statement. Considering the longstanding experience of Massachusetts people with scarcity of cash, this unanimity is not surprising. Throughout the eighteenth century the scarcity of money had caused serious problems. While merchants could rely to a degree on their own credit facilities, debtors risked imprisonment because, though willing to pay, they could not get cash. Sale of lands under such conditions meant considerable loss of property because of severely depressed prices. Foreclosures would be the result. "And what the consequence would be of so sudden a shock and such a convulsive change of the whole course of our business and Subsistence to the peace of the Province, We tremble to consider." In addition, the constitutional grievances, taxation without representation and, in certain cases, trial without jury, were considered invasions of fundamental rights. Such invasions were the more likely, since the Vice Admiralty judges were biased against the defendants through "pecuniary temptation." Whenever they condemned a seizure, they would receive a part of the proceeds from the sale of the property. This was one of "the most mischievous of all customs." At the same time, newspapers reported that Great Britain was restricting American fishing so that British boats could engross all there was. The British, it seemed, were bent on destroying the colonists economically, politically, and constitutionally.[18]

On 12 August the *Gazette* reported a meeting of the Sons of Liberty in Providence, Rhode Island, that had dealt with the Stamp Act. On this day large crowds of Bostonians celebrated the birthday of the Prince of Wales, and, according to the

[18]*BG*, 29 July 1765; *BNL*, 10 Oct., 28 Nov. 1765; Hutchinson, *History*, 3:86. Braintree instructions: *BG*, 14 Oct. 1765; John Adams, *Diary and Autobiography of John Adams*, ed. L. H. Butterfield, 4 vols. (Cambridge, Mass., 1961–66), 3:282; Samuel A. Bates, ed., *Records of the Town of Braintree, 1640 to 1793* (Randolph, Mass., 1886), pp. 404–406.

newspapers, loyal toasts were drunk and "re-thundered thro' every street in the city." Somewhat less loyal were the epithets hurled at Jared Ingersoll, stamp distributor for Connecticut, who, accompanied by Andrew Oliver, stamp distributor for Massachusetts, left Boston on the same day. In Roxbury the two had to evade another crowd. Oliver, whose hospitality to Ingersoll "occasioned murmuring among the people" (Hutchinson), was compared to slave drivers on plantations. For the sake of gaining the favor of their white masters, it was said, they treated their fellow slaves with special brutality. The British government, in this comparison, behaved like white slave owners.[19]

The conspicuous behavior of the two stamp distributors, or stamp masters, as they were now called, the example given by the Providence Sons of Liberty, and the crowded celebration of the Prince of Wales's birthday prompted some Bostonians to organize a protest demonstration against Andrew Oliver.[20] The home government, in a move to make the colonial elites swallow the new taxes, had offered the lucrative positions of stamp distributors to men from the colonies. What seemed to have been a shrewd calculation—there was a run for the offices—now turned out to be a crucial weakness. Contrary to the intent of Parliament and the ministry, the distributors were as susceptible to direct action as the customs officials had been throughout the earlier decades of the century. The reasoning was simple: If the agents did not distribute the stamps, the act could not go into effect; hence, the problem of further opposition or resistance was solved. For officials and merchants dealing daily or almost daily with legal documents, this was essential. Once the "enraged multitude" had forced the distributor to resign, there was no need for them to stick their necks out. From the tradition and the point of view of the rioters, an equally important argument probably was that one man attempted to profit from a hardship imposed on the whole community. While everybody would have to pay additional taxes, the stamp distributor would skim off a luxurious salary. His turning against his fellow colonials allowed them to turn against him. The sneer about the "reputable office" and the designation "placeman" pointed in this direction.[21]

Late in July two petitions were circulated in Boston to demand a town meeting on account of the Stamp Act. Such a meeting might have been used for preventing direct action, but, whether intentionally or not, none was called.[22] Instead, the Loyal Nine, one of the many political and social clubs, made plans for a demonstration against the act and the stamp distributor. The men usually met at William Speakman's Southend distillery, "Liberty Hall," as these self-styled Sons of Liberty called it. John Adams once visited them and "heard nothing but such Conversation as passes at all Clubbs among Gentlemen about the Times. No Plotts, no Machinations." One glance around the "Compting Room" of the distillery in-

[19]*BG*, 5 Aug., 12 Aug., 19 Aug. 1765; Hutchinson, *History*, 3:87.

[20]Date and connection have been suggested by William V. Wells, *The Life and Public Services of Samuel Adams*, 3 vols. (Boston, 1865, 1888), 1:61. It is possible that the plans had been in the making earlier.

[21]*BG*, 19 Aug. 1765. The debate about "placemen" later climaxed in a pamphlet addressed to Hutchinson, *A Ministerial Catechise, Suitable to Be Learned by All Modern Provincial Governors, Pensioners, Placemen etc.* (Boston, 1771).

[22]Misc. Unbound Papers, 1765, BCH.

formed him about their social and economic standing: "A very small Room." As employers, the Loyal Nine ranked considerably above those men whom they intended to be the participants in the direct action, journeymen, *le menu peuple*. Compared to the large importing merchants and capitalists, on the other hand, they were not important men. The difference becomes graphically clear when we turn to John Adams's diary entry for the next day, when he dined at the home of the wealthy merchant Nicholas Boylston. As much impressed with pomp and circumstance as his archenemy, Thomas Hutchinson, he rapturously described

> An elegant Dinner indeed! Went over the House to view the Furniture, which alone cost a thousand Pounds sterling. A Seat it is for a noble Man, a Prince. The Turkey Carpets, the painted Hangings, the Marble Tables, the rich Beds with crimson Damask Curtains and Counterpins, the beautiful Chimny Clock, the Spacious Garden, are the most magnificent of any Thing I have ever seen.[23]

The nine were small businessmen.[24] John Avery, who was to become known as "mob secretary," was junior partner of John Avery & Son, merchants and distillers. In the group he was the only one with a college education (Harvard, 1759).[25] Benjamin Edes—together with John Gill—was proprietor, printer, and editor of the *Boston Gazette,* in which the group usually published its announcements.[26] Thomas Chase, a distiller, and Henry Bass, a merchant and shipowner, were members of the Northend Caucus, a voting organization under the influence of Samuel Adams.[27] Thomas Crafts, painter, George Trott, jeweler, and John Smith and Stephen Cleverly, braziers, were the other members. Economically the men came from the lower ranks of property owners, with some real estate and moderate investments in stores or ships.[28]

Politically the group had numerous connections with the leadership of the town. John Avery, Sr., was town official in 1765. He and William Speakman were good friends of John Rowe, leading member of the Merchants' Club's standing commit-

---

[23]John Adams, *Diary*, 15–16 Jan. 1766, 1:294–295.

[24]Lists of the members have been given by William Gordon, *The History of the Rise, Progress, and Establishment of the Independence of the United States of America,* 4 vols. (London, 1788), 1:175, and by John Adams, *Diary*, 1:294. They were John Avery, Jr. (Adams omitted the "Jr.," but a letter from John Avery, Jr., establishes the identity beyond doubt); Thomas Crafts; John Smith; Thomas Chase; Stephen Cleverly; Henry Bass; Benjamin Edes (named by both Gordon and Adams, but a letter written by Henry Bass suggests that Edes did not attend the meetings regularly, though he closely cooperated with the group); George Trott (not in Gordon's list); Henry Welles (omitted in Adams's list); William Speakman (mentioned by neither Adams nor Gordon, but acted with the group and was part owner of the house in which they met—Rowe, *Letters and Diary*, p. 157); Joseph Field (listed by Adams, but being a master of a vessel, he was probably only a guest).

[25]"Manuscript about the Boston Sons of Liberty, Prepared to Be Inserted in a London Newspaper in the Spring of 1775," *MHSP* 2.12:139–142 (1899); John L. Sibley and Clifford K. Shipton, "John Avery," *Biographical Sketches of Those Who Attended Harvard College,* vol. 14 (Cambridge, Mass., 1968), pp. 384–389.

[26]In 1757 the two partners had been accused of printing pamphlets that tended "to destroy the Principles of the Christian Religion." When the selectmen threatened not to let the firm do any more of the town's printing, Benjamin Edes promised to "publish nothing that shall give any uneasiness to any Person whatever." *BTR* 19:54–55.

[27]On the Northend Caucus, see Alan Day and Katherine Day, "Another Look at the Boston 'Caucus,'" *J. Am. Studies (GB)* 5:19–25 (1971).

[28]Edward Blake Robins, "Col. Thomas Crafts, Jr., 1740–1799," *Bostonian Soc. Proc.* (1914), pp. 31–38. Only Crafts, Bass, and Edes have been identified in the tax and valuation list for 1771. MA 132:92–147.

tee. Henry Bass was an acquaintance and later the son-in-law of Samuel Ph. Savage, former selectman and active Merchants' Club member. Through Edes and Gill's printing office, close relations existed with the more vocal Whigs, who not only wrote for the *Gazette* but had their club (the Long Room Club) one floor above the printing shop. Samuel Adams, who occasionally spent an evening with the Loyal Nine, was also a member of the Monday Night Club, which comprised a number of influential and generally wealthy Whigs.[29] The Loyal Nine became a kind of clearing house between top leadership and crowd. Their strength was the organizational talent with which they arranged crowd action or responded to it. The informality of their connections gave them large discretionary powers.

The Loyal Nine signed their notifications "M.Y. Sec'y." Whigs often used initials of political leaders as aliases. "P.P." stood for Pascal Paoli, the Corsican freedom fighter, "O.C." for Oliver Cromwell. The origin of "M.Y." has not been solved. Possibly it stood for "*M*obility," a contemporary term for crowds and for voters who did not belong to the better sort. Elisha Cooke, Jr., leader of the Popular party in the 1730s, had been contemptuously called "his mobility" by crown officials. Possibly John Avery took up this tradition. They realized, in 1765, the necessity for direct action.[30] The crowd, according to their plans, was to come from the lower classes, the Pope's Day constituency. The Northend and the Southend, Boston's two low-income sections, had developed a rivalry that made the customary Pope's Day parades and effigy burnings a rather riotous affair. A contemporary diarist described the custom of "the lower class of people" celebrating the evening

> in a manner peculiar to themselves, by having carved images erected on stages, representing the Pope, his attendant, etc. and they were generally carried thro' the streets by negroes and other servants, that the minds of the vulgar might be impressed with a sense of their deliverance from popery, and money was generally given them, to regale themselves in the evening, when they burnt the images.[31]

In 1764, Boston's civil magistrates attempted to head off violence by sending sheriffs, justices, and militia officers into the areas to destroy the effigies of the Pope. In the Northend they seemed successful. The Southend, however, had sufficient manpower immediately present to fight off the authorities. The latter "could not conquer" and withdrew. Meanwhile the Northenders assembled and repaired their Pope, and the day continued as usual. Subsequently, 19 men were arrested for rioting and had to find bondsmen for their appearance in court. Five of them were minors but had trades or were learning them.[32] These men and the owner of the barn

[29]Robert F. Seyboldt, *The Town Officials of Colonial Boston* (Cambridge, Mass., 1939); Rowe, *Letters and Diary,* pp. 84 *passim;* Long Room Club: Francis S. Drake, ed., *Tea Leaves. Letters and Documents Relating to the Shipment of Tea to the American Colonies in the Year 1773* (Boston, 1884), p. 66; Rowe, *Letters and Diary,* 1 Aug. 1768, pp. 171–172. Members of the Monday Night Club were Otis, Cushing, Wells, Pemberton, Gray, Austin, Daniel and Joseph Waldo, Inches, and Dr. Parker; John Adams, *Diary,* 23 Dec. 1765, 1:270–271. As no records or membership lists of the Southend and Middle Caucuses exist, no connections with these two organizations can be established.

[30]George P. Anderson, "Pascal Paoli: An Inspiration to the Sons of Liberty," *CSMP* 26:206ff. (1924–1926). On Elisha Cooke, Jr., see Jonathan Belcher to R. Waldron, 4 March 1734, *MHSC* 6.7:22–24 (1894).

[31]James Freeman, Notebook, 1745–1765, 5 Nov. 1764, MHS; *Acts and Resolves,* 3:647–648, 1752–1753, Ch. 18.

[32]Rowe, *Letters and Diary,* 5 Nov. 1764, 7 Feb. 1765, pp. 67–68, 76; Freeman, Notebook, 1764, MHS; Boyle,

Figure 1.   Tightly clustered houses of mechanics along Boston's waterfront. From here, many of the rioters of 14 August 1765 came. In the background, the larger mansions of merchants and Beacon Hill with the staff to alert the country about moves of the British. From Burgis' view of Boston.

in which the Northend Pope was prepared came from the maritime trades (8), the leather trades (3), provision handling (4), and miscellaneous other trades (5). The bondsmen came from similar trades. Four of the rioters and eight bondsmen were identified in the 1771 tax and valuation list. Seven of them met the property qualifications for voting. Of the five who had no property listed, four—two shipwrights, a cordwainer, and a joiner—came from the Northend. By contrast, the one witness called and his bondsman came from the center of the town, each owning about five times as much property as the average rioter.[33] Each section had a "captain." Henry Swift, from the Northend, was a shipwright, like his father, James. Nothing else is known about him. In the southern part, Ebenezer Mackintosh, aged 28 and a shoemaker by trade, was the leader. He was a member of the crew of a fire engine and a minor town official, one of five sealers of leather, who controlled the quality and size of hides sold in Boston. He was familiar with Pascal Paoli's role in the Corsican struggles for liberty, and during the Stamp Act period his reputation spread fast. Political leaders in Rhode Island inquired about him, and he even won the respect of Justice Peter Oliver, an outspoken critic of the Whigs who despised crowds.[34]

Swift and Mackintosh were to be the links between Loyal Nine and crowd. Possibly Samuel Adams tried to get control over Mackintosh, who owed taxes. Two days before the planned crowd action, Tax Collector Adams took out a warrant against Mackintosh and one Benjamin Bass for £10.12 lawful money. This was a rather unusual action for Adams, who had neglected or been unable to collect about £8000 in taxes and who usually did not pressure tax defaulters into paying. The warrant against Mackintosh and Bass ordered the sheriff or his deputy to collect the money or confiscate their property or imprison them for debt. When the goal of the leaders, combination of the sectional crowds, had been achieved, Adams ordered the deputy sheriff to return the warrant to the court, although neither Bass nor Mackintosh had paid the debt or even a part of it. Since the evidence is circumstantial, however, this interpretation remains hypothetical.

The Loyal Nine brought about an agreement between Swift and Mackintosh—whether others were involved is not known—to let the sectional rivalries subside and to form a "union" for the purpose of crowd action against the stamp master. When they felt sure of the support of the people from the Northend and the Southend, they decided on symbolic action against the stamp distributors and simulation

---

"Journal," 5 Nov. 1764, p. 167; *BG,* 12 Nov. 1764; *BNL,* 8 Nov. 1764; Council Records, 15:339, MSA; Hutchinson's charge to the grand jury, March 1765, in Samuel M. Quincy, ed., *Reports of Cases Argued and Adjudged in the Superior Court of Judicature of . . . Massachusetts Bay, 1761–1772, by Josiah Quincy, Junior* (Boston, 1865), pp. 113–114; Bernard to Pownall, 26 Nov. 1765, Sparks MSS., 10.1:97, HHL; SCF 100493, 100494. The indictments were for rioting and assault on 31 October, 2 November, 3 November, and 5 November 1764. Two members of the Loyal Nine vouched for two of the rioters.

[33]The trades of the rioters were as follows: shipwright (4), caulker (1), ropemaker (1), sailmaker (1), lighterman (1); cordwainer (2), leather dresser (1); baker (3), distiller (1); hatter (1), chaise maker (1), housewright (1), bricklayer (1), tallow chandler (1). In addition to the tradesmen, who gave bond, one gentleman appeared as surety for a relative, to judge by the identical last names.

[34]On Swift, SCF 100494. George P. Anderson, "Ebenezer Mackintosh, Stamp Act Rioter and Patriot," *CSMP* 26:15–64, 348–361 (1924–1926); Oliver, *American Rebellion,* pp. 54–55; John Adams, *Diary,* 1:300.

of conditions under the operation of the Stamp Act. Involvement of large numbers of people to increase political awareness was also planned. They then prepared the effigies.[35]

RIOT AGAINST ANDREW OLIVER, PLACEMAN

On a normal weekday, Boston bustled with activity. John Adams noted:

> My Eyes are so diverted with Chimney Sweeps, Carriers of Wood, Merchants, Ladies, Priests, Carts, Horses, Oxen, Coaches, Market men and Women, Soldiers, Sailors, and my Ears with the Rattle Gabble of them all that . . . I cant raise my mind above this mob Croud of Men, Women, Beasts and Carriages. . . .

Those going to work early in the morning of Wednesday, 14 August, discovered two effigies hanging from the branches of a large old elm. "Liberty Tree," as it was to be known, stood in the Southend, on Orange (later Washington) Street, the thoroughfare from the Neck, the town's entrance, to the center, the docks, markets, and warehouses. Every weekday it was busy with countless incoming and outgoing teams and carts, carriages and stage coaches, farmers, visitors, townspeople. Incoming teamsters spread the rough verse affixed to one of the effigies:

> A goodlier sight who e'er did see?
> A Stamp-Man hanging on a tree!

Soon "vast numbers of Spectators" from all quarters assembled. They were joined by country people to whom outgoing passengers had carried the tale. The "surprise and joy of the public" were interrupted briefly when the owner of the tree attempted to cut down the effigies in defiance of a label affixed to them: "He that takes this down is an enemy to his Country." It turned out that the effigies were guarded by men from the Northend, who advised the intruder to desist, "lest it should occasion the Demolition of his [imported glass] Windows, if nothing worse." Later, upon orders of the lieutenant governor, the sheriff appeared. In the words of bystanders, the "Common Hangman" with other officers came and "asked liberty to take it dow[n] but to no purpose." The advice to desist, Hutchinson thought, came from "some of the graver persons present" and was accompanied, said the sheriff, by threats to his life. In the next days, newspapers proudly reported that the "Spectacle continued the whole Day without the least Opposition."

The crowd of spectators continued to grow. "So much were they affected with a Sense of Liberty, that scarce any could attend to the Task of Day-Labour; but all seemed on the Wing for Freedom." One of those leaving work was George R. T. Hewes. Arriving at the corner, he saw not only the stamp master's effigy pending from the tree but also a huge boot. "The Boot was old, and had a new . . . Green-

---

[35]Bass was a cordwainer too, and probably a business associate of Mackintosh. From 1760 to 1762, he had been a member of the same fire engine crew as Mackintosh. The warrant is in SCF 86536. Adams's list of deficient taxpayers is among Misc. Unbound Papers, 1768, BCH. On the role of the Loyal Nine, see Gordon, *History,* 1:175, and Samuel Mather to his son, 17 Aug. 1765, Letters from Rev. Samuel Mather to His Son, 1759–1785, 1 vol., MHS.

vile sole.'' The pun, on the Earl of Bute and George Grenville's soul, was accompanied by a devil peeping out of the boot. The image had a very direct meaning to people accustomed to biblical allusions. But not everybody knew that the legal formula ''not having God before his eyes, but being instigated by the devil'' was used in indictments for such choice crimes as murder, manslaughter, and fornication. Now Bute, adviser of George III, and Oliver, the stamp master, stood—or hung—''indicted.'' Some highly placed crown officials sourly noted that the insult was directed against the third-highest official in the colony, since Oliver was secretary of the province and councillor. In addition to his political station, his economic motivation and the betrayal of the community became a subject of reflection. His designation as placeman had already sounded the note. Now popular poems enlarged on it. One had Oliver say that he ''quitted'' the common cause and ''betrayed'' his country ''for the sake of Pelf.'' Another noted that he ''hated'' his country, ''sold'' his allegiance, and had his heart ''set on gain.''[36]

Reflections like these probably agitated the ''vast numbers'' of spectators, 2500 to 5000 during the day and some 3000 in the evening. One-third of Boston's schoolboys, from the South Writing School, were sent to see the spectacle as an educational experience. John Avery of the Loyal Nine later told a friend, ''you would have laughed to have seen two or three hundred little boys with a Flagg marching in Procession on which was King, Pitt & Liberty for ever, it ought to have been Pitt, Wilks & Liberty.'' While the boys were waving flags, adults could participate in simulating the harassment that would result from the act. No farmer or teamster was allowed to enter or leave Boston without stopping and getting his goods stamped. In an ''enthusiastic spirit'' the people good-humoredly mock-stamped all goods on the passing carts and wagons. It was relatively unimportant that the act referred to paper only and not to other goods. What was important was to reach large segments of the population, and teamsters and farmers, not accustomed to these delays, would definitely spread the story. Not a single complaint was received that any goods had been damaged or lost in the process. No cargo was left in disarray.[37]

Toward evening the Northenders were relieved by men from the Southend, who cut down the effigy of stamp master Oliver, placed it on a bier, and carried it through the town accompanied by a cheering multitude shouting, ''Liberty and

[36]*BNL,* 22 Aug. 1765; *BEP,* 19 Aug. 1765; *BG,* 19 Aug. 1765, Supp.; Bernard to Halifax, 15 Aug. 1765, in Morgan, ed., *Prologue to Revolution,* pp. 106–108; Cyrus Baldwin to his brother, 15–16 Aug. 1765, Misc. Bound Papers, vol. 13, MHS; Andrew Oliver to Andrew Oliver, Jr., 18 Jan. 1769, Hutchinson and Oliver Papers, 3 vols., vol. 2, 1761–1774, MHS; Jonathan Mayhew to Thomas Hollis, 19 Aug. 1765, *MHSP* 69:174–175; Freeman, Notebook, Aug. 1765, MHS; Boyle, ''Journal,'' p. 169; letters from Hutchinson, 6 Aug., 26 Oct. 1765, Letterbooks, MA 26:145, 167–168. Betrayal and pensioner motif: Frank Moore, ed., *Songs and Ballads of the American Revolution* (Pt. Washington, N.Y., 1855), pp. 17, 18; John Adams, *Diary,* 1:80–81, 259–261; Hutchinson, *History,* 3:87, 101; Gordon, *History,* 1:175; George R. T. Hewes, *Traits of the Tea Party: Being a Memoir of George R. T. Hewes,* ed. Benjamin B. Thatcher (New York, 1835), pp. 67–68; *Liberty, Property, and No Excise: A Poem* (Boston, 1765), Mass. Broads. 1348; poem quoted in G. B. Warden, *Boston, 1689–1776* (Boston, 1970), p. 165; Arthur M. Schlesinger, ''Liberty Tree: A Genealogy,'' *NEQ* 25:435–458 (1952).

[37]John Avery, Jr., to John Collins, 19 Aug. 1765, in Ezra Stiles, *Extracts from Itineraries and Other Miscellanies of Ezra Stiles, 1755–1794, with a Selection from His Correspondence,* ed. Franklin B. Dexter (New Haven, Conn., 1916), pp. 435–437; *BTR* 16:142; *BG,* 19 Aug. 1765, Supp.

property for ever," "No stamps," "No Placemen." "The greatest order" and "solemn manner" were preserved. At the townhouse, where the governor and council were assembled, the people "gave three huzzas by Way of Defiance." There were no restrictions on joining the procession. A contingent of 40 or 50 master craftsmen, who usually would not participate in crowd action, marched in a solid body. They were joined by some gentlemen of "highest Reputation" disguised as tradesmen. This gave increased respectability to the whole affair, especially in the eyes of those who looked down on journeymen as rabble and who feared every spontaneous unguided action of the lower sort. To those of the journeymen who accepted the tradition of deference to social superiors, this was a gratifying show of sympathy. The master craftsmen's position at the head of the procession suggested a leading role and the strength of unity.[38]

The actual managers, however, were still the Loyal Nine and Mackintosh, acting according to one report "visibly under the direction of persons much his Superiors." At the townhouse a brief discussion ensued on whether to follow the customary Pope's Day route to the Northend or to burn the effigies immediately.[39] Mackintosh, however, directed the throng down King Street into Kilby Street, where Andrew Oliver was erecting a new building, designed—in the opinion of the assembled people—to be used as a stamp office. At this point the symbolic action, designed to suggest resignation to Oliver and to build up public involvement in and support for the demand, was temporarily replaced by direct action aimed at destroying the means, or one of the means, to be used for executing the act. Property, widely distributed among freeholders, according to the prevailing ideology was the basis of liberty. By using his property—and increasing it in the process—to deprive others of some of their property and thereby of their liberty, Oliver violated the social responsibility to the community that was inherent in property ownership. Accordingly, the community, for purposes of self-protection, had to destroy that part of his property with which he oppressed them. The crowd quickly leveled the building, taking time, though, to "stamp" the bricks and beams.[40]

The demonstrators then turned to Fort Hill to end the day with a bonfire. "Unfortunately," as some said, Oliver's private house was on a lot adjacent to the hill, and a few panes of glass were broken. But the main action was symbolic again. In front of the house, the crowd beheaded the stamp distributor's effigy by sawing off its head. Thus, "A. O. Stamp man was seasonably taken out of this troublesome

---

[38]Hutchinson, *History*, 3:87: "Forty or fifty tradesmen, decently dressed, preceeded; and some thousands of the mob followed. . . ." In Governor Bernard's words, "there were 50 Gentlemen Actors in this Scene disguised with trousers and Jackets on, besides a much larger Number behind the Curtain." Sparks MSS., 4.4:142, HHL. Gordon, *History*, 1:175. A few months later Hutchinson asserted that the "rabble" headed by Mackintosh was "some what controuled by a superior set consisting of master masons carpenters etc.," Hutchinson to Pownall, 8 March 1766, in Morgan, ed., *Prologue to Revolution*, pp. 122–126.

[39]Bernard to Halifax, 15 Aug. 1765, Sparks MSS., 4.4:139, HHL, to Pownall, 26 Nov. 1765, *ibid.*, 10.1:97. Rowe noted that the crowd marched "through the Town House," *Letters and Diary*, p. 89. This is confirmed by a poem on the Stamp Act resistance.

[40]"Liberty, Property, and No Excise." James Henretta, "Economic Development and Social Structure in Colonial Boston," *WMQ* 3.22:85 (1965); R. E. Brown, *Middle-Class Democracy and the Revolution in Massachusetts, 1691–1780* (Ithaca, N.Y., 1955), p. 50.

World by an ignominious Death,'' a less than subtle hint. When the fire was lighted on the hill with the wooden parts of the destroyed stamp office, the remains of the effigy were committed to the flames. This ''noble Fire,'' explained the *Evening Post*, was meant to be ''a Burnt-Offering of the Effigies [of Oliver and Bute] for those Sins of the People which had caused such heavy Judgements as the STAMP-ACT etc. to be laid upon them.'' Then the ''gentlemen'' actors and probably the Loyal Nine left, ''supposing all, that was proper to be done, was completed.'' No property unconnected with the Stamp Act had been destroyed, and no persons were hurt, not even the stamp master.[41]

When the fire burned down and new fuel was needed, some of the crowd returned to Oliver's estate and tore railings off the fence. Although Oliver and his family had left, his friends were barricaded inside. Coach house and coach became targets of the crowd too, and the men inside began to use ''some irratating Language,'' which ''Indiscretions, to say the least . . . so enraged the People . . . tho' hitherto no Violence had been offered to any Person and [tho'] the utmost Decorum had been preserved,'' that they now broke the remaining windows of the house and forced their way into it. First they searched for Oliver and organized search parties to check neighboring houses, but they failed to find him. No complaints were registered that any property was damaged during the search. In Oliver's house ''they bravely shewed their Loyalty, Courage, and Zeal, to defend the Rights and Liberties of Englishmen,'' as the *Newsletter* reported. This explanation, however, did overlook the essential features of the action.

The rights of Englishmen had receded into the background. The men from the small, crowded quarters of the Northend and Southend, who, if laborers, earned approximately 2s. or 3s. per weekday, perhaps £40 per year, suddenly came into the estate of a man who with his income could surround his house with a well-kept garden, barn, stables, and coach house. His style of living was evident from the rich furniture, wine cellar, and—as one newspaper disapprovingly noted—even silver plate. To all this his handsome salary as stamp master would add further luster, while burdening others. The rioters attempted to burn his coach and damaged garden and furniture in accordance with the tradition of crowd action against outsiders breaking economic norms of the community. Additionally, they integrated part of their social superiors' tradition: They drank some of the expensive wine. Nothing was stolen.[42]

Wealth itself—stocks and capital, position and investments—was not destroyed or taken away. The targets of crowds were symbols of wealth. Thus, Oliver suffered material losses but kept his political, social, and economic power and influence. The stamp agent, placeman of the British government, was also a high provincial official, a plural officeholder at that, one of a haughty clan of families that monopolized lucrative offices. In all this he was hardly different from other provin-

[41]*BEP*, 19 Aug. 1765; Avery to Collins, 19 Aug. 1765, in Stiles, *Itineraries*, pp. 435–437; Bernard to Halifax, 15 Aug. 1765, Sparks MSS., 4.4:139, HHL; Mayhew to Hollis, 19 Aug. 1765, *MHSP* 69:174–175 (1947–1950); Gordon, *History*, 1:176.

[42]*BG*, 19 Aug. 1765, Supp.; *BEP*, 19 Aug. 1765; *BNL*, 22 Aug. 1765; Gordon, *History*, 1:176; Freeman, Notebook, 14 Aug. 1765; Cyrus Baldwin to his brother, 15–16 Aug. 1765, Misc. Bound Papers, vol. 13, MHS.

cial officials who had little or no direct connection with the crown, Parliament, or the Stamp Act. Second, he belonged to a section of society that could afford a different kind of rioting than the members of the crowd. They could "riot in luxury," as the contemporary expression had it. Andrew Oliver, over the next 10 years, used his wealth and position in such a way that at his death an unparalleled instance of crowd action occurred. When his coffin was lowered into the grave, a group of uninvited bystanders cheered. For the present, however, the rioters merely did not follow the subtle distinction made by the Loyal Nine and other well-placed Bostonians between Oliver the abhorrent British placeman and Oliver the wealthy merchant and official, deference-commanding part and partisan of the colonial establishment. Private gain was the motive in all three cases, according to the popular reasoning. This we can infer from the contemporary popular songs quoted earlier.[43]

The rioters had not been in the house for long when some of the gentlemen who had left earlier returned. After some persuasion the rioters left the house, went back to the bonfire, and toasted the "UNION" between Northend and Southend. When the crowd seemed to grow quiet, Hutchinson, belonging to the same social section, to the same group of officials, to the same family clan even, attempted to reassert his authority and help his relative. Together with Sheriff Greenleaf, he appeared and ordered the crowd to disperse. This was what they were just about to do anyway. However, as soon as Hutchinson began to speak, "a Ringleader cried out, the Governor and the Sheriff! to your Arms, my boys!" The boys got busy, and Hutchinson found himself the target of a "volley of Stones." He and the sheriff escaped through backyards and alleys under cover of the night. Left alone, the crowd dispersed.[44]

Except for a few minor interferences and the disdain of the better sort for the attack on Oliver's home, the day's proceedings had the more or less open approval of all spectators, and, during the next days, some of the Boston ministers gave their blessing. Governor Francis Bernard, who issued a proclamation against the rioters, offering a reward of £100 lawful money for information, was answered by an anonymous note asserting "that the Persons *at the Head* of the late insurrection are in all respects as good and respectable Men as the Governor and Council."[45]

OTHER GRIEVANCES TOO: RIOTS ON 15–26 AUGUST

The governor, who had fled to Castle Island for fear of violence against his person, officially explained that he did not want to suffer the indignity of witnessing insults to His Majesty's government. That had been the reason when Governor Shirley, in 1747, had left town after a two-day impressment riot. He had promptly

[43]Sibley and Shipton, "Andrew Oliver," *Harvard Graduates,* 7:383–413.

[44]Bernard to Halifax, 15 Aug. 1765, Sparks MSS., 4.4:139, HHL; Hewes, *Memoir,* p. 69; Hutchinson (*History,* 3:87) remained silent about his defeat.

[45]Bernard to Halifax, 22 Aug. 1765, Sparks MSS., 4.4:144–148, HHL; anonymous note (emphasis added), in Bernard to Pownall, 18 Aug. 1765, *ibid.,* pp. 11–15; Cyrus Baldwin to his brother, 15–16 Aug. 1765, Misc. Bound Papers, vol. 13, MHS; *BEP,* 2 Sept. 1765; MA 88:176–178.

and politely been asked by a town meeting to return. In 1765, nobody thought of inviting the governor to return, and Bernard knew that. He wrote to his friends and superiors in Great Britain lamenting that all civil power had come to an end. Angrily he accused the council of conniving with the popular leaders. Sitting in his candlelit room at the castle, he looked into the dark night "towards Boston." There, beyond the water, "I saw a Bonfire Burning on Fort Hill: by which I understand that the Mob is up and probably doing Mischief."[46]

He was correct. The Loyal Nine and other Whig leaders were taken by surprise. The "amazingly inflamed" people acted on their own. Thursday being market day, their ranks were swelled by persons from neighboring towns. In the early evening the rioters, planning a bonfire on Fort Hill, "erected a Number of Stages with Tar Barrels, etc. in the Form of a Pyramid, in the Centre of which was a Flag Staff, and a Union Flag Hois[t]ed." Andrew Oliver had sent word via a friend to some of the important men in town declaring that he would not act as stamp distributor. He did not appear himself to resign, a humiliation difficult to bear for one of the better sort, who were used to deference. Friends had read the statement to the public in the center of the town. It was now read to the crowd on Fort Hill and around Oliver's house. In town-meeting manner some gentlemen, in part magistrates, in part members of the group at the head of the previous day's procession, moved that Oliver receive the thanks of those present for his compliance with the sense of the town. The crowd cheered him for resigning. Regarding his position as stamp distributor, no more direct action was to be expected. By his resignation he gained readmittance into the community. Instead of a placeman, he was one of the townsmen again, as a town meeting emphasized, and a newspaper explicitly pointed out that now he had retrieved his status as "gentleman."[47]

However, the opposing positions were no longer simply defined as community versus outsider. There were the latent tensions between different groups of the community that had surfaced already the previous evening. When magistrates demanded that the people disperse after cheering Oliver, they were disregarded. The bonfire was extinguished, but then the crowd went to see Lieutenant Governor Hutchinson, who according to a rumor had assisted in drawing up the Stamp Act "by recommending it as an easy Method of gulling the People of their Liberty and Property." Passing Province House, the governor's official residence, the crowd broke some windows and asked for Bernard. A few minutes later they arrived at the mansion of Hutchinson, who considered the request to answer their questions from his balcony—that is, not even face to face with the crowd—to be "an indignity to which he would not submit." He lived in the Northend, the oldest section of the

---

[46]Bernard to Halifax, 15 Aug. 1765, Sparks MSS., 4.4:141, HHL; Bernard to Colville, 1 Nov. 1765, *ibid.*, p. 84 William Shirley to Duke of Newcastle, 1 Dec. 1747, *Correspondence of William Shirley, Governor of Massachusetts and Military Commander in America, 1731–1760,* ed. Charles H. Lincoln, 2 vols. (New York, 1912), 1:412–419.

[47]Avery to Collins, 19 Aug. 1765, in Stiles, *Itineraries*, pp. 435–437; Oliver to Whately, 20 Aug., 2 Sept. 1765, House of Lords MSS., 209:96, 104–106; note by Oliver announcing his resignation to Waterhouse, 15 Aug. 1765, *ibid.*, p. 102, printed in Samuel G. Drake, *History and Antiquities of Boston, from Its Settlement in 1630, to the Year 1770* (Boston, 1856), p. 695n; *BG*, 19 Aug. 1765, Supp.; *BEP*, 19 Aug. 1765; BTR 16:152; Rowe, *Letters and Diary*, p. 89; Gordon, *History*, 1:176; Hutchinson, *History*, 3:88.

town, where his mansion dominated the tightly clustered artisans' and journeymen's houses, many of whom had probably experienced his conceit and arrogance in their daily contacts with him, or in the lack of them. Northenders were now among the crowd. They wanted to inquire about his role in drawing up the Stamp Act and in sending depositions about smuggling to England. Getting no response from Hutchinson, who listened from behind the carefully bolted door, the leader asked "whether they should begin with coach house or stables." The men began to lay hands on the fence, but "one grave elderly tradesman," whom Hutchinson privately called a "demagogue," asked what they were doing and received the short reply "Pull [it] down." As "a noted speaker in town meetings," he asked them to give reasons. They repeated the rumor, adding that they wanted to question the lieutenant governor about the circumstances. Just as Oliver's acquaintances had spoken for him, the tradesman now shielded Hutchinson, and after about an hour of argument the crowd left, patrolled the streets, and "quietly" went home.[48]

Two days later the selectmen dismissed 10 additional watchmen, arguing that since "the quiet of the Town seems now to be restored, . . . the Inhabitants may be eased of this burden." An uneasy calm continued for a few days. Captain Daverson was due from London and was expected to have stamps on board. Accordingly, great numbers of people assembled when a ship was sighted on 21 August. It turned out to be a false alarm, and the crowd dispersed. A Bostonian who made it publicly known that no "mob" would intimidate him if he were stamp distributor almost immediately saw cause to reconsider and withdrew his imprudent statement. The tradesman who had talked to the crowd at Hutchinson's house, the commanding officer of Castle William, and the customs house were said to be in danger of crowd action. It seems that the rioters transferred their expectation to be free from official interference on Pope's Day to the anti-Stamp Act actions.[49]

A second component of the Pope's Day tradition (as well as of many popular holidays) that was part of the anti-Stamp Act activities was the collection of money. For once, not the gentlemen of property and standing, whether in private or public capacities, collected, but the lower sort. The rudimentary criticism of existing societal relations implied in this kind of collective behavior seems to have been combined during the crowd action of August 1765 with the discontent voiced periodically by crowds in response to displays of wealth and luxury.[50] In the rumors about further riots, the residence of a customs official, Benjamin Hallowell, popped up with disturbing (or inviting) frequency. On 23 August three men forced their way into the house. Whether they came with intent to steal or whether they believed the rumors and expected to be the vanguard of a crowd is not clear. The crowd, at any rate, did not come. Contemporaries agreed that it was a lucky surprise for Hallowell

---

[48]*BEP,* 19 Aug. 1765; *BNL,* 22 Aug. 1765; *BG,* 19 Aug., 26 Aug. 1765; Bernard to Halifax, 15–16 Aug. 1765, Sparks MSS., 4.4:137–144, HHL; Hutchinson to ———, 16 Aug. 1765, Letterbooks, MA 26:145a–145b; Hutchinson, *History,* 3:88.

[49]*BTR* 20:172; *BG,* 26 Aug. 1765. More windowpanes were broken in Province House on 18 August. Bernard to Pownall, 19 Aug. 1765, Sparks MSS., 4.4:10, HHL; Bernard to ———, 16 Oct. 1765, Add. MSS., 33030, p. 98, British Museum (LC transcripts); Bernard to Halifax, 22 Aug. 1765, Sparks MSS., 4.4:144–148, HHL.

[50]Cf. Chapter 1, pp.71–78 . On the tradition, dating back to Plough Monday in England, see A. F. Young, *From Ritual to Rebellion.*

that only three men showed up. Later a jury took the same view, and no indictment was entered. Hallowell's house had just been built, and its size and lavish interior accounted for the cost, £2000 sterling. This, of course, was known not only to the governor, who reported the figure, but also to the local craftsmen who had done the work. Hallowell, as customs official, lived on fees—in the opinion of large sections of the society, small shopkeepers, artisans, farmers, not a very honorable way to make a living. While the colonial elite certainly did not agree with this viewpoint in general, it did have some reservations about customs fees. For mechanics, the sum spent by Hallowell on his mansion equaled the total earnings of a lifetime.[51]

Over the weekend before Monday, 26 August, indications of an impending riot multiplied. It was said that several wealthy and high-ranking officials would be attacked. Cautiously a court clerk notified the public that he had *not* favored the Stamp Act. The selectmen, in an unusual move, met on Sunday, 25 August, and called a town meeting, often used to head off potential violence, but on Monday they decided not to call the meeting. One Bostonian heard from a soldier of a British warship then in the harbor "that there was to be a mob in Boston that night, with intent to pull down the Lieut.-Governor's house, and that their ship's crew was sent for." By noon both governor and lieutenant governor were informed, and in the early evening an unusual number of people from neighboring towns were on their way toward Boston.[52]

At twilight some "Boys and Children" started a bonfire on King Street. One of the fire wardens interposed but was warned by "several Whispers from a Person unknown" not to interfere. Confident of his authority, he persisted, but a blow ended his endeavors rather abruptly, and he had to depart under "Insult and Outrage." Thus ended the interference of the civil magistrates. There is no evidence that soldiers or sailors from the man-of-war were called or actually attempted to counteract the riot. Of course, they may have received private communications, but the military could act only when called for by the civil authorities.[53]

The crowd first went to Charles Paxton, marshall of the Court of Admiralty and surveyor of the port. These two positions left him sufficient leisure to desire a third office, a royal appointment to the council of Massachusetts. The council at that time was annually elected by the representatives. Since this state of affairs did not suit Placeman Paxton's interest or his opinion about how a colonial government should be run, he simply suggested to his protector, Lord Townshend, the leading British minister, that the Massachusetts charter be altered and the council be made appointive. On 26 August he too had had notice of what was to happen and had left the

[51]The average of a laborer's daily earnings has been estimated at 2s. lawful money, or £30 per year. The pound sterling compared to the pound lawful money as 3:4; Brown, *Middle-Class Democracy*, pp. 12, 24. Main, *Social Structure of Revolutionary America*, p. 274, suggested annual earnings of up to £50. Throughout this study an intermediate figure of £40 is used. Richard Dana, Pleas, 1760–1767, 24 Aug. 1765, no. 51, Dana Family Papers, MHS.

[52]*BTR* 20:173; Ebenezer Parkman, Diary, 10 vols., photostat, vol. 7, 26 Aug. 1765, MHS; Bernard to Halifax, 31 Aug. 1765, Sparks MSS., 4.4:149–158, HHL; Hutchinson to Jackson, 30 Aug. 1765, in Morgan, ed., *Prologue to Revolution*, pp. 108–109. For the sailor's account, see Justin Winsor, ed., *The Memorial History of Boston, Including Suffolk County, Massachusetts, 1630–1880*, 4 vols. (Boston, 1880–1881), 3:14, notes 4 and 5, from papers in the "Charity Building"; these papers seem to be lost now.

[53]*BPB*, 2 Sept. 1765; *BNL*, 5 Sept. 1765.

dwelling with his family and his most valuable belongings. The owner of the house, a Mr. Palmer, argued with the rioters, explaining that he should not be made to suffer in Paxton's place. Over a barrel of punch, the rioters agreed.[54]

The next target was William Story, deputy registrar of the Court of Vice Admiralty. The Stamp Act included a provision that breaches of the act were to be tried in the Courts of Vice Admiralty, which, according to Story, made him a particular object of resentment to the people. It "diffused a general uneasiness in persons of almost every rank they being thereby deprived of the invaluabel priviledge of trials by Juries." To contemporaries the deputy registrar, "by various malpractices, had made himself highly obnoxious," and access to his office was made easier when the crowd forced open the door, "making a thorow fare from the Street" to his office. The hated files of his office were used as "fuel to revive the expiring Flames" of the King Street bonfire. Story resigned soon afterward.[55] At the same time another crowd visited Benjamin Hallowell, who was obnoxious to merchants and seamen because of his attempts to enforce the British trade regulations.[56] Whether artisans who had built his residence were among the rioters we do not know. At his estate, fences and windows were broken, his "rich" furnishings and "China" partly destroyed, his desks broken open, some of his large wine supply consumed, and clothing and about £30 sterling taken away.[57]

Small groups of rioters went through the town "committing outrages, threatening the customhouse, and several dwelling houses" and, according to another report, the dwelling of a Mr. Richardson, probably the customs informer. The attorney general of the province and one of Boston's overseers of the poor, both merchants, suffered minor damages. Governor Bernard had sent away his plate for the second time and gone to the castle. Passing by his official residence, some of the crowd suggested attacking it. The rioters, "inflamed monsters" in the opinion of their adversaries, according to the same adversaries coolly argued that the official residence of the governor would be restored with tax money, their money, which would not be the case for private property. They then turned to Lieutenant Governor Hutchinson's private residence.[58]

Hutchinson had been assured by his friends that "he was become rather Popular," but it seems that his friends did not have very close connections with prospective crowd members. He left at the last minute. Not finding him in his house, the

[54]Parkman, Diary, 27 Aug. 1765, MHS; Paxton to Townshend, 22 Dec. 1764, Paxton Letters, MHS; Gordon, History, 1:176; Charles Paxton, "Letters of Charles Paxton," ed. G. G. Wolkins, MHSP 56:343–352, esp. 345–349 (1922–1923); John Adams, Diary, 6 Sept., 19 Oct. 1769, 1:343–344.

[55]BG, 26 Aug., 30 Sept. 1765; BNL, 23 Sept. 1765; Story's petition, 19 Oct. 1766, MA 44:604–606; Gordon, History, 1:177.

[56]The accounts vary on the division of the crowd into two task forces, one group attacking Story's house, a second group taking on Hallowell's house [Josiah Quincy, Jr., "Extracts of the Diary of Mr. Quincy," MHSP 4:47 (1858–1860)]. Such a division would be a notable instance of allocation of resources and of strategy. The two crowds had to unite afterward for the attack on Hutchinson's house. While most sources do not mention this division, it is plausible, considering the short time in which Story, Paxton, and Hallowell were visited.

[57]Benjamin Hallowell's account of 14 August and 26 August, House of Lords MSS., 209:199–203; John Tudor, Deacon Tudor's Diary, 1732–1793, ed. William Tudor (Boston, 1896), p. 18; Henry Lloyd to William Butler, 29 Aug. 1765, Letterbook, pp. 151–152, HBS.

[58]Freeman, Notebook, 28 Aug. 1765, MHS; Parkman, Diary, 27 Aug. 1765, MHS; Hutchinson, History, 3:90;

rioters organized search parties, as they had done two weeks earlier in the case of Oliver.[59] The "Northend Raggamuffins" and others wrought havoc among his possessions, destroying many, scattering others over the town, stealing considerable amounts. His house, which he prided himself as being one of the most elegant mansions in the province, was severely damaged: cupola cut down, part of the roof uncovered, partitions torn out. All this was done while a crowd of "some hundred" spectators from Boston and other towns watched without interfering, as a Boston justice of the peace noted.[60]

Numerous, partly contradictory explanations for this violent action against Hutchinson were advanced by contemporaries, including Hutchinson himself. It was said that the rioters still resented his attempt to intervene on behalf of Oliver late in the evening of 14 August. His refusal to talk to the crowd and his neighbors on 15 August may have singled him out, since other officials and house owners did talk with the men from the crowds. Or the action may have been meant as intimidation. As chief justice, Hutchinson could charge the grand jury, scheduled to convene on 27 August, to prosecute the rioters. Second, as to his participation in provincial politics, many people resented his relentless quest for more offices and the gain associated with them. His conduct as an official was the perfect example of "covetousness" and "ambition," traits against which Puritan divines had thundered from the pulpit for a century and a half, always calling upon the people to prevent such men from gaining their ends. He was lieutenant governor, councillor, chief justice, captain of the castle guard, judge of probate.[61] Hutchinson himself thought that his role as spokesman for the hard money interests in the late forties, which had brought about crowd action at that time, was still remembered by many and that animosities persisted: "The lower class cursed him." Sailors and merchants had a longstanding grievance against Hutchinson for supporting the customs and trade regulations, and more recently for taking depositions about illicit trading and allegedly sending them to Great Britain. A third and very important explanation blamed private economic interests among some wealthy persons:

Hutchinson to Conway, 1 Oct. 1765, Letterbooks, MA 26:154–156; Bernard to Lords Commissioners, 22 Aug. 1765, House of Lords MSS., 209:348–356; Bernard to ———, 16 Oct. 1765, Add. MSS., 33030, p. 98, British Museum; Bernard to Barrington, 23 Nov. 1765, *Barrington–Bernard Correspondence,* ed. Edward Channing and Archibald C. Coolidge (Cambridge, Mass., 1912), p. 102; Governor Bernard's proclamation, 28 Aug. 1765, published in *BEP,* 2 Sept. 1765; Sibley and Shipton, *Harvard Graduates* 12:13, 210.

[59]Hutchinson to Jackson, 30 Aug. 1765, Letterbooks, MA 26:146–147; Tudor, *Diary,* pp. 19–20; Esther Forbes, *Paul Revere and the World He Lived In* (Boston, 1942), p. 105.

[60]Nathan Bowen, "Extracts from the Interleaved Almanacs of Nathan Bowen, Marblehead, 1742–1799," ed. W. H. Bowden, *EIHC* 91:190 (1955). A list of Hutchinson's stolen or lost possessions was published in *BEP,* 2 Sept. 1765. Quincy, ed., *Reports,* pp. 170–173; Hutchinson, *History,* 3:92, 113–115. Hutchinson's claim not to have countenanced the Stamp Act is correct. For Hutchinson's conduct through the whole of this period, see Morgan and Morgan, *Stamp Act Crisis,* Ch. 12, and Bernard Bailyn, *The Ordeal of Thomas Hutchinson* (Cambridge, Mass., 1973), pp. 35–69.

[61]His brother Foster Hutchinson was justice of the peace and on the bench of the Inferior Court. His brother-in-law, Andrew Oliver, was secretary of the province; Andrew's brother Peter sat on the Superior Court bench too. Among the two Olivers' sons were two representatives, a justice of the peace, and an Inferior Court judge. A nephew of Thomas Hutchinson was registrar of the Probate Court and Andrew Oliver's deputy. Ellen E. Brennan, *Plural Officeholding in Massachusetts, 1760–1780* (Chapel Hill, N.C., 1945), pp. 32–49, and Chs. 1 and 2 in general. Sibley and Shipton, "Thomas Hutchinson," *Harvard Graduates,* 8:149–217.

the mob was led on to the house by a secret influence, with a view to the destruction of certain papers, known to be there, and which, it is thought, would have proved, that the grant to the New Plymouth Company on Kennebec River [Maine], was different from what was contended by some claimants.

The case was up for trial at the oncoming session of the Superior Court.[62]

How did this diversity of interests affect the internal and external restraints of crowd action? It has already been noted that the selectmen intentionally by-passed the chance to use community control by calling a town meeting. Nor did town officials, present during the anti-Hutchinson action, interfere, "though they saw the danger from this assumed power in the populace, yet they would give no aid in discountenancing it, lest they should become obnoxious themselves; for there were whisperings of danger from further acts of violence."[63] As to the composition of the crowd and internal restraints, several factors combined to distinguish this riot from tradition. The New Plymouth Company had lined up numerous witnesses for its claims—mostly sailors from Maine—and the *Evening Post* explicitly charged that "foreign villains" were the perpetrators of the violence. It seems that private interests sent men with orders into the riot and probably paid them. Hutchinson maintained that John Rowe, member of the Merchants Club's executive committee, admitted as much.[64] It is difficult to evaluate the impact of a second unusual group, those people coming from the country, since neither the specific motivation nor the degree of their active participation can be ascertained. Third, according to the reports, young persons were extraordinarily active. Without support from powerful individuals, they could not have lighted the bonfire in King Street or defied the firewarden's orders to extinguish it. Because of the danger to the town, with its many wooden buildings, such fires were prohibited by law, and crowds generally avoided such action because of the safety hazards.[65] The "Boys and Children," probably indentured servants and apprentices, were considered difficult to restrain, and town-meeting votes frequently forbade their participation in celebrations and crowd action. On the other hand, they were intentionally used when some interests wanted violence without being hampered by the internal restraints inherent in the traditional crowd action.[66] Finally, contrary to the tradition of rioting, property was not only damaged but stolen.[67] This may be explained partly by the crews of men

---

[62]Parkman, Diary, 26 Aug. 1765, MHS; Bernard to Lords of Trade, 31 Aug. 1765, House of Lords MSS., 209:376–399; Bernard to Halifax, 31 Aug. 1765, Sparks MSS., 4.4:149–158, HHL; Hutchinson, *History*, 3:89–90, and *The Diary and Letters of His Excellency Thomas Hutchinson*, ed. Peter Orlando Hutchinson, 2 vols. (London, 1883–1886), 1:67; Caleb H. Snow, *A History of Boston* (Boston, 1825), marginal note on merchant involvement in author's copy, BPL; Oliver, *American Rebellion*, p. 52; Gordon, *History*, 1:180; Warden, *Boston*, p. 166, note 34; John Adams, *Diary*, 1:259–261; *BEP*, 2 Sept. 1765. Hutchinson on hard money animosity and lower-class curses, *Diary and Letters*, 1:54. Rhode Islanders thought that the intent of the riot had been the destruction of material that Hutchinson had collected for his *History;* John Adams, *Diary*, 20 Jan. 1766, 1:300.

[63]*BTR* 20:173; Tudor, *Diary*, p. 20; Hutchinson, *History*, 3:89.

[64]Hutchinson, *Diary and Letters*, 1:67; *BEP*, 2 Sept. 1765; *BNL*, 7 Nov. 1765; Tudor, *Diary*, p. 19; Bowen, "Almanacs," pp. 189–190.

[65]Shirley to Lords of Trade, 1 Dec. 1747, *Correspondence*, 1:413.

[66]See Chapter 8, pp. 216–223.

[67]For the thief, Magnus Mode, see note 85.

sent to get at Hutchinson's papers, partly by the participation of many strangers who could not easily be recognized. None of the opponents of this action blamed all of the rioters for the extraordinary proceedings. Story spoke of "some ill minded persons" using the occasion for private purposes, and a Boston merchant firm informed its correspondents that now the rioters had gone too far, "Robbers and Vialins [villains] having joined them for Plunder."[68]

Almost all witnesses present at Hutchinson's house agreed that the action was influenced by consumption of large quantities of alcohol by the rioters. This, in all probability true, has to be seen in the perspective that regular consumption of rum during work was very high compared to today's standards. Thus, the barrel of punch at Palmer's house (Paxton) was nothing extraordinary, and the rioters departed without damaging the house. The action at Story's office and, with the exception of some stealing, also the action at Hallowell's house are readily explainable by misconduct of the two officials; they themselves were conscious of this. The rational argument among the rioters when passing Province House suggests that a large part of the crowd was not overly influenced by alcohol.[69] Hallowell's and Hutchinson's liquor stores seem to have been considerable, however. As the participants in the direct action were swayed by arguments at Palmer's house and at Province House, they had been willing to defer action for discussion at Oliver's place and at Hutchinson's quarters on 15 August. This suggests that as long as they were accepted in a dialogue about grievances and about fears concerning the stamp taxes, the crowd members were ready to stay within the limits of nonviolent political debate. Only when they were refused participation, as Hutchinson attempted to do on 15 August, were they ready to assert their claims by using other than the obviously closed political channels.

Thus far we have been concerned with the extraordinary aspects of the riot, outside participants and private interests, rather than with the men of 14 August, the Pope's Day constituency from the poorer classes. They seem to have become aware of the possibility of using their combined powers against extravagant luxury and arrogant officials during the confrontation at Oliver's house late in the evening of the first riot. From that time onward there was a continuing and open emphasis on the union between Northend and Southend. There was also a seemingly rational selection of targets for further action from among wealthy inhabitants and influential but disliked officials. Seeing Hutchinson one day after the riot, some of the participants remarked without the slightest trace of deference: "There he is!" "If such men are by God appointed, the Devil may be the Lord's anointed," quipped Bostonians in later years.

All those who had been targets of crowd action had ready explanations of why they had been selected. One of the Loyal Nine, John Avery, after witnessing the first spontaneous action, simply remarked: "There are a great many other imposi-

---

[68]Petition of William Story, MA 44:604–606; Jonathan and William Powell to Christopher Champlin, 2 Sept. 1765, Letters of Boston Merchants, 1732–1790, 4 vols., 1:72, HBS.

[69]Abolition of the free distribution of rum was still considered reason enough for a strike in 1817 (Medford, Mass.), Province House argument: Hutchinson to Conway, 1 Oct. 1765, Letterbooks, MA 26:154–156.

tions that desire as much Notice of in their Order."[70] In the decades before 1765 during the successive stages of crowd action against wealthy inhabitants hurting the community, against rival interest groups, against displays of wealth, the nature of the action had changed from attacking the actual means of economic power to destroying symbols of wealth. The latter was merely an expression of resentment. In the course of the intense action from 14 August onward, this possibly changed into a consciousness of distinct interests among the mechanics.

After 10 days of intermittent direct action and rumors, Jonathan Mayhew, minister of the West Church, preached on 25 August about Gal. 5:12–13, "I would they were even cut off which trouble you. For brethren, ye have been called unto liberty; only use not liberty for an occasion of the flesh, but by love serve one another." The sermon was widely believed to have contributed to the riot on the next day, and, Mayhew's disclaimers notwithstanding, one of the rioters, according to Hutchinson, declared "that he thought he was doing God service."[71]

Among the wealthy or well-to-do inhabitants, fear of economic "leveling" and social "licentiousness" was widespread. Some hid their plate and other valuables in the houses of poorer neighbors and friends or in their country homes. A merchant reported that the "almost Infernal Mob," acting "without controul," had threatened "many of the most respectable Inhabitants with destruction to their Houses Furniture etc." The governor had information that 15 houses of "the most respectable persons" were to be attacked on 27 August. He suspected that a "war" was being fought for "taking away the Distinction of rich and poor." Though the fears were probably exaggerated, their general acceptance, the extent of the crowd action, the selection of actual targets, and the somewhat frantic Whig reaction to spontaneous crowd action suggest that there was some truth in them.[72] General Gage in New York summarized the information he had received fairly accurately when he said: "The Boston Mob, raised first by the Instigation of Many of the Principal Inhabitants . . . rose shortly after of their own Accord." On the other hand, the motives that he imputed to the crowds ("Plunder," "Rapacity") and his opinion about the character of the action ("Fury") merely reflected his class bias. The leadership retracted, according to Gage, when they realized that they could not guide the crowd. This experience of the Massachusetts Whigs was repeated in other colonies, and there "has been as much Pains taken since, to prevent Insurrections, of the People, as before to excite them." William Gordon, Whig historian, shared this view, noting that size and intention of crowds may have gone far beyond what Whig leadership intended. He also admitted the danger from "crafty men"—that is, Boston merchants—attempting to use the crowd for their own purposes. Neither the view of crowd action as savage violence nor the view of rioters as Whig-inspired

---

[70]Hutchinson to Jackson, 30 Aug. 1765, *ibid.*, pp. 146–147, and *History,* 3:90; Avery to Collins, 19 Aug. 1765, in Stiles, *Itineraries,* pp. 435–437; *BG,* 29 Feb. 1768.

[71]Memorandum on the sermon, folder 91, Mayhew MSS., Boston Univ., Boston, Mass.; Mayhew to Hutchinson, 27 Aug. 1765, *ibid.;* Mayhew to Richard Clarke, 3 Sept. 1765, *NEHGR* 46:16–20 (1892); Hutchinson, *History,* 3:89; Charles W. Akers, *Called unto Liberty: A Life of Jonathan Mayhew, 1720–1766* (Cambridge, Mass., 1964), pp. 198–207.

agents of politics by other means is correct. The crowd had a tradition of its own, an ideology of its own, and interests of its own.[73]

THE REACTION OF OFFICIALS AND MERCHANTS

On the morning after the riot of 26 August, the authorities got busy. The selectmen, the council, militia officers, and justices met to take steps to suppress further crowd action. A large number of inhabitants declared in a hurriedly called town meeting that they had "an utter detestation of the extraordinary and violent proceedings of a number of Persons unknown against some of the Inhabitants . . . the last Night." Such votes were a customary ritual to reaffirm community cohesion after differing interests, usually submerged in notions of a common interest, had been brought into the open by direct action. In addition, and dangerous to all sections of the community, came the experience that wealthy individuals appropriated a community tradition for their own private purposes. In the conceptual and institutional framework of the corporate townships, this not only threatened anomie. It was anomie. The only means to counteract institutionally uncontrollable private interest was crowd action, just that instrument of public redress that had been usurped by the private interests. The careful limitation of the town-meeting vote to the "last Night" excepted the anti-Stamp Act violence of 14 August, which had been done under the guidance of Whig leaders and seems to have met with general approbation. The inhabitants voted unanimously "to use their utmost endeavors agreable to Law to suppress the like disorders for the future" and, according to the newspapers, "to have a Military Watch, till the present unruly Spirit shall subside."[74]

The councillors met. This they had done on 14 August too, treating the whole affair first as "a Boyish sport," but later explaining "that it was a preconcerted business in which the greatest Part of the Town was engaged" and that they had no power to oppose it. The governor then tried to call out the militia but was told by the top officers that "as soon as the drum was heard, the drummer would be knocked down, and the drum broke . . . [and] that probably all the drummers of the Regiment were in the Mob."[75] Now, after the disorders of the twenty-sixth, the council reacted strongly and ordered out a military guard. To reassert their authority over town officials and rioting Boston militiamen, the councillors threatened to call in a militia force from the country. But they advised against asking for British troops.

[72]James Gordon to William Martin, 10 Sept. 1765, *MHSP* 2.13:393–396 (1900); Henry Lloyd to William Butler, 29 Aug. 1765, Letterbook, 1765–1767, pp. 151–152, HBS; letters from John Hancock, Aug. 1765–Jan. 1766, Letterbooks, NEHGS; Herbert S. Allan, *John Hancock, Patriot in Purple* (New York, 1948), pp. 88–89; W. T. Baxter, *The House of Hancock: Business in Boston, 1724–1775* (Cambridge, Mass., 1945), pp. 232–239; Bernard to Halifax, 31 Aug. 1765, Sparks MSS., 4.4:153, HHL.

[73]Gage to Conway, 23 Sept. 1765, *The Correspondence of General Thomas Gage*, ed. Clarence E. Carter, 2 vols. (New Haven, Conn., 1931–1933), 1:67–68; Gordon, *History*, 1:177.

[74]*BTR* 16:152; *BEP*, 2 Sept. 1765; *BG*, 2 Sept. 1765; Tudor, *Diary*, p. 21; Boyle, "Journal," p. 170 (1930); Samuel Adams to Smith, 20 Dec. 1765, *The Writings of Samuel Adams*, ed. Harry A. Cushing, 4 vols. (New York, 1904–1908), 1:60, cf. 89–96.

[75]Council Records, 16:31–33, MSA; Bernard to Halifax, 15–16 Aug. 1765, Sparks MSS., 4.4:137–139, HHL.

Privately Bernard had sent information off to the military authorities a day earlier because "all civil power ceased in an instant, and I had not the least authority to oppose or quiet the Mob."[76]

Military measures were only the most immediate step to restore order. Those who saw their position threatened were by no means satisfied with the four militia companies. The selectmen ordered the crews of two fire engines to turn out and "assist the Civil Magistrates." But these, too, came from the same ranks as the rioters. Upper-echelon Bostonians therefore went on duty themselves; the Cadet Company mustered. A volunteer force of gentlemen and some master craftsmen, it was geared to ceremonial duties for the governor and exempt from training with the lower-class militia. Its ranks were increased by "gentlemen-volunteers." Cadets and volunteers now mounted guard to protect—not wholly disinterestedly—order and property. Boston gave the impression of a garrison.[77]

A number of the rioters, however, were not ready to give in. The Anglican minister who had condemned the rioting was threatened with violence. So was someone who had talked about the necessity for calling British troops into the town. Supporters of Hutchinson were fearful that expressions of sympathy would bring about the "Resentment" of the rioters. On the evening of the twenty-seventh, a crowd did in fact assemble. Not surprisingly, the Cadets rather than the militiamen took action. One of them was knocked down by a stone. They "were obliged to present their Pieces; but did not fire." This show of force dispersed the crowd, but the watch continued for three weeks and even then was ordered to be ready to muster on short notice.[78]

The judicial institutions brimmed with activity too, to subdue the "unruly spirit." In another of his many offices, that of chief justice, Hutchinson, loyal adherent to British rights, instructed a grand jury to bring indictments against the rioters. A local justice of the peace, Richard Dana, staunch defender of the colonies' position, issued warrants against them. The politically singularly colorless county sheriff, Stephen Greenleaf, made arrests.[79] All political factions united against the lower-class crowd. In the Superior Court, Hutchinson made it absolutely clear that it was necessary to indict the rioters, who "hurt the Peace of the Community, and disturb the Order of Society." Grand jurors were not only *custodes legum* but also *custodes morum* of the people. Riots, burglary, and treason were mentioned in the chief justice's charge. Burglary included actions "done when a great Number are pre-

---

[76]Council Records, 16:37–39, 66, MSA; *BEP*, 2 Sept. 1765; Gordon to Martin, 10 Sept. 1765, *MHSP* 2.13:393 (1900). Bernard quoted in Anderson, "Ebenezer Mackintosh," pp. 35–36. General Gage wrote to Barrington on 16 January 1766 (*Correspondence*, 2:334): "No Requisition [for troops] has been made of Me for assistance, which I must acknowledge I have been sorry for, as the disturbances which have happened, have been so much beyond riots, and so like the forerunners of open Rebellion, that I have wanted a pretence to draw the troops together." Cf. Bowen, "Almanacs," 26 Aug. 1765, p. 190.

[77]BTR 20:174; Bernard to Halifax, 31 Aug. 1765, Sparks MSS., 4.4:153, HHL. Council Records, 16:47, MSA.

[78]Bernard to Lords Commissioners, 22 Aug. 1765, House of Lords MSS., 209:348–356; Bernard to Halifax, 31 Aug. 1765, Sparks MSS., 4.4:149–158, HHL; Mayhew to Hutchinson, 27 Aug. 1765, folder 91, Mayhew MSS., Boston Univ.; Sibley and Shipton, *Harvard Graduates*, 11:465–466; John Osborne to Hutchinson, 28 Aug. 1765, Letterbooks, MA 25:28–31; Joshua Henshaw to ———, 27 Aug. 1765, *NEHGR* 32:269 (1878).

[79]Quincy, ed., *Reports*, pp. 175–179; Superior Court of Judicature, Minute Books, vol. 14, no. 81, p. 17, Records, 1764–1765, f. 259, SCCH; Dana, Pleas, 1760–1767, 30 Aug. 1765, Dana Family Papers, MHS.

sent.'' ''If the Intention of riotous Assemblies is to redress Grievances of a publick Nature, and such Intention is executed, it is a levying War against the King, and Treason.'' Though the conservative Hutchinson admitted that rioting ''indeed does not strike the Mind with so much Abhorrence, as some other Offences,'' he continued, ''yet on the Discouragement and Suppression of these, all Peace of Society depends . . . because such Assemblies, when not restrained, generally resist all Opposition, and tend to the Subversion of all Government: There is no knowing where they'll end.''[80]

Only 11 participants in direct action and a few spectators have been identified.[81] The three of them present on 14 August considered the proceedings highly entertaining but mainly emphasized the necessity for opposition to oppressive British officials. They felt that they shared this opinion with all others present. Cyrus Baldwin was a captain and merchant from Woburn who lived in Boston only temporarily. James Freeman and Robert Hewes were both politically conscious persons, but the former also seems to have had a liking for brawls. Hewes was present during the King Street riot (1770), the tea riot (1773), and a riot against a customs official (1774).[82] Seven men were arrested for entering Hutchinson's house on 26 August; some of them admitted their guilt.[83] A merchant from the Northend, Andrew Hall, was accused of ''reviling'' Hutchinson. He had promoted passive resistance to the Sugar Act.[84] A sailor, Magnus Mode, was arrested, released, but arrested again in 1766 because several things belonging to Hutchinson and missing since August 1765 were found on him or had been sold by him.[85]

This judicial onslaught to mete out punishment to the rioters came to nothing. The first to be arrested had been Ebenezer Mackintosh, leader of the men from the Southend and suspected of having been at the head of the riot of 26 August. He could have raised a crowd against the official within minutes but did not even bother to do so. Sheriff Greenleaf had barely seized him when several gentlemen interposed. Afraid that Mackintosh might not be willing to take the blame for the whole affair and decide to divulge the names of those officials and merchants who participated in the planning, they demanded his release. As in the whole of the opposition

---

[80]Quincy, ed., *Reports,* pp. 175–179.

[81]Cyrus Baldwin, James Freeman, George R. T. Hewes (14 August); Patrick Murray (23 August); Christopher Barrett, Stephen Greeley, J. Johonnot (distiller), Joseph Snelling (mariner), Samuel Taylor (merchant), Will Moore (26 August); Andrew Hall, merchant. Among the spectators were Deacon John Tudor and a Mr. Miller from Chauxit. Several more men were in prison at this time for breach of peace or other offenses, but in all cases participation in the riots can be ruled out because of contrary evidence. Bernard to Hillsborough, 29 Aug. 1768, Sparks MSS., 4.7:26, HHL; Hutchinson, *Diary and Letters,* 2:228; Tudor, *Diary,* p. 19; Parkman, Diary, 31 Aug. 1765, MHS; SCF 172951.

[82]Cyrus Baldwin to his brother, 15–16 Aug. 1765, Misc. Bound Papers, vol. 13, MHS; Freeman, Notebook, MHS; Superior Court of Judicature, Minute Books, vol. 14, Suffolk, March 1766, SCCH; Hewes, *Memoir,* pp. 67, 96, 179.

[83]SCF 172947; Superior Court of Judicature, Minute Books, vol. 14, Suffolk, p. 24, SCCH; Dana, Pleas, 29–31 Aug. 1765, nos. 55–58, Dana Family Papers, MHS.

[84]Dana, Pleas, 3 Sept. 1765, no. 59, *ibid.* BG, 24 Sept. 1764; *BEP,* 24 Sept. 1764.

[85]Mode came from Bristol and was taken up on 26 June 1766. Neither the Court of General Sessions of the Peace nor the Superior Court of Judicature, Minute Books, mention any action against him. In 1765 he was arraigned for leaving his ship. Dana, Pleas, 16 Sept. 1765, no. 66, Dana Family Papers, MHS. In 1767 he was indicted and convicted for counterfeiting, and in 1768 he was accused of burglary. *BPB,* 30 June 1766; SCF 87706; Superior Court of Judicature, Minute Books, vol. 13, Middlesex, no. 78, SCCH; *A Few Lines on Magnus Mode* (Boston, 1767), *Mass. Brds.* 1407.

to the Stamp Act, the division into Whigs and Tories was not yet operating. Nathaniel Coffin, who interposed, later chose the Tory side. When Coffin threatened to cancel the agreement according to which armed gentlemen would patrol the streets at night to protect their property, Mackintosh was released. Arrests of other, less important participants were made, and more were expected.[86] But instead, further crowd action, a rescue riot, set most of the arrested men free.[87] The last three imprisoned men had to be discharged when the grand jurors refused to prosecute the rioters. In sum, the clampdown on crowds notwithstanding, they still engaged in independent action, though at the levels of before 14 August.

Officials in at least two other New England colonies faced the question of how to put the rioters in their place. In Newport, Rhode Island, the first Stamp Act riots were generally approved. But when a crowd leader of Mackintosh's rank began to act on his own, he was imprisoned by the attorney general. The influential townsmen agreed with this procedure, although the attorney general had been stamp master until the crowd had forced him to resign. The governor of Connecticut, trying to disperse a crowd demanding Stamp Distributor Ingersoll's resignation, was told ''that they lookt upon this as the cause of the people, and that they did not intend to take directions from any body.'' This self-assertiveness is typical of goal-directed crowd action and has been described as characteristic of seventeenth-century and eighteenth-century European crowds too. In New York anyone who favored the act was labeled ''traytor,'' coaches were attacked, and the usual patterns of deliberate action were found.[88]

This review of the reaction of officialdom to the Stamp Act riots was intended to show the actual methods used to control the crowds. Before turning to the further development of this relationship in the months before the repeal of the act, two problems that have surfaced repeatedly in the preceding description and analysis of the rioting need further attention. Whigs as well as crown supporters condemned the violence committed on 26 August. In order to achieve a balanced perspective, this attitude has to be related to the violence and application of force practiced by the upper strata of colonial society. Second, it has to be asked whether the Whig leadership reacted to crowd action on the spur of the moment only or whether basic notions about popular sovereignty and direct action were involved.

A critique of contemporary attitudes toward the use of violent coercive measures is the more necessary since historians have tended to present merely the opinions of leadership and highly placed targets of crowd action. This, of course, is insufficient. It has already been noted that resorting to individual acts of violence was common to all groups of colonial society. Second, it has been shown that the specific actions of

---

[86]Hutchinson, *Diary and Letters*, 1:70–72, and *History*, 3:91; *BEP*, 2 Sept. 1765; Bernard to Halifax, 31 Aug. 1765, Sparks MSS., 4.4:149–158, HHL.

[87]*BEP*, 7 Oct. 1765; *BNL*, 3 Oct. 1765; Council Records, 16:52–54, MSA; Hutchinson to Jackson, Sept. 1765, Letterbooks, MA 26:150–153.

[88]*BNL*, 5 Sept. 1765; Captain Leslie on the arrest of the crowd leader in Rhode Island, Misc. Bound Papers, vol. 13, MHS. Beverly McAnear, ''The Albany Stamp Act riots,'' *WMQ* 3.4:496 (1947); *N.Y. Gaz.*, 7 Nov. 1765; Jesse Lemisch, ''New York's Petitions and Resolves of December 1765: Liberals vs. Radicals,'' *N.Y. Hist. Soc. Q.* 49:313–326 (1965).

26 August were due in large part to a variety of conflicting interests of some merchants or mercantile groups, who brought about an anomic situation. The most recent study of one of the protagonists of the Stamp Act period, the biography of Thomas Hutchinson by Bernard Bailyn, still refers to the crowd action against him as "savage," a term that is used again and again in the course of the book. George Minot, giving one of the earliest descriptions, reported the affair exclusively on Hutchinson's own terms. The "intoxicated rioters," he wrote, attacked the lieutenant governor when he was having dinner with his loved ones. His "domestic happiness in the enjoyment of his children at once formed a striking contrast to their diabolical employment, and furnished desirable victims for their malice. The family circle was instantly dispersed. . . . All was now delivered up to a triumphant democracy, which exercised its force effectually until daylight. . . ."[89] Hutchinson's sufferings have furnished material for many melodramatic accounts.

It has never been asked how Hutchinson, the victim of violence in this case, conducted himself when he was in a position to administer violence or when it lay in his power to save others from suffering violent treatment. The description of the following incident is based on a source published in 1865 and open to use by historians ever since. Five months before his house was destroyed, Hutchinson, in his charge to the grand jury, represented the Boston jail as "a most shocking, loathsome Place . . . a dark, damp, and pestilential Room." In short, the conditions were against the law and violated the prisoners' rights and health. The chief justice, being a man of "Sensibility or Humanity" had "the most tender and exquisite Sensations" for those he and others sent there. Hutchinson did cite a case in which a sheriff had been indicted and hanged for similar negligence, and he did show genuine concern for the prisoners. But he refused to blame those officials responsible or the prison keeper, whom he knew "to be a Man of great Tenderness." "Hellish crew," he shrieked when talking about rioters. If his anguish about the destruction of his home arouses sympathy; the rioters' anguish about his arrogance should do the same. Otherwise, historians are nothing but partisans of the better sort.[90]

Hutchinson, of course, did not stand alone among his contemporaries in his

---

[89]Bailyn, *Ordeal of Thomas Hutchinson*, pp. 36 *passim*; George R. Minot, *Continuation of the History of the Province of the Massachusetts Bay*, 2 vols. (Boston, 1798, 1803), 2:215; Hutchinson, *History*, 3:90–91. The tendency to condemn violence when used by those of the lower sort, to excuse it when used by those of the better sort, and to accept it when it is in the laws can best be illustrated by a literary example, Kenneth Roberts's fast-selling pseudohistorical novel *Oliver Wiswall* (New York, 1940). Though written with "the generous assistance" of more than a dozen well-known librarians and historians, the book contains a note, not without reason, that the cumulative efforts of author, historians, and librarians for historical accuracy may be summarized: "All characters in this book are fictional and any resemblance to persons living or dead is purely coincidental." The book pictures the senseless brutalities of the lower classes, the unfeeling rabble, against Loyalists, whose heroic violence in turn shines as manly and great. Members of the rabble "scurry"; Loyalists "stride." The rabble steals from malice; Loyalists have lower-ranking factotums who "obtain" for them the necessities of life. Loyalists observe and think; the rabble wails in chorus. A "threatening, exulting, wolfish" mob cuts out a tarred and feathered horse's tongue; tough and heroic Oliver Wiswall rides a horse almost to death. The extensive theoretical and empirical literature on the use of, justification for, and revolutionary or counter-revolutionary character of violence has had little influence on the historiography of the American Revolution (Arendt, Merleau-Ponty, Neumann, Sartre, Fanon, and others, as well as the countless evaluations by advocates of specific ideologies).

[90]Quincy, ed., *Reports*, pp. 111–112.

one-sided view of violence. Boston gentlemen rejected the violence of some of the rioters who had been armed with nothing but clubs, and then patrolled the streets armed with guns. Without mentioning that leading merchants were responsible for parts of the robberies committed, Samuel Adams lamented the "mobbish" transactions in the town, and the newspapers thundered against the "rude fellows."[91] John Adams developed the theoretical underpinning for this point of view. He took the stratification of society for granted and was mainly concerned with the maintenance of the dignity of officials and of deference among the people. Concerning the widely approved and supported symbolic action against Andrew Oliver on 14 August, he asked, "has not the blind, undistinguishing Rage of the Rabble done him irreparable Injustice?" To be exhibited in effigy, to be carried around in "insolent Tryumph," to be molested in one's home, was "a very attrocious Violation of the Peace and of dangerous Tendency and Consequence." This was and remained the basis of Adams's attitude toward the people and their action. Similarities to legal punishments—stocks, whipping, execution—escaped his attention. He admitted the necessity of opposing some British policies and, more so, Thomas Hutchinson, who held all those offices that Adams would have liked to hold. "Is not this amazing ascendency of one Family, Foundation sufficient on which to erect a Tyranny?" Since he was suspicious, he admitted that the "Vulgar" might be suspicous too. To avoid "ignominous" violence, Adams suggested that it might have been prudent "and a Condescention that is due to the present Fears and Distresses of the People" to resign some of the offices, provided this could be done "in some manner consistent with the Dignity of their stations and Characters."

Two months later, as "Humphry Ploughjogger," he took a public stand against violence in the *Boston Gazette*. He lumped together "thieves and robbers and rioters, ay and liars, too," and advocated opposition by mere nonconsumption of British goods. However, he seems not to have been quite convinced himself that this would do, and he came forward with a suggestion as revealing as it was scurrilous. If riots there need be, should the Spittlefield weavers in London riot against Parliament to protest their unemployment caused by the American nonimportation. In fact, there was one incident of disorder in Great Britain. Not the lowly weavers but American merchants, respectable gentlemen, assembled in the lobby of Parliament on the day of repeal of the Stamp Act, 18 March 1766, and shouted, huzzahed, and hissed at Grenville.[92]

The other end of the spectrum of Whig attitudes toward crowd action was represented by an article in the *Boston Gazette*, reportedly from New York. The author, in his opening sentence, made it clear that he was taking the opposite attitude toward the demands for deference and dignity of class voiced by John Adams. "As all Men sprang from the same common Parent, they were all originally equal, and all equally free." From this principle is derived the basic argument of the article, that government was instituted for the public good and for nothing else. Property rights are

[91]Samuel Adams to John Smith, 20 [Dec.] 1765, *Writings*, 1:60, cf. 89–96; *BG*, 2 Sept. 1765.
[92]*Ibid.*, 14 Oct. 1765; John Adams, *Diary*, 1:260–261; William Baker, "William Baker's Account of the Repeal of the Stamp Act," ed. D. H. Watson, *WMQ* 3.26:259–265 (1969).

limited by this principle: "Whatever one acquired, *without Injury to others,* was his own Property; which none had a right to take from him" (emphasis added). The "Regard to the Rights of others" demanded the establishment of "prudent Rules for the Determination of Property." The state of nature was changed into the corporate society, with rights and duties and protection for all members:

> When Strength or Cunning were employed to violate or encroach upon the Rights of others, it became necessary for *Many* to unite in *Defence* of their Properties against these invaders. Hence Government arose. By common Consent some were chosen to act for the Service of the Rest, and by each Individual invested with his power, to render that Service effectual. *The sole End of Government was the publick Good.*

As Jefferson did a decade later in the Declaration of Independence, the anonymous author of this article proceeded to examine the consequences of misuse of power, a frequent occurrence: "those who are invested with Power and Authority to be employed for the publick Good, make use of it to injure and oppress their Brethren, in direct Opposition to the Design of their Appointment." If the rulers "cannot be removed, nor Redress be obtained by the ordinary Methods of proceeding," if discontent is general and a continuance under the present government would mean imposition of greater "Evils" than the dissolution of government, "then there always resides a power in the sacred Body of the People, sufficient to suspend and dissolve the powers they have given, or oblige those, who hold them to perform their Duty." As to popular action, "It is needless to give Cautions against this Recurrance to the first Principles of Government."

The Stamp Act, the argument continued, would destroy liberty unless repealed. Since direct action had been necessary, and would continue to be so until a repeal was achieved, some advice on the conduct of "popular Meetings" seemed appropriate: Nobody should receive any injuries unless there was sufficient evidence. Second, participants were advised

> to consider that while they are thus collected, they act as supreme uncontroulable Power, from which there is no Appeal, where Trial, Sentence and Execution succeed each other almost instantaneously—and therefore they are in Honour bound to take Care that they do no injustice, nor suffer it to be done by others, lest they disgrace their Power, and the Cause which occasioned its Collection.

Third, no other secondary complaints should be mingled with the great cause, especially since "many Men of bad Principles will take the Opportunity of publick Commotions to perpetrate their base or villanous Designs, to indulge Revenge, or prey upon private Property." While thus far the argument had been based on the equality of all, the author, in his last sentences, showed his class position when he called for the "Leaders and Directors of the rest" to take greatest care "to keep an undisciplined irregular Multitude from running into mischievous Extravagencies: And if any Enormities are committed, it damps the Spirits of all concerned and perhaps may not leave them Courage enough for the necessary Defense of their Liberties."[93]

Whig opinion about crowd action, then, was essentially placed between the two poles of no crowd action because it violated deference[94] and the acceptance of popular direct action as the means for redress of grievances when the public good could by no other means be protected against encroachments. John Adams was to change his opinion somewhat in later years, as did the advocates of popular action. Temporarily both converged toward the middle between the two opposites. None of the Whig leaders ever considered the question of public good from the viewpoint of those strata of society from which the rioters· were recruited. Nor did anyone consider the diversification and stratification of society, together with the concentration of economic power and the resultant thrust for liberalist–individualist notions of property usage. Accordingly, Whig ideology, as developed up to the early eighties, remained a political ideology. Measures to accommodate differences of interest between economic groups remained makeshift. It is with this frame of reference that we return to the actual measures taken in Boston to ensure continued opposition to British policies without concomitant social action within colonial society.

Established officialdom, which opposed the Stamp Act, faced the serious dilemma that in its moves to reassert its power and position it had to act against the rioters, its allies, albeit temporary ones. Until the repeal they were still needed. On the other hand, 5 November, Pope's Day, was also not far off, and the rival sections in Boston had taken the union seriously and had enormous potential for independent action. To achieve control, the Loyal Nine, backed by money from John Hancock and other merchants, attempted to bribe the rioters and especially their leaders. Mackintosh and Swift were furnished with stately uniforms and speaking trumpets to hand down orders. The uniforms were blue with red and included a gold-laced hat, a "gilt gorget" over the breast, and a "rattan cane," sign of a gentleman. Other men, distinguished by their laced hats, acted as underofficers. Important and wealthy men publicly paraded with Mackintosh through town in hopes of wooing him to their side. Finally, they gave a dinner for the most influential leaders of both sections. Mackintosh, who had been locally known as "Captain," was now addressed as "General" by his superiors. These, according to Bernard, later "expressed a kind of shame" for mixing with the lower classes.[95]

Contrary to military and judicial suppression, the bribes proved effective, at least temporarily. No violence occurred on 5 November. Both parties began a common rally at the townhouse, complete with the usual stages—effigies and slogans, parading through the town, North and South exchanging grounds, and finally reuniting to

---

[93]*BG,* 2 Dec. 1765.

[94]This position was more conservative than that of Hutchinson, who admitted that some crowd action is constitutional. Hutchinson to Grant, 27 July 1768, Letterbooks, MA 26:317.

[95]Bernard to Pownall, 1 No|v|. 1765, Sparks MSS., 4.5:16–21, HHL, to Pownall, 5 Nov. 1765, *ibid.,* pp. 21–25, to Pownall, 26 Nov. 1765, *ibid.,* 10.1:97, to Board of Trade, 30 Nov. 1765, *ibid.,* 10.2:2; Boyle, "Journal," 5 Nov. 1765, p. 171; Freeman, Notebook, 1 Nov. 1765, MHS; *BNL,* 31 Oct., 7 Nov. 1765; *BEP,* 11 Nov. 1765; William H. Sumner, in "Reminiscences by General William H. Sumner," *NEHGR* 8:191 (1854), stated that Hancock was master of ceremonies and spent more than $1000 on it, and that Samuel Adams gave an "eloquent speech."

burn the trappings of their pageantry together. The Pope's Day collection this time netted a sum exceeding "all expectations; many contributed from affection, much more from fear," reported the governor, whose own household had been tapped for this purpose. Probably under prodding from the Loyal Nine and their new friends, the wealthy merchants, the two captains, Mackintosh and Swift, agreed to spend this money for a public entertainment. It was held on 11 November, under the name of Union Feast, at the Royal Exchange Tavern. Admission was limited to 200 persons, and to imbue due notions of rank and deference, the printed tickets provided for five different classes. "The Conductors having discriminated the Company" in this manner, they provided separate rooms for each rank, and "while those of the first class were enjoying themselves in Conversation, those of the Class who had formerly been at Varience [the Northend and Southend people] were joining together with heart and Hand in flowing Bowls and bumping Glasses." Thus, behavior conformed to class too, at least according to the reporter.[96] Whether the mechanics could be bought off for long and packaged into the custom of the better sort remained to be seen.

[96]Bernard to Pownall, 1 Nov., 5 Nov., 26 Nov. 1765, Sparks MSS., 4.5:16–21, 4.5:21–25, 10.1:97, HHL; *BEP*, 11 Nov. 1765; *BNL*, 7 Nov. 1765; Freeman, Notebook, 5 Nov. 1765, MHS.

Massachusetts Defies the Stamp Act 3

While the Stamp Act was to take effect on 1 November, Oliver's resignation notwithstanding, the example of the Boston crowds was catching on. To the south of Boston, Hingham people threatened their minister for preaching submission and accused him of hiding stamps. To the north, crowds assembled in Marblehead, Salem, Newburyport, and Portland. Gloucester's inhabitants took advantage of the situation to act on another economic grievance. They refused to pay taxes not only to the British but to the provincial authorities as well.[1] In Newburyport, 500 people rioted on 25 September, 2000 on the next day. Here too, fears about direct action to redress social and economic grievances arose among the wealthy, who bargained with the crowd to obtain a promise that property would not be endangered. Newburyport's representative, who had used his influence to direct the crowd, soon after was instructed by a town meeting to use it now to suppress riots.[2] Massachusetts newspapers informed their readers that dozens of towns throughout the colonies were joining the opposition. The *Boston Newsletter,* in a single issue enlarged from four to six pages, reported direct action from nine towns in six colonies. Men from all ranks were united in the opposition, complained James Murray, a Massachusetts justice of the peace. General Gage concurred for New York: The riotous "Sailors" had found help from "the people from the Country" and from "many people of substance." New England sailors instigated antistamp riots as far away as the West Indies.[3]

[1]*BNL,* 6 Feb., 20 March 1766. Hingham: John Adams, *Diary and Autobiography of John Adams,* ed. L. H. Butterfield, 4 vols. (Cambridge, Mass., 1961–1966) 1:279. Falmouth (Portland): Thomas Smith and Samuel Deane, *Journals of the Rev. Thomas Smith, and the Rev. Samuel Deane, Pastors of the First Church in Portland,* ed. William Willis (Portland, Me., 1849), pp. 206–207. Salem: Alexander Fraser, ed., *United Empire Loyalists: Enquiry into the Losses and Services in Consequence of Their Loyalty—Evidence in the Canadian Claims,* Second Report of the Bureau of Archives for the Province of Ontario, 1904 (Toronto, 1905), Pt. 1, p. 491; James B. Connolly, *The Port of Gloucester* (New York, 1940), p. 45; Samuel Roads, *The History and Traditions of Marblehead* (Boston, 1880), p. 75.
[2]Nathan Bowen, "Extracts from the Interleaved Almanacs of Nathan Bowen, Marblehead, 1742–1799," ed. W. H. Bowden, *EIHC* 91:266 (1955); John Adams, *Diary,* 1:295; Vale E. Smith, *History of Newburyport from the Earliest Settlement of the Country to the Present Time* (Newburyport, Mass., 1854), pp. 69–70; Joshua Coffin, *A Sketch of the History of Newbury, Newburyport, and West Newbury, from 1635 to 1845* (Boston, 1845), pp. 230–231; John J. Currier, *History of Newburyport, Mass., 1764–1905,* 2 vols. (Newburyport, Mass., 1906–1909), 1:47–48.
[3]*BNL,* 5 Sept. 1765; James Murray to John Murray, 13 Nov. 1765, *Letters of James Murray, Loyalist,* ed. Nina M. Tiffany and Susan I. Leslay (Boston, 1901), pp. 154–155; Gage to Conway, 4 Nov. 1765, *The Correspondence of General Thomas Gage,* ed. Clarence E. Carter, 2 vols. (New Haven, Conn., 1931, 1933), 1:70–71; James T. Adams,

While Massachusetts people thus learned that "Affairs seem to be ripening to an universal mob," the fame of the Boston crowd was still spreading.[4] Far out at sea, a vessel from London was hailed by a Boston ship. Its captain, Thomas Hulme, was incorrectly told that crowds had taken Boston's Castle William and were waiting for the stamps. Captain Hulme was less than pleased; he had the stamps on board. One of his passengers began musing about whether he would be mistaken for a stamp distributor. The captain cautiously put into Marblehead to reconnoiter, mooring his vessel so that it could leave at a moment's notice and posting a double watch on board (20 September). On shore, everything was quiet, except for a rumor: A contingent of Boston rioters was said to be on the march to Marblehead, a distance of approximately 20 miles. Hulme decided to move into the lion's den and, off Boston, was met by a messenger from the ship's owner, announcing that the ship was in danger of being burned by a crowd. A guard of the British navy was put on board, and later the cargo was stored in the castle without further opposition (2 October).[5]

The decision to store the stamps had been preceded by a power struggle over their protection from violent destruction. The effort to keep the crowd in its (Whig-assigned) place meant that extraordinary care was taken to limit any direct action to anti-British aims. The effort to repudiate those officials who favored, if not the Stamp Act, at least its temporary execution, meant that the initiative could not be left to crown officials. The attempt to control the crowd thus brought about a struggle for control over degree and form of repression and opposition among the provincial leadership. Those of the Whig leaders who suggested that direct action might occur again had the advantage of not having to rely on it. The image of the formidable power and perseverance of Boston crowds had become so persuasive that frequently it was sufficient to threaten crowd action or to spread a rumor that the potential rioters were getting restless to influence decision-making processes in political institutions and to hurry reluctant officials into compliance. Since the elite could control rumors more easily than lower-class rioters, it increasingly relied on them. The question of what was to be done with the stamps provoked the following series of bids for control over the situation. First, the provincial council voted to store the stamps in Castle William (21 August). Second by 29 August, crowd action was threatened against the commanding officer of the castle, and there were suggestions to take the whole castle. The council, still certain of its power, in response voted to increase the garrison by 60 men. The fourth move, still on the institutional

---

Revolutionary New England, 1691–1776 (Boston, 1923), p. 336. For a list of resignations by stamp distributors, see Lawrence H. Gipson, *The Coming of the Revolution, 1763–1775* (New York, 1954), pp. 92–93.

[4] Smith and Deane, *Journals,* p. 206.

[5] *BG,* 26 Aug., 23 Sept., Supp., 30 Sept., 7 Oct. 1765. Some more stamps, brought a fortnight later by Captain Hunter, were also stored in the castle. *BG,* 21 Oct. 1765, Supp. *Journals of the House of Representatives,* 1765–1766, pp. 124–126; Council Records, 16:49, 57–60, 137–139, MSA. For the return of the stamps to Great Britain, see John Boyle, "Boyle's Journal of Occurrences in Boston, 1759–1778," 27 July 1766, *NEHGR* 84:250 (1930). Deposition of William Angar, clerk (passenger on the stamp ship), 1 Oct. 1766, SCF 87255, in *Fitch v. Peat.* Mr. Fitch, the ship's owner, and Captain Hulme, under pressure from the townsmen, demanded reimbursement by the crown for the delay caused by anchoring under guard outside Boston until the stamps were stored. They demanded personal security from the governor and had a navy officer arrested in a suit for damages.

level, a motion in council to rescind the order, was voted down 16 to 4. Fifth, a crowd in Haverhill, Essex County, not controlled by the edgy Boston leadership, stopped Colonel Saltonstall's attempt to enlist the men. The colonel found it prudent to declare to the 300–400 men assembled around his house that he abhorred the Stamp Act and that he would not execute his order to enlist men. Five days later, after a vehement editorial in the *Boston Gazette,* the council retreated too: As the stamped paper was not due to arrive for some time and, as it discreetly said, "there being an alteration in other circumstances of affairs," it withdrew its order and thereby its claim to power (11 September). The governor had declared six days earlier that he was powerless; the House of Representatives rejected any responsibility.[6]

In sum, rumors of crowd action determined the course of the ship with the stamps, the course of several council votes, and, together with an actual riot in Haverhill, the conduct of a high militia officer as well as the retreat of the council. Boston town magistrates, on the other hand, still had influence, as the following incident, happening on the day before the council's retreat, proved. George Messervey, stamp distributor for New Hampshire, arrived in Boston on 10 September on a ship from Great Britain. He too had learned what was waiting for him. Two hundred leagues off the American coast, the story about Boston crowds had reached him. Accordingly, he was ready to resign when the crowd on the wharf demanded his pledge not to act. Rumors of a possible repeal occasioned extensive celebrations in the evening, including the dedication of Liberty Tree to the glorious memory of the action of 14 August. Whig leaders prepared on two levels. The Loyal Nine saw to it that the tree was illuminated; the magistrates stationed a military guard around the corner.[7]

While the "long-dreaded First of November" was drawing nearer, Boston inhabitants in a series of town meetings sent letters to sympathetic persons of influence in Britain criticizing the "arbitrary unconstitutional Innovations." Innovations in this tradition-bound society were still regarded with suspicion. After 1776 this was to change. In 1765 the town meeting only extolled the town's efforts in defense of the empire and stressed the rights of the British subjects. Protected by these rights, they felt that it was "extraordinary" on the part of Parliament not even to admit their "Decent Remonstrance," sent while the act was still pending. Then they ordered their representatives in the Massachusetts legislature "by no Means to Join in any publick Measures for countenancing and assisting in the Execution" of the act.[8]

---

[6]*BG*, 26 Aug., 9 Sept. 1765; Council Records, 16:36, 39–40, 42–43, 45–46, MSA; Bernard to Lords Commissioners, 22 Aug. 1765, House of Lords MSS., 209:348–356. Six weeks later, still without any clear notion about the situation in the colony, the commissioners in London were "pleased to direct your Excy [Gov. Bernard] to see that the stamps be duly distributed." Cowper to Bernard, 8 Oct. 1765, *ibid.,* p. 116.

[7]Messervey to Lords Commissioners, 7 Sept. 1765, *ibid.,* pp. 206–208; *BNL*, 12 Sept. 1765; *BEP,* 16 Sept. 1765; *BG,* 16 Sept. 1765; James Freeman, Notebook, 16 Sept. 1765, MHS. On 7 October the *Gazette* printed a skull and crossbones in the lower right corner of its first page and explained, "Hereabouts will be the Place to affix the Stamps." No disorders occurred during the celebrations of the accession anniversary of George III. *BG*, 28 Oct. 1765.

[8]*BTR* 16:152–153, 156–157, 177–179; Lord Adam Gordon, "Journal of Lord Adam Gordon," in *Travels in the American Colonies,* ed. Newton D. Mereness (New York, 1916), pp. 451–452; Gordon to Martin, 10 Sept. 1765, *MHSP* 2.13:396 (1900). For the town's argument, see Edmund S. Morgan and Helen M. Morgan, *The Stamp Act*

Some Boston merchants began to discuss nonimportation measures, and a few took such steps on their own initiative. The majority, however, followed only after news of such agreements was received from New York (October 1765) and Philadelphia (November 1765).[9]

On 1 November American liberty was symbolically carried to the grave. "About break of day, the melancholy blast of the Cong Shell with a funeral Tolling of Bells, ushered in the important Epoch." Solemn, with flags at half-mast and shops closed, a "vast Concourse of People repaired in the Forenoon to the Royal Elm [Liberty Tree], some with Weeds in their hats, others with downcast Eyes, uttering . . . Sorrow and Wonder," "Lamentation[s] and Mourning." The two effigies on the tree bore the following inscriptions: "Vox Populi est Vox Dei," "Good Order and Steady," and "Honi soit qui mal y pense" (He is a fool who thinks this is bad). The last slogan was the supreme irony because it was also the official imprint of the stamps. In the afternoon "innumerable people from the Country as well as the Town" (Governor Bernard) carried the effigies to the center of the town, where the assembly was sitting. The funeral procession then toured the Northend and the principal streets of the town. Back at the Neck, the "People of all Ranks" hung the effigies of George Grenville and John Huske on the gallows. Finally, "the justly enraged Multitude" cut the effigies down and tore them to pieces. The Stamp Act was in force but could not be executed.[10]

Before the town turned its attention to such questions as whether and how to proceed in business without stamps, some inhabitants and high officials felt it necessary to take precautionary measures against the possibilities of renewed rioting on 5 November, Pope's Day. The council voted to reinstitute a military watch till 6 November, "for if the Mob was once allowed to assemble, it might soon grow incontrollable." The governor called Boston's selectmen and admonished them to prevent any violence. Upon a petition of concerned townsmen, a town meeting was called for the express and only purpose of preventing "Disorders." The result for anyone but the town officials was a fiasco. The governor's intervention was not even made public, and the petitioners were induced to withdraw their demand for a peace-keeping force. Instead, it was said that the town's militiamen "were not

---

Crisis: Prologue to Revolution (Chapel Hill, N.C., 1953), pp. 211–219; Edmund S. Morgan, "Thomas Hutchinson and the Stamp Act," *NEQ* 21:459–492 (1948).

[9]*BEP*, 23 Sept., 9 Dec. 1765; *BPB*, 9 Dec., 16 Dec., 23 Dec. 1765; *BG*, 25 Nov. 1765; Boyle, "Journal," 3 Dec. 1765, p. 171. Thomas Hutchinson, *The History of the Colony and Province of Massachusetts Bay,* ed. Lawrence Shaw Mayo, 3 vols. (Cambridge, Mass., 1936), 3:99–100; Charles M. Andrews, "The Boston Merchants and the Non-Importation Movement," *CSMP* 19:198–201 (1916–1917); Arthur M. Schlesinger, Sr., *The Colonial Merchants and the American Revolution, 1763–1776* (New York, 1918), pp. 80–82; Edmund S. Morgan, ed., *Prologue to Revolution: Sources and Documents on the Stamp Act Crisis, 1764–1766* (Chapel Hill, N.C., 1959), pp. 106, 130–131. The agreement excepted certain commodities necessary for fishing or prerequisites for manufactures. J. & J. Amory to ———, 20 Dec. 1765, in William B. Weeden, *Economic and Social History of New England, 1620–1789,* 2 vols. (Boston, 1890; reprint ed., 1965), 2:719.

[10]*BPB*, 4 Nov. 1765, "Extraordinary," *BEP*, 4 Nov. 1765; *BNL*, 7 Nov. 1765; Boyle, "Journal," 1 Nov. 1765, pp. 170–171; Freeman, Notebook, 1 Nov. 1765, MHS. For reprints of the stamps with the motto, see Justin Winsor, ed., *The Memorial History of Boston, Including Suffolk County, Massachusetts, 1630–1880,* 4 vols. (Boston, 1880–1881), 3:12, and *CSMP* 26:50. Bernard to Pownall, 1 Nov. 1765, Sparks MSS., 4.5:18–21, HHL.

obliged to obey'' the commander in chief's orders—that is, the governor. Colonel Joseph Jackson of the militia announced that the men refused to obey orders, ''that the Men which had mustered, declared they would go off, and that he should soon have none left but his Officers.'' ''We found ourselves obliged to revoke the orders,'' noted the governor, who was then informed by some councillors that ''upon diligent inquiry'' they found no reason to expect disorders. Council and governor had not only lost the authority to keep order and enforce laws but others had already taken over, at least de facto.[11]

Courts and port had been closed since 1 November. No stamps were to be had. No official dared execute the act, and the *Gazette* asked, ''who would desire to increase his property, at the expense of liberty?''[12] The question was not as rhetorical as it sounded. Among the better sort there was a definite weakening of opposition for political and economic reasons. According to sources as different as the governor's letters and the *Boston Gazette,* the expected economic stagnation might exacerbate social tensions to a degree that social upheaval could result. Large-scale unemployment was certain, and a famine was feared because the closing of the ports put a stop to the grain imports from Maryland and Pennsylvania. ''Necessity will soon oblige and Justify an insurrection of the Poor against the rich; those that want the necessaries of Life against those that have them.'' Bernard continued that ''persons of property and Consideration'' began ''to cool in their Zeal.'' The question asked by the *Gazette* posed a false alternative. The real question was at whose expense and loss of property, with whose suffering, was liberty to be maintained. Bernard even considered, if only theoretically, an equal distribution of provisions among the people ''without regard to Property.'' Famine and unemployment might ''be the Occasion of great uneasiness and Tumult,'' admitted the *Gazette,* adding that this was causing a great deal of concern. But, hinted the writer darkly, ''an Expedient will be attempted to keep this valuable Set of People [sailors] honestly employed.''[13]

To the breakdown of trade the closing of the courts would add the breakdown of government; ''terrible will be the Anarchy and Confusion.'' Andrew Oliver reported that ''some Considerate Men in the opposition'' had second thoughts. James Otis began to assert the rights of Parliament.[14] However, decision making no longer lay fully in the hands of the better sort. The ''lower sort of People'' were so alarmed that use of stamps was out of the question, whatever the thoughts of the leadership; ''The people would rise upon the Government.'' Oliver's opinion of August 1765 was corroborated by John Adams in December. ''The People, even to the lowest

[11]*BTR* 16:158, 20:183 ; Council Records, 16:61–63, 66, 68, MSA; Bernard to Pownall, 1 Nov. 1765, Sparks MSS., 4.5:18–21, HHL.

[12]*BG,* 26 Aug. 1765.

[13]Bernard to Halifax, 7 Sept. 1765, Sparks MSS., 4.4:158–161, HHL; *BG,* 23 Sept. 1765, Supp. For a thorough investigation of the problem of unemployment with heavy emphasis on New York, see Jesse Lemisch, ''Jack Tar in the Streets,'' *WMQ* 3.25:371–407 (1968). Oliver M. Dickerson, *The Navigation Acts and the American Revolution* (Philadelphia, 1951), p. 191.

[14]Bernard to Halifax, 7 Sept. 1765, to Pownall, 1 Nov. 1765, Sparks MSS., 4.4:160, 4.5:17, HHL; Oliver to Whately, 20 Aug. 1765, House of Lords MSS., 209:104–106. For Otis's stand, see Chapter 2, note 15.

Ranks have become more attentive to their Liberties, more inquisitive about them, and more determined to defend them, than they were ever before known or had occasion to be.'' Otis had realized this a few months earlier when he was up for reelection as representative for Boston. Sensing that the voters were uneasy, he asked for an occasion to explain his position, a move unheard of in Boston, where elections were arranged so smoothly that no more than one or two election pamphlets had been published in 20 years. He was reelected with only 61 percent of the vote; the average vote cast for him in the annual elections was 94 percent. The better sort adjusted to the situation by developing the theoretical justification for open breach of the law. Referring to Coke, they argued that an act of Parliament inconsistent with the Magna Charta was ipso facto void.[15] Defiance meant redirection of the potential for internal violence into united action against British authority and authorities.[16]

The incapability of the crown officials in the colonies to take any steps to enforce the act bore a strong similarity to parts of what has been described as a weakness syndrome in any *ancien regime* (Tocqueville, Brinton). Those representatives of British authority in Boston who were the focal persons for any attempt to open the port without stamps were Comptroller Benjamin Hallowell, crowd target in August, and Collector William Sheaffe. Conscious of their difficult situation, they applied for advice to the top customs official. Surveyor General John Temple, not willing to take the responsibility, referred them to other crown officials. Upon application to the governor and the designated stamp distributor, they were given the runaround again. While on other questions the officials moved with a ponderous slowness, they now became rather agile in passing the buck. The whole process of applying to Oliver, waiting for his refusal, explaining the situation to the governor, and waiting for his written answer was finished in a single day with enough time left to submit the whole correspondence to Attorney General Trowbridge and Advocate General Auchmuty. But the two hapless customs officials were disappointed again. The advocate general did not answer at all, and the attorney general referred them back to Surveyor General Temple, where the circle had started.[17]

For a while the merchants watched, perhaps amused at the helplessness of the officials. Less amusing to them must have been the refusal of the Massachusetts General Court to act.[18] The decision of the Rhode Island assembly, ordering all governmental officials to continue business as if the act did not exist, remained the only open defiance of Parliament on the level of colonial legislatures. Anticipating this situation, merchants had taken out clearances before 1 November for ships that were to sail weeks later.[19] By December, however, they began to debate further

[15]Oliver to Whately, 20 Aug. 1765, House of Lords MSS., 209:104–106; John Adams, *Diary,* 1:263; Hutchinson to ————, 12 Sept. 1765, Letterbooks, MA 26:153–154.

[16]For a different view, see William A. Benton, *Whig–Loyalism: An Aspect of Political Ideology in the American Revolutionary Era* (Rutherford, N.J., 1969). Benton neglects the socioeconomic reasons for unity in favor of an exclusively political explanation. The doctrine of legislative independence in the colonies is seen as cause for unity.

[17]Morgan and Morgan, *Stamp Act Crisis,* pp. 134–139.

[18]*Journals of the House of Representatives,* 1765–1766, pp. 143, 155; Bernard to Pownall, 20 Oct., 1 Nov. 1765, Sparks MSS., 4.5:13–14, 16–21, HHL; text in House of Lords MSS., 209:506–508.

[19]Hutchinson, *History,* 3:100; cf. Morgan and Morgan, *Stamp Act Crisis,* p. 160, for similar procedures in Philadelphia.

action. Neither petitions to the official authorities, king and Parliament, nor renewed reliance on unofficial authorities, the crowd, appealed to them. As at the time of the arrival of the stamps, rumors of crowd action were considered sufficient. John Rowe, member of the merchants' committee, informed his friend customs official William Sheaffe that a crowd was preparing to seize the customs house. One detail of the rumor casts a revealing light on how Whig merchants thought about crowd motivation. The customs house had been selected, it was said, because £6000 sterling were stored there—a good target for plunder. Sheaffe informed the surveyor general, who informed the governor, who informed the councillors. Whether intentionally or because of lack of experience in inventing rumors, the riot was scheduled for the evening of 11 December, the council meeting to take countermeasures for the morning of 12 December. Since nobody had cared to inform the prospective rioters, no crowd showed up. The councillors then, in acrimonious language, repudiated the overapprehensiveness of the customs officials and suggested storing the money in the castle. The port was still closed.[20]

Crowd action was necessary again to bring about a change in affairs. Oliver had received his official commission as stamp distributor at the end of November. Two weeks later the printers of the *Gazette* sent him an anonymous letter that, they said, had been left at their office. In it Oliver was requested to state his position. On 16 December the letter, together with Oliver's answer, was published in the *Gazette*. Almost immediately he was informed by the Sons of Liberty, probably the Loyal Nine, that his statement was insufficient and that he was to appear under Liberty Tree the next day at noon for a public resignation. The ritual of public confession may have provided the stimulus for this type of crowd action. Oliver was promised polite and gentlemanly treatment but was threatened in case he should refuse to appear. Oliver tried to negotiate, sending "one of his neighbors, a tradesman of the first character," for an appearance in the townhouse only. In town-meeting manner his communication was transmitted to the people waiting at Liberty Tree but was deemed insufficient. Mackintosh then acted as escort, and by 12 o'clock Oliver was present. In front of 2000 people, waiting in cold and rain, he resigned and affirmed his resignation by oath to a justice of the peace. Town officials, together with "many other persons of condition," watched. The crowd dispersed immediately after the end of the ceremony. Mackintosh was credited with arranging the proceeding, but the Loyal Nine had also been active. As a consequence of the action, the officials opened the customs house and port without stamps.[21]

[20]Council Records, 16:74–75, MSA; House of Lords MSS., 283:73–74. The evidence for John Rowe's activity in this affair is circumstantial. He is named in the council records and by Hutchinson (to Pownall, 8 March 1766, Letterbooks, MA 26:207–214). Cf. Morgan and Morgan, *Stamp Act Crisis,* p. 137.

[21]*BG,* 16 Dec., 23 Dec. 1765; Oliver to John Brettel, 13 Dec. 1765, postscript 19 Dec., House of Lords MSS., 221:127–136; Henry Bass to Samuel P. Savage, 19 Dec. 1765, *CSMP* 26:355–356; Bernard to Board of Trade, 10 Jan. 1766, Sparks MSS., 4.4:184–189, HHL. According to Bernard, the customs house opened when "it was known that the two Mob Captains had fixed upon a Day for rising." Hutchinson, *History,* 3:100–102; John Adams, *Diary,* 1:265. Later Samuel Waterhouse, to whom Oliver's first note of resignation was sent on 15 August, was accused of intending to become stamp master upon Oliver's recommendation (*BG,* 3 Feb. 1766). Hallowell to Commissioners of Customs, 17 Dec. 1765, House of Lords MSS., 221:159. While the Sons of Liberty celebrated their success, Hallowell explained the hazards of his onerous office and humbly added, "I beg leave to ask your Honors Interest in some

Next the inhabitants addressed themselves with unfailing energy to the opening of the civil courts. (Criminal prosecution was not affected by the act.) In fact, they did so with amazing speed. On the same day on which Oliver resigned and the customs house was opened, a petition for a town meeting on the courts was drawn up, signed by 17 men, and presented to the selectmen. These met at once and called the meeting for the next morning, and overnight Edes and Gill printed the notifications. In the town meeting a memorial demanding the opening of the courts was passed and a committee of the most important town leaders sent to present it to the governor immediately. Neither governor nor councillors were ready to act with equal speed. Upon leaving the council chamber with no decision made, they found that somebody had left some Boston poetry for them:

> Open your Court & let Justice prevail
> Open your Offices & let not trade fail
> For if these Men in power will not act,
> We'll get some that will is actual fact.[22]

On the next day the "Men in power" heard three lawyers argue the demands of the town. James Otis declared dramatically that a "Stop to all Justice . . . is *ipso Facto* a Dissolution of Society," that parliamentary authority has limits, and that the king "unkings himself" when his law courts are closed. Jeremiah Gridley assisted: "Government is subverted if the Law is not open. . . . The People must return to a State of Nature." He expounded the rights of property and repeated the fears that hunger would cause tumults. The third lawyer was John Adams, later somewhat of an expert on constitutional questions. Instead of outlining his argument in council, I quote from his private diary. Something must be done about the situation, he wrote, for the "Debtors grow insolent."[23]

While the inhabitants were awaiting the results of their memorial, they learned that the demand for opening the courts was not unanimous. While some felt grieved by the suspension of legal procedures, others disliked exactly these procedures and the fees involved. Both Sheriff Greenleaf and his deputy, Benjamin Cudworth, had received threatening letters. Greenleaf was told to dismiss Cudworth, who was guilty of "many bad actions . . . [and] of taking two much fees and adviseing other to Sue." Court suits, of course, meant further fees. Cudworth was told to resign and to do it quickly, or "you must Expect a Visit which may be more fatal then any that has been in this town Lately . . . or Leave the town amediately—for the true Sons of Liberty are inraged against you." The author or authors explained that Cudworth's

---

method to secure Officers in the Execution of their Office." Letters and depositions about the inactivity of the officials are in *ibid.*, 238:64–139.

[22]*BEP*, 23 Dec. 1765; John Adams, *Diary*, 1:264; petitions in Misc. Unbound Papers, 1765, BCH; the signatures give no clue to any specific group from which the move might have originated; *BTR* 16:158–159, 20:189–190; Bernard to Conway, 18 Dec. 1765, postscript 19 Dec., Sparks MSS., 4.4:183–184, HHL.

[23]Samuel M. Quincy, ed., *Reports of Cases Argued and Adjudged in the Superior Court of Judicature of . . . Massachusetts Bay, 1761–1772, by Josiah Quincy, Junior* (Boston, 1865), pp. 200–214; John Adams, *Diary*, 18–20 Dec. 1765, 1:265–267.

actions had "brought great Defficulty on many poor people which theire is a great Number in town are Ready to Declare." This discontent, voiced from the bottom of the society against local authorities, could not prevail in the town meeting. Those who met the property requirements to participate, having just applauded the opening of the courts in defiance of the Stamp Act, now "Voted, unanimously that said Letters were highly abusive and inflamitery, and tending to the distruction of all good Order and Government" and that their authors should be prosecuted. Never had a similar blast been directed at placemen or other crown officials. The letters were filed as "Seditious Letters" in the town papers. The qualified voters were not willing to discuss complaints by the "poor people." Threats against the lives and property of officials were acceptable only when the official Sons of Liberty issued them.[24]

While the town meeting took effective action to quell discontent from below, it adjourned from day to day watching the incapability of the top provincial leadership to deal with the discontent about the closed courts. Councillors and governor had listened to the doctrines of constitutional and natural rights, from which was to grow the political ideology of the struggle with Great Britain. But the political elite showed little interest in these doctrines.

On 26 December Thomas Hutchinson, this time in his capacity as probate judge, gave in. Reportedly, he had been told "to do business without stamps, to quit the country, to resign . . . or—." He asked the governor to name his brother, Foster Hutchinson, as deputy for one year. So the fees from the lucrative office were not lost to the family. This Bernard did, on unstamped paper. The somewhat shaky argument for not using stamps was that "After further examining the act he [Bernard] was satisfied he could make an appointment not exceeding 12 months without a stamp."[25]

After this victory, court after court opened. First, hints about riots induced the judges of the Inferior Court of Common Pleas and the sheriff to resume the execution of their offices. Next, it was the turn of the courts in the country and the Superior Court of Judicature. Again the threat of direct action was used. The *Newsletter* published a report of the crowd action against the chief justice for North Carolina. In its next issue it mentioned that a court in Frederick County, New York, had decided to proceed without stamps and jailed the clerk "for contempt" when he refused to comply. A crowd that happened to be around then buried the Stamp Act in a coffin bearing the inscription "aged 22 days." In Massachusetts, pressure from the town meeting and newspapers caused the Superior Court judges to meet. They had no opinion—the next session of the court was still five weeks off. At that time Chief Justice Hutchinson happened to be absent from Boston; Peter Oliver was ready to act for fear of violence; Judge Lynde confined his opinion to "we are here." The farce became worse when none of the lawyers, including Otis, dared to

[24]Both letters are in Misc. Unbound Papers, 1765, BCH; *BTR* 16:161.

[25]*BTR* 16:160–161; Council Records, 16:76–78, 81, MSA; John Adams, *Diary*, 1:268–270; *BNL*, 26 Dec. 1765, 2 Jan. 1766; Hutchinson to Bollan, 20–21 Dec. 1765, Letterbooks, MA 25:22, cf. *ibid.*, 26:193, and Hutchinson to ———, 15 Jan. 1766, Cushing Papers, MHS; Bernard to Lords Commissioners, 22 Aug. 1765, House of Lords MSS., 209:348–356; Hutchinson, *History*, 3:102–103.

plead for an opening of the court. It seems that the judges and lawyers agreed with Andrew Oliver's statement that the "alarm" of the people had risen to such a degree that it could not be defied. To avoid the resentment of the people, Whig lawyers and crown justices compromised. Two actions originating before the Stamp Act were tried, and then the court quickly adjourned for six weeks, hoping that by then the current rumors of repeal would have proved true. This was not to be the case, and on 29 April the whole farce was repeated. As yet, Whig leaders were often as undecided what to do as were the crown officials.[26]

While most of the business relating to the opening of the courts was transacted in the town meeting and by threats of crowd action only, the crowd was still active and still enjoyed its reputation of power. In March a rescue riot freed a female criminal from jail. The surprised Sons of Liberty (that is, the Loyal Nine) expressed their "detestation" ·of the affair and offered a reward for the discovery of the rioters— which, however, was not collected. At about the same time the councillors debated whether to jail Edes and Gill for printing a piece by "Freeborn Armstrong" with animadversions on the council and a virulent attack on Lieutenant Governor and Chief Justice Hutchinson. But Edes and Gill could not be committed to jail, so some councillors argued, because they would be rescued by a crowd. All the council could do was to publish a defense.[27]

Within the four months from 14 August to 17 December, five large-scale riots or mass actions and several minor incidents had terrified officials and opened the port of Boston. Town-meeting votes combined with threats of further direct action forced the judicial establishment to act without stamps. Thus, all stipulations of the Stamp Act were effectively nullified. While opposition to the act was widely diffused through all ranks of society, the action was made possible by the Pope's Day crowd, the artisans and journeymen. The presence of better-situated persons was limited to a small group on 14 August and to some town officials on 17 December. Rioters from other provinces, who did not share the internal restraints of the crowd, were present only late in the evening of 26 August. The homogeneity of the crowd as far as class goes also explains the ambivalent attitude of the Whig leadership toward their allies ever since they realized that the lower sort was capable of self-determination and had their own interests. The crowd was highly politicized. This is attested not only by the slogans and rituals but also by the perseverance of opposition among the "people" when men of substance began to waiver. That the crowd had an ideology of its own is suggested by its reaction to Mayhew's sermon, the omnipresence of the image of the devil as instigator of evil deeds, the selection of symbols of wealth for destruction, and the adaptation of rituals for the purpose of protest. Among the last were the execution of Oliver's effigy, the solemnity of the

[26]*BNL,* 26 Dec. 1765, 2 Jan. 1766; Quincy, ed., *Reports,* p. 215; town meeting, 16 Jan. 1766, *BTR* 16:161–162; *Journals of the House of Representatives,* 1765–1766, pp. 186ff., 214–215; Bernard to Board of Trade, 18 Jan., 10 March 1766, postscript of 12 March, quoted in Quincy, ed., *Reports,* pp. 211–212, 216–217; John Adams, *Diary,* 1:305, 310–311; Hutchinson, *History,* 3:104–106.

[27]*BEP,* 10 March 1766; *BG,* 27 Jan., 3 Feb. 1766; Legislative Council Records, 26:141, MSA; Bernard to Pownall, 31 March 1766, Sparks MSS., 4.5:100–101, HHL; Bernard to Board of Trade, 10 March 1766, in Quincy, ed., *Reports,* pp. 212–213; Hutchinson to ———, 27 Feb. 1766, Letterbooks, MA 26:199–200; Hutchinson to Pownall, 8 March 1766 (not sent), *ibid.,* 26:200–206.

Figure 2.   The devil, prompting British politicians once again to encroach on American liberties. Effigies prepared for the crowd action on 20 February 1766 in Boston. Contemporary cut, published in the *Boston Gazette*.

mock funeral on 1 November, and the similarity of the 5 November parades by Northend and Southend crowds to militia exercises.[28]

In the months before the repeal, one more institution was adapted to popular direct action, the judicial process. The "United Free-Born Sons of Liberty," according to the *Evening Post* meanwhile operating on an intercolonial level, had fixed 20 February for burning stamps throughout the colonies. Bostonians erected a stage under Liberty Tree as an open-air courtroom. Gallows with the devil sitting on the top beam were put up and effigies of Bute and Grenville chained to them. When "judge" and "jury" had taken their seats, the accused, a chained stamp, heard its indictment: "the said Prisoner did on the first of November last, endeavour to make its Appearance in a forcible Manner, and in Defiance of the known and established Laws of the British Constitution, to deprive the Subject of his Rights and Privileges." The two-hour trial was watched by 2000–3000 people.

> After many learned debates, the Evidence was so clear, that the Jury without going out of Court found the said Prisoner guilty of a Breach of Magna Charta, and a Design to subvert the British Constitution, and alienate the Affections of His Majesty's most loyal and dutiful Subjects in *America* from his Person and Government.

Sentence was passed, and the convicted effigies were paraded through town and finally burned under the gallows.[29] A few days later Captain Thacher arrived from Jamaica with a stamped clearance for his ship. A "warrant" was issued to procure "Those Marks of Creole slavery." Thacher delivered the clearance form, and the rioters, who definitely had a knack for arranging impressive mock procedures, then "fixed it on a Pole, and carried it to the lower End of the Court-House, where they put the Pole in the Stocks, and exposed the Paper to publick View until the Time appointed for Execution," which was effected after a reading of an execution warrant.[30] Similar action was taken by crowds in Salem, Marblehead, Falmouth, Casco Bay, and Plymouth.[31]

When the news of repeal finally arrived, bonfires as big as houses—"tremendous blazes"—were reported from western Massachusetts.[32] In Boston the celebrations

[28] In imitation of Governor Bernard's title as chief militia commander, Mackintosh was styled "Captain General of the Liberty Tree." Alfred F. Young, "Pope's Day, Tar and Feathers, and 'Cornet Joyce, jun.': From Ritual to Rebellion in Boston, 1745–1775" (Paper prepared for the Anglo-American Labor Historians' Conference, Rutgers Univ., April 1973), pp. III–18–20 (forthcoming as *From Ritual to Rebellion*).

[29] *BG,* 24 Feb. 1766; *BEP,* 24 Feb. 1766; *BNL* (20 Feb. 1766) had suggested that "there is no Doubt but all will be done without Tumult or Rioting." Several Sons of Liberty met later that day at their apartment in Hanover Square. Their toasts did not have the refinement of those made in higher circles: "A perpetual Itching without the Benefit of Scratching to its [the Stamp Act's] Friends."

[30] *BEP,* 3 March 1766.

[31] Salem: *BEP,* 3 Feb. 1766. Marblehead: *BPB,* 10 Feb. 1766; *BG,* 10 Feb. 1766. Falmouth, Plymouth: *BNL,* 20 March 1766. Boston: *BEP,* 3 March 1766.

[32] George F. Clark, ed., "Stow and John Gates' Diary," *Worcester Soc. Antiq. Coll.* 16:273 (1899); Boyle, "Journal," 21 July 1766, p. 250. Portland: Smith and Deane, *Journals,* 18–20 May 1766, p. 209. Salem: Henfield Diary, 21 May 1766, quoted in Joseph B. Felt, *The Annals of Salem from Its First Settlement* (Salem, Mass., 1827), p. 467. Newburyport: Coffin, *History of Newbury,* p. 232; Peter Oliver, *Peter Oliver's Origin and Progress of the American*

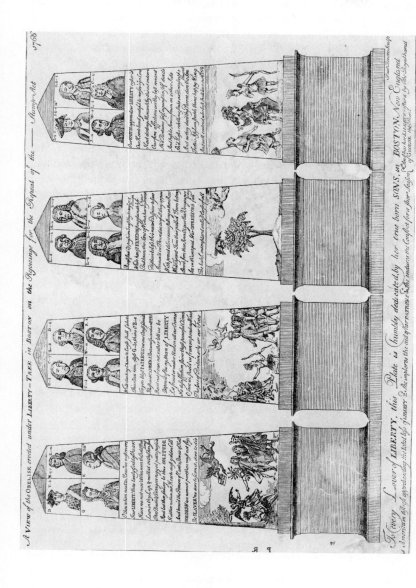

Figure 3.   Paul Revere's engraving of the obelisk erected on Boston common for the celebration of the Stamp Act repeal.

customary for victories of His Majesty's armies were appropriated for this matter. Every inhabitant was asked to illuminate his house, with the exception of persons who were too poor to afford the cost or too sick or who had religious scruples. A dinner, again separated according to class, was held. Hancock provided a "grand and elegant" festivity at his residence for "the genteel Part of the Town." The Sons of Liberty had their repast in the workhouse. The "Populace," who had provided the manpower for the direct action, were treated to a pipe of wine outside. It seems that unless they forced entrance into the houses of the wealthy and powerful, they would not be admitted.[33]

RIOTS IN WESTERN MASSACHUSETTS

While symbolic anti-Stamp Act measures permitting or demanding popular participation continued in Boston and other towns until the repeal festivities in May 1766, other crowd action occurred in the country. Economic problems merged with Stamp Act rhetoric and the expected constitutional and legal consequences. Riots were used to redress alleged or real grievances in Massachusetts' two westernmost counties, Hampshire and Berkshire, and in Maine, then part of Massachusetts. In Westfield, Hampshire County, a group of men had banded together with the intent to protect any one of their number should he be apprehended for debt. They could be arrested on unstamped warrants issued before 1 November, but no stamped paper would be available to give bail, to recover debts from their debtors, or to sell land for discharging of debts. Arrest, in short, would mean being "kept in as close custody as felons," with any "lawful" relief barred. When one of the group was arrested, the others assaulted the sheriff and rescued him. A second riot happened in Lanesborough, Berkshire County, where several men confederated to prevent any arrest for debt. The majority of the male inhabitants joined the agreement. They drove off a sheriff and his posse, who had come to arrest one of them. Near Northampton, Hampshire County, a crowd of lumberjacks seized a British-paid surveyor of the King's Woods who had tried to seize their logs, detained him, and forced him to resign.[34] Subsequently, they excused their proceedings, stating that

Rebellion: A Tory View, ed. Douglass Adair and John A. Schutz (Stanford, Calif., 1961), p. 56; Ballantine's Journal, May 1766, Judd MSS., Rev. Matters, pp. 144, 146, Forbes Library; Henry Lloyd to Aaron Cleveland, 22 May 1766, Letterbook, pp. 366–367, cf. p. 368, HBS; Hancock's letters, May–June 1766, Letterbooks, pp. 182ff., NEHGS.
[33]*BEP,* 7 April 1766; *BNL,* 22 May 1766; *BG,* 26 May 1766; *BTR* 16:175, 20:213–214; Mayhew to Hollis, n.d. [1766], *MHSP* 69:188 (1947–1950); Dennys de Berdt to Samuel White, 17 March 1766, "Letters of Dennys de Berdt, 1757–1770," ed. Albert Matthews, *CSMP* 13:315 (1910–1911); Joshua Henshaw to William Henshaw, 31 May 1766, *NEHGR* 23:451 (1869); Samuel Mather to his son, 21 May 1766, Letterbook, MHS; John Rowe, *Letters and Diary of John Rowe, Boston Merchant, 1759–1762, 1764–1779,* ed. Anne Rowe Cunningham (Boston, 1903; reprint ed., 1969), pp. 90, 95–96; Boyle, "Journal," 19 May, 21 June 1766, pp. 249–250; George R. T. Hewes, *Traits of the Tea Party: Being a Memoir of George R. T. Hewes,* ed. Benjamin B. Thatcher (New York, 1835), p. 72; *Glorious News,* Brds. (Boston 1766), Evans 10317; Alden Bradford, *Memoir of the Life and Writings of Jonathan Mayhew* (Boston, 1838), pp. 414–427.
[34]*BEP,* 5 Jan., 19 Jan., 6 July, 13 July 1767; Superior Court of Judicature, Records, 1767–1768, f. 282–285, SCCH; Quincy, ed., *Reports,* pp. 248–250; Hutchinson, *History,* 3:113–115, and *The Diary and Letters of His Excellency Thomas Hutchinson,* ed. Peter Orlando Hutchinson, 2 vols. (London, 1883, 1886), 1:72–73; Hutchinson to Cushing, 30 July 1767, *MHSP* 44:524 (1911); William V. Wells, *The Life and Public Services of Samuel Adams,* 3 vols.

they happened "at a time when peoples minds were greatly fretted and unsettled." This reference to the impact of the Stamp Act on other social issues was preceded by a long, elaborate, and explicit statement of the causes that led to the action. The petition of the Westfield men to governor and legislature, asking for remittance of the fines imposed on them for their direct action, is a valuable example of the influence of imperial problems on local thought and concepts of deference. Their words are therefore quoted at length:

> Within the Time of the late general Troubles, and Confusions that arose ... by Means of the Stamp Act ... We viewed and Considered ourselves as well as many of our fellow subjects to be much agrieved, and subjected to Extream Hardships and Distresses, as to our Persons, Estates and Properties, in the Practice and Proceedings that then was used in sueing and recovering Debts. . . . In this situation immagining the Conduct of the Executive Officers, to be an Invasion of Liberty and concluding they had in Fact no Right or Authority by Law to execute such Writs and Processes, because made Void as we conceived by the Act of the British Parliament; moved with Fear of oppression, and looking [at] all order and Government as being in a Manner at an End, thought ourselves concerned to Consult our own safety and defend ourselves against what we called and then really supposed to be oppression in the executive Officers ... and Loss of Liberty ... we concerted and resolved on a rash and imprudent (and as we are now fully sensible) unwarrantable Method of obtaining Redress from ... supposed Grievance and oppression, and that not from any Principle of Disloyalty or Disaffection to his Majesty's government, but rather from an ill-judged and mistaken zeal for Liberty and the Common Peace and accordingly determined to resist and oppose such Executive Officers as by Virtue of such Writs and Executions ... should arrest or attempt to arrest the Body of any of us for Debt. . . .[35]

The men from Westfield had been represented in court by Joseph Hawley. When the case was lost in the Superior Court, where Hutchinson presided, Hawley, member of the House of Representatives, demanded that a clause pardoning all rioters who had participated in direct action in the period from 1 August 1765 to 1 May 1766 be inserted in a bill intended to grant compensation to those officials who had suffered. Hawley questioned whether it would be just to subject men who had acted in defense of the Constitution to punishment while the lieutenant governor, who was "a person of unconstitutional principles," received a compensation. The bill was referred from session to session as representatives consulted their constituents, and numerous towns that had not been actively engaged in opposition to the Stamp Act now had to face the issue and pass resolutions on it. In its final form the bill granted compensation to four riot targets and pardon to the riot participants. Because the power to pardon was reserved to the king, the act was disallowed, and the Massachusetts council ordered that the persons concerned should "govern them-

---

(Boston, 1865, 1888), 1:127; Ernest F. Brown, *Joseph Hawley, Colonial Radical* (New York, 1931), pp. 64–68, 107–110.

[35]MA 88:210–212.

selves accordingly.'' The four officials, Hutchinson, Hallowell, Oliver, and Story, otherwise advocates of strict submission to the laws, did not comply; their private interests would be hurt, for the compensation would have to be paid back.[36]

The action and petition of the Westfield rioters revealed the opinions of an agrarian community, as the actions and letters of the Boston lower sort reflected the greater socioeconomic stratification of a populous mercantile seaboard town. The riots in Scarborough, Maine, took place in a relatively small mercantile and artisanal center in a region where subsistence farming dominated. Together with the previous and subsequent litigation, they give some insights into the subordinations and dependencies within the community and into the ideological concepts of the inhabitants. Numerous depositions of rioters, riot target, and witnesses provide a picture of the structures in a socioreligious unit, the second parish of Scarborough, and of the thinking of the antagonists, Richard King, richest merchant and former treasurer of the parish, and a number of the inhabitants, small but independent property holders. In this case the Stamp Act provided merely the final spark, or rather the pretense, for the riots.[37]

Briefly, the crowd action against King comprised the following separate riots: In the evening of 19 March 1766, rioters broke into his house and his warehouse, destroyed part of his belongings, took a substantial number of deeds, notes of hand, and the like, and later burned them in the home of one of the rioters. A threatening letter was sent to one of King's tenants ordering him off the land, and later a crowd twice damaged the place (May 1766) and finally rendered it irreparable (March 1767). When one of the rioters was arrested, a barn and a shed belonging to King were burned at night and two of his cattle killed (May 1767). Resistance to prosecution, ranging from threatening letters and smashed windows to assembling of a crowd to rescue arrested men, took place throughout the period.[38]

At the time of the first riot, it was said that King favored the Stamp Act, that he had been offered or even accepted the office of stamp master. Some asserted that he had the stamps already in his house. The rioting in other towns was pointed out as showing the proper course to be taken. King himself unsuccessfully petitioned the General Court for relief under the Compensation Act, stating that the riot had "origenated under a Notion of Publick Utility." In the courts the attorneys for the

---

[36]A. C. Goodell *et al.*, eds., *Acts and Resolves, Public and Private, of the Province of the Massachusetts Bay*, 21 vols. (Boston, 1869–1922), 4:903–904, 1766–1767, notes, pp. 931–945; Hutchinson received £3194.17.6; Hallowell, £385.6.10; Oliver, £172.4; Story, £67.8.10. Mary F. Pierce, ed., *Town of Weston*, 3 vols. (Boston, 1893–1897), 1:127; Roads, *History of Marblehead*, p. 75; Lucius R. Paige, *History of Hardwick, Massachusetts* (Boston, 1883), pp. 65–66; Barnstable voted that riots, "Especially Those Whereby private property has been affected," were of "Bad and Dangerous Tendency" and instructed its representative to "disavow the Governments having any hand in them," SCF 172942; Bernard to Shelburne, 14 Nov. 1766, *Acts and Resolves*, 4:939–940; BTR 16:187–188; William T. Davis, ed., *Records of the Town of Plymouth, 1636–1783*, 3 vols. (Plymouth, Mass., 1903), 3:167. Hutchinson, *Diary and Letters*, 1:73; Hawley Papers, 1709–1804, folder 1767, NYPL.

[37]William S. Southgate, "The History of Scarborough from 1633 to 1783," *Maine Hist. Soc. Coll.* 1.3:182–186 (1853). Trial of the rioters: *King* v. *Stewart*, case 2, in John Adams, *The Legal Papers of John Adams*, ed. L. Kinvin Wroth and Hiller B. Zobel, 3 vols. (Cambridge, Mass., 1965), 1:106–140; Bernard to Pownall, 31 March 1766, Sparks MSS., 4.5:100–101, HHL.

[38]King's petition to the General Court, 4 Jan. 1768, in John Adams, *Legal Papers*, 1:108–111.

rioters pleaded "Prov[ince] in an Uproar, on Account of Stampd Papers," obviously considering this as extenuating circumstances.[39]

The rioters, however, had other scores to settle. And so had King. Distrust of his conduct as parish treasurer had led to his dismissal. At this point he held that the parish owed him money, while the parishioners held exactly the opposite to be true—the parish account book was lost or misplaced. King took the issue to court, then found the missing book. He refused to return it to the parish, hoping to pressure the parishioners into paying. A jury later decided the case partly in King's favor.[40]

As to his private business, he was the wealthiest merchant in town. People depended upon him for imported goods, and many were indebted to him. King vigorously used the courts to collect outstanding money. He was accused of numerous misdeeds. Altogether, townspeople had resented this conduct "for many yers post," considered him "a bad man," and argued that he treated his clients arbitrarily and unrighteously, indeed cheated them outright; that he had "destroyed the poor and taken away Peoples Estates"; that he still "took all advantages of people." In short: He "will ruin us all, if he goes on at this rate; if something or other is not done with him, if he is not humbled, it is not worth while for any of us to live here; and he is hard hearted to the widow and orphan."[41] Connecting this vein of argument with the Stamp Act was the observation that King had "done as much hurt to people here, as Bute [the favorite of George III] had done to the people at home."[42] The timing of the first riot coincided with a report "that he had said he would fill Falmouth Goal with Debtors next C[our]t." The people who entered his house called themselves the "Suns of liburty" and took time that evening to gather around an elm and baptize it "Tree of Liberty."[43]

As one of the Boston rioters reportedly said that his doings on 26 August were in line with the Bible's commands, one Scarborough man explicitly told his prospective companions that this rioting was "no Sin." Moral improvement was among the rioters' avowed aims. It was necessary to "humble" him, as the saying went. Since the purely moral aim could be achieved without destruction of property, some participants thought it would be sufficient to whip King. This would make him a "better man." Considering that his health was not of the best, it was even suggested that he be whipped with small sticks only. Public whipping, it should be remembered, at that time was the legal punishment for the breaking of numerous moral norms and criminal laws. The community opinion that King had grown arrogant is corroborated by King's own blunt statement: "[I am] The Greatest Benefactor in Trade that Ever Dealt in the Place." This attitude may explain to a degree why the

---

[39]Deposition of Silas Burbank, *ibid.*, pp. 121–122; King's petition, *ibid.*, pp. 110–111; witnesses Silas Burbank and Jonathan Wingate, *ibid.*, pp. 129, 130; lawyer James Sullivan, *ibid.*, p. 134.

[40]*Richard King* v. *Second Parish of Scarborough*, and vice versa, Superior Court of Judicature, Records, 1767–1768, ff. 219–220; SCF 119624 *passim*, 139251, 139254, 139590, 139642, 139645.

[41]Deposition of Silas Burbank, in John Adams, *Legal Papers*, 1:121–123; deposition of John Newbegin, *ibid.*, p. 124; deposition of Jonathan Wingate, *ibid.*, p. 125.

[42]Deposition of Silas Burbank, *ibid.*, p. 121.

[43]Witness Benjamin Carl, *ibid.*, p. 130; *BEP*, 31 March 1766; *BPB*, 14 April 1766.

resentment of him was widespread not only among small debtors but among "Men of Estates and Character" too. These, however, were few. Aside from the property of the wealthy Richard King, only 39 houses in town "will Rent for any Thing or more to Pay the anual Repairs." The rest, added the assessors, "are no more than Shells or huts." In property King was king.[44]

Those who were content to "humble" King without hurting his "interest" were few. Obviously, to many, the moral default was intimately connected with his wealth. The majority of the rioters and, to judge from the extensive participation in the subsequent cover-up, the majority of the inhabitants felt that his economic position had to be attacked too. Bonds, deeds, and notes were destroyed. A barn, a shed, and a tenant's farmhouse were burned. Some cattle were killed, tools taken away, parts of his dwelling destroyed. This action had obvious similarities to the Boston riot against Oliver. A wealthy inhabitant, in the Scarborough case the wealthiest, had offended against norms by using his position as official and merchant to behave "high-handedly" toward clients and fellow townsmen. However, there were obvious differences too. While the Bostonians destroyed the symbols of wealth and position, the people in Scarborough aimed mainly at the economic base of social position. Stores, farms, and investments were concentrated in one spot and accessible to the rioters. Deeds to King were burned, and the previous owners reentered the deeded lands. A tenant whose labor added to King's profits was chased off. This lessened King's economic influence and increased the rioters' economic independence. In other words, it equalized—to a degree—economic opportunities.[45]

Additionally, the rioters, after entering King's house, also wrought havoc in the kitchen. Kitchen and cooking utensils were evidently no luxury items. Was this, then, a proof of wantonly destructive action on the part of the rioters? To some it may be. But there is a specific tradition of patterns of action that does furnish a plausible explanation for this kind of destruction. Throughout colonial history border riots had occurred, stemming from claims of two neighboring colonies for the same strip of land. Sometimes the border line had simply not been laid out clearly; sometimes deliberate attempts to extend borders were behind the difficulties. Whatever the case, two colonial governments would grant the same land to different (groups of) settlers. Both depended on the land for their subsistence and/or economic position. One side would then riot against the other with the intention of driving the latter off. This, of course, meant destruction of the means of living, for which kitchen and tools are the symbols. Since Scarborough men had said that unless King changed his methods many people would have to move away, it is possible that the alternative had occurred to them too—if King could be forced to leave, the others could stay. The destruction of his barn and tools points in this

---

[44]Deposition of Silas Burbank, in John Adams, *Legal Papers*, 1:121; deposition of Jonathan Wingate, *ibid.*, p. 125; King to Silas Burbank, *ibid.*, p. 119; witness Silas Burbank, *ibid.*, p. 129. Assessors' statement in tax list, MA 134:122–124. Cf., for dozens of King's suits for debt, vol. 753, SCF, nos. 119562ff.

[45]King's petition, in John Adams, *Legal Papers*, 1:108–111; deposition of John Newbegin, *ibid.*, pp. 123–124; deposition of Silas Burbank, *ibid.*, p. 122; deposition of Jonathan Wingate, *ibid.*, p. 125; witness Silas Burbank, *ibid.*, p. 129.

direction.[46] This was no commitment to a classless society, no blind leveling. All the evidence points to an explicit and pragmatic concept of some opportunity for all social classes.[47]

Prosecution of the rioters lagged because they went out armed, intimidated witnesses, locked their doors to officials and threatened them, or retreated into the woods. At least some officers agreed with the rioters' doings. The easiest way to prevent any further action, said the rioters, was for the King "to Submit to Provadences, and behave beter for the futer." They called a special meeting shortly after the riot and "proposed the whole Parish should go to the Justices, and let him take whom he pleased." To find out the identity of the offenders, they suggested, King had only "to go to his Books and see who he had wronged." A man who had not participated in the first riot declared that

> if there was ever another he would be in it. For it was justifiable in the sight of God and Man. The Common Law could not take hold of a Mob. If a man was injured and could not get his Remedy at common law, he might take it himself.

If this interpretation of the common law was not altogether correct from a lawyer's viewpoint, it reflects thinking in earlier traditions and sometimes formerly existing laws concerning equity. In the English peasant uprisings of 1381, the peasants stormed an abbey to search for the old lawbooks, where their rights were supposedly fixed. The eighteenth-century English food rioters acted in accordance with a "Book of Orders" of 1630. The defense lawyer of the Scarborough rioters also took up the notion of equity and justified the riot by charging that King would have "beggared, and reduced to Distress for Life" one of the rioters, who was indebted to him.[48]

John Adams, lawyer for King when the case came up for review in 1773–1774, argued along different lines. He did not mention the connection to the political scene, admitted by plaintiff and defendants. Instead, he dwelt upon King's private sufferings and those of his family. He did not mention King's high-handed attitudes as creditor. He had the same fears about social and economic uprisings that Governor Bernard had voiced in his report on the riot. He extensively expounded the sanctity of (King's) property and based his whole argument on a distinction between public and private "mobs," a distinction Otis made in a Boston town meeting too. This meant that he rejected the colonial tradition of rioting, indeed more so than did the former chief justice and then royal governor, Thomas Hutchinson. Adams made one exception: "Popular Commotions can be justifyed, in Opposition to Attacks upon the Constitution." In plain words, this meant that he accepted crowd action only in support of his political point of view, Whig thought. Later, as president of

---

[46]Witness servant Robert, *ibid.*, p. 131; witness John Newbegin, *ibid.*, p. 130.

[47]James Sullivan, *ibid.*, p. 134.

[48]King's petition, *ibid.*, pp. 108–111; deposition of John Newbegin, *ibid.*, pp. 124–125; deposition of Jonathan Wingate, *ibid.*, p. 126; deposition of John Sayward, *ibid.*, pp. 127–128; threatening letter sent to King [April 1766], *ibid.*, p. 126; witnesses John Newbegin, Benjamin Carl, Paul Thompson, and John Porry, *ibid.*, pp. 130–132; James Sullivan, *ibid.*, p. 134; SCF 87726.

the United States, he attempted to outlaw direct action on constitutional principles too. In his plea in 1774, he outlined the depravity of crowds and laid open his social bias toward men of King's status. "There are Levellers, but they disgrace Jurys," he thundered. The jury awarded King one-eighth of the £2000 that he had demanded.[49]

CELEBRATING RESISTANCE: THE SONS OF LIBERTY AS MIDDLE-CLASS DINING CLUB

When the immediate aim of resistance had been achieved, many colonials regularly celebrated the events of 1765 and 1766 to cultivate the sentiments of liberty and to foster a spirit of opposition to encroachments on their rights. Two more days were added to the already long list of "patriotic" festivities. They were neither as imperial-minded as the celebration of the king's birthday nor as provincial-centered as the festivities around council election time. They were distinctly American in that they commemorated Boston's first step of opposition to the Stamp Act, the riot of 14 August, and, second, the retreat of Parliament before the united colonies' demands, the repeal on 18 March 1766. The latter celebration, exuberant in 1767, was somewhat dimmed when the Townshend Acts had been passed and customs commissioners were in town. In the evening a crowd broke some windows in their houses. From 1769 onward, the day was no longer celebrated because the victory over Parliament had proved illusive.[50]

The celebration of the resistance of 14 August lasted longer and followed a different pattern. In the first two years, attendance was thin. A "few individuals," as a conservative observer noted, toasted "Paoli" and "Liberty for Spain," but also the "Union between America and Great Britain."[51] This changed suddenly in 1768. In March the repeal had been toasted for a last time. In August, Bostonians were ready to emphasize resistance again. The customs commissioners had seized Hancock's vessel *Liberty,* new duties were to be paid, British troops were to garrison the town. In contrast, somewhat paradoxical at first sight, the celebration consisted of nothing but a dinner. This pattern was followed in the next years too. The dinner was held at Roxbury or Dorchester, several miles from Boston. The feasts were opulent: Once the tables broke down under the load. The diners, numbering between 250 and 400, came in chaises and carriages and sometimes had to buy admission tickets in advance. Entertainers and "liberty songs" enlivened the scene.

---

[49] John Adams's outline of the argument (*Legal Papers*, 1:136–140) was almost identical to governor Bernard's report that King's "Crime was . . . being richer than his Neighbors . . . [who wanted] to bring him upon their own level." Bernard to Pownall, 31 March 1766, Sparks MSS., 4.5:100–101, HHL; John Adams to Abigail Adams, 7 July 1774, *Legal Papers,* 1:140. Otis speech: *BEP,* 23 Nov. 1767; Superior Court of Judicature, Records, 1773, f. 92, 1774, ff. 229–231; Minute Books, vol. 15, York County, Me., SCCH.

[50] *BTR* 16:205; Rowe, *Letters and Diary,* pp. 125–126; Nathaniel Ames, "Diary of Dr. Nathaniel Ames," 18 March 1767, ed. Sarah Breck Baker, *Dedham Hist. Reg.* 2:97 (1891); Hutchinson, *History,* 3:107; *BEP,* 23 March 1767.

[51] Andrew Oliver to ———, 7 May 1767, in Israel Mauduit, *A Short View of the History of the Colony of Massachusetts Bay* (London, 1769), pp. 31–36; Boyle, "Journal," p. 250; *BNL,* 14 Aug. 1766; *BEP,* 18 Aug. 1766; *BG,* 18 Aug. 1766. About 60 men met in 1767: Bernard to Shelburne, 24 Aug. 1767, Sparks MSS., 4.6:223–229, HHL; Rowe, *Letters and Diary,* p. 139; *BEP,* 17 Aug. 1767.

The seeming paradox is easily explained when the differences between crowds and leaders are remembered, when the stratified character of the province's society, especially strong in Boston, is taken into account. The removal of the dinner from Boston made attendance difficult for people who did not own a chaise or at least a horse. This protected the well-to-do participants from noisy and unruly crowds of spectators, who furthermore might find it debatable whether this feasting was appropriate to their spirit of 1765.[52] The celebration was for "respectable" people and for them only. In fact, they were so thoroughly respectable that after 14 toasts at Liberty Tree and another 45 during the dinner, John Adams "did not see one Person intoxicated."

"This is cultivating the Sensations of Freedom," he wrote, "Otis and [Samuel] Adams are politick, in promoting these Festivals, for they tinge the Minds of the People, they impregnate them with the sentiments of Liberty." It was indeed a success: In 1769, 86 percent of the richest Bostonians but only 1 percent of the propertyless men attended. Even the property-owning Sons of Liberty were over-proportionately recruited from the wealthier classes (percentages for the whole of the property-owning taxpayers in parentheses): small and middle 42 (46) percent, well-to-do 30 (42) percent, wealthy 28 (12) percent. The diners went to their lavish feast in 139 chaises; the Boston "Sons of Liberty" became a middle-class dining club after 1768.[53] Only a few of them are known to have participated in riots, and those few as much attempted to keep them within narrow limits as they initiated them. Others were charged with monopolizing or selling at extortionate prices in subsequent years. Several became Tories. The Boston Sons of Liberty never were a mechanics' association, as were their namesakes in Charlestown. In other colonies too, the Whig politicians and merchants, who gave the impression that they had copyrighted the name "Sons of Liberty," came mainly from the ranks of independent artisans or higher-ranking groups. They were "men of standing," as Pauline Maier found. Within this group, influence was concentrated among a small number of men, outspoken and eloquent pamphleteers, influential governmental officials, and active committeemen. It seems that from these men large sections of the post-1776 colonial elite were drawn.[54]

Neither the Scarborough "Sons of Liberty" nor the Boston rioters would have had much chance if they had applied for admission to this exclusive circle. Occasional attempts to break the Whig leaders' monopoly on the use of the term "Sons

---

[52]Rowe, *Letters and Diary*, p. 191; Boyle, "Journal," p. 259; *BPB*, 21 Aug. 1769; *BEP*, 21 Aug. 1769; unsigned advertisement of the Sons of Liberty, *BG*, 6 Aug. 1770.

[53]William Palfrey named 345 Bostonians and a few guests from other towns and colonies as diners in 1769; 60 percent of the men have been located in the valuation list for 1771. List of Sons of Liberty, *MHSP* 1.11:140–142 (1869); Rowe, *Letters and Diary*, p. 191; John Adams, *Diary*, 14 Aug. 1769, 1:341–342.

[54]Richard Walsh, *Charleston's Sons of Liberty: A Study of the Artisans, 1763–1789* (Columbia, S.C., 1959); Pauline R. Maier, *From Resistance to Revolution: Colonial Radicals and the Development of American Opposition to Britain, 1765–1776* (New York, 1972), p. 304; Herbert Aptheker, *The American Revolution, 1763–1783 . . . An Interpretation* (New York, 1960), p. 62; Philip G. Davidson, "Sons of Liberty and Stamp Men," *N.C. Hist. Rev.* 9:38–56 (1932); Staughton Lynd and Alfred F. Young, "After Carl Becker: The Mechanics and New York City Politics, 1774–1801," *Labor History* 5:215–276 (1964); Charles S. Olton, "Philadelphia Artisans and the American Revolution" (Ph.D. diss., Univ. of California, 1967).

of Liberty'' remained unsuccessful. ''Trueborn Sons of Liberty'' some opponents called themselves, referring to their social origin, the lower classes. But without difficulty the Whigs, in Boston the Loyal Nine, usurped this addition to what they considered their registered trademark. By making the Boston celebration of 14 August a social rather than a political event, Samuel Adams and James Otis succeeded in drawing a large number of usually inactive members of the community to the side of the Whigs, or at least in neutralizing them for a time. The diners, according to the *Boston Post Boy,* ''established the sacred character, that the Enemies to *usurpation* and *oppression* are the great Examplers of *Order* and *Decency.''* Order and decency are easily kept when no action is taken and when whole social groups are excluded.[55]

Those who actually engaged in the riots could drink to their own achievements on 5 November, Pope's Day. The day was no longer as noisy and tumultuous as it was before the union between Northenders and Southenders was established. With the rivalries submerged, the day kept its distinctly lower-class flavor. The Loyal Nine did not try to usurp it anymore, nor was it supported by contributions from John Hancock and others. The celebrations of 5 November were more politicized than those of 14 August. The customary effigies of the Pope were sometimes replaced by effigies of disliked crown officials, and signs with political slogans were carried about town. The expression of political sentiments on the day did not automatically lead to anti-British riots. In 1767 the marchers carried posters reading ''Liberty and Property and no Commissioners,'' but three of the commissioners could land that very evening, after arriving from London, without being molested; they had not yet become personally obnoxious. When the brawls between inhabitants and soldiers were at their greatest height, in 1769, no violence occurred on that day. Once a soldier tried to stop the procession, but only one young man fought him off; the other participants watched or continued on their course. It seems that part of the anti-British spirit fostered by the Whig leadership had taken root among the lower sort of the Northend and Southend. But the political leadership and the crowds kept apart. The attempt to take over the Pope's Day customs for merely political purposes had failed. Social differences and differences of purpose between the groups could not be bridged, at least not in the way the Loyal Nine and other leaders had attempted, by the imposition of authority.[56]

Further evidence for the wide gulf between the majority of the participants in the direct action and the majority of the Sons of Liberty is found in the different directions in which the Loyal Nine and Ebenezer Mackintosh turned after 1766. During the Stamp Act they had formed the crucial link between social and political

---

[55]*BPB,* 16 Aug. 1773. For descriptions of the day throughout the years, see John Rowe's diary, John Boyle's journal, and the newspapers.
[56]Rowe, *Letters and Diary,* 5 Nov. 1766, p. 114; *BNL,* 6 Nov. 1766. Loammi Baldwin, Diary, 5 Nov. 1767, Essex Institute; Rowe, *Letters and Diary,* 5 Nov. 1767, p. 145; *BG,* 9 Nov. 1767; letter from Anne Hulton, 17 Dec. 1767, *Letters of a Loyalist Lady* (Cambridge, Mass., 1927), p. 8; Bernard to Shelburne, 14 Nov. 1767, Sparks MSS., 4.6:252–253, HHL. The complaints of the customs commissioners were placed in the context of colonial practices by Governor Bernard, who said that the evening passed without ''any Affront whatsoever.'' See also A. F. Young, ''Pope's Day.''

strata that usually did not interact or cooperate intensively. Peter Oliver, subsequently a Loyalist who described most Whig leaders in vitriolic terms, in 1765 said of Mackintosh that he was sensible, manly, and well dressed for his position. In order to convince the public of the crowd's power, Peter Oliver continued, "he paraded the Town with a Mob of 2000 Men in two Files, and passed by the Stadthouse, when the general Assembly was sitting." He named his first son in honor of the Corsican Pascal Paoli, thus showing his familiarity with and respect for other liberty struggles.

In 1765, Rhode Island leaders inquired about his capabilities and "Whether he would probably rise, in Case this Contest should be carried into any Length." Mackintosh did not rise; in fact, he became so obscure that even his role in crowd activities is no longer traceable. He was not among the Sons of Liberty dining on 14 August. He was dropped from his office as sealer of leather, and, according to an informer for the crown officials, "he *was* one that attended their Night Meetings" and, because he knew all, had "already been threatened with Death in case he should inform." About the same time, 1769, merchants reverted to violence to enfore the nonimportation agreements, but carefully avoided involvement of artisans and Pope's Day celebrators. The death threat was only the first hint that there were differences between Mackintosh and those higher up. None of the numerous accounts of the King Street riot in 1770, in which Samuel Maverick, half-brother of his wife, Elizabeth, was killed, even mentions him. Later in the year he was imprisoned for debt, but none of his wealthy "superiors" helped him out. According to tradition, Mackintosh was one of the leading men in the Tea Party, and a few months later the *Massachusetts Spy*—incorrectly—reported that Hancock, Rowe, Adams, and Mackintosh would be transported home in irons for trial because "the latter has been very active among the lower order of people, and the other among the higher." Seemingly, the Whig leaders feared his intimate knowledge of their proceedings and his power over crowds. Soon the rumor spread, or was spread, that he was dead, though he had only left town. He was no longer needed or wanted when emphasis changed from opposition to British rule to order under Whig rule.

Both Thomas Hutchinson and Peter Oliver, the high-ranking and well-informed officials, compared Ebenezer Mackintosh to Tomaso Aniello, "Massaniello." A simple fisherman, his articulation of his townsmen's grievances brought about a colonial and social revolt. He wrote no tracts. He spoke in the marketplace of Naples in 1647 against the oppressive *gabelle,* a kind of sales tax, imposed by the Spanish "motherland." The tax was collected by local men from the nobility, and within a day the *rivolta antispagnola* turned into a *rivolta proletaria*. There was an attempt to establish a popular monarchy that would be dependent on Spain, but with Aniello as local king. The nobility of Naples had profited as "placemen" while attempting to contain popular aspirations (*speculazioni finanziarie e ripresa*). Now it was deemed necessary to assassinate Tomaso Aniello, and in a second phase the revolution was turned to concern about relations within the Spanish empire and to a leadership-mapped *ribellione republicana*. The people had proved capable of administering the city on their own, of maintaining distribution of food and goods, of containing any excesses—private enrichment from those luxuries that were to be committed to the flames. In the name of republicanism and anti-Spanish feeling, the poor people's government was quelled.

Just as the shoemaker Mackintosh was compared to a plebeian, educated contemporaries in 1768 compared the better-placed Loyal Nine and their trademarked Liberty Tree with its copper plate to the better-placed Jack (that is, John) Cade and his "Oak of Reformation." Cade was a leader in the rising of 1450 in Kent, England, against double-dealing officials who had the support of the king. As Boston merchants mixed their private interests with those of the Boston crowd, so had some of Cade's men after the masses had marched to London and entered the town. While the oppressive sheriff of Kent was executed, while imprisoned fellow rioters were freed, while some began to perceive the possibilities for social change, others began to plunder. As in Boston on 27 August, London's "propertied classes" took to arms to suppress the rising. In a fracas Cade was wounded and captured.[57]

The career of the Loyal Nine also followed a very different pattern from that of Mackintosh. They had advocated symbolic action but opposed direct action; they had approved organized demonstrations but restrained or counteracted spontaneous activities. Thus, they too lost influence during the violent period from 1767 to 1776. They dined with the Sons of Liberty in 1769. Two of them, Henry Bass and Thomas Crafts, became members of the Boston Committee of Correspondence.[58] Crafts and Trott studied such political literature as Swift's essay on the dangers of the "Encroachments" of "the Many," which disturbed the balance between institutions and classes and inevitably led to tyranny. Distinctions of rank were necessary and had to be institutionalized, so that the balance between classes could be maintained. The "Many" were apt to be misled in their blind toil and half-witted existence by "Popular Orators, Tribunes, or, as they are now stiled, Great Speakers, Leading Men, and the like."[59] Some thought that members of the Loyal Nine, as other Sons of Liberty, had become Loyalists. After 1776, when the Loyalists had left, the Loyal Nine and loyal others reemerged in power and in office.[60]

The Stamp Act, as we have seen, was an imperial issue that did more than merely induce colonial political leaders and pamphleteers to reconsider the colonies' posi-

[57]George P. Anderson, "Ebenezer Mackintosh, Stamp Act Rioter and Patriot," *CSMP* 26:15–64, 348–361 (1924–1926); Oliver, *American Rebellion,* p. 54; Hutchinson to Pownall, 8 March 1766, in Morgan, ed., *Prologue to Revolution,* p. 125; John Adams, *Diary,* 1:300; Bernard to Shelburne, 11–16 June 1768, Sparks MSS., 4.6:320, HHL; informer's statement, *ibid.,* 10.3:40 (emphasis added); *Mass. Spy,* 7 April 1774. On Aniello: Walter Wallace, "'Massaniello of Naples' and the Image of the Stamp Act Mobs in Boston" (Seminar paper, Northern Illinois Univ., Jan. 1973, with a bibliography of English-language literature on Aniello); Antonio D'Ambrosio, *Masaniello: Rivoluzione e controrivoluzione nel reame di Napoli (1647–1648)* (Milan, 1962); Nicola Napolitano, *Masaniello e giulio genoino, mito e coscienza di una rivolta* (Naples [1960]), with a bibliography on the revolt of 1647; Michelangelo Schipa, *Masaniello* (Bari, 1925); Rosario Villari, *La rivolta antispagnola a Napoli: Le origini (1585–1647)* (Bari, 1969). On Cade: George Kriehn, *The English Rising of 1450* (Strasbourg, 1892).

[58]John Adams, *Diary,* 2:72; Palfrey's list of the Sons of Liberty, *MHSP* 1.11:140–142 (1869); *BTR* 18:233, 271.

[59]Jonathan Swift, *A Discourse of the Contests and Dissentions Between the Nobles and the Commons in Athens and Rome with the Consequences They Had upon Both of Those States,* ed. Frank H. Ellis (Oxford, 1967), p. 116.

[60]John Adams, *Diary,* 2:72. Avery became the first secretary of the Commonwealth of Massachusetts; Crafts, colonel of a regiment established for the temporary defense of Boston; Edes, assessor; Cleverly and Crafts, fire wardens.

tion in the empire. The opposition also provided training for large sections of Bostonians and people in inland communities in direct and symbolic action against officials and wealthy persons, regardless of affiliation with the British or of colonial descent. It brought into the open the differences between leaders and crowds and shaped the leaders' attitudes toward their unwelcome allies, the rioters. It set in motion the development of increasing political awareness among those social groups from which the rioters came, without giving it a definite shape. The direct action, on the other hand, gave definite political force to new constitutional principles.

New Duties but No Crowds

4

CUSTOMS OFFICIALS, COLONIALS, AND THE TRADITION OF RESCUE RIOTS

Late in 1766 Charles Townshend, chancellor of the exchequer in the Pitt mininstry, took up the problem of American revenues again. Seizing on the distinction made by some Americans during the Stamp Act controversy between internal and external taxes, he decided to levy more of the latter. Among customs officials, unable to collect the customary duties, this move created some surprise. Measures to extend their powers seemed to them more necessary than laws to enlarge the revenues. Townshend sought to solve this pivotal problem by establishing an American Board of Customs, which was to be based in Boston. High-level decisions could then be made in America with no need for the time-consuming and cumbersome process of appeals to Britain.[1]

Customs officials had never had an easy position in colonial America. In 1701 a customs informer in South Carolina was beaten by the attorney general and told that he would "ruin the country." In 1724 a writer in the *New England Courant* stated that they were outsiders, not accepted by the community: "Foreigners who come to take the Bread out of the Natives mouth." Benjamin Hallowell, customs official in Boston, had his house ransacked in August 1765, was prevented from searching for smuggled goods in September 1766, was beaten up after the *Liberty* seizure in June 1768, was threatened with destruction of his house in September 1768, was pelted in May 1773, and narrowly escaped another assault in September 1774. These were experiences with crowds. Affrays and disputes with individuals were in addition. Opposition to or at least discontent with the customs establishment was not limited to advocates of colonial rights against Parliament. Samuel Curwen, Salem merchant and later Loyalist exile, remitted a few dollars to a business partner and explained that this was all "I can possibly rescue from the all devouring jaws of our Custom House." Ashley Bowen of Marblehead, inveterate opponent of Whigs and anti-

---

[1]Arthur M. Schlesinger, Sr., *Colonial Merchants and the American Revolution, 1763–1776* (New York, 1918), Ch. 3; Henry Hulton to ———, 21 April 1772, Letterbooks, 1:44, HHL; Hallowell to Commissioners of Customs, 17 Dec. 1765, House of Lords MSS., 221:159, LC transcripts; D. H. Watson, ed., "Joseph Harrison and the *Liberty* Incident," *WMQ* 3.20:593 (1963) (hereafter cited as Harrison to Rockingham).

British crowd action, complained that "our Streets [are] full of the Tide Wa[i]ter and other offesers."[2]

The attitudes of the colonists toward an individual official depended on his personal conduct; toward customs officials in general, it was negative. Commissioner John Temple remained on good terms with most Boston merchants and sailors. During the height of the tensions of 1768, when the troops called by the commissioners began to arrive, he named a son Grenville, held the baptism at the Episcopal King's Chapel, and invited as sponsor the leading general of the British troops. Nobody published invectives; no crowd assembled. James Cockle, the collector for Salem, on the other hand, by his successful racketeering induced the *Boston Gazette* to include under "Ships Cleared" a note, "Now riding at Anchor and ready for Sailing, the Idiot of full Freight, with Ignorance, no Commission, few Guns." Then again came the charge that such placemen and their underlyings were fattening themselves to the detriment of the community. Stories propagated repeatedly about obnoxious customs officials also cropped up during the collection of the controversial provincial taxes. This is another example of how easily opposition to one set of officials, either provincial or imperial, could be shifted to another. It had happened in 1765, from the British placeman to other officials, and was to happen again and again in the next decades. Imperial and local issues were closely interwoven.[3]

When customs officials did effect seizures of goods or ships or when offenses against the trade laws were tried in court, crowds frequently assembled, hooted or pelted the officials, or rescued the seized goods. Massachusetts merchants tried to reduce the powers of the officials with their petition against writs of assistance. When their motion failed, the legislature passed a law designed to harass the customs collectors. The governor, who, by the way, profited from the sale of condemned seizures, refused to sign the bill. In Rhode Island the first documented rescue riot occurred in 1719. By 1764, the king's cutter *St. John* was fired upon from the provincial fort upon orders of several councillors, who, together with a crowd, appeared to help the gunner. The captain of the *St. John* had been deputized as a customs official; the sailors allegedly had stolen provisions from the inhabitants. Impressment had been attempted. According to the new trade laws, the captain could not be held responsible for malfeasance in his office. The sailors could not be held responsible either, because the captain refused to allow the local sheriff on board to serve a warrant on the accused men. In Falmouth, Maine, the house of the collector was surrounded and attacked after a seizure, while another group of

[2]Pauline R. Maier, "Popular Uprisings and Civil Authority in Eighteenth-Century America," *WMQ* 3.27:10 (1970); *New Eng. Courant,* 1 June 1724; Samuel Curwen, Letterbooks, 1754–1771 (Salem), 2 vols., 30 May 1965, Essex Institute; Ashley Bowen, "Personal Diary of Ashley Bowen of Marblehead," *Mass. Mag.,* vols. 1–3, 5 (1908–1912), June 1774, 3:242–245; for Hallowell, see Chapter 2.

[3]John Rowe, *Letters and Diary of John Rowe, Boston Merchant, 1759–1762, 1764–1779,* ed. Anne Rowe Cunningham (Boston, 1903; reprint ed., 1969), 23 Oct. 1768, p. 178; for Temple's conduct in general, see Samuel M. Quincy, ed., *Reports of Cases Argued and Adjudged in the Superior Court of Judicature of . . . Massachusetts Boy, 1761–1772, by Josiah Quincy, Junior* (Boston, 1865), App. 1, p. 466, and, for Cockle, see *ibid.,* pp. 422–424; *BG,* 10 May 1762, 29 April, 23 Sept. 1765, 26 April, 9 Aug. 1773; *BEP,* 23 Sept. 1765; *BTR* 18:94–108; Paul S. Boyer, "Borrowed Rhetoric: The Massachusetts Excise Controversy of 1754," *WMQ* 3.21:328–351 (1964).

men carted off the goods. In Newbury, Massachusetts, inhabitants manned half a dozen boats, surrounded the local officer with his haul of seized goods, took the goods and the officer's boat, and left him overnight on the beach of an uninhabited island.

Early in 1765 the captain of the sloop *Polly* was suspected of having declared only part of her cargo. John Robinson, customs collector for Newport, and Captain Charles Antrobus of *HMS Maidstone* boarded the sloop at Dighton, Massachusetts, found twice the quantity of molasses on board that had been declared, and seized goods and ship. Left in the custody of two minor officals, the ship was first taken from them and at night unloaded by about 40 persons in disguise. Another crowd barred Captain Antrobus and his crew from coming to recover the ship. He and Robinson then assembled 70 armed men and set out for another try. This time no crowd but a justice of the peace waited for them, who arrested the customs collector because the owner of the sloop had sworn out a warrant for damages. Accompanied by a crowd of armed men, he was marched off to jail. Governor Bernard issued a proclamation but found the Massachusetts people "temperate" and "orderly" compared to the Rhode Islanders with whom Antrobus and Robinson had to deal most of the time. People there resented the disorderly conduct of the *Maidstone's* sailors, the rise of prices, and the scarcity of wood caused by the refusal of sellers to come to town for fear of impressment. Merchants also resented the rise of sailors' wages. Merchants, captains, and sailors were antagonized because every entering boat, even coasters, was searched. After a particularly severe impressment, 500 men burned one of the *Maidstone's* boats.[5]

In all these cases the crowd's role was not limited to opposition but resembled the work parties of the countryside, men assembling for a common task. Seized ships were unloaded by collective endeavors in a single night and even fitted out again and put off to sea. Since many colonial magistrates were merchants, they usually cooperated with such direct action. Among the little people, support was broad, especially after the deputizing of navy officers welded impressment and customs grievances. Up to 1763, incidents seem to have been few because duties and regulations could easily be evaded. After the beginning of strict enforcement of the trade laws, crowd action increased to nullify their effects by assault of individual officers, by rescue of seized goods and ships, and by the sinking of vessels in the customs service. Governor Bernard summarized the situation adequately when he wrote about a rescue that "People do not wonder at the Goods being rescued, but at

[4]Maier, "Popular Uprisings," p. 10; Quincy, ed., *Reports,* App. 1, pp. 395–540; "Petition of Lechmere," case 44, in John Adams, *Legal Papers of John Adams,* ed. L. Kinvin Wroth and Hiller B. Zobel, 3 vols. (Cambridge, Mass., 1965), 2:106–146. St. John: Edmund S. Morgan and Helen M. Morgan, *The Stamp Act Crisis: Prologue to Revolution* (Chapel Hill, N.C., 1953), pp. 43–44; John R. Bartlett, ed., *Records of the Colony of Rhode Island and Providence Plantations in New England,* 10 vols. (Providence, R.I., 1856–1865), 6:428–430; *Newport Mercury,* 16 July 1764, Falmouth: *BG,* 25 Aug. 1766; Council Records, 16:145, MSA; Bernard to Comptroller and Collector of Falmouth, 18 Jan. 1766, Sparks MSS., 4.5:195, HHL. Newbury: *BG,* 17 March 1766; Hutchinson to Pownall, 8 March 1766, Letterbooks, MA 26:214; Bernard to Conway, 17 March 1766, Sparks MSS., 4.4:217–218, HHL; Quincy, ed., *Reports,* App. 1, p. 445.
[5]Morgan and Morgan, *Stamp Act Crisis,* pp. 40–52; Carl W. Ubbelohde, *The Vice Admiralty Courts and the American Revolution* (Chapel Hill, N.C., 1960), pp. 95–97; Bernard to Pownall, 10 Feb. 1764, Sparks MSS., 4.3:128–130, HHL. *Maidstone: BG,* 17 June 1765; Bartlett, ed., *Records of the Colony of Rhode Island,* 6:444–446; MA 56:442–452, 66:280–301, 305 *passim.*

an Officer's being so hardy and foolish as to seize them and think he would be able to retain them."[6] While the *Polly* incident illustrates active participation of crowds, an attempted search in the fall of 1766 in Boston is an example of mere passive presence of a crowd as sufficient safeguard to prevent action by officials. Customs officials, town magistrates, and governor took depositions about this affair, and from them the argument about the right to search can be reconstructed in detail.[7] Constitutional and economic arguments, pragmatic concepts, and emphasis on principles were combined into a distinct whole.

On 24 September, Collector William Sheaffe and Comptroller Benjamin Hallowell, upon information from an unknown informer, procured a writ of assistance to search the cellar of Captain Daniel Malcom for smuggled goods.[8] Accompanied by a deputy sheriff and two tidewaiters, they went to Malcom's house in Bennet Street and searched it in the presence of the owner. A bystander described the confusion and grief of Malcom's family stemming from the officers' search as vividly as Hutchinson had described his family's grief over the intrusion of a crowd in August 1765. Nothing was found, but a part of the cellar was partitioned off, with Captain William Mackay named as leasee. He was sent for and upon arrival disconcertedly noted that "it appeared to be War Times, . . . his House was beset by the whole Possey of the Custom House Officers and Mr. Cudworth the Deputy Sheriff."[9] In the following debate Malcom and Mackay stated that they considered it "very extraordinary Proceedings to break open private Dwellings," that according to "the Laws of England and Ireland" the officers had no right to do so, that they "always understood a Man's House was his Castle," and that if "such Things were allowed of there was an end of every thing."[10] This was a position taken by many merchants throughout the colonial period, but it had been rejected in the Massachusetts Superior Court in the writs of assistance case in 1761. Mackay and Malcom also followed colonial tradition in demanding to know who had been the informer. Disclosing the name would make prosecution for willful misinformation possible, but it would also lay open the former to intimidation. Accordingly, customs officials had always refused to name their informants.

The argument then evolved onto a more pragmatic and personal level. Malcom told the officers that their behavior was ungentlemanly. They ought to have let him know a day earlier that they were coming. He added that he thought they came for his money rather than from any other motives. Everybody knew, of course, that the officials were rewarded with a part of the value of the goods for each seizure. Sheaffe and Hallowell explained that they were only doing their duty and produced

[6]Morgan and Morgan, *Stamp Act Crisis*, pp. 40ff.; Quincy, ed., *Reports*, App. 1, pp. 436–437; Bernard to Conway, 17 March 1766, Sparks MSS., 4.4:218, HHL.

[7]The relevant documents have been published in George G. Wolkins, "Daniel Malcom and the Writs of Assistance," *MHSP* 58:5–84 (1924–1925). *BTR* 16:187–194; Rowe, *Letters and Diary,* 24 Sept., 25 Sept., 10 Oct. 1766, pp. 111–112; *BG*, 27 Oct. 1766; Bernard to Shelburne, 10 Oct. 1766, Sparks MSS., 4.4:251–255, HHL.

[8]The name has variously been spelled "Malcom" or "Malcolm." Daniel Malcom himself signed several petitions as "Malcom." This spelling is used in this text.

[9]The page numbers in this and the subsequent notes on the Malcom affair refer to Wolkin's publication of the documents unless otherwise noted. Deposition of Mackay, p. 43.

[10]Deposition of Mackay, pp. 43–44; Turner and Vincent, p. 81.

the writ. Well aware of the belief that they acted from motives of personal gain, both officials offered to give up their reward if any contraband was found in the cellar, provided the locked part was opened without further resistance. Even to his own superiors, Hallowell had to point out that their "principle aim was a faithfull execution of their trust, and not Lucretive motives." He thought that since he could not execute the trade laws by force, his compromise proposal would best "Save the Honour of the Office."[11]

When no positive response was forthcoming, a test of strength ensued. Hallowell stressed his official authority and threatened to break open the door. Malcom answered that he was not "satisfied of that Authority." Hallowell snapped that in that case Malcom would have to be tried for treason, just as was one of the border rioters during the New York–Massachusetts boundary controversy. Mackay in turn lectured Hallowell that if they wanted to search the cellar, "they must break every Lock and Door 'till they come at it, and then People would know what foundation they stood on."[12] The next part of the argument cannot be reconstructed because the existing versions disagree completely. The customs officials reported that Malcom threatened them with "the Mob." Malcom, however, stated that he had accused them of behaving like a mob by violently intruding into his house. Mackay, more specific, reported that Malcom had asked Hallowell whether he was treating Malcom's house as the mob had treated Hallowell's house in August 1765.[13] At any rate, Malcom armed himself with two pistols and a sword. He and Mackay later stated that the pistols were not loaded. However, it seems that they forgot to apprise the customs officials of this when ordering them to leave. At the door Malcom saw the deputy sheriff, who was rather uneasy. Malcom told him, "do your Duty, only mind to do nothing but according to Law." Since the controversial point was exactly the question of what the law was, and since the deptuy was not willing to solve a problem that others had failed to solve, he simply answered, "[I] don't know what the Officers brought me here for."[14]

This lengthy argument, especially on Malcom's side interspersed with strong epithets, was basically a discussion of the legality of the officers' procedure and the right to resist the search. While Malcom and Mackay argued for secure property as a basis of liberty, the officials defended the crown authority and with it their own. Outside, a crowd of 50–100 persons stood and listened to the arguments, keenly awaiting the outcome of the debate, which ended only after an hour and a half when the two customs officers left, while the tidewaiters remained to watch the house. During the "noon recess" Hallowell went to the council. As the crowd has listened to the debate in the house without interfering, the administration now listened to the officials' pleas for help without interfering except for an order to the county sheriff.

[11]Deposition of Mackay, p. 43; Turner and Vincent, p. 81; Sheaffe and Hallowell, p. 27; Malcom, p. 42; Hallowell to Commissioners, 14 Nov. 1766, pp. 79–80.
[12]Deposition of Malcom, p. 40; Mackay, pp. 43–44.
[13]Depositions of Sheaffe and Hallowell, p. 27; Malcom, pp. 41–42; Mackay, p. 44.
[14]Deposition of Mackay, p. 43; Malcom, p. 40.

Angrily, Hallowell wished for "a Regiment of Soldiers here to assit them in doing their duty."[15]

In the afternoon the crowd reassembled, numbering most of the time between 25 and 60. They seemed "concerned" but quiet and orderly. The absence of complaints about rudeness from the customs officials, who usually reacted to even minor incidents, testifies to this. Later, when the North Writing School dismissed classes for the day, it grew a little more lively, but the boys soon dispersed. From those assembled, 20 have been located in the valuation list of 1771. They belonged to a middling group of property owners between the little people and the well-to-do. This sample is probably biased toward the middling sort because only the names of those men are known who were later called to testify about the affair. Most of those identified, among them Paul Revere, happened to pass by and stopped for a time to inquire what the matter was. Less than a third came intentionally after hearing about the search. All thought of themselves as spectators, and many came from the immediate neighborhood. Their sympathies were with Malcom, but only once did some of them have thoughts about ringing the bells of the North Church to assemble a larger crowd. Malcom did not ask the people to assist him, but in the afternoon several friends came and closed and secured all doors and windows from the inside. "In a merry humour," they waited as prospective witnesses in a court action, which Malcom intended to bring in case the officers entered forcibly.[16]

About 3 P.M. the two customs officials reappeared, accompanied by Sheriff Greenleaf. They knocked at the door, peered into the backyard, and yelled for Malcom without gettting an answer. Then they began to look for reinforcements. Constables "would be of Little Service." As to justices of the peace, one merely gave them another warrant; a second was ill. At the third, they consulted. The fourth decided that he would not "Disgrace the Dignity of a Justice So Much" as to assist in person. Well-informed, he pointed out that there was no mob, just a few people standing around, who had even been urged to go home by Malcom.[17] An hour or two later, the officers were back in Bennet Street. Sheriff Greenleaf talked with the people. "Some of them said very Pleasantly they Came to see how Affairs was like to go." Others felt "that no admission into Capt. Malcom's house would be suffered" unless—and this point was repeatedly stressed—the customs officials named the informer. This, the people thought, they were obliged to do by law. When Greenleaf mentioned their duty to assist him, the answer was that "they hoped no body would hurt him." They added that they knew he was only doing his duty, but that Malcom thought "himself in the right Cause, and . . . if any Person went to break open his Doors without first showing him legal Authority, that he'd fire upon them." Greenleaf, in grand prose, declared that he could die but once and would

[15]Depositions of Sheaffe and Hallowell, pp. 27–28; Greenleaf, pp. 34–35; Malcom, p. 41; Mackay, pp. 44–45; Council Records, 16:157, MSA.

[16]Deposition of Goodwin, pp. 46–47; Wimble, pp. 32, 57; Hopkins, p. 51; Revere, p. 52; Pidgeon, p. 55. Valuation list, 1771, MA 132:92–147.

[17]Deposition of Greenleaf, pp. 35–39; Tudor, p. 30; Wimble, p. 32; Nichols, p. 31; Ruddock, p. 30.

willingly do so in the execution of his office. When the only response was an ironical voice from the rear saying, "Aye we'll assist you," he returned to the customs officers. The warrant was valid only until sunset, and since it would be dark soon, sheriff and justice advised letting matters rest and "went home." So did the others.[18]

Among the crowd, now numbering between 300 and 400, the "melancholly" state of mind gave way to "a good deal of laughter and merriment," apparently augmented by journeymen returning from work. In the afternoon Malcom had declined to give any wine to the crowd, arguing that "it might possibly be understood to be done to influence the People and make them disorderly." Upon the advice of his friends, several buckets of wine mixed with water were now distributed, and Malcom asked the people to disperse. After finishing the wine, they "hollowed out 'Good Night to You Gentlemen we thank you,'" and left. Some of "the Boys made a talk about the Informer and said it was one Richardson." They went to his house and shouted and threatened, but did no harm.[19]

Political concepts and legal knowledge expressed by Mackay and Malcom were also debated among the crowd. They were conscious of the rights of individual citizens against the magistrates. Courts indicted rioters because they "unlawfully, routously and riotously assembled themselves together." The crowd discussed why "so many of the Officers had gathered themselves together in such an unusual manner" and reflected about "breaking open a mans house which thing was not common in this Country."[20] The crowd knew that they were obliged to assist the sheriff when he had a warrant to raise the posse. To avoid this, they exaggerated Malcom's threats and the general danger.

Malcom had been one of the merchants who challenged the legality of writs in 1760–1761. While at that time the decision was in favor of the writs, Malcom was by no means convinced, nor was anybody else, for that matter. Even the attorney and solicitor general in Great Britain, when reviewing the attempted action against Malcom, found the opposition legal "inasmuch as the Writ of Assistance . . . was not in this Case a legal Authority." According to Governor Bernard, crowd actions, violent or nonviolent, were "the natural and certain Consequences of a Seizure, and the Effect of a predetermined Resolution that the Laws of Trade shall not be executed." Proclamations had become a "meer farce." Into this situation came the Townshend duties.[21]

THE TOWNSHEND DUTIES: NONCONSUMPTION AND NONIMPORTATION

As he had recorded the news about the Stamp Act in his diary, John Boyle, Boston printer, in October 1767 noted the arrival of the Townshend Revenue Act. In

---

[18]Deposition of Tudor, pp. 30–31; Greenleaf, p. 38; Goodwin, pp. 46–47; Barber, pp. 32–33.

[19]Deposition of Mackay, p. 45; Hopkins, p. 51; Pidgeon, p. 55; Malcom, p. 41; Rust, p. 49; Harris and Aves, p. 53; Goodwin, p. 47; Ruddock, p. 30.

[20]Deposition of Hopkins, p. 51.

[21]Treasury minutes, 6 Feb. 1767, *ibid.*, p. 73; Bernard to Lords of Trade, 18 Aug. 1766, Sparks MSS., 4.4:245–247, HHL.

1765 Boyle had added no comments. This time he was sure that an "Opposition . . . will take place." Customs Officer Harrison mused:

> It's astonishing to me: after the Warning and Experience of the Stamp Act Times; that any new Impositions should be laid on the Colonies, till the Powers of Government were strengthend, and a Reformation made in the Constitution of those, founded on the popular Plan, or at least, that some precautions should not have been previously taken, to preserve the Peace of the Country.

The essential features of the acts were levying of certain specified duties (external taxation) and appropriation of the funds thus raised (1) for "defraying the charge of the administration of justice," (2) for "the support of civil government, in such provinces as it shall be found necessary," and (3) for "further defraying the expenses of defending, protecting and securing the said dominions." The administration of the revenues was to be in the hands of the crown. To facilitate the collection of the duties, each colony's superior or supreme court was empowered to issue writs of assistance. Additionally, a Board of Customs Commissioners was established in Boston.[22] For colonials, this meant an infringement on some cherished principles: violation of the right of self-taxation by imposing taxes granted by Parliament and violation of the rights of self-government by making the executive and judiciary potentially independent of popular influence via legislative appropriations. On top of this, provision was made for a standing army, anathema to the defenders of the popular militia system.[23]

Having learned from the experience gained in the opposition to the Stamp Act, the colonial leadership was more self-assured. The new attitude was a change from evasion of duties by smuggling to outright opposition to Parliamentary authority. The acts were to go in force on 20 November 1767. Plans for opposition were primarily concerned with defeating the purpose of the acts, producing revenue. Nonconsumption (October 1767) and nonimportation (March 1768 and later) were debated and carried into effect. The former was concerted in the town meeting, the latter by the Merchants' Society. Violence against customs officials was explicitly and repeatedly discouraged. The *Gazette* printed the following exhortation: "No Mobs or Tumults, let the Person and Properties of our most inveterate Enemies be safe—Save your money and you save your Country."[24] That popular direct action was not easily controlled was another lesson the leadership had learned from the Stamp Act period.

Accordingly, a town meeting was called before the acts went into effect and before any friction might result from the arrival of new officials. The "very large and full" town meeting heard an address by *Philo Patria* and then considered the

---

[22]Extracts of the acts are in Henry S. Commager, ed., *Documents of American History*, 2 vols. (6th ed., New York 1958) 1:63–64; Harrison to Rockingham, 17 June 1768, *WMQ* 3.20:593; John Boyle, "Boyle's Journal of Occurrences in Boston, 1759–1778," 5 Oct. 1767, *NEHGR* 84:253 (1930).

[23]The third act, the suspension of the New York assembly, had at this time very limited impact in the other colonies.

[24]*BG*, 9 Nov. 1757, 14 March 1768; Harrison to Rockingham, 17 June 1768, *WMQ* 3.20:588 (1963); Eliot to Hollis, 10 Dec. 1767, *MHSC* 4.4:418–421 (1858). Cf. Edmund S. Morgan, "The Puritan Ethic and the American Revolution," *WMQ* 3.24:10 (1967).

"present distressed state of this Town," which was caused by "the excessive use of Forreign Superfluities" and which would soon be aggravated by "the late additional burthens and impositions on the Trade of this Province which threaten the Country with poverty and ruin." The inhabitants decided to discourage the use of certain enumerated imports: luxury goods, wearing apparel, hardware. Frugality and economy were advocated again, and the selectmen were directed to send copies of this agreement to all towns in Massachusetts and to the principal towns of the other colonies. A Connecticut man later stated that the people there had "given more implicit Observance to a Letter from the Select Men of Boston than to their Bibles for some Years." Spinning bees were recorded again; local manufacturers exhibited their products and were "much approved of." By permission of the town, they used the town's poor as their labor force without paying wages. The quick changes of markets and consumption were possible because "homespun and workshop industries expanded and contracted with a minimum displacement of labor and capital." However, their effects were limited because of the comparatively high cost of labor.[25]

The question of nonimportation became the subject of merchants' meetings. More or less formal cooperation among merchants had resulted in the establishment of a "Society for the Encouragement of Trade" in the early sixties. In its seven-year existence it had charged the crown with squandering moneys belonging to the province and had rebuked the General Court for spending too many tax funds to honor the parting governor, Thomas Pownall. It had challenged the legality of writs of assistance (1761) when Pitt ordered the enforcement of the Navigation Acts, and supported enactment of a law that would have wrecked the information system of the customs officials (1762). Measures against the Sugar Act had been passed in 1764, and against provisions of the Stamp Act in 1765. The society concerted judicial steps against a customs collector, and the Malcom affair was a subject of discussion.[26] Active members held a large number of the seats on town committees, elected by town meetings.

In 1767 the nonconsumption resolves came before the Society. In three meetings on 1, 4, and 9 March 1768, the Society decided on a nonimportation agreement for economic as well as political considerations. Reportedly, Daniel Malcom was among the most impatient supporters of this step, though he was not a member of the Society's standing committee. The scarcity of money, aggravated by the outflow caused by the duties, and the unfavorable trade balance were listed as economic reasons, the threat posed by the Townshend Acts to colonials' enjoyment of "many Inestimable Blessings and advantages of the British Constitution" as the political one. The merchants agreed not to import any British goods except certain enumer-

[25]BTR 16:220–225; *BEP*, 2 Nov., 9 Nov. 1767; *BNL*, 5 Nov., 19 Nov. 1767; Rowe, *Letters and Diary*, 28–30 Oct. 1767, pp. 144–145; John Adams, *Diary and Autobiography of John Adams*, ed. Lyman H. Butterfield, 4 vols. (Cambridge, Mass., 1961–1966), 26 June 1770, 1:351; Peter Oliver, *Peter Oliver's Origin and Progress of the American Rebellion: A Tory View,* ed. Douglas Adair and John A. Schutz (Stanford, Calif., 1961), pp. 63–64. Victor S. Clark, *History of Manufactures in the United States,* 3 vols. (rev. ed.; New York, 1929), 1:215–232.

[26]Charles M. Andrews, "The Boston Merchants and the Non-Importation Movement," *CSMP* 19:168ff. (1916–1917); Samuel A. Drake, *History and Antiquities of Boston, from Its Settlement in 1630, to the Year 1770* (Boston, 1856), p. 257; Caleb H. Snow, *A History of Boston* (Boston, 1825), p. 248; *BNL*, 7 Aug. 1760; Quincy, ed., *Reports*, App. 1, pp. 495–499; *Paxton* v. *Gray,* Superior Court of Judicature, Records, 1761, f. 235, SCCH.

ated articles and at the same time to encourage colonial manufacture. Corresponding British merchant houses were to be informed at once, but the agreement was to become binding only when other trade centers in the colonies accepted similar measures. A committee of correspondence was elected to effect this by attempting to concert measures throughout the colonies and by informing the local merchants about steps taken elsewhere. Finally, the agreement was to be voluntary, but to encourage adherence, preferential treatment was to be given to co-signers in intracolonial and intercolonial trade.[27]

The merchants' meetings were usually attended by 50–100 men, and the procedures were limited to recommendations and gentlemen's agreements. It seems that the question of cooperation by nonsubscribers, small inland traders, and the town's shopkeepers was not debated at all. By May, proposals from New York merchants were received. It was voted to concur and not to write for goods after 1 June 1768 and not to receive any shipments after 1 October. This left sufficient time to import large stocks, which could later be sold at high profits when supplies became scarce and prices high. While the merchants were coordinating the oppositional economic measures, the Massachusetts General Court sent out a circular letter to the other colonies, stating the grievances caused by the new acts and suggesting united remonstrances. It seemed as if the anti-Stamp Act measures were to be repeated, with the one important exception of direct action that would again necessitate involvement of the lower classes.

OPPOSITION TO CROWD ACTION

Together with the vote for nonconsumption, the Boston town meeting had voted that only "prudent and legal Measures" should be pursued. A week after the town meeting, on 4 November, Captain Watts arrived from London with "a most unwelcome Cargo," three of the five new customs commissioners. On 5 November the Pope's Day crowds carried their effigies around, "more numerous and Stately" than ever. They lamented the impending ruin of trade and the appointment of new officials: "Liberty and Property and no Commissioners." Passing one of the bonfires, the commissioners received no abuse, however. This did not keep them from complaining to their superiors in Great Britain about insults from the populace.[28]

Remembering the mass attendance at the funeral rites for the Stamp Act almost exactly two years earlier, the selectmen called another town meeting for 20 November to divert people from demonstrations and to reiterate the town's opposition to the duties that would become effective on that day. The selectmen either knew, or anticipated correctly, that the commitment to mere passive resistance was by no means unanimous. Early in the morning, papers were found to have been posted in town, and particularly on Liberty Tree, advocating an armed rising of the

---

[27]Schlesinger, *Colonial Merchants*, pp. 103–131; Bernard to Shelburne, 21 March 1768, Sparks MSS., 10.2:78, HHL; Samuel Ph. Savage Papers, 1702–1829, 8 vols., 2:142–145, MHS.

[28]*BTR* 16:221; Boyle, "Journal," 6 Nov. 1767, p. 253; Loammi Baldwin, Diary, 1767–1768, 5 Nov. 1767, Essex Institute; Harrison to Rockingham, 17 June 1768, 3.20:587 (1963); Bernard to Shelburne, 14 Nov. 1767, Sparks MSS., 4.6:252–253, HHL; Anne Hulton, *Letters of a Loyalist Lady* (Cambridge, Mass., 1927), 17 Dec. 1767, p. 8.

Sons of Liberty. The magistrates were quick to act, and by the time the inhabitants were assembled in Faneuil Hall, they could already vote thanks to the selectmen for suppressing the call to arms. As in the case of the anonymous letters against the sheriff and his deputy in December 1765, the town then condemned the "scandalous and threatning Papers . . . tending to excite Tumults and Disorders" and their unknown author, "some evil minded Person or Persons, Enemies to its peace." By the time that the representative of the British crown, the governor, heard about the threat of an uprising and a forced resignation of the commissioners under Liberty Tree in imitation of Stamp Distributor Oliver's resignation, the Whig law-and-order forces could inform him that measures had already been taken to prevent disturbances. While lower-class Bostonians were prevented from showing their displeasure about the new set of placemen, top crown officials took up the typical crowd complaint against luxury. The commissioners' salaries, and even those of some of their clerks, were "sufficient to support equipages and elegant tables." Hutchinson, as a result, began to lobby for a higher salary for himself. The lower orders opposed luxury; the top officials tried to outdo one another.[29]

The town meeting instructed the representatives "carefully to inspect" every act of Parliament binding on the colonies. "It is without controversy the natural right of every Man, and the constitutional Right of every British Subject solely to dispose of his own property either by himself in Person, or by his Representatives of his own free Election." It was also stressed that the government officials had so far been supported well enough without interference from London and that, in voting the necessary appropriations, the taxpayers and their representatives demanded "the privilege of taking into Consideration our own ability and the merit of their [the officials'] Services."[30]

The most notable feature of the meeting was, however, a speech by James Otis, the moderator. He advocated a reasonable and balanced approach to solve the grievances. The duties and the commissioners were different things, and the latter should not be held responsible for the former. Measures of redress from the burdensome duties should be "proper and legal," "humble and dutiful." Petitions would doubtless achieve a repeal. This argument and the assertion that "access to the throne was always open," of course, were the reverse of the Stamp Act experience. In 1766 there had been in Massachusetts alone three instances of resistance to customs officials, two of them rescue riots. But, Otis now emphasized, the colonials "had from the first, and for a long course of time acknowledged the authority of the custom house officers appointed by the crown." The Board of Commissioners was a great advantage for the trade, he continued, because complaints would no longer have to take the time-consuming course to Great Britain. This was true; there had in fact been demands for a kind of board of appeals in the colonies. The assertion that the board would effect "immediate redress" in case the colonists felt "oppressed by any undue severities of the subordinate officers," however, was as yet unproved. It

---

[29]*BTR* 16:225, *BG,* 16 Nov., 23 Nov. 1767; Council Records, 16:263–264, MSA; Bernard to Shelburne, 21 Nov. 1767, Sparks MSS., 4.6:254–256, HHL; Hutchinson to Bollan, 31 Oct. 1767, Letterbooks, MA 25:209–210, to [Jackson], 14 Feb. 1768, MA 26:288; Bernard Bailyn, *The Ordeal of Thomas Hutchinson* (Cambridge, Mass., 1973), p. 146.
[30]*BTR* 16:226–230; cf. pp. 230–232.

also raised the question of whether only subordinate officers were unduly severe, their superiors inevitably just. Otis was evidently concerned not only with customs officers but with the dangers of revolution. For a period of 15 years, he said, their forefathers had opposed the reign of Charles I merely by prayers to "their God" and petitions to "their king." Only then did they "betake themselves to any forceable measures." The same prudent course, he continued, had been taken during "the revolution which placed King William on the throne." There were "no tumults or disorder and When the whole city of London was in motion, only a single silver spoon was stollen," and at this the Londoners became so angry that the thief was hanged on the spot. The lesson for 1767 was that "let our burthens be ever so heavy, or our grievances ever so great, no possible circumstances, tho' ever so oppressive, could be supposed sufficient to justify private tumults and disorders, either to our consciences before God, or legally before men."[31]

The newspaper reporter present concluded his account by stating that "This speech was much to his honor, and greatly applauded, and is thought would have a very good effect." On whom? is the almost inevitable question. The participants in the Pope's Day activities obviously had escaped the control imposed on them by the Loyal Nine and the merchants who had footed the bill. They were acting again, in union, politicized, but without disorders or damage to property. Nevertheless, there seems to have been uneasiness among the better sort, and an exhortation that all "assist the civil magistrates in preserving peace and good order" was deemed necessary.[32] That there was a split among the inhabitants was evidenced by the "incendiary" papers that had been stuck up overnight. Otis, by his reference to *private* tumults, admitted that there were separate social interests, which in his opinion could not claim to act for the whole. Or did he simply refer to robberies and hidden influences similar to those of the New Plymouth Company in 1765? Neither seems to be the case; robberies had always been punished by normal legal procedures, and the interests of the most important merchants would not be restrained, or even dealt with, in a town meeting. Rather, the hint that some people might think direct action justified by God or by (common) law directs attention to those who had voiced such concepts in 1765–the lower sort, the Pope's Day constituency. It seems, then, that Otis and those who agreed with him were ready to accept British impositions, economic and constitutional, rather than face direct action by the lower classes and its implications for the internal social structure. A mere nine years later, Bostonians from the Southend would tell the imperious Whigs of the Committee of Correspondence that their tyranny was as bad as that of the British.[33]

In 1767 the town remained quiet. Several letters of Bostonians confirm that there were efforts to suppress riots, should any occur. But the old suspicions about placemen were also voiced: "we shall be obliged to maintain a parcel of pitiful sycophants, court parasites, and hungry dependents, in luxury and extravagance." Samuel Waterhouse, who had been accused of hoping to become stamp master in

[31]*BEP*, 23 Nov. 1767; Rowe, *Letters and Diary*, 20 Nov. 1767, p. 146; Bernard to Shelburne, 21 Nov. 1767, Sparks MSS., 4.6:254–256, HHL.
[32]*BEP*, 23 Nov. 1767; *BTR* 16:225.
[33]William Knox to Henry Knox, 24 July 1776, Henry Knox Papers, 1770–1828, 55 vols., reel 2:173, MHS (MF Edition).

Oliver's place in 1765, was now writing articles in support of British policies. To one Bostonian, at least, his intentions were clear. The "Political Water-house Rat" was writing in the "Expectation of Gain by a Post." The call of the *Gazette*, "No Mobs or Tumults," has already been reported. The same paper called the posting of the papers calling for an uprising a "dirty Trick" done "under Cover of the . . . Night." Early in 1768, "Populus," probably Samuel Adams, summed up that "the people have listened with attention" to the *Gazette*, which "has been incessantly calling upon all to be quiet; and patiently to wait for their political salvation—NO MOBBS—NO CONFUSIONS—NO TUMULTS." He then concluded:

> Let this be the language of ALL—We know who have abused us—We owe them Contempt, and we will treat them with it in full measure: But let not the hair of their scalps be touched: The time is coming, when they shall lick the dust and melt away.[34]

Why these incessant calls? Because the situation in town was not as quiet as some or all leaders would have liked it. For a brief period after the acts came into force, little happened besides the nonconsumption drive. The five commissioners were kept socially isolated. Henry Hulton could not rent a house from anybody. Owners of houses feared the resentment of the people. The commissioners began to give entertainments "to wear off the prejudice of the people and to cultivate their Acquaintance," though, as the sister of one of them disconcertedly noted, "there are no fortunes there." Some Bostonians set up a rival "Liberty Assembly," and the commissioners continued to be isolated.[35]

During the symbolic action against the Stamp Act, its provisions had been extended to apply to farmers' goods and building materials. Now, Anne Hulton reported, the "Common people" believed that the commissioners had "unlimited power . . . to tax even their land" and that the revenue would be used to support "a Number of Bishops." Accordingly, there was "an enthusiastic Rage for defending their Religion and liberties." As to merchants, their interests were no longer served by law-abiding payment of duties, as advocated in the town meeting, and their discontent began to mount. After customs officials had effected a seizure in February 1768, William Molineux, a petty merchant who was politically very active, abused them publicly and accused them of acting from profit motives rather than from intent to enforce laws. A few days later Daniel Malcom appeared in the customs house and explained that he expected a ship carrying wine and wanted to

[34]Eliot to Hollis, 10 Dec. 1767, *MHSC* 4.4:419–420 (1858); Joshua Henshaw, Jr., to William Henshaw, 10 Dec. 1767, *NEHGR* 23:451–452 (1869); Bernard to Barrington, 4 March 1768, *Barrington–Bernard Correspondence*, ed. Edward Channing and Archibald C. Coolidge (Cambridge, Mass., 1912), p. 149; Harrison to Rockingham, 17 June 1768, *WMQ* 3.20:588 (1963); Thomas Cushing to Stephen Sayer, 21 Dec. 1767, John Davis Papers, 3 vol., 3:30 (partly mutilated), MHS; *BG*, 9 Nov., 16 Nov., 23 Nov., 1767; "Populus," in *BG*, 14 March 1768.

[35]Anne Hulton, *Letters*, 15 Feb. 1768, 10 April 1769, pp. 9–10, 17–19; Henry Hulton, Letterbooks, 1:5–9, HHL; Henry Hulton, Some Account of the Proceedings of the People of New England from the Establishment of a Board of Customs in America to the Breaking Out of the Rebellion in 1775, p. 94, Princeton Univ. Library, Princeton, N.J.; *Am. Gaz.* (London), 10 Dec., 23 Dec. 1768, quoted in William Tudor, *The Life of James Otis of Massachusetts: Containing Also Notices of Some Contemporary Characters and Events from the Year 1760 to 1775* (Boston, 1823), p. 339n.

discuss what "indulgence" he might expect concerning the duties. When no deal could be made, his schooner, *Friendship,* was unloaded at night. About 60 pipes of wine were carried to different hiding places, each load guarded by about 35 "stout fellows" armed with clubs. The whole affair was done with so much noise that it was public knowledge, but nobody dared interfere, not even when the captain finally appeared at the customs office and swore that he had come in ballast.[36]

The commissioners did not improve their position when they openly showed their personal thoughts about town meetings and representative government. Charles Paxton, who had escaped the Stamp Act crowds and was now back as commissioner, complained that government was "quite ineffectual and impotent." It was "as much in the hands of the people as it was in the time of the Stamp Act, and there is still not one single soldier within 250 Miles of Boston nor a Ship of War in any part of the Province." Together with his colleagues, he lamented that at town meetings "mechanics discuss upon the most important points of government." They then dismissed Timothy Folger, customs searcher at Nantucket and friendly to mercantile interests, from his office. As representative in the legislature, he had voted for a resolve "encouraging Industry and suppressing Vice," a nonconsumption declaration. Dismissing someone for voting to suppress vice as unfit for the customs service was indeed a way to raise whatever prejudices there were to higher levels.[37]

Rumors about riots against the commissioners began to spread. By February, Paxton had been burned in effigy, and his house had been surrounded by about 100 boys. The same group, with drums and horns, paraded through town and yelled at the town house, where the governor was holding council. Another group, about half the number, crowded around the house of Commissioner William Burch. After a merchants' meeting a "small mob with a drum" roamed the streets. The houses of several board members were beset, but no violence against persons or property ensued. Inspector General William Wooton was threatened with violence. The newspapers during this time reported on the Wilkes riots in Great Britain.[38]

[36]Anne Hulton, *Letters,* 30 June 1768, p. 13. Molineux: Rowe, *Letters and Diary,* 11 Feb. 1768, pp. 150–151. Malcom: Thomas Hutchinson, *The History of the Colony and Province of Massachusetts Bay,* ed. Lawrence Shaw Mayo, 3 vols. (Cambridge, Mass., 1936), 3:136; Bernard to Barrington, 4 March 1768, *Barrington–Bernard Correspondence,* pp. 147–150; Bernard to Shelburne, 21 March 1768, Sparks MSS., 10.2:78, HHL; Harrison to Rockingham, 17 June 1768, *WMQ* 3.20:588 (1963); *Mass. Gaz.,* 24 Nov. 1768.

[37]Paxton to Townshend, 24 Feb. 1768, *MHSP* 56:348–349 (1922–1923); Commissioners of Customs to Lords of the Treasury, 12 Feb. 1768, *MHSP* 55:265 (1921–1922); Hutchinson to Pownall, n.d., Letterbooks, MA 26:417–419; *BG,* 14 March, 11 April 1768. For an extensive account of Folger's case and other reasons for his dismissal, see *Folger* v. *Sloop* Cornelia, case 45, editors' note, in John Adams, *Legal Papers,* 2:147–157. George G. Wolkins, "The Boston Customs District in 1768," *MHSP* 58:433–435 (1924–1925).

[38]Paxton was disliked more than the other commissioners because he was a native of Massachusetts who had turned against—"betrayed"—his fellow colonials and because he constantly suggested the creation of new salaried offices to his protector, Lord Townshend, to which he could be appointed. In September 1769 he attempted to obstruct justice. John Adams, *Diary,* 6 Sept. 1769, 1:343–344; Paxton to Townshend, 24 Feb. 1768, *MHSP* 56:348–349 (1922–1923); Harrison to Rockingham, 17 June 1768, *WMQ* 3.20:589 (1963); Bernard to Shelburne, 19 March, 21 March 1768, Sparks MSS., 10.2:74, 78, HHL; Bernard to Barrington, 4 March 1768, *Barrington–Bernard Correspondence,* p. 148; Commissioners of Customs to Lords of the Treasury, 28 March 1768, *MHSP* 55:268–271 (1921–1922); affidavit of William Wooton, House of Lords MSS., 252:115; Pauline Maier, "John Wilkes and American Disillusionment with Britain," *WMQ* 3.20:373–396 (1963).

When 18 March, the anniversary of the Stamp Act repeal, drew near, the commissioners had information that on this day "of Triumph over Great Britain" they would be forced to resign under Liberty Tree. In good tradition the day began with the discovery of two effigies. Commissioner Paxton and Inspector General Williams were hanging from the branches of the elm. But here the similarity to 1765 ended. Law and order was still the watchword. Enraged at this spontaneous action of men whom they had considered their wards, three members of the Loyal Nine took down the "ragged images" before selectmen and councillors could even assemble. The council then voted that the effigies had been put up "by some insignificant people," a designation that probably reflected not only the desire to play down the importance of the incident but also the actual attitude of the councillors toward those who had prepared the effigies. The *Gazette,* a radical, rabble-rousing paper according to many historians, simply blamed "this piece of Buffoonry" on those crown officials who needed "mobs and riots" for "their next letters to their Masters" in Great Britain.[39]

While councillors and *Gazette* writers were attempting to create the impression that nothing did happen, the selectmen were facing a celebration that was definitely exuberant. The town reverberated with the sound of guns, the beating of drums, and the ringing of bells. Colors were flying, and numerous toasts were drunk, one of the latter a new variation on the placeman theme: "Halters for Parasites."[40] Unimpressed, the selectmen grimly pursued their course, trying to find out who had fixed a staff with flags to the town pump, "as it would have a tendency to Colect a Number of people together at Night." Their connections with the crowd were at least better than those of Hutchinson's friends on 26 August 1765. When suspicion fell on 23-year-old Loammi Baldwin, who had been active in the Stamp Act crowds too, it did not hit an innocent inhabitant. When the constable arrived at Baldwin's quarters with a rather direct suggestion to take the staff down, Baldwin held a council with four friends. They disagreed with the selectmen about the dangers inherent in a flagstaff and decided to let it stand. Neither constables nor selectmen had sufficient authority left to take the staff down themselves, but they were not yet ready to concede defeat. Loammi Baldwin was called into the selectmen's meeting. He opened the interview with the defiant statement that he was a stranger—his family lived in Woburn—and that he was not the head of the group that had raised the staff. He concluded by voicing the suspicion that the selectmen wanted to blame the affair on him because he was from out of town. Except for a suggestion from the selectmen to take the staff down, the interview ended with Loammi's statement. When he went back to his friends, they voted the suggestion down.[41]

---

[39]Commissioners of Customs to Lords of the Treasury, 28 March 1768, *MHSP* 55:268–271 (1921–1922); Bernard to Shelburne, 19 March 1768, Sparks MSS., 10.2:74, HHL; Hutchinson to Jackson, 23 March 1768, Letterbooks, MA 26:295–296; Rowe, *Letters and Diary,* 18 March 1768, pp. 156–157; Hutchinson, *History,* 3:136; "M. Y." (signature of the Loyal Nine), in *BG,* 21 March 1768. John Avery, Thomas Crafts, and William Speakman had cut the effigies down. Council Records, 16:298–300, MSA.

[40]*BG,* 21 March 1768.

[41]Baldwin, Diary, 18 March 1768, Essex Institute. The selectmen's minutes, as often happened when matters became crucial, do not even contain a note that the meeting was held.

From among the higher circles 50 gentlemen assembled in the British Coffee House for an elegant dinner. Rather cheerful after many toasts, the gentlemen nevertheless decided to use their influence to prevent any kind of disorder. Outside the tavern and all over town, the people set off rockets and fireworks, and the worthy diners stepped out into "prodigious Noises and throng[s] of people." The gentlemen found that their influence did not reach very far, as did those Sons of Liberty who had pledged "there should be no riots." Eight hundred people assembled in King Street, and almost like militia companies, with "Drums beating, and Colours flying," they paraded through the town, with special salutes at the houses of governor and commissioners. Contrary to earlier reports, they did not harm William Wooton, inspector general for the customs, but they went to the house of John Williams in the Northend, whose effigy had been hung in the morning. Williams, together with his neighbors, suceeded in dispersing the crowd and suddenly found that "the greatest part of the Gentlemen in Town" were rather grateful to him, the customs official.[42]

While the Sons of Liberty, selectmen, and gentlemen had been unsuccessful in trying to prevent any assemblies, they successfully controlled the reporting about those who had assembled. The "great number of people of all kinds, sexes and ages" (Governor Bernard) became "a few disorderly persons mostly boys" (Samuel Adams) or "sailors and apprentices" (*Newsletter*). The *Gazette* topped this kind of news by reporting that there was *no* apprehension of "mob" action and that a number of gentlemen "unanimously agreed to use their influence" for preventing it.[43] Basically, the evaluation of the councillors was correct. They stated that the frolics were "trivial, and could not have been noticed to the disadvantage of the Town, but by persons inimical to it: especially as it happened in the Evening of a day of recreation." Lieutenant Governor Hutchinson concurred, and the governor merely added that the evening's crowd had produced some "terror" but no "actual mischief." The commissioners, however, thought the situation far more serious. They spoke about an "Attack" of "the Mob" on Williams and demanded protection by British troops. They were to succeed in their calls for assistance. In June the secretary of state of the colonies, Earl of Hillsborough, received the news of the March "disorders" and instructed General Gage to send two regiments to Boston. But June was far away, and the actual arrival of the troops even farther. Before then many incidents happened, finally inducing the ministry to double the number of regiments sent to Boston[44] and inducing Bostonians explicitly to reject Otis's plea for submission and humble petitions as the only means of protest.

[42]*BG*, 21 March 1768; Rowe, *Letters and Diary*, 18 March 1768, pp. 156–157; Baldwin, Diary, 18 March 1768; Essex Institute; Hutchinson to Jackson, 23 March 1768, Letterbooks, MA 26:295–296; Commissioners of Customs to Lords of the Treasury, 28 March 1768, *MHSP* 55:268–271.

[43]*BG*, 21 March 1768; *BNL*, 24 March 1768; Bernard to Shelburne, 19 March 1768, Sparks MSS., 10.2:74, HHL; Convention of Massachusetts Towns to Dennys de Berdt, 27 Sept. 1768, in Samuel Adams, *Writings*, 1:241–247.

[44]Councillors' address to General Gage, 27 Oct. 1768, Gay Transcripts, State Papers, 12 vols., 11:119, MHS; Hutchinson to Jackson, 23 March 1768, Letterbooks, MA 26:295–296; Bernard to Shelburne, 19 March 1768, Sparks MSS., 10.2:75, HHL; Commissioners of Customs to Lords of the Treasury, 28 March 1768, *MHSP* 55:268–277 (1921–1922); Paxton to Townshend, 24 Feb. 1768, *MHSP* 56:348–349 (1922–1923); Hillsborough to Bernard, 11 June 1768, Sparks MSS., 4.11:187–193, HHL; Henry Hulton, Account, pp. 111–118.

On 17 June, less than seven months after his speech, Otis presided over a town meeting in which he and the other three Boston representatives were told that the customs commissioners did not arrange redress when subaltern officers acted oppressively. The "multitude of Placemen and Pensioners, and an enormous train of Underlings and Dependants, . . . we have seen already: Their injurious temper, their rash inconsiderate and weak behavior, are well known." And instead of improving, the situation was getting worse:

> We have the mortification to observe one Act of Parliament after another, passed for the express purpose of raising a Revenue from us; to see our money continually collecting from us, without our consent, by an authority in the constitution of which we have no share, and over Which we have no kind of influence or control; to see the little circulating cash that remained among us for the support of our trade, from time to time transmitted to a distant Country [Great Britain], never to return, or what in our estimation is worse if possible, appropriated to the maintainance of swarms of Officers and Pensioners in idleness and luxury, whose example has a tendency to corrupt our morals, and whose arbitrary disposition will trample upon our rights.

While the inhabitants were "Waiting with anxious expectation for a favourable answer to the Petitions and sollicitations of this Continent for Relief," the commissioners had called a ship of war "with design to over awe and terrify the Inhabitants of this Town into base compliances, and unlimited submission." With "Officers and Pensioners to suck the life blood of the body politick," with "still severer restraints upon our trade," there had to be an end to "passive obedience."[45]

45.*BTR* 16:257–259.

PART II

From Merchants to Crowds: Resistance from 1768 to 1770

In the following four chapters we will mainly be concerned with the attempts of the British government to enforce the new trade regulations, to make enforcement more efficient, and to collect the newly imposed duties. On the side of the colonists, this meant an extension of resistance, first against external taxation, then against quartering of troops, a "standing army," in Boston.

Relations between customs officials and merchants had never been very cordial. But the ineffectiveness of the imperial customs service meant that little real friction occurred. Smuggling was widespread, and the few local officers could usually be bribed without much difficulty. They were often deputies for better-paid favorites of influential ministers in Great Britain who never left there. All this changed rather abruptly when customs officials were ordered to reside at their places of duty, when navy officers were deputized as customs officials, when a crackdown on petty smuggling, a popular pastime for low-paid sailors, was ordered, and when duties were increased and remedies against unreasonable seizures decreased.

From some points of view, nonimportation seemed the ideal solution. It erased causes for friction and thus possible violence. It stopped the drain of money from the colonies to British merchants. It helped overstocked merchants to get rid of their inventories and at the same time put out of business all those small-scale traders who in recent years had begun to import for themselves and, aided by the extension of British credit, had become considerable competition for the large importing houses. On the other hand, the nonimportation agreements resulted in suffering for small shopkeepers, unemployment for artisans and laborers, a split among the large merchants, and, in the later stages, increasing distrust by the country people of Boston's merchants. There were also suspicions that the whole nonimportation plan had been cooked up by overstocked merchants. These suspicions increased when, with growing scarcity, those who still had imported goods to sell began to mark up their wares considerably. Moreover, there were a number of large merchants who opposed the plan for political reasons or because they felt it was simply a scheme to drive them out of business. Finally, in a kind of involuntary counterboycott, British merchants stopped ordering new ships or having old ones repaired, since they used to pay for this work by their exports.

I will argue in this part that the strict enforcement of the trade laws, the increased number of seizures effected by customs officials, led to increased friction with colonists along the seaboard, and soon to rescue riots or violence against customs officials. The "No Mobs" policy was shelved because the crowds were needed to oppose the customs officers. In addition, the harassment of customs officials brought troops to Boston for their protection. The leadership reneged on the oppositional rhetoric when the merchants preferred to do business with the army. Mechanics, on the other hand, felt the additional burden of increased labor competition. Soldiers were allowed to work for wages in their off-duty hours. Finally, with soldiers present, the merchant supporters of British policies felt safer to continue to import.

As a result, crowd action moved to the forefront of resistance again. Merchants needed crowds for rescue riots when their goods had been seized or for intimidation to prevent seizures. The crowds came mainly from the waterfront community—sailors, dock workers, perhaps artisans from the shipbuilding and outfitting trades—but were joined by one middle-class group, the merchant–captains who had a smaller operational margin and were therefore most vulnerable to seizures by customs officials. Merchants also needed crowds to force the nonimportation agreements on opponents. They did not rely on the mechanics from Boston's poorest quarters, as they had during the Stamp Act period, but on school-boys, country people, and probably shopkeepers. For a variety of reasons, this crowd composition made for fewer internal restraints but easier external control. The Loyalist importers thus became targets for action ranging from picketing to terrorizing. A crisis developed at the end of 1769, when the original agreements terminated.

At the same time, lower-class suffering reached a high, and mechanics' opposition to the troops increased. Here again we find—in my opinion—the customary forms of crowd action: crowds forcing magistrates to make soldiers conform to the law, crowds attacking soldiers who in their opinion had trespassed on their rights, and, finally—in consequence of an incident concerning labor competition—the King Street riot, commonly called the Boston Massacre. These antisoldier crowds were again, as in the Stamp Act period, one class rather than many, they acted spontaneously and were self-led, and they forced the leadership to sanction *ex post facto* their achievements.

By March 1770, crowds had driven the troops out of town and forced the leaders to provide employment. By the middle of the year, the merchants had "deserted" the "cause" and were importing again. With these two developments the second period of resistance came to an end.

Local Grievances and Imperial Issues [5]

CUSTOMS OFFICIALS, IMPRESSMENT, AND THE CROWD

By spring 1768, a number of merchants were no longer willing to accept the enforcement of the customs and trade laws. John Hancock, one of the most important Massachusetts merchants and a representative, repeatedly stated in the House of Representatives that he would not allow any customs officers on board his ships. Merchant–captain Daniel Malcom, one of a group of substantial but not large traders, had defied the customs officers in February. John Oakes, master of a lighter and engaged merely in coastal trade, was to do so in April 1768. In each case, sailors and dock workers were involved in the opposition. They not only supported their employers, but had definite grievances of their own. The actions of customs officers and their deputies threatened not only the job security of these men but also their daily work and their persons. When, on 8 April, John Hancock's ship *Lydia,* captained by James Scott, arrived, one of his workers who went down to the wharf to unload the ship later noted in his diary, "meet with some difficult about getting them [the goods] out on account of the Commissioners." Two tidesmen, minor customs officials, had boarded the *Lydia.* Instead of staying on deck, as was the law, they were down in the steerage. The workers had to call on Hancock to come down himself. They were glad when, as they said, "[he] Resolutely ordered them" to get back on deck, and his workers manhandled them up there. From the wharf came a shout, "Damn them throw them overboard." Hancock's stand "pleased the people much"; they escorted him back to town, and he had "to intreat them not to huzza him through the town."[1]

A week later John Oakes's lighter passed the H.M.S. *Hope,* commanded by

[1]Hutchinson to [Rogers], 17–18 April 1768, Letterbooks, MA 26:299–300; Bernard to Barrington, 4 March 1768, *Barrington–Bernard Correspondence,* ed. Edward Channing and Archibald C. Coolidge (Cambridge, Mass., 1912), p. 148; Commissioners to Lords of the Treasury, 28 March 1768, *MHSP* 55:268–271 (1921–2911). *Lydia* incident: Loammi Baldwin, Diary, 8 April 1768, Essex Institute; Treasury Papers, 1/465, ff. 348, 351–352, 354–358, 1/466, f. 275, 1/468, ff. 164–166, PRO; Herbert S. Allan, *John Hancock, Patriot in Purple* (New York, 1948), pp. 102–104; Oliver M. Dickerson, ed., "Opinion of Attorney General Jonathan Sewall of Massachusetts in the Case of the *Lydia,*" *WMQ* 3.4:499–504 (1947).

George Dawson, who was a deputized customs officer. Dawson sent a crew of mariners to search the lighter for contraband goods. The harassment of local shipping was a constant source of irritation to captains, sailors, and senders and consignees of the shipped goods, many of whom claimed that the customs laws did not apply to coastal trade. John Oakes and his three-man crew warned the mariners, according to depositions by the latter, to keep off or he would "blow our brains out with a Musquett." Captain Dawson thereupon armed his men, seized the lighter, and detained Oakes and his three men over the weekend under the pretense that he could not spare a boat to send them ashore. Oakes, once ashore, sued Dawson for £300 damages and had the sheriff arrest the British official. The latter in turn brought action against the lighter and its cargo of molasses. The judge of vice admiralty, crowd target in August 1765, restored the lighter but sustained the reasonableness of the seizure.[2] Reports of such incidents spread quickly along the coast. An incensed Boston town meeting ordered the selectmen to see to it that customs officials were excluded from the annual election day dinner given by governor and council. Piqued, the governor and councillors protested but were simply refused their customary banquet room in Faneuil Hall.[3] With feelings already high against the conduct of customs officers, the situation became worse when the Royal Navy came on the scene.

On 17 May the H.M.S. *Romney* cast anchor in Boston harbor. Since the *Romney* was short of sailors, as was almost every navy ship, Captain Corner planned to get additional men by impressment. On a Lord's Day, 5 June, he sent out a press gang. Immediately sailors on the endangered ships got into their boats to escape to the shore. The afternoon was sunny and warm, and large numbers of people were promenading along the waterfront and on the wharves. When the hotly pursued sailors landed, the people made way for them. Curses of the press-gang officers were answered by volleys of stones and brickbats. The navy boats were prevented from landing, and for this day their purpose was thwarted. Crown officials, as usual, blamed the incident on the mobbish temper of the town. That this disturbance was merely a reaction to the impressment is attested by the character of the numerous days of public celebration that fell during these two weeks. The town was quiet on 25 May, election day, on 4 June, the king's birthday, and on 6 June, Artillery Election Day. Captain Corner, however, continued to provoke the waterfront community. A sailor was impressed from an outgoing vessel. This procedure was illegal and created particular resentment, since insufficient numbers of sailors on a seagoing vessel meant increased danger to the rest of the men. Then a man was impressed from another vessel. He in turn, paid another man to go in his place, releasing himself from forced duty. Contrary to custom, Captain Corner refused to accept the other man. As yet, no town officials had interposed, and on 9 June another crowd rescued a sailor from the impressment gang. While sailors and others en-

[2]*Dawson* v. Dolphin, case 51, in John Adams, *Legal Papers of John Adams,* ed. L. Kinvin Wroth and Hiller B. Zobel, 3 vols. (Cambridge, Mass., 1965), 2:223–237; SCF 101809; Treasury Papers, 1/465, f. 256, PRO, LC transcripts.
[3]*BTR* 16:250—a conciliatory motion to reconsider was rejected "almost unanimously," p. 253; *BTR* 20:292; Council Records, 16:310, MSA.

dangered by impressment could gain no redress from officials, Captain Corner got a special committee of the council appointed immediately after some officers complained about having been abused by townsmen.[4]

Meanwhile the customs officers were brooding over the customs declaration of Hancock's sloop *Liberty*. On 10 May, the day after the sloop arrived, its master, Nathaniel Barnard, had paid duties for a mere 25 pipes of wine. Hancock had again been heard boasting that he would land cargo without paying duties, and it was common gossip in town that the sloop had had a larger quantity of wine on board. The two tidesmen who had guarded the vessel swore, however, that no illegal measures had been taken to land any undutied cargo. Hancock meanwhile used the *Liberty* for storage. This was unlawful, since a permit to load was technically required, but the practice was common and had always been tolerated. As to the wine, the officials were helpless. They lacked evidence—until one of the two tidesmen decided to change his oath. Thomas Kirk now declared that after he had boarded the vessel on 9 May, one of the merchant-seamen, Captain Marshall, had come on board in the evening and tried to bribe him. "I peremptorily refused; upon which Capt. Marshall took hold of me, and with the Assistance of five or six other Persons unknown to this Declarent, they forcibly hove me down the Companion into the Cabin, and nailed the cover down." After three hours, during which in Kirk's opinion "many People" were hoisting out goods, Captain Marshall came down, set him free, and told him that if he informed about "this Frolick" his property would be destroyed and his life endangered. However, Marshall died soon afterward, and Kirk now thought it safe to file his deposition under oath with Collector Harrison.[5]

The official immediately went to check with the second tidesman but got no answer. The man, drunk, had gone home to sleep on the crucial day. Whether Kirk's deposition was true cannot be ascertained. Dickerson, in his study of the methods of the customs officers, contended that it was a device to engross, to put Hancock in his place, to punish him for his political stand and for his insults to the commissioners.[6] At any rate, the latter decided to have the vessel seized. Considering "that the Populace at Boston, had long before this shewn a great Disaffection to the Revenue Laws," they further directed that the sloop be removed from Han-

[4]Hiller B. Zobel, *The Boston Massacre* (New York, 1970), pp. 73–74; *BEP,* 20 June 1768; *BG,* 20 June 1768; Council Records, 16:313, MSA.

[5]George G. Wolkins, "The Seizure of John Hancock's Sloop *Liberty,*" *MHSP* 55:239–284 (1921–1922); D. H. Watson, ed., "Joseph Harrison and the *Liberty* Incident," *WMQ* 3.20:589 (1963) (hereafter cited as Harrison to Rockingham, 17 June 1768); *Sewall* v. *Hancock,* case 46, in John Adams, *Legal Papers,* 2:173–210; Hutchinson to Jackson, 16 June 1768, *MHSP* 55:281–284; deposition of Thomas Kirk, 10 June 1768, in *Letters to the Ministry from Governor Bernard, General Gage, and Commodore Hood, and Also Memorials to the Lords of the Treasury, from the Commissioners of the Customs* (Boston, 1769), pp. 90–91. Peter Oliver, *Peter Oliver's Origin and Progress of the American Rebellion: A Tory View,* ed. Douglass Adair and John A. Schutz (Stanford, Calif., 1961), p. 69; Henry Hulton, Some Account of the Proceedings of the People of New England from the Establishment of a Board of Customs in America to the Breaking Out of the Rebellion in 1775, p. 127, Princeton Univ. Library, Princeton, N.J.; John Mein, Key to a Certain Publication, Sparks MSS., 10.3:45–47, HHL.

[6]Oliver M. Dickerson, *The Navigation Acts and the American Revolution* (Philadelphia, 1951), pp. 231–250; Hancock to Hill, Lamar & Bissett, 20 Jan. 1767 [1768], *MHSP* 55:262–263; Joshua Henshaw to William Henshaw, 15 June 1768, *J. Am. Hist.* 18:245–247 (1924).

cock's wharf near the Northend with the help of the sailors from the warships and be moored directly under the guns of the *Romney*. The officials who received these orders were well aware of the "utmost Risque and Danger" they were to incur. What actually happened was noncommittally described as "some Commotions" by the writers of the *Gazette,* who continued their policy of playing down any direct action.[7]

Between 6 and 7 P.M. on 10 June, Harrison and Hallowell seized the sloop by painting the king's broad arrow on the main mast. This stirred interest. Harrison saw that "the People began to muster together on the Wharf, from all Quarters," at the same time that the boats from the *Romney* were coming. Among the crowd were merchant seamen, Captains Matchet, Malcom, and Hopkins, and sailors, who, remembering the previous days' impressments, "were suspicious of an Intention to put them on board the Ship." Benjamin Goodwin came to watch because—as he explained a few days later—a seizure after sunset was something extraordinary, and he wanted to know what was going to happen. (Warrants were valid only from sunrise to sunset.) When the *Liberty* was delivered to an officer of the *Romney,* the crowd, numbering 300–400, became active. Threats and insults gave way to rough treatment of the officials and to an attempt to get on board before the *Liberty* could be towed off. The navy men, seeing the danger, cut the ropes and got the ship clear before they could be overpowered. While Captain Corner sent two more boats, the men on the wharf tried "every Means in their Power" to prevent the seizure but finally could only cover the officers and men in the boats with abuse mingled with stones. The customs officials got off "without any Insult or Molestation" because the people were so "eagerly engaged" in the scuffle, but they were soon pursued. Hallowell was accosted "by a numerous mob," using rather foul language and throwing first dirt and then stones and bricks at him and his son. He received several blows, one on the back of his head, and "verily" believed "that if some friendly People had not interposed . . . he should have been murthered in the Street." Harrison and his son met a similar fate.[8]

While the "friendly people" succeeded in helping Hallowell, two crowds assembled: "Several principle Gentlemen of the Town" to discountenance violence; and about 2000 others, "chiefly sturdy boys," to vent their resentment about impressment, about the behavior of customs and navy officials, and about the consequences, "a Prospect of the Trade and Business of this and other Towns being in a Manner ruined," which meant rising unemployment or underemployment and

[7]Case of the *Liberty, MHSP* 55:273–276 (1921–1922); Harrison to Rockingham, 17 June 1768, *WMQ* 3.20:589–590 (1963); *BG,* 13 June 1768.

[8]Depositions of Benjamin Hallowell, Joseph Harrison, Richard Acklom Harrison, *Letters to the Ministry,* pp. 91–93; further depositions in House of Lords MSS., 252:288–312; sunset was at 7:33 P.M., John Adams, *Legal Papers,* 2:175, note 8; *BEP,* 20 June 1768; John Rowe, *Letters and Diary of John Rowe, Boston Merchant, 1759–1762, 1764–1779,* ed. Anne Rowe Cunningham (Boston, 1903; reprint ed., 1969), 10 June 1768, p. 165; Samuel Mather to his son, 8 Sept. 1768, Letterbook, MHS; Gage to Hillsborough, 28 June 1768, *The Correspondence of General Thomas Gage,* ed. Clarence E. Carter, 2 vols. (New Haven, Conn., 1931, 1933), 1:182–183, cf. 2:488; Bernard to Barrington, 18 June 1768, *Barrington–Bernard Correspondence,* pp. 160–161; Palfrey to William Holt, 13 June 1768, in John G. Palfrey, *History of New England,* 5 vols. (Boston, 1876–1905), 5:387; William Gordon, *The History of the Rise, Progress, and Establishment of the Independence of the United States of America,* 4 vols. (London, 1788), 1:231–233.

higher prices. The crowd of gentlemen went to the houses of customs officials to protect them; the other townsmen searched for the offending officers. First they looked for officers of the man-of-war at their meeting place, the Coffee House, but found none. Then they decided to visit customs officials Hallowell, Harrison, and Williams. On their way they came across Customs Inspector Irving, "who used some harsh language . . . upon which they seized [him] and made him repent of his expression" until two "meanly dressed" men from among the crowd took pity on him and prevented further violence. At Hallowell's house the crowd demanded "satisfaction" but was told that Hallowell was not there. At Harrison's lodgings influential gentlemen, the owner of the house, and Mrs. Harrison argued with the crowd. Harrison was not there, nor was the house his property. At Williams's place, the same story: Mrs. Williams told them that her husband was out of town, and the rioters left. In all three cases some windows were broken, however. Returning to the wharf, the crowd then searched for boats from the man-of-war. Finding none, they took a "particular and elegant" pleasure boat belonging to Harrison, pulled it ashore, and dragged it to Liberty Tree. There the crowd held a mock Vice Admiralty Court, condemned the seizure, and then proceeded to the common and burned it. At this point a man with wig and hat was suspected of attempting to identify the rioters. He was forcibly deprived of these two attributes of status and "kicked out of the Common." The crowd, asked by "some Gentlemen" to disperse, debated the proposal, voted on it, and left about 1 A.M. Somebody, in a concluding speech, shouted, "We will defend our Liberties and property, by the Strength of our Arms and the help of our God; to your Tents O Israel."[9]

The reactions of officials and other leading inhabitants varied widely. Some of their measures would have far-reaching consequences, while others would have little impact beyond indicating the mentality of the leaders. Governor Bernard, probably over a glass of good wine, mused about how lucky it had been that the rioters did not procure large quantities of liquor, or the "fury" would have been worse. However, if the rioters had wanted liquor, there would have been no difficulty in procuring it. Most officials had well-stocked wine cellars, and in Hallowell's house people knew their way around. On the other side, William Molineux, vociferous Whig and less judicial in some of his means than crowds, wrote a letter to his friends the customs officials. He was sorry that Hallowell had incurred the displeasure of the people and expressed regret that Harrison's boat had been burned in the "Frensey" of the night. But—among friends—"Such Sort of People Inhabit Every Great City Perhaps in the World." However, he seems to have had some inkling that "such people" knew how to choose their target, since he asked Harri-

[9]*BG*, 20 June 1768; *BEP*, 20 June 1768; Hutchinson to Jackson, 16 Oct. 1768, *MHSP* 55:281–284; Bernard to Hillsborough, 11–18 June 1768, Sparks MSS., 4.6:311–324, HHL; deposition of Thomas Irving, *Letters to the Ministry*, pp. 93–94; John Boyle, "Boyle's Journal of Occurrences in Boston, 1759–1778," 10 June 1768, *NEHGR* 84:255 (1930); "An Appeal to the World . . . ," 4 Oct. 1760, in Samuel Adams, *The Writings of Samuel Adams*, ed. Harry A. Cushing, 4 vols. (New York, 1904–1908), 1:396–445; William V. Wells, *The Life and Public Services of Samuel Adams*, 3 vols. (Boston, 1865, 1888), 1:187; Joshua Henshaw to William Henshaw, 15 June 1768, *J. Am. Hist.* 18:245–247 (1924); Anne Hutton, *Letters of a Loyalist Lady* (Cambridge, Mass., 1927), 30 June 1768, pp. 11–14; Harrison to Rockingham, 17 June 1768, *WMQ* 3.20:591 (1963).

son to keep his letter secret. As to the customs commissioners, they seem to have had clear opinions at best inside the walls of their meeting room. Once outside, confronted with the reality of opposition and potential as well as real direct action, they flinched. In this case they spread a rumor among the ropewalk mechanics that collector and comptroller had effected the seizure on their own authority and against the instructions of the board.[10]

The top customs officials expected more rioting. The crowd certainly had not reached its objectives, satisfaction from the officials and punishment of the navy officers. They, with numerous clerks and underofficers, often family members in need of employment, fled to the *Romney,* a move they were to repeat in March 1770 and again in December 1773. Harrison, when he was able to walk again, followed early one morning, before anybody else was up. Altogether, the *Romney's* captain had to deal with a sudden invasion of 67 persons. Later they moved to Castle William. To make the ostracism complete, several persons who visited them were threatened with having their houses pulled down.[11] As to measures against rioting, the councillors answered Bernard's questions by saying "that they did not desire to be knocked on the Head." Applications to the Boston justices of the peace would be of no use, the crown officials thought, because they either favored the riot or were afraid of crowd action if they issued warrants for apprehending rioters. The sheriff, finally, would need the posse for any effective countermeasures, and the men necessary for that were again rioters or their sympathizers. While nothing could be accomplished in this respect, both houses of the General Court joined to denounce the customs officers for provoking the riot. They had acted "in a manner unprecedented" by effecting the seizure "a little before sunset." Worse, there had been a "preconcerted plan" with the navy's officers. This last "conspiracy charge" was usually leveled by crown officials against magistrates conniving at anti-British direct action.[12]

The legal aftermath turned out to be a fiasco for the prosecution. The council had directed the attorney general to recommend indictment of the rioters to a grand jury. This he did, but no witnesses could be found. The matter subsided.[13] The litigation about the seizure took more time to settle. First Hancock proposed a compromise to Harrison, offering bond if the vessel would be returned to him until a verdict could be obtained in the courts. Joseph Warren, one of the most prominent Sons of Liberty, functioned as go-between for the merchant and the customs officials. Harrison and Hallowell, realizing their own weak position, agreed to return the *Liberty.* However, over the weekend, leading men of the caliber of James Otis and Samuel Adams held council with Hancock and Warren, and in consequence the

[10]Bernard to Shelburne, 11 June 1768, Colonial Office 5/766, quoted in Zobel, *Massacre,* p. 76; ――― to John Powell, 13 June 1768, Sparks MSS., 10.3:2, HHL; Molineux to Harrison, 15 June 1768, *ibid.,* p. 1.

[11]*BG,* 20 June 1768; Harrison to Rockingham, 17 June 1768, *WMQ* 3.20:592 (1963); Anne Hulton, *Letters,* 30 June 1768, 10 April 1769, pp. 11–14, 17–19; Zobel, *Massacre,* p. 76. For the return of the commissioners to the town, see Council Records, 16:360, MSA; *BNL,* 10 Nov. 1768; Bernard *et al.* to Commissioners, 22 Dec. 1768, *MHSP* 55:279–280 (1921–1922).

[12]Bernard to Hillsborough, 11–18 June 1768, Sparks MSS., 4.6:311–324, HHL; Council Records, 16:319–320, 333–345, MSA; Hutchinson to Jackson, 16 June 1768, *MHSP* 55:282–283 (1921–22).

[13]Bernard to Hillsborough, 12 Dec. 1768, Sparks MSS., 10.3:3, HHL.

agreement was called off. They "did not choose to let go their Hold of an affair so well adapted to keep up the Ferment." In the suit the allegedly smuggled wine was no longer mentioned at all. After months of legal battles, Advocate General Jonathan Sewall asked leave to withdraw the information and entered a nolle prosequi. In the course of the proceedings, Hancock and others were to be arrested. The night before, all army officers were ordered to hold their men in readiness, "as a large mob was then expected." Hancock, as intent as the crown officials on preventing direct action, "prudently" gave bail of £3000 sterling before the news had reached large numbers of townsmen.[14]

As a consequence of the riot, the commissioners sent out further urgent requests for troops. They were to arrive at the end of September. Among the townspeople there was talk of more direct action. Among the town leaders, once their concern over the Hancock–Hallowell compromise had been settled, there were debates on how to prevent the people from taking to the streets, for which purpose they called a series of town meetings.

LOCAL CONSEQUENCES OF THE CROWD ACTION: A CHANGE OF LEADERSHIP

On Monday Bostonians "were in great agitation," as one of the newspapers reported. This should come as no surprise, for the town officials still had done nothing about the impressment and its consequences for the economy of the town. Since sections of the leadership were still opposing direct action, "the Consequences whereof would be very prejudicial," as was darkly said, they had to consider some action. Accordingly, a meeting of the Sons of Liberty was called for the next day at Liberty Tree. In addition, the officials examined the town's legal position in relation to impressment and conferred with governor and council about the situation. It turned out that, as sailors had always claimed, impressment was illegal, as was the granting warrants for it by civil magistrates. Two laws, dating from 1707 and and 1746, exempted sailors on vessels employed in the American trade from impressment. The acts had been forgotten by the officials, whose social position exempted them from impressment. To appease the people, reports were spread about Captain Corner's gentlemanly behavior. But he shattered this reputation quickly by continuing to harass boats, even pleasure boats, by stopping them, firing upon them, and detaining and insulting the men.[15]

Amid rumors about whole series of mass action, the inhabitants assembled on

---

[14]*Sewall v. Hancock,* case 46, in John Adams, *Legal Papers,* 2:173–210; "Case of the *Liberty,*" *MHSP* 55:275 (1921–1922); Samuel M. Quincy, ed., *Reports of Cases Argued and Adjudged in the Superior Court of Judicative of . . . Massachusetts Bay, 1761–1772, by Josiah Quincy, Junior* (Boston, 1865), pp. 456–464; O. M. Dickerson, ed., *Boston under Military Rule (1768–1769) as Revealed in a Journal of the Times* (Boston, 1936), 3 Nov. 1768, p. 18; Richard Frothingham, *Life and Times of Joseph Warren* (Boston, 1865), pp. 59–60.

[15]*BEP,* 27 June 1768; *BNL,* 23 June 1768; *BG,* 4 July 1768; *BPB,* 20 June 1768; Rowe, *Letters and Diary,* 13 June, 16 June 1768, pp. 165(166; *BTR* 20:296; depositions, House of Lords MSS., 252:291–292. For the impressment laws, 6 Anne c. 37, § 9 (1707) and 19 Geo. 2, c. 30, § 1 (1746), see John Adams, *Legal Papers,* 2:278, 283; extracts are among the Misc. Unbound Papers, 1768, BCH, and in the instructions to the representatives, 17 June 1768, *BTR* 16:259.

Tuesday. An innkeeper reported having heard talk about an armed uprising including thousands of men from the countryside. The customs officials were told to expect something dreadful should they dare to come back to town. As in 1765, storming the castle was suggested. In addition, the men-of-war in the harbor should be taken. Whether these reports, one by a "trusty Hand" to the commissioners, are to be taken seriously may be doubted. Only some minor harassment of officials did actually take place.[16] Why, with violence seemingly imminent, the meeting of the inhabitants was called for Tuesday and not for Monday was not explained by contemporaries. Two reasons may be suggested. Probably the leadership needed time to decide on a policy. Second, even during this tense period action did not occur as a preventive measure. The three days of celebration just before the *Liberty* seizure and during the first impressments had passed peacefully. As long as no provocation would happen on Monday, no violence would occur either. The expectation of a legitimate forum for expressing grievances also helped to keep the town quiet and was consciously used for that purpose.[17]

While the people were trudging through a drizzle to Liberty Tree, the governor grumbled about "the Impropriety of the Sons of Liberty appointing a Meeting to secure the Peace of the Town where the Governor and Council were sitting upon that Business, and seemingly to little purpose."[18] At the Southend, thousands assembled. Since the stories about customs harassment and impressment had spread, angry countrymen had flocked into town too. Those "principal Gentlemen" present "attended in order to engage the lower People to concur in Measures for Peace and Quiet" and proposed that the "vast numbers" adjourn to Faneuil Hall, a mile's walk. Once there, it was proposed to dissolve and call a regular town meeting. This procedure consumed energy, prevented spontaneous action, and excluded the country people, who would have been harder for the Boston leaders to influence. Nevertheless, in the afternoon men got down to business. Hutchinson, not subject to impressment by the royal navy, as usual sneered at the "thousands of the Rabble." That men spoke up to express their interest and had views untempered by theories about the subordinate position of colonies in an imperial system was evidenced by a proposal "that every Captain of a [British] Man of War that came into the Harbour should be under the Command of the General Court." Later a petition to the governor was accepted "after very cool and deliberate Debates upon the distressed Circumstances of the Town, and the present critical Situation of the Affairs."[19]

It was decided that a sizable committee should immediately proceed with the "humble" petition to the governor at his country seat. Merchant leader John Rowe

[16]Information of Richard Sylvester, 23 Jan. 1769, Sparks MSS., 10.3:12, HHL. Joshua Henshaw, Jr., to William Henshaw, 22 June 1768, *NEHGR* 23:452–453 (1869); "Trusty Hand" to Commissioners, 7 July 1768, Admiralty Papers, Sec. Office, 483:179, PRO.

[17]*BEP,* 20 June 1768.

[18]Bernard to Hillsborough, 11–18 June 1768, Sparks MSS., 4.6:311–324, HHL.

[19]*BEP,* 20 June 1768; Hutchinson to Jackson, 16 June 1768, *MHSP* 55:281–284 (1921–1922); Bernard to Hillsborough, 11–18 June 1768, Sparks MSS., 4.6:311–324, HHL; Bernard, "State of Disorders," *Barrington–Bernard Correspondence,* p. 273; *BTR* 16:253–255. Zobel (*Massacre,* pp. 78–79), gives a different interpretation of the adjournments, in my opinion not supported by the evidence.

considered the petition "a very smart" one, which is not surprising, as he had been among the members drafting it. But he was correct. The petition began with the usual submission to the British Constitution. Though the colonies' rights under it had been violated, they had peacefully waited for their "most gracious" sovereign's answer to the "Dutiful Petitions," which, Otis had assured his townsmen eight months earlier, would surely be forthcoming. But, instead, the peaceful atmosphere had changed to desolation: ". . . [we] find ourselves invaded with an armed force, Siezing, impressing . . . our fellow-Subjects . . . Menaces have been thrown out, fit only for Barbarians which . . . threaten us with Famine and Desolation." There was, however, hope for relief, continued the petition, as the commissioners "have thought fit, of their own motion to relinquish the exercise of their Commission here." A smart interpretation indeed of the flight to the *Romney*.

His Excellency the governor, whose "tenderness to this People" had been lauded in the petition, outsmarted the committeemen by being very tender to them. Politely he bid them welcome and served wine. In this congenial atmosphere, which, as Bernard realized, impressed them very much, he managed to satisfy them with a rather evasive answer. Though he promised to talk with Captain Corner about the impressment, the basic idea of the answer was "All I can say is, that I shall not knowingly infringe any of your Rights and Privileges, but shall religeously maintain all those which are committed to me as a servant of the King." Bernard must have served a very good wine to make them swallow that answer. The committee returned to town in their 11 chaises in exact order according to rank—town-meeting moderator, representative, and selectmen at the head, the men without office and little wealth at the end. They celebrated their "success" at Hancock's and in the town meeting the next day steered the answer clear of the cliffs of opposition by acquainting "the Town with the manner in which they had been received."[20]

In short, the leadership had accomplished nothing. However, while they were off, the townsmen had continued to do business. While the 21 men sent to the governor were drinking wine, the inhabitants elected a three-man committee to draft a vote expressing the town's dislike of the customs officials and the "armed force" that was in the harbor. Contrary to the acceptance of the noncommittal report from Bernard, the three men reported a resolve outspoken to a degree that it was not even recorded in the minutes. Instead, "after considerable debate thereon and the propriety of a Towns passing Resolves," the meeting only elected a new committee, this time to instruct the representatives.[21]

Almost every aspect of these procedures was unusual: the size of the petition committee, the smallness of the resolve-drafting committee, the acceptance of the report about the conference, the rejection of the draft resolve, the debate on the town's right to pass such resolves. It seems advisable, therefore, to take a closer look at the proceedings and at the members of all town committees relative to the new revenues. From the first town meeting in opposition to the Townshend duties to

[20]Rowe, *Letters and Diary*, pp. 165–166; Bernard to Hillsborough, 11–18 June 1768, Sparks MSS., 4.6:311–324, HHL; *BTR* 16:254–257.
[21]*BTR* 16:255–256.

the meetings immediately preceding the *Liberty* seizure and the impressment, five committees had been elected.[22] Two of them were important, making policy in regard to the duties. Two were less important, executing the votes of the former. One was to deal with internal social problems arising from the boycott of British goods. The policy-making committees were to draw up a general nonconsumption agreement and to instruct the representatives for the legislature. Both were comparatively large, presumably because of the importance of the subject. Dominating in all committees were the merchants. The nonconsumption committee was chaired by John Rowe, and its members came almost exclusively from the Merchants' Society and from the top town officialdom. Four of these men also sat on the instruction committee. Among the other three was the influential and Whig-inclining justice of the peace Richard Dana, a regular member of these committees since 1764. The two committees to put decisions into effect were to procure subscriptions for the agreements. Of their 24 members, two came from the original nonconsumption committee; the other 22 seats were held by 22 different men. The fifth committee (seven members) was elected to consider measures for employing the poor—that is, to alleviate economic and social tensions. Four of its members again came from the nonconsumption committee; the three others were much less distinguished men. This committee's power was derived from its connections with the overseers of the poor, who controlled substantial amounts of tax money.

These findings have several analytical implications. First, the policy-making committees were controlled by men from the mercantile town hierarchy. Second, the members of the policy-making committees in turn influenced the other committees by plural committee assignments. Third, to broaden the base of active support, other, less involved men were elected to related committees of limited importance. The men from the mercantile hierarchy were in control of the anti-Townshend policies from October 1767 until June 1768 (that is, during the period of nonviolence and—later—minor incidents that prompted attempts at suppression in keeping with the "no mobs" policy). Two members of the mercantile community who provoked incidents went, however, unrebuked. Daniel Malcom (February 1768) and John Hancock (April 1768) had probed the rigor of the commissioners. Their firm stand and the customs officials' ineptness has exacerbated the tensions caused originally by the reluctance of merchants to sacrifice their business interests to the navigation and customs acts and by the militancy of those men whose immediate economic standing would be imperiled by a recession resulting from nonconsumption and nonimportation. These issues were to lead to a crisis in fall 1769. In the week from 5 June to 11 June 1768, the impressment, whether legal or not, and the failure of the leadership to take vigorous counteraction to protect those liable to lose their freedom created the potential for direct popular action. The fuse was then provided by the actions of the commissioners, their subalterns, and the British navy officers. The seizure of the *Liberty* with the help of the *Romney* effectively welded mercantile and impressment grievances. Nonviolent measures, petitions, town meetings, and nonconsumption and nonimportation agreements had failed to afford redress from

[22]*Ibid.*, pp. 221, 225–226 *passim*.

the consequences of the Townshend Acts. Neither repeal nor an end to the "harassment" by the customs officers had been accomplished by the opposition policies of the leadership. The economic outlook for all sections of the society continued to be bleak.

The result was the election of new men, seemingly more responsive to the acute problems, to the committees during the first town meeeting after the *Liberty* and impressment riots on Tuesday, 14 June. The exceptional size of the petition committee (21 members) was necessary because the concept of township politics demanded consistency of political structures and coherence of leadership. It did not allow for factionalism. Of the committeemen, nine came from the old-guard committeemen. Among the new were the two oppositional merchants, Hancock and Malcom; two representatives, Samuel Adams and James Otis; Thomas Young, and Joseph Warren, physicians and political activists with connections to the Sons of Liberty in other towns. Two selectmen, a councillor, a justice of the peace, and two lawyers completed the list. The three-man committee, which had been elected in the absence of the leadership, especially of Moderator James Otis, consisted of new men only. Samuel Adams, Benjamin Church, a doctor, and Joseph Warren were promptly defeated. But during the future months these new men were to play a vital role in the conduct of affairs.

To gauge the exact differences between the two groups of committeemen, a brief study is required of all committees concerning the Townshend duties (that is, the relationship between colonies and mother country) from the first move for nonconsumption to the last, a report on the promotion of arts and agriculture. The focus will be on the question of whether the change meant a radicalization of leadership. In the period under consideration, 85 men held 277 committee seats. To distill a power elite from these, the merely supportive committees have to be deducted. In them, six men from policy-making committees formed the link to leadership; the other 41 seats were held by 35 persons, an average of 1.2 seats for each. The rest, 236 posts, were shared by 50 men, 19 from the old guard, 12 elected on 14 June, and the rest added in the following years before the repeal of the duties. From June 1768 to the end of 1769, old-guard and new leadership shared the committee seats about equally. Within the old guard a concentration of seats was registered for those sympathizing or siding with the more radical men. From March 1770 onward, after the King Street riot (Boston Massacre), the town meeting eliminated the men from the old guard almost altogether.

In social composition the new men were not a sharp break with the past. The number of professional men increased, compared to men from the merchant groups, though the former never outnumbered the latter. The change is important because the professional men were among the most active politicians in the caucuses and clubs. In economic background the old guard averaged £1398 in property per person, the new men of June 1768, exclusive of the rich Hancock, only £567. This reflects the shift to the professions. The significant difference vanishes when Hancock and the men elected in the following months are included: The average of property per committeeman jumps to £1808, topping the average of the old guard by

£410. Among the merchants a slight shift from the large importing houses to the merchant–captains, operating on a more limited scale, is registered. They had been active during the Malcom affair, 1766, and the *Liberty* seizure, 1768.[23] Thus, the typical committeeman came from a well-to-do or wealthy segment of the population, even when elected by rioters/voters.

No broadening of political participation can be traced. In fact, distribution of committee seats became more hierarchical. The 19 men of 1767 held 102 seats (5.4 per member) in 36 months, the 12 men of June 1768 85 seats (7.1 per member) in 28 months (June 1768 to September 1770).[24] Hierarchical structures existed also within the two groups. Men serving on five committees or fewer averaged 2.2 seats, while those serving on six or more averaged 9.2 seats. The highest total of seats among the old leaders amounted to 13 seats, from among the new to 17.

The composition of the town's leadership was thus decisively influenced by two riots, which were set off by local grievances: impressment and the quartering of soldiers (King Street riot). Only indirectly were they aimed at Parliamentary authority or against a system of colonial government. The new men were elected into the important committees because their approaches to these grievances promised more success in alleviating them than those of the more moderate old leaders. The achievement of the new men was to connect the local grievances and resulting remedial direct action with imperial relations—to realize, conceptualize, and propagandize the uncontrolled power of king and Parliament as the source of these grievances. Internally they attempted to redirect the discontent of the lower sort from local leaders to crown officials. Awareness of the sovereignty of the people, or at least of their powers, was forced on the leaders when the sovereigns exercised their powers in direct action combined with town-meeting activity, thereby upsetting complacent power structures behind the scenes.

The new men favored neither increased popular participation nor a decrease in social distinctions. To avoid overemphasis on the power of the rioters/voters, it has to be stressed that their interest in policy changes toward a more clear-cut stand against British impositions coincided with a split in the mercantile community, which had its roots in the adoption of a nonimportation policy in early March 1768. In the next town meeting, on 14 March, John Hancock, one of the selectmen, made the unprecedented proposal of punitive taxation of those merchants who refused to sign the nonimportation agreement. After two months of haggling among officials and in the town meeting, the motion was voted down.[25] Other merchants from the new committee leadership actively participated in violent enforcement of nonimportation during the next two years. It seems that the nonimportation faction among the merchants and in the committees, though opposed to blurring of social and economic distinctions, was ready to rely on lower-class crowds and to court mechanics' votes consciously. The former will be discussed in detail with the analysis of the

---

[23]Tax and valuation list, 1771 (MA 132:92–147), contains 63 of the 85 committeemen—that is, 74 percent.
[24]The weighted average for the new men amounts to 9.1 seats per person.
[25]*BTR* 16:241, 243, 250, 20:293. Hancock absented himself from the selectmen's meeting for two months after the defeat of his motion. Mein, Key to a Certain Publication, Sparks MSS., 10.3:45–47, HHL.

nonimportation enforcement. The latter was evidenced by an issue that came up in the town meeting of March 1768.

Samuel Adams, as tax collector far in arrears, had petitioned the town for a stay of legal execution. The selectmen, when putting the issue on the town-meeting agenda, also notified the townsmen that at this meeting admission would not be handled as tolerantly as it usually was: "A strict Scrutiny will be made as to the qualification of Voters." After several heated debates Adams's petition was granted. John Rowe, merchant leader and selectman, sadly noted in his diary that the "gentlemen" could not prevail in the meeting.[26] Over the tax issue, Adams's petition, and the town's stance against customs officials and their supporters among the magistrates, deep dissentions arose among the top town officials. Four of the seven selectmen resigned; one—John Rowe—reconsidered.[27] The split among the leadership had sociopolitical implications. Those tending toward accomodation with Britain and adherence to traditional forms of political conduct and leadership by a "natural" mercantile social and economic elite considered themselves the "gentlemen." It seems that among the "faults" of the other side, mainly gentlemen too, was political innovation, stooping to the "rabble"—that is, to those men on whose direct action much of the opposition had to rely.

While Boston's town meeting was moving toward a more pronounced opposition to the British influence and to particular acts, the customs commissioners had sent Hallowell to London to support their demands for troops, "to put a stop to the Seditious Spirit and daring threats of Rebellion so prevalent in this Country."[28] When the nature of Hallowell's errand became known in Boston, new threats to pull down his house were uttered, and reportedly a tentative date was set for Saturday, 17 September. But only a few windows were broken in his house on that day. Possibly the "patriot leaders of the opposition," who, according to a British visitor, "were much more concerned at any mobs that happened than the government people," discountenanced any direct action.

Samuel Adams, for one, was concerned that an impression might be created "that we are in a state of confusion." Though he accepted crowd action under Whig leadership, confusion was the opposite of what he wanted. "One general scene of tumult," however, was the state of affairs in the mother country, involving "the Weavers mob, the Seamens mob, the Taylors mob, the Coal miners mob, and some say, the Clergys mob." Such confusion was another sign of "misrule of the empire's governors," since the people never rose in "Mobs and Tumults . . . but thro' Oppression and a scandalous Abuse of Power." Boston Whigs, by suppressing or discountenancing crowd action, also demonstrated to the world that under their rule there was no abuse of power. "Government people," on the other hand, could use any kind of rioting to demand more military protection.[29]

[26]*BTR* 16:241, 243, 20:287; John C. Miller, *Samuel Adams, Pioneer in Propaganda* (Boston, 1936), pp. 58–60, 101–102; Rowe, *Letters and Diary,* p. 157.

[27]*BTR* 16:252, 20:291; Rowe, *Letters and Diary,* May 1768, pp. 162–165; cf. John Adams, *Diary and Autobiography of John Adams,* ed. Lyman H. Butterfield, 4 vols. (Cambridge, Mass., 1961–1966), 4 Sept. 1769, 1:343.

[28]Hillsborough to Gage, 30 July 1768, State Papers, 11:33–36, Gay Transcripts, MHS; orders for the 64th and 65th Regiments, 27 July 1768, House of Lords MSS., 252:316.

[29]Hallowell's examination before the Lords of the Treasury, *ibid.,* pp. 273–280; Gage to Barrington, 28 June 1768,

IMPERIAL CONSEQUENCES ON THE LOCAL LEVEL: THE ARRIVAL OF TROOPS IN BOSTON

The possibility of British troops being stationed in Boston to force submission to trade and customs regulations and deference to the officials collecting the duties had been a recurrent topic in town ever since the Stamp Act riots. And not without foundation: The governor had been instructed in October 1765 to call troops if necessary. The customs collector had publicly demanded supporting military units in 1766. The customs commissioners, ever since their arrival in November 1767, had sent out calls for military help, and by June 1768 the calls had become rather frantic. By that time, apprehension was so general that Bostonians wanted "a Parliamentary enquiry" in the Massachusetts House of Representatives into the matter. Should anybody be detected who "really wrote or solicited for Troops," he was to be labeled "an Enemy to this Town and Province, and a disturber of the peace and good order of both." The legal punishment for disturbing the peace was sitting in the stocks exposed to the resentment of the people.[30]

Meanwhile, the colonists received a foretaste of having soldiers in town by having men-of-war in the harbor. The impressment, the hailing and searching of the boats, and the support given to customs officials resulted in strong antipathies. The newspapers, especially the *Gazette,* published acid attacks on the navy officers, and accounts of their impertinent behavior spread. The harassment of coasters and even of boats out merely for hunting fowl occasioned discontent among inhabitants of country and coastal settlements who would never see a soldier or British sailor.[31] Crowds continued to assemble for direct action and to debate the issues at stake. When the *Romney* fired on an incoming lighter (10 August), a crowd on shore immediately interposed.[32]

Correspondence, 2:479–480; Knox to Grenville, 23 July 1768, *The Grenville Papers, Being the Correspondence of Richard Grenville Earl Temple, K.G., and the Right Hon. George Grenville, Their Friends and Contemporaries,* ed. William J. Smith, 4 vols. (London, 1852–1853), 4:319–321; Hood to Grenville, 11 July 1768, *ibid.,* pp. 306–307; Captain Corner's Diary, 14 Sept., House of Lords MSS., 253:19; Samuel Adams ("Determinatus"), in *BG,* 8 Aug. 1768, reprinted in *Writings,* 1:236–237, speech in Parliament, 1737, quoted in Pauline R. Maier, *From Resistance to Revolution: Colonial Radicals and the Development of American Opposition to Britain, 1765–1776* (New York, 1972), p. 191. British visitor: London *Chronicle,* 22 April 1769; Frothingham, *Joseph Warren,* p. 76.

[30]Instructions to Governor Bernard, 24 Oct. 1765, Instructions to the Governors, transcripts, p. 2340, MHS; deposition of William Mackay, 20 Oct. 1766, in George G. Wolkins, ed., "Daniel Malcom and the Writs of Assistance," *MHSP* 58:45 (1924–1925); *BTR* 16:259; Rowe, *Letters and Diary,* 29 July 1768, p. 171; John Powell to Christopher Champlin, 23 Oct. 1769, *MHSC* 69:246 (1914).

[31]John Shy, *Toward Lexington: The Role of the British Army in the Coming of the American Revolution* (Princeton, N.J., 1965), pp. 267–320 for the years 1768–1770 in Boston and pp. 248–258 for the Quartering Acts and New York. Some of the resentment against the British army may have stemmed from the previous wars. Only in 1758 did the British king "grant to the Officers of his American Forces a Rank and Command equal to the Officers of his British Forces." Within a rank, however, any British officer was to be considered senior to American officers. Proclamation by Pownall, 23 March 1758, in A. C. Goodell *et al.,* eds., *Acts and Resolves, Public and Private, of the Province of Massachusetts Bay,* 21 vols. (Boston, 1869–1922), 4:136–137. Whig opposition to "standing armies" was expressed in the resolves of the Boston town meeting, 13 Sept. 1768, *BTR* 16:263; by the convention of Massachusetts towns, which called a standing army quartered without the town's consent an "unlawful assemblage," a legal term that presupposed bad intent, William Tudor, *The Life of James Otis of Massachusetts: Containing Also Notices of Some Contemporary Characters and Events from the Year 1760 to 1775* (Boston, 1823), p. 332; by Samuel Adams as "Vindex" in *BG,* 26 Dec. 1768. For incidents, see *BG,* 4 July, 18 July, 29 Aug. 1768; memorial by the council, MA 66:438–441, by the House, *ibid.,* 110:336.

[32]*BEP,* 15 Aug. 1768.

The inhabitants' impression of the army was as bad as their experiences with the navy.[33] It began in November 1766, when a transport ship with troops put into Boston harbor because of weather conditions. The House of Representatives had recessed, and the governor made provisions to accommodate troops at Castle William. This was in accordance with the Quartering Acts of 1765 and 1766 but not in accordance with how Massachusetts people felt their taxes should be spent.[34] While some of Boston's town leaders wined and dined the navy and artillery officers, rumors began to circulate that William Molineux with 500 men from Boston would attempt to take over the castle. This issue had hardly been resolved when reports in the newspapers announced that the lower house of the New York legislature had been dissolved by the king in council for not complying with the Quartering Acts.[35] In January 1767 an army captain was arrested in Boston for debt, "which occasioned much noice etc. in Town." In August 1767 the *Evening Post* reported a riot from Elizabeth-Town, New Jersey, after military officers to be arrested for debts had attacked the sheriff.[36]

People in western Massachusetts got their foretaste of the presence of standing armies from troops quartered in upstate New York. A storehouse for the troops' provisions in Albany was destroyed in a riot late in 1766 after a petition to remove it had been unsuccessful. Troops turned out to fight the rioters. Next, the large landlords of New York used British troops to enforce their claims on Massachusetts settlers. One of the settlers demanded help from the Massachusetts militia, explaining, "there are a Number of armed Men lye incamped in Noblestown who call themselves the Kings Troops, but who seem to conduct themselves like a number of Banditi or Collution of Robbers." While the militia did not march officially, rioters did. Once, when the troops tried to cross into Massachusetts, a sheriff raised a posse to repel them. During the Malcom incident in Boston, the brutal treatment of the settlers by troops and courts, or—from the viewpoint of the crown officials—their treasonous conduct, was part of the debate.[37]

When rumors about the coming of troops began to multiply, resistance was contemplated, and preliminaries began with what may be called the tar-barrel affair. On the morning of 11 September 1768, Bostonians saw a tar barrel affixed during the night to a staff on the top of Beacon Hill. Though it was a Sunday, governor, council, and selectmen went into emergency sessions, since the barrel was accompanied by a hint about crowd action reminiscent of Stamp Act times. The barrel, the story went, would be lighted if British troops arrived. Tens of thousands of militiamen from the country towns would then converge on Boston. Upon communi-

---

[33]Shy, *Toward Lexington*, pp. 267–320.

[34]Zobel, *Massacre*, p. 61.

[35]Shy, *Toward Lexington*, pp. 248–258.

[36]Rowe, *Letters and Diary*, 2 Dec. 1766, 7 Jan., 8 Jan. 1767, pp. 116–117, 119; Thomas Hutchinson, *The History of the Colony and Province of Massachusetts Bay*, ed. Lawrence Shaw Mayo, 3 vols. (Cambridge, Mass., 1936), 3:121–123; *BEP*, 10 Aug. 1767.

[37]Storehouse riot: Gage to Shelburne, 11 Nov., 23 Dec. 1766, *Correspondence*, 1:114, 117. Border riots: *ibid.*, pp. 101–103, 107; Mark Hopkins to William Williams, 15 Aug. 1766, MA 56:488–489, cf. *ibid.*, pp. 490–494; Wolkins, ed., "Malcom and Writs of Assistance," p. 40; Oscar Handlin, "The Eastern Frontier of New York," *N.Y. Hist.* 18:50–75 (1937); Irving Mark, *Agrarian Conflict in Colonial New York, 1711–1775* (New York, 1940).

cations from the top provincial officials, the Boston selectmen and the town meeting merely intimated that a tar barrel was too insignificant to be worthy of their attention. After four days of deliberations, the council ordered the sheriff to take down the barrel. It was empty, and gleefully the townspeople ridiculed the governor's apprehensions. But sightseers visiting Boston were told by the same townspeople that the beacon "is lighted in case of surprize, and at this signal all the militia of the country rally."[38] Next, 3000 inhabitants, in a town meeting, took more direct steps in response to the expected arrival of troops. They drew attention to a law ordering every male inhabitant to be armed "with a well fixed" gun. The explanation, "there is at this Time a prevailing apprehension, in the Minds of many, of an approaching War with France," was received with "a general Smile." A plan to take the castle was also reported—for the third time, at least, since 1765. Under these circumstances both Bernard and Hutchinson expected strong resistance to the landing of the troops, and Captain Corner of the Royal Navy commented on the sullen discontent and abusive behavior of the inhabitants.[39]

The attention that an empty barrel received from the officials and the attention that only the shadow of a rumor about troops received among the inhabitants were symptomatic of the apprehensions on both sides. The town, as always in such circumstances, proceeded via a town meeting. A demand was sent to the provincial governor for information, who had suggested guardedly to his superiors that he experienced a certain want of power. He admitted to "private" intelligence of the coming of troops. The inhabitants in response passed a report drawn up by the new committeemen, among them William Molineux, who was to become one of the most important figures in the resistance to troops and the enforcement of nonimportation. In rather strong terms the principle of no taxation without representation was enlarged to "no Law of the Society can be binding on any Invididuals, without his consent, given by himself in Person, or by his Representative of his own free Election." In this situation "the raising or keeping a standing Army, without their [the inhabitants'] consent . . . would be an infringement of their natural, constitutional and Charter Rights." No consent could be given by the provincial assembly. The General Court had been dissolved, according to instructions from London, for voting 92 to 17 not to rescind the letter sent in February to the other colonies and demanding a joint opposition to the duties.[40] Town meetings bitterly criticized this move, but so did crown officials. Their salaries could not be paid without legislative appropriation. More important, when the troops arrived, no commissioner could be

[38]Council Records, 16:350–352, MSA; *BTR* 16:260, 20:307–308; Rowe, *Letters and Diary*, 11 Sept. 1768, p. 174; deposition of Richard Sylvester, Sparks MSS., 10.3:12, HHL; Diary of Captain Corner, 13 Sept. 1768, House of Lords MSS., 253:19; *BG*, 19 July 1773; "Diary of a French Officer 1781, Presumed To Be That of Baron Cromot du Bourg," 7 May 1781, *Mag. Am. Hist.* 4:209 (1880); Robert Honyman, *Colonial Panorama, 1775: Dr. Robert Honyman's Journal*, ed. Philip Padelford (San Marino, 1939), 21 March 1775, pp. 42–43; William Gregory, "A Scotchman's Journey in New England in 1771," ed. Mary G. Powell, *New Eng. Mag.*, n.s. 12:344–345 (1895).

[39]*BTR* 16:264; Information to the Governor, Sparks MSS., 10.2:81, HHL, cf. *ibid.*, p. 18; Bernard to Hillsborough, 16 Sept. 1768, *Letters to the Ministry*, pp. 52–56; extract of a letter from a Gentleman of Character, 14 June 1768, House of Lords MSS., 252:269–270; Captain Corner's Diary, 7–26 Sept. 1768, *ibid.*, 253:19.

[40]*BTR* 16:259–264; *BEP*, 19 Sept. 1768; *BPB*, 12 Sept. 1968; *BNL*, 15 Sept. 1768; Rowe, *Letters and Diary*, 30 June 1769, pp. 167–168; Hutchinson, *History*, 3:141–144.

appointed for supplying them, nor could funds be provided, because these rights belonged to the House of Representatives. Any attempts by the governor to circumvent the provisions of the laws were rebuffed by the councillors, who pointedly informed him that he would have to call a session of the House.[41]

While Bernard had to abide by his instructions, the town was by no means going to be inconvenienced. They renamed their representatives a "Committee in Convention" and invited the other towns of the province to attend this convention on 22 September in Faneuil Hall. This was a revolutionary step, as the lieutenant governor noted: "The inhabitants of one town alone took upon them to convene an assembly from all the towns, which in every thing but in name, would be a house of representatives; which, by the charter, the governor had the sole authority of convening." The delegates were responsible only to the constituents and had no connection with the crown or its officials. It was an extralegal, perhaps illegal body taking over by implicit consent of local officialdom the powers lawfully belonging to the legislature. The measure was devised by men from the new leadership *and* by the old guard of Boston's committeemen. The surprising consent of the latter was explained by one of them with fears of internal upheaval. They were for "driving out" governor and lieutenant governor, if necessary, to call the assembly, because actions by the representatives might prevent more violent proceedings of the people. The reasoning was derived from experience. The convention, they continued, would also be more moderate than Boston's new leadership. Thomas Cushing, Speaker of the House and one of the old guard, was elected chairman of the convention. The proceedings were indeed moderate. The 70 delegates disclaimed any intentions of usurping established authority. With little accomplished, they broke up somewhat hurriedly, as a hostile observer noted, on 29 September, the day after the arrival of the first British soldiers, ordered to discipline Boston.[42]

Troops thus came to Boston less than a year after the arrival of the customs commissioners and the effective date of the new duties. They were to remain there till March 1770. The soldiers were carried by navy transports and men-of-war. Masters of private ships refused to carry the troops because they were threatened with crowd action on departure as well as upon arrival. Lieutenant Colonel William Dalrymple, the commanding officer, received an express from headquarters in New York intimating that plans of resistance to the landing of the troops existed. In consequence, both regiments were immediately stationed in the center of the town instead of outside it. But the armed "Fracas" expected by many did not occur; "the Novelty of a military Parade served but to amuse a vast Rabble; and even some of the Leaders of Faction [the opposition to the crown] went out and saluted the commanding Officer."[43]

[41]Andrew Oliver to Richard Jackson, 8 Nov. 1768, Letterbooks, 1:47–50, MHS; Council Records, 16:336–343, 353–356, MSA.

[42]Richard D. Brown, "The Massachusetts Convention of Towns, 1768," *WMQ* 3.26:94–104 (1969); John C. Miller, "The Massachusetts Convention of 1768," *NEQ* 7:445–474 (1934); Hutchinson, *History*, 3:148–153, 356–358; Henry Hulton, Account, pp. 91–92; deposition of Nathaniel Coffin, 6 Feb. 1769, Sparks MSS., 10.3:19, HHL; Cooper to Pownall, 18 Feb. 1769, *AHR* 8:302–305 (1902–1903); Ballantine's Journal, 20 Sept., 26 Sept. 1768, Judd MSS., Rev. Matters, p. 147, Forbes Library. The authors of this move probably referred to the Convention of 1689 in England.

[43]Gage to Hillsborough, 26 Sept. 1768, *Correspondence*, 1:195–197; Hutchinson to Whately, 5 Oct., 17 Oct. 1768, to

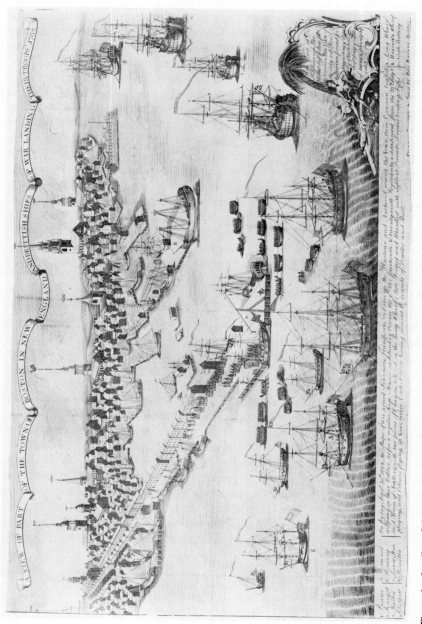

Figure 4.   Landing of the troops in fall 1768 as seen by Paul Revere. From Stokes Collection.

The second problem, quartering, created more difficulties. With the exception of the governor, who had no authority to act on his own, no official was willing to do anything. The council, in session since the middle of September, debated for nine days before even inquiring of the selectmen which method of quartering would be least disagreeable to the inhabitants. The selectmen, having used the time to scrutinize the Quartering Acts, had found a flaw that worked to the inhabitants' advantage. Only when all barracks in town were filled could troops be quartered in public or private houses. The law simply referred to towns, as in Britain, the selectmen to the New England townships, which comprised the whole surrounding countryside. The town's barracks were empty, and they were on Castle Island, three miles by water, seven miles by land and ferry. Selectmen, constables, justices of the peace, and councillors refused one after another to quarter a single soldier. The resolution spread, and Nantucket inhabitants refused to accommodate a customs official, Samuel Proctor. "If quarters are to be provided by the people for Custom-House officers, who are daily increasing upon us, as well as for Majesty's troops, we shall quickly perceive that we are without quarters ourselves," asserted a newspaper writer. Meanwhile the 14th and 29th Regiments stood on the Boston common waiting and lacking the necessary equipment to encamp.[44]

The description of awed spectators watching the troops is not quite correct, however. Small affrays between inhabitants and soldiers began immediately, the first on the day of landing, when after darkness the soldiers on the common met with abuse and had some stones thrown at them.[45] While some opposition thus occurred on the lower level, the opposition on the top levels began to cave in. The selectmen permitted the troops to take shelter in Faneuil Hall over the weekend, and the State House was opened for them. By Monday, when Faneuil Hall was to be relinquished, one of the selectmen, merchant John Rowe, was already functioning as messenger between the commander of the troops and the town officials. Neither selectmen nor other officials took offense when the military simply told the town that Faneuil Hall would remain their quarters until others were ready.

Dalrymple continued to accuse the magistrates of sabotaging the quartering. However, unperceived by him, a total reversal of roles had taken place. Crown officials, led by the governor, attempted to get the troops out of town to the castle. "[P]erpetual feuds and affrays" would happen if the soldiers remained in town, and only in the castle could "frequent Desertion, for which no encouragement would be wanting," be prevented.[46] The local officials meanwhile began to make plans for finding quarters in town. They permitted the erection of barracks and guardhouses on town lands, and one of the selectmen demanded severe punishment for opposition to the troops.

Jackson, 5 Oct., 19 Oct. 1768, Letterbooks, MA 25:281–284; Oliver, *American Rebellion*, pp. 70–71; Hutchinson, *History*, 3:154–155; Dickerson, ed., *Journal of the Times*, 1 Oct. 1768, pp. 1–2.

[44]Council Records, 16:354, MSA; *BTR* 20:309–311; Gage to Hillsborough, 10 Oct. 1768, *Correspondence*, 1:200–201; Henry Hulton, Account, p. 93; Dickerson, ed., *Journal of the Times*, 3 Oct., 10 Oct. 1768, pp. 2–4; Justices of the Peace to Bernard, House of Lords MSS., 256:56. Quartering and multiplication of offices were among the grievances later enumerated in the Declaration of Independence.

[45]Deposition of Gilbert Carter, State Papers, 12:138–140, Gay Transcripts, MHS.

[46]*BTR* 20:311, 313; Bernard to Gage, 24 Sept. 1768, State Papers, 11:102–105, Gay Transcripts, MHS.

What had become of the often invoked "noble spirit of opposition"? Had Selectman Rowe been converted to law and order? The explanation for his and other officials' behavior was that they had realized their chance to profit from the troops' presence. The call for opposition, allegedly justified by natural rights, had been superseded by expectations of private gain. While Rowe was conspicuously absent from all selectmen's meetings since the arrival of the troops, except when the commanding military officer sent him with an errand to his colleagues, he and other wealthy Whigs were busy soliciting the friendship of the officers. Thomas Young, political radical and not commercially interested, complained that provisioning navy or army was an "alluring bait" to merchants, including Otis and Hancock. They courted General Gage, commander of His Majesty's troops in America, they dined with the officers, and they rented fashionable houses to them. They overlooked insults, admired the good discipline of the troops, and occasionally borrowed the military "Brass Bands of musick" for their own use. Smaller shopkeepers profited by the soldiers' spending wages in town, especially from the large sales of rum. Economic advantage for some of the inhabitants was an important factor in the collapse of the plans for resistance.[47]

Still, there were people who saw more problems than benefits in the presence of the troops. A week after their arrival, a small crowd cut down the frames for a large guardhouse on the Neck. A crown official ordered prosecution of the rioters; a town official and merchant called them "scoundrels."[48] Crowd action also ensued when the council assigned the province-owned Manufactory House for the troops and when the tenant, John Brown, who did not belong to the merchant-officer dinner circle, refused to leave. Sheriff Greenleaf tried to expel Brown but had to send for soldiers, "finding the people gather fast about the gate." A double "siege" began. The military guards denied supplies to Brown and his workers. They in turn were beleaguered by a crowd of spectators, who repeatedly broke the circle to get provisions to the "children at the windows crying for bread." Crowds also threatened direct action against the sheriff, and a military guard had to protect his house. New York crowds burned governor and sheriff in effigy when news of the siege was received. Disorders against governor and proadministration tutors broke out at Harvard. When the troops finally did succeed in entering Manufactory House, the tenant immediately sued the sheriff for unwarranted forcible entry. Crowds now threatened to riot if the council granted the sheriff's request for legal counsel at the cost of the province. The council gave in and instead rebuked the governor for the use of troops. The newspapers pointedly charged the military with breaking "the laws of the country," which they had been sent to project. Thus, they introduced "that anarchy and confusion it was pretended they were sent to suppress."[49]

The tenant of the province-owned Manufactory House had the support of several

---

[47]Rowe, *Letters and Diary,* Oct.–Nov. 1768, pp. 174–177; Boyle, "Journal," Oct. 1768, p. 256; Dickerson, ed., *Journal of the Times,* 15 Oct. 1768, p. 6; *BTR* 20:310–311; Thomas Young to Hugh Hughes, 21 Dec. 1772, Misc. Bound Papers, vol. 14, MHS; Gage to Hillsborough, 5 Jan. 1769, *Correspondence,* 1:208–209.

[48]Rowe, *Letters and Diary,* 10 Oct. 1768, p. 177; Dickerson, ed., *Journal of the Times,* 9 Oct. 1768, p. 4; Council Records, 16:366–367, MSA.

[49]*BG,* 24 Oct. 1768; Boyle, "Journal," 12 Oct. 1768, p. 256; Dickerson, ed., *Journal of the Times,* 6 Oct., 20 Oct., 21 Oct., 25 Nov. 1768, pp. 9, 26–27; Hutchinson, *History,* 3:155; Council Records, 16:386–387.

men from Boston's "new leadership." Some of them had no financial interests in the affair. But the support of others had rather ambiguous motives. Unlike the crowd members who wanted to get the soldiers out of the town, they wanted to profit from renting private quarters to them. A few weeks earlier Boston innkeepers had decided to give up their licenses rather than quarter soldiers in their houses. Now profiteers rented private houses to the officers and warehouses for the use of the ranks. Molineux, chief supporter of the "siege" among Whigs, offered storehouses for an exorbitant rate. The British officers were so much in fashion that they were in a position to select with whom to dine, a far cry from the social ostracism that had greeted the customs commissioners, who had no lucrative contracts to offer. Only some Loyalists, who from the beginning had supported the troops and had rented stores to them, were criticized by the Whiggish newspapers. "[W]hat do you think of the Patriotism of [the Whig leaders]?" crown supporters now asked. They suggested to one another, "I don't see why you may not put in for something either by way of Contractor [or] Agency." Proudly Dalrymple reported his success to Commodore Hood: "I am . . . visited by Otis, Hancock, Rowe, etc., who cry peccavi, and offer exhortations for the public service."[50]

Nevertheless, the troops were unable to fulfill their mission of enforcing imperial regulations. Two factors contributed to this development: the colonists' dislike for standing armies and the legal prescription that use of troops to curb internal disorders had to be authorized by local civil magistrates. Hardly any of them would dare to do so. Colonial officials knew this, and after two years of experience with the troops in Boston, the commander of the British forces in the American colonies knew it too. He reported to the home authorities that at first "the People were kept in some awe" by the troops. But they soon discovered that "Troops were bound by Constitutional Laws, and could only Act under the Authority, and by the Orders of the Civil Magistrates." He erred when stating that the latter "were all of their Side." His final assessment, never fully understood by the British ministry, was that the people "recommenced their Riots, Tho' two or three Regiments were in the Town with the Same unbridled Licentiousness as before."[51]

---

[50]Bernard to Gage, 24 Sept. 1768, State Papers, 11:102–105, Gay Transcripts, MHS; Oliver to John Spooner, 28 Oct. 1768, Letterbooks, 1:41–45, MHS; Dickerson, ed., *Journal of the Times*, 4 Oct. 1768, p. 3; Dalrymple to Hood, 4 Oct. 1768, House of Lords MSS., 253:12–14.

[51]Gage to Hillsborough, 7 July 1770, *Correspondence*, 1:262–264.

Enforcement and Defiance of the Trade Laws | 6

CROWDS AGAINST CUSTOMS OFFICIALS

The combined anticustoms and antiimpressment action of 10 June 1768 had ended the period during which the Townshend duties were opposed merely by petitions. In the subsequent months direct action rapidly spread along the coastline, and revenue officers had a difficult time. The one exception was Boston. There the anticrowd Whig leadership decided to show that it was still in control and opposed to direct action. A schooner seized for smuggling molasses was unloaded by a crowd of 30 men on 8 July. To avoid a second *Liberty* incident, the customs officers had left the vessel at the wharf, though the governor wearily remarked that "it was easy to see what would be the Event of this." However, the selectmen met immediately to take a rather unusual decision: They upheld the crown officials. The town had declared a month earlier that the *Liberty* would have been absolutely safe on the wharf, and the present rescue doubtless cast a shadow of suspicion on the truthfulness of the assertion. They peremptorily ordered the surprised master of the vessel, not a powerful merchant but "a poor simple Irishman," to replace the molasses immediately. He began to play the usual "know nothing" game, but the selectmen only hinted at "the Displeasure of the Town." The molasses was back on board the same day. Customs commissioners, judge of Admiralty, chief justice, or governor could not have achieved a similar submission to authority. "So we are not without a Government," wrote the governor; "it is in the Hands of the People of the Town." On another occasion he had noted that "gentlemen of fortune profess to have the Command." With these statements Bernard was much closer to the truth than he was with his periodical lamentations about anarchy and disorder. The Whig press, reporting that the inhabitants had "expressed their resentment" about the rescue, thus called a decision of the leadership the general opinion of the inhabitants. It would be interesting to know whom the selectmen would have mobilized had the captain of the ship or his men refused to return the molasses.[1]

[1] Bernard to Hillsborough, 9–11 July 1768, Sparks MSS., 4.6:335–340, 4.7:1–2, HHL; *BTR* 20:301; O. M. Dickerson, ed., *Boston Under Military Rule (1768–1769) as Revealed in a Journal of the Times* (Boston, 1936), 26 Dec. 1768, p. 40. There is no evidence for such assertions as "a state of virtual anarchy apparently existed in Boston" in summer 1768, as in Lawrence H. Gipson, *The Coming of the Revolution, 1763–1775* (New York, 1954), p. 180.

A second incident, a week later, sheds additional light on the crowd–leadership relations. It showed the unwillingness of the leaders to act as openly as they expected crowds to act and the limitations under which crowd members labored for want of being articulate in the way officials were. The target of the action was Customs Inspector John Williams. He had been hung in effigy once. After the *Liberty* seizure his house had been surrounded, but the crowd had left because Williams was out of town, though they promised to come back when he returned. On 15 July 1768 the fire bells rang to signal the news of his return. The crowd ordered Williams to come to Liberty Tree, there to resign his office and swear never to resume it. Three years earlier the stamp distributor had done so, and the commissioners lived in constant fear that they would be forced to follow the same course. Williams, however, took a different approach. He categorically refused to resign, but he did speak with the rioters and finally announced that he would be on the Exchange, in the center of the town, the following day and answer any charge against him. No damage was done to his house, and on Saturday probably as many as 1500 men assembled at the townhouse. Williams came, but he did not mingle with the people. Instead, he appeared on the balcony of the council chamber together with several councillors. From there he offered to answer any objections to him. None was brought forward. He repeated his offer. Again "nothing was said." Ill at ease, the crowd dispersed.

The Sons of Liberty, who had not dared to appear on the Exchange to speak out against Williams, officially disavowed the proceedings and ordered the printers not to mention the affair. But they agreed with the intent of the crowd action and privately told Williams to resign. Williams refused again and was now sustained by men from the crowd. Annoyed that the leaders had so little courage to stick their necks out, that the action was disavowed and hushed up, they and "particularly the Captain" assured Williams that nothing would happen to him.[2]

Even the pattern of resistance to customs officials shows vestiges of increasing deference on the part of the rioters with higher rank of the officials. While the commissioners were threatened, insulted, but only in rare instances attacked personally, their underlings fared worse. These had closer contacts with merchants, captains, and sailors, and accordingly there was much more occasion for friction. The lower the rank, the harder the punishment: Beatings were frequent, and many petty officials were tarred and feathered. Similarly, legal punishments were more violent with decreasing social status. Whipping or sitting in the stocks was replaced

<hr/>

[2]John Rowe, *Letters and Diary of John Rowe, Boston Merchant, 1759–1762, 1764–1779*, ed. Anne Rowe Cunningham (Boston, 1903; reprinted, 1969), 16 July 1768, p. 170; Bernard to Hillsborough, 18 July 1768, Sparks MSS., 4.7:8–10, HHL; Knox to Grenville, 23 July 1768, *The Grenville Papers, Being the Correspondence of Richard Grenville Earl Temple, K. G., and the Right Hon. George Grenville, Their Friends and Contemporaries*, ed. William J. Smith, 4 vols. (London, 1852–1853), 4:319–321; Hutchinson to ———, 21 July 1768, Letterbooks, MA 26:315–316; cf. John Adams, *Diary and Autobiography of John Adams*, ed. L. H. Butterfield, 4 vols. (Cambridge, Mass., 1961–1966), 19 Oct. 1769, 1:344. Hutchinson [*The History of the Colony and Province of Massachusetts Bay*, ed. Lawrence Shaw Mayo, 3 vols. (Cambridge Mass., 1936), 3:146] suggested that the incident was staged by the Sons of Liberty to prove that it was safe for customs officials to stay in town. The evidence does not point to this conclusion.

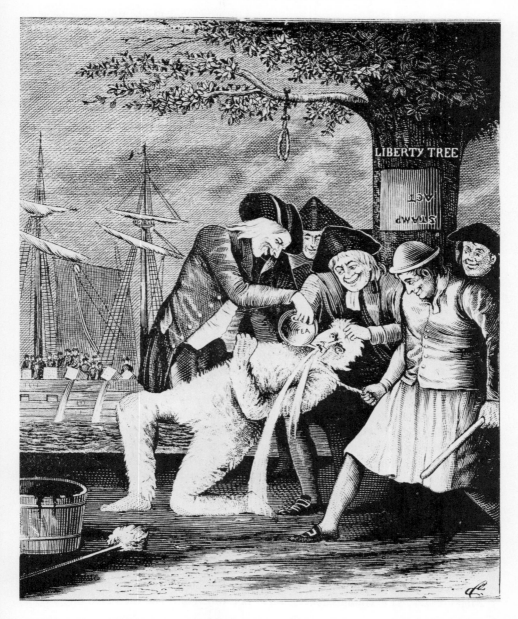

Figure 5.   Bostonians paying the exciseman, or tarring and feathering. A cartoon published in London 1774.

by fines for the better sort, and these were frequently remitted later. Whipping, once executed, could not be mitigated later.

The commissioners remained at the castle, "frightened at their own Shadows," as one Bostonian noted. When no direct action happened, when no seizures aroused the townsmen, the well-paid commissioners found other reasons for complaints and for nettling the inhabitants. They felt themselves above paying taxes, and, when the town threatened "compulsive measures" according to law, the commissioners demanded special status from their superiors in Britain. Disregarding the opinion of the crown's attorney general as well as of the governor of Massachusetts, the Board of Trade acceded. As a result, Bostonians had one more grievance against the placemen, and representatives from all over the province condemned the decision as "surprizing and alarming." They boldly declared: "We know of no Commissioners of his Majesty's Customs, nor of any Revenue his Majesty has a right to establish in North America." Less boldly, Hutchinson and later his successor, Gage, tried to work out compromises, so that "the honour of Government can be saved" and "our quiet here" as well.[3]

Quiet was not easily kept. On the evening of 6 July 1768, about 50 or 60 men marched three miles from Boston to Roxbury, where Commissioner John Robinson had his country seat. The crowd split into two groups and with diligent planning arrived at the same time from different sides at his house. Robinson, still at the castle, had his fences, garden, and orchard destroyed. A few weeks later Robinson went to Newport, Rhode Island, where he had been stationed and had met with opposition. Upon arrival, he found posters all over town quoting him as saying that the Rhode Island people would willingly support him. A crowd soon assembled to disprove it. The *Boston Gazette* pointedly described the crowd's search through the house in which Robinson was suspected to be in terms of searches conducted by customs officials. It was undertaken "not by Virtue of any Writ of Assistance, but by Candle Light." During the "diligent Search . . . of the House, Out-Houses, Bales, Barrels, Meal Tubs, Trunks, Boxes, Packs and Packages, packed and unpacked, and in short of every Hole and Corner sufficient to conceal a Ram Cat, or a Commissioner, they could find neither." Robinson had left in a hurry. A year later, he got involved in a brawl with James Otis and had to leave the continent in a hurry to avoid presecution.[4]

Further seizures in Boston created more ill feeling. The brig *Triton* was seized in October after lying in the harbor for more than four months; she belonged to Solomon Davis, a politically very active merchant. Another vessel was seized with the help of soldiers (26 December 1768) but had to be released soon. John Rowe, contracting for the army, said bitterly that the "insolent" behavior of "their high Mightinesses," the commissioners, was "not to be born, and for which they may

[3]Palfrey to William Holt, 13 June 1768, Palfrey Family Papers, vol. 5, no. 2, HHL. Commissioners to Hutchinson, 15 Dec. 1769, Hutchinson to Hillsborough, 20 Dec. 1769, printed with other relevant documents in A. C. Goodell *et al.*, eds., *Acts and Resolves, Public and Private, of the Province of Massachusetts Bay,* 21 vols. (Boston, 1869–1922), 5:53–55, 363–364, cf. *ibid.*, pp. 5–20, Hutchinson to ———, 17–18 July 1771, Letterbooks, MA 27:199–202. For an attempt by Paxton to obstruct justice, see John Adams, *Diary,* 6 Sept. 1769, 1:343–344.
[4]Bernard to Hillsborough, 9 July 1768, Sparks MSS., 4.6:335–340, HHL; *BG,* 5 Sept. 1768, 11 Sept. 1769.

hear more about." Did he mean crowd action? There was no other means. In his "no violence" speech, Otis had asserted that the commissioners would afford immediate relief if any of the underofficers violated the laws and harassed colonists. He had wanted to keep the lower classes quiet. Now he himself, Rowe, and other well-placed men were seething, and Otis was soon insulting and abusing the commissioners in a manner that would have brought men of lower rank to the pillory for "profane swearing."[5]

In September 1768 a crowd in Salem seized a petty officer, Robert Wood, for informing against a vessel loaded with molasses and tarred him and rolled him in feathers. As an example to others, he was carted through the town with a halter around his neck. Finally, before the crowd left, they banished him for six weeks from the town.[6] In Newburyport two informers, Joshua Vickery, a carpenter, and Francis Mignot were taken up on a Saturday, put in the stocks, and carted about the town. In order not to profane the coming Lord's Day, the inhabitants imprisoned them till Monday, when they were tarred and feathered, carted again, and finally committed to gaol for breach of the peace.[7]

During the same day a Gloucester crowd went in search of Samuel Fellows, a petty customs official. He escaped. A year later he was indicted and fined for rescuing a fellow official, Josiah Merill, from the hands of a sheriff and for attacking and shooting at Deputy Sheriff Jacob Parsons. The governor remitted one-half of the fine, proving to the colonists that it was useless to rely on courts and fines.[8] The crowd in search of him in 1768, suspecting that he might be hidden in the house of Jesse Saville, another customs official, searched the house without success and then retired to the meeting house to eat and drink by courtesy of one of the deacons. Among the rioters were two merchants and a physician, according to a later indictment, but also a cooper, a cordwainer, a bricklayer, a yeoman, and a tinman. For their business they had chosen a clerk in town-meeting manner. Late at night the crowd got hold of Jesse Saville, and during the following weeks there were continuous rumors in town that his house would be pulled down. He did not dare show himself outside unless it was dark or the Sabbath. Next, Gloucester people rescued some seized molasses (October), and Saville, who meanwhile had been manhandled

---

[5]*Sheaffe* v. Triton, case 48, in John Adams, *Legal Papers of John Adams*, ed. L. Kinvin Wroth and Hiller B. Zobel, 3 vols. (Cambridge, Mass., 1965), 2:213–215. Davis's political activities: member of merchants' standing committee [Charles M. Andrews, "The Boston Merchants and the Non-Importation Movement," *CSMP* 19:164 (1916–1917)]; cooperation with other leaders (Hutchinson to Pownall, 8 March 1766, Letterbooks, MA 26:207–214; Rowe, *Letters and Diary*, pp. 76, 144, 145, 148, 151, 156, 213, 265); accused of smuggling [Thomas Hutchinson, *The Diary and Letters of His Excellency Thomas Hutchinson*, ed. Peter Orlando Hutchinson, 2 vols. (London, 1883, 1886), 1:67]; John Adams reported Davis as having said, "Country man I dont see what Occasion there is for a Governor and Council and House" (*Diary*, 16 Jan. 1766, 1:295). Dickerson, ed., *Journal of the Times*, pp. 40, 45; complaint of a shipowner, Sparks MSS., 10.3:22, HHL. Rowe, *Letters and Diary*, 15 Dec. 1768, p. 181; *BEP*, 23 Nov. 1767; narrative about Otis's speech in the House of Representatives, Sept. 1768, Sparks MSS., 10.2:81, HHL.

[6]Benjamin Lynde and Benjamin Lynde, Jr., *The Diaries of Benjamin Lynde and of Benjamin Lynde, Jr.*, ed. F. E. Oliver (Boston, 1880), p. 192; *BEP*, 12 Sept. 1769; *Boston Chron.*, 12 Sept. 1768; Council Records, 16:351–352, MSA.

[7]*BEP*, 19 Sept. 1768; *BNL*, 15 Sept, 1768; *Essex Gaz.*, 27 Sept. 1768. Two sailors were indicted and found guilty, Superior Court of Judicature, Records, 1769, ff. 72–73, SCCH.

[8]*Ibid.*, ff. 71–72; Jacob Parsons's petition, MA 44:673–676, and council proceedings thereon, Records, 16:407–408, MSA; *BEP*, 22 May 1769. In August 1771, Fellows was sentenced and whipped for stealing, *BG*, 2 Sept. 1771.

at Providence, was seized again in March 1770. He was carted through the streets, and, after acknowledging that he was an informer, he had "to swear that he would never more inform against any Person in that or any other Town." A justice of the peace trying to disperse the rioters was also attacked. Juries stalled or refused to indict the rioters.[9]

Many more riots happened against customs officials. Merchants openly threatened them. Convicted rioters were rescued from prison. These riots were always reactions to acts of the officals and were confined to redressing specific grievances. Since certain men again and again became targets of action while hosts of others were left unmolested, it seems safe to suggest that the crowd picked its targets according to their conduct in office. The rioters had no confidence that customs officials or any other placemen would be punished in the courts. Placemen not only from Massachusetts but from all colonies were rewarded by the king, whether former stamp distributors, customs officials, or governors. Offenders were pardoned, and fines were remitted. Tarring and feathering, introduced to mete out punishment where all-too-lenient courts would not act, was soon called "feathering one's nest" because the victims were granted pensions by the crown in many instances.[10] An informer to the crown officials reported that this further alienated the Sons of Liberty from the crown. "The common Argument they make use of is this, that the People make the King, and that whenever they think it proper to dispose him, they act Constitutionally."[11] Whether those whom the informer had overheard were sailors and mechanics we do not know. The term "Sons of Liberty," as used in Boston, was usually applied to the men from the middle class. By fall 1769, when the informer made his report, middle-class Bostonians had realized that they needed the people from the lower orders to make resistance effective.

LIMITED RESISTANCE TO TROOPS

Besides the civil placemen of the customs service, Bostonians had to deal with

[9]Jesse Saville's report, MA 88:220–223, printed in *EIHC* 42:36–39 (1906); Superior Court of Judicature, Records, 1769, ff. 210–211, SCCH; remission of fines, MA 44:680–681. Rescue: Council Records, 16:375–377, MSA. *A Proclamation,* Boston, 3 Nov. 1768, *Mass. Brds.* 1454. March 1770: *BEP,* 26 March 1770; *BG,* 26 March 1770; Prosecution of the rioters: Hutchinson to ———, Nov. 1768, Letterbooks, MA 26:324–325; Superior Court of Judicature, Records, 1770, ff. 235–236, SCCH; SCF 89791; *BG,* 19 Nov. 1770; *Essex Gaz.,* 13 Sept. 1770. No white man was found guilty. But the only black man among those indicted, a servant, was sentenced to sit on the gallows, to be whipped, to two years' imprisonment, and to give bond for seven years' good behavior. Hutchinson, *History,* 3:203–204, 365–370.

[10]*BEP,* 1 Aug. 1768; William Tyng to Bernard, 17 July 1768, MA 56:552; Council Records, 16:343, 598–599, 605–606, MSA; proclamation, MA 44:668, 669; Thomas Smith and Samuel Deane, *Journals of the Rev. Thomas Smith and the Rev. Samuel Deane, Pastors of the First Church in Portland,* ed. William Willis (Portland, Me., 1849), 28 Oct., 13 Nov. 1771, p. 220. On placemen and the law, see Pauline R. Maier, *From Resistance to Revolution: Colonial Radicals and the Development of American Opposition to Britain, 1765–1776* (New York, 1972), pp. 174, 186. On feathering one's nest: George R. T. Hewes, *Traits of the Tea Party: Being a Memoir of George R. T. Hewes,* ed. Benjamin B. Thatcher (New York, 1935), p. 134; Frank Moore, ed., *Songs and Ballads of the American Revolution* (Pt. Washington, N.Y., 1855), p. 42; James Murray to his sister, n.d. [1769], *Letters of James Murray, Loyalist,* ed. Nina M. Tiffany and Susan I. Leslay (Boston, 1901), p. 169: John Mein, "He goes home in hopes to make their mischievous intensions turn out to his Emolument"; John Adams, *The Works of John Adams,* ed. Charles Francis Adams, 10 vols. (Boston, 1850–1856), 4:76 (Novanglus V), on John Malcom, 1774; Ezra Stiles, *The Literary Diary,* ed. F. B. Dexter, 3 vols. (New York, 1901), 1:466–467, on the Reverend Mr. Peters from Hebron, Conn.

[11]Report from George Mason, 20 Oct. 1769, Sparks MSS., 10.3:40, HHL.

the military, and though opposition to both sometimes coincided, its patterns differed. Politicized and strongly enforced nonimportation agreements were aimed at the duties, direct action at officials. Harassment, accompanied by political statements and intensified by economic grievances, was the method used against the troops. When the lieutenant governor, the town watch, and the commanding military officer stated that the situation was under control, the pronouncement was true only when measured against the amount of resistance expected or when compared to the incidents in the months to come, climaxing in the fatal affair of 5 March 1770.

It seems that immediately after the arrival of the troops the built-up hostility gave way to some sympathy for the simple soldiers because of the treatment they received from their officers and because of the brutal punishments common in the army (and navy). Whipping, as a legal punishment in Massachusetts, was limited to 39 lashes. Everything above that was considered unchristian, a breaking of the Bible's commands. Bostonians were aghast when they witnessed the hundreds of lashes to which soldiers were condemned. At least one incident in which a small "mob" accosted an officer was credited by contemporaries to anger over the punishment of a soldier on the same day.[12] But compassion gave way to contempt over the soldiers' submission to such treatment. "Bloody backs" or "lobsters" they were called.

Numerous grievances reinforced this negative attitude. Military officers, at first, were the chief culprits. Quartered in private houses all over the town and often drunken, they made it clear that they despised the inhabitants, the "rebels." Relieving the guards on Sundays with military music disturbed public worship and tended to attract crowds of spectators. In 1769 one of the wardens, special magistrates to enforce the quiet of Lord's Day, attempted to disperse people watching the changing of the guard. Among them was one of the governor's sons, who was promptly invited by the military officers to stay around, the orders of the magistrate notwithstanding. Bernard Junior did so and was indicted for loitering.[13]

In other instances too, officials were obstructed when doing their duty. Not only did robberies and assaults increase, but the sheriff, his deputies, and the constables reguarly met with difficulties when serving warrants on soldiers or officers. Other grievances included the burden placed on taxpayers by the numerous poor persons following the army, the criminal neglect some officers showed for preventive measures against spreading of smallpox, and the presence of a military force when justice was administered and when representatives were elected. "The election of members of Parliament ought to be free."[14]

Singularly disturbing to some Bostonians was the thought of slave rebellion. Newspapers, officials, and some mercantile groups showed strong concern, while,

---

[12]Eliot to Hollis, 7 Sept. 1769, *MHSC* 4.4:444 (1858); Dalrymple to Gage, 19 Aug. 1769, quoted in John Shy, *Toward Lexington: The Role of the British Army in the Coming of the American Revolution* (Princeton, N.J., 1965), p. 313; "Queries of George Chalmers, with the Answers of General Gage," *MHSC* 4.4:370 (1858); deposition of Gilbert Carter, State Papers, 12:138–140, Gay Transcripts, MHS; Dickerson, ed., *Journal of the Times*, pp. 3, 6, 35.
[13]*Ibid.*, 17 Oct. 1768, pp. 7, 31, 37, 118–119; Eliot to Hollis, 29 Jan. 1769, *MHSC* 4.4:437–440 (1858). John Adams, *Works*, 2:213; Boston wardens to General Mackay, 17 June 1769, Misc. Bound Papers, vol. 13, MHS.
[14]Dickerson, ed., *Journal of the Times*, 3 Oct., 1 Nov. 1768, 6 Jan., 12 May, 30 May, 3 June 1769, pp. 2–3, 17, 46, 97, 104–106; selectmen's records, 1768–1770, *BTR*, vols. 20 and 23, especially 23:19; instructions to the representatives, 8 May 1769, *ibid.*, 16:285–289; Bernard to Gage, 15 May 1769, Gage to Bernard, 22 May 1769, State Papers, 11:141–146, Gay Transcripts, MHS.

according to the evidence available, racism had no influence on selection of targets by those men who engaged in brawls with soldiers. As to the whipping of soldiers, the *Evening Post* pointedly noted that white "Britons [were] scourged by Negro drummers." A justice of the peace watching a brawl did not interfere except to tell a Negro soldier to keep out, since this was a white man's affair. After a British officer was overheard inducing several Negro slaves to revolt against their masters, however, Boston's officials were in an uproar. The watch was put on special alert, the selectmen held emergency meetings, justices of the peace heard witnesses. "[T]he property" of several inhabitants, as it was expressed, had been encouraged to revolt. This endangered the social structure and tended "to excite an insurrection." Joshua Henshaw, selectman, Son of Liberty, and slave owner, thought it "prudent" to keep the affair "as secret as possible." A series of articles, printed not only in Boston but also in other colonies and representing a mercantile point of view, repeatedly assailed the attitude of the British toward freeing blacks and slaves and suggested, after two more regiments arrived in Boston, "that the aid and countenance of our Negro gentry may now be dispensed with."[15]

Most trouble-prone was the military guard system, which placed sentries all over town for military ceremonious and protective reasons. The guards gave ample occasion for resentment and incidents to the inhabitants, who rarely answered challenges, were stopped with bayonets, and then complained about armed assaults. In return, sentries were often abused and harassed till they lost their tempers. When a sentry attempted to strike his tormentors, they left off and went to swear out a warrant against him for breach of the peace. The top military officers complained to governor and councillors, but to avoid further incidents, they had to suspend the practice of challenging. This, however, at the same time aggravated an internal problem of the military—desertion. Especially the ferry guards and Neck guards were to prevent deserting soldiers from leaving the town.[16]

The newspapers again and again pointed out that disorders were the natural consequence when troops were injudiciously quartered in populous towns. The readiness of military officers fearing riots to put troops on alert each time the fire bells were rung led to an article in the *Gazette* coldly informing the officers that the town was governed by its own laws and those of the province, and informing the local people that, so far, military officers had to march the troops back to the barracks when "properly spoke to by the Town Officers." Brawls between inhabitants and soldiers and discussions among inhabitants in taverns became increasingly politicized in 1769, according to reports by informers to crown officials and depo-

[15]Dickerson, ed., *Journal of the Times*, pp. 3, 6, 16–17, 18, 21; *BTR* 20:313–314; Henshaw to Henshaw, 2 Nov. 1768, *J. Am. Hist.* 18:243–245 (1924); indictment, 15 March 1769, in Samuel Adams Papers, NYPL; deposition of John Hill, in Frederic Kidder, ed., *History of the Boston Massacre, March 5, 1770: Consisting of the Narrative of the Town, the Trial of the Soldiers and a Historical Introduction* (Albany, N.Y., 1870), p. 50. In 1775 a white middle-class woman expressed more fears about "Neagros" than about British soldiers, though the latter and not the former had repeatedly abused women. Helena Bayard to Meletiah Bourn, 7 June 1775, Bourn Papers, 3:29, HHL.
[16]Dickerson, ed., *Journal of the Times*, 2 Nov., 13 Dec. 1768, pp. 6, 34; "Vindex" [Samuel Adams], in *BG*, 5 Dec. 1768, *The Writings of Samuel Adams*, ed. Harry A. Cushing, 4 vols. (New York 1904–1908), 1:255–259; Council Records, 16:381–382, MSA; depositions of William Godson, Cornelius Murphy, James McKaan, and Henry Collins, State Papers, 12:102–103, 105–107, 115–117, 131–132, Gay Transcripts, MHS.

sitions by soldiers about incidents. Opposition to the troops and the authorities who sent them was voiced more clearly, and abuse of soldiers was mingled with statements that the king had no authority to send them.[17]

In 1768 the affrays had been unconnected and mainly unimportant. With increasing grievances, disaffection, and questioning of the right of the soldiers to be in town, the brawls began to follow certain patterns; they became intentional harassment rather than occasional incidents caused by the inconveniences of living in a garrisoned town. Small crowds assembled frequently, but until the end of August 1769 no large riot happened. The direct action fell into several different methods: harassment of individual soldiers on duty, gang warfare against off-duty soldiers, sabotage, encouragement of desertion. The soldiers were ready to strike back if insulted, and no restraints placed on them by officers could prevent it.

The harassment of soldiers on guard has already been mentioned. Small groups or crowds also attacked off-duty men and tried to beat them up. The soldiers' hats, side arms, and swords were valued as trophies by the assailants. Once, when a soldier was to be punished by his officers for being concerned in an affray, even Whig leaders interposed because he had been intentionally provoked. The soldiers sometimes fought back in groups and once attacked the house of a Bostonian particularly obnoxious to them. They also threatened to burn the town. Among the inhabitants the Ruddock brothers, Abiel and John, Jr., were, together with others, an especially active group. They dared take on soldiers on duty too. Whenever they got into trouble, their father, Justice Ruddock, arrested the attacked soldiers.[18]

Continuous action was taken to encourage desertion. In taverns the inhabitants treated soldiers to drinks and in this congenial atmosphere explained that they would furnish them with money and clothes. Deserters were conveyed out of town and hidden by farmers, who valued them as farm hands. Sometimes they were told that they would have a chance to acquire their own land. One countryman offered a soldier an annual salary of £50 if he would desert and drill the country militia. People caught inciting soldiers to desert were hauled into court, but the juries refused to indict. Many soldiers left their companies on their own impulse, as did sailors their crews. To guard "against the Mischievous humour of the populace, as well as to prevent Desertion," no boat from the warships was to come ashore without one officer who would solely "attend to the keeping her Crew together." Commodore Hood of the navy soon advertised for the return of 40 to 50 seamen. In the army 21 men left in a single night; 70 left during the first two weeks after the landing.[19] A concerted plan to increase desertion, proposed by townsmen, accord-

---

[17]*BG,* 26 Dec. 1768. Rowe, *Letters and Diary,* 31 Jan. 1769, p. 182; "Urbanus," in *BG,* 6 Feb. 1769; "Sallust," in *BNL,* 9 Feb. 1769; *BG,* 13 Feb. 1769; Richard Sylvester's information, 23 Jan. 1769, Sparks MSS., 10.3:12, HHL; deposition of George Smith, State Papers, 12:94, Gay Transcripts, MHS.

[18]Depositions, *ibid.,* pp. 81–82, 84–85, 90, 107–109, 124–125; SCF 88852, 89161, 101569; Peter Oliver, *Peter Oliver's Origin and Progress of the American Rebellion: A Tory View,* ed. Douglass Adair and John A. Schutz (Stanford, Calif., 1961), pp. 71–72; Daniel Chamier, Jr., to Bob ———, 18 June 1770, *Maryland Hist. Mag.* 4:284 (1909); Dickerson, ed., *Journal of the Times,* 27 Feb., 6 March 1769, pp. 71, 74–75; Superior Court of Judicature, Records, 1769, ff. 251–252, SCCH; Court of General Sessions of the Peace, Minute Book, 1769–1773, SCCH.

[19]Henry Hulton, Some Account of the Proceedings of the People of New England from the Establishment of a Board of Customs in America to the Breaking Out of the Rebellion in 1775, p. 93, Princeton Univ. Library, Princeton, N.J.;

ing to an informer's report, was aborted. While some officials supported the drive to reduce the troops by encouraging desertion, a substantial section opposed this policy, which could have seriously crippled army and navy. The Whig–mercantile-oriented series of articles, quoted earlier for its racist leanings, now again espoused a law-and-order stand and discouraged the inhabitants' activity. The army offered large rewards for any information about attempts to seduce soldiers to desert but seemingly with little result. Search parties were sent into the country to recapture deserters. But they were preceded by letters from Boston warning the farmers of their coming. One such detachment, which did find and capture two deserters, was surrounded by a crowd of countrymen and forced to release the prisoners.[20]

Sabotage was less frequent, according to the sources. The destruction of the guardhouse frame in October 1768 and two attempts to damage sentry boxes at the governor's official residence, the only incidents reported, were executed by small crowds, mainly boys. In 1769 an effort to evict the troops from the town's lands, granted them for temporary use by the selectmen without consent of the town meeting, did not materialize.[21]

Inhabitants aiding the soldiers were punished and intimidated by rioters. A woman calling for help when a soldier was beaten up was pushed over, "damned for a whore," and told to keep quiet. A man who had lured a girl into the barracks, where she was abused by the soldiers, was carried by a crowd to the docks and ducked several times. He escaped but was caught again in Charlestown and tarred and feathered. Persons giving shelter to soldiers harassed by inhabitants were threatened by crowds with having their houses pulled down. Justices of the peace were intimidated, and large crowds attended judicial interrogations of soldiers. Petitions to the governor demanding retention of a regiment ordered to withdraw were voted "inamical" to the town in a town meeting.[22]

By fall 1769 there was a clear and vocal opposition to soldiers among large sections of the inhabitants. This opposition was undercut by the interests of shopkeepers, by large merchants, and by law-and-order forces among the leadership.

THE ECONOMICS OF NONIMPORTATION AND THE QUARTERING OF TROOPS

Nonimportation has frequently been considered as an economic weapon in a

Superior Court of Judicature, Records, 1768, f. 370, SCCH; depositions by John Croker and James Corkrin, State Papers, 12:117–118, 121, Gay Transcripts, MHS; Dickerson, ed., *Journal of the Times*, 3 Oct., 12 Oct., 15 Oct., 1 Nov. 1768, pp. 3, 5, 6, 17; Gage to Hillsborough, 18 Aug. 1768, *The Correspondence of General Thomas Gage,* ed. Clarence E. Carter, 2 vols. (New Haven, Conn., 1931, 1933), 1:186–188; Henshaw to Henshaw, 2 Nov. 1768, *J. Am. Hist.* 18:243–245 (1924); instructions to Captain John Corner, 2 May 1768, *MHSP* 55:271–272 (1921–1922).

[20]Dickerson, ed., *Journal of the Times*, 3 Oct., 12 Oct., 15 Oct. 1768, 16 Jan., 2 Feb., 14 Feb. 1769, pp. 3, 5, 6, 51, 59, 64; Hutchinson to Whately, 17 Oct. 1768, Letterbooks, MA 25:283; informer's statement, Sparks MSS., 10.3:18, HHL; Dalrymple to Gage, 1–29 Oct. 1769, State Papers, 11:181–189, Gay Transcripts, MHS.

[21]Rowe, *Letters and Diary,* 10 Oct. 1768, p. 177; Council Records, 16:391–392, MSA; Dickerson, ed., *Journal of the Times,* 9 Nov. 1768, 13 Jan. 15 March, 4 April 1769, pp. 21, 50, 78, 87, *BTR* 16:273, 274, 277.

[22]Depositions of John Shelton *et al.* and John Timmons, State Papers, 12:89–90, 128–140, Gay Transcripts, MHS; *BEP,* 3 July, 10 July 1769; *BG,* 6 Nov. 1769; petition for a town meeting, signed by 146 persons, Misc. Unbound Papers, 1769, BCH; *BTR* 16:296.

political struggle to obtain constitutional ends. Until recently, students had to go back to Arthur M. Schlesinger's treatise on the colonial merchants, first published in 1918, for a comprehensive survey of mercantile interests and strategies during the revolutionary period. Now James A. Henretta and Joseph A. Ernst have inquired into economic and related social developments with much greater sophistication. A close reading of the innumerable memorials and petitions concerning the tightening of the trade regulations after 1763 reveals that political, constitutional, and economic arguments were deeply interwoven in contemporary thinking. The emphasis placed on political ideology since Bernard Bailyn's publication of the *Pamphlets* therefore represents only one section of the complex play of social and economic, political, and constitutional forces that shaped ideology or were reflected in it. Egnal and Ernst have added an interpretation of the merchant position in the empire and as a class. Works on the lower classes, particularly artisans and sailors, give some glimpses of their perspective. Shopkeepers, small merchants, large-scale artisans, and early manufacturing entrepreneurs, important because they furnished a link between lower and upper classes, economically, socially, and ideologically, have not yet been the subject of similar studies.[23]

The economic position of the colonies in the empire, legally defined by the trade laws, was changing long before the new imperial policy was mapped out. The increase in imports in the fifties and the resulting deficits in the balance of trade brought about a growing dependence on British credits. Governmental military spending during the Seven Years' War briefly eased the situation, but after the end of the hostilities British expenses slumped, and provincial governments rapidly retired their war currency issues. In the subsequent recession numerous merchant houses went bankrupt. For many this meant a dip below subsistence level and dependence on charities. When the British credit contraction had passed its peak, goods began to flow into the colonies at a rate that resulted in accumulation of large overstocks among the well-to-do and wealthy merchants and in extension of direct sales to small merchants, even shopkeepers. Under these conditions a nonimportation period was useful to redress the balance of trade, to encourage local manufactures, and, for large merchants, to reduce stock. They could regain control over the shopkeepers and sell off their high inventories, often with considerable markups because after a few months of no shipments demand for British goods outstripped supply. Small entrepreneurs benefited too. Their products, often inferior to British imports, suddenly found a ready market. In Boston the stationing of troops complicated the situation because mechanics and laborers were faced with competition from off-duty soldiers in a labor market in which supply of labor already outstripped demand.[24]

---

[3]Arthur M. Schlesinger, Sr., *The Colonial Merchants and the American Revolution, 1763–1776* (New York, 1918); Marc Egnal and Joseph A. Ernst, "An Economic Interpretation of the American Revolution," *WMQ* 3.29:1–32 (1972); Joseph A. Ernst, *Money and Politics in America, 1755–1775: A Study of the Currency Act of 1764 and the Political Economy of the Revolution* (Chapel Hill, N.C., 1973); E. James Ferguson, "Currency Finance: An Interpretation of Colonial Monetary Practices," *WMQ* 3.10:153–180 (1953); James A. Henretta, "Economic Development and Social Structure in Colonial Boston," *WMQ* 3.22:75–92 (1965), and *The Evolution of American Society, 1700–1815: An Interdisciplinary Analysis* (Lexington, Mass., 1973); Allan Kulikoff, "The Progress of Inequality in Revolutionary Boston," *WMQ* 3.28:375–412 (1971). For further literature, see the essay by Egnal and Ernst.

[24]Egnal and Ernst, "An Economic Interpretation," pp. 10–24; town-meeting records, Boston, 1767–1770, *BTR*, vols. 16, 18; Esther Forbes, *Paul Revere and the World He Lived In* (Boston, 1942), pp. 141–142.

For a 10-month period, from the end of September 1768 to the end of July 1769, the Boston merchants and the allied politicians had their own mouthpiece, the *Journal of the Times,* a series of articles written in Boston but published originally in New York, then in other colonies and Boston too. It has frequently been called one of the most radical and rabble-rousing publications during the controversy with Britain, because it minutely listed any affray between soldiers and inhabitants in Boston, any "misdeed" of crown officials, and because it usually accompanied these by less than friendly comments. O. M. Dickerson has pointed out that its content was intended to raise sympathies of three distinct audiences, the Massachusetts people, Americans in general (including the South), and the British. This analysis has to be modified. From all three groups only those who bought or read newspapers were reached. The *Journal* appealed to a section of the population that can be described as somewhat unpolitical and conservative, respectable and upper class. It supported mercantile or planter interests for social stability. No radical schemes ever appeared in its columns. Spinning bees were the means for redress. The North Carolina Regulators, who had many sympathizers among Bostonians, were considered "very alarming." Impressment of sailors were mentioned only as a burden on merchants, since wages increased. When Boston merchants were falling over one another to get contracts for supplying the troops, the *Journal* noted that in Halifax, where the troops came from, trade would decline seriously, because its main support was army and navy contracts. Then the *Journal* explained the relations between patriotism and business. To get back the army and business, Halifax "patriots were about erecting a liberty pole, and employing some boys to sing the Liberty Song." Troops would then have to return "to quell such disturbances." As to the Boston situation, direct action was discountenanced. Army officers, according to the *Journal,* improved their conduct upon mere admonishing by civil magistrates, though judicial prosecution might be necessary in the case of rank-and-file soldiers. The dangers arising to constitutional liberties were mentioned, but only drunken officers' suggestions for a slaves' revolt caused real concern. Labor competition and similar lower-class problems never entered its distinguished columns.[25]

Once nonimportation had become official policy, the Merchants' Society coordinated the efforts. At first, merchants solved difficulties by gentlemen's agreements or recommendations. When tensions mounted and compulsory measures were proposed, Otis, Samuel Adams, and other Whig politicians gained influence. They seem consciously to have sought this influence because they distrusted the merchant mentality, suspecting them of being ready to end nonimportation whenever it would help their short-term business interests. They belonged to the new committees elected after the *Liberty* incident and could thus either use the votes of the town meetings to pressure the merchants or restrain voters from antagonizing the old guard too much.

[25]Dickerson, ed., *Journal of the Times,* pp. vii–xiii. On slave insurrection, *ibid.,* pp. 16–17, 84 , 91–92. On Halifax, *ibid.,* pp. 5–6. On spinning bees, *ibid.,* p. 6. On Regulators, *ibid.,* p. 29. Frothingham named William Cooper as author; Governor Bernard named Samuel Adams. The line of reasoning in the *Journal* points to Cooper rather than Adams.

The Merchants' Society also needed the cooperation of small traders and shop-keepers to make the nonimportation effectual. These allies naturally demanded and acquired a voice in further proceedings once they had signed the agreement. The merchants' meetings were expanded, their name was changed to "meeting of the trade" or "the Body," and Town Clerk William Cooper kept the minutes. To some alert observers, these changes were an ill omen. "It appears to me to carry the most threatning Aspects on the Authority of G. Britain of anything that has been yet attempted: the combination of Journeymen Weavers and Taylors are in my opinion Trifling Affairs compared with this ... ," wrote Andrew Oliver to Governor Bernard.[26]

The "patriotism" of the merchants, so revealingly exposed by their publication, the *Journal of the Times*, and by their actions, contracting with the army, was not only suspect to mechanics whose earnings fell while prices rose. It was criticized by the shopkeepers who in prosperous times could make a living but now lost the capability to support themselves "honestly." It was viewed with misgivings in the countryside, where the drive against luxuries, bringing about a reduction of the specie outflow and an easing of the currency shortage, had been taken up with enthusiasm. When the agreement collapsed in 1770, a man in Worcester stated his criticism in very strong terms to John Adams:

> He is very bitter vs. the Town of Boston. I Hate 'em for my Soul says he.—Great Patriots—were for Non Importation, while their old Rags lasted, and as soon as they were sold at enormous Prices, they were for importing—no more to be heard about Manufactures—and now, there is a greater Flood of Goods than ever were know—and as to Tea, those who were most strenuous against it are the only Persons who have any to sell.

In 1774 and later, the low reputation of the merchants deepened east–west cleavages. Many Whig politicians, James Warren and Josiah Quincy, Samuel and John Adams, the Reverend Charles Chauncy, were fearful that their "mercenary" spirit would contribute to enslaving the country.[27]

The shopkeepers' position was ambiguous too. They profited from the increased purchasing power of the community, brought about by free-spending officers and by soldiers' wages. The ambiguity of the Puritan morality, its condemnation of vice and approbation of worldly success, became evident when a town committee was "to Consider what steps can be taken to give a check to the progress of Vice and

---

[26]Rowe, *Letters and Diary*, Feb.–March 1768, pp. 152–155; Hutchinson, *History*, 3:145–146; Hutchinson to Bernard, 8 Aug. 1769, Letterbooks, MA 26:361–362, to Whately, 24 Aug. 1769, *ibid.*, pp. 367–368. Oliver to Bernard, 21 Nov. 1769, Letterbooks, 1:118, MHS. Hillsborough, in his instructions to Bernard, had demanded information on "Town Meetings, and Meetings of the Merchants, (which appear to me to be of far greater moment than the less deliberate Proceedings of a Mob)." Instructions to Governor Bernard, 11 June 1768, Instructions to the Governors pp. 2405–2407, MHS.

[27]Army contracts: see Chapter 5, note 47. Criticism in the country: John Adams, *Diary*, 26 June 1770, 2 June 1771, 1:351, 2:20. There is no monograph on the deep distrust and suspicion that Whig politicians harbored for merchants. But see Stephen E. Patterson, *Political Parties in Revolutionary Massachusetts* (Madison, Wis., 1973), pp. 113–114. Charles Chauncy to Richard Price, 30 May 1774, "Price Letters," *MHSP* 2.18:266–268 (1903).

Immoralities in this Town, and to promote a Reformation of Manners.'' After a noncommittal report and long debates, the town was unable even to curb the sale of rum to soldiers. The only measure taken was an attempt to prevent ''unlicensed Strangers'' from peddling liquors. Thus, profits could be kept in town. Finally the army took action, refusing to pay the soldiers' subsistence money to prevent them from spending it on rum and distributing meat bought with the retained wages instead. When it became known that butchers and other suppliers overcharged the army to the damage of the individual soldiers, the merchants' mouthpiece, the *Journal of the Times,* noted threateningly, ''the inhabitants are far from interesting themselves in this dispute.''[28]

Late in 1769, tensions between shopkeepers and hucksters on the one hand and merchants on the other began to grow. Overstocked merchants argued for continued nonimportation, and in consequence ''great numbers of smaller Traders are to be sacrificed to the Interest of a few.'' The situation became trouble prone when those dependent on their daily business began to realize that patriotism in the guise of nonimportation meant profits for some merchants. ''The Advanced price put upon the old Stock begins to open the eyes of some.'' The treatment of those whose livelihood depended on their daily business was similar to that of the poor. But as these men had known better times, they were more conscious of the deterioration of their economic situation and accordingly more restless. Many small traders were inclined to break off from the agreement, especially ''shopkeepers, whose daily bread depends on that business, unable to stand the shock, would willingly depart therefrom.'' But in the ensuing ''hard struggle,'' the ''principle people,'' ''land-holders,'' ''most substantial people,'' as far as they were Whigs or could gain from the policy, stood firm. The expansion of the merchants' meetings to include shop-keepers thus not only gave the latter some say but also provided opportunities for the economically more powerful and politically more influential merchants to guide the shopkeepers' stand on policies.[29]

The political course of the mechanic population, because of their social and economic position, also differed from the merchants' politics. They took a more radical stand on the presence of troops in town. But on nonimportation they were more cautious than the Whig leadership. They, too, watched Whig merchants profit. They, too, paid higher prices. They watched the changes being made in the nonimportation agreements to accommodate the business interests of individual merchants. But when they petitioned to exempt certain goods so as to permit shipbuilding and to decrease unemployment, they were turned down by imperious Whig magistrates. Had not angry resolves against the king and Parliament been passed for not admitting the petitions of the colonies? It was also noted that other

[28]*BTR* 16:273–274, 18:17, 19; Dickerson, ed., *Journal of the Times,* pp. 28, 35, 48.
[29]Oliver to Bernard, 10 Jan., 21 Nov. 1769, Letterbooks, 1:119, 135–136, MHS; John Montresor ''Journals of Capt. John Montresor, 1757–1778,'' ed. G. D. Scull, *N.Y. Hist. Soc. Coll.* (1881), pp. 115–544, 14 Sept. 1770, ''what is wanted becomes exorbitant'' (p. 403); Oliver, *American Rebellion,* p. 65; Jonathan Trumbull to William S. Johnson, 29 Jan. 1770, *MHSC* 5.9:400–404 (1885); John Powell to Christopher Champlin, 23 Oct. 1769, *MHSC* 7.9:294 (1914); *Boston Chron.,* 23 Oct. 1769; Schlesinger, *Colonial Merchants,* p. 166. Because of the difficult economic situation, three tax collectors refused to serve. *BTR* 16:299, 301, 303.

towns were ready to take the problems of mechanics into account. A fortnight after the Boston mechanics had been rebuffed, news arrived that the ships for which orders had been received were now being built in Newburyport.[30]

Sailors continued to be exposed to impressment. The leadership brought about no lasting change after the impressment riots in the wake of the *Liberty* seizure. From the end of 1768 to the middle of 1769, impressment occurred frequently, though no press gangs were sent on shore. Sometimes it seems to have been used as a means of retribution against Whig merchants. All of Captain Dashwood's men were pressed in one incident, while usually only a few men were taken from each ship. Dashwood was an active member of the Merchants' Society and a supporter of the nonimportation agreements. Neither navy officers nor merchants seem to have been the least bit concerned that this part of their vendetta was carried on the backs of the sailors and their families. Merchants were merely concerned because impressment meant scarcity of men and rising wages or delayed the sailing of ships. The revolutionary potential of the sailors' discontent was never recognized or used by contemporary leadership; their class position made them blind to it, or they were afraid of its internal consequences. At the time of the Stamp Act, social upheaval had been feared if the sailors were laid off, but surviving sources record no similar explicit apprehensions for the years 1768–1770, when trade declined.[31]

The sailors' consciousness of their rights and the politicization and mobilization consequent upon increased impressment came to the attention of the better sort in April 1769. Action in a special Court of Admiralty against Michael Corbet, a sailor from a Marblehead vessel who had killed a British navy officer, Lieutenant Panton, in self-defense against impressment, aroused widespread concern. Of the 12 members of the bench, six came from Massachusetts. Five of these, Governor Bernard, Lieutenant Governor Hutchinson, Province Secretary Oliver, Admiralty Judge Auchmuty, and Customs Collector Harrison had been targets of crowd action in the years immediately preceding the trial; Collector John Nutting of Salem became so later. The judges rejected a plea for trial by jury, but several of them privately conferred with one of the interested parties, the Royal Navy. The prosecutor charged murder.

On the other side were the sailors who had resisted impressment. They had hidden themselves in the forepeak when Panton with a number of marines boarded their vessel. Though it was later claimed that the navy men came as customs officers, Panton immediately asked the captain for the men. He was willing not to impress favorites of the captain and American men, or at least married American men. When the four Irish crew members did not choose to submit to impressment, Panton threatened to take the Americans, or all men on board, though originally he had wanted only two men. The resisting crewmen argued that "they did not want to

[30]Journal of Transactions, Sparks MSS., 10.3:55–56, HHL; *Advertisement* (Boson, 1769), *Mass. Brds.* 1473.
[31]Council Records, 16:313, MSA; Dickerson, ed., *Journal of the Times,* 7 Oct. 1768, p. 3, cf. pp. 23, 51, 90; Rowe, *Letters and Diary,* 5 Dec. 1768, p. 181; Nathaniel Ames, "Diary of Dr. Nathaniel Ames," ed. Sarah Breck Baker, 7 June 1768, *Dedham Hist. Reg.* 2:149 (1891); Jesse Lemisch, "Jack Tar in the Streets," *WMQ* 3.25:393 (1968).

hurt him or his Men, they only wanted their own Liberty.''[32] In the ensuing abuse and argument, one of the marines fired into the forepeak, wounding Michael Corbet in the face. To Corbet's angry protests, Lieutenant Panton jauntily answered that he had not given any orders to shoot, that once on the man-of-war Corbet could demand satisfaction of the sniper. When Panton approached the forepeak, Corbet threw a harpoon, which unintentionally killed him. He and the other crewmen were arrested and carried on board the man-of-war. One of the Marblehead sailors, considering himself impressed, asked the vessel's master to deliver his chest and belongings to his wife.[33]

Accounts of the affair spread rapidly along the coast. John Adams, defense counsel for Michael Corbet and deeply impressed by his political understanding, gave the following report about the reaction of the waterfront community on the trial: "No trial had ever interested the community so much before, excited so much curiosity and compassion, or so many apprehensions of the fateful consequences of the supremacy of parliamentary jurisdiction, or the intrigues of parliamentary courts. No trial had drawn together such crowds of auditors from day to day. . . ." Corbet was acquitted, officially because Panton had neither an impressment nor a customs search warrant. But there were other reasons for acquittal. It saved the court from ruling on two British laws that seemed to forbid any impressment in the American colonies, an interest dear to the bench and particularly to one of its members, Commodore Samuel Hood of the British Navy, who had ordered the pressing of sailors.[34]

The impression this case left was strong enough that when several years later a murky case of murder on the high seas came up for trial many were ready to charge the British navy with the crime.[35] Another consequence of the trial's outcome was a restriction of impressment. About that time, bread prices began to fall in Boston, although in Philadelphia, one of the major supplying ports for Boston, they had already gone down in the preceding harvest season.[36]

In a town meeting in March 1769, the inhabitants explicitly acknowledged that the small shopkeepers, mechanics, and sailors were hit hardest by nonimportation when they elected a committee "To Consider of some Suitable Methods employing

[32]For the legal proceedings and witnesses' despositions, see *Rex* v. *Corbet,* case 56, in John Adams, *Legal Papers,* 2:276–335. The other six judges were Commodore Samuel Hood (Royal Navy); the governor, two councillors, and a customs collector from New Hampshire; and a Vice Admiralty judge from Rhode Island. On the Vice Admiralty Courts, see Carl Ubbelohde, *The Vice-Admiralty Courts and the American Revolution* (Chapel Hill, N.C., 1960), and David S. Lovejoy, "Rights Imply Equality: The Case against Admiralty Jurisdiction in America, 1764–1776," *WMQ* 3.16:459–484 (1959). John Boyle, "Boyle's Journal of Occurrences in Boston, 1759–1778," 22 April, 23 May, 17 June 1769, *NEHGR* 84:258–259 (1930); Hutchinson, *History,* 3:166–167; Dickerson, ed., *Journal of the Times,* 4 May 1769, pp. 94–95; *Boston Chron.,* 1 May 1769; witness accounts by Peter Bowen and Thomas Power, in John Adams, *Legal Papers,* 2:296–297, 313.

[33]Witness Thomas Power, *ibid.,* p. 315.

[34]*Ibid.,* p. 280; Adams to Jedediah Morse, 20 Jan. 1816, in John Adams, *Works,* 10:204, 209–210; Hiller B. Zobel, *The Boston Massacre* (New York, 1970), pp. 121–131.

[35]*Rex* v. *Nickerson,* case 57, in John Adams, *Legal Papers,* 2:335–351; Hutchinson, *History,* 3:299–303; Rowe, *Letters and Diary,* Nov.–Dec. 1772, pp. 236–237, 247 *passim; BPB,* 9 Aug. 1773; *BG,* 2 Aug. 1773.

[36]Assize for bread, flour, and wheat, selectmen's records, 1767–1768, *BTR,* vol. 20. Anne Bezanson, Robert D. Gray, and Miriam Hussey, *Prices in Colonial Pennsylvania* (Philadelphia, 1935), pp. 12–15.

the Poor of the Town, *whose Numbers and distresses are dayly increasing by the loss of its Trade and Commerce."* The overseers of the poor reported that they expected a large increase in expenses. While the normally self-sufficient groups could at least voice discontent, the poor had no such possibility. Many still received out-relief, but those who had no other support were quartered in the almshouse or workhouse. These, subject to the regulation of the authorities, against which there was no appeal, were to become the first of legally free people to be forced into manufacture work, a process that achieved its full momentum only decades later.[37]

A "Society for encouraging Industry and employing the Poor" had already been founded in 1764, when the first measures had been introduced to reduce reliance on British imports and to encourage local manufactures. In 1767, after adoption of a nonconsumption agreement, a committee elected to employ the poor in linen manu-facture first advised against production in a factory, then for it, provided the inhabi-tants would defray the necessary charges. It rejected the offer by one John Brown to undertake the manufacture and the employment of the poor. Then, upon its recom-mendation, the town voted a subscription to encourage "John Barrett Esq. and others," who had begun the manufacture. John Barrett and those modestly termed "others" were five of the seven members of the committee that had rejected Brown's application and demanded money from the town. Ezekiel Goldthwait, Edward Payne, Henderson Inches, and Meletiah Bourne were members of the Merchants' Society. Barrett was overseer of the poor; Inches and Bourne had held the same office till 1766. The overseers controlled the town's budget for poverty relief, which since the postwar depression and the 1764 smallpox epidemic had averaged 54 percent of the town's total annual tax budget, or more than £3000 lawful money per year. The inhabitants perceived that these incipient entrepreneurs acted from self-interest, and no financial support could be found, though Barrett and Co. protested, "Our design in pursuing this Business is not to enrich ourselves, but for employing the many Poor." Without taking notice, the town passed to the next issue on the agenda. The *Boston Chronicle,* mouthpiece of the opposition to nonim-portation, reported dissensions among Whig officials about the funds for charity as well as financial irregularities.[38]

The committee of 1769 included John Barrett again, William Molineux, and others. They reported that 230 persons were in the almshouse and another 40 in the

---

[37]*BTR* 16:273, 275; cf. "Marcus Aurelianus," in *BNL,* 6 Feb. 1772. For the position of the poor in later decades, see David J. Rothman, *The Discovery of the Asylum: Social Order and Disorder in the New Republic* (Boston, 1971), and Paul G. Faler, "Workingmen, Mechanics and Social Change: Lynn, Massachusetts, 1800–1860" (Ph.D. diss., Univ. of Wisconsin, 1971).

[38]*BTR* 16:222, 225, 226–227, 230–231, 239–240, 249–250. The group of 1767 demanded £300 for initial investment and £300 annually for a period of five to seven years. Edward Payne had been connected with the similar Linen Manufactury Company, which had been unable to repay sums lent to it by the town. *BTR* 18:138–139. In 1769 there was dissent among the Whig leadership about the town's funds for the poor. John Mein, Key to a Certain Publication, Sparks MSS., 10.3:45–47, HHL. The percentage of the total budget used for poverty relief may be understating the case, since the nominal sum, voted by the town to be collected as taxes, decreased by abatements made at the discretion of the assessors later. This bias is probably offset by the parts of fines levied for a number of legal offenses that were used for the poor. The figures given here compare the total expenses of the overseers of the poor, as audited annually, to that year's nominal total amount of taxes.

workhouse. These and children, "proper Objects of such Charity," should be employed for spinning. A "responsible Gentleman" was willing to execute this proposal provided the town raised £500 for the overseers, £200 of which were to be granted to the gentleman, the other £300 lent to him. The overseers' expenses had already jumped to more than 70 percent of the budget, approximately 26 percent above the 10-year average (1764–1773). The gentleman to be supplied with funds was committeeman William Molineux, who requested the town in 1772 to change the £300 loan into a grant. But after considerable debate and after hearing the lawyers, the town refused and attempted to recover the loan in 1773. The available evidence for the two plans to employ the poor suggests that a few well-to-do and clever men attempted to exploit the political and economic situation. Belonging to or closely connected with the town officialdom, they used their position, the lowly place assigned by society to the poor, and the money raised by the inhabitants to further their own advantage. Both plans failed. The relationship of the men to their workers, the poor, evidently fell into the workhouse tradition of getting work out of women and children, who are in no bargaining position to prevent exploitation.[39]

The opposition to the Townshend duties and the troops brought about two important internal developments. First, the failure of nonviolent measures led to a change in political leadership. Men who were more responsive to popular grievances replaced the old merchant leaders. Second, on an intermediate level the merchant–captains consolidated their position and emerged as a group. They were men of good political knowledge and not averse to the use of violence against "harassment" by officials. The best-known example is Daniel Malcom. In business he was not averse to smuggling; in a town meeting he moved that a vote of thanks be passed in honor of the author of the *Farmer's Letters*. In his dealings with customs officials, he could chose between constitutional arguments and rough abuse, between bribery, compromise, and evasion. Economically these men were medium property owners. They met at the Long Room Club at Edes and Gill's printing office, and via Paul Revere they were connected with St. Andrew's Lodge, which met next door in the Green Dragon Tavern. The 15 men who jointly commissioned Paul Revere to make the silver bowl commemorating the legislators' vote not to rescind the Massachusetts circular letter were from this group. The same men sometimes appeared together in riots or drew up and signed petitions.

While the troops and nonimportation caused dislocation among many occupations that could not be redressed by town-meeting action, the inhabitants tried at least to put their own house in order by addressing themselves to a number of thorny economic problems. Samuel Adams's tax arrears were debated. The franchise for the mills was revoked. This conditional monopoly had long been due to review, since the owners of the franchise, respectable townsmen, had stopped fulfilling their obligations. The result was that the inhabitants had to cart their grain out of town for

---

[39]*BTR* 16:275–277, 18:70–73, 139. A month before the lawyers argued against granting Molineux the money, he reportedly wanted "to destroy" two of the Whig lawyers, Josiah Quincy and Benjamin Kent. *Rowe, Letters and Diary*, 5 Feb, 1772, p. 224.

grinding.[40] Only in retrospect do such problems appear insignificant. To the townspeople, they were different aspects of one question, how to improve Boston's economic situation, or at least how to ward off new impositions, whether originating from local men or imperial authorities.

---

[40]*BTR* 16:271–272 (Adams's tax arrears), 279–282, 294–295 (mills), 301–302 (forestalling of the market), 293 (loan arrears of the Manufactory Company), 290–292 (state of town's finances). As for the tax issue, a thorough analysis of Samuel Adams's notebook of deficient taxpayers would increase our understanding of the methods of collection and their economic and possibly political aspects. The book is in Misc. Unbound Papers, BCH. Daniel Malcom on *Farmer's Letters:* Commissioners of Customs to Board of Trade, 28 March 1768, *MHSP* 55:268–271 (1921–1922); cf. *BTR* 16:241–243. For the Long Room Club, see Chapter 2, note 29.

Merchants' Violence: Compulsory Nonimportation

THE FAILURE OF NONVIOLENCE

In June 1768, lower-class Bostonians realized that, the leadership's protestations notwithstanding, orderly remonstrations led nowhere. Their life and liberty were endangered by impressment. Therefore they took action. The mercantile groups realized a year later that voluntary nonimportation did not solve their problems or suit their interests. For them, neither life nor liberty was endangered but pocketbooks were. Accordingly, they took to direct action. During the Stamp Act period, opposition to British measures had been so widespread among the population that no policies for preventing internal sabotage of the resistance were necessary. Opposition after 1765 was of three kinds: British taxes, duties, and troops. While resistance sometimes could be successful with support from parts of the community, other measures needed the support of the majority of the population. When, after 1768, different interests came into the open, and when some were willing to abide by British regulation, the character of the opposition had to change. Side by side with nonviolent pressure and violence against interference by the British ministry, this policy had to be enforced on dissenting members of the local communities in provincial Massachusetts.

Nonconsumption and nonimportation were effective only if generally adhered to; otherwise, those who continued to import would take over the business of the nonimporters. An additional problem arose when the old tradition of ostracizing outsiders proved ineffectual. While the commissioners of customs, who collected money without providing business opportunities, had been isolated for a while, intensive socializing took place between merchants and army officers. Profiteering was common and probably more successful than any racketerring of the customs officials. Because of the structure of governmental institutions and the mercantile background of many magistrates, nothing was undertaken to prevent cooperation with the troops. Thus the removal of the troops, if intended, had to be effected by inhabitants who suffered more from the presence of the troops than they gained. Nonimportation, on the other hand, was enforced by Whig town officials and by patriot merchants whose business interests were seriously affected.

The moves to reduce reliance on British imports had begun in October 1767 (Phase 1, Oct.–March) by a drive for nonconsumption, mainly restricted to New England. Phase 2 comprised the efforts for a tri-city, nonimportation agreement, March–June 1768; Phase 3, independent agreements. In October 1769, Phase 4, the most decisive phase began with the extension of the scope of the nonimportation agreements. The last two phases—the movement to terminate the agreements, April–October 1770, and the actual collapse, October 1770–July 1771—will be dealt with later. After the agreements became effective in Boston, the Merchants' Society was busy preventing breaches of faith by the signers. At the same time the continued importation of nonsigners began to create discontent. Handbills were distributed by the "Sons of Liberty And Supporters of the Non-Importation Agreement," threatening that anyone who insulted or menaced the committees concerned with drawing up or enforcing the agreements, or opposed their press releases, would be chastised. "As a warning," one of the handbills was to be "posted up at the Door or Dwelling-House of the Offender." In April 1769 a "committee of seven" for the inspection of all arriving ships was appointed. Inadvertent violations resulted in constant bickering among the signers. Of greater importance were the repeated intentional importations by some Sons of Liberty, who finally had to agree to store their goods under supervision of the committee. Thomas Young, one of the patriot political leaders, admitted that proscribed goods had been carried in the vessels of the chief patriot merchants, but he shrugged the affair off, stating that if they had not carried them, others would have.[1]

The efforts of the merchants and their political allies also were applauded by the inhabitants. At town meetings, votes of thanks were passed in honor of "our Merchants [who] have so strictly adhered to their Agreement." It was then recommended to the inhabitants not to buy from importers but to "use their Influence to promote in the way of Trade the Interest of those Gentlemen, who have nobly preferred the future welfare of their Country and all North America to any present advantages of their own." At another town meeting the inhabitants could not "but express their Astonishment and Indignation that any of its Citizens should be so lost to the feelings of Patriotism, and the common Interest, and so thoroughly and infamously selfish as to obstruct" the execution of the agreement. It was "solemnly" voted to enter those still refusing to sign the nonimportation agreement into the town records that posterity might remember them for deserting their country, for opposing it, and for preferring their private advantage to the common interest. The names of the importers were also published on the first page of the *Gazette* by order of the town meeting. The merchants alone had not dared take this measure for fear of legal prosecution.[2]

[1]Arthur M. Schlesinger, Sr., *The Colonial Merchants and the American Revolution, 1763–1773* (New York, 1918), Chs. 3–6; *The True Sons of Liberty*, Brds. (Boston, 1768), Evans 11097; BG, 24 April 1769; John Rowe, *Letters and Diary of John Rowe, Boston Merchant, 1759–1762, 1764–1779*, ed. Anne Rowe Cunningham (Boston, 1903; reprinted, 1969), 4 Aug. 1769, pp. 190–191; Bernard to Hillsborough, 8 May 1769, Sparks MSS., 10.3:24, HHL; Thomas Young to Hugh Hughes, 21 Dec. 1772, Misc. Bound Papers, vol. 14, MHS; Gage to Hillsborough, 26 Sept. 1768, *The Correspondence of General Thomas Gage*, ed. Clarence E. Carter, 2 vols. (New Haven, Conn., 1931, 1933), 1:197.

[2]John Boyle, "Boyle's Journal of Occurrences in Boston, 1759–1778," 4 Oct. 1769, NEHGR 84:260 (1930); BG, 12

One additional nonviolent measure, proposed by John Hancock, had been the attempt to force nonsigners into compliance by arbitrarily raising their taxes. The motion was attached as a rider to an order for preventing fraud in the sale of hay and wood. This unusual method resulted in the resignation of two-thirds of the members of the respective committee. Opposition rallied, and the report of the committee chairman was not even recorded in the town records. The assessors, bound by oath to value the inhabitants impartially, refused to deliver the tax lists and were sustained by the selectmen. They had always been somewhat separated from the wealthy top officialdom, to which they belonged by rank, because Boston's voters took care to elect only small and middling property holders to his office. Finally the town reconsidered Hancock's motion and repealed its earlier vote.[3]

While the movement spread, while other towns elected committees of inspection, while meetings voted to "Expose to shame and Contempt all persons" attempting to sell British goods, Boston's merchants realized that shame and contempt were less effective punishments than violence. Small-scale violence that had been practiced on soldiers was now used against importing merchants. On their own, crowds began to act more deliberately against British soldiers and against judicial magistrates who seemed too lenient with military offenders.

Large-scale crowd action began on 1 August 1769 with an exuberant celebration of Governor Bernard's departure from Massachusetts. Nine years earlier, upon his arrival, Bernard had been greeted with deference. Now he had to watch the "Flag hoisted on Liberty Tree," bonfires, shooting of squibs and rockets. Bernard "that Enemy to American Liberty," heard all church "Bells Ringing Great Joy to the People." Two weeks earlier Rhode Islanders had expressed their opposition to the current British trade policies more drastically. After the customs sloop *Liberty* had seized a vessel, the people were so "exasperated" that they burned the sloop, and for good measure even burned the charred hulk when it drifted ashore.[4]

On 5 September, Customs Commissioner John Robinson, who had taken offense at a rather critical article Otis had published in the *Gazette,* seriously injured Otis by hitting him over the head with a cane during an affray in the Coffee House. Otis was sufficiently popular in town that he had regularly been elected moderator of the town meetings, and this incident created an uproar against the commissioners. When a Mr. Brown was arrested as an accessory to the affair, people crowded into Faneuil Hall to witness his examination before Justices Dana and Pemberton. James

March 1770; *BTR* 16:289, 297–298. Entered into the town records were the names of John Bernard, Nathaniel Rogers, Theophilus Lillie, James McMasters & Co., John Mein, Thomas Hutchinson, Jr., and Elisha Hutchinson. The papers added Deblois, Selkrig, and Benjamin Green & Sons. Bernard to Hillsborough, 8 May 1769, Sparks MSS., 10.3:24.

[3]"The Boston Patriots Characterized," *Boston Chron.,* 26 Oct. 1769, and [John Mein,] Key to a Certain Publication, Sparks MSS., 10.3:45–47, HHL; *BTR* 16:241, 250, 252, 20:293. Inhabitants were "doomed" by the assessors when they did not hand in their property statement.

[4]Town records of Haverhill, in George W. Chase, *The History of Haverhill, Massachusetts, from Its First Settlement, in 1640, to the Year 1860* (Haverhill, Mass., 1861), p. 369. Bernard: Bernard to Barrington, 7 Aug. 1760, Sparks MSS., 4.1:272, HHL; Boyle, "Journal," 20 July, 1 Aug. 1769, p. 259; Rowe, *Letters and Diary,* 1 Aug. 1769, p. 190; Hiller B. Zobel, *The Boston Massacre* (New York, 1970), pp. 133–134; *The Tom-Cod Catcher: On the Departure of an Infamous* B[a]r[one]t (Boston, 1769), *Mass. Brds.* 1505, cf. 1526. *Liberty* incident: Boyle, "Journal," 17 July 1769, p. 259; *BEP,* 24 July, 7, Aug. 1769.

Murray—justice, merchant, and Loyalist—attended, although he knew he was resented for importing and aiding the troops. He had hardly entered when some of the crowd attempted to throw him out again. Selectman Jonathan Mason, Whig opponent of direct action, yelled at the men, "... do not behave so rudely," and protected Murray. Murray offered bail for Brown but prudently stated that by no means did he intend to vindicate Brown. The justices then asked the people to disperse, but to no avail. When Murray and Dana left the hall, Murray's wig was pulled off. Some men, often connected with riots, announced, "No violence, or you'll hurt the cause." But this was not sufficient; together with Loyalists, they had to guard Murray to prevent people from poking him or trying to trip him. The crowd followed, parading his wig on a staff.[5]

Late in September the two sons of Acting Governor Hutchinson signed the nonimportation agreement after the shop "of his Honor's two Children" had been "besmeared." Malignantly the *Gazette* asked: "May this not be worth representing Home?" "Pacificus" reflected on the sneer with which "the TWO CHILDREN" had treated the message that the "respectable body condescended to send." Others who had originally refused to sign now agreed to store their goods, because their signs, doors, and windows had been "daubed over in the Night with every kind of Filth, and one of them particularly had his Person treated in the same manner."[6] This kind of direct action was obviously very different from the spontaneous assemblage of people at Faneuil Hall and from Pope's Day crowds that collected in the evening so no wages were lost. It was done secretly, late at night, by small groups. Two explanations are possible but remain speculative, since the rioters were never identified. The actors may have been shopkeepers, who had no experience in crowd action but whose potential for violence was high because of their constantly declining position. They suffered while the importers benefited. Or perhaps Whig merchants sent dependent laborers to do the job, just as they had sent men into Hutchinson's house on 26 August 1765. The different patterns of action at a time when customary forms of crowd activity were maintained against soldiers suggest that the participants were different too.

RIOTS

By fall 1769 the number and extent of the riots and affrays between soldiers and inhabitants had grown steadily, and in October several persons living near the guardhouse on the Neck complained about continual disturbances and thefts. In

---

[5]SCF 89392, 102135; Rowe, *Letters and Diary,* 5 Sept. 1769, p. 192; John Adams, *Diary,* 2–4 Sept. 1769, 1:342–343; . *Essex Gaz.,* 12 Sept. 1769; *Boston Chron.,* 11 Sept. 1769; *BPB,* 11 Sept. 1769; *BG,* 11 Sept. 1769, 14 Sept. 1772; Hutchinson to Bernard, 5 Sept. 1769, Letterbooks, MA 26:372–373; Murray to ———, 30 Sept. 1769, *Letters of James Murray, Loyalist,* ed. Nina M. Tiffany and Susan I. Leslay (Boston,'1901), pp. 159–162; Clifford K. Shipton, "James Otis and the Writs of Assistance," *Bostonian Soc. Proc.* (1961), pp. 17–25 ("Legend of the Martyrdom of James Otis"); William Tudor, *The Life of James Otis of Massachusetts: Containing Also Notices of Some Contemporary Characters and Events from the Year 1760 to 1775* (Boston, 1823), p. 365, App. 2, p. 503, contains extracts from the court records; John J. Waters, *The Otis Family in Provincial and Revolutionary Massachusetts* (Chapel Hill, N.C., 1968), p. 177.

Great Britain, magistrates even refused to call on troops to quell disorders because troops only caused further grievances. Bostonians requested a town meeting. The selectmen, legally bound to call the meeting, may have been apprehensive about the bellicose temper of the inhabitants. They decided that a special guard stationed near the house of Robert Pierpoint, one of the complainants, at the Southend, would be sufficient. Earlier in the year they had refused his demand to eject the soldiers from town lands, which he had leased, but which the selectmen had granted for military use without either consulting him or the inhabitants, as was customary.[7]

"Further Insults and injuries" that Pierpoint soon reported were part of the most serious incident since the arrival of troops. In the evening of 23 October, Pierpoint and about 20 men, seemingly from the neighborhood, appeared at the Neckguard and demanded to talk to the officer, complaining that soldiers regularly stole firewood from people living near the guardhouse. The next morning a constable came to arrest the officer on duty, Ensign Ness, for stealing wood and assaulting Pierpoint the preceding evening. Ness denied the charges but agreed to surrender once relieved from duty. A crowd then abused and threatened the sentinels. When the crowd closed in, the whole guard fixed bayonets. The crowd continued to increase.

A short time later, when the guard was relieved and marched back to the barracks, an abusive crowd showered them with stones and broke into the ranks. A musket discharged accidentally without hurting anybody. The soldiers had almost reached the barracks when a blacksmith, Obadiah Whiston, struck one of the soldiers, William Fowler, in the face so that he began to bleed. When Whiston threatened a second blow, Sergeant Hickman stopped him with a lowered halberd. For this Hickman was later indicted, had to post bail, and at his trial was threatened by an infuriated crowd.[8]

William Fowler succeeded in obtaining a warrant against Whiston, whom he carried before a justice of the peace. But Whiston brought a crowd along, including Richard Gridley, a blacksmith, whose shop had been hit by the bullet fired accidentally. The judge wanted to postpone the hearing, but the crowd demanded that the affair be settled at once. There was no reason for the judge to grant a warrant to a soldier, anyway, and they all wanted to hear "what that Rascal of a soldier had to say." If standing armies were a danger to liberty in general, the soldiers certainly were a danger to the lives of particular inhabitants. Becoming apprehensive of violence, the justice of the peace acceded. When evidence indicated that Whiston hurt Fowler with a brickbat, the court decided that evidence exclusively from soldiers was insufficient.

Ensign Ness, after reporting to his commander, appeared at the house of Justice Dana. The crowd was waiting. When Ness complained about the crowd, the justice

[6]*BG,* 18 Sept., 9 Oct. 1769; George Mason to Joseph Harrison (informer's report), 20 Nov. 1769, Sparks MSS., 10.3:40, HHL; Nathaniel Rogers to ———, 25 Oct. 1769, *ibid.,* p. 44.

[7]*BTR* 20:312, 23:39–40- 42, 45–46. For Great Britain, see John H. Bohstedt, "Riots in England, 1790–1810, with Special Reference to Devonshire" (Ph.D. diss., Harvard Univ., 1972), pp. 297ff.; O. Teichman, "The Yeomanry as an Aid to Civil Power, 1795–1867," *J. Soc. Army Hist. Research* 19:75–91, 127–143 (1940).

[8]Depositions of James Hickman, Michael Graves *et al.* William Fowler, and John Park *et al., State Papers,* 12:60–68, 73–75, Gay Transcripts, MHS; SCF 89244.

answered that he was deaf. Two days later Ness was apprehended again, this time on the charge of having ordered the guard to fire. Justices Dana, Ruddock, and Pemberton demanded another £100 bail. Both charges against Ness were later dismissed. In the first case Pierpoint did not appear in court, and three soldiers testified that he had tried to bribe them to give evidence sufficient to convict Ness. In the second case Ness was acquitted by the unanimous verdict of the jury.[9]

Four days later, in the evening of 28 October, between 1000 and 1500 men seized a seaman from the customs sloop *Liberty,* which had been burned in Rhode Island in July. The seaman, suspected of being a customs informer, was placed in a cart and led by the customs house, where the crowd smashed windows as a warning to customs officers. The seaman was then tarred and feathered, and a sentry on duty at the customs house was threatened with the same treatment. Next the crowd stopped at the office of John Mein, the printer and outspoken critic of the Whigs and their double-dealing on nonimportation. The house was damaged, but the doors were broken open only after a shot had been fired from the house. Some of Mein's belonging were destroyed, but nothing was taken away.

The seaman in the cart repeatedly had to acknowledge his misdeeds. On the way to Liberty Tree, the crowd ordered the house owners along the street to put candles in their windows as a show of sympathy. Only one, Mr. Silvester, refused. His windows were broken. Probably the crowd did not know that he too was an informer. His reports to top crown officials about anti-British sentiments were somewhat exaggerated, to judge from those that remain, and even the recipients of the reports seem to have had difficulty believing them, since they never relayed them to London. The crowd released the sailor after three hours and returned home around 9 P.M.[10]

John Mein, whose house the crowd had visited briefly, was probably the most hated man in town, at least as far as the merchants were concerned. Bookseller and publisher, he had opened the first circulating library in the colonies. Loyal to British policies and opposed to the nonimportation agreements, he had hit upon a device as simple as it was ingenious to expose the gap between the high-sounding rhetoric and the actual performance of Whig merchants. Instead of publishing long articles against nonimportation in his *Boston Chronicle,* he simply published the customs house entries. This created deep distrust among and against Boston merchants. They charged and countercharged one another with violation of the agreements and then denied any breaches to the public. To achieve the same effect on an intercolonial level, Mein printed the lists separately and distributed them in other towns.[11]

[9]*BTR* 16:286; SCF 89239; Superior Court of Judicature, Records, 1769, f. 252, SCCH; depositions of John Ness, James Hickman, William Fowler, and Thomas McFarland *et al.*, State Papers, 12:54–64, 66–68, 70, Gay Transcripts, MHS.
[10]Geyer had possibly informed in Newport, Rhode Island, as three of the most active men in the crowd came from there. *Gailer* [that is, *Geyer* or *Galer*] v. *Trevett* et al., in John Adams, *Legal Papers of John Adams,* ed. L. Kinvin Wroth and Hiller B. Zobel, 3 vols. (Cambridge, Mass., 1965), 1:41–42; Superior Court of Judicature, Records, 1771, f. 209, SCCH; Minute Books, no. 91, 95 (Suffolk), March 1770, Aug. 1771; deposition of Thomas Burgess, State Papers, 12:122–124, Gay Transcripts, MHS; Rowe, *Letters and Diary,* 28 Oct. 1769, p. 194; Hutchinson to Hillsborough, 31 Oct., 11 Nov. 1769, Letterbooks, MA 26:400–403; George Mason to ———, 28 Oct. 1769, Sparks MSS., 10.3:47, HHL; Council Records, 16:437–438, MSA; proclamation, MA 88:223 ½; *BEP,* 30 Oct. 1769; *BG,* 6 Nov. 1769.
[11][John Mein], *A State of the Importation from Great Britain* (Boston, 1769, 1770), Evans 11336, 11744; vindications by the Boston committee of merchants, in *BEP,* 28 Aug., 4 Sept. 1769; cf. *ibid.,* 29 Jan. 1769; John E. Alden, "John

Mein was unwelcome to others besides merchants. His paper tried to exculpate the navy officer who had been killed during an impressment in April 1769. Had the court followed this line of argument—and the king's counsel did present it—the sailors could have been sentenced for murder.[12] Mein, criticized by the *Boston Gazette* for a long time, had retaliated by assaulting the printer John Gill. After the fight between Otis and Robinson, Mein angered a crowd by offering surety for the customs commissioner. By mid-October he had become so obnoxious that he felt obliged to go armed whenever he left his house, and one night a man mistaken for Mein was beaten.[13]

In the tense atmosphere after the Neckguard riot (23–24 October 1769), Mein published a devastating attack on the principal Whig leaders and merchants of the town. He charged them with frauds, embezzlement of public funds, duplicity, and other offenses; exposed internal dissentions; and ridiculed all of them. The publications caused "great uneasiness," and Mein "was spoken to by Capt. Dashwood," as one of the derided merchants noted. This was somewhat of an understatement. Merchant leaders, who condemned the lower class crowd action against the customs informer Geyer then in progress, accosted Mein and his business partner, John Fleeming, in King Street. One merchant hit him with a cane, another with an iron shovel that caused a lengthy gash and slit Mein's clothes from shoulder to hip. Drawing a pistol, Mein retreated to the nearby Mainguard and slipped into the guardhouse. Miss Elizabeth Cummings, a small shopkeeper and proscribed importer, described the scene: "we was alarmed with a violent Skreeming Kill him Kill him, . . . I saw Mr Meen at the head of a large Croud of those who Call themselves Gentelman, but in reality they ware no other then Murderers for there designe was certinly on his life." The "gentlemen" pestered the guard and sent for a warrant against Mein—a civil officer an official business had the right to enter the guardhouse. It was rumored that their intention was to take Mein to prison and have him "rescued" by a crowd for instant punishment. The "gentlemen" had rioted on their own and had not communicated with the anticustoms crowd. Mein was probably correct in suspecting that they intended to deal with him themselves and then blame "the boys and negroes." The iron shovel assault supports this view. But Mein was so well hidden that the deputy sheriff, assisted by Samuel Adams and William Molineux, could not find him. During the night Mein, clad in a uniform, was secretly conveyed on board a man-of-war.[14]

As to the "gentlemen" rioters, Acting Governor Hutchinson instructed the justices of the peace and the sheriff to do their duty and take action. But they feared attacks on their persons, and one of the justices argued that if the proceedings were not legal, they were "laudable being necessary for the Public good." Justice Dana,

---

Mein: Scourge of Patriots," *CSMP* 34:571–599 (1942).

[12]*Boston Chron.*, 1 May 1769.

[13]*Ibid.*, 21 Dec. 1767; *BG*, 18 Jan., 25 Jan. 1768; *Gill* v. *Mein*, case 5, in John Adams, *Legal Papers*, 1:151–157.

[14]"The Boston Patriots Characterized," *Boston Chron.*, 26 Oct. 1769, and [John Mein,] Key to a Certain Publication, Sparks MSS., 10.3:45–47, HHL; Boyle, "Journal," 28 Oct. 1769, pp. 260–261; Rowe, *Letters and Diary*, 28 Oct. 1769, p. 194; Elizabeth Cummings to ———, 28 Oct. 1769, James Murray Robbins Papers, vol. 2 (1769–1770), MHS; *BEP*, 30 Oct. 1769; Mason to Harrison, 28 Oct. 1769, Sparks MSS., 10.3:47, HHL; Mein to Joseph Hamson, 5 Nov. 1769, *ibid.*, p. 51.

who had issued the warrant against Mein, predicted that no further steps against Mein would be taken in the courts. He had probably been informed by his son, a witness of the riot, that Mein had not been the aggressor. Hutchinson himself had asked the commander of the troops to keep the soldiers under arms and ready to act, but even conservative inhabitants were "thanckful" that no Loyalist justice of the peace was in town: "[T]hings might have ben wors for the Solders ware all ordred under Arms but no justis to reed the Roit act, so they could do nothing." Hutchinson himself did not dare call upon the troops. During the whole incident he had proven so weak and timid that Mein, had he ever published another issue of the *Chronicle,* would probably have selected Hutchinson as the next target for ridicule.[15]

On 24 October Mein had informed Hutchinson that he had received anonymous threatening letters and was apprehensive of violence. His customs house information about the patriot merchants had been circulated for several weeks, and the skit on the patriots was to appear two days later. Mein intended to lay a memorial before the council, but Hutchinson objected. Mein then asked whether the justices of the peace could be reached in case of a riot. Hutchinson evasively and untruthfully declared they would do their duty. Mein finally asked directly whether Hutchinson himself would come to his aid. Hutchinson would not say. This Mein contemplated while hiding in the Mainguard. He then asked the governor's brother Foster, a justice of the peace, to take depositions. Foster Hutchinson refused. Next Mein asked Thomas Hutchinson for help. The governor refused. In a second letter Mein declared that he was willing to surrender if he was granted a guard against the crowd. The governor again refused. Exasperated, Mein stated in a third message:

> to the second, the Gentleman who presented it, requested an Answer in Writing; which you declined. It is readily granted that you declared to him I might appear with safety, but it ought also to be remembered that you mentioned, that I must be sensible of the Weakness of Government: This I have been already fully convinced of; I only wish to see one proof of the contrary.[16]

Hutchinson could haggle with the General Court or explain British policies, but he was helpless when action came from social groups that, according to his notions, it was not supposed to come, or when political action took forms that did not fit his concepts. The temporizing and incapability of the representatives of the *ancien régime,* their absolute lack of understanding for changed circumstances contributed as much to the rise of town-meeting influence and the power of crowd action as did fear about infringements on liberties and growing political awareness. One week after the riot, the Pope's Day crowd hanged Mein in effigy, and in a suit for debt, "Johny Dupe Esq.," as Mein had called John Hancock, attached Mein's printing press. Hutchinson watched passively.[17]

---

[15]Hutchinson to Gage, 29 Oct. 1769, State Papers, 11:179–181, Gay Transcripts, MHS; Cummings to ———, 28 Oct. 1769, James Murray Robbins Papers, vol. 2 (1769–1770), MHS.

[16]Hutchinson, in a letter to Gage (25 Feb. 1770, Letterbooks, MA 26:445, 448), stated that there was no "Justice of Peace in town who will appear" to suppress a riot.

[17]Mein to Hutchinson, three letters, 20 Oct. 1769; *ibid.,* 25:455–459; *Boston Chron.,* 9 Nov. 1769; Hutchinson to

OTHER PATTERNS OF RESISTANCE

While violent resistance against the troops grew from a trickle to a torrent of incidents, culminating in the Neckguard riot, sections of the population engaged in the affrays also used the judicial apparatus against soldiers and officers as extensively as possible and voiced objections to the military presence in other ways. The merchants at the same time stepped up enforcement of the nonimportation agreement, although on a somewhat selective basis.

The judicial drive against the military had several causes. Drunken army officers repeatedly and impudently attacked the town's watchmen. The selectmen, instead of prosecuting, mildly reproached and "cautioned them." The attorney general's lax prosecution of offenses by military persons was resented, and even more so the practice of officers' assigning accused soldiers to units in other towns before they could be brought to punishment. Anger flared up when soldiers were freed on £20 bail, while the "Worshipful Mr. Gridley," Loyalist justice of the peace, set an unusually high bail for a Medfield militia captain and Son of Liberty, who, accompanied by a crowd, had forced another inhabitant to sign a nonconsumption agreement. Gridley exacerbated the situation by refusing men from out of town as securities "upon orders," thereby raising suspicions that the judicial system was weighted against Whig colonists. He also reportedly boasted that he had locked up a Son of Liberty.[18]

While the military authorities could remove accused soldiers from town before trial, the justices could do so after trial. Debtors sentenced but unable to pay could be sold as servants for a limited period of years to work off their debts. Having already to cope with the high rate of desertion, the officers now found that their men were sent off by the courts. Their rage was not quieted when legal authorities advised them that the procedure was within the letter of the law.[19] While Loyalist Justice Gridley had arbitrarily refused some men willing to be securities for the Medford Son of Liberty, the Whig justices Dana, Pemberton, and Hill soon developed the same methods against arrested soldiers. Other judges followed under the pressure from crowds.

The case of John Timmons provides a good example of the difficulties soldiers met when seeking legal redress. He had been assaulted by three wigmakers when on duty at the Mainguard and later applied for a warrant to Justice Quincy. The justice

Hillsborough, 11 Nov. 1769, Sparks MSS., 10.3:53, HHL; Murray to his sister, n.d., *Letters*, p. 169, Mein to Murray, 11 Jan. 1775, *ibid.*, pp. 171–172; *Longman* v. *Mein,* case 12, in John Adams, *Legal Papers,* 1:199–200. The *Chronicle* was continued by Fleming till 25 June 1770, with an intermission when Hancock had the press attached. Then Fleming was forced to leave too. Fleming to Mein, 1 July 1770, Sparks MSS., 10.4:5, HHL. Mrs. Barnes to Elizabeth Smith, 29 June 1770, in Murray, *Letters*, p. 178; Murray to Smith, 12 March 1770, *ibid.*, pp. 169–170.

[18]*BTR* 16:286, 20:317; *BG,* 27 Feb. 1769; Palfrey to Wilkes, 4 Nov. 1769, Palfrey Family Papers, vol. 4, no. 89, HHL; John Shy, *Toward Lexington: The Role of the British Army in the Coming of the American Revolution* (Princeton, N.J., 1965), p. 315.

[19]Mackay to Gage, 12 June 1769, State Papers, 11:155–158, Gay Transcripts, MHS; cf. *Rex* v. *Moyse and Reader,* case 61, in John Adams, *Legal Papers,* 2:436–437. Usually the legislature passed acts to prevent soldiers and sailors from being arrested for debt in wartime. See A. C. Goodell *et al., Acts and Resolves, Public and Private, of the Province of the Massachusetts Bay,* 21 vols. (Boston, 1869–1922), 4:73, 5:614.

suggested dropping the charges if the three men would make a "restitution," arguing that the suit would be postponed from one court session to the next to protect the inhabitants, raising the costs above the means of the soldier. Timmons, suspecting the justice's motives, demanded the warrant nevertheless. Quincy told Timmons that he was too busy but that he could come back in the evening. When Timmons returned, Quincy told him "to make it up" with the wigmakers, to whom he had meanwhile granted a warrant against Timmons.[20]

After another affray Quincy's doors were beleaguered by two crowds: inhabitants angry at a soldier who had been involved in a brawl with a Cambridge butcher, and soldiers who came to watch how their comrade fared. When Quincy decided to commit the soldier to jail because he was unable to procure bail, the soldier attempted to flee and was seized by a constable, but in the general melee that followed, the soldier did manage to escape to the barracks. During the subsequent trial the justices told the soldiers, including the officers, that they had no right to be in Boston at all.[21] The crowds in the streets pushed guards aside with the remark that inhabitants had as much right to stand there as Redcoats. What authority had sent them? No authority had a right to garrison Boston. The soldiers were abused and hated as protectors of customs officials—the swarms of locust-like placemen, in contemporary imagery. The honor guard of the governor was harassed, as were soldiers protecting the houses of importers. Customs seizures jumped, and importers felt reassured. The presence of the soldiers forced Bostonians to submit while Rhode Islanders burned a customs sloop.[22]

In many of their attacks on soldiers, the assaulting inhabitants swore that they would serve the officers the same way if they could get hold of them. They never did. As in the case of customs officials, the lower the rank of officer or soldier, the more violent the treatment (even though there was more friction with drunken officers than with soldiers). Many a soldier was beaten as a scapegoat for those higher up, whom the crowds did not want to or could not attack. During the fights the rioters were expressing their dislike of commissioners, governor, and British ministry.

Samuel Adams obtained letters of the governor, the two principal military officers, General Gage and Commodore Hood, and the principal customs officials, the commissioners. A town meeting ordered that the letters be publicly read and then "Resolved, That many of the Letters and Memorials aforesaid are false scandalous and infamous Libels . . . of the most virulent and Malicious, as well as dangerous and pernicious tendency." The selectmen were instructed to complain "to proper

[20]Deposition of John Timmons, State Papers, 12:128–130, Gay Transcripts, MHS.

[21]*Rex* v. *Ross,* case 60, in John Adams, *Legal Papers,* 2:431–435; Shy, *Toward Lexington,* p. 314; depositions of Alexander Ross, Charles Fordyce, John Phillips, Samuel Heale, and Jonathan Stevenson, State Papers, 12:41–54, Gay Transcripts, MHS.

[22]O. M. Dickerson, ed., *Boston under Military Rule (1768–1769) as Revealed in a Journal of the Times,* (Boston, 1936), pp. 59, 85; *BEP,* 27 Feb. 1769; *Boston Chron.,* 1 May 1769, report of a seizure, which was so unreasonable that the governor interposed on behalf of the owners (21 Feb. 1769); Rowe, *Letters and Diary,* 7 March, 30 Sept. 1769, pp. 183, 193. *Liberty:* Boyle, "Journal," 17 July 1769, p. 259; *BEP,* 24 July, 7 Aug. 1769. *BTR* 18:1–2; Narrative of Proceedings at Boston, Feb. 1770, Sparks MSS., 10.3:70–71, HHL; Murray to Smith, 12 March 1770, *Letters,* pp. 162–163.

authority, that the wicked Authors of these incendiary Libels, may be proceeded with According to Law, and brought to condign punishment.'' The jury indicted ''said Thomas''—that is, ''his Excellency Thomas Gage, Esq Commander in chief of His Majestys forces in North America.'' Although according to Chief Justice Hutchinson there was sufficient legal reason to declare this bill of indictment and those found against the others void, the Superior Court judges did not dare take public notice of them but privately ordered the clerk neither to enter them nor to issue summons. Months later, upon order of the king, the attorney general entered a *nolle prosequi* on each bill.[23]

Information is scarce about participants in brawls and affrays and about their connection with the leadership. From soldiers' depositions, brawls were most frequent in the Northend and Southend. Only one deposition specifically mentioned that the men who abused a soldier were well dressed. And only in this case no physical violence occurred. The action against judges proved that relations between crowd and better sort were less than cordial. Not without reason, crowds appeared at trials to question judges about their granting warrants to soldiers. Robert Pierpoint and William Molineux were suspected of encouraging incidents. Molineux during this period was the ''bully'' of the merchants and worked to enforce nonimportation. Pierpoint lived in the Southend, had several personal and justified grievances against the soldiers, and could easily raise crowds or voting blocs. Presumably he held an important position in the informal power structure of the town. He was a coroner and after the beginning of the war became commissioner of prisoners. A possible explanation of his influence would be a prominent position in the Southend Caucus. But no records of this organization have survived. He was a close associate of Samuel Adams, whose bondsman he was—ironically, together with Andrew Oliver, Jr.—when Adams was tax collector. When Adams defaulted, Pierpoint was elected but later informed the town ''that there is no probability'' that the debts, amounting to £1150, would be collected.[24] Samuel Adams showed a certain interest in the affrays and kept copies of some indictments among his papers. As evidenced by his articles and co-authorship of town resolves, he clearly realized the possibilities for propaganda that the stationing of troops meant. As clerk of the House of Representatives, he maneuvered to stop withdrawal of part of the troops, but he was not supported by the House. Did popular pressure bring this about, as it contributed to the stand of the justices?[25]

The merchants during this period, the second half of 1769, tried to keep themselves in line with their own nonimportation regulations. Rumor after rumor circu-

[23]*BTR* 16:297–301, 303–325, 23:48; indictment, State Papers, 11: 194–195, 12:1–2, Gay Transcripts, MHS; Hutchinson to Hood, 25 Dec. 1769, Letterbooks, MA 26:422, *The History of the Colony and Province of Massachusetts Bay*, ed. Lawrence Shaw Mayo, 3 vols. (Cambridge, Mass., 1936), 3:189; Hillsborough to Hutchinson, 26 April 1770, Instructions to the Governors, p. 2459, MHS.

[24].*BTR* 16:273, 18:69, 20:312, 23:23, 39, 40, 42 *passim*; *Acts and Resolves*, 1769–1770, 5:27. On Molineux, see Chapter 8, note 17.

[25]Samuel Adams Papers, NYPL; Bernard to Hillsborough, 7 July 1769, Sparks MSS., 10.3:31–32, HHL; Gage to Hillsborough, 22 July 1769, *Correspondence*, 1:228–229; Hutchinson, *History*, 3:173–174; cf. Samuel Adams to James Warren, 25 March 1771, *Warren–Adams Letters: Being Chiefly a Correspondence among John Adams, Samuel Adams, and James Warren*, 2 vols. (Boston, 1917, 1925), 1:9, *MHSC*, vols. 72–73.

lated in town that signers had imported contrary to the rules and that the inspection committee did not act as impartially as it should have. In October, goods came from London for a Mr. Smith, who at that time was out of town. A committee consisting of Molineux and other Whig merchants ordered the goods to be sent back, showing affidavits that Smith had agreed to reship. However, Smith had had no intention of doing so, had not signed a declaration to that intent, and was somewhat surprised to find his goods gone when he returned to town.[26] The motives of those merchants who claimed in the town meeting to prefer the public good over their private gain were somewhat dubious. While most nonsigners were forced to reship, many signers only had to store goods imported contrary to the agreement. Once the agreement terminated, they could sell in a market where demand had accumulated and prices were high, while the other merchants had to send for goods, which took at least three months.

Miss Elizabeth Cummings, a Boston shopkeeper, and Henry Barnes, a Marlborough merchant, received some proscribed goods in November and were at once requested to store them. Neither of the two had signed the agreement. Mrs. Barnes resignedly wrote that only the "daring Sons of Liberty" were permitted to import. The consignment for Miss Cummings, worth £300, was already sold when the committee came to demand storage. Miss Cummings pointed out that "it was verry trifling owr Business but that littil we must do to enabel us to Suport our family; . . . [and we did not expect] they would tack Notis or try to injur two industrious Girls who ware Striving in an honest way to Get there Bread. . . ." The committee members listed her with other importers in the public prints. This, Miss Cummings stated defiantly, "far from being a Disadvantage to us Spirits up our friends to purchess from us I wish we had Sent for Sixtimes the Sum."[27] Nonimportation was running into difficulties.

---

[26]Extract from a letter, 23 Oct. 1769, Sparks MSS., 10.3:43, HHL; Rowe, *Letters and Diary,* 4 Aug. 1769, pp. 190–191; William Gordon, *The History of the Rise, Progress, and Establishment of the Independence of the United States of America,* 4 vols. (London, 1788), 1:277. Peter Oliver [*Peter Oliver's Origin and Progress of the American Rebellion: A Tory View,* ed. Douglass Adair and John A. Schutz (Stanford, Calif., 1961), pp. 61–62] reported that trunks and bales belonging to importing signers of the agreement were secretly emptied of the proscribed goods and refilled with bricks when they had to be sent back.

[27]Barnes to Smith, 20 Nov., 23 Dec. 1769, Murray, *Letters,* pp. 122, 123; Cummings to Smith, 20 Nov. 1769, James Murray Robbins Papers, vol. 2 (1769–1770), MHS.

Crowds against Importers and Troops $\boxed{8}$

VIOLENCE AGAINST IMPORTERS

The economic distress and social tensions added to the political conflicts already existing and led to a crisis in January 1770. Merchant dominance and the split within the merchant community between adherents to and opponents of nonimportation help to explain the crowd action to enforce the agreements, which was substantially different from the patterns of spontaneous action. Merchant-led groups, among them schoolboys and country people, were used to intimidate the importers. The original agreement expired on 31 December 1769. Political opponents of the policy saw their chance to reverse it. Small shopkeepers who had been hurt economically had reason to support termination, and the mechanics needed work.

A move by mechanics to exempt some goods from the agreement so ships could again be built in Boston, and unemployment in shipbuilding trades lowered, was ruthlessly quashed by Whig authorities. The mechanics had drawn up a petition and were considering how to present it, when Justice of the Peace and Selectmen Ruddock, accompanied by other magistrates, burst into their meeting, tore the petition to shreds, and told the men that they were the ruin of their country. These were big words, especially since the only ones ruined so far were the mechanics assembled. No resistance to Justice Ruddock's intrusion is recorded by our high-placed sources. This does not necessarily mean that there was none, since those low-placed mechanics who might have offered it were articulate enough.[1]

More is known about the opposition of importing merchants to the nonimportation group. After the lapse of the agreement, Hutchinson's sons and the firm of Benjamin Green & Sons took their goods out of the storage places supervised by the merchants' committee, hoping to induce others to follow. Some of the members of the committee to enforce the agreement were not well stocked and demanded that the goods be kept stored till other merchants had had reasonable time to import. No one defended the nonimportation policy until politicians rallied to call a series of

[1]Journal of Transactions in Boston, Sparks MSS., 10.3:55–56, HHL; *Advertisement* (Boston, 1769), *Mass. Brds.* 1473.

216

mass meetings "to consider some legal and spirited measures."[2] These meetings, according to reports, were similar to the meetings of the Merchants' Society enlarged by the town's shopkeepers. Since many tradesmen were out of work, it is possible that they too attended. Four meetings, held within seven days, were attended by from 1200 to 2000 men each. Attendance at the last meeting on 23 January was larger than ever, a sign of how deeply affected the townspeople were. Usually interest in mass meetings following so close upon each other began to sag after the second or third. In better times, shopkeepers and tradesmen would have been busy earning their livings during work hours.

The last meeting was the first to meet with official intervention from acting governor. So far Hutchinson's endeavors had been unsuccessful because of the councillors' obstruction: no opinion (18 January), no decision (19 January), no quorum (20 January). On 22 January, Hutchinson, whose sons were among the importers, explained to the council not altogether credibly that no member of his family had any private interest in suppressing the meetings but that "such Assemblies are of dangerous Tendency." The councillors, not altogether credibly either, snapped back that the meetings were only "legal measures for obtaining the performance of disputed contracts between a Committee of Merchants and sundry Persons" and opposed all proposals for intervention. Hutchinson next threatened the moderator of the meeting, merchant William Phillips by saying that "he and the other Men of property would answer for it with their Lives and Estates" should any violence occur. Finally Hutchinson instructed the county sheriff to deliver an official letter to the meeting ordering its dispersal. The sheriff first prevailed upon Hutchinson to address the letter to the moderator only, then prevailed upon the people at the meeting not to consider him an "accomplice" to the sender. The meeting "calmly considered" the letter and decided to proceed with its business.[3]

However, the unanimity among the Whig leadership was not as strong as it might seem from the determined rejection of intervention. Leadership split as usual when crowd activity was considered. When a march to the importers was proposed, Josiah Quincy, lawyer and son-in-law of the presiding merchant, declared that such a march, especially to the house of Hutchinson, whose sons Elisha and Thomas, Jr., had withdrawn their stored goods, would amount to high treason. Quincy, who had opposed crowd action during the Stamp Act period, also opposed rioting against soldiers. His opinion was the same as that of John Adams, outlined earlier. At the meeting Quincy called upon Justice Dana and lawyer Otis to support his opinion. Dana remained silent. Otis spoke so confusedly that nobody knew whether he

[2]Hutchinson, *History of the Colony and Province of Massachusetts Bay,* ed. Lawrence Shaw Mayo, 3 vols. (Cambridge, Mass., 1936), 3:191–193; Eliot to Hollis, 25 Dec. 1769, *MHSC* 4.4:446–447 (1858); *BEP,* 22 Jan. 1770.

[3]Council Records, 16:444–450, MSA; Cooper to Pownall, 30 Jan. 1770, *AHR* 8:314–316 (1902–1903); Journal of Transactions in Boston, Sparks MSS., 10.3:55–56, HHL; cf. Hillsborough to Hutchinson, 24 March 1770, Instructions to the Governors, p. 2454, MHS; *BEP,* 29 Jan. 1770; Hutchinson to ———, n.d., Letterbooks, MA 25:373; John Rowe, *The Letters and Diary of John Rowe, Boston Merchant, 1759–1762, 1764–1779,* ed. Anne Rowe Cunningham (Boston, 1903; reprint ed., 1969), 23 Jan. 1770, pp. 196–197; Thomas Hutchinson, "Additions to Thomas Hutchinson's *History of Massachusetts Bay,*" ed. Catherine Barton Mayo, *AASP* 59:17 (1949).

agreed. Samuel Adams, still thinking of corporate communities, argued that non-signers and importers were like sheep broken out of the fold. If not brought back (by Whig shepherds), others would follow. Dr. Thomas Young supported him by violently rebuking Quincy. But the leading men were fearful; moderator Phillips, John Hancock, and James Otis expressly refused to lead a march to the importers. Probably 1500 people then watched a dramatic culmination of dissension among the leaders. William Molineux jumped on a table, declared that the glorious cause was deserted, and, making for the door, exclaimed that he would commit suicide. But he was restrained, and after a brief conference directed by Young, two merchants (Phillips and Austin) and two politicians (Otis and Adams) agreed to act as a committee to head the crowd under the leadership of Molineux.[4]

As agreed, the "Body" was to remain silent throughout the march. Negotiations were to be conducted by committeemen. But on the first day, nothing was achieved. William Jackson refused to admit the committee to his house and was lectured by Molineux, who had expected his rank and file followers to wait in the street, that it was "beneath the dignity of this committee to be parlied with in the street." On the second day, Elisha and Thomas Hutchinson, Jr., were the first targets. Mixing politics with business as usual, the acting governor and "acquisitive bourgeois" (Bailyn) spoke for his sons. The negotiations remained inconclusive and the "Body" proceeded to the other importers, most of whom did not accede to the demands. When the crowd began to huzzah, Molineux silenced the men by telling them that so far they had behaved like gentlemen. Obediently the men dispersed quietly. The conduct of the "Body" suggests that the control exerted by the leadership was much stronger than that exerted over the Stamp Act crowds. Merchants and magistrates were among the people, and many of the shopkeepers were economically dependent on the merchants. They and any mechanics in the crowd would also be dependent on the magistrates for support from the town's poor funds. Finally, the mechanics from the shipbuilding trades had been unsuccessful when acting as a cohesive group against nonimportation. They had even less chance for success when mingled with other groups of different interests and subjected to a barrage of high-sounding rhetoric about political principles. No action was attempted against Whig merchants; all violence was directed against Loyalist importers.[5]

A day later the acting governor reversed his position. The Hutchinsons, who were considered the spearhead by the nonsigners, thus angered their supporters as well as the crowd, the latter by their long resistance and by Hutchinson's attempt to use political office to protect the business interests of his sons. Once again his acquisi-

---

[4]Journal of Transactions in Boston, Sparks MSS., 10.3:55–56, HHL; Council Records, 16:444–450, MSA; George Mason to ———, 24 Jan. 1770, Sparks MSS., 10.3:63, HHL; Rowe, *Letters and Diary,* 17 Jan., 18 Jan. 1770, p. 196; *BEP,* 22 Jan. 1770.

[5]Journal of Transactions in Boston, Sparks MSS., 10.3:55–56, HHL; George Mason to ———, 24 Jan. 1770, *ibid.,* p. 63; Nathaniel Rogers to Hutchinson, 19 Jan. 1770, Letterbooks, MA 25:351–351a; *BEP,* 22 Jan. 1770; deposition of Hutchinson's sons, MA 88:226–228; *William Jackson an Importer,* Brds. (Boston, 1770), *Mass. Brds.* 1523, desiring "the Sons and Daughters of Liberty" not to buy from Jackson. Frederic Kidder, ed., *History of the Boston Massacre, March 5, 1770* (Albany, N.Y., 1870), p. 214.

tiveness led him into political troubles, and his refusal to fight for political principles demonstrated his weakness.[6]

That there was a potential for violence against Loyalist importers is shown by the increasing amount of direct action outside of the tightly controlled marches. At Jackson's house, arson was attempted; Rogers's windows were broken; others were subject to nightly attacks; one was excluded from community help against accidental fires. Some left town, while others slept with guns beside their beds. Rogers received a guard of British soldiers. Reportedly the guard had orders to fire and was promised £10 as a reward for any dead rioter, £50 for any prisoner. When the commanding officer during one of the "Body" meetings kept the troops under arms, ready to intervene, the incensed meeting ordered those having any business dealings with the troops to collect outstanding debts immediately.[7]

At the merchant–shopkeeper meetings, the importers were labeled "delinquents," thus stressing a quasi-legal function of the crowd to enforce contractual obligations. As stampmasters and customs officials had been, they were called "strangers" and excluded from common civility and business connections. A broadside distributed "in this and every other colony" declared that the importers "deserve to be driven to that obscurity from which they originated, and to the hole of the pit from whence they were digged." Subsequent accounts indicate that importers were hardly safe in any town. Crowds chased them from taverns where they lodged, burned them in effigy, and threatened friends who provided them shelter.[8]

To sever business connections demanded constant attention. The stores of the importers were "picketed" on market days (Thursday), when countrymen were in town and when schoolboys could participate because schools closed. Both groups were more violence-prone than others. Schoolboys had always been excluded from crowd activities when violence was imminent but not wanted. The countrymen, acting against Boston importers, were not subject to community restraints. For the merchants both groups had the advantage of not having distinct socioeconomic interests within the community. Accordingly, there was no danger of a repeat of the spontaneous action that had occurred during the Stamp Act period.

The chief agents behind these "combination riots" to enforce the nonimportation combination were William Molineux and merchant–captains. The latter had less room to maneuver than large mercantile firms. They were frequently present during the picketing. The four market days from 8 February to 1 March saw basically

[6]Hutchinson, *History,* 3:192–193; Bernard Bailyn, *The Ordeal of Thomas Hutchinson* (Cambridge, Mass., 1973), p. 154.

[7]Journal of Transactions in Boston, Sparks MSS., 10.3:55–56. HHL; George Mason to ———, 24 Jan. 1770, *ibid.,* p. 63; Hutchinson to Bernard, 28 Feb. 1770, Letterbooks, MA 26:450–451; *BTR* 18:1–2, 14; William Gordon, *The History of the Rise, Progress, and Establishment of the United States of America,* 4 vols. (London, 1788), 1:277–278.

[8]*BEP,* 24 Jan. 1770; *At a Meeting of the Merchants and Traders* (Boston, 1770), *Mass. Brds.* 1542; *Essex Gaz.,* 19 June 1770. The news of these crowd actions created "great uneasiness among our friends" in Great Britain. *BEP,* 8 Oct. 1770. Rogers to Hutchinson, 19 Jan. 1770, Letterbooks, MA 25:351–351a. Rogers's fame spread, and when he visited New York, reportedly to induce the merchants to break the agreement, he was burned in effigy, and he fled from town at night. *The Dying Speech of the Effigy of a Wretched Importer,* Brds. (New York, 1770), Evans 11639.

similar action. "Importer" signs were posted in front of one or more shops. Their houses were bespattered with mud and dirt, sometimes feces. "Hillsborough treat," this was called. Some windows were broken. Once a carved wooden head was set up on a pole in front of one of the shops, an allusion to the old custom of exhibiting the heads of executed criminals on the town gates. Customers of the ostracized merchants met with abuse and were pelted with dirt by crowds assembling on the streets. Attempts to take down the signs were opposed whether undertaken by the importers themselves or by soldiers. Rumors that effigies of the commissioners and of minor customs officials would be added to the show proved to be unfounded.[9]

The interference of Ebenezer Richardson, customs informer, who had been suspected of giving information against Daniel Malcom in September 1766, achieved what the crowds had been unsuccessful in doing—involving the customs service in the "combination violence." Richardson attempted to take down the crowd's decorations at an importer's shop on 22 February, and dozens of boys began to abuse and pelt him. A number of merchants watched without interfering. Richardson retreated to his nearby house, and a growing crowd followed, milling around his door and smashing his windows. When he ordered them off, the rioters answered that "they would not, Kings high Way." Richardson, aided by George Wilmot, who reportedly had served on the customs schooner *Liberty,* then aimed a gun at the crowd and threatened to shoot. The crowd broke the frames of the windows, and Richardson fired, killing a boy named Christopher Snider and wounding two others. The crowd in response stormed his house and arrested him. A guard of several influential townsmen, including Molineux, had to intervene for Richardson's protection to prevent immediate punishment, while the sheriff did nothing. It has been suggested that the leaders wanted to prevent a lynching of Richardson. But no crowd had ever killed during a riot. And the punishment, most likely tarring and feathering, would have been executed by a different, fast-assembling crowd of sailors and mechanics. It was exactly these two groups that the leaders had tried to keep out of the combination riots.[10]

Richardson could not expect much help from anybody. His employers gave out that he and his fellow-accused, George Wilmot, had never been in the customs service, just as they had dissociated themselves from the *Liberty* seizure 18 months earlier.[11] To Bostonians, Richardson was a wretched outsider. He came from

[9]Narrative of Proceedings at Boston, Sparks MSS., 10.3:70–71, HHL; extract from a letter from Boston, 14 March 1770, *ibid.,* pp. 69–70; Lillie's account, *Mass. Gaz.,* 11 Jan. 1770; cf. the cut entitled *The Life and Humble Confession of Richardson, the Informer,* (Boston, 1772), *Mass. Brds.* 1630, p. 221; Hutchinson to Hood, 23 Feb. 1770, Letterbooks, MA 26:444–445.

[10]The term "combination riots" was a contemporary expression for direct action enforcing the nonimportation agreements (merchants' combinations). Hutchinson to Bernard, 29 June 1773, Letterbooks, MA 27:502–503. *Rex v. Richardson,* case 59, in John Adams, *Legal Papers of John Adams,* ed. L. Kinvin Wroth and Hiller B. Zobel, 3 vols. (Cambridge, Mass., 1965), 2:417; *BEP,* 26 Feb. 1770; *BG,* 26 Feb. 1770; *BNL,* 1 March 1770; John Boyle, "Boyle's Journal of Occurrences in Boston, 1759–1778," 22 Feb. 1770, *NEHGR* 84:262 (1930); extract of a letter from Boston, 14 March 1770, Sparks, MSS., 10.3:69, HHL; Hutchinson to Gage, 25 Feb. 1770, Letterbooks, MA 26:445–448, to Hood, 23 Feb. 1770, *ibid.,* pp. 444–445; Council Records, 16:454–456, MSA.

[11]*Boston Chron.,* 5 March 1770; *BNL,* 8 March 1770. Both papers stated that they had been "authorized" to print the disclaimer. The *BNL* added some comments. Cf. *BG,* 26 Feb., 5 March 1770.

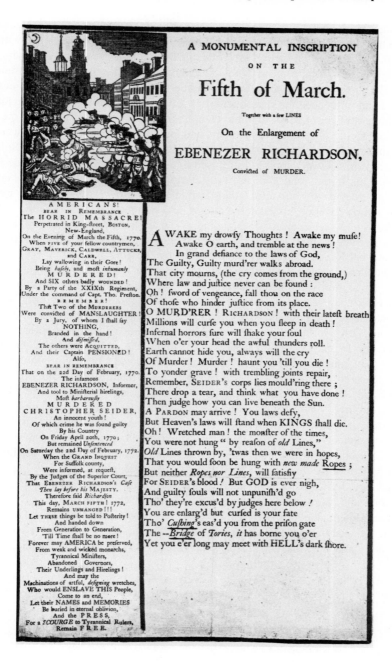

Figure 6.   A broadside on Ebenezer Richardson, customs informer.

Woburn, was involved in a scandal about an illegitimate child, and in the customs service had not only given information about smuggled goods but had sided with the disliked Paxton in a struggle to oust Collector Benjamin Barrows in 1760, who was well liked for his compromises with smugglers. During Richardson's examination before the justices, a menacing crowd numbering 1000 gathered. Crowds closely watched and influenced the subsequent trial. Contrary to their intentions, the judges of the Superior Court had to submit to clamors for punishment and to call up the trial during the spring session before tempers had had time to cool. They were afraid of being subjected to violence from the crowds, and so was everybody else. Nobody dared act as his lawyer, constables refused to summon his witnesses, and the jailer prevented his friends and counsel from talking with him. At the trial, when the judges instructed the jury for manslaughter, the crowd attempted to punish Richardson on the spot, hissed at the judges, and shouted threats at the jury: "damn him—hang him—Murder no Manslaughter." To applause from the crowd, the jury brought in their verdict: guilty of murder. The court adjourned without passing a sentence, and Richardson was later pardoned by the king.[12]

But he had become so infamous that crowds as far away as Philadelphia assembled to punish him when he came to town. He was dismissed from Boston gaol in March 1772 and escaped from town without a tarring and feathering only because the inhabitants were engaged in a town meeting. When "the infamous murderer" visited a relative in Stoneham, he was jailed, and abusive articles appeared in the newspapers. In May 1773 "that execrable Villain, the condemned Vagabond; the rank, bloody, and as yet unhanged" Richardson received a post in the Philadelphia customs establishment from Charles Froth, "a Wretch, who from his earliest Puppy-hood, thro' the lingering progress of a too long protracted Life" heaped "eternal Infamy" on his head. In Philadelphia Richardson narrowly escaped "many well wishers to peace and good order" who intended to tar and feather him. Back in Boston in January 1774, "A Great Concourse of People were in Quest of the Infamous Richardson this night—they could not find him, very lucky for him."[13]

The funeral of the dead boy, Christopher Snider, took place on 26 February. Five hundred boys from Boston schools preceded the coffin. The streets were lined with spectators, and about 2000 women and men followed the hearse. While the status-conscious Hutchinson grumbled that "the son of a poor German" received a "grand funeral," the equally status-conscious John Adams, though usually opposed to processions and crowds, was deeply impressed. "My Eyes never beheld such a

[12]Hiller B. Zobel, *The Boston Massacre* (New York, 1970), pp. 54–55; Palfrey to Wilkes, 5 March 1770, *CSMP* 34:415–417 (1937–1942); Cooper to Pownall, 26 March 1770, *AHR* 8:316–318 (1902–1903); Gordon, *History,* 1:276–277; *Rex v. Richardson,* case 59, in John Adams, *Legal Papers,* 2:396–430; Hutchinson, *History,* 3:206; *BNL,* 23 April 1771; *BEP,* 8 April 1771; Narrative of Events in Boston, Sparks MSS., 10.3:76–77, HHL; Peter Oliver, *Peter Oliver's Origin and Progress of the American Rebellion: A Tory View,* ed. Douglass Adair and John A. Schutz (Stanford, Calif., 1961), p. 86; Boyle, "Journal," 20 April 1770, p. 265.

[13]Boston: *BG,* 16 March 1772; *A Monumental Inscription on the Fifth of March: Together with a Few Lines on the Enlargement of Ebenezer Richardson, Convicted of Murder* (Boston, 1772), *Mass. Brds.* 1631, Evans 12302; cf. *BEP,* 28 Oct. 1771, 16 March 1772. Stoneham: *Mass. Spy,* 26 March 1773, cf. 27 Feb., 26 Nov. 1773; cf. *Essex Gaz.,* 25 May 1773; *BG,* 1 Nov. 1773. Philadelphia: *BG,* 24 May, 1 Nov. 1773. Boston: *BNL,* 27 Jan. 1774; Rowe, *Letters and Diary,* 26 Jan. 1774, p. 261; cf. James H. Stark, *The Loyalists of Massachusetts and the Other Side of the American Revolution* (Boston, 1910), pp. 422–423.

funeral. . . . This Shewes, there are many more Lives to spend if wanted in the Service of their Country. It Shews, too . . . that the Ardor of the People is not to be quelled by the Slaughter of one Child and the Wounding of another." Adams did not care to clutter his vista of heroic events with details. Snider had not intended to die for his country. Nor is it likely he wished to include his own life among those that could be "spent." Neither did the mourners contemplate the circumstances of the victim's demise except as a symbol of the times.[14]

KING STREET RIOT

While attention in Boston seemed to center almost exclusively on the importing merchants, there were still the troops to contend with. The Whig merchants had no grievances against them, although other groups in town did. On 2 March, an incident centering on conflict between a soldier and ropemakers led to a riot that became the prelude for large-scale violence, finally forcing removal of the two remaining regiments from town.[15] A soldier, Patrick Walker, was busy in a yard adjacent to John Gray's ropewalk in the Southend. One of the ropemakers, William Green, asked Walker whether he wanted to work for them. When the soldier answered yes, the mechanics sent him to clean their "Necessary House." A hot dispute ensued, and Walker demanded satisfaction, was knocked down by one of the ropemakers from the adjoining workshops, and had his sword taken away. The ropemakers displayed their trophy, and the soldier limped to the nearby barracks. He returned with reinforcements. With their own reinforcements the ropemakers beat them off. In a third wave, eight or nine more soldiers "fell upon the ropemakers, who being accidentally well provided for their reception, made it necessary for the whole body to march in quest of auxiliaries." In a fourth assault, 30 or 40 soldiers turned out from the barracks, among them a tall Negro drummer. A justice of the peace, who had watched the battle from his window and then from his doorstep, interposed for the first time. He told the "black rascal" to keep out of "white people's" quarrels. The soldiers finally retreated.[16] Several other, but small incidents occurred on the same day.[17]

[14]*BEP*, 26 Feb., 5 March 1770; *BG*, 5 March 1770; Hutchinson, *History*, 3:194; Rowe, *Letters and Diary*, 26 Feb. 1770, p. 197; Narrative of Proceedings at Boston, Sparks MSS., 10.3:70–71, HHL; Henry Hulton to de Walmoden, 5 May 1770, Letterbooks, 1:19–28, HHL; John Adams, *Diary and Autobiography of John Adams*, ed. L. H. Butterfield, 4 vols. (Cambridge, Mass., 1961–1966). 1:349–350. During the procession a man who was thought to look supercilious was beaten.

[15]Harry Hansen, *The Boston Massacre: An Episode of Dissent and Violence* (New York, 1970); Zobel, *Massacre*. For a critical appraisal of Zobel's hostile interpretation of crowd action, see Jesse Lemisch, "Radical Plot in Boston (1770): A Study in the Use of Evidence," *Harvard Law Review* 84:485–504 (1970–1971) and Pauline Maier, "Revolutionary Violence and the Relevance of History," *J. Interdisc. Hist.* 2:119–134 (1971–1972). The relevant documents have been collected by Kidder, ed., *Massacre;* by L. Kinvin Wroth and Hiller B. Zobel, eds., *The Boston Massacre Trials*, vol. 3 of John Adams, *Legal Papers* (Boston, 1965); and by Frederick L. Gay, State Papers, Gay Transcripts, MHS, cited in this chapter as State Papers.

[16]Kidder, ed., *Massacre*, pp. 48–50, 56; State Papers, 12:142–144; *BEP*, 5 March 1770; *BNL*, 8 March 1770; *Essex Gaz.*, 6 March 1770; Gage to Hillsborough, 10 April 1770, *The Correspondence of General Thomas Gage*, ed. Clarence E. Carter, 2 vols. (New Haven, Conn., 1931, 1933), 1:248–251; A Narrative of the Late Transactions at Boston (enclosure in a letter from Dalrymple), House of Lords MSS., 258:51–57; "Reminiscences of a Bostonian," Hezekiah Niles, ed., *Principles and Acts of the Revolution in America* (Baltimore, 1822), pp. 15–17.

[17]State Papers, 12:109–110, 110–111, 136–137.

On the following day, Saturday, small groups of soldiers attacked inhabitants and vice versa. Ensign Gilbert Carter was told that within a short time the inhabitants would not leave any soldier alive in Boston. The feeling was mutual. Soldiers reportedly had threatened to knock down any inhabitant they could lay hands on. Their tempers were probably inflamed by a report that during the ropewalk fights one soldier had been killed. The officers even sent a party to John Gray's ropewalk to search for the corpse. Hearing about this, Gray immediately complained to Lieutenant Colonel Dalrymple, the commanding military officer in Boston. In the short conference, concern about the dangers of such spontaneous riots soon superseded the original topic. The ropewalk owner and the officer decided to combine energies to prevent further riots. Gray did so by firing the mechanic who had first called Walker over to the ropewalk. The army officers merely told the men not to go out of the barracks unless in groups strong enough to defend themselves.[18]

On Monday morning several soldiers warned friends among the inhabitants to stay off the streets that evening,[19] and others posted a handwritten notice:

> Boston March ye 5th 1770
>
> This is to Inform ye Rebellious People in Boston that ye Soldiers in ye 14th and 29th Regiments are Determend to Joine to Gether and Defend them Selves against all Who shall Opose them   Signed ye Soljers of ye 14th & 29th Regiments.[20]

It was probably too late to have any effect on the soldiers, but the supposedly dead sergeant, "represented as a sober Man," was found drunk "in a House of Pleasure" during the day.[21]

When it grew dark, affrays began.[22] Small crowds of inhabitants knocked down soldiers. Robert Pierpoint met a corporal and told him that soldiers were murdering inhabitants and must be driven out of town. He was going to start with the corporal. The latter escaped, only to be attacked by other inhabitants. Pierpoint went his way and came across another corporal, who had a bayonet in his hand. This he thought an offense, so he hit the corporal with a cudgel. In a deposition he declared that he

---

[18]Kidder, ed., *Massacre*, pp. 50–51, 53; State Papers, 12:111–112, 135–136, 138–140; *BEP*, 5 March 1770; *BNL*, 8 March 1770; *Essex Gaz.*, 6 March 1770.

[19]Kidder, ed., *Massacre*, pp. 52–54.

[20]The mutilated original is among Misc. Unbound Papers, 1770, BCH. John Cary, in *Joseph Warren: Physician, Politician, Patriot* (Urbana, Ill., 1961), p. 92, suggested that it was written by patriot leaders. I do not agree with this interpretation. Boston's leaders were unlikely to encourage this kind of crowd action, and when crowd members themselves stuck up papers, they usually did so in several places to alert people.

[21]Kidder, ed., *Massacre*, pp. 50–51; *BG*, 12 March 1770.

[22]In addition to Kidder, ed., *Massacre*, Wroth and Zobel, eds., *Trials*, and State Papers, see for 5 March 1770: House of Lords MSS., 258:51–57, 71ff.; Colonial Office, Sec. Dept., 5/759:119ff., PRO; Mellen Chamberlain Collection, pp. 186–228, BPL; Sparks MSS., 10.3:69–71; Henry Hulton, Letterbooks, 1:24 *passim*, HHL; Gage to Hillsborough, 10 April 1770, *Correspondence*, 1:248–251; Preston's account, *BNL*, 21 June 1770, and elsewhere; John Adams, *The Works of John Adams*, ed. Charles Francis Adams, 10 vols. (Boston, 1850–1856), 2:229–230, 322; Hutchinson, *History*, 3:194–201, "Additions," pp. 18–19, Letterbooks, MA 26:452–455 *passim*; Gordon, *History*, 1:282–290; "List of the Officers of the 14th and 29th Regiments," *Edes & Gill's North American Almanac, 1770*; Randolph G. Adams, "New Light on the Boston Massacre," *AASP* 47:259–354 (1937).

had been attacked while on his way to visit a sick neighbor, but in the town meeting he explained that "he had disarmed a Soldier who had struck down one of the Inhabitants." Other incidents occurred at the Southend and the Northend.[23] From both sections, men began to converge on the town center. Weather conditions were partly favorable (bright moonlight), partly not ("we looked for stones or bricks but could find none, the ground being covered with snow"). This saved the soldiers from volleys of stones, which the sailors of the *Romney* had experienced two years earlier. Instead the soldiers were pelted with snowballs and ice, not considered "hard objects" by the jury during trials in the following months. The soldiers presumably saw less difference.[24]

About 9 P.M. the opening skirmish occurred in Boyleston's Alley, a narrow passage leading from the townhouse to Murray's barracks on Brattle Street. After a short fight, reinforcements were called, and during the next quarter of an hour the alley changed possession several times. Groups of soldiers that did not join the alley fight roamed the adjoining streets, shouting, "Where are your sons of liberty? Where are the damned boogers, cowards, where are your liberty boys?" On Corn-hill, people could not retreat fast enough into their houses as a dozen or so soldiers descended on them, abusing, threatening, and assaulting. One who went to get an officer from the Mainguard was told that none was there, and two soldiers attacked him. Sailors coming from the harbor received their share of the soldiers' rage. They had neither houses to retreat to nor officers to call. So they fought back.[25]

Inhabitants meanwhile abused and assaulted soldiers wherever possible. One officer living in private quarters heard the noise and opened his door to inquire, but seeing armed men pass, he quietly and prudently closed the door again. He "had reason to believe people in a military character were not agreable," he said. "I never heard such abuse in my life," Captain Goldfinch put it more directly. "I found that any Man that wore the K[ing]'s Com[missio]n was lyable to be insulted any Hour of the Night."[26]

The crowd gathered around the gates of Murray's barracks, from where the first groups of soldiers had come. This was not merely to drive soldiers back into their quarters. Some of the approximately 70 people declared that "if the soldiers did not come out and fight them, they would set fire to the four corners of the barracks, and burn every damned soul of them." Several officers were engaged at the gates to keep the soldiers in and the inhabitants out, though some officers would rather have seen the townsmen get a thorough beating. When they had sent the soldiers back, they found themselves surrounded by inhabitants who wished the military to hell or at least wanted to lecture them on proper behavior in Boston. When the inhabitants had been quieted, one soldier rushed out, presented his musket, damned the people, and threatened to shoot a lane through them. Although ordered back into the bar-racks, he returned minutes later, aimed the musket, and was knocked down by an

---

[23]Kidder, ed., *Massacre*, pp. 55–56; State Papers, 12:118–119, 119–120, 140–142; *BTR* 18:1.
[24]Kidder, ed., *Massacre*, p. 61.
[25]*Ibid.*, pp. 56–57, 57–58, 58–60, 61–62, 67–68, 74–75.
[26]*Ibid.*, pp. 194, 197; Wroth and Zobel, eds., *Trials*, p. 187.

officer. Then the town bells began to ring. Most of the crowd left, but small groups remained, and several incidents occurred there during the next two hours.[27]

The crowd went to the Mainguard at the townhouse. Earlier a man walking from the center of the town to the Southend had seen about 50 armed men. Another, walking down to the docks, met numerous people with "pretty large sticks, rather too large for walking sticks." There were shouts: "town born, turn out," "Fire," "King Street forever." What had been a trickle of men before the bells began to ring became a steady inflow.[28] The better sort, especially the magistrates, stayed away. Only one of the 16 annually elected fire wardens was later heard as a witness. He lived next door to the customs house in King Street and saw nothing unusual when he came home about 9 P.M. He heard the noise of the alley fight, chased off some boys who were pestering the customs house sentry, then went into his own house. When the cry of fire became general, "I had a mind to get my staff and go out, but I had a reluctance, because I had been warned not to go out that night . . . ," so he just stood at his door and watched. Others reacted similarly. The guests in the Green Dragon were told not to bother, there was no fire, only a rumpus with the soldiers. And a company at the Southend was informed by one of their number "not to be uneasy, for he had heard it was only to gather people to fight the soldiers."[29]

Others reacted differently. Crews of the fire engines soon abandoned their gear to have their hands free. A sailor, boarding his ship, excitedly told the other men that he "believed there would be mischief that night. . . ." Just at that moment the bells began to ring, which deprived him of his audience. The sailors hurried off. Inhabitants coming with fire buckets began to deposit them in nearby houses. Others went back to arm themselves: "[I] could find no stick, but I cut the handle of my mother's broom off." Many had left their fire equipment home and came armed. Later they became somewhat coy when questioned about their arms. Benjamin Burdick, Jr., a barber, engaged in an affray with a soldier, who "pushed at me with his bayonet," which, he said modestly, "I put by with what I had in my hand." Question: "What was it?" Answer: "A Highland broad sword."[30]

The people who had earlier crowded around the gates of Murray's barracks went down to the townhouse and to Dock Square. In both places large crowds, broken up into smaller groups, discussed the situation. Accounts of affrays were passed on, rumors circulated, and debates were held on what to do next. A bleeding oysterman graphically described how soldiers had assaulted him. Some inhabitants had seen soldiers under Liberty Tree. Others feared that they might plan to cut down his symbol of opposition. A man on the payroll of the customs commissioners reported

[27]Kidder, ed., *Massacre,* pp. 61, 62–63, 98–99, 101, 191–194, 197, 207–208, 209, 214; Wroth and Zobel, eds., *Trials,* pp. 181, 182. Deposition of James Kirkwood (Kidder, ed., *Massacre,* pp. 62–63), contradicted by Richard Hirons (*ibid.,* pp. 191–194), confirmed by an indictment against Mall (Mellen Chamberlain Collection, p. 228, BPL). "Vindex" [Samuel Adams], *BG,* 24 Dec. 1770.

[28]Kidder, ed., *Massacre,* pp. 142–143, 191, 195, 207, 212–215; Wroth and Zobel, eds., *Trials,* p. 188.

[29]Kidder, ed., *Massacre,* pp. 66–67, 156–157 (cf. Wroth and Zobel, eds., *Trials,* pp. 50–51), 189 (cf. C.O. 5/759:157–160, PRO), 190.

[30]Kidder, ed., *Massacre,* pp. 68–69, 85–86, 144, 152, 186–187, 195, 208–209; Wroth and Zobel, eds., *Trials,* pp. 56, 134–135.

later that an attack on the customs house was mentioned. Such plans had always been reported in times of disturbance, in this case with the addition that the rioters wanted to distribute the large amounts of money lodged there. The payment of customs duties meant a serious drain of specie from the country, compounding the perennial problem of insufficient circulating currency, and was a major colonial grievance. One importer, William Jackson, had his windows smashed. But attention centered on the soldiers. Among the people "the cry was, damn the rascals. Some said this will never do, the readiest way to get rid of these people is to attack the main-guard, strike the root, there is the nest." All over town, groups of men huzzahed for the Mainguard.[31]

The soldiers at the Mainguard had received several calls for help, had been surrounded by passing crowds, and were told of imminent danger.[32] The calls for help came from a lone soldier, Hugh White, who was on duty as customs house sentry. Half an hour earlier he had overheard several boys insulting an officer. They were apprentices of Mr. Piemont's barber and peruke shop, which was a kind of news exchange for the town. While the officer thought it best to pass without taking notice of the allegation that he did not pay his bills, Hugh White began to defend the captain, at first verbally, then physically by attempting to strike the boys with the end of his gun. Similar incidents had led to crowd action in 1769, and did so again in 1774. The boys soon dispersed and spread their story. Some returned with help to pelt the soldier; others began to tear down the stalls in the market to get sticks. At least one soldier had to be rescued out of their hands by an inhabitant.[33]

In King Street the number of people continued to increase, and so did the demands at the Mainguard for help. Finally, a group of seven soldiers accompanied by Captain Thomas Preston marched down to the customs house. On their way through the crowds, some pushing and shoving was necessary to clear the way, or—seen from the other side—to keep the soldiers off. The reinforcement was accompanied and followed by a large crowd. At the customs house the soldiers drew up in a half-circle. There was a shout: "here is old Murray [a Loyalist justice of the peace] with the riot act." Turning around, most people only saw a man fleeing before a shower of snowballs, and they continued to center their attention on the soldiers,[34] who had to put up with more than snowballs. Ice and any kind of rubbish or coal that could be found in the snow were hurled, and within a few minutes the soldiers were ordered to level their guns to ward off the pressing crowd.[35]

---

[31]Kidder, ed., *Massacre,* pp. 80–81, 85–86, 182, 183, 184, 199, 210–211, 214, 217, 218–219; *BG,* 26 March 1770.

[32]State Papers, 12:112–114. Preston's account (*BNL,* 21 June 1774): "I was soon informed by a Townsman [that] their Intention was to carry off the Soldier from his Post, and Probably murder him."

[33]Kidder, ed., *Massacre,* pp. 56, 57–58, 64, 80, 80–81, 132–134, 135–137, 194–195, 196–197, 209–210; Wroth and Zobel, eds., *Trials,* p. 64.

[34]Kidder, ed., *Massacre,* p. 204; Wroth and Zobel, eds., *Trials,* p. 70. James Murray was also owner of the barracks. Riot Act: A. C. Goodell *et al.,* eds., *Acts and Resolves, Public and Private, of the Province of the Massachusetts Bay,* 21 vols. (Boston, 1869–1922), 3:544–546. This was the only attempt by civil magistrates to interfere. Earlier in the evening Justice of the Peace John Ruddock had met about 20 armed young men but said that he found nothing unusual about it. Kidder, ed., *Massacre,* p. 202.

[35]*Ibid.,* pp. 77–78, 80, 87–88, 208, 216–217.

Estimates of the size of the crowd vary between 50 and thousands. The eyewitnesses whose depositions were later recorded by the town named 50 to 100 persons.[36] Witnesses asked immediately after the event about their estimates thought thousands had been there. At least 85 persons testified that they had seen the soldiers level their guns, 200 or more had come from Dock Square, at least another 100 from Cornhill. In addition, sailors from the docks and the constant stream of men from Northend and Southend have to be included. Probably between 1000 and 2000 people were assembled in King Street. Around the soldiers the throng was so thick that people climbed on posts on the other side of the street to see what was going on. Robert Williams, a propertyless man from Ward 6, reported, "I tried to press into the midst of them to know what they were about." Dozens of others attempted to get in too. Williams gave up and stood back, as Andrew, a black servant, did. Andrew saw that a "number were jumping on the backs of those that were talking with the officer, to get as near as they could." Since this impeded his view, he jumped down from his post and "Crowded through." Those present were described as "mostly sailors and other persons meanly dressed." This is supported by the evidence that streams of men came from the wharves, the Northend, and the Southend.[37] Among them were, however, some better-dressed persons, to whom historians have devoted much attention. A tall "gentleman" with a white wig and a red cloak talked to some people in Dock Square, and a gentleman in dark blue clothes was seen at the customs house.[38] A detailed analysis of the depositions about the affair shows that the men closest to the soldiers were mainly mechanics and sailors from the Northend, that the men farthest away (on the other side of the street) were merchants, often simply standing at their doors. In their depositions almost all merchants stated explicitly that they had been present accidentally, as spectators only, or because they lived there.

With the crowd so close to the soldiers, pelting was no longer possible. Some men, seemingly from the waterfront, suggested, "let us burn the sentry box, let us heave it over-board." Others abused the soldiers and dared them to fire.[39] Men talking to Preston, the officer present, were better dressed than those who dealt with the soldiers. The one man who attempted to strike Preston, immediately described as "a man like a sailor," was in fact a petty merchant.[40] In this case, the description was probably the usual attempt to consider the better sort as being above violence. Shouts were directed at the eight soldiers from all directions—front, flanks, even from behind their backs. Shoving in the crowd increased when 20 or 30 men armed

---

[36]The low estimates of the number of people in King Street, which the town subsequently published, were obviously dictated by the intent to exculpate the townsmen from the charge of rioting and provoking the soldiers.

[37]Wroth and Zobel, eds., *Trials*, pp. 70, 136–137; Kidder, ed., *Massacre*, pp. 90, 142, 153, 204.

[38]Man in the red cloak: *ibid.*, pp. 183, 187–188; William V. Wells [*The Life and Public Services of Samuel Adams*, 3 vols. (Boston, 1865, 1888), 1:313] doubted that it was William Molineux; Caleb H. Snow (Scrapbook, BPL) suggested Justice Ruddock; Nathaniel Dearborne [*Boston Notions: Being an Authentic and Concise Account of That Village, from 1630 to 1847* (Boston, 1848), p. 131] suspected Samuel Adams. Man in blue cloak: Wroth and Zobel, eds., *Trials*, pp. 76, 77–78. The extraordinary attention paid by historians to those two men meant focusing on .2 percent of those present, very moderately estimated at 1000.

[39]Kidder, ed., *Massacre*, pp. 87–88, 190–191, 202.

[40]*Ibid.*, pp. 77–78, 90–91, 93–94, 142.

Figure 7. The King Street riot or Boston Massacre. Detail from Revere's rendering of the event.

with sticks, among them Crispus Attucks, came running from Dock Square, where a barber's apprentice had told them that the soldiers were going to fire on the inhabitants. They joined those standing directly in front of the bayonets of the soldiers.[41] Benjamin Burdick, Jr., and John Hickling attempted to knock a gun out of a soldier's hand or to wrest it from him.[42] One soldier was knocked down, got up, and his gun went off, followed by several more shots.

Most men in the crowd turned to run for shelter, but dozens stayed, thinking that the soldiers had loaded powder only and no balls. Then they saw the dead and wounded lying in the snow. A few men counterattacked. Robert Patterson, a sailor active in the riot against customs informer Richardson 10 days earlier, attempted to grab the muskets. So did Nathaniel Fosdick, one of the ropemakers active in the riot at the Southend ropewalks on 2 March. Theodore Bliss, a carpenter, closed in on the soldiers. Richard Palmes, who had been talking to Preston, threw a stick at the soldiers. The assault proved unsuccessful, and the soldiers stood their ground. Several streets off, a councillor who reluctantly had agreed to come and talk to the crowd to disperse them headed back home when he heard the shooting. Nathaniel Fosdick, the ropemaker, on the other hand, decided that determined action was needed. He retreated to the main body of the crowd, told the people to seal off the streets, and went to get his gun and a party of men. Soon after, some militia drummers began to beat to arms. A man walking from the Northend to the center of the town met many rushing to get guns.[43]

It is certain that Preston did not give an order to fire. He had accompanied the soldiers but was not in command. Soldier Hugh Montgomery, struck and stumbling, fired first; the others followed. In the noise and confusion, the constant taunts from the crowd, "Fire!" may have been mistaken by one or several of the soldiers for an order from the officer. Four men were killed immediately, and eight were wounded. Of the latter, Patrick Carr died a few days later. All of them had a trade or, were apprentices. A quarter of the rioters on 5 March were men without property, and many others probably were sailors who happened to be in port, since an exceptionally high percentage of them were not in the tax list for 1771.[44]

With 1000–2000 people already assembled in the town center, hundreds more now hurried to the townhouse. The guards had been drawn up between townhouse and Mainguard and had been reinforced. The captain of the *Rose* man-of-war kept his men up all night ready to intervene but was disappointed not to receive any

[41]*Ibid.*, pp. 65, 129–131, 137–141, 142–143.

[42]*Ibid.*, pp. 73–74, 94–95, 152; Narrative of Proceedings at Boston, Sparks MSS., 10.3:70–71, HHL.

[43]Kidder, ed., *Massacre*, pp. 75–76, 77–78, 91–92, 148, 216–217; Gage to Barrington, 24 April 1770 (enclosure), *Correspondence*, 2:536–537; deposition of Joseph Belknap, Belknap Papers, box labeled "Misc. Dated and Undated Papers," p. 69 (two slightly differing copies), MHS.

[44]Killed: Samuel Gray (ropemaker, employed), Crispus Attucks (Small Deer) (sailor), James Caldwell (mate), Samuel Maverick (ivory turner, apprentice), Patrick Carr (leather breeches maker, employed). Wounded: Christopher Monk (shipwright, apprentice), John Clark (apprentice), Edward Payne (merchant), John Green (tailor), Robert Patterson (sailor), David Parker (wheelwright, apprentice), Benjamin Burdick, Jr. (barber). *BG,* 12 March 1770; *Boston Chron.*, 8 March 1770; coroner's reports, Mellen Chamberlain Collection, BPL, and Colburn Collection, MHS; *BTR* 18:45–46, 49, 120, 215, 269, 23:212, 25:113, 26:2; Misc. Unbound Papers, 1771, BCH; tax and valuation list, 1771, MA 132:92–147. On Small Deer (Attucks), see Lerone Bennett, Jr., *Pioneers in Protest* (Chicago, 1968), pp. 3–9.

orders to that effect.[45] Town officials were sent for, and Acting Governor Hutchinson was asked by some inhabitants to prevent more bloodshed. On his way from the Northend, he met many of his neighbors with cutlasses and sticks and was soon obliged to hide and then continued by back alleys. Arriving at the townhouse, he began to talk to an officer but was suddenly hustled by some friends into the building. He was not safe outside, he was told. Later he heard that one man in the crowd had lifted a club over his head, but that someone had seized the rioter's arm before he could hit. Negotiations between leaders and the crowd then continued, with the former appearing at the windows of the council chamber and the latter remaining in the street. Hutchinson asked the people to disperse, but was told that the soldiers would have to go first. Molineux and other popular Whig leaders, addressing the crowd from the balcony, toned down the demand that the troops had to go; they were to be ordered back into the barracks. An hour earlier the rioters had threatened to set fire to the barracks unless the soldiers came out. Even for removal of the troops to the barracks, however, the leaders needed the pressure of the crowd. Some promises were made, the first witnesses were heard, and the soldiers who had fired were committed to gaol.[46] About 11 P.M. the people began to leave; the last 100 drew off about 3 A.M. after intently following the negotiations and the taking of depositions.[47] Several incidents occurred during the night, but none had important consequences.[48]

Looking back on the events of the night, John Adams decided, "that night the foundation of American independence was laid." A Loyalist coldly noted that the shooting "set the People in a great fury not being used to such skirmishes." Both the Whig and the Loyalist joined in despising the victims, "the most obscure and inconsiderable [persons] that could be found upon the continent" (Adams), "none of note except Mr. Edward Payne" (Murray). Payne was a merchant who had been standing on his doorstep.[49] Historians have joined the chorus. When the Massachusetts General Court in 1887 resolved to commemorate the victims, distinguished Boston historians decided that a "monument to perpetuate the fame of rioters was preposterous" (Abner Goodell) and meant placing "the martyr's crown ... upon the brow of the vulgar ruffian" (Charles Deane) or, worse, on "Crispus Attucks—that half Indian, half negro and altogether rowdy." A "typical mob group," found Longley, writing during the New Deal, when people were striking for better wages and less oppression by company thugs.[50] Only minority

[45]Kidder, ed., *Massacre*, pp. 98, 102–103; Hutchinson to Gage, 18 March 1770, *AASP* 47:286–287 (1937).

[46]Hutchinson to Bernard, 22 May, 23 May 1770, Letterbooks, MA 26:491–492; deposition of Joseph Belknap, Belknap Papers, box labeled "Misc. Dated and Undated Papers," p. 69, MHS.

[47]Hutchinson to Hillsborough, March 1770, *MHSP* 6:484–487 (1862–1863); Hutchinson to Gage, 6 March 1770, *AASP* 47:270–272 (1937); John Tudor, *Deacon Tudor's Diary, 1732–1793*, ed. William Tudor (Boston, 1896), pp. 31–32.

[48]Kidder, ed., *Massacre*, pp. 96, 100–101, 101–102; SCF 101646; on Goldfinch, see also State Papers, 12:84, and Colonial Office 5/759:161ff., PRO.

[49]John Adams to James Burgh, 28 Dec. 1774, *Works*, 9:350–352, to Matthew Robinson, 2 March 1786, *ibid.*, 8:384; Murray to Smith, 12 March 1770, *Letters of James Murray, Loyalist*, ed. Nina M. Tiffany and Susan I. Leslay (Boston, 1901), p. 163.

[50]R. S. Longley, "Mob Activities in Revolutionary Massachusetts," *NEQ* 6:119 (1933); MHS May meeting, 1887, in Randolph G. Adams, "New Light," p. 262; James R. Gilmore, "Nathaniel Emmons and Mather Byles," *New Eng. Mag.* 16:735 (1897).

groups, who had to resort to direct action themselves for recognition of their claims, accepted Attucks, "Small Deer." Black orators named Attucks as one of their notable brothers after emancipation, as do Indians today in their struggle for equality. Contemporaries had no idea about the attitudes that Adams and Murray expressed in their letters or diaries and that historians were to perpetuate.

On the day after the riots, several meetings were held to effect the removal of the troops from town and to commemorate the victims. In council the advice was removal, and the councillors "did not judge from the general temper of the people only," but were certain that it was "the determination" of the people, including the "principle inhabitants." The latter certainly had been reluctant to leave the safety of their houses on the preceding evening, but now that the crowd had acted, had suffered the casualties, they dared to speak up too.[51] Councillor Royal Tyler did this so strongly that crown officials tried to make him admit treasonous conduct by the Boston Whig leaders. Perhaps they had to speak up, since it would have been impossible to lead and control the crowds had they stayed behind and kept quiet.

The town crier announced a general meeting of the inhabitans for 11 A.M., where depositions were taken and the demand to remove the troops reiterated. At a regular town meeting in the afternoon, 3000 people assembled and via messengers negotiated with Hutchinson. To the first request he answered that he had no power to remove the troops, but that the commanding officer in council had agreed to send the 29th regiment, the one involved in the shooting, to the castle and to withdraw the Mainguard until further orders from General Gage in New York. The town voted the answer unsatisfactory, only one of the 3000 disagreeing, and sent the committee straight back to demand removal of the 14th Regiment too. Hutchinson laid the town's vote before the council, which supported it and thus pressured Lieutenant Colonel Dalrymple to give his word of honor to remove both regiments without "unnecessary delay."[52] At the adjournment of the meeting, several motions were made to speed up the removal. Letters were ordered sent to friends in Great Britain, assurances of help from other towns read, and votes of thanks passed. The inhabitants debated the erection of a monument to the victims and castigated the supporters of the troops. They voted their "greatest abhorrence" of Samuel Waterhouse, one-time candidate for the office of stamp master, who had rented his house in King Street to the troops "and thereby basely prostituted a once respectable Mansion House to the use of the Main Guard."[53] Did people also think of those Whig merchants who had prostituted a once respectable business to provisioning of the troops?

As after the spontaneous riot of 26 August 1765, there were considerable apprehensions about further violence. The selectmen, in their only recorded action

---

[51]Hutchinson to Hillsborough, March 1770, *MHSP* 6:484–487 (1862–1863); Council Records, 16:457–461, MSA, and depositions on the meetings, MA 50:360, 361–367; cf. *BNL*, 27 Sept. 1770.

[52]*BTR* 18:1–2, 3–4; *BEP*, 12 March 1770; Rowe, *Letters and Diary*, 6 March 1770, p. 198; Palfrey to Wilkes, 13 March 1770, *MHSP* 6:480–483 (1862–1863); Hutchinson to Gage, 6 March 1770, Sparks MSS., 10.3:66, HHL. When Gage later stated that "both regiments were withdrawn at the *request* of the civil authorities," Hutchinson strongly disagreed. See also Gage, *Correspondence*, 1:255.

[53]*BTR* 18:4–21; Hutchinson to Hillsborough, 12 March 1770, Sparks MSS., 10.3:68.

concerning the disturbances, for once attempted to cooperate with Hutchinson. They demanded safety measures. Hutchinson immediately thought of a guard but declined to take action, "as it would be Reported on the other side of the Water that he had raised the Militia to drive the Soldiers out of the Town." But he did suggest to the colonel of the militia to act on his own. This, however, was not what the town leaders wanted. The militiamen, as in 1765, had been among the rioters. About 100 "respectable" inhabitants volunteered for guard duty, and an elite unit, the Artillery Company, was called out. Individual inhabitants accosted soldiers and ordered them to give an account of themselves, so that the town's watchmen had to interpose for their protection.[54]

On 8 March, four of the "unhappy Victims" were buried. From each of their homes, a procession started, and all converged on King Street, "the Theatre of that inhuman Tragedy," to form one funeral march. Directly behind the four coffins were the nearest relatives and the selectmen. Then thousands followed in ranks of six, and the carriages of the principal gentlemen formed the rear. Most shops in town closed, and the bells of Boston and the neighboring towns joined "to toll a solemn Peal." "The aggravated Circumstances of their Death, the Distress and Sorrow visible in every Countenance, together with the peculiar Solemnity with which the whole Funeral was conducted, surpass Description." Multitudes of country people, estimated at 10,000 or more, had come to town. Patrick Carr died on the fifteenth and was buried two days later in the same grave after another procession beginning at Faneuil Hall.[55]

Meanwhile, Lieutenant Colonel Dalrymple began to embark the troops for Castle Island. He had promised that no unnecessary delay would occur, but he found it necessary to move slowly to gain time to inform General Gage and to await his orders. Several times the town sent to him for information about the withdrawal and to press for a more speedy removal. Each time it was William Molineux who conferred with Dalrymple and who reported to the town. Once, when Dalrymple had to march two companies through the whole town, he informed Hancock that the inhabitants might attempt to attack the soldiers. Hancock informed Molineux, who marched alongside the soldiers from the west part of the town to the embarkation point on Wheelwright's wharf. The troops had come to protect the king's officials from the riots of the inhabitants. Now riots had forced their withdrawal, and the king's troops had to ask the leaders of His Majesty's most loyal but rioting inhabitants for protection. When the removal of the troops was finally completed on 27 March, the town "sincerely hoped we shall never be visited with them again."[56]

Many considered the King Street riot and earlier frays to have been a precon-

[54]*BTR* 23:57–58; George R. T. Hewes, *Traits of the Tea Party: Being a Memoir of George R. T. Hewes,* ed. Benjamin B. Thatcher (New York, 1835), p. 115; Tudor, *Diary,* p. 33; orders of Colonel Jackson to Captain Paddock, Mellen Chamberlain Collection, 1.7:83, BPL; State Papers, 12:68, 92–93, 97, 137–138; deposition of Lieutenant James Vibart, Colonial Office 5/759:191ff., PRO.

[55]*BG,* 12 March 1770; *BNL,* 15 March 1770; *BEP,* 12 March 1770; Boyle, "Journal," 8 March, 15 March 1770, p. 264; Rowe, *Letters and Diary,* 8 March, 17 March 1770, p. 199; Palfrey to Wilkes, 13 March 1770, *MHSP* 6:480–483 (1862–1863).

[56]Dalrymple to Gage, 7 March 1770, *AASP* 47:277–279 (1937); Boyle, "Journal," 27 March 1770, p. 264.

certed affair. According to the commanding officer, Councillor Tyler had said "That the people in general were resolved to have the troops removed." Should other measures fail, "they were determined to effect their removal by force." He reportedly added that this was supported by "people of the best characters and Fortunes in the Province and Men of Religion," that "the same Sentiments were adopted in the Towns adjacent," and that "10,000 men would be assembled on the Common of Boston." The councillors and others present disputed this version. Probably Tyler reported hearsay from among the crowds. Some townspeople, on the other hand, supposed that the military had made secret plans to force them into submission by "a general if not universal massacre." From the available evidence, it seems that indeed no definite plans similar to those for the riot of 14 August 1765 had been made. None of those who sometimes attempted to lead or incite crowd action was on the scene. After the fight between ropemakers and soldiers on 2 March, both sides "privately agreed for a general Engagement" on the following Monday. When in the evening of that day the bells began to ring, many soldiers and inhabitants alike knew that this was not a fire. Furthermore, in Charlestown and Roxbury the bells began to ring too, many people armed, and some Roxbury militiamen went off to Boston. John Adams, who in later years suspected that "certain busy characters" had been inciting quarrels "between the inhabitants of the lower class and the soldiers," had noted in 1770 after carefully reviewing all evidence that aside from constant bickering no concerted plan had existed on either side. But there was a tacit agreement between some sections of the people and the soldiers to fight it out. To control lower-class independent action, men of great influence were once again elected as wardens, an office designed to watch over the keeping of Lord's Day. The prestigious office had been conveted by men of top rank after its establishment in 1761. But tired of having their Sundays spoiled and not always receiving deference, they had soon retired, and the office became a domain of middle-class men. During the elections, three weeks after the riot, the top people were suddenly ready to serve and be elected. After order was reestablished, their ardor lasted only till lower-ranking men could replace them at the elections a year later.[57]

AFTERMATH

In the months after the troops had been forced from town, Bostonians still had to deal with trials of soldiers, with the crumbling nonimportation agreements, and, of course, with the customs officials. In the second half of April, the news was received that all Townshend duties with the exception of the duty on tea had been repealed. Efforts to continue nonimportation to force Parliament to retreat on the tea

[57]Depositions on council meetings, MA 50:360, 361–367; Kidder, ed., *Massacre,* pp. 47–48, 103, 189–190; State Papers, 12:98–102; Whitwell to Vernon, 10 April 1774, *MHSP* 22:122 (1885–1886). Eliot to Hollis, 28 June 1770, *MHSC* 4.4:451–452 (1858); Preston's account, *BNL,* 21 June 1770; Narrative of the Proceedings at Boston, Sparks MSS., 10.3:70–71, HHL; John Adams, *Works,* 2:229–230. Notes in John Davis Papers, 3 vols., 3:31, MHS; David Hall, Diary, 1740–1784, 2 vols., 11 March 1770, MHS. On wardens: Dirk Hoerder, *Society and Government, 1760–1780: The Power Structure in Massachusetts Townships* (Berlin, 1972), p. 47.

duty were pursued for several months, but the high unemployment rate among the mechanics, the precarious position of the small shopkeepers, and the interest of merchants in doing business again combined to doom all measures taken.

Compared to the nonimportation-connected direct action and the deep-reaching social tensions, the action against customs officials and the remaining soldiers remained marginal. The spontaneous King Street riot was followed by a series of three town meetings concerning the nonimportation agreements. A committee was elected "to strengthen the Hands of the Merchants" in these matters, to debate a nonconsumption agreement for tea and other foreign luxuries, and to employ the poor by home manufacture. This sounded noncommittal enough but was in fact a guise for a sharp reversal of leadership policies. John Ruddock, who had destroyed the tradesmen's petition for shipbuilding and jobs in January, was on the committee, which now admitted that the mechanics' situation was extremely serious and that the course demanded by the tradesmen was appropriate. "The best method of employing the Tradesmen and poor People in this Town is in the natural branch of Ship building," the town's main industry. Probably from fear of more direct action that could not be controlled, the committee also saw to it that the building of three ships began immediately.[58]

Since hundreds of families had been left without subsistence by the economic policies, the effects could not be reversed on short notice. By the middle of the year, the situation of the poor was still so distressing that fears of an uprising disturbed well-to-do importers and Whig merchants alike. A Loyalist justice of the peace and merchant of Boston thought that if the social and economic situation did not improve soon, "the poor People, many of whom are almost starving for want of Employment, [are] going to plunder the Rich and then cutting their throats." Mrs. Barnes, wife of an importing merchant, noted that the Sons of Liberty were disturbed by such prospects too. She reported that the goods temporarily seized and stored by the merchants' committee to enforce nonimportation might be lost to their owners, "For they begin to talk of selling them at vendue, and distributeing the money to the poor." This was intended not only to help the poor but also to take some of the pressure off taxpayers, who were faced with skyrocketing costs for poor relief. Moreover, it would enlist the suffering people on the side of those who still favored nonimportation and make them "very assidious in seizing everything that comes in their way."[59]

The distress had been foreseen by merchant John Powell, who touched on another sore point, the feeling against minorities. He called the agreements "a Self Denying Ordinance to starve one half of the Inhabitants of this good Town." The method was to be "not to admit Scot's Goods." It was Scottish merchants who extended credit to small shopkeepers thus breaking the power of the large importing firms in the colonies. It seems that the Whig leaders realized the potential for social unrest

---

[58]Anne Hulton, *Letters of a Loyalist Lady* (Cambridge, Mass., 1927), 25 July 1770, p. 26; *BTR* 18:12–20. Cf. *Mass. Brds.* 1473.

[59]Murray to Smith, 8 June 1770, *Letters*, pp. 132–133; Barnes to Smith, June–July 1770, *ibid.*, pp. 176–179; cf. Hutchinson to Whately, 3 Oct. 1770, Letterbooks, MA 27:11–12.

and undertook to direct it against outsiders. John Mein had been blamed for being a Scot, and throughout the following years Scotsmen and sometimes Irishmen were used as scapegoats or had to bear the burden of the difficulties together with the poor. Samuel Adams attempted to discredit the evidence of several men about the King Street riot by mentioning that they were Scottish. Later, in 1774, tea was more readily seized when it belonged to poor peddlers or Scotsmen. One of the importing merchants who was attacked in the summer of 1770 was a Scot, and care was taken that this became well-known. Some ministers occasionally included Jews in the list of undesirables.[60] The Sandemanians, a religious sect, also met with hostility. John Mein had belonged to this sect. Shortly after the leaders' riot against him, another member of the sect, Colburn Barrell, condemned rioting in a sermon to the small congregation. For this inflammatory talk, the town leaders, Mein's attackers, who torpedoed every one of the governor's moves to get rioters indicted, managed to get Barrell punished in court.[61]

In June two Scottish merchants, the McMasters, were the main target for violence. They applied to Hutchinson for protection after they had received numerous threats and had finally been warned to leave town within three days or expect to be tarred and feathered. Hutchinson could or would do nothing, except to mention the case to a "Gentleman of Character and influence." This did not help: Patrick McMaster was seized by a crowd, carted to the gallows, and forced to swear never to return to the town. At the town limits the crowd formed a lane through which he had to pass, the men spitting in his face. He escaped but had to evade several dozen men from Roxbury who came in his pursuit. Missing him, the men broke several windows in Commissioner Hulton's house. The *Gazette* began its report on the proceedings: "The bold and generous spirit of Freedom encreases every day among us. . . ." The affair happened in broad daylight, but none of the magistrates interfered.[62]

Those importers who had held out longest against the pressure were now used as scapegoats for the slow crumbling of the nonimportation. Hate and action had to focus on concrete objects or persons rather than on abstract principles, agreements, or faraway institutions and officials in Great Britain. The last importers "begged with tears" that their signatures to agreement might be accepted. Mr. Rogers, a relative of the governor, was several times assaulted by "the most diabolical crew that are upon the face of the earth," set on him by the merchants. He became well-known as a target for destruction, and in August his house was even vandalized without any political motivation.[63]

[60]Powell to Champlin, 23 Oct. 1769, *MHSC* 69:294 (1914); "Vindex" [Samuel Adams], in *BG*, 24 Dec., 31 Dec. 1770, reprinted in *The Writings of Samuel Adams*, ed. Harry A. Cushing, 4 vols. (New York, 1904–1908), 2:99–100, 122–123; John Andrews, "Letters of John Andrews," 1 Aug., 8 Sept., 5 Nov. 1774, *MHSP* 8:335, 356, 383 (1864–1865); Ezra Stiles, *The Literary Diary*, ed. F. B. Dexter, 3 vols. (New York, 1901), 31 March 1770, 1:53–54, cf. 151, 270; Nathaniel Noyes to William Henshaw [Aug. 1774], *NEHGR* 43:144–145 (1889).
[61]Indictment, 21 Nov. 1770, Mellen Chamberlain Collection, 1.7:20, BPL; Hutchinson to Whately, 5 Oct. 1768, Letterbooks, MA 25:281–282.
[62]Fleming to Mein, 1 July 1770, Sparks MSS., 10.4:5, HHL; *BG*, 4 June 1770; *Essex Gaz.*, 5 Feb. 1771; Council Records, 16:487–488, MSA; Anne Hulton, *Letters*, 25 July 1770, p. 27; cf. Wells, *Life of Samuel Adams*, 1:299–300.
[63]Hutchinson to Bernard, 12 Aug. 1770, Letterbooks, MA 26:534–535; Gordon, *History*, 1:277.

When Whig merchants recommenced their meetings in April 1770, one of the Loyalist importers thought that the whole agitation was undertaken by others envious of their good business. Another demanded: "Pray inquire where the biggest shops in Town [that is, those of some Whigs] get their assortments." The merchants, after the repeal of the duties, met separately again, to be independent of politicians of the type of Otis and Adams and to stop lowly shopkeepers from having a say in policy making. They could then appear with one line of argument in subsequent "Body" meetings, which were held mainly for purposes of agitation, since few were left to counteract the Whig merchants. Perhaps because there were some lingering doubts that the "Body" meetings were legal, the votes were often repeated in the town meeting.[64]

Merchants outside Boston were under pressure too, with the original impetus for action sometimes coming from Boston. Henry Barnes, government-supporting justice of the peace in Marlborough, was discovered in June 1770 conveying goods out of Boston. More than 1000 people assembled and threw some of his goods on the street and carried others off—an unusual procedure, lending further credibility to the reports that the impoverished people were desperate. A few days later a crowd, supposedly led by a youth from Boston, attacked his house, destroyed his coach, tarred and feathered his horse in lieu of him, and let it loose with his effigy. Finally they hung and burned the effigy. Next a threatening letter was left at his house, declaring that unless he closed his shop, he would be tarred or killed, or both, and his house and shop would be burned. A Marlborough town meeting chose inspectors to watch Barnes's customers. The young men in town were invited to hold a special meeting of their own to make the same resolutions and, "fond of their new-gotten power, hastened to put it in execution."[65]

In the same month a Worcester shopkeeper, Ebenezer Cutler, bought two wagon loads of British goods, including a quantity of tea from Lillie, an importer. Although Cutler could have rested now in his effort to bring the wrath of the Committee of Inspection upon him, he freely talked about his purchase. The Southwatch unsuccessfully attempted to stop the wagons, and Cutler left a rather agitated community in his wake. A number of men, variously estimated from 20 to 150, pursued him and seized the bridles of the teams. Cutler unwillingly agreed to return. At every public house the men stopped to raise the people, so that they could watch. On the Neck, where 200 people were waiting, they halted at the house of John Dennie, Jr., to whom they had announced their visit on leaving the town, because he sold tea. Asked for his tea, Dennie told them that was none of their business. After some

[64]Gilbert Deblois to Elizabeth Smith, 10 May 1770, James Murray Robbins Papers, vol. 2, MHS; Martha Curtis to William Cooper [Jan. 1770], Samuel Adams Papers, transcripts, reel 1, NYPL; Hutchinson to Hillsborough, 24 Jan. 1770, Sparks MSS., 10.3:64, HHL; Powell to Champlin, 10 July 1770, Letters of Boston Merchants, 2:103, HBS; Rowe, *Letters and Diary*, April 1770, p. 201; Hewes, *Memoir*, pp. 139–140; *BG*, 18 June 1770; *BEP*, 29 Jan. 1770; Narrative of Events in Boston, Sparks MSS., 10.3:76–77, HHL.

[65]*Essex Gaz.*, 12 June 1770; *BG*, 2 July 1770; proclamation, MA 88:229–230; Barnes's petition, Council Records, 16:489–493, MSA; Barnes to Smith, June 1770, in Murray, *Letters*, pp. 175–179; Charles Hudson, *History of the Town of Marlborough, Middlesex County, Massachusetts, from Its First Settlement in 1657 to 1861* (Boston, 1862), pp. 156–157. The goods on the wagon were at least in part material necessary for potash and pearlash manufacture. Both commodities were important export articles of the colony. No tea was found in the load.

altercation the crowd left, threatening to come back and pull down or burn his shop. In the center of the town, the Committee of Inspection told Cutler that he could store his goods "of his own free will." Cutler refused, and several committeemen tried to pacify the crowd. Their endeavors yielded such meager results that Cutler felt compelled to declare in writing that he would store. On the way the crowd pulled him from his horse and threw him on one of the wagons. One of the two wagoners coming back to Oxford, Worcester County, had to justify his conduct to his fellow inhabitants. He declared that he did not want to help importers and gave or had to give his hire to the town for the use of the poor. (Most legal fines were—at least partly—to be used for the poor.) The issue was kept alive for years when Cutler commenced suit against Pierpoint and Davis, two men from the crowd and the merchants' committee. In 1775 he was arrested and sent as a Loyalist to the Provincial Congress for examination, where he requested and obtained the "privilege of going into the town of Boston, without his effects."[66]

A man carting tea and other goods bought from Jackson was more careful than Cutler. He can back to Marblehead by a back way late in the evening. However, the Boston committee informed its sister body in Marblehead, and by 3 A.M. the same night the wagoner received a letter saying that he would be cut off from any employment unless he returned the goods, which he did immediately.[67] In other towns of the province, meetings and crowds acted on the nonimportation problem too. In Marblehead, offenders were forced to recant if they wanted to continue in business. In Salem, on the other hand, importers threatened to tar and feather supporters of the agreement coming from Boston. Haverhill voted to use only lawful means to prevent importation but to expose importers to public shame. The state of hate and pressure under which the importers lived is evidenced by the following item from a contemporary newspaper about a country town, where "they keep in Readiness in some convenient Place near the Center of the Town (to wit, near Execution Dock, and not far from Liberty Oak,) a sufficient Quantity of Tar and Feathers." They were reserved for "those atrocious V[illain]s, those vile Miscreants, who . . . thro' the avaricious Humour of raising a private Fortune on the Ruins of the Public, have perfidiously broke through the general and salutary Non Importation Agreement."[68]

Two months after the repeal of most of the Townshend duties became known in

[66]*BNL*, 5 July 1770, 17 Nov. 1772; *BG*, 2 July, 9 July, 27 Aug. 1770, 29 April, 23 Sept. 1771, 21 Sept. 1772; *Mass. Spy*, 25 Aug. 1770; *Essex Gaz.*, 2 July, 28 Aug. 1770; Superior Court of Judicature, Records, 1771, f. 140, 1772, ff. 124–125, SCCH; SCF 152615, 152686; Fleming to Mein, 1 July 1770, Sparks MSS., 10.4:5, HHL; John Adams, *Diary*, 25 April 1771, 2:8; Memorial of Cutler, B. F. Stevens, Transcripts of American Loyalist Claims, NYPL, microfilms of vols. 13 and 14, "Massachusetts Claims," in MHS, 14:469–472; William Lincoln, ed., *The Journals of Each Provincial Congress of Massachusetts in 1774–1775 . . .* (Boston, 1858), 24 May 1775, p. 253, MA 138:72–73; Northborough Committee to General Ward, 17 May 1775, in Peter Force, ed., *American Archives,* 9 vols. (Washington, D.C., 1837–1853), 4.2:632.
[67]*BNL*, 18 Jan. 1770; *BEP*, 22 Jan. 1770.
[68]Samuel Roads, *The History and Traditions of Marblehead* (Boston, 1880), 10 May 1770, p. 86. *BNL*, 23 Aug. 1770. George W. Chase, *The History of Haverhill, Massachusetts, from Its First Settlement, in 1640, to the Year 1860* (Haverhill, Mass., 1861), p. 367; *Essex Gaz.*, 21 Aug. 1770; *Mass. Spy*, 25 Aug. 1770 (from *Conn. Courant*): "an Importer drinks the Blood of his Country."

April 1770, the efforts to continue nonimportation collapsed. Abusive publications about nonsigners and merchant-led terrorizing of opponents ended. The last mass action was a meeting of the "Body" on 24 July. A group of participants paraded the streets, Thomas Young at their head, with a horn and "Flags Flying." No violence ensued; rather, it was a farewell parade, awakening reminiscences but remaining an empty form. Town-meeting action also ended unimpressively, when a report to promote agriculture and home manufactures was shelved without being read because of disinterest, though Samuel Adams was among its authors.[69]

Sections of the people of Boston continually pressed for a speedy trial of the soldiers, while the judges, in accord with the leadership, as persistently postponed it. The inhabitants ordered a committee to help—or to put pressure on—the king's attorney and the selectmen to hire lawyers to assist the prosecution. A petition to the governor demanded special judges to replace those not able to attend for "bodily Indisposition." The petition was unsuccessful, and threats followed. To divert the anger of the people, the trial of informer Richardson was held, and large crowds attended. The trials of Preston and the soldiers finally began in November. The jury had been packed with government men, many of whom had to pay later for serving: Crowds repeatedly abused and harassed them. The defense lawyers, John Adams and Josiah Quincy, had been advised by the whole Whig leadership of the town to take the case. The sentiments of the leaders had cooled so far that even Molineux agreed. Hutchinson charged that Adams repeatedly kept evidence that reflected negatively on the town of Boston from being used by the defense. Whether this was in fact done or was the reason for Whig-inclined defense counsels remains in doubt. What is certain is that Quincy and Adams were both strong opponents of crowd action and highly critical of the rioters of 5 March. Thus, while care was taken that the soldiers had good lawyers, Quincy's and Adams's role meant, at the same time, a repudiation of the rioters.[70]

Preston was found innocent; the soldiers pleaded benefit of the clergy, a legal device to avoid punishment in the case of offenses committed the first time. Preston rejoiced at the "complete victory obtained over the knaves and foolish villains of Boston." The inhabitants were rather discontent and mused about the report that the king had granted Preston a pension and that "the Murderers of our innocent fellow-Citizens are still permitted to go unpunished." During the trial the well-to-

---

[69]Rowe, *Letters and Diary*, 24 July 1770, pp. 204–205; Gage to Barrington, 6 Oct. 1770, *Correspondence*, 2:561–562.
[70]Wroth and Zobel, eds., *Trials*, 3:31, note; Wade Millis, "A Monument to the American Sense of Justice," *Mich. Law Rev.* 25:143–168 (1926); *A Proclamation* [concerning an anonymous letter] (Boston, 1770), *Mass. Brds.*, 1535; *BTR* 18:13–15, 23:70; Memorial of the Town of Boston, Misc. Unbound Papers, 1770, BCH, and Samuel Adams, *Writings*, 2:7–8; Oliver, *American Rebellion*, pp. 92–93; Narrative of Events in Boston, Sparks MSS., 10.3:76–77, HHL; Palfrey to Wilkes [23–30 Oct. 1770], *CSMP* 34:418–426 (1937–1942); Josiah Quincy to Josiah Quincy, Sen., 26 March 1770, in Josiah Quincy, *Memoir of the Life of Josiah Quincy, Jun., of Massachusetts* (Boston, 1825), pp. 32–45; Quincy's plea to the jury, *ibid.*, p. 46. For Adams's and Quincy's opinions on crowds, see John R. Howe, Jr., *The Changing Political Thought of John Adams* (Princeton, N.J., 1966), pp. 11–14, 106–107, 171–172, and George H. Nash, III, "From Radicalism to Revolution: The Political Career of Josiah Quincy, Jr.," *AASP* 79:255, 258–259, 260–261 (1969); cf. Samuel M. Quincy, ed., *Reports of Cases Argued and Adjudged in the Superior Court of Judicature of . . . Massachusetts Bay, 1761–1772, by Josiah Quincy, Junior* (Boston, 1865), pp. 170–171, 173–174; Hutchinson, *History*, 3:205, "Additions," pp. 31–32.

do Justice John Cushing had commented, "It is odd the Town should think of doing Justice by a Mob." But the people knew that lax prosecution, remitting of fines, and pardons obstructed justice as they understood it. John Adams, convinced of the soldiers' innocence, nevertheless decided that the verdict "is no Reason why the Town should not call the Action of that Night a Massacre,"[71] and the inhabitants annually commemorated this "most horrid and inhuman Massacre on the Fifth of March." A special oration was delivered by one of the town leaders in the Old South meeting house from a pulpit draped in black. "That large Church was filled and crouded in every Pew, Seat, Alley, and Gallery, by an Audience of several Thousands of People of all Ages, and Characters and of both Sexes." King Street taverns exhibited pictures and relics of the riot, and visitors were shown the place where "the massacre was." The commemoration was held for the last time in 1783 and then replaced by the celebrations on 4 July.[72]

During the summer of 1770, soldiers occasionally came from the castle to town on business. Several of them were mistreated by the townspeople. On 29 May, the day before election day, several soldiers were insulted on the common near the military hospital that had remained in town. They were told that no soldiers would be tolerated on the common. One of them reported having heard that while King George and his ministers were damned, a toast was proposed to King Hancock.[73]

The town assiduously attempted to link the customs commissioners to the massacre, on the basis that not all shots had been fired by soldiers, that some had come from the customs house windows. These attempts ended rather pitiably, although several low-ranking customs officials were repeatedly imprisoned under suspicion of having fired into the crowd. A town committee tried to prevent their release, but numerous witnesses appeared in their defense. Of the town's two witnesses, one gave unclear evidence and was probably deranged, and the other was a servant boy belonging to an accused customs official. The poor boy was alternately threatened and beaten by his master and those town leaders attempting to get the official indicted. He was later sentenced to the pillory and 25 lashes for "not having the fear of God in his heart being moved and seduced by the Instigation of the devil [read: the town leaders] and wickedly and maliciously minding and Contriving to Cause and procure a Verdict" against the customs employees. The crowd showed more sympathy for him than master, leaders, judges, or jury. When he was led to the pillory, a crowd rescued him from the sheriff.[74]

The customs commissioners had fled to the castle again. Paxton had been threatened with death; Hulton's residence in Brookline was attacked in June 1770.

[71]Preston to Gage, 31 Oct. 1770, *AASP* 47:338–340 (1938); *Mass. Spy*, 24 Oct. 1771; Boyle, "Journal," 29 Oct., 5 Dec. 1770, p. 267; John Adams, *Diary*, 5 March 1773, 2:79, *Legal Papers*, 3:97.

[72]Boyle, "Journal," 5 March 1770, p. 263; John Adams, *Diary*, 5 March 1773, 2:79; William Gregory, "A Scotchman's Journey in New England in 1771," ed. Mary G. Powell, *New Eng. Mag.*, 29 Sept. 1771, n.s. 12:344 (1895). For later celebrations, see newspapers; Boyle, "Journal"; Rowe, *Letters and Diary; BTR.*

[73]Soldiers' depositions, State Papers, 12:86, 86–87, 91, 94–95, 95–96; Kidder, ed., *Massacre*, p. 98.

[74]Superior Court of Judicature, Records, 1771, ff. 40–41, SCCH; Journal of Transactions in Boston, Sparks MSS., 10.3:56, HHL; Narrative of Events in Boston, Sparks MSS., 10.3:76–77; Rowe, *Letters and Diary*, 28 March 1771, p. 213; *BNL*, 13 Dec. 1770; *BEP*, 17 Dec. 1770; *BG*, 1 April 1771. Oliver M. Dickerson, in "The Commissioners of Customs and the 'Boston Massacre,'" *NEQ* 27:307–325 (1954), overemphasizes the commissioners' involvement.

He had prepared for such emergencies by keeping firearms in the house and by fixing an alarm bell to the roof to arouse sympathetic neighbors. A few days later another small group of men smashed his windows.[75] In Boston a crowd seized a customs tidewaiter, Owen Richards, after he had given information about smuggling of goods on 18 May 1770. He had been manhandled in 1768, when he poked through Hancock's vessel *Lydia* without proper authority. Now the crowd carried him to the customs house, where his wig and clothes were taken off. Then, as an example to all officials inside, he was tarred and feathered. A sign bearing the word "importer" was fixed on his breast, a halter around his neck. He had to acknowledge his misdeeds and was carted around town for two hours, until three or four men from the approximately 120 men in the crowd took him off. During the same time another group of men rescued the seized goods from the ship about which Richards had given information. The riot had been planned during the afternoon, right after the smuggling had been detected. It seems that the merchant–captains had a hand in it or were at least considered sympathetic to the action, since the crowd did not carry Richards to the gallows at the Southend but through Ward 9, stopping at the houses of these men. John Hancock seemingly had some interest in the affair, since he paid the fees of the defense lawyer. Prosecution began only after the justices had been lectured by the council on their duties. The rioters were described as "disorderly men and boys and Negroes" by Richards. But of 67 persons who later gave evidence, only one was a Negro. Three were women. Indicted were a minor and four adults, one of them a wheelwright, one a peruke maker. The occupations of the other two are not known. Present were at least four men who had been active in the King Street riot three months earlier, most conspicuously the barber's apprentice who had pestered the customs house sentry. Lendall Pitts, later reportedly one of the leaders of the tea riot, was among the witnesses.[76]

A review of the nonimportation policies and their consequences from 1767 to 1770 shows the following developments. A period of leadership-imposed policies of "no mobs and tumults" opened the struggle. But the customs establishment called in troops, and Bostonians of different classes were plagued by impressment, seizures, and the presence of soldiers. The emphasis on economic measures temporarily served to unite the people through joint efforts to establish local manufactures and to support nonconsumption drives. It widened the breach between America and Great Britain. Economic distress among mechanics and shopkeepers resulting from this policy soon put severe strains on the alleged unity. The merchants were helpless without the support of the shopkeepers and the crowds. They did not even dare to

[75]Anne Hulton, *Letters,* 21 Dec. 1770, pp. 28–30, 38–47; *BEP,* 30 Oct. 1769; *Essex Gaz.,* 3 July 1770; *BNL,* 21 June 1770; Council Records, 16:448–449, MSA; proclamation, MA 88:224–225; Cooper to Pownall, 2 July 1770, *AHR* 8:318–320 (1902–1903).

[76]Memorial of Owen Richards, Sparks MSS., 10.4:1, HHL; Memorial of John Woart, *ibid.,* p. 2; *BPB,* 28 May 1770; *BEP,* 21 May 1770; *BNL,* 24 May 1770; *BG,* 21 May, 24 Dec. 1770, 5 Aug. 1771; *Essex Gaz.,* 5 Aug. 1771, 21 Jan. 1772; Rowe, *Letters and Diary,* 18 May 1770, p. 202; Boyle, "Journal," 18 May 1770, p. 265; Hutchinson to Hillsborough, 21 May 1770, Letterbooks, MA 26:488; Council Records, 16:481, MSA; *Richards* v. *Doble,* in John Adams, *Legal Papers,* 1:39–41; SCF 89791, 102127, 102288, 102532; Samuel Salisbury to ———, quoted in Esther Forbes, *Paul Revere and the World He Lived In* (Boston, 1942), p. 209; Edward A. Jones, *The Loyalists of Massachusetts, Their Memorials, Petitions, and Claims* (London, 1930), p. 243.

publish importers' names for fear of legal counteraction and, later, charges of treason. The people from among whom crowds were recruited, on the other hand, could act on their own, and did so first in June 1768. The political consequence of the action, directed at redressing local grievances, was the replacement of moderate leadership in merchants' and town meetings with politicians more responsive to popular demands.

After a relatively quiet period from fall 1768 to summer 1769, explained partly by precautionary measures against spontaneous crowd action and by the merchants' defection from the antitroop movement, violence recommenced with new vigor in fall 1769 on two levels. Lower-class crowds began an active campaign against the troops and compliant leaders, while merchants directed a series of intimidating acts of violence against those merchants opposing the nonimportation. The coercive measures against the latter remained for several months on a limited scale, with the one exception of the leaders' anti-Mein riot. But in the crisis at the beginning of 1770, the coercion expanded to carefully planned terrorizing of all nonsigning importers. At the same time spontaneous crowd action succeeded in bringing about the removal of the troops and then in forcing concessions from the leadership regarding the economic plight of the lower classes, sailors, mechanics, and shop-keepers. The immediate interests of the last had been sacrificed to the political interests of the country as interpreted by the leadership, which was partly elective, partly deriving its influence from economic and social position. Some of the leading Whig merchants also furthered their own private interests to the detriment of the community, especially its poorer sections. In this situation a grouping occurred that approached a kind of class alignment. The prevalent ideology of deference, though in conflict with the actual social stratification, succeeded in preventing the lower classes not from acting consciously and openly as a separate group, but from doing so continuously on a sufficiently high level to influence day-to-day political deci-sion making. Ultimately the leadership could direct most opposition and violence against outsiders, customs officials, soldiers, Scots and other minorities, and a group hurting the professed common good of the community, the importers. But during and after the antiimpressment riot in June 1768 and the antitroops riots in March 1770, the hard-hit lower classes asserted their interests and position.

The years from 1767 to 1770 also saw a development that has not been sufficiently explored to warrant definite conclusions, the increasing militancy of country towns. It has received little attention because compared to Boston's it seemed submerged, almost unnoticeable. But the ambiguous character of political, social, and economic thought in the countryside had briefly appeared in 1765 already. The riots connected with the Stamp Act in Berkshire, Maine, and elsewhere evidenced immediately much more open expressions of economic conflict than the slow maturation of concepts about socioeconomic conflict in Boston in August 1765. Still, at that time most towns repudiated the property destruction done in Boston. But during the nonimportation period the spirit of opposition caught on. By 1768, at the time of the arrival of the troops, the tar barrel on Beacon Hill was taken seriously by administra-tion officials—the farmers might indeed march into town to repel the British forces.

After the massacre, again, a rumor circulated that thousands of countrymen would come to attack the British Regulars. As to seaboard towns, nowhere had the inhabitants heeded the ''no mobs, no tumults'' policy of the Boston leadership.

Thus, when Samuel Adams and his political allies were to establish the Committee of Correspondence in fall 1772, their calls for participation in opposition measures fell on receptive ground; receptive not because all countrymen had learned John Locke by heart and now thought exclusively in Whig terminology, but because the ground had been prepared by the debates about and practice of nonimportation. The British were dangerous to public virtue because they inundated the country with foreign luxuries—and Boston merchants could be dangerous too. Their interest, the way they earned their living, was commerce with these luxuries. In consequence, the militancy and radicalism of the country were different from those in Boston, so different, in fact, that the Boston Committee of Correspondence sometimes failed to understand it. The attitudes developed in this period explain the surge of activity in the tea duty controversy and the anti-British crowd and militia action in 1774–1775, as well as the critical stance toward the leadership in Boston, which in these years became that of the province.

PART III

From Direct Action to Mass Movement in the Country, 1770-1775

In this part the important change from urban crowd action to rural mass and militia action will be traced. After a temporary lull in activities, partly explainable by imperial economic developments and merchants' interests, partly explainable by the economic decline and resulting loss of independence by Boston's lower classes, the next high point of riotous activity was the mainly leadership-controlled destruction of the tea in Boston harbor. When British punitive legislation singled out Boston by stationing troops in large numbers, the country took over. The military governor was soon happy to deal with the "quiet" Boston people, but he got nervous when the country towns merely sent a committee of perhaps 10 men or so. Less leadership-influenced than Boston's population, country people often came down on crown officials, by contingents of hundreds from each town, who on their way elected a leader or a committee to approach the offenders, but expected any decisions made by the delegates and crowd targets to be publicly announced by the offenders and then be ratified by popular vote. Within three weeks British influence was limited to the peninsula of Boston, though by law the new capital was Salem. It even became impossible to send troops out. The refugees in Boston were afraid of any loss of protection; the commanders feared that small detachments might be met by large crowds and did not want to lead the latter into temptation. In short, the tea riot precipitated a harsh reaction by the British government, which in turn precipitated an increase in opposition that nullified any British measures and effectively brought about independence. When militia units and then the army took over from crowds after Lexington and Concord, this by no means signified the end of crowd action. In some parts of the state, it intensified. The opposition to the British had had the effect of increasing militancy, difficult to curb for the Boston-centered provincial leadership, who had considerable problems in getting from the rear guard of the action back to the lead positions. The crowd members certainly were not very helpful in getting them back there. Their loss of control will be dealt with in this part, and their attempts to assert their power as well as the opposition to it will be treated in the last part.

Crowd Action against the Duty on Tea

9

LACK OF MILITANCY, FALL 1770 TO FALL 1773

With the repeal of the Townshend duties, excepting only the duty on tea, the issue shifted from general nonimportation to tea or no tea. In preceding years separate tea nonconsumption agreements had occasionally been reported, and a committee consisting of rather unimportant men had been elected. In March 1770, 212 Boston shopkeepers agreed not to sell tea.[1] In September a last-ditch effort to salvage the general nonimportation agreements failed, and agitation as well as activities, whether mass meetings, demonstrations or riots, declined sharply and remained on a low level for the next three years.[2] In town meetings, letters purloined from crown officials were discussed; crown grants replacing legislative appropriations of officials' salaries were opposed. A proclamation by the governor, November 1771, giving thanks for the "Continuance of our *Privileges*" was termed "a prophane Mockery of Heaven." Crowd action prevented ministers from reading it in public. The issue of a nonconsumption agreement for tea totally vanished from the agenda till November 1773.[3] Newspapers asserted that tea was replaced by some kind of beverage made of Labrador shrubs, but private diaries, customs house entries, and public advertisements all prove that no reduction of tea consumption was effected or even actively pursued. Confiscation or destruction of tea was rare and involved only small quantities. John Hancock and his clerk, William Palfrey, once threatened a small shop but took no action. "The Spirit of Liberty still keeps up, but the People are more moderate than formerly," reported a contemporary.[4]

[1]*BNL*, 6 Oct. 1768, 29 June 1769; *BTR* 18:12, 17, 20.

[2]John Rowe, *Letters and Diary of John Rowe, Boston Merchant, 1759–1762, 1764–1779*, ed. Anne Rowe Cunningham (Boston, 1903; reprint ed., 1969), Sept. 1770, pp. 206–207.

[3]*BTR*, 1770–1773, vol. 18; Richard D. Brown, *Revolutionary Politics in Massachusetts: The Boston Committee of Correspondence and the Towns, 1772–1774* (Cambridge, Mass., 1970), pp. 52–54; Samuel Adams as "Candidus," in *BG*, 11 Nov. 1771, *The Writings of Samuel Adams*, ed. Harry A. Cushing, 4 vols. (New York 1904–1908), 2:271, to Arthur Lee, 13 Nov. 1771, *ibid.*, 2:274–276; Cooper to Pownall, 14 Nov. 1771, *AHR* 8:325–326 (1902–1903).

[4]Jolley Allen, "Jolley Allen's Account," ed. C. C. Smith, *MHSP* 16:70 (1878); Nathaniel Ames, "A Page for Ladies," *Almanack, 1772* (Boston, 1771); Henry Bromfield to Robert Crafton, 30 July 1772, Bromfield Letterbook, HBS; Samuel Adams to James Warren, 25 March 1771, *Warren–Adams Letters: Being Chiefly a Correspondence among John Adams, Samuel Adams, and James Warren*, 2 vols. (Boston, 1917, 1925), *MHSC*, vols. 72 and 73, 1:9; Benjamin Labaree, *The Boston Tea Party* (New York, 1964), App. Table 1, "English Exports of Tea to America 1750–1774."

In the whole province no tax had to be raised in 1771 because of a surplus in the treasury. In Boston the merchants severed their connections with the political leadership and the shopkeepers. The latter were no longer admitted to the meetings; the former lost influence with the demise of the nonimportation agreement. Opposition to Great Britain with its need for intergroup cooperation, contrary to customary political and economic behavior, had not yet become normality. When Hutchinson received his commission as governor, 106 merchants presented a congratulatory address to him, customary on such occasions. Never had so many assembled for a nonimportation meeting. Among other inhabitants a shift to local issues was also noticeable, and a petition for removal of the powder house from Boston, received more signatures than any petition concerning imperial issues. This suggests that imperial questions were still perceived largely in local terms, that the attention they received depended on their local impact. It has recently been said that the developments of the 1780s and 1790s ''cannot be understood in essentially ideological terms'' (Bailyn). The impact and function of the ideology before 1776 also seem to be in need for reconsideration. Did it just provide a useful and plausible terminology behind which differences of interest could be hidden, while the discontent about imperial regulation could be expressed all the better?[5]

In the Massachusetts of the early seventies, economic elements of ideology were reformulated during struggles between different economic factions of a community. The language employed was influenced by the debate of natural rights and the formulation of a political ideology as well as by remnants of the old Puritan tradition of just prices and equity or by propositions to move toward a more liberalist society. For illustration, two petitions and a report to the General Court concerning Boston, Marblehead, and Kittery (York) will be used. These arguments during the revolutionary period in Massachusetts never reached the intensity of earlier and later years and were never printed, the last prerevolutionary ones being *Massachusetts in Agony* (1750), its *Appendix* (1751), and those of the excise controversy.[6]

In Boston the Merchants' Society concentrated its energies in the early seventies on attempting to force the auctioneers out of business.[7] Reversing their argument of the nonimportation years, they stated ''That the Importation of British Goods is what gives life and spirit to every other branch of Trade and Commerce among us.'' If the nonimportation policy was intended, as many contemporaries suspected, to drive competitors out of business, then the merchants now reversed the argument but not the policy. They succeeded in severely restricting the number of auctioneers

[5]G. B. Warden, *Boston, 1689–1776* (Boston, 1970), pp. 243–246; John Adams, *Diary and Autobiography of John Adams*, ed. Lyman H. Butterfield, 4 vols. (Cambridge, Mass., 1961–1966), 13 Aug. 1771, 2:49–50; *BG*, 10 Sept., 17 Sept. 1770; *BTR* 16:279–282, 18:44, petition in *MHSC* 71:106–107; Bernard Bailyn, ''The Central Themes of the American Revolution: An Interpretation,'' in J. H. Hutson and S. G. Kurtz, eds., *Essays on the American Revolution* (Chapel Hill, N.C., 1973), p. 19.

[6][Vincent Centinel], *Massachusetts in Agony* (Boston, 1750), [Cornelius Agrippa], *Appendix* (Boston, 1751), Evans 6475, 6626. Paul S. Boyer, ''Borrowed Rhetoric: The Massachusetts Excise Controversy of 1754,'' *WMQ* 3.21:328–351 (1964); the pamphlets of the excise controversy are listed in Evans (1754).

[7]A. C. Goodell *et al.,* eds., *Acts and Resolves, Public and Private, of the Province of the Massachusetts Bay,* 21 vols. (Boston, 1869–1922), 5:248–250, 1772–1773, Ch. 44, notes, pp. 282–283, 300–301, 1773–1774, Ch. 10, notes, pp. 357–362.

and in curtailing the range of their sales, and they finally attempted to confine them to one day of business per week.

The auctioneers countered with a masterful petition, convincing the General Court that the merchants planned to monopolize British imports and colonial sales. It was "contrary to the nature of the British Constitution [or rather to corporate communal responsibility] to trample on the Liberty of one Subject to the Emolument or agrandizing of another." The auctioneers argued about the dangers of supporting one class, the "wealthy few," to the detriment of a "Free People." Auctions were necessary when people with no large capital but in urgent need of funds had to get their stores or properties sold quickly. Limitation of auctions to one day per week was in direct opposition to the command of the Bible—"Six Days shalt thou labour"—and would bring poverty to the auctioneers and their familes, who would then become a burden to the other inhabitants. As to the economic side of the question, they were ready to admit the truth of the merchants' maxim "That Trade is the great mean of Wealth, and that Wealth is essentially necessary to a vigorous and successful Opposition to arbitrary Power." Then they continued:

> but we contend, that the more generally the Wealth of the Community is diffused, the better enabled will it ever be to exert its whole Strength upon every occasion; and that nothing can be more alarming to a Free People, than to see the Riches of the State running in a narrow Channel, and into a few hands, because by such means the *wealthy few* are frequently enabled to arrogate to themselves the *Power,* as well as the Wealth of the State.

As constitutional arguments they advanced public good and equal rights. In a final blast against the merchants, the auctioneers quoted the proverb "That the love of Riches, increases with the increase of Riches," that commerce has ever suffered most from "those, who having gained immense Riches in Trade, have become jealous of their less successful Brethren." Though a flourishing trade benefited the community, the auctioneers could not find one example in history where the merchants and great trading companies have not "amply compensated themselves by their exclusive and exorbitant Gains."[8]

Just as the General Court acceded to the demand of the auctioneers not to restrict their business further, but if necessary regulate it in a way that no abuse and fraud might happen, the court supported fishermen and inhabitants of the poorer sort against impositions by the wealthy inhabitants of Kittery, York County [Maine]. In 1772, 76 inhabitants complained that seines were being introduced for fishing in the Piscataqua River by those of the townsmen who could afford to buy them. The "poorer Sort of people" merely used dip nets and could not "advance the money necessary to purchase" better equipment, but needed the catch for "a greater part of their Sustenance" when other provisions were scarce. On the other hand, "the Engrossers of said fish having no Occasion to consume them in their families commonly barrel [them] up and send them out to Town to market." The local price

---

[8] "The Answer of the Auctioneers," *ibid.,* pp. 360–362.

for fish had tripled, and overfishing had severely depleted the stock. The community was not yet ready to change from a subsistence to a market economy. In the moral economy of the poorer sort, the principle that individuals are created equal, to have any practical usefulness, had to be supplemented by the principle of equal opportunities. The General Court agreed to this reasoning of the 76, rejecting a counterpetition signed by 13, and outlawed the use of seines.[9]

In Marblehead, Essex County, economic tensions came into the open during a smallpox epidemic in 1773. Upon a petition for an inoculation hospital, a town meeting voted strict safety regulations and granted leave to build the necessary accommodations. Among the proprietors were Jonathan Glover, selectman in 1771–1773; his brother John, member of the Committee of Correspondence since 1772; Elbridge Gerry, the town's representative; and Azor Orne, holder of various town offices. All four enhanced their extensive influence by family ties. In 1772, for example, three Gerrys and two Ornes were members of the eight-man Committee of Correspondence. The inhabitants remained uneasy about dangers arising from inoculation. Rumors circulated that the Essex Hospital was a money-making scheme that would scare away trade, that townsmen and farmers coming to the market might be infected. Reportedly the selectmen, closely connected with the proprietors, did not enforce the safety regulations or even relaxed the rules, contrary to the vote of the town meeting. On 10 January 1774 an indignant inhabitant of Marblehead noted in his diary, "Sarah Broodstreet Come from Catt Island [the location of the hospital] as Sick as Shee was." After that, riots lasted till the end of March. Crowds sometimes consisting of Salem and Marblehead militia companies enforced the regulations, held trials, voted on procedures, tarred and feathered offenders, and paraded them through the streets. The proprietors' houses were beset. Reportedly one of them had a small cannon erected in his doorway and threatened to shoot into the crowd. Finally a crowd burned down the hospital. When two men were arrested for arson, a crowd of 400–500 men rescued them. This emphasizes the broad community support. Such riots were usually executed by only a few dozen persons. The proprietors, under further threats form the crowd, agreed not to prosecute anybody. But the county sheriff set out with an armed posse comitatus of several hundred men to recapture the two rescued prisoners. When 600–800 men gathered for resistance, the sheriff ordered a posse from Newburyport to come to his assistance. But the people were reluctant to assemble, and the sheriff had to negotiate a "compromise": No judicial action was to be taken.[10]

[9]*Acts and Resolves*, 5:173, 1771–1772, Ch. 15, notes, pp. 184–186; petition reprinted *ibid.*, pp. 184–185. Many petitions and laws of a similar nature were on the books; Hutchinson to Board of Trade, 8 May 1772, *ibid.*, p. 186. Cf. *ibid.*, vols. 1–5, and MA volumes. See also Carl Bridenbaugh, *Cities in the Wilderness: The First Century of Urban Life in America, 1625–1742*, 2nd ed. (New York, 1955), p. 383, for a riot about fishing rights in the Schuylkill River, 1738.

[10]Richard W. Searle, "History of Catta Island off Marblehead," *EIHC* 83:308–352 (1947); George A. Billias, "Pox and Politics in Marblehead, 1773–1774," *EIHC* 92:43–58 (1956); Gerard H. Clarfield, "Salem's Great Inoculation Controversy, 1773–1774," *EIHC* 106:277–296 (1970); *Narrative of the Late Disturbances* (Salem, Mass., 1774), *Mass. Brds.* 1769; "A Lover of Truth," *Essex Gaz.*, 1 March 1774; Ashley Bowen, "Diary of Ashley Bowen," 10 Jan. 1774, *Mass. Mag.* 2:114 (1909); Tristam Dalton to Samuel White, 5 March 1774, *EIHC* 71:9–11 (1935); Gerry to

What looked like a small-scale civil war caused by prejudices against inoculation and fear of smallpox was in fact a violent outbreak of sociopolitical and class conflict. A committee of the General Court, sent to investigate, "after hearing the account of the Matter from Numbers of Persons of all Rank," assigned the following causes. (1) Disdain of the wealthy proprietors and patients for the public good—that is, apprehensions and "perhaps Satisfactory Proof" of a violation of the safety regulations. (2) Refusal of the top magistrates to obey town-meeting votes—that is, the selectmen's defiance of the regulations as voted by the inhabitants. (3) Economic conflict—that is, "A loss of Confidence of the poorer sorts of which the majority of the Town is composed" in the proprietors and staff of the hospital "at a time when the poorer sorts were all at home [for example, sailors], and out of Business." They feared "not being able to bear the expense of Inoculation," that the inoculation of the more wealthy inhabitants would expose them, leaving them "to Suffer the Small Pox in the natural way, at the great Hazard of their Lives." In Boston it had long been the custom that doctors who had received permission for inoculation offered to inoculate poor persons free of charge for a limited time. (4) Furthermore, the lower classes' standard of living would deteriorate even further because farmers as well as coasters would be reluctant to come to town for fear of infection, and accordingly prices for provisions and firewood would rise.

The political and social rifts were so deep that the rioting had repercussions on more than a local level. The Salem Committee of Correspondence complained that the local grievances had taken precedence over every other matter, including the relations with Great Britain. The Marblehead Whig Committee resigned because the disorders "have put an End . . . to all Order and Distinction, and rendered publick Officers of every Degree obnoxious." In other words, Whig magistrates were as disliked as their Loyalist colleagues when they remained unresponsive to local grievances. By 1774 and 1775, part of the imperial conflict, the opposition to Tories, became local struggles against the wealthy and powerful. Country people began to act against symbols of wealth, coaches and riding horses, as Boston's lower classes had done earlier.[11]

In addition to the local economic questions and tensions, the one imperial issue that continued to hurt the economic elite was the trade regulations and customs duties. Boston merchants proved willing to pay (if they could not smuggle) rather than rely on crowd action to rescue seized goods and ships. John Rowe noted five seizures in his diary for 1771, adding that this might "Raise the Minds of the People." It obviously did not raise the merchants'. People in other towns were less submissive. In Salem a customs informer was chased off a wharf by a crowd, and in

Adams, 16 Feb. 1774, Gerry–Knight Papers, 1772–1779, MHS; Samuel Roads, *The History and Traditions of Marblehead* (Boston, 1880), p. 128. For a similar incident in Virginia, see Patrick Henderson, "Smallpox and Patriotism: The Norfolk Riots, 1768–1769," *Va. Mag. Hist. Bio.* 73:413–424 (1965), and Pauline R. Maier, "Popular Uprisings and Civil Authority in Eighteenth-Century America," *WMQ* 3.27:7 (1970).

[11]Report of the committee, 18 Feb. 1774, MA 87:384–385; Stephen E. Patterson, *Political Parties in Revolutionary Massachusetts* (Madison, Wis., 1973), pp. 132–141; on riding horses as symbols of wealth, see Chapter 13.

Falmouth (now Portland) a naval officer was attacked by enraged militiamen.[12] Rhode Island crowds rescued a seized vessel in February 1772 and on 6 June burned the British schooner *Gaspée*. A captain of the Royal Navy, active in procuring witnesses to the affair, soon afterward visited Boston, where he barely escaped the sheriff, who under some pretense planned to arrest him if necessary with the help of a posse (crowd) or the militia. Armed crowds went in search of witnesses and threatened to pull down their houses should they dare give evidence before the Royal Commission.[13] A Boston newspaper extolled "the Wisdom" of the burning of the *Gaspée* and of not permitting "Monsters"—that is, officials—"to prowl their Streets for Prey."[14]

There are several clues to the reasons for the lack of militancy among the lower classes. A gentleman said to be familiar with the people reported that the events during the nonimportation period and the acquittal of the soldiers who had shot into the crowd during the King Street riot had opened people's eyes to the duplicity of the leaders, and that they had no intention of doing the dirty work for them and bearing the brunt of subsequent difficulties too.[15] This explicit rejection of leadership was similar to that of 1768, after the leaders' refusal to speak up publicly against Customs Inspector Williams. Distrust of Whig officialdom was also expressed in an article by "Marcus Aurelianus." Want and misery were still widespread among artisans and tradesmen, who had suffered badly during the preceding four years, and the author suggested a strict inquiry into how the town funds were spent, since the enormous sum of £8000 had been raised as annual tax.[16]

Several popular leaders were accused of mismanagement of public funds. John Hancock promoted a reopening of the case of Samuel Adams's deficiencies as tax collector and added demands for an inquiry about Thomas Cushing's conduct as manager of the town's lotteries. Robert Pierpoint was criticized for leasing town lands below value. William Molineux had used town funds for a workhouse employing those sinking to poverty "from the great decay of Trade, and the consequent want of employ" during nonimportation. Taxpayers and those who had been forced to rely on the town's charity witnessed Molineux's pitiable efforts to extricate himself from charges that he had enriched himself on the plight of his fellow townsmen. He was accused by partners and master craftsmen in his employ of having cheated them and of having promoted a scheme that was "a meer Bubble for a Considerable time." A jury ordered Molineux to repay the town funds; a town

---

[12]Rowe, *Letters and Diary*, 16 June, 17 June, 7 Dec. 1771, pp. 217, 222. Salem: *BEP*, 25 Nov. 1771. Falmouth: Thomas Smith and Samuel Deane, *Journals of the Rev. Thomas Smith, and the Rev. Samuel Deane, Pastors of the First Church in Portland*, ed. William Willis (Portland, Me., 1849), 28 Oct., 13 Nov. 1771, p. 220; Council Records, 16:598–599, 605–606, MSA; Thomas Hutchinson, "Additions to Thomas Hutchinson's *History of Massachusetts Bay*," ed. Catherine Banton Mayo, *AASP* 59:45 (1949).

[13]William R. Staples, *The Documentary History of the Destruction of the* Gaspée (Providence, R.I., 1845); John R. Bartlett, *A History of the Destruction of His Britannic Majesty's Schooner* Gaspée... *Accompanied by the Correspondence Connected Therewith*... (Providence, R.I., 1861), pp. 81–88; Rowe, *Letters and Diary*, Aug. 1772, p. 233.

[14]*BG*, 26 April 1773.

[15]Anne Hulton, *Letters of a Loyalist Lady* (Cambridge, Mass., 1927), 21 Dec. 1770, 21 Nov. 1772, pp. 29, 55.

[16]"Marcus Aurelianus," *BNL*, 6 Feb. 1772.

meeting debated the matter for days, because Molineux was unable or unwilling to pay. Handbills exposing his misdealings were distributed. Never choosy about his means, Molineux raged against Whig-inclined lawyers who did not support him. He was notorious in other towns of the province too. In 1768 a crowd in Falmouth attempted to rescue a debtor from jail because they were of the opinion that the debt was not a just one. The creditor was Molineux. In 1770, Salem importers could threaten to have Molineux chased out of town by a crowd.[17]

The first change from concern and anger about Whig leaders to renewed attention on the crown officers became noticeable four weeks after customs officials had searched several warehouses for smuggled goods in a particularly provoking manner. On election day, 1773, the town, as in 1768, refused to permit use of Faneuil Hall by the council if the "Justly obnoxious" commissioners should be invited. The council moved the dinner to a private hall of a crown supporter serving as the office for the commissioners. The selectmen refused to attend, but a crowd of spectators came. Commisioner Burch was hissed at when he left by the front door, which hardly anybody had expected. Commissioners Hallowell and Hulton tried to sneak out by the back door, but this had been anticipated, and the crowd was there to waylay them. Hissing soon gave way to pelting. Two members of the Corps of Cadets, the honor guard, left the ranks at the front door to riot at the back door. Dissensions arose among the leadership, on how to handle this incident of direct action. John Hancock, colonel of the corps, in the face of heated opposition expelled the two men from the unit. In its next issue the *Gazette* reported "this indignity" suffered by men who had shown their "just resentment" as a rumor and added, "Quere, Would it not be for the honor of the Cadet Company to Vindicate themselves from the above aspersion?"[18] Hancock understood the message. When in November, during the agitation against the landing of the tea, the governor ordered the company under arms to suppress any riots and tumults, he did not respond. Just to make sure, the newspapers issued a reminder by openly questioning "whether Mr Hancock will think himself obliged or even authorized by any law in this province to pay the least regard to so very extraordinary a Mandate." This was the distribution-of-power situation when the East India Company began to ship dutied tea to selected consignees.[19]

THE MOBILIZATION OF OPPOSITION

In October 1773 an anonymous address to the prospective tea consignees compared them to stamp distributors, commissioners, and crown officials in general,

[17]Molineux: *BTR* 16:275–277, 18:70–73, 139, 168–169; Thomas Mewse to ———, 23 Sept. 1770, Daniel Brooke to Joseph Otis, 24 Nov. 1770, Otis Papers, 1770–1800, 3:7–8, MHS; SCF 90898; Rowe, *Letters and Diary*, 5 Feb. 1772, p. 224; *BG*, 16 March 1772. Cushing, Adams: Hutchinson, "Additions," p. 43. Pierpoint: *BTR* 18:168–169. General: *Boston Chron.*, 26 Oct. 1769, "The Boston Patriots Characterized," and [John Mein], Key to a Certain Publication, Sparks MSS., 10.3:45–47, HHL.

[18]*BTR* 18:139; Rowe, *Letters and Diary*, 27 May 1773, p. 245; *BG*, 31 May, 7 June 1773; Cadet Company, Records, 28 May, 31 May 1773, Boston Univ.; Hutchinson, "Additions," p. 60; Thomas Newell, "Diary for 1773 to the End of 1774, of Mr. Thomas Newell, Boston," 26 May 1773, ed. R. Frothingham, *MHSP* 15:338–339 (1876–1877).

[19]*BG*, 15 Nov. 1773; Cadet Company, Records, 11 Nov. 1773, Boston Univ.

thus making them outsiders liable to coercion by the community. Nevertheless, actual opposition to the scheme began to manifest itself only very late. The Boston Committee of Correspondence merely pitied the East India Company, which, by act of Parliament, had its "sacred Charter Rights . . . arbitrarily taken from them." A circular sent by the Massachusetts committee mentioned the tea shipments only in passing. The expectation that the duties would be paid by the company in London and the fear that nonimportation votes would merely raise the price of tea may have contributed to the unwillingness to propose strong countermeasures.[20]

Another, probably more important reason was the decision by Whig politicians to leave as little action as possible to crowds or merchants, because of doubts about the reliability of the latter and a desire to prevent a repetition of the economic distress and social tensions caused by the policies of 1768. The politician-dominated Committee of Correspondence was to be the pivotal institution for developing opposition measures. Among the committee's papers is a note entitled "Agreement not to be Recorded," in which 15 men promised "to support and vindicate each other" should they or others be held responsible "for any noble Effort they have made to serve their Country by defeating the operation of any Act of the British Parliament expressly designed to extorte a Revenue from the Colonies ag[ain]st their Consent." Samuel Adams headed the list; others were Pierpoint, Young, and Molineux, who had gained experience in violent direct action during the "combination riots" and the antitroop actions. John Bradford, influential merchant–captain of the Long-Room Club, belonged to the group, as did Dr. Benjamin Church, a vociferous but double-dealing Whig who had been accused of having "cheated and backbitten" any number of his acquaintances and two years later was caught spying for the British. Several other men came from the officialdom: a selectman, an overseer of the poor, the town clerk, and John Pitts, one of the most influential councillors. The rest of the signers became officials in subsequent years.[21]

These men were the steering committee for the opposition to the tea duty in November and December 1773. They collected information about other towns that expected tea, examined the owners of vessels coming to Boston, organized the guard on board the tea ships after their arrival, and planned mass meetings.[22] They derived their strength from their connection with master artisans, petty merchants, and tavern keepers organized in the Northend Caucus, who provided the connections with journeymen mechanics and had considerable influence in town meetings.[23] By the end of October 1773, the tea consignees had heard of "several nightly meetings" but could find out nothing more.

---

[20]Circulars in *MHSP* 13:158–159, 160–162; Hutchinson to Dartmouth, 4 Nov., 6 Nov. 1773, Sparks MSS., 10.4:47–49, HHL. Labaree, *Tea Party;* Francis S. Drake, ed., *Tea Leaves: Letters and Documents Relating to the Shipment of Tea to the American Colonies in the Year 1773* (Boston, 1884). Anonymous letters quoted by the tea consignees, *ibid.,* pp. 279–289. Brown, in *Revolutionary Politics,* pp. 156–157, note 15, suggested that the news of the duty arrived only in the middle of October.

[21]Minute Books, 26 Oct. 1773, 3:230 *passim,* Committee of Correspondence Papers, NYPL; agreement printed in William V. Wells, *The Life and Public Services of Samuel Adams,* 3 vols. (Boston, 1865, 1888), 2:126–127.

[22]Labaree, *Tea Party,* pp. 149–150. But see Brown, *Revolutionary Politics,* p. 166. Since the associates agreed to vindicate "each other," it seems safe to assume that they were decisively involved in the opposition to the Tea Act.

[23]"Proceedings of the Northend Caucus," in Elbridge H. Goss, *The Life of Colonel Paul Revere,* 2 vols. (Boston, 1891), pp. 635–644.

In fact, the Northend Caucus members had met on 23 October and had voted to oppose the landing of the tea with their "lives and fortunes" and to concert measures with other interested groups in town. To implement the vote, a letter signed "O.C.," possibly "Oliver Cromwell," was delivered to the consignees at night, desiring them to resign their offices under Liberty Tree on 3 November. Throughout the the the town, handbills by "O.C." announced that the consignees would not only resign but also swear to send the tea back by the first ship sailing for London. The second edition of the handbills contained the self-conscious addition "Shew me the Man that dare take this down."[24] At noon on 3 November, Bostonians, including many town officials, and people from the neighboring towns assembled at the Southend. The consignees "did not obey the Summons." This had been expected by the steering committee and the caucus members, who on the preceding evening had ordered Young, Church, and Warren to draft a vote for this situation. The resolution was now read to the crowd and passed. The consignees, "by neglecting to give satisfaction," as had "justly" been expected from them, had "intolerably insulted this body." Unless they would appear at once and resign their "destructive" office, they would be esteemed enemies to their country and would feel the resentment of their fellow citizens.

The expression of resentment came fast. A committee headed by Molineux was sent to the consignees and found them assembled at Richard Clarke's store, unwilling to discuss their consignment. The customary pattern of town-meeting action, vote and election of a committee to execute it, had thus been adapted to the exigencies of the situation. But about 500 men from the crowd had considered it necessary to accompany the committee. They remained quiet as long as negotiations took place. When no agreement was reached, some of them rushed into Clarke's store, defied a justice of the peace (a relative of one of the consignees), but were ejected by force. The people then dispersed peacefully. In the evening "O.C." was at one of his nightly meetings again, and "pr. order" wrote threatening letters to merchants, including the sons of the governor and prominent members of the Merchants' Society.[25]

For 5 November, Pope's Day, a town meeting was called "to know the minds of the inhabitants in this matter" and to head off violence from celebrating crowds. The petition for the meeting argued that the company's plan would destroy colonial trade and that the duty would destroy liberty. But it turned out that this was by no means the unanimous opinion in Boston. Socioeconomic tensions and factionalism among the leaders surfaced once again. First a printed sheet was handed around, entitled "The Tradesmens Protest against the Proceedings of the Merchants Relative

---

[24]Clarke & Sons to Abraham Dupuis, Nov. 1773, in Drake, ed., *Tea Leaves,* p. 282; *BNL,* 4 Nov. 1773; Hutchinson to Dartmouth, 4 Nov., 6 Nov. 1773, Sparks MSS., 10.4:47, 49, HHL; "O. C." to consignees, 1 Nov. 1773, in Drake, ed., *Tea Leaves,* p. 282; Rowe, *Letters and Diary,* 2 Nov. 1773, p. 252; Thomas Newell, "Diary," 2 Nov. 1773, p. 343.

[25]"Proceedings of the Northend Caucus," pp. 641–643; Rowe, *Letters and Diary,* 3 Nov. 1773, pp. 252–253; Thomas Newell, "Diary," 3 Nov. 1773, p. 343; John Boyle, "Boyle's Journal of Occurrences in Boston, 1759–1778," 4 Nov. 1773, *NEHGR* 84:367 (1930); Hutchinson to Tryon, 21 Nov. 1773, Letterbooks, MA 27:572–574; Henry Pelham to Charles Pelham, 5 Nov. 1773, *MHSC* 71:202 (1914); extract of a letter from Boston, 4 Nov. 1773, in Drake, ed., *Tea Leaves,* p. 262; Narrative of Events in Boston, Sparks MSS., 4.8:229–243, HHL; Council Records, 16:739, MSA; *Mass. Spy,* 4 Nov. 1773; *BNL,* 4 Nov. 1773; *BEP,* 8 Nov. 1773.

to the New Importation of Tea.'' It emphasized the economic consequences for the little people.

> Avoid the Trap. Remember the iniquitous Non-Importation Scheme . . . Whereas we have repeatedly been imposed upon by the Merchants of the Town of Boston, and thereby incurred heavy Taxes upon us, . . . And as it is now proposed by said Merchants to prevent the Importation of Tea from the India Company, whereby that Article may be sold for less than half the Price they can afford it [by smuggling] . . . it is our humble Opinion that it is subversive of that *Constitutional* Liberty we are contending for [to support the antitea policy].

Immediately after it had been read, an attempt was made to discredit it. Someone mentioned that he had seen Commissioner Paxton of the customs establishment distribute it. Then the tradesmen present were asked to assemble on the south side of the hall. Supervised by the town leaders, 400 of them disavowed the protest and, reunited with the other inhabitants, voted their detestation of Paxton and the printer. Suspicions that merchants intended to further their own interest remained current, however, perhaps justifiably because smugglers of Holland tea saw their profits decline.[26]

Second, there was tension among Whigs because of the breaches of the earlier tea nonimportation agreements by Whig merchants. It was admitted that ''by reason of the peculiar circumstances . . . some quantities tho very small in proportion to what had been usual before'' had been imported; the customs entries showed that from 1768 to summer 1773 about 500 chests had been imported yearly by 60 different persons. Samuel Adams proposed to condemn *all* importers of tea as enemies to their country. William Cooper, town clerk and factotum for the merchants, strongly opposed such a vote. It was true, he argued, that several Whig merchants had imported and sold dupe tea, but they were ''otherwise worthy Citizens,'' and that at this critical juncture it was not opportune to expose their conduct. Adams persisted, saying that since Whigs had imported ''to the Shame and Scandal of this Province and to the just and great Grief'' of others, it ought to be confessed and changed. After a hot debate Cooper finally settled on the concession from Adams that some merchants had ''inadvertantly'' imported.[27]

More consensus was obtained when the meeting turned from the domestic scene to the British impositions. The inhabitants debated ''largely on the nature and tendency'' of the tea shipments and continued to call the consignees ''commissioners.'' This implied more than a reference to the customs board. ''Commissioners'' were men sent from the outside to impose certain views, decisions, or laws on the

---

[26]Tradesmen's protest, signed ''True Sons of Liberty,'' *MHSC* 71:203, *Mass. Brds.* 1695, Evans 13046; *BTR* 18:141–144; John Adams, *Diary,* 26 June 1770, 1:351; Thomas Newell, ''Diary,'' 5 Nov. 1773, pp. 343–344; Boyle, ''Journal,'' 4 Nov., 5 Nov. 1773, pp. 267–268; Rowe, *Letters and Diary,* 5 Nov. 1773, p. 254; *BNL,* 11 Nov. 1773; *Mass. Spy,* 11 Nov. 1773. The town of Boston had rejected a tax on tea in 1750, arguing that it would hurt the many persons in indigent circumstances who sold tea. *BTR* 14:180–181.

[27]Labaree, *Tea Party,* Table 1, p. 331; L. F. S. Upton, ed., ''Proceedings of ye Body Respecting the Tea,'' *WMQ* 3.22:295–296 (1965); ''Q,'' in *BPB,* 15 Nov. 1773; Copley to Clarke [1 Dec. 1773], *MHSC* 71:211–212 (1914); Scollay to Lee, 23 Dec. 1773, *MHSC* 4.4:379–386 (1858); *BTR* 18:144.

colonies. Already in 1665 the colonists had sent an address to the king complaining about the high expenses incurred for inimical commissioners. "These things occasioned in the hearts and minds of the people a deepe sence of the sad events threatning this colony, in case the commissioners should improove their power in such manner as they feared they would." The commissioners, in investigating the burning of the *Gaspée* in 1772, had aroused strong opposition. The consignees were now placed in this tradition.[28] The resulting distinction between public (colonial) and private (placeman) interest was stated in the town meeting and, more bluntly, in one of the threatening letters to the consignees: "mad dogs, whom the public safety obliges . . . to destroy."[29]

Also raised was the question of equity in the treatment of thieves and mercantile profiteers. The people of Massachusetts had lately seen "a *penitential* thief suffer death for pilfering a few pounds from scattering individuals." The impenitent consignees "boldly avow a resolution to bear a principal part in the robbery of every inhabitant in this country, in the present and future ages, of every thing dear and interesting to them." In the words of the Bible and of Mayhew's 1765 sermon, the question was then raised, "Are there no laws in the Book of God and nature that enjoin such miscreants to be cut off from among the people, as troublers of the whole congregation?" While the scene was thus set for confrontation, a last effort was made to prevail upon the consignees to give in. The town called the duty on tea a "tribute" and the whole scheme a plan to enslave America. A committee was then sent to the consignees to ask them to resign "from a regard to their own character and the peace and good order of this Town." In the afternoon the evasive answers of the tea agents were read, debated, and voted "Daringly affrontive."[30]

MASS MEETINGS AND THE DESTRUCTION OF THE TEA

In the morning of 17 November, Captain Scott arrived from London and brought the news that the tea ships were on their way. Only a few hours later the selectmen received two petitions to call a town meeting as soon as possible. This they did for 18 November. In a further step to prevent violence, they ordered all town arms to be returned to the armory, which proved to be a necessary precaution; already bullets were sold out in town—"they were all bought up, with a full determination to repel force by force." In the papers "A Transient Person" lauded the performance of the Artillery Company, and "A Ranger" was ready to march against the English, as he had done against the Indians and French "when they attempted to enslave us." A motion in the town meeting for the inhabitants to arm themselves was received with applause.[31]

[28]Nathaniel B. Shurtleff, ed., *Records of the Governor and Company of the Massachusetts Bay*, 5 vols. (Boston, 1853–1854), 4(2):168; for the *Gaspée*, see note 13.

[29]"O. C." to Benjamin Faneuil, 4 Nov. 1773, in Drake, ed., *Tea Leaves*, pp. 292–293.

[30]On Mayhew's sermon, see Chapter 2, note 71; *BTR* 18:145–147; committee report, Mellen Chamberlain Collection, p. 74, BPL; Clarke & Sons to Dupuis, Nov. 1773, in Drake, ed., *Tea Leaves*, p. 289; Scollay to Lee, 23 Dec. 1773, *MHSC* 4.4:379–386; *BEP*, 8 Nov. 1773; *BNL*, 11 Nov. 1773. The thief was Levi Ames. Rowe, *Letters and Diary*, 21 Oct. 1773, p. 252, cf. *Mass. Brds.* 1640–1648.

[31]Petitions, Mellen Chamberlain Collection, p. 86, BPL; *BTR* 23:202; Rowe, *Letters and Diary*, 17 Nov. 1773, p. 254;

In the evening after Scott's arrival, about 250 persons surrounded the houses of two consignees, Hutchinson's sons and Richard Clarke. In the latter's house a party was given that evening for the junior Clarke, who had negotiated the tea contracts. A town official tried to disperse the rioters by explaining that they could vent their grievances at the meeting. Some people left, but a guest at the party yelled insults at the crowd, who returned the compliments. Violence was initiated by the consignees and their friends. They fired a pistol, and the crowd in turn smashed the front windows. The official continued his peacemaking mission at Clarke's back door, advising them to keep cool. No direct negotiations got underway; the crowd outside demanded resignation, while the crowd inside refused to deal with "such people."[32] During the next weeks business partners broke off connections with the tea agents. Neither councillors nor selectmen were willing to do anything for their protection.[33]

The town meetings called to debate the situation were soon extended into "Body" meetings as in 1769, to broaden participation and to shift responsibilities to a body not legally defined or limited as to its participants. "Provincial meetings," in which men from every town could participate, were the next step, again at once broadening the basis of support and enlarging the circle of people against whom retaliatory measures would have to be directed. When the ships with the tea sailed into the harbor,[34] handbills called Bostonians and inhabitants of other towns to attend a meeting on 29 November. "Friends! Brethren! Countrymen! . . . the hour of Destruction or manly Opposition to the Machinations of Tyranny stares you in the face." "Altho' this Meeting or Assembly consisted principally of the lower Ranks of the People, and even Journeymen Tradesmen were brought to increase the Number and the Rabble were not excluded," noted Governor Hutchinson", yet there were divers Gentlemen of Good Fortune among them." The "general muster" began at 9 A.M. on Monday and by adjournment was continued till Tuesday

John Andrews, "Letters of John Andrews, Esq. Boston 1772–1776," ed. Winthrop Sargent, 1 Dec. 1773, *MHSP* 8:325 (1864–1865); Hutchinson to ———, 24 Nov. 1773, Letterbooks, MA 27:575; *BEP,* 6 Dec. 1773; *BNL,* 9 Dec. 1773.

[32]Hutchinson to Dartmouth, 2 Dec. 1773, Letterbooks, MA 27:577–578; Anne Hulton, *Letters,* 25 Nov. 1773, pp. 62–65. Hulton noted that guards had been placed along the streets from Clarke's house to prevent him from escaping. *BNL,* 18 Nov., 1773; *BG,* 13 Dec. 1773; Boyle, "Journal," 17 Nov. 1773, p. 368; Rowe, *Letters and Diary,* 18 Nov. 1773, p. 254; Thomas Newell, "Diary," 17 Nov. 1773, p. 344.

[33]Scollay to Lee, 23 Dec. 1773, *MHSC* 4.4:379–386 (1858) and in W. P. Parker, ed., "Some Facts about the Boston Tea Party," *Nantucket Hist. Assoc. Proc.* 28:31–37 (1922); *BG,* 22 Nov. 1773; petition to council, in Drake, ed., *Tea Leaves,* pp. 309–310; council proceedings, *ibid.,* pp. 310–320; Thomas Hutchinson, *The History of the Colony and Province of the Massachusetts Bay,* ed. Lawrence Shaw Mayo, 3 vols. (Cambridge, Mass., 1936), 3:306–308; *BTR* 23:202–203; Clarke to East India Company, 1 July 1773, in Drake, ed., *Tea Leaves,* pp. 209–211; Boston tea consignees to Philadelphia tea consignees, 4 Dec. 1773, Henry Drinker Papers, Hist. Soc. of Penn.

[34]*BTR* 18:203–206; Committee of Correspondence, Minute Books, 6:452ff., NYPL; Leslie to Haldimand, 16 Dec. 1773, in John Montresor, "Journals of Capt. John Montresor, 1757–1778," ed. G. D. Scull, *N.Y. Hist. Soc. Coll.,* 1881, pp. 531–532; Hulton to ———, 8 Dec. 1773, Letterbooks, 1:76–78. One ship was cast ashore at Cape Cod. As for Captain Hall's ship, Hutchinson claimed that she anchored below the castle, where she was not obliged to declare cargo to the customs officials, but was ordered to come up to town by the Committee of Correspondence. Labaree (*Tea Party,* pp. 126–132) convincingly argued that this achievement of the Whig leaders precipitated the crisis. In other ports the ships did not enter the harbor. Bernard Knollenberg, "Did Samuel Adams Provoke the Boston Tea Party . . . ?" *AASP* 70:493–503 (1960).

afternoon. The assembled people left Faneuil Hall for the larger Old South; the consignees left Boston for the safer castle.[35]

The opening move was the by now familiar vote that the tea should not be landed. An armed watch of 25 men was ordered to guard the ships at Griffin's wharf. When Hutchinson inquired of the chief militia officer, by whose authority the armed men were on board the ships, he was merely told that the militia officers could do nothing about them. The captains of the watch on 29 and 30 November were both members of the Northend Caucus. John Hancock later participated as captain of the cadets. Reportedly the Train of Artillery and possibly militia units stood guard. The setup of the watch was informal. Each evening's captain was to prepare a list of watchmen for the following night; the Committee of Correspondence was to take care of difficulties.[36] In case of any molestation, the watch had to alarm the inhabitants of Boston and the country.[37]

The crown officials no longer had any authority to take preventive measures. The Cadets guarded the tea ships but defied orders of the governor to protect officials threatened by crowds. Hutchinson correctly estimated his position: "I am in a helpless state" because the council as well as the merchants in general "profess to disapprove of the tumultuous violent proceedings of the people but they wish to see the professed end of the people . . . attained in a regular way. . . ."[38] He admonished the justice of the peace to do their duty in suppressing riots, but on a similar occasion in 1769 he himself had refused to do so. On the day of the first "Body" meeting, 29 November, his attempts to disperse the crowd were defeated in council. When Hancock, as moderator, reported "the restless Machinations of that Tool of Power and Enemy of his Country," those assembled censored the governor. A third defeat followed on the next day. After having retreated to his country seat, Hutchinson sent Sheriff Greenleaf with a letter to the meeting, to be read "if they will give him leave." The sheriff gone, Hutchinson brooded gloomily, "This may possibly cause me to take my lodgings at the Castle also." At the Old South Church Greenleaf's appearance occasioned a "confused Noise," but he finally did obtain leave to read his message. It was answered by loud and general hissing and a vote not to disperse but to continue business as normal. Hutchinson would have to order justices and sheriff to raise the posse, but he knew that "no Justice dare[d] to do it and no other Posse except the Meeting itself would have appeared."[39]

[35]Hutchinson to Dartmouth, 2 Dec. 1773, Letterbooks, MA 27:577–578; Warren and Church to committees of neighboring towns, 28 Nov. 1773, *MHSP* 13:167–168. Dorchester, Roxbury, Brookline, Cambridge, and Charlestown were invited.

[36]"Minutes of the Tea Meetings, 1773," *MHSP* 20:10–17 (1882); Commissioners to Lords of the Treasury, 4 Jan. 1774, House of Lords MSS., 266:387–389. Watch: lists of watchmen for 29 and 30 Nov., in Drake, ed., *Tea Leaves*, p. xlvi; Thomas Newell, "Diary," 3 Dec. 1773, p. 346; Hutchinson to his son, 30 Nov. 1773, Hutchinson Family Correspondence, Egerton MSS., 2659, p. 50, Brit. Museum, LC transcripts, p. 65; Narrative of Events in Boston, Sparks MSS., 4.8:241; *BTR* 23:204–205.

[37]Upton, ed., "Proceedings," p. 294.

[38]*BG*, 15 Nov. 1773; Hutchinson to Hancock, 11 Nov. 1773, in Drake, ed., *Tea Leaves*, p. xxxiii; Hutchinson to Dartmouth, 15 Nov. 1773, Letterbooks, MA 27:570–571, cf. *ibid.*, pp. 572–578.

[39]Hutchinson to his son, 30 Nov. 1773, in *The Diary and Letters of His Excellency Thomas Hutchinson*, ed. Peter Orlando Hutchinson, 2 vols. (London, 1883, 1886), 1:94–95; Hutchinson to Dartmouth, 2 Dec. 1773, Letterbooks, MA 27:577–578; Upton, ed., "Proceedings," p. 292; *BEP*, 6 Dec. 1773.

At the meeting Samuel Adams countered Hutchinson's assertion that it was "unlawful." A free people had a right to assemble and consult, especially if they were injured and did so for their own safety. Furthermore, these proceedings were as regular as those of the House of Representatives or the House of Commons. Finally, said Representative Adams, the Riot Act had expired and would not be reenacted. After the applause had died down, Dr. Young argued, citing Blackstone's *Commentaries* as authority, that there was nothing "unlawful" about this meeting. If a subject could not find redress of his grievances by law or constitutional means, he was in a state of nature. And, like the Commons at Runnymede, this assembly was in that state.[40]

The rest of the afternoon was spent waiting for the answer of the consignees, who had earlier refused to accede to the town's demands because their correspondents in Great Britain had "entered into penal engagements" in their behalf. No answer came. "The Meeting out of great Tenderness to these persons, . . . notwithstanding the Time they had hitherto expended upon them to no purpose," reassembled the next morning. The proposals of the tea agents finally came, addressed to the lawful authority, not to the extralegal meeting, but the crowd permitted them to be read nevertheless. The consignees declared their willingness to store the tea but refused to send it back. Richard Clarke's son-in-law asked whether the agents would be treated civilly "though they might be of differing sentiments with this body." The meeting voted that it would be safe, but in a turnabout the consignees refused to leave the castle. Their "mulish obstinacy" contributed much to the inflexible reaction of the townspeople.[41]

The meeting then addressed itself to the owners and masters of the tea ships, ordering them to return the tea in the same bottom in which it had come. To this, Rotch, owner of the *Dartmouth*, objected, because his ship was liable to be stopped by the castle guns or the Royal Navy or be seized on arrival in Great Britain. Samuel Adams mentioned that it was common for captains and owners of vessels to enter a protest at the customs house for goods lost or damaged by accidents or storms, and now a "Political Storm" was blowing, compelling him to send the tea back. Rotch complied when told not to "further incence" the several thousand people present, who had the power in their hands and would execute their resolutions.[42]

John Rowe, part-owner of Captain Bruce's ship and rather uneasy about its cargo, is an example of how reluctant merchants suddenly found themselves among the Whigs. In order to quiet the minds of the people, Rowe told the "Body" that he was sorry that the "detestable and obnoxious" tea was loaded in the ship. Carried away by the applause, he dwelt further upon the subject and finally asked "Whether a little Salt Water would not do it good. . . ." The crowd shouted and clapped. Someone on the floor remarked to a friend that they had brought a good Tory over to their side. To keep him there, Rowe was elected to a committee to transmit a vote to

[40]Upton, ed., "Proceedings," pp. 292–293.
[41]*BEP*, 22 Nov., 6 Dec. 1773; *BNL*, 26 Nov. 1773; Thomas Newell, "Diary," p. 345; Boyle, "Journal," pp. 368–370; James Bowdoin to John Temple, 13 Dec. 1773, *MHSC* 6.9:327–330; Andrews, "Letters," p. 324.
[42]Upton, ed., "Proceedings," p. 290.

Great Britain not to import any tea until the "unrighteous act" was repealed. The other members were Hancock, Adams, William Phillips, and Jonathan Williams. Rowe angrily noted in his diary: "was Chose a Committee Man much against my will but I dare not say a word." He had reason to be displeased: Behind the scenes he was author of an attempt to get the duties paid.[43] This would have meant acknowledging the right of Parliament to impose duties and to confine trade in specific commodities to designated consignees. It would have brought about some dislocation among merchants and shopkeepers and might have lowered the price of tea.

The neighboring colonies were informed about these meetings, and a group of men collected news about the state of affairs in other towns. Rumors spread once that the tea would be landed and stored, but "The People" contradicted them in the *Evening Post*. Tea was the general topic of all conversations. "The flame [of opposition] is kindled and like lightning it catches from Soul to Soul." For the next mass meetings on 14 and 16 December, large numbers of men flocked in from the country. Samuel Phillips Savage from Weston, formerly Boston merchant and selectman, was chosen moderator of the "Provincial meeting." He had always had a keen interest in political developments and via his son-in-law Henry Bass had connections with the Northend Caucus and the Loyal Nine.[44]

The tea consignees, who had boasted that, "being surrounded with cannon, we have [given] them such answers as we should not have dared to do in any other situation," were not even mentioned. All attention of the "mobility" (Hutchinson) centered on Rotch and Hall, owner and captain of the first ship that had arrived. Their 20-day period to pay the duties expired on the sixteenth. A motion for reconciliation was not acted upon. Instead, Rotch was called. He retracted his promise to reship, saying that he had acted from fear of crowd action. He was ready to do as much as anybody else for his country, "but he could not see the Justice or Patriotism of his being put in the Front of the Battle." Only if the merchants agreed to bear the loss of ship and tea together would he willingly pay his portion. Josiah Quincy, Jr., sustained Rotch. As the reshipping of the tea was a public concern, its losses should be shared equally by the people; the treatment Rotch had received was inhuman rather than patriotic. He had hardly finished when he was accused of having been bribed by Rotch. Nothing further came of the proposal. The meeting ordered Rotch to apply at once to the various officials for the necessary clearances.

Adams announced that the tea must not be landed under any circumstances, because some would always prefer their own gain to even the ruin of the country. Furthermore, "he could not trust the private Virtue of his Countrymen in refraining

[43]*Ibid.*, pp. 294–295; Hutchinson, *Diary and Letters*, 1:97; Proceedings of the Town of Boston, in Drake, ed., *Tea Leaves*, pp. 320–321; Rowe, *Letters and Diary*, p. 256. A few months later Rowe wrote, "The People have done amiss and no sober man can vindicate their Conduct" (p. 274).

[44]Andrews, "Letters," 29 Nov. 1774, p. 324; Nathaniel W. Appleton to Eliphalet Pearson, 14 Dec., 21 Dec. 1773, *CSMP* 8:291–297 (1902–1903); Abigail Adams to Mercy Warren, 5 Dec. 1773, *Warren–Adams Letters*, 1:18–19; John Adams to James Warren, 22 Dec. 1773, *The Works of John Adams*, ed. Charles F. Adams, 10 vols. (Boston, 1850–1856), 9:334–336; Samuel Phillips Savage, Diary, 14 Dec., 16 Dec. 1773, MHS; Leslie to Haldimand, 16 Dec. 1773, *N.Y. Hist. Soc. Coll.*, 1881, pp. 531–532.

from the Use of it, but he had rather trust their publick Virtue.'' He referred to the corporate concept that the individual must be watched and controlled by the community and that public necessity was to be placed before the private interests of the consumers as well as the consignees. Occasionally the speeches were interrupted by shouts from the galleries: The tea should be burned on the common. If everybody present would help, it would soon be accomplished. Or the people should get axes and then throw the tea into the harbor. But none of the leaders except Thomas Young once hinted that such action might be a last expedient.[45]

When Rotch came back to inform the meeting that his ship had not been cleared, a group of men left the meeting house. The noise made John Andrews, a Boston merchant, get up from his cup of tea, which he was quietly enjoying at home. But he found the Old South still so packed that he could not get in, so ''I went contentedly home and finished my tea.'' About a quarter of an hour later, wild yelling and boatswains' whistles were heard. At the meeting, people rushed out, although Adams and Young tried to prevail upon them to stay. Most went down to Griffin's wharf.[46]

Activity there had begun about half-past six, led by two groups, one of which had disguised itself at Edes and Gill's printing office and consisted of 17 members of the Long Room Club, mainly masters and shipbuilders from the Northend. The second party came from the corner of Essex and Orange Streets (that is, Liberty Tree), in the Southend. These may have been the men to whom Mackintosh is said to have referred as ''my Chickens.'' Other men joined on the spur of the moment when the first group passed the Old South or later on the wharf. Several of those who claimed to have participated had come from other towns. Those who joined spontaneously came undisguised or quickly blackened their faces. St. Andrew's Lodge, where the tea shipments had been discussed and to which several of the rioters, most prominently Paul Revere, belonged, closed on the evening of the sixteenth because hardly any members were present.[47] Hancock, probably not a party to all plans, sent a teamster who loaded at his warehouse down to the wharf. One of his captains was sufficiently well informed that Hancock could refer his London agent to him for particulars about the riot. Molineux was probably active in the actual direction of the riot. He was named as a participant, and unlike all other Whig leaders, was not present in the Old South during the afternoon.[48]

[45]Thomas Hutchinson, Jr., to Elisha Hutchinson, 14 Dec. 1773, *Diary and Letters,* 1:96; conciliatory motion in the town meeting by Timothy Prout, 14 Dec. 1773, Massachusetts Misc., vol. 5, LC; Upton, ed., ''Proceedings,'' pp. 296–299; fragment of Quincy's speech, in Drake, ed., *Tea Leaves,* pp. lix–lx.

[46]''Minutes of the Tea Meetings, 1773,'' pp. 15–17; Hutchinson to Mauduit, Dec. 1773, *MHSP* 13:170–171; Hutchinson to Dartmouth, 17 Dec. 1773, Letterbooks, MA 27:589; Andrews, ''Letters,'' 18 Dec. 1773, p. 326; Upton, ed., ''Proceedings,'' p. 298.

[47]William Gordon, *The History of the Rise, Progress, and Establishment of the United States of America,* 4 vols. (London, 1788), 1:339, 341; Statement of Peter Edes (1836) and estimates of the number of rioters, in Drake, ed., *Tea Leaves,* pp. lxiv–lxx, lxxxix–xciv; Justin Winsor, ed., *The Memorial History of Boston, Including Suffolk County, Massachusetts, 1630–1880,* 4 vols. (Boston, 1880–1881), 3:49; George P. Anderson, ''Ebenezer Mackintosh, Stamp Act Rioter and Patriot,'' *CSMP* 26:53 (1924–1926); Hutchinson to East India Company, 19 Dec. 1773, Letterbooks, MA 27:597–599; ''Records of St. Andrews Lodge,'' *Proc. in Masonry,* 1:249ff. (1895).

[48]Thompson Maxwell, ''Account Given by Major Thompson Maxwell to the Late General James Miller,'' ed. J. Colburn, *NEHGR* 22:57–58 (1868); Hancock to his agent, 21 Dec. 1773, *John Hancock His Book,* ed. A. E. Brown (Boston, 1898), p. 178; Upton, ed., ''Proceedings,'' p. 300.

At the wharf the men from the Northend and the Southend and those who had joined them divided into three groups, each with a commander and a boatswain, who took up their roles with the tacit consent of the others. They boarded the ships, ordered the crew members and customs officials off, and assured Captain Coffin, who had come to the wharf only a few days earlier, that his cargo other than the tea would be handled with utmost care. The hatches were opened, and the groups on the ships divided the work among themselves, some going into the hold, others to the winches. Some opened the chests, and the rest emptied them. The work was finished in about two hours, or according to the meeting's well-informed moderator in 110 minutes. The men worked fast and did not destroy any property besides the tea. They even replaced a padlock that had been broken. The riot was a combination of planned and spontaneous action, during which the participants showed themselves capable of coping with any unexpected difficulty.[49]

From among the crowd of 2000–3000 spectators, a few tried to pocket some of the tea, but they were designated "East Indians" and manhandled. Adams's doubts about "private virtue" were justified. In fact, armed guards had been posted at the head of Griffin's and the neighboring wharves. When the job was done, about 9 P.M., the men marched back to town. All were "well pleased" that "the ships are thus cleared," reported printer Boyle, while merchant Rowe noted, "I am sincerely sorry for the Event."[50] The moderate Benjamin Franklin declared that the destruction of private property, even "in a Dispute about Public Rights," was carrying matters too far.

Several historians have determined the names of a total of 123 participants.[51] However, the authenticity of the lists cannot be ascertained, for their sources, recollections many decades after the event, are dubious. Further research has revealed the names of a few more men, but most of them were spectators only. Of the 123 men, 14 came from other towns, and another 16 were apprentices—that is, not in the tax list. Of the other 93 men, 34 have been identified in the tax list (1771): One-third had no property, one-third were small property holders, one-sixth owned up to £100, and the last sixth owned more than that. As to the men named in

[49]George R. T. Hewes, *Traits of the Tea Party: Being a Memoir of George R. T. Hewes*, ed. Benjamin B. Thatcher (New York, 1835), pp. 177–184, and "Log of the *Dartmouth*," pp. 260–261; depositions by captains and mates of the tea ships, House of Lords MSS., 266:406–414, and Colonial Office, Sec. Dept., 5/133:211, 213, 215, PRO; Andrews, "Letters," 18 Dec. 1774, p. 326; Samuel P. Savage, Diary, 16 Dec. 1773, MHS; *BEP,* 20 Dec. 1773; *Mass. Gaz.,* 23 Dec. 1773.

[50]Andrews, "Letters," p. 326; *Mass. Gaz.,* 23 Dec. 1773; *BEP,* 20 Dec. 1773; Upton, ed., "Proceedings," pp. 298–299; Boyle, "Journal," p. 371; letter from Boston, 17 Dec. 1773, in Drake, ed., *Tea Leaves,* p. lxxxiv; Rowe, *Letters and Diary,* 16 Dec. 1773, pp. 257–258.

[51]"Minutes of the Tea Meetings, 1773," pp. 11, 13; Drake, ed., *Tea Leaves,* pp. xcii–xciii (from Hewes) and pp. xciii–xciv (family traditions); Caleb A. Wall, *The Historic Boston Tea Party* (Worcester, Mass., 1896), pp. 21–22. Other sources are Samuel Dyer's deposition, 30 July 1774, Admirally Papers, Sec. Dept. 1.484:535–538, PRO, LC transcripts; Upton, ed., "Proceedings," pp. 289–300. Thomas Young, named by all there, and Hancock, named by Hewes, have been excluded from the total because they were definitely not present. Only one of the spectators was willing to give evidence, provided it could be done in Great Britain. "Queries of George Chalmers, with the Answers of General Gage," *MHSC* 4.4:367–372; Cooper to Franklin, 17 Dec. 1773, *ibid.,* pp. 373–392. There is no evidence for R. S. Longley's assertion ["Mob Activities in Revolutionary Massachusetts," *NEQ* 6:123 (1933)] that a Mr. Eckley was imprisoned and that the informer against him was tarred and feathered.

contemporary accounts as present at any of the tea meetings since 2 November (that is, mainly speakers and committeemen), they came from many different organizations, clubs, and town officialdom. Many of them were wealthy. This representation of all economic groups of the society is also found in the actions during the subsequent months.

On the next morning Hutchinson attempted to assemble the council, but no quorum could be obtained. To those who came, he heatedly pointed out that the tea riot was high treason and that Attorney General Sewall would explain the laws to them. Hearing about this, John Hancock, who knew the present seat of power, said, "he was for having a Body Meeting to take off that" attorney general. The councillors obviously were active elsewhere; John Adams at least suspected that something was behind "the Marching and Countermarching of Councillors." Only five days later did the council meet, and then Hutchinson settled for "what we call New England Burglary, that is, breaking open a shop or ship." The troops at Castle William did not intervene, although Colonel Leslie kept them under arms. Admiral Montague complained that "neither the Governor, Magistrates, Owners or the Revenue Officers of this place ever called for my assistance," though he could easily have prevented the destruction of the tea "by Firing upon the Town."[52]

Looking back on the preceding evening, John Adams wrote on 17 December:

> The die is cast. The people have passed the river and cut away the bridge. . . . This is the grandest event which has ever yet happened since the controversy with Britain opened. The sublimity of it charms me! . . . All things were conducted with great order, decency, and *perfect submission to government*.

For once he did not rail against the rioters. But then, though the action was in part spontaneous—no man from the waterfront community needed directions about how to unload a ship—the destruction of property remained within the limit set by the leadership. This impressed John Adams.[53]

RESISTANCE BECOMES GENERAL

In the following months the tea boycott was vigorously enforced. On numerous occasions, tea was publicly burned. Crowds searched houses and stores and examined peddlers. Taverns serving tea were ransacked, and the *Gazette* suggested that licenses should be denied to those innkeepers. Committees watched the roads for wagons, wharves for ships carrying tea.[54] Vessels with the obnoxious herb were

[52]John Adams, *Diary*, 2:87, to James Warren, 22 Dec. 1773, *Works*, 9:334–335; Council Records, 16:748–749, MSA; Leslie to Haldimand, 20 Dec. 1773, *N.Y. Hist. Soc. Coll.*, 1881, p. 532; Leslie to Barrington, 6 Dec., 17 Dec. 1773, House of Lords MSS., 266:206–207; Montague to Stevens, 17 Dec. 1773, Admirally Papers, Sec. Dept., 1.484:497–498, PRO.

[53]John Adams to James Warren, 17 Dec. 1773, *Works*, 9:333–334.

[54]Peter Force, ed., *American Archives* 9 vols. (Washington, D.C., 1837–1853), 4.4:1288. Marshfield: Tercentenary Committee, *Marshfield . . . The Autobiography of a Pilgrim Town* (Marshfield, Mass., 1940), pp. 114–115. Lexington: *BG*, 20 Dec. 1773. Plymouth: *BEP*, 26 Sept. 1774; *BG*, 3 Oct. 1774. Charlestown: Rowe, *Letters and*

Figure 8. The opposition to the tea duty, December 1773.

usually sent back and sometimes prevented from obtaining supplies. Once, in Maryland, a ship was even burned. Sometimes all European goods found were confiscated, a sign that general considerations about importation, luxury, and drain of money motivated some of the rioting.[55] People found possessing tea often had their windows broken and in repeated instances were tarred and feathered, even women.[56] Boston tea dealers subscribed to an agreement not to sell tea, though some wanted to exempt smuggled (undutied) tea. Prices for the latter should be fixed, so as to prevent high profits for monopolizing merchants or those importing from other colonies. On 20 January several hundred pounds of tea were burned in King Street "amidst the loud Acclamations of a vast Concourse of People."[57] While the nonconsumption of tea had been debated in 1767, a sign of consciousness about women's rights had appeared. Some "Matrons of Liberty" held a meeting and decided that they had a right to drink tea and would not stop doing so unless their husbands stopped drinking alcohol in the taverns. Now the *Gazette* reported that in Newport, Rhode Island, it was known that the "Ladies in Boston, to their immortal honour," subscribed to a no-tea association.[58]

The tea from the fourth tea ship, Captain Loring's brig that had been cast ashore at Cape Cod, was carried to Castle William. The Salem skipper who accepted this "infamous Employment" was visited by a crowd but was not punished because he was ill. Later a town meeting resolved that his misdeed had been "unintentional." Two of the chests were sold at Provincetown. But the buyer had more trouble from crowds and committes than profit from selling.[59] In March 1774 Captain Gorham came from London with several chests of tea. The Boston Indians reassembled on 7 March and threw the load overboard. This crowd action overtook the committee action. The brig arrived on Sunday, 6 March. On the following day the Boston Committee of Correspondence examined the owner and invited the committees of the neighboring towns for the eighth. But on that day they voted that they would

Diary, 31 Dec. 1773, p. 259; Thomas Newell, "Diary," 31 Dec. 1773, p. 347; *BG* and *BEP*, 3 Jan. 1774, Charlestown, Nov. 1774: Andrews, "Letters," 5 Nov. 1774, p. 383; *BEP*, 7 Nov. 1774. Dorchester: Thomas Newell, "Diary," 1 Jan. 1774, p. 347. Newbury, Portsmouth: *BEP*, 23 Jan. 1775. Providence: *BEP*, 13 March 1775; *Mass. Spy*, 17 March 1775. Salem: *BPB*, 4 July 1774. Weston: *Essex Gaz.*, 5 May 1774. Leominster: *BG*, 5 Sept. 1774. Montague: *BEP*, 7 Feb., 14 Feb. 1774. Provincetown: *BEP*, 17 Jan. 1774. Newburyport: *BEP*, 29 Aug. 1774; *BG*, 7 March 1774. Boston: Rough Drafts of Protests, Ezekiel Price Papers, Boston Atheneum. Other incidents and report of a more general nature: *BG*, 20 Dec. 1773, 17 Jan. 1774; *BEP*, 12 Sept. 1774; Andrews, "Letters," p. 358.

[55]Andrews, "Letters," 7 Sept., 10 Sept., 14 Sept., 1 Nov. 1774, pp. 356–358, 382; Force, ed., *Archives*, 4.2:309–311. In Salem a Marblehead crowd threatened to burn a ship with tea on board. Samuel Curwen, Letterbook, 29 Aug. 1774, Essex Institute; Ezra Stiles, *The Literary Diary*, ed. F. B. Dexter, 3 vols. (New York, 1901), 1:448; Committee of Correspondence, Minute Books, 9:788–789, NYPL.

[56]*BG*, 5 Sept. 1774; *BPB*, 4 July 1774; *BEP*, 18 July 1774.

[57]Tea dealers' meetings, 21 Dec. and 23 Dec. 1773, *BEP*, 27 Dec. 1773. Participants: S. L. Boardman, ed., *Peter Edes, Pioneer Printer in Maine: A Biography* (Bangor, Me., 1901), App. 4; Minutes of a meeting held by Boston tea merchants, MSS., BPL; *BNL*, 20 Jan., 27 Jan. 1774; *BEP*, 24 Jan. 1774; Thomas Newell, "Diary," 20 Jan. 1774, p. 348; Boyle, "Journal," 20 Jan. 1774, p. 372; anonymous proclamation, Colburn Collection, 3:161, MHS.

[58]*BEP*, 28 Dec. 1767; *BG*, 10 Jan. 1774.

[59]Andrews, "Letters," 19 Dec. 1773, p. 327; Boyle, "Journal," 30 Dec. 1773, p. 372; *BEP*, 17 Jan. 1774; *BNL*, 20 Jan., 27 Jan. 1774; Jonathan Clarke to Richard Clarke, 31 Dec. 1773, Misc. Bound Papers, vol. 14, MHS; *BG*, 20 Dec. 1773, 17 Jan. 1774; cf. Labaree, *Tea Party*, p. 150.

Figure 9.   French report of the crowd action against John Malcom, printed in 1784.

have exerted their influence to have the tea sent back "had not the unexpected destruction" made further efforts unnecessary.[60]

The tea consignees, "those odious Miscreants and detestable Tools to Ministry and Governor, . . . those Traitors to their Country, Butchers, who have done and are doing every Thing to Murder and Destroy all that shall stand in the Way of their private Interest," did not lead an easy life. The "Chairman of the Committee for Tarring and Feathering" warned them not to come to Boston. Elisha Hutchinson was chased out of Plymouth early one morning in the middle of a snowstorm after the local committee had succeeded in convincing the crowd to let him stay at least overnight. Consignee Clarke embarked for London; the others emigrated later.[61]

When a large group of men in Worcester petitioned the selectmen for a town meeting to condemn the rioting, they were outvoted. The sympathizing town clerk nevertheless entered the protest and published it. He was forced to dip his fingers in ink and cross out the protest in the records. Other men had to recant or to take shelter in Boston. But there too, crowds were ready to deal with them.[62] Bostonians closely followed the proceedings in the other colonies. When Revere came with the news from New York that Governor Tryon had promised to send the tea back, the bells were set ringing. The other colonies in turn watched Boston. A letter from John Andrews to Philadelphia with an account of the Tea Party was "thumbed and worn."[63]

At Piscataqua the collector and comptroller of customs were summoned before a town meeting and ordered to ship back tea that had been stored because the owner could not pay the duties. The commissioners, by that time safe under the protection of troops, reprimanded the two harassed officials for attending "the Summons of the People assembled for the avowed Purposes of opposing the operation of an Act of Parliament."[64]

At the same time another customs official became the target of crowd action in Boston. John Malcom, although only a minor employee, had brought forth from the *Gazette* the exasperated comment "When such Creatures are employed in publick Affairs, it gives us great Reason to think there is some rotten Planck in our Constitution." In 1763 he had been apprehended in Boston for debt and counterfeiting. He was a tidewaiter in Newport in 1770, fought against the Regulators in North Carolina, and in 1773 was tarred and feathered in Pownalborough by 30 sailors for giving information about the brig *Brothers*. Back in Boston in 1774, he beat a boy who had offended him. Such incidents had given rise to riots twice before. This time

[60]*BG*, 7 March 1774; *BNL*, 10 March 1774; *BEP*, 14 March 1774; Thomas Newell, "Diary," 7 March 1774, p. 350; Rowe, *Letters and Diary,* 8 March 1774, p. 264; Boyle, "Journal," 10 March 1774, p. 373; Hutchinson to Dartmouth, 9 March 1774, *Diary and Letters,* 1:138–139; Committee of Correspondence, Minute Books, 9:726–728, NYPL.

[61]"Joyce, jun.," *BG,* 17 Jan. 1774; *BNL,* 20 Jan. 1774; *BEP,* 24 Jan. 1774; Hutchinson, *Diary and Letters,* 1:97–98, 107; Rotch to Consignees, 6 Jan. 1774, in Drake, ed., *Tea Leaves,* pp. 350–351.

[62]Albert A. Lovell, *Worcester in the War of Revolution* (Worcester, Mass., 1876), pp. 31–33; *BG,* 4 July 1774; *BPB,* 4 April 1774.

[63]*BPB,* 22 Nov., 29 Nov. 1773; *BEP,* 10 Jan., 17 Jan. 1774; Thomas Newell, "Diary," 28 Dec. 1773, p. 347; Boyle, "Journal," 27 Dec. 1773, p. 273; Andrews, "Letters," p. 325, note.

[64]Commissioners to ———, 26 July 1774, Copy of Orders, MHS.

G. R. T. Hewes interposed. According to one account, Malcom told Hewes not to presume to talk to him because he was too poor, at which Hewes retorted that he was at least honest enough never to have been tarred and feathered. Blows ensued, people assembled, and Hewes swore out a warrant.

Some men tried to stop the violence, referring to the warrant and insisting that justice should be done lawfully. But they were answered by the crowd, according to the newspapers, "that, in case they let him go, they might expect as little satisfaction as they had received in the cases of Richardson [the customs official who had killed Snider] and the soldiers, and the other friends of government." So Malcom was tarred and feathered, carried through the streets for four hours, and beaten severely. Hewes followed the crowd with a blanket to shelter Malcom from the cold once he was released. Many Bostonians disapproved of the riot because its immediate cause was no special act on Malcom's part against the public interest but a fight, a private affair. One of the underlying reasons for the riot as well as for its condemnation by well-to-do inhabitants was Malcom's role in the war against the Regulators, for which he had just been publicly rewarded and which had been reported in Boston newspapers. The economic groups from which crowds were recruited sympathized with the Regulators as much as wealthy Bostonians abhorred them. The latter even tried to suppress the riot, a step that had not once been taken when riots were aimed only at British officials and had no intrasocietal implications.[65]

This reaction among the better sort of the Whig leadership differed markedly from the reaction to the tea riot, which had been described as "the most magnificent Movement of all. There is a Dignity, a Majesty, a Sublimity, in this last Effort of the Patriots" that should be admired. Nevertheless, some were concerned about the "Attack upon Property." John Adams probably exaggerated when he envisioned further violence: There were many who wished that "as many dead Carcasses were floating in the Harbour, as there are Chests of Tea." Considering the "malicious Pleasure" with which governor, consignees, and customs officials watched the "distresses of the People, and their Struggles," Adams himself found the feeling understandable. He provided the theoretical justification for the destruction of the tea. It would have been a weapon in "the hand of tyrants and oppressors, who want to do violence with it to the laws and constitution, to the present age and to posterity." Whigs were acutely aware of the possible consequences of the action. The "Noble stand," wrote William Palfrey, Son of Liberty and clerk to John Hancock, will "either involve us in Civil War or emancipate us from the taxation so unjustly exercised over us by the British Parliament."[66]

[65]Frank W. C. Hersey, "Tar and Feathers: The Adventures of Captain John Malcolm," *CSMP* 34:429–473 (1941); Edward A. Jones, *The Loyalists of Massachusetts, Their Memorials, Petitions, and Claims* (London, 1930), pp. 208–209. *BG,* 9 Aug., 15 Nov. 1773, 31 Jan., 4 Feb., 20 Feb. 1774; *BNL,* 20 Jan., 27 Jan., 3 Feb. 1774; *BEP,* 31 Jan., 14 Feb. 1774; *Mass. Spy,* 27 Jan., 17 Feb. 1774; *Mass. Gaz.,* 3 Feb. 1774; SCF 84397; Council Records, 16:740, MSA; Thomas Newell, "Diary," 25 Jan. 1774, p. 348; Rowe, *Letters and Diary,* 25 Jan. 1774, p. 261; Hewes, *Memoir,* pp. 127–133; Anne Hulton, *Letters,* 31 Jan. 1774, pp. 69–72; John Adams to Abigail Adams, 5 July 1774, *Adams Family Correspondence,* ed. L. H. Butterfield, 2 vols. (Cambridge, Mass., 1963), 1:124–125; Hutchinson, *Diary and Letters,* 1:164; Joyce's advertisement (Boston, 1774), *Mass. Brds.* 1738, Evans 13359.

[66]John Adams, *Diary,* 17 Dec. 1773, 2:85–86, *Works,* 9:334–336; Samuel Adams, *Writings,* 3:72–73 *passim;* Palfrey

Because of such dangers, many moderates and conservatives alike condemned the riot. Some suspected tea-smuggling merchants of being involved because they could not undersell the low-dutied tea and because its sale was confined to specific consignees. Numerous Massachusetts towns disapproved of the destruction of the company's property. They demanded punishment of the rioters and, if called for, compensation by the inhabitants of Boston.[67] John Andrews, a moderate Boston merchant, hoped that the other colonies would ship back their tea, or "poor Boston will feel the whole weight of ministerial vengeance." And he continued with a striking and rather persuasive reason for the action on the night of 16 December: "However, its the opinion of most people that we stand an equal chance now, whether troops are sent in consequence of it or not; whereas, had it been stored, we should inevitably have had 'em, to enforce the sale of it."[68]

The troops arrived in Summer 1774. Resistance began at once, and, by April 1775, crowd action changed to war. Opposition to the punitive legislation, the Regulating Acts, passed by Parliament in response to the riot, also began in summer 1774 and resulted in the destruction of old institutions, their reestablishment, and the creation of new ones.

to Peacock, 24 Jan. 1774, Palfrey Family Papers, vol. 4, no. 63, HHL; Franklin to Cushing, 2 Feb. 1774, *CSMP* 5:57–58 (1897–1898).

[67]Rowe, *Letters and Diary,* 18 Dec. 1773, p. 258; *BG,* 20 Dec. 1773; extract of a letter from New York, 5 Nov. 1773, in Drake, ed., *Tea Leaves,* p. 269; Tercentenary Committee, *Marshfield,* pp. 114–115; J. E. A. Smith, *The History of Pittsfield,* 2 vols. (Boston, 1869, 1876), 1:184–186.

[68]Andrews, "Letters," 18 Dec. 1773, p. 325.

Resistance to the "Intolerable Acts" (1774-1775)

10

THE EROSION OF THE OLD ORDER UNDER GOVERNOR HUTCHINSON

During the first large-scale violent opposition to the new imperial policies in August 1765, Governor Bernard had lamented his lack of power. People talked "familiarly of turning out the Governor, (for adhering to King and Parliament)." Differentiating the "minister's creatures" according to rank, crowds physically attacked those coming from "low life"—tidewaiters, informers, soldiers, sailors. Those coming from "higher life"—commissioners, army and navy officers, governors—were mainly slandered in the papers. In 1765, friends of the government still judged it a "Strainge Delusion! that Such bare faced Contempt of Government Should be expected to affraight the English Parliament." They proved to be wrong.

Parliament relied on crown officials. But the system of patronage politics dominated by country gentry and town patricians was coming to an end. A new merchant elite relying on economic power moved to the fore together with a new brand of politicians replacing patronage by "majorities." In 1769 even the Loyalist secretary of the province demanded: "The Committee of Merchants are now become the grand assertors of Liberty. We wish to know whether the government at home asserts their own authority, or whether we are to submit to the powers now in being."[1] In 1771 the Massachusetts House of Representatives began to style itself "his Majesty's Commons." Criticism of laws by the Board of Trade in London was answered by the representatives with the assertion that they were "no incompetent Judges what the circumstances of this Province require." In 1772 Great Britain was referred to as "an exterior power." In the following year the *Evening Post* carried an advertisement on its front page entitled "The Revolution in New-England." In

[1]Bernard to Pownall, 26 Nov. 1765, Sparks MSS., 4.5:46, HHL; *A Ministerial Catechise, Suitable to Be Learned by All Modern Provincial Governors, Pensioners, Placemen, etc.*, dedicated to T——— H———, Esq. (Boston, 1771); Nathan Bowen, "Extracts from the Interleaved Almanacs of Nathan Bowen, Marblehead, 1742–1799," ed. W. H. Bowden, 26 Aug. 1765, *EIHC* 91:266 (1955); Oliver to Bernard, 15 Nov. 1769, in Thomas Hutchinson, *The Diary and Letters of His Excellency Thomas Hutchinson*, ed. Peter Orlando Hutchinson, 2 vols. (London, 1883, 1886), 1:21–22; Hillsborough to Bernard, 11 June 1768, Sparks MSS., 4.11:190, HHL.

small print it referred to a book about 1689. ''Locke'' called for an American Commonwealth, and Otis was ready to ''defy the whole Legislature of Great Britain.''

In 1775 such thoughts were propagated in many households by almanacs: ''A People may forsake their King, and still continue a people; but if a King loses his people, he is no more King. . . . When the King changes ministers and not measures, he is like a sot who only changes his liquors, and not his manner of living.'' One Bostonian mused, ''I have often wondered that so much difficulty should be raised about *declaring* independence, when we have actually got the *thing* itself. Who or what are we afraid of?''[2]

Rigidly paternalist attitudes patterned by and designed for a deferential society made an adjustment to popular demands impossible for Hutchinson. He preferred strong social and political barriers between rulers and ruled. The Whig leadership, demanding deference too, was able to communicate with the people of the lower sort and to picture the royal governors as the intractable placemen of an exterior power attempting to make its power over the lives and property of the colonists absolute.[3]

The attempts to involve the whole province in the controversy with the British authorities included emphasis on the economic burdens for all inhabitants as well as extensive use of personal connections by Boston's leaders—skillful extension of Whig influence in official institutions as well as circumventing them with new ad hoc bodies. The British policy, to prevent further growth of ''unruly'' lower houses by excluding new towns from representation, carried the struggle for representative government and against oppressive British decrees into many communities that otherwise would have been marginally concerned at best.[4]

Since the legislature needed popular support as much as Boston leaders needed the crowd, galleries were built in the House. The council permitted publication of its proceedings and barred the lieutenant governor from taking a seat in council. When, by British punitive regulation, the General Court was not in session, Boston took over the governor's sole right to call the assembly and invited all towns to join in a convention. When, during assembly recesses, its Committee of Correspondence continued to sit, Hutchinson expressed disapproval but took no steps to regain initiative and authority.[5]

[2]Message to the Governor, 25 April 1771, A. C. Goodell *et al.*, eds., *Acts and Resolves, Public and Private, of the Province of the Massachusetts Bay*, 21 vols. (Boston, 1869–1922), 5:58–59; proceedings concerning an act about fees, *ibid*, 4:352–354; cf. [Pownall], State of the Government of Massachusetts Bay in 1757, Mass. Misc., 1620–1864, LC; Bernard to Shelburne, 27 July 1767, Sparks MSS., 10.2:63, HHL; *BTR* 18:83; *BEP*, 22 Feb. 1773; *BG*, 31 May, 23 Aug., 27 Sept. 1773; report of a speech by James Otis, Sparks MSS., 10.2:81, HHL; *Essex Gaz.*, 1 Nov. 1768, printed the story of Wilhelm Tell; [Benjamin West], ''Maxims for a Prince,'' *Bickerstaff's Boston Almanac 1775*, (Boston, 1774); Winthrop to Adams, 1 June 1776, *MHSC* 5.4:306 (1878).

[3]James Warren to John Adams, 20 July 1775, to Samuel Adams, 4 Aug. 1775, in *Warren–Adams Letters: Being Chiefly a Correspondence among John Adams, Samuel Adams, and James Warren*, 2 vols. (Boston, 1917, 1925), 1:84, 2:418; Samuel Adams to James Warren, 13 Oct. 1775, *ibid.*, 1:141.

[4]*Mass. Gaz.*, 11 July 1765; *BG*, 22 July 1765; *Acts and Resolves*, 5:419, 511, 1775–1776. See also the catalogue of grievances in the Declaration of Independence.

[5]Thomas Hutchinson, *The History of the Colony and Province of Massachusetts Bay*, ed. Lawrence Shaw Mayo, 3 vols. (Cambridge, Mass., 1936), 3:113, 127, 149, 285–288, 307; *BTR* 16:260–261, 263–264; Thomas Newell, ''Diary for

Hutchinson's notion of his social position and of his role in government in the sixties and seventies centered around "dignity" and "respect." These were constantly endangered by criticism, or, in his words, "contemptuous Disrespect" and "Licentiousness which is worse than Tyranny." The dignity of his station, he was certain, increased with income. The Morgans commented, "a cool man this, who could swallow half the offices in the province and look as though they belonged to him by divine right." He reconciled his private interest with the public good by mentally shaping the latter to suit the former. Personally he could freely forgive a lawyer who, he felt, had insulted him, but there was the dignity of the court to preserve. Personally he had no ambition for the governorship, but the best interests of the colony required that he be named.[6] Torn between two powerful concepts, that of the acquisitive bourgeois and that of the elevated aristocrat, he was unable to decide which to follow, becoming almost paralyzed in the agony of not being able to reconcile them. He was too much the aristocrat to stoop to speaking to the crowd (1765). He was too acquisitive not to speak to the crowd when business interests were at stake (1770). In the latter case the crowd had merely asked for his sons and found itself faced with the acting governor.[7]

Vigorous action was irreconcilable with seignorial dignity. Thus, he retreated to his country estate when the going got rough. During the anti-Mein riot he squirmed and finally refused protection for his most valuable and active ally among the Loyalists. His erratic course concerning nonimportation not only increased the hostility of his opponents but also alienated the loyal merchants. A Loyalist justice of the peace in 1770 offered his assistance to the troops, intentionally by-passing Hutchinson, who would stall rather than act. When faced with a request from the military, his main concern was "to save appearances." As chief executive officer, he remained inefficient because he could think only in terms of patronage, not of political alliances or popular support. The General Court, removed from Boston to Cambridge in a punitive move for an anti-British vote and for allegedly being under the influence of Boston's "licentious and unrestrained Mob," refused to do business. The constituents, angered by the quibbling about location, demanded immediate action on such important questions as fee tables, choice of jurors, laws relating to usury and recovery of debts, and the "Exorbitant Tax." The governor, then Bernard, who had identical intentions, literally overlooked his potential allies,

---

1773 to the End of 1774, of Mr. Thomas Newell, Boston," 26 Jan. 1774, ed. R. Frothingham, *MHSP* 15:348 (1876–1877); Samuel M. Quincy, ed., *Reports of Cases Argued and Adjudged in the Superior Court of Judicature of... Massachusetts Bay, 1761–1772, by Josiah Quincy, Junior* (Boston, 1865), pp. 214, 270.

[6]Hutchinson's charge to the grand jury, Aug. 1767, *ibid.*, pp. 241–248; *A Ministerial Catechise; Edmund S. Morgan and Helen M. Morgan, The Stamp Act Crisis: Prologue to Revolution* (Chapel Hill, N.C., 1953), p. 208. Hutchinson lamented that Bernard had left the governorship "without any material addition to his private fortune" (*History*, 3:208); his demand for a seat on the council was considered by the representatives to be "a new and additional instance of ambition and a lust of power" *ibid.*, pp. 126–129. Governorship: Hutchinson to Bernard, Sept. 1769, Letterbooks, MA 26:374. Lawyer: Quincy, ed., *Reports*, pp. 246–250, 270; Hutchinson to Cushing, 30 July 1767, *MHSP* 44:524; Ernest F. Brown, *Joseph Hawley, Colonial Radical* (New York, 1931), pp. 67–68. Cf. Malcolm Freiberg, "Thomas Hutchinson: The First Fifty Years, 1711–1761," *WMQ* 3.15:35–55 (1958); Bernard Bailyn, *The Ordeal of Thomas Hutchinson* (Cambridge, Mass., 1974).

[7]See Chapter 2, p. |102|, and Chapter 8, p. 218.

the voters. When a storm arose about crown grants replacing legislative appropriations for the sustenance of the top officials, it did not occur to Hutchinson to mobilize loyal colonists, as well as tax-conscious ones, by publicly pointing out that some years earlier the representatives had suggested crown grants in order to ease provincial taxes. He returned a bill to the House with angry complaints because in the traditional opening lines an "etc." was missing, though he knew that "by the body of the people" his conduct would be "considered to proceed from mere humour." Many a colonist must have shaken his head in disbelief over the "etc." affair. Was Hutchinson still in his right mind? He was. The "etc." was the traditional abbreviation for a list naming all the dominions of the king, including North America.[8] But he was above explaining political and constitutional questions to the people, the rabble.

Hutchinson was thus the perfect man to supervise his own burial as politician, which happened to include that of British domination. While crowds and town meetings acted, he complained about his lack of power or merely watched the actions of his opponents, preferably from his country seat. Bostonians meanwhile amused themselves by reading the governor's letters and those of other crown officials in town meetings. These "ex parte" accounts were considered detrimental to the colony's interests; a jury indicted the top officials for slander. A captain, refusing to accede to the demand of a Boston merchant that he open those letters of Hutchinson that he was forwarding, was censored in a town meeting and lost his job.[9]

When Governor Hutchinson left Boston for Great Britain on 1 June 1774, a petition for his removal preceded him. In Philadelphia he was hanged in effigy, carted, and burned for attempting to incense Britain against the colonies. Crowd violence against his supporters became so widespread that they "led a devil of a life" and had to recant in large numbers.[10] At the same time the British secretary for

---

[8]John Mein to Hutchinson, n.p., n.d., Letterbooks, MA 25:455–459; John Montresor, "Journals of Capt. John Montresor, 1757–1778," ed. G. D. Scull, 14 Sept. 1770, *N.Y. Hist. Soc. Coll.*, 1881, pp. 399–400; Murray to Dalrymple, 27 Aug. 1770, in *Letters of James Murray, Loyalist*, ed. Nina M. Tiffany and Susan I. Leslay (Boston, 1901), pp. 166–167. General Court: D. C. Lord and R. M. Calhoon, "The Removal of the Massachusetts General Court from Boston, 1769–1772," *JAH* 55:735–755 (1969); Hutchinson, *History*, 3:170 ff.; William Lincoln, *History of Worcester, Massachusetts, from Its Earliest Settlement to 1836* (2d ed.; Worcester, Mass., 1862), pp. 100|–104, 210; George W. Chase, *The History of Haverhill, Massachusetts, from Its First Settlement, in 1640, to the Year 1860* (Haverhill, Mass., 1861), p. 368; Instructions to the Governors, pp. 2422–2427, 2439–2440, MHS. Crown grants: *Acts and Resolves*, 4:860, 1032–1033, 5:34, 57–60, 139–140; Thomas Hutchinson, "Additions to Thomas Hutchinson's *History of Massachusetts Bay*," ed. Catherine Barton Mayo, *AASP* 59:47–48; the governor's salary was increased in the process to £1500 annually. "Etc. affair": *Acts and Resolves*, 5:346–347; for another ridiculous struggle (about repairs to Province House), see *ibid.*, pp. 60–61.

[9]Cooper to Pownall, 18 Feb. 1769, *AHR* 8:302–305; *BTR* 16:297, 18:15; report on the town meeting, 4 Oct. Sparks MSS., 10.3:37, HHL; *BEP*, 9 Oct. 1769. Further letters were published in 1773. *Mass. Brds.* 1477, 1652. John Andrews, "Letters of John Andrews," 4 June 1773, *MHSP* 8:323; Thomas Newell, "Diary," 16 June 1773, p. 339; John Adams, *Diary, and Autobiography of John Adams*, ed. L. H. Butterfield, 4 vols. (Cambridge, Mass., 1961–1966), 22 March 1773, 2:79–80; Henry Hulton to ———, 8 Oct. 1773, Letterbooks, 1:66–69, HHL; Hutchinson, *History*, 3:282–298, *Diary and Letters*, 1:81–93, Letterbooks, MA 26:520; *BEP*, 21 June, 28 June 1773.

[10]*Mass. Spy*, 2 Nov. 1774; *Mass. Gaz.*, 2 June 1774; Jeremy Belknap, Diary, 1774, MHS; *Penn. Gaz.*, 4 May 1774, reprinted in *CSMP* 12:86–87 (1908–1909); Peter Force, ed., *American Archives*, 9 vols. (Washington, D. C., 1837–1853), 4.1:646–647, cf. pp. 358–365, 626–628, 4.3:625–627; Gage to Hillsborough, 6 Oct. 1770, *The Correspondence of General Thomas Gage*, ed. Clarence E. Carter, 2 vols. (New Haven, Conn., 1931, 1933), 1:271.

Figure 10.   Governor Hutchinson as seen by his countrymen in 1774.

the colonies, Dartmouth, termed the tea riot and its related activities criminal anarchy and usurpation. He ordered Hutchinson's successor, General Thomas Gage, to prosecute the offenders, especially their "ringleaders," *if* the prejudices and sympathies of the people would allow a successful indictment. Failure would cast an unfavorable light on British authority. Gage did not prosecute. Instead, he later proclaimed a general pardon excepting only Samuel Adams and John Hancock, both out of his reach at that time. He explained that strong measures against the leadership would have been necessary and effective long ago, "but at present it would be the Signal for Hostilities."[11]

GOVERNOR GAGE, THE COERCIVE ACTS, AND BOSTON WHIGS

Vast numbers of people assembled at Long Wharf on 13 May 1774 to watch the arrival of General Gage, the new governor. None of the customary celebrations took place. An address was presented to him by some and resented by others. The first message of the council contained what Gage considered a "censure" of his predecessor, and he retorted, "I consider this Address as an Insult upon His Majesty and the Lords of his Privy Council, and an Affront to myself."[12] Attempts of moderate merchants to bring about a compromise about the tea duty failed. They realized that the closing of the port of Boston, one of the punitive measures passed by Parliament, would hurt their short-term interests, so they circulated a subscription list for raising money to pay for the destroyed tea. Their efforts were opposed in the town meeting, and when further British restrictions were announced they retracted their offer. Large numbers of troops were to be quartered in town to enforce the so-called Regulating Acts. Instead of protesting or lamenting this, a letter from another colony congratulated Boston "upon her late great Deliverance" and continued, "The Time is come, so dreaded by Great Britain, that we are independent."[13]

In the years from the King Street riot to 1774, a number of incidents had kept the resentment against the British army and navy aflame among Bostonians. In 1772, after rumors that troops would again be quartered in town, the selectmen received

[11]Dartmouth to Gage, 9 April 1774, in Force, ed., *Archives,* 4.1:245–246. At that time Thomas Pownall suggested bringing Samuel Adams and William Molineux to trial in Britain. Hutchinson, *Diary and Letters,* 1:183, 191, 219. Edmund Burke, *On the American Revolution: Selected Speeches and Letters,* ed. Elliott R. Barkan (New York, 1966), p. 126; Gage to Dartmouth, 25 Sept. 1774, *Correspondence,* 1:375–376. Three days after the Massachusetts Provincial Congress received Gage's pardon, it published a "counterpardon" (16 June 1775), excepting only General Thomas Gage, Admiral Samuel Graves, and several mandamus councillors. William Lincoln, ed., *The Journals of Each Provincial Congress of Massachusetts in 1774–1775 . . .* (Boston, 1858), pp. 330–331, 344–347.

[12]John Boyle, "Boyle's Journal of Occurrences in Boston, 1759–1778," 17 May, 18 Aug. 1774, *NEHGR* 84:374, 378; Thomas Newell, "Diary," 17 May 1774, p. 352; John Rowe, *Letters and Diary of John Rowe, Boston Merchant, 1759–1762, 1764–1779,* ed. Anne Rowe Cunningham (Boston, 1903; reprint ed., 1969), 17 May 1774, pp. 270–271; John Andrews, "Letters of John Andrews, Esq., Boston, 1772–1776," ed. Winthrop Sargent, 16 Aug., 17 Aug. 1774, *MHSP* 8:342–343 (1864–1865); address of the council, 9 June 1774, and Gage's answer, *CSMP* 32:469–470 (1937); *BEP,* 23 May, 22 Aug. 1774; *BG,* 29 Aug. 1774.

[13]Rowe, *Letters and Diary,* 2 June, 14 July 1774, pp. 274, 278; Andrews, "Letters," 18 May 1774, p. 329; Boyle, "Journal," 3 June 1774, p. 375; Thomas Newell, "Diary," p. 353; Silas Downer to Palfrey, 12 July 1774, Palfrey Family Papers, box 3, no. 60, HHL.

two petitions for a town meeting. One was drawn up by William Mackay, of the group of merchant–captains, the other by Samuel Adams: "We shall not like to see again our streets stained with the Blood of our Brothers." The first regiments sent to discipline the inhabitants for the tea riot arrived in June 1774 and landed without molestation. The calm was deceptive, however, and there was little reason for Dartmouth "to suppose that the people [of Boston] will quietly submit to the Correction their ill conduct has brought upon them, and lay a foundation, by their future behaviour for a re-establishment of their Commercial Privileges."[14]

Of the four Coercive Acts, the Port Bill was designed specifically to punish Boston for the "dangerous commotions and insurrections" by closing its port and thus ruining the town economically. The Quebec Act granted tolerance for Catholics in Quebec and extended the province to include large territories west of the Alleghenies. This was a considerable grievance to the intolerant Calvinists and to land-hungry colonists in many other colonies. The other two acts attempted to curb the rise and progress of popular institutions in Massachusetts.[15] The Government Act condemned the "open resistance" and made the council appointive by the king. The councillors were to hold their offices "for and during the pleasure of his Majesty." This design to get a loyal executive body as well as upper house of the legislature was supplemented by a move against the participatory features of the political institutions in Massachusetts. Town meetings were outlawed except for the annual March and May meetings for election of town officials and representatives, because "a great abuse has been made of the power of calling such meetings, and the inhabitants have, contrary to the design of their institution, been misled to treat upon matters of the most general concern, and to pass many dangerous and unwarrantable resolves." The Administration of Justice Act was designed to remedy the popular influence on the third branch of government, the judicature, which had played an important role in the resistance to British authority:

> It is of utmost importance . . . to the re-establishment of lawful authority . . . , that neither the Magistrates acting in support of the laws, nor any of his Majesty's subjects aiding and assisting them therein, or in the suppression of riots and tumults . . . should be discouraged from the proper discharge of their duty.

If local juries were biased against magistrates who were sued for acts done in the execution of their duty, the trial could be moved to any other colony or to Great Britain.

Changes as outlined in the laws had been demanded by conservatives for a long time. Customs official Charles Paxton had called for an appointive council and recommended himself for a seat on it in 1764. "River God" Israel Williams, from

---

[14]Petitions, 28 June 1772, by Adams, Misc. Unbound Papers, 1772, BCH, by Mackay, HHL. *BTR* 23:133. Incidents: *BG,* 11 Nov. 1771, 24 Feb. 1772; *BEP,* 24 Feb. 1772, 17 April 1773; *Essex Gaz.,* 12 Nov. 1772, Dartmouth to Gage, 3 June 1774, *Correspondence,* 2:167–168; W. Glanville Evelyn. *Memoir and Letters of Capt. W. Glanville Evelyn, of the 4th Regiment ("King's Own") from North America, 1774–1775,* ed. G. D. Scull (Oxford, 1879), p. 27.

[15]Acts: Force, ed., *Archives,* 4.1:35–225. R. T. H. Halsey, *The Boston Port Bill as Pictured by a Contemporary London Cartoonist* (New York, 1904), including a chapter on women's reactions.

the Connecticut River Valley, hoped for more royal control in 1770 and expected "an alteration in the Constitution." A visitor from Britain was told by the "better kind of people" that they "lament their present Plan of Government, which throws too much weight into the popular scale." Governor Bernard had been told the same thing by "the thinking part" of the people.[16] Loyalist groups in other colonies were also faced with Whig politicians and merchants who advocated far-reaching self-determination for the colonies. Both sides feared the "lower sort."

The immediate danger was that the lower classes in Boston, which would suffer most from the Port Bill, since they were economically most vulnerable, might voice discontent and demand social and economic equality or policy changes that would help prevent starvation. To work out a policy concerning imperial relations in general and the Regulating Acts in particular that would ensure that existing structures would not be endangered, Boston leaders moved in a town meeting to elect a committee for considering "our Conduct in the present Exigency." After some debate the meeting was adjourned until the afternoon. Thus, time was gained to work out compromises, to rally voters, and to iron out differences among the leaders. The afternoon meeting brought forth an 11-man committee, obviously on a prepared slate: It was not elected, but it was "Moved and Voted, Nem. Cont., that . . . [these 11 men] be and hereby are appointed a Committee." The unanimity of the vote was achieved by making the committee nonpartisan. Samuel Adams headed the list, but two moderate merchants followed. The other eight were prominent men, of whom only Joseph Warren and William Molineux belonged to the avant-garde of the Whigs.[17]

This heterogeneous membership made it difficult to agree on a policy. Time elapsed, and the other colonies, whose attention was focused on Boston, were merely informed "that we are not idle." The direction of the committee's deliberations changed from "Ways and Means" of resistance to "employing the poor" and finally merely to "supplying the Poor." In the end the committee in a political masterstroke came up with an invitation to all colonies and towns to send donations for the Boston poor. This gave colonists from New Hampshire to Georgia the chance to participate in supporting resistance and at the same time prevented, or was intended to prevent, local social discontent. Innumerable meetings throughout America discussed whether relief should be sent; thousands contributed. General Gage blamed the success on "Those Demagogues," but Whigs felt that "kind Providence has raised up the whole Continent."[18]

---

[16]Paxton to Townshend, 22 Dec. 1764, Paxton Letters, MHS; Williams to Hutchinson, 8 May 1771, MA 154:90; Lord Adam Gordon, "Journal of Lord Adam Gordon," *Travels in the American Colonies,* ed. Newton D. Mereness (New York, 1916), Aug.–Sept. 1765, p. 449; Bernard to Barrington, 15 Dec. 1761, Sparks MSS., 4.2:23, HHL; Leslie to Haldimand, 20 Dec. 1773, *N.Y. Hist. Soc. Coll.,* 1881, p. 532. For moves to get royal governments in other colonies, see Morgan and Morgan, *Stamp Act Crisis,* pp. 16, 50–52, 150, 243 (Rhode Island); James H. Hutson, *Pennsylvania Politics 1746–1770: The Movement for Royal Government and Its Consequences* (Princeton, N.J., 1972).

[17]*BTR* 18:173, 175–178, 193 *passim.*

[18]Gage to Dartmouth, 26 June 1774, *Correspondence,* 1:357–358; Noyes to Henshaw, 13 July 1774, *NEHGR* 43:143–144 (1889). Richard D. Brown, in *Revolutionary Politics in Massachusetts: The Boston Committee of Correspondence and the Towns, 1772–1774* (Cambridge, Mass., 1970), p. 195, presents a different view of the "success" of the committee.

Boston's lower classes had a different idea. Instead of referring to "Demagogues" or "Providence," they suspected that part of the donations was gobbled up by the better-placed committeemen. When the port was closed to incoming ships on 1 June and to outbound vessels on 15 June 1774, distress became intense among many inhabitants. Some Bostonians left town to find work elsewhere; others were offered temporary work near Boston. But unemployment among "all classes of mechanics and labourers" rose alarmingly, and aside from attending to its extensive correspondence with the donating towns and individuals, the committee had two functions in Boston: to find employment for those out of work and to distribute the donations. Its well-to-do members decided to let the unemployed and poor do menial work to get the benefit of the donations. They were to build a wharf and houses on town lands, to clean docks, to dig a well, or to work on a brickyard. The selectmen employed the poor to repair and pave streets and fixed their wages. People from other towns complained that their donations paid for the repair of Boston streets. The suffering laborers in Boston "grumble[d] that they are obliged to work hard for that which they esteem as their right without work." The laborers at the brickyard were paid very little or not at all, and they decided to destroy the works. Boston's selectmen asked the British governor for a military guard against the laborers—and received it.

It was the implicit task of the committee to prevent discontent that would endanger the social structure, "to keep our poor from murmuring," as Samuel Adams put it. Some of the unemployed thought of working for the troops, which paid higher wages, but the tight rein of the committee and the dishonor associated with such work prevented that. Murmuring increased because of the autocratic conduct of the committee; indeed, its members had to publish two declarations in their own defense. Many unemployed people had applied for help—"great numbers of various classes . . . especially mechanics and laborers; of the latter the circumstances of much the greater part called for immediate relief." Reports spread among the applicants that the committee members received fees for their attendance and commissions on the donations, that they employed the poor to work for themselves or for their well-to-do friends. It is characteristic of the distrust of the poor toward the rich that the accounts found such willing ears. The committee succeeded, however, in keeping the social and economic tensions within limits. Admiral Graves admitted the failure of the British attempt to put economic pressure on those people whose economic situation was unstable, expecting that they in turn would pressure the Whig leadership. The opposite happened: The deferential character of the society, and especially the weak position of the laborers, permitted the officials to remain in office almost unmolested and to use the hard conditions to get cheap labor for public (or private) use. The other colonies stabilized this setup by their donations. The British lost their game, just as many little people lost what economic independence they hitherto had.[19]

---

[19]"Donations to Boston during the Siege," *MHSC* 2.9:158–166 (1822); "Correspondence in 1774 and 1775 between a Committee of the Town of Boston and Contributors of Donations for the Relief of the Sufferers by the Boston Port Bill," *MHSC* 4.4:15–16, 35, 66–67, 275–277, 277–278 (1858); William Cooper to New York, 12 Sept. 1774, in

While merchants and Whigs could agree on a policy demanding help from the other colonies to smother the mounting discontent of the lower classes, they could not agree on a policy toward Great Britain. A similar impasse in 1768 had led to crowd action and subsequent replacement of the old leadership. Always reluctant to rely on the people, Whig leaders this time managed to oust the moderates via a nominating committee, consisting of six men each from the populous Northend and Southend and 12 from the wealthy middle part of the town. The members, partly from the top of the town hierarchy but mainly from its middle section, reported a list of additional members for the committee for employing the poor. The town accepted the slate and named the nonpartisan group the Donations Committee.[20] Next, its predecessor, the original committee "relative to our Conduct in the present Exigency" reappeared as a separate body and, having failed to develop a policy, was dissolved. Then Samuel Adams, as moderator, turned the townsmen's attention to the next article in the warrant: "To determine on the Expediency of appointing a Committee of Seven by Ballot for the Purpose of Consulting proper Measures to be adopted for the common Safety, during these Exigencies of our public Affairs." Thus, the old committee had hardly been dissolved when a new exigency committee was proposed. Opposition was expected: Ballots were hardly ever mentioned in a warrant and rarely used for committee elections, but they had the advantage that they could be prepared beforehand. After considerable debate Samuel Adams, Joseph Warren, and John Adams were elected. So were William Philipps and Josiah Quincy. The first had chaired the nonimportation meeting that defied Hutchinson's orders to disperse; the latter was an ardent Whig and ardent in his adherence to legal forms, his opposition to crowds, and his distrust of merchants. The new members were James Bowdoin, under whose lead the council had shifted from supporting the governor to supporting the Whigs, and John Hancock, wealthy, popular, and pliable. The moderates were ousted.[21] But even before the new men, radical only in their attitude toward Great Britain, could act, the inhabitants of the province were acting on their own to defy the Coercive Acts, and soon Boston's leaders, especially the Committee of Correspondence, attempted to moderate them and to induce them to accept social distinctions.

DEFIANCE OF THE ADMINISTRATION OF JUSTICE ACT

Parts of the judicial branch of provincial government had been under popular pressure before the arrival of the Coercive Acts. Lenient attitudes toward soldiers in

---

Force, ed., *Archives,* 4.1:784–785, cf. 35–66; *BTR* 18:181, 182, 186, 188–189, 23:223; Graves to Stevens, 8 Aug. 1774, Graves Papers, 1:8–13, Gay Transcripts, MHS; Andrews, "Letters," 1 Aug., 2 Aug., 5 Aug. 1774, pp. 335, 337; Rowe, *Letters and Diary,* 1 June, 14 June 1774, p. 273; Henry Hulton to ———, 7 May 1775, Letterbooks, 1:146–153, HHL. Whether irregularities in fact occurred cannot be determined. The committee did employ men of dubious renown, Barrett and Molineux, in its financial transactions. "A British Officer [i.e., John Barker] in Boston in 1775," ed. R. H. Dana, *Atlantic Monthly* 39:389–401, 544–554 (1877), 20 Nov. 1774, p. 391 (hereafter: Barker, "Diary").
[20]*BTR* 18:177, 181–183, 193.
[21]*Ibid.,* pp. 183–185.

1769 and 1770 and pardons and compensation for convicted royal officials had reduced confidence in the legal process and provoked crowd action. In 1772 the governor and judges of the Superior Court of Judicature had been granted fixed stipends by the crown, making them independent from the provincial legislature's annual appropriation of salaries. Colonials were infuriated also because the salaries were paid by the commissioners from the customs revenues; a town meeting called this practice a dangerous innovation.

Whig leaders chartered the course of counteraction: "There is to be no riot." The judges wanted to accept the crown grants, arguing that they had to hand down unpopular decisions, as in the soldiers' trials in 1770. Should the court "differ in Judgement from the Mob what Sallery would the Judges have next Year!" Under popular pressures, including a crowd visit to Judge Nathaniel Ropes's home in Salem, and under prodding from the General Court, all judges with the exception of the chief justice finally declined to accept the crown grants. Chief Justice Peter Oliver was impeached, and jurors refused to serve while he remained on the bench.

When the Administration of Justice Act went into effect, opposition increased. Lawyers were told not "to appear in Court, or otherwise to do any Business with the Judges."[22] Officials executing these "unconstitutional" provisions were taught adherence to the old laws by crowds. Jurors, according to the new acts, were no longer chosen by the inhabitants but selected by sheriffs, who in turn were appointed by the governor. The clerks of the Suffolk and other courts were forced not to send out venires for jurors. The sheriff of Braintree, who had delivered court warrants, was visited twice by crowds. Before the rioters left, they voted "whether they should huzza, but it being Sunday evening," they remained quiet.[23]

To prevent any litigation from coming to court, county conventions devised arbitration measures, and the Committees of Correspondence took over judicial functions. In Newbury, criminal offenders were seized by crowds and paraded through town. A drummer preceded, and the offender had to proclaim his offenses.[24] In civil actions, debtor–creditor tensions did not increase after the courts were closed. "Any one who avails himself of the times, and keeps a creditor from his just due, ought to be despised by every good man."[25] Towns or regions with a relatively high percentage of debtors usually showed more zeal for closing the

[22]*Ibid.*, pp. 88–92, 133; Superior Court of Judicature, Minute Books, no. 98, Suffolk, 2 Sept. 1774, SCCH; jurors' declaration, in Force, ed., *Archives*, 4.1:747–749; Thomas Aylwin to ———, 23 Oct. 1772, William Cushing Papers, 1 vol. (1664–1780), MHS; Peter Oliver, *Peter Oliver's Origin and Progress of the American Rebellion: A Tory View*, ed. Douglass Adair and John A. Schutz (Stanford, Calif., 1961), pp. 107–111; James D. Phillips, *Salem in the Eighteenth Century* (Boston, 1937), pp. 317–318; Quincy, ed., *Reports*, pp. 340–342; Hutchinson, *History*, 3:317–326, "Additions," *AASP* 59:50–51 (on social composition of opponents); Noyes to Henshaw, 30 Aug. 1774, *NEHGR* 43:146–147; Andrews, "Letters," 30 Aug. 1774, p. 349; Thomas Newell, "Diary," 30 Aug. 1774, p. 357; advertisement of 1 Sept. 1774, Graves Papers, 1:16, Gay Transcripts, MHS; cf. Ballantine's Journal, 27 April 1774, Judd MSS., Rev. Matters, p. 160, Forbes Library; *BG*, 5 Sept. 1774, Supp.

[23]*Mass. Spy*, 1 Sept. 1774; Price's declaration, *MHSP* 2.14:52 (1900); Abigail Adams to John Adams, 2 Sept., 14 Sept. 1774, *Adams Family Correspondence*, ed. L. H. Butterfield, 2 vols. (Cambridge, Mass., 1963), 1:146–148, 151–152; *BG*, 12 Sept. 1774.

[24]Joshua Coffin, *A Sketch of the History of Newbury, Newburyport, and West Newbury, from 1635 to 1845* (Boston, 1845), p. 243.

[25]Andrews, "Letters," 13 Aug., 4 Sept. 1774, pp. 341, 355.

courts than others. But in these subsistence farming areas animosity against high fees and other inadequacies of the judicial process had a long tradition. Though some debtors in fact remained in arrears, these were often merchants from coastal towns who let their British creditors wait.

Proceedings against other courts involved more direct action than those against the Superior Court. In August 1774 a meeting in Pittsfield, Berkshire, decided to petition the justices of the Inferior Court not to sit. Fifteen hundred men, some from Connecticut, occupied the courthouse and adjoining streets, so that the justices could not enter. This was the basic pattern of most of these actions. The crowd reasoned that it would "be of dangerous consequences to do any business in the law" while the Regulating Acts were in force, because it would "imply some degree of submission to them." A Bostonian thought this crowd action "rather premature," but the complicated and costly court system was so hated in the west that people seized the opportunity without waiting for deadlines.[26]

Three hundred men from this crowd, coming from Litchfield, Connecticut, arrested David Ingersoll, lawyer and land speculator, who was particularly obnoxious because of his business dealings as well as his professed loyalty to Great Britain. A few days later he fled to Salem, but his reputation preceded him, and on his way he was set upon two or three times by crowds. His fellow townsmen laid waste to his enclosures to prevent his return. Eight "ringleaders" of the riot were arrested "without resistance," as a contemporary letter noted. But its author had hardly finished this sentence when he had to add: "But this minute there is entering the town on horseback, with great regularity, about fifty men, armed each with a white club; and I observe others continually dropping in." The prosecution accordingly remained unsuccessful.[27]

A convention for Hampshire County on 26 August ordered a court not to sit under the "new establishment." On the morning of 30 August, the day the court was to open at Springfield, the bells were set ringing, and soon judges and convention delegates were no longer the only guests in town. Bodies of men marched in with white staves. Many, from the west, had marched a whole day. Some Tories, whose homes they passed on their way, got a "trimming," among them a Captain Bancroft, who was apprehended two years later for aiding escaped British prisoners of war. Between 1500 and 3000 men occupied the courthouse and demanded from justices and lawyers an explicit and signed declaration not to accept any commission under the Regulating Acts.[28]

[26]J. E. A. Smith, *The History of Pittsfield (Berkshire County), Massachusetts, from the Year 1734 to the Year 1876*, 2 vols. (Boston, 1869, 1876), 1:194–197; George Sheldon, *A History of Deerfield*, 2 vols. (Deerfield, Mass., 1896), 2:681–682; letter from Great Barrington, 18 Aug. 1774, in Force, ed., *Archives*, 4.1:724; Andrews, "Letters," 23 Aug. 1774, p. 346.

[27]Ballantine's Journal, Aug.–Sept. 1774, Judd MSS., Rev. Matters, p. 152, Forbes Library; Aaron Burr to Mathias Ogden, 17 Aug. 1774, *Memoirs of Aaron Burr, with Miscellaneous Selections from His Correspondence*, ed. Matthew L. Davis, 2 vols. (New York, 1837–1838), 1:48–49; Frank Moore, ed., *Diary of the American Revolution from Newspapers and Original Documents*, 2 vols. (New York, 1860; reprint ed., 1969), 1:38. Ingersoll had been dismissed twice from offices for dishonesty: in 1749 as town clerk of Great Barrington and in 1755 as justice of the peace. Charles J. Taylor, *History of Great Barrington (Berkshire County), Massachusetts* (Great Barrington, Mass., 1882), p. 33; *Acts and Resolves*, 15:378; Andrews, "Letters," 6 Nov. 1774, p. 383.

[28]Ballantine's Journal, 29–31 Aug. 1774, Judd MSS., Rev. Matters, p. 152, Forbes Library; Westfield Committee

An eyewitness, one of the lawyers, described the further proceedings. A Deerfield Tory was forced to recant. One of the powerful landowners, John Worthington, resigned his office. "He attempted to harangue them in mittagation of his conduct, but was soon obliged to desist. The people were not to be dallied with." Lawyer Jonathan Bliss asked their pardon for any acts "contrary to their opinions." Accusations against his brother Moses proved unfounded. The sheriff got off with some reproaches. Then Colonel Israel Williams, a longstanding friend of Hutchinson and a beneficiary of his patronage, vindicated himself of the charges against him and promised compliance with all popular measures. A Captain Merrick had to appear next "for uttering imprudent expressions." Another offender, Mr. Stearns, did not come voluntarily, and Colonel Worthington's house was searched for him. The lawyer reported:

> No man received the least injury, but the strictest order of justice were observed. The people of each town being drawn into separate companies marched with staves and musick. The trumpets sounding, drums beating, fifes playing and Colours flying, struck the passions of the soul into a proper tone, and inspired martial courage into each.

There was probably more to the people's courage than military music.[29]

In the wake of the Springfield crowd action, smaller groups threatened Tories in the neighboring towns. Samuel Field of Greenfield "felt very low, as he expected to be mobbed." A crowd from Montague planned "to correct the Tories" of Deerfield, but there the inhabitants decided to take "measures to prevent these petty Mobbs," which broke with the tradition of united action for the public good. They sometimes mixed public with private motivations and were therefore discountenanced.

An action similar to the Springfield mass meeting, but larger, took place in Worcester on 6 September, when the courts were scheduled to open there. Nearly 5000 men assembled to prevent it. Middlesex men convened in Concord on 13 September and forced the justices to sign a declaration not to open the court and the sheriffs to sign a recantation of delivering the warrants for the session.[30] At a mass meeting in Barnstable, the people adopted customary town-meeting procedures— they chose a moderator, passed resolves, and voted on a variety of questions. They demanded a reorganization of the militia and asked the lawful councillors to attend

---

against Captain Bancroft, 20 June 1776, in Force, ed., *Archives*, 4.6:998; Sheldon, *Deerfield*, 2:682–683; Andrews, "Letters," 3 Sept. 1774, pp. 353–354.

[29]Joseph Clarke to ———, 30 Aug. 1774, in James R. Trumbull, *History of Northampton, Massachusetts*, 2 vols. (Northampton, Mass., 1902; 1st ed., 1898), 2:346–348; Jonathan Judd, Diary, 28 Aug. 1774, Judd MSS., Rev. Matters, p. 159, Forbes Library; same, undated entry, quoted in John Hoyt Lockwood, *Westfield and Its Historic Influences, 1669–1919*, 2 vols. (Springfield, Mass., 1922), 1:516; Ballantine's Journal, Aug.–Sept. 1774, Judd MSS., Rev. Matters, p. 152, Forbes Library; report from Hartford, 1 Sept. 1774, in Force, ed., *Archives*, 4.1:747; Judges of the Inferior Court for the County of Hampshire to Gage, 20 Sept. 1774, House of Lords MSS., 284:166–175; Account of the Proceedings against the Inferior Court at Springfield to Gage, 20 Sept. 1774, *ibid.*, pp. 177–180; Henry A. Booth, "Springfield during the Revolution," *Conn. Valley Hist. Soc. Papers and Proc.* 2:289 (1904).

[30]Quoted in Sheldon, *Deerfield*, 2:683–684; *BG*, 19 Sept. 1774.

the General Court at Salem to endeavor to achieve constitutional proceedings.

Their main target, however, was the Inferior Court. They gave the following reasons for their actions: (1) The new acts were unconstitutional, (2) appeals would come before the Superior Court, where an impeached chief justice was presiding, and (3) judicial decisions would be executed by unconstitutional sheriffs, while unresolved cases would be unavoidably delayed, which meant increased costs for the litigants. Thus, suspension of all action was the best solution. The judges, who were informed of this resolve by a committee, had a different opinion: Not the people, but only a representative, even if unconstitutional, body could determine whether the courts should be closed. (The judges lost their fees when they did not sit.)

> Therefore, we the said justices, express our utmost concern that the said courts of justice, in this, or any other county, should be turned out of their ordinary, or constitutional course, by people of this province, until the minds of the continental or a provincial congress can be fully known.[31]

The mass meeting peaceably received the justices' opinion, debated it "thoroughly," and outlined the characters of those who had given it: Two justices were addressers to Hutchinson; one of them was an "old Recinder";[32] two had voted against a general congress; one or more of them had assisted in vending the East India tea of Captain Loring's brig last winter; and "another [was] concerned in endeavouring to procure a mob to destroy private property, on purpose, as they apprehended, to bring an odium on the friends of liberty." This was sufficient to discredit any opinion. The justices remained dissatisfied, but they submitted, and several of them recanted. Officials in other branches of government did not fare better. The people were not going to permit any magistrate to act under the unconstitutional Regulating Acts—they might become too fond of their position and the concomitant material rewards.[33]

DEFIANCE OF THE GOVERNMENT ACT

Town meetings were designed to deal with "any business of public concernment to the town," but interpretations of what concerned the public varied. The intention had been the regulation of local affairs, but occasionally, and since the late sixties with increasing frequency, the meetings acted on provincial and imperial questions. The Government Act restricted them to the choice of town officers.

---

[31]*BG*, 31 Oct. 1774.

[32]"Rescinders" were those 17 representatives who in 1768 had obeyed Hillsborough's order to the Massachusetts House of Representatives to rescind the letter sent to the other colonies to coordinate measures against the Townshend duties.

[33]In New York in 1775, proceedings against a court led to bloodshed, the "Westminster Massacre." A crowd had assembled in Westminster (Cumberland County) and occupied the courthouse. The sheriff succeeded in raising a posse, and in the ensuing battle one rioter was killed and several were wounded. The hostilities arose in part from the manor lord–tenant tensions. Abner Sanger, "Ye Journal of Abner Sanger," *Repertory*, vols. 1–2 (1924–1927), 13 March 1775, 1:74–77; *BEP*, 27 March 1775; cf. reports from New York, 23 March 1775, in Force, ed., *Archives*, 4.2:214–218; Moore, ed., *Diary of the Revolution*, 1:50–52.

On 13 August Gage read the Government Act to the Boston selectmen, emphasizing the clause that forbade meetings without the special permission of the governor. He was going to leave town soon, and, as one of the selectmen reported with obvious gusto, he "chose to give us this Information" so that if any meetings were wanted and "if he should Judge it expedient he would allow one to be called." The selectmen politely informed him that his efforts were unnecessary, because two meetings stood adjourned and the law did not cover adjournments of meetings called before it went into effect. "On this information he looked serious and said 'he must think upon that,' adding 'that by thus doing we might keep the Meetings alive for ten years.'" This was exactly their intention, but they were counting on fewer than 10 years. They retorted that there was nothing to think about, that the law was the law and they, as lawfully chosen officers, were bound to obey it. Gage replied ("we thought with some degree of temper") that he would enforce the new acts of Parliament.[34]

The clause relating to town meetings was either not observed at all or simply rendered ineffectual by endless adjournments. Boston continued its May meeting 14 times till 1 January 1775, the Port Bill meeting 26 times. Additionally, to exhaust all possibilities, the selectmen called separate meetings for the purpose allowed by the act—election of officials. These meetings proceeded to other business when the elections were finished, without leave or interference by the governor. Other towns were not intimidated either. No week passed without a town meeting held somewhere "in direct contempt of the Act; which they regard as a blank piece of paper and not more." A Marblehead town meeting convened to consider the "alarming situation" and to resolve measures "that appear to be constitutional," which the Regulating Acts were not, and then adjourned 46 times till April 1775.[35]

Noncompliance was to be expected in the towns out of reach of the troops. But even Salem, the new seat of government, where troops were quartered, held a meeting. On 22 August the townsmen, or those who had enough courage, assembled and elected five delegates for an extralegal county convention, the purpose of which was to determine arbitration procedures to circumvent the courts and thus the Administration of Justice Act. General Gage ordered the troops to march to the townhouse. In Marblehead and other adjacent towns, armed men assembled, 3000 according to one account, to assist the people in Salem. Gage ordered the soldiers back. He then summoned the Committee of Correspondence, charged the members with "high crimes and misdemeanoures" for calling the meeting, and threatened to arrest them. The committeemen refused to give bail and dropped a hint that the militia was assembling in the country. Gage dropped the matter, "seeing them resolute and the people so determinate." The civil magistrate who had attempted to execute Gage's order to arrest the committee soon resigned "all his posts of *honor* and *profit*" because country people refused to sell provisions to him and because the

---

[34]*BTR* 23:224–225; Andrews, "Letters," 13 Aug. 1774, p. 341; *BEP,* 15 Aug. 1774; Gage to Dartmouth, 27 Aug. 1774, *Correspondence,* 1:365–368.

[35]*BTR* 18:166–224; Andrews, "Letters," 28 Aug. 1774, pp. 347–348; Henry Hulton to ———, 24 Aug. 1774, Letterbooks, 1:102–103, HHL; Samuel Roads, *The History and Traditions of Marblehead* (Boston, 1880), pp. 97–98.

inhabitants did not help his starving family. His recantation appeared a few days later in the *Boston Gazette*.[36]

On 29 August, rumors spread in Boston that Gage had sent one or two companies to Roxbury to break up a town meeting. But without being disturbed, the inhabitants forced two crown officials to resign or leave. A Danvers meeting was held "directly under his [Gage's] nose," his show of force in Salem notwithstanding. The townsmen "continued it two or three howers longer than was necessary, to see if he would interrupt 'em. He was made acquainted with it, but reply'd—'Damn 'em! I wont do any thing about it unless his Majesty sends me more troops." The town meetings were supplemented by a form of regional government, county conventions from which "we promise ourselves great benefitt." They drew timid towns into the opposition and were agents of stabilization and unity through concerting local measures against courts and officials.[37]

Opposition was not limited to specific institutions. Government officials all over the country were ordered to renounce their commissions by committees, conventions, and crowds. The high sheriffs for Middlesex, Essex, and Cumberland were forced to resign. Many of their deputies followed suit. The governor had "all his Cabinet papers, Ministers' Letters, &c., and his Correspondence all stole" from Province House. A reward had to be offered to get the stolen province seal back. Gage summarized the failure of the acts in a letter to Lord Dartmouth: The Regulating Acts have been "published here, and People have had Leisure to consider Means to elude them, in doing which they are very expert."[38]

While Bostonians often confined their hopes for strong resistance to their diaries, people farther from the reach of the troops had no need to restrain themselves: "The little Town of Marlborough has had the Audacity to burn the Genl in effigy." The representatives simply locked the doors from the inside when a messenger from the governor came to dissolve the General Court. While the province secretary stood outside with the proclamation, the representatives elected delegates to the extralegal Continental Congress.[39]

The council, which had been elective throughout the colony's history, was made appointive by the Government Act. The town-meeting clause of the act had been opposed by civil disobedience; the dislike of the "Mandamus Council" manifested

[36] Andrews, "Letters," 23 Aug., 9 Sept. 1774, pp. 345, 357; John White, "Extracts from the Interleaved Almanacs Kept by John White of Salem," 24 Aug. 1774, *EIHC* 49:92 (1913); Palfrey to Samuel Adams, Sept. 1774, Cadet Company, Records, Boston Univ. *BG*, 5 Sept., 12 Sept. 1774; Salem town meeting, 24 Aug. 1774, in Force, ed., *Archives*, 4.1:730.

[37] Andrews, "Letters," 29 Aug., 6 Sept. 1774, pp. 348, 355. Andrews added that these meetings, as well as assemblies of armed men ("riots" by law, or even treason), observed "as much good order decorum . . . as when attending church on Sundays."

[38] Thomas Smith and Samuel Deane, *Journals of the Rev. Thomas Smith and the Rev. Samuel Deane, Pastors of the First Church in Portland*, ed. William Willis (Portland, Me., 1849), 21 Sept. 1774, 8 April 1775, pp. 335–336; Joseph B. Felt, *The Annals of Salem from Its First Settlement* (Salem, Mass., 1827), p. 490; Belcher Noyes, Diary, 17 April 1775, AAS; Oliver, *American Rebellion*, pp. 153–154; Gage to Dartmouth, 27 Aug. 1774, *Correspondence*, 1:365–368; Boston Committee of Donations to Norwich, 27 Aug. 1774, *MHSC* 4.4:46–47.

[39] Andrews, "Letters," 10 Sept., 11 Sept., 22 Sept. 1774, pp. 358, 365–366; *BG*, 24 Oct. 1774; Ashley Bowen, "Diary of Ashley Bowen," June 1774, *Mass. Mag.* 3:243 (1910); Anne Hulton, *Letters of a Loyalist Lady* (Cambridge, Mass., 1927), 8 July 1774, p. 74; Gage to Dartmouth, 26 June 1774, *Correspondence*, 1:357.

itself in crowd action and violence against the individual councillors. They were ostracized in their communities. Their families were threatened, and the shops of their relatives were boycotted. One of the "unconstitutional Councillors" was ousted from his position as church deacon, and the appearance of another caused the parishioners to leave the service. A third, returning from Connecticut to his home town, was ill-treated by several crowds. News of his coming was relayed from town to town until he finally "freely and solemnly" declared his resignation. "They hunt the new Councillors," noted one observer.[40]

The action against Councillor Timothy Paine exemplifies the complicated logistics necessary to execute these mass actions. Notice was given to assemble on the common of Worcester on 26 August. Men from the surrounding towns began to converge on Worcester, marching in companies with elected leaders, often militia officers. By 9 A.M. more than 2000 had arrived. Each company elected two or three men to a central committee. The group thus constituted found itself too numerous and in turn chose a subcommittee, which summoned Paine. He had to resign, hat in hand, before the crowd. Five hundred men then continued to Rutland, where John Murray lived. While they entered the town, another 1000 men from three other townships arrived. Most were armed only with sticks; the others stacked their guns at the town entrance to prevent accidents. A committee searched Murray's house, but he had escaped even though sentries had been placed around town. The crowd left a note informing him that they had come "to converse with him upon his new and unconstitutional Appointment and Acceptance as a Councellor." He was ordered to publish a written resignation in the Boston papers by 10 September, or the people would return. His son, who expostulated with the men, telling them that the consequences of their actions would be "Rebellion, Confiscation and Death," was curtly informed that rebellion is better than slavery.[41]

Before the men marched on toward Hardwick to "converse" with Councillor Ruggles, scouts returned and reported that he had fled. Upon this news, they left for their home towns, but not without sending riders off to inform the people along the route Ruggles was taking that he had not yet resigned. By the time he reached a friend in Freetown, 3000 men from seven surrounding townships were getting ready to march. This precipitated his departure for Boston, where the British troops could protect him.[42]

[40]Albert Matthews, ed., "Documents Relating to the Last Meetings of the Massachusetts Royal Council, 1774–1776," *CSMP* 32:460–504 (1937); *BEP*, 29 Aug. 1774; Andrews, "Letters," 23 Aug., 24 Aug. 1774, p. 346; Ezra Stiles, *The Literary Diary*, ed. F. B. Dexter, 3 vols. (New York, 1901), 26 Aug. 1774, 1:455; Ballantine's Journal, Aug.–Sept. 1774, Judd MSS., Rev. Matters, p. 152, Forbes Library; Thomas Hutchinson, Jr., to Elisha Hutchinson, 22 Sept. 1774, Hutchinson–Oliver Papers, MHS, 4 reels from originals in Egerton MSS. and Add. MSS., Brit. Museum, 1:100, i.e., Egerton MSS., 2659, p. 100; Ellis Gray to Thomas Dolbeare, 15 Sept. 1774, *MHSP* 14:315–316 (1876); report from New London and Taunton, Aug.–Sept. 1774, in Force, ed., *Archives*, 4.1:731–732; *BG*, 5 Sept. 1774.

[41]*BPB*, 29 Aug. 1774; *BG*, 5 Sept. 1774, Supp.; William Paine to Gage, 27 Aug. 1774, *CSMP* 32:476–478; Daniel Murray to his father, 28 Aug. 1774, *CSMP* 32:478–479; Edward A. Jones, *The Loyalists of Massachusetts, Their Memorials, Petitions, and Claims* (London, 1930), pp. 216–217; unsigned notice to printers of the *Mass. Gaz.*, Walcutt Papers, 1671–1866, 2 vols., 1:38, MHS; Albert A. Lovell, *Worcester in the War of Revolution* (Worcester, Mass., 1876), pp. 43–45; William Thomas, "Memoranda," Aug.–Nov. 1774, *EIHC* 14:265 (1877).

[42]Gage to Dartmouth, 27 Aug. 1774, *Correspondence*, 1:365–368; Oliver to Ruggles, 19 Aug. 1774, *CSMP* 32:476;

When the news of these incidents spread, some councillors did not wait for the people to act as a crowd. Thomas Hutchinson, Jr., resigned at Milton. Isaac Winslow appeared at an illegal Roxbury town meeting, apologized for having accepted the seat, and resigned. Another councillor from Roxbury, "the drunken Commodore" Joshua Loring, asked for a period of grace. This was granted. In the evening a crowd surrounded his house, but only to inform him pleasantly that they too would give him 24 hours to consider resignation before taking action against him. Loring left for Boston without resigning. Angered, 200 men threatened to pull down his house unless he published a recantation within 48 hours.[43]

Action by the British troops in Charlestown and Cambridge on 1 September[44] triggered the largest and most successful mass action against councillors and other officials. William Brattle, whose information about unrest in the militia had prompted General Gage to order the troops out, was visited by a small crowd, which then visited Attorney General Sewall's house. Mrs. Sewall silenced them, explained that her husband was away, and asked for civil treatment for herself and her children.[45] The crowd was of "indifferent spirits," but violence increased after friends of Sewall accidentally fired a gun from inside his house. Those besieged went out and explained that the shot had not been fired intentionally. This satisfied the crowd. Someone told the defenders that they "had fought like brave fellows," and after some debate and a few glasses of wine, the rioters left.[46]

The accounts of the military action spread overnight, and early the next morning, on 2 September, thousands from surrounding towns approached Cambridge. Nervous Whigs from the Cambridge and Charlestown Committees of Correspondence attempted to prevent this "extraordinary Movement," at the same time sending urgent messages to Boston asking the leaders to help prevent "immediate acts of violence as incredible numbers were in arms." Those passing Attorney General Sewall's house and seeing the broken windows from the previous evening's action expressed their dislike of such behavior. They had no intention of proceeding in a disorderly fashion or of relinquishing control to faint-hearted committees of established Whigs. An observer, one of the defenders of Sewall's house, "had not the least Reason" to suspect similar violence from the 4000 men present.[47] Waltham, Watertown, Concord, Charlestown, and Framingham were represented. Somewhat

---

letter from Taunton, in Force, ed., *Archives*, 4.1:732; evidence of Timothy Ruggles, B.F. Stevens, Transcripts of American Loyalist Claims, NYPL, "Massachusetts Claims," 13:321, MF in MHS.

[43]Andrews, "Letters," 30 Aug. 1774, p. 349; Noyes to Henshaw, 30 Aug. 1774, *NEHGR* 43:146–147 (1889); Loring's narrative, and Pepperell to Gage, 31 Aug. 1774, *CSMP* 32:480–481, 482–483.

[44]For the military action, the powder seizure, see Chapter 11.

[45]Untitled paper with marginal notation "Tea Notes, 1774," in Sewell Papers, Public Archives of Canada, partly published in L. S. F. Upton, ed., *Revolutionary versus Loyalist: The First American Civil War, 1774–1784* (Waltham, Mass., 1968), pp. 4–6.

[46]Ward Chipman, who had the gun, later explained to the Royal Commission in support of his claim that he had fired intentionally. B. F. Stevens, American Loyalist Claims, 14:397, 401, MHS. Cf. Joseph Warren to Samuel Adams [4 Sept. 1774], in Richard Frothingham, *Life and Times of Joseph Warren* (Boston, 1865), pp. 355–357.

[47]Tea Notes, 1774, pp. 7629–7637, Sewell Papers, Public Archives of Canada; William Tudor to Abigail Adams, 3 Sept. 1774, *Adams Family Correspondence*, 1:149; Thomas Newell, "Diary," 2 Sept. 1774, p. 357; Rowe, *Letters and Diary*, 2 Sept., 3 Sept. 1774, p. 284; Andrews, "Letters," 2 Sept 1774, pp. 351–352; Hannah Winthrop to Mercy Warren, 27 Sept. 1774, *Warren–Adams Letters*, 1:32–33.

later the men from Marlborough arrived after an all-night march (30 miles). Each company delegated one or two men for a joint committee to negotiate with the officials. The primary target, William Brattle, had fled. Lieutenant Governor and Councillor Thomas Oliver was sent to Boston to stop General Gage from ordering out troops.[48]

About 10 o'clock the committee began to negotiate with Councillors Danforth and Lee at the latter's house. The crowd waited on the common; some men with horses acted as messengers. The committee of 10 or 12 men, "very serious and rather pensive," advised them to resign and to do so publicly, since decisions behind closed doors would not be accepted by the people. The companies drew up before the courthouse; the committeemen joined their respective companies and did not direct the resignation procedure. When Danforth asked the men what they wanted, "a Bystander" answered that the two councillors should resign their seats "on the new Plan." Both did so. Danforth declared that "he could not be suspected of accepting from Views of Honor or Profit," as he had been on the council for 40 years and of late the post seemed to be regarded as dishonorable. This note, sounded in other mass meetings, evidenced an important shift in the attitudes of the people. For years the principal point of contention had been that the rulers profited from their positions. Now the position itself—rank and honor—were deemed inconsistent with the people's liberties. Danforth had to repeat his declaration to the companies further off because they had not been able to hear him. Each of the two answers was accepted by separate votes. Upon a question from the crowd about whether they had treated Lee and Danforth as respectfully as promised, Lee admitted that they were "the most extraordinary People that he ever saw for Sobriety and Decency etc." on such an occasion.[49]

At this point the Boston Committee of Correspondence arrived: Warren, Cooper, Young, Molineux, Bradford, and Greenleaf. Contrary to what the ad hoc committeemen of the companies did, they stood on the steps of the courthouse. William Cooper addressed the people. In the name of the committee and the town of Boston, he thanked them "for their Readiness to serve the Cause of the Country . . . [and] for discovering such a Spirit of Jealousy over their Rights and Priviledges." Having thus complimented them, he began to show his real concern: their spontaneous and determined action. As he had attempted to hush up the discontent about the tea importation by Whig merchants in 1773, he now hushed up the military action, seizure of the province's powder stores. The captain general of the province, Gage, had a right to take the powder, so the Bostonians could not and did not oppose him. Besides, the powder was old and wet. Molineux spoke to the same effect. Captain Bradford, on the other hand, tugged at Cooper's sleeve to stop him and was in turn told to keep quiet. He spoke up when Molineux had ended and disputed Cooper's and Molineux's opinion. The seizure was illegal because it was done without the advice of the legal, (that is, the old) council. Then Mr. Devans of Charlestown, one

---

[48]Edward Hill's report, 4 Sept. 1774, *Adams Family Correspondence*, 1:149; Hutchinson, *Diary and Letters*, 1:320–321.

[49]Lee to Gage, 1 Sept. 1774, *CSMP* 32:483; Tea Notes, 1774, p. 7630, Sewell Papers, Public Archives of Canada.

of those who early in the morning had attempted to persuade the companies to return to their towns, quickly stepped in to contradict Bradford: "his Excellency had a Right to take it and by that Charter which they [the crowd] were constantly striving to preserve and defend." (The "state of nature," often referred to even by men as moderate as John Andrews, was not once mentioned.) Either Young or Cooper then put an end to the haggling by proposing that the men vote "that they abhorred and detested all petty Mobs, Riots, Breaking Windows and destroying private Property." The vote was unanimous; the men had said so earlier anyway and conducted themselves accordingly. But the Bostonians' biggest blunder was still to come. Cooper, revealing his total lack of understanding of the situation, suggested that the crowd go to the common, while the Boston committee would sit at Captain Stedman's inn, since the day was very hot. He "would be very glad if they would chose a Committee (1 or 2 from each Company)" to come to the tavern "to confer about the Situation." He was drily informed that committeemen had been elected hours earlier.[50]

This surprising failure to understand the situation and the intentions of the "fine body of respectable freemen" (Warren) is easily explained by the nature of the "radicalism" of the Boston leadership. Their constitutional doctrines were more developed than those of the crown officials, but the stratification and deferential character of Bostonian society made them blind to the social implications of the theory of popular sovereignty. They acted as they were accustomed to at celebrations: The gentlemen drank toasts inside Faneuil Hall, and the people huzzahed outside. Now in Cambridge the action had been done by "the people," and elected spokesmen were literally overlooked by the Boston "radicals" because they did not separate from their constituents, because they did not act like the dignified and elevated "better sort." The Boston leaders, on the other hand, attempted at once physically and politically to separate from the people. They would rather sustain their avowed enemy, the British general, than accept the spontaneous action of the Massachusetts farmers.

In the course of the proceedings, Colonel Phips, county sheriff for Middlesex, and Thaddeus Mason, clerk of the Middlesex court, had to promise not to act under the new "tyrannic Parliamentary Edicts." The Bostonians unsuccessfully tried to convince the people that the officials had so far acted legally and under orders. When Lieutenant Governor Oliver came back from Boston, he too was advised to inform the people on the common directly about his conference with the governor. He reported that he had explained to Gage that the crowd was not a mob, but consisted of freeholders and had convinced him of this. A long debate ensued about his offices. Finally he had to sign his resignation as councillor.[51]

While Oliver's case was under consideration, customs official Hallowell passed through Cambridge in a carriage followed by a mounted and liveried servant. Two

---

[50]*Ibid.*, pp. 7632–7634. *BG*, 5 Sept. 1774.

[51]Tudor to Adams, 3 Sept. 1774, *Adams Family Correspondence*, 1:149; Andrews, "Letters," 4 Sept. 1774, p. 354; Graves to Stevens, Sept. 1774, Graves Papers, 1:16–18; Gay Transcripts, MHS; Oliver, *American Rebellion*, p. 153; accounts of Thomas Oliver *et al.*, in Force, ed., *Archives*, 4.1:762–766, his letters, *CSMP* 32:488, 489, 492.

of the customs commissioners had gone through town on that day, but little notice had been taken. The hotheaded Hallowell commented on the crowd, and within minutes 160 men were ready on horses to pursue him. The Boston leaders interposed, explaining that business with the councillors should be finished first to avoid confusion. Thomas Young, more sympathetic to the mass action than his colleagues Cooper and Molineux, "delivered his mind very fully," probably to gain time and permit Hallowell to escape. One man disagreed, set out in pursuit, and stopped Hallowell. After a scuffle Hallowell mounted the horse of his Negro servant and fled toward Boston. Driven too hard, the horse collapsed just inside the town gates. No pursuer was in sight. But without even turning to look, Hallowell ran directly into the military camp, shouting that he was pursued by large numbers of armed men who could arrive any minute. The camp was thrown into confusion. Observant Bostonians sent messages to Cambridge that troops were getting ready to march. Then, watching the nervous bustle in the camp, they told the soldiers to settle down—there were merely two boys in Cambridge playing the fife. Hallowell had been exaggerating once again. Soon scouting soldiers returned to substantiate that no countrymen were coming toward Boston.

Among the crowd in Cambridge, rumors spread at the same time that Hallowell had shot a man—he pulled the trigger of his pistol but no shot went off—and that the troops were opening fire on the inhabitants. Drums beat the alarm, patrols were sent out, a detachment rode off to fetch the arms from where they had been stored in the morning, and a bridge was taken away to prevent the passing of the Regulars. But the scouts came back and contradicted the rumors, and the debates were resumed, "sober" and without "the least Flurry of Passion." The people in the crowd took their measures as a matter of fact. Joshua Green, from Boston, dispassionately noted, "Went to Cambridge—Lt: Govr: &c ther resign'd actg: as Councellors, thousands present." Resistance had become normal.[52]

Late in the afternoon most companies departed. About 100 men remained and, on the next day, ordered a few more officials to resign. In Weston, Deputy Sheriff Elijah Harrington had to recant on the same day, and 300 men crowded around the house of their representative. They "made his Mightiness walk through their Ranks with his Hat off and express his Sorrow for past Offenses, and promised not to be guilty of the like for the future." A few more councillors were visited by crowds: William Brown in Salem, Nathaniel Ray Thomas in Marshfield by 2000 "of the substantial Yeomanry" of several neighboring towns. Two of the famous "River Gods," Israel Williams and Colonel Worthington, afraid of crowd action, resigned.[53]

[52]Tea Notes, 1774, p. 7637, Sewell Papers, Public Archives of Canada; Andrew, "Letters," 2 Sept., 3 Sept. 1774, pp. 352–353; *BG*, 5 Sept., 3 Oct. 1774; Henry Hulton to ———, 8 Sept. 1774, Letterbooks, 1:104–107, HHL. Joshua Green, Interleaved Almanacs, 1766, 1770–1774, 2 Sept. 1774, NEHGS; letters from Gage and Oliver, *CSMP* 32:484–487. Oliver first spoke of the "landholders of this Country" when talking about the crowd; after his forced resignation, he changed the tune to the "lower class." Three customs officials passed Cambridge on that day. As on many other occasions, only Hallowell was molested. He seemingly had a particular talent for antagonizing people; contemporaries called him a "hot-spur."

[53]Andrews, "Letters," 6 Sept. 1774, p. 356; *BG* and *BEP*, 12 Sept. 1774. Representative Jones of Weston was one of the most important men in town. He had been selectman, overseer, assessor, and representative. Letter from Williams,

By 5 September, 20 of the 36 mandamus councillors had resigned or refused to be sworn. Many had fled to Boston, but even there, under the protection of the troops, they were not altogether safe. Disguised men surrounded their houses at night. Four of them lodged in Quaker Lane and had soldiers quartered in their houses to defend them against nightly molestations. In the same lane several Whig craftsmen had their shops. Each had a bell installed at his house, and whenever one of the refugee councillors passed, the inhabitants knew for whom the bells tolled. The town of Boston refused to do any business with them and enforced this resolve on individuals in its service.[54]

When Governor Gage called the council, or what was left of it, to assemble at Salem, he "found a shyness in several towards giving an opinion." They informed Gage that it would be dangerous for them to go to Salem. Some asked that their appointments be kept secret. Gage had to meet them at Boston, contrary to the law, and reportedly put them under "town arrest" because he was afraid that once they left they would comply with popular demands. They were so obnoxious to the people for having betrayed their country that the governor avoided them as much as possible, because "their Advice would add no weight to the authority of Government, but rather be an argument for disobedience."[55]

Thus, by the beginning of September both houses of the legislature were unable to act in their old institutional framework. The executive officials, from governor to sheriff's deputies, were paralyzed. On the other hand, locally elected town magistrates, from selectmen to constables, continued to function. Crowd and town-meeting action in defiance of the Government and Administration of Justice Acts had begun about 20 August. Disturbed by the extent of it, the governor began to make plans to hold the courts under protection of troops, which—so he thought—could at the same time protect the councillors. But the councillors were already fleeing to Boston in droves, and even if the judges could have been protected, little would have been achieved, since jurors would refuse to appear. The frightened councillors suggested that for their protection it would be best to keep all troops at hand. Six days after he had decided to send troops into the country, Gage had to fortify Boston Neck and to increase the guards at the ferries. There were rumors that the countrymen "intend to fling in about fifteen thousand [militiamen] by the way of the Neck, and as many more over the ferry." Resignedly the governor reported, "the Flames of Sedition had spread universally throughout the Country, beyond conception." He had to admit that "there was no knowing where to send them [the troops] to be of Use." Furthermore, if the troops were divided into small detachments, the people might be tempted "to fall upon them." On 10 September, three weeks after the first mass action, most troops were withdrawn from Salem, Massachusetts' capital according to the Government Act. The governor, other officials,

concurred with by Worthington, 10 Aug. 1774, *MHSC* 4.10:715–716. As in the case of the importers in 1768–1770, inhabitants of other towns were on the lookout for the councillors. Cf. *Legion,* Brds. (New York, 27 Oct. 1774).

[54]*BG,* 5 Sept. 1774; Gage to Dartmouth, 27 Aug. 1774, *Correspondence,* 1:365–368; Graves to Stevens, 31 Aug. 1774, Graves Papers, 1:14–16, Gay Transcripts, MHS; Andrews, "Letters," 12 Sept. 1774, p. 359; *BTR* 23:245.

[55]Gage to Dartmouth, 25 Aug., 2 Sept., 15 Dec. 1774, *CSMP* 32:473–474, 474–475, 493; Andrews, "Letters," 4 Sept., 19 Nov. 1774, pp. 354, 385–386; Percy to Harvey, 21 Aug. 1774, *Letters of Hugh Earl Percy from Boston and New York, 1774–1776,* ed. Charles K. Bolton (Boston, 1902), pp. 35–37.

and the Board of Customs commissioners all returned to Boston, the last foothold of the British.[56]

At the beginning of October, the representatives convened in Salem for the session of the General Court in defiance of the governor's orders. In accordance with their constituents' instructions, they immediately decided to adjourn to Watertown and there reconstituted themselves into a Provincial Congress. All officials who received commissions under the new acts were ordered to renounce their "disgraceful" and "detestable" appointments within 10 days after publication of the resolve. By that time, none was left to resign; the crowds had seen to that. The representatives were merely rubber-stamping spontaneous actions in hopes of changing from followers of the people back into their leaders. With the customary condescension they could not forbear advising "the good people of this province" not to molest those officials who resigned.[57]

The crowds had very clear notions about what they were intending and how they went about it. From the description of the actions the deliberate and discriminating nature should be clear. At the Worcester mass meeting the case of each official was weighed and decided on its individual merits. In Pittsfield and Springfield, the crowds explained their reasons for preventing the courts from sitting. At Barnstable the crowd, before dispersing, gave a plain statement of what they considered their role to be in the frame of provincial society, institutions, and ideas:

> And this body have not met together in a riotous, wanton or disorderly manner, with a design of injuring the person or property of any body, nor passed the above votes and resolutions in opposition to good government, or disloyalty to our sovereign; but from a painful necessity of exerting ourselves, in a serious, steady and determined manner, to prevent the total extirpation of liberty, justice and religion from our land.[58]

In this and their resolutions, the assembled people at once showed their opposition to disorder, as committed by "*petty* mobs," which had no backing of the community, though they might be leadership dominated; and their opposition to compromises about their constitutional rights as they, in contrast to judges and other magistrates, understood them. The period of riots against individual officials who had violated their trust was past, as was the time of deferential waiting for decisions to be made by authorities. Crowds acted against thieves and judges, against disorders and perverted institutions. They intended "to procure a due submission to the laws of the land" by everyone. "Government has now devolved upon the people; and they seem to be for using it."[59]

---

[56]Andrews, "Letters," 2 Sept., 10 Sept. 1774, pp. 352, 358; Anne Hulton, *Letters*, 8 July 1774, p. 74; cf. "Hugh Finlay['s Journal] in 1773," 11 Oct. 1773, in G. F. Dow, ed., *Two Centuries of Travel in Essex County* (Topsfield, Mass., 1921), p. 78; Gage to Dartmouth, 27 Aug., 2 Sept. 1774, *Correspondence*, 1:365–368, 369–372; Council Records, 31 Aug. 1774, *CSMP* 32:475–476; Hutchinson, *Diary and Letters*, 1:224.

[57]Lincoln, ed., *Journals of Each Provincial Congress*, 21 Oct. 1774, pp. 24–25.

[58]*BG*, 31 Oct. 1774.

[59]Ballantine's Journal, 7 Sept. 1774, Judd MSS., Rev. Matters, p. 152, Forbes Library. "This must bring on confusion," added the prejudiced commentator, more active in filling the pages of his diary than the ranks of crowds.

Resistance against Troops: Noncooperation and War

11

THE TRIGGER—A MILITARY EXPEDITION TO CHARLESTOWN

The mass action of about 4000 men at Cambridge on 2 September was only a small part of the total consequences of the first and only successful British military action in Massachusetts. Its main consequences were a spontaneous mobilization of tens of thousands of militiamen and, in the subsequent weeks, an acceleration of the reorganization of the militia, begun by the rank-and-file militiamen, to secure its independence from the royal governor and his appointees.

On 29 August Brigadier William Brattle, who in 1765 had paraded the streets of Boston arm in arm with Mackintosh, sent a letter to General Gage, warning him of possible disloyalty of the militia and informing him that many towns had taken their powder out of the province powder house at Charlestown. Within two weeks almost 2000 barrels of powder had been carried off. Only the small quota belonging to the province remained. To seize the remainder, Gage sent 200 soldiers up Mistick River on 1 September. A detachment of the troops went to Cambridge and captured two cannons. Accounts of the affair spread rapidly and magnified with growing distance. The most frequently repeated story was that the powder had been taken and that the troops had fired on the inhabitants and killed six. Some versions added heavy artillery fire, and a messenger arriving in Deerfield reported 106 persons killed.[1]

About 1 A.M. on the night of September 2, the account reached Shrewsbury,

[1]Brattle to Gage, 29 Aug. 1774, vol. 2, Ward Papers, 6 vols., MHS; *Copy of a Letter, Said to Be Wrote by Gen. Brattle* (Boston, 1774), *Mass. Brds.* 1714–1717; John L. Sibley and Clifford K. Shipton, "William Brattle," *Biographical Sketches of Those Who Attended Harvard College*, vol. 7 (Cambridge, Mass., 1945), pp. 20–23; John Rowe, *Letters and Diary of John Rowe, Boston Merchant, 1759–1762, 1764–1779*, ed. Anne Rowe Cunningham (Boston, 1903; reprint ed., 1969), 1–3 Sept. 1774, pp. 283–284; Abigail Adams to John Adams, 2 Sept. 1774, *Adams Family Correspondence*, ed. L. H. Butterfield, 2 vols. (Cambridge, Mass., 1963), 1:146–148; Noyes to Henshaw, 30 Aug., 1 Sept. 1774, *NEHGR* 43:146–147 (1889); John Andrews, "Letters of John Andrews, Esq., Boston, 1772–1776," ed. Winthrop Sargent, 18 Sept. 1774, *MHSP* 8:363 (1864–1865); Ashley Bowen, "Diary of Ashley Bowen," 31 Aug. 1774, *Mass. Mag.* 5:30 (1912); Ebenezer Parkman, Diary, 10 vols., photostat, 2–3 Sept. 1774, vol. 9, MHS; *BG* and *BEP*, 5 Sept. 1774; George Sheldon, *A History of Deerfield*, 2 vols. (Deerfield, Mass., 1896), 2:684.

about 40 miles west of Boston. A traveler, Mr. McNeil, lodging in a local tavern, was awakened by a violent rapping at the door. A messenger told the "doleful" story and added that the people between Shrewsbury and Boston were "arming and marching down to the Relief of their Brethren." Within half an hour, "fifty men were collected at the Tavern . . . equipping themselves and sending off Posts every Way to the neighboring Towns." McNeil was asked "to tell the Story of the Springfield Affair," the anticourt meeting of 29 August, which most of the men had not yet heard. He "had to repeat and tell the story over and over again to New Comers till day." As fast as the men were equipped, they set off for Boston on foot or on horseback. Women and children everywhere were packing provisions and getting equipment ready.[2]

Ezra Stiles, minister and librarian, later traced the spreading of the news. To the northwest, accounts came to New Hampshire, and 2000 men were ready to march at Bennington. Westward, in Albany, New York, the Dutch sent off wagons with provisions, and from beyond the Hudson River an honorary sachem of the Mohawks, Colonel William Johnson, set out for Boston with 50 or 60 Indians. In the southwesterly direction the report reached Colonel Putnam in Pomfret, Connecticut, at 11 A.M. Saturday (3 September). Before he set out, he sent a letter further to the south desiring the people to dispatch the militia. Only 30 miles before Boston, he was informed that the alarm was false. By that time his letter had been printed and spread all over Connecticut. On Sunday the meeting houses of many towns were shut up after the letter had been read from the pulpits. Militia musters were held instead. Colonel Putnam had been followed by 1500 men, and Colonel Saltonstall was to come with more regiments.[3]

Ministers who opposed the movement were assaulted by crowds. The Episcopal minister of Hebron, Connecticut, Samuel Peters, had to appear under the Liberty Pole and humbly confess his errors. He and his parishioners were repeatedly harassed by crowds, damaging particularly insignia of the Episcopal church. Peters, who later took refuge in Boston, thought that the riot had been encouraged by the governor of Connecticut and denounced "the rage of the puritan Mobility." Elsewhere the accounts of the powder seizure increased anxieties and insecurity too and prompted action against supporters of British authority. When reports spread that men from "all the western world" were coming to act against the "River Gods" from the Connecticut River Valley, other towns set out to protect them. When the anti-Tory crowd met with the "protective crowd," they joined, heard a militia colonel vindicate himself, and dispersed.[4]

Rhode Islanders were ready to send 10,000 men to "inquire" about "the account of the Powder's being stolen by Gage's orders," and Ezra Stiles continued his chronicle:

[2]Ezra Stiles, *The Literary Diary*, ed. F. B. Dexter, 3 vols. (New York, 1901), Nov. 1774, 1:479–480.

[3]*Ibid.*, pp. 479–485; Putnam's letter, *ibid.*, p. 483; Nathaniel Ames, "Diary of Dr. Nathaniel Ames," ed. Sarah Breck Baker, 4 Sept. 1774, *Dedham Hist. Reg.* 3:72 (1892); BG, 12 Sept. 1774.

[4]Peters to Auchmuty, 1 Oct. 1774, in Stiles, *Diary*, 1:466–467; Sheldon, *Deerfield*, 2:684–685; John W. Shy, "A New Look at Colonial Militia," *WMQ* 20:175–185 (1963); Don R. Gerlach, "A Note on the Quartering Act of 1774," *NEQ* 39:80–88 (1966).

Figure 11.   A "daughter of liberty" ready to support the men in the militia, 1774.

The news flew like Lightning, reached N. York on Monday Evening—and in 70 hours from the Date of Col. Putnam's Letter, it reached the Congress sitting at Philadelphia—where the City convened and were meditating something very weighty, which the Congress prevented. In 100 hours it reached the 3 Delaware Counties, where they instantly armed to the No of 1000 Men. The News proceeded to Maryland and Virginia before it was overtaken by the Contradiction. Thus in about 5 or 6 days the Alarm spread thro' above a Million of People. . . . had the News not been contradicted, Ten Thousand Men would have been instantly raised in Virginia.

Estimates were that 30,000 men were on the march in Massachusetts and New Hampshire, 20,000 in Connecticut.[5]

Three major consequences arose from this military and mass action. Politically, the imperial administrators lost any authority that had been left to them outside of Boston. Internally, all over Massachusetts measures for surveillance and control of supporters of British policies, the Tories, were taken. Militarily, General Gage decided to guard and fortify Boston Neck, while the militia units of the towns in the country began regular exercises. The feeling that an armed clash or prolonged conflict was unavoidable became prevalent.[6]

BRAWLS AND OPPOSITION IN BOSTON

In Boston the situation was materially different from the conditions in the country and from the situation in 1768, when troops had first been quartered there. The presence of the troops was so impressive that riotous resistance with intent to drive the troops out of town was impossible. Opposition concentrated on encouraging desertion, refusal to work for the troops, refusal to supply the troops, and intelligence gathering to inform other communities about possible troop movements. In order to prevent violence between troops and inhabitants, selectmen and many of the better sort, including leading Whigs, exerted themselves to arrange in accommodation. Such moves caused dissensions and were opposed by some Whig politicians and particularly by many mechanics, who also carried the burden of the resistance activities.

The discontent of the inhabitants showed itself in the wish that the "infernal Wretches" would perish and in the popularity of jokes about dumb soldiers, especially if they contained comparisons favorable to the colonists. The soldiers, in turn, despised the Bostonians. "I can only say, from the short acquaintance I have with the holy men of Massachusetts, I firmly believe that so execrable a set of sanctified villains never before disgraced the human species."[7]

---

[5]Stiles, *Diary,* 1:485; cf. John Adams, *Diary and Autobiography of John Adams,* ed. Lyman H. Butterfield, 4 vols. (Cambridge, Mass., 1961–1966), 6 Sept. 1774, 2:124.

[6]*BG,* 12 Sept. 1774; Stiles, *Diary,* 1:457, 460; Donations Committee to East Haddam, 1 Sept. 1774, *MHSC* 4.4:58–59; W. Glanville Evelyn, *Memoir and Letters of Capt. W. Glanville Evelyn, of the 4th Regiment ("King's Own") from North America, 1774–1775,* ed. G. D. Scull (Oxford, 1879), pp. 34–35.

[7]Noyes to Henshaw [Aug. 1774], *NEHGR* 43:144–145; Andrews, "Letters," 21 Aug., 1 Oct., 20 Oct. 1774, 2 Jan. 1775, pp. 345, 371–372, 378–379, 393; Evelyn, *Memoir and Letters* [n.d.], p. 36; Palfrey to Adams, Sept. 1774, Cadet Company, Records, Boston Univ.; *BG,* 5 Sept. 1774.

The situation in town deteriorated quickly. Letters of the inhabitants, as well as the orderly book of the military commander, mentioned affray after affray. As in 1768, it was mainly officers, quartered in private houses, who, when drunk, sallied through town and insulted, assaulted, and infuriated inhabitants by breaking almost any custom, regulation, and law in existence. Only the interposition of sober officers prevented large-scale rioting when several drunken officers attacked the town watch. General Gage accused the latter of having ''Afforded the Kings Enemys the very Advantage they seek.'' From gaming and drinking ''ill must arise,'' and ''Attacking the Watch of any Town, in all parts of the World, must be attended with bad Consequences.''[8] Nevertheless, the ''houses of ill fame'' flourished, and with exasperating frequency disturbances happened at the Neckguard and the ferries. Incoming and outgoing people refused to stop; soldiers then used force. Passengers of stage coaches, manhandled by the guards, expected ''some desparate affair'' if the troops remained. John Hancock's house was attacked twice by soldiers, so that Gage was obliged to send his aide-de-camp to disperse the rioting soldiers. Inhabitants were impressed or arrested and held without trial.[9] Three incidents illustrate the grievances concerning bawdy houses, interference by soldiers with town officials doing their duty, and the treatment of inhabitants who complained to officers about abuse by soldiers.

Several officers living in the house of ''a family noted for their hospitality and kindness to strangers, in admitting all comers to their b-d and board'' sallied out drunk and began to abuse some inhabitants, threatened them, and committed ''enormous indecencies.'' They used their weapons to clear the street but were subdued by some bystanders and a quickly assembling crowd. As in the years from 1768 to 1770, the inhabitants began a trophy hunt and took swords and epaulets from the officers. On another occasion the selectmen ordered an innkeeper, David Wiswall, to be warned out for selling large quantities of liquor to the troops, especially to guards on duty, and his wife for keeping a whorehouse. When a constable did so, army officers sent soldiers against the magistrate.[10] The third case

[8]Rowe, *Letters and Diary,* 27 July 1774, 21 Jan., 24 Jan. 1775, pp. 280, 289; Nathaniel Noyes, ''Letters of Nathaniel Noyes to William Henshaw, 1774–1775,'' ed. Harriet E. Henshaw, 13 July 1774 to 22 March 1775, *NEHGR* 43:140–149 (1889); Helena Bayard to Meletiah Bourne, 7 June 1775, Bourne Papers, 11 vols., 3:29, HHL; Andrews, ''Letters,'' 20–21 Sept., 29 Oct. 1774, 21 Jan. 1775, pp. 364, 380, 395–396; Stiles, *Diary,* 1:512; John Boyle, ''Boyle's Journal of Occurrences in Boston, 1759–1778,'' 31 March 1775, *NEHGR* 85:8; Eliot to Belknap, 30 Jan. 1775, *MHSC* 6.4:74–79; *BTR* 18:208–211, 23:223, 240–241; Thomas Gage, General Orders, 21 Jan., 24 Jan. 1775, MSS., BPL; John Barker, ''A British Officer in Boston in 1775,'' ed. R. H. Dana, 21 Jan., 24 Jan., 1 Feb. 1775, *Atlantic Monthly* 39:395–396; Frederick Mackenzie, *Diary of Frederick Mackenzie Giving a Daily Narrative of His Military Service . . . During the Years 1775–1781 in Massachusetts, Rhode Island and New York,* 2 vols. (Cambridge, Mass., 1930; reprint ed., 1968), 24 Jan. 1775, etc., 1:4–5.
[9]Committee of Donations to Worcester County, Maryland, 10 Oct. 1774, *MHSC* 4.4:79–82; Andrews, ''Letters,'' 25 Sept. 1774, 2 Jan., 18 March 1775, pp. 367, 392, 401; Bowen, ''Diary,'' 26 Sept. 1774, p. 31; George R. T. Hewes, *Traits of the Tea Party: Being a Memoir of George R. T. Hewes,* ed. Benjamin B. Thatcher (New York, 1935), pp. 208–209; *BPB,* 23 Jan. 1775; Lovell to Quincy, 3 Nov. 1774, *MHSP* 50:472–473 (1917); John Simpkins to Wallcutt, 24 Jan. 1775, vol. 1, Wallcutt Papers, MHS; Barker, ''Diary,'' Jan.–Feb. 1775, pp. 396–397; Robert Honyman, *Colonial Panorama, 1775: Dr. Robert Honyman's Journal,* ed. Philip Padelford (San Marino, 1939), 18–21 March 1775, pp. 39–43; Lord Harris, *The Life and Services of General Lord Harris, G.C.B., during His Campaigns in America, the West Indies and India,* ed. S. R. Lushington (London, 1840), letter dated 7 Aug. 1774, pp. 42–44.
[10]Andrews, ''Letters,'' 1 Aug., 2 Nov. 1774, pp. 333–335, 382; Lovell to Quincy, 3 Nov. 1774, *MHSP* 50:472–474; *BTR* 23:231; *BG,* 7 Nov. 1774.

involved a court martial of soldiers upon the complaint of a shopkeeper who had been abused by them. Angrily, the inhabitants heard that in court the plaintiff was told by one of the officers that if he had been called a "rebel," it was no insult but the truth, that all rebels, and that were nine tenth of Boston, would be soon hanged. One of the witnesses, whose father was a member of the Committee of Correspondence, was insulted by the military judges. This denial of justice was considered another instance proving that the Bostonians were "reduced to a state of nature," and one Bostonian ominously noted that Captain Scott "seasonably" arrived with a quantity of powder.[11]

The town's economic prospects were gloomy. Prices rose, and town expenses had to be cut. Merchant John Andrews, who considered himself of the middling interest and who considered "20 to 40 dollars" the amount he usually carried home in the evening after "an ordinary day's work," analyzed the prospects:

> [T]he burthen falls heaviest, if not *entirely,* upon the middling people among us; for the poor (who always lived from hand to mouth, i.e. depended on one day's labour to supply the wants of another) will be supported by the beneficence of the colonies; and the rich, who lived upon their income either as landholders or usurers, will still have the same benefit from their wealth.

There were always new tenants if one was "incapacitated to pay the annual rent," and "the money-lenders will rather be benefitted by our calamities." Those, on the other hand, who had been considered "good livers," as he had himself, would neither be the objects of charity nor be able to continue their trade, since the port was closed. They would have to borrow money to the "emolument" of others, who would even like to be thought of as "benefactors."

As to the lower classes, the lessons of social discontent voiced by artisans during the nonimportation period, 1768–1770, were still fresh in the minds of the leadership. A work program for the men from the shipbuilding trade was launched.[12] But the leadership's attempts to negotiate concessions from General Gage met with rebuffs from the townsmen. In 1768 rioting inhabitants had temporarily stopped construction of a military guardhouse on the Neck approved by the selectmen. Now they answered a similar request, probably under the pressure from irate townsmen, that "they could not consent to any such improvement of the Towns Estate." When, on 3 September, after the mass action in response to the powder seizure, General Gage ordered the troops to fortify the Neck, the selectmen were ordered to remonstrate with Gage. They were content with a rather evasive answer. Others were less content, and the selectmen had to go back to Gage to explain the apprehensions of Bostonians *and* countrymen. The "Fortress" on the Neck would reduce the "Metropolis" to a garrison. This might "hurry the Province into Acts of

[11]Andrews, "Letters," 21 Sept. 1774, pp. 364–365; affray of soldiers versus butchers (similar to contentions about food prices in 1768–1770), *ibid.,* 21 Jan. 1775, p. 396; *BG,* 3 Oct. 1774.

[12]For the Donations Committee, see Chapter 10, notes 18 and 19. *BTR* 23:221–222, 226; Andrews, "Letters," 1 Aug., 20 Aug., 9 Nov. 1774, 16 Jan. 1775, pp. 335, 343–345, 383, 394–395; Henry Hulton to ———, 11 Oct.–29 Nov. 1775, Letterbooks, 1:156–166, HHL. Port bill: Peter Force, ed., *American Archives* 9 vols. (Washington, D.C., 1837–1853), 4.1:35–66.

Desparation,'' especially hungry Bostonians and countrymen deprived of their market. The country–town alliance proved successful when Gage later ordered the officers of the Neckguard to stop detaining wagons with provisions and helping themselves at the expense of farmers and townsmen.[13]

Aside from desertion, the inhabitants did not facilitate anything for the military or for conciliatory magistrates. When the selectmen granted certain privileges to the troops "so long as no inconveniences attended," inconveniences came rather soon for the selectmen. Only one day later, they reconsidered their vote and withdrew the permission. Among the townsmen political consciousness was further developed than during the earlier years of opposition. A contemporary traveler noted that "all sorts of Political writings are bought up with amazing avidity." People proudly noted that even the youth had caught the spirit: When a servant of General Haldimand sanded a skating place of theirs, "they chose a committee to wait upon the General to remonstrate against . . . the invasion of their rights," and obtained redress.[14]

In a town meeting a member of the Loyal Nine, as always concerned about order, demanded steps "to prevent Bickerings and Disputes" between inhabitants and soldiers. The small number of townsmen present mildly voted that "Whereas Affrays may happen," a committee was to consult with the governor "to preserve Peace and good Order." Upon its report that the governor was willing to promote peace, "considerable debate" ensued. Accepting the governor's proposals might have "an air of agreeing to being garrisoned," argued Whig politicians. A moderate merchant angrily commented that "a discontented few" used "their influence among the popularity" and "raised a party," with the result that the matter was set aside. In a move to gather support for an agreement with the garrison, a new and larger committee was elected two days later, ensuring representation to more factions within the leadership and including popular Whig leaders. After the usual diatribe against the Coercive Acts and the presence of the troops, the committee recommended an increase in the town watch and peaceable behavior to the inhabitants. Although the committee did not officially report again—for fear of opposition?—it did negotiate on accord with the governor. But relations remained far from friendly, and the orderly books of Generals Gage and Howe reveal the reasonableness of the townsmen's complaints.[15]

The inhabitants, particularly the mechanics in the Northend, concentrated on refusing to work for the troops, spying on the military, and, most important, encouraging desertion. In June printed handbills had been distributed to the soldiers. But the relatively greater social equality of colonial society was already an induce-

---

[13]*BTR* 23:221, 227–228; Convention of Suffolk County Towns, 9 Sept. 1774, in Force, ed., *Archives*, 4.1:779–782.
[14]Barker, "Diary," 20 Nov., 18 Dec. 1774, pp. 391–392; *BTR* 23:231; Honyman, *Colonial Panorama*, p. 58; Eliot to Belknap, 30 Jan. 1775, *MHSC* 6.4:74–79; Andrews, "Letters," 28 Jan. 1775, p. 399.
[15]*BTR* 18:193–195, 23:224, 231; Andrews, "Letters," 31 Oct., 1 Nov., 17 Nov., 19 Nov. 1774, pp. 381–382, 385–386; Lovell to Quincy, 3 Nov. 1774, *MHSP* 50:472–474; Eliot to Belknap, 8 Nov. 1774, *MHSP* 6.4:60–62 (Belknap Papers). Gage, General Orders, MSS., BPL; Sir William Howe, *General Sir William Howe's Orderly Book at Charleston, Boston and Halifax, 17 June 1775 to 26 May 1776*, ed. Benjamin F. Stevens (London, 1890), see 20 May, 27 May, 6 June, 18 June, 7 July, 15 Nov., 18 Nov. 1775, 14 March, 22 April 1776.

ment by itself. Samuel Dyer, an illiterate seaman, was caught by officers while attempting to induce soldiers to desert. He was pressed for navy service to be kept as a witness. In a deposition given while in the custody of the British, he told the following story: In June Samuel Adams and Thomas Young asked him to get shipwrights, carpenters, and other men from the Northend to meet at specified taverns. Expenses were paid "by people who stiled themselves Sons of Liberty." The two leaders needed the men "to collect a Mob" on "a Minutes warning." Furthermore, he was to encourage desertion and to send deserters to an innkeeper near Mill Bridge, who would have horses ready for them. Half of this story was probably invented by the officers taking the deposition. Mechanics did encourage desertion, and they did form groups to watch the movements of the troops and, if necessary, alert the country. On the other hand, leaders discouraged crowd action wherever possible, Dyer was called an "Audacious Villain" by merchant leader John Rowe, and getting deserters on horseback in the middle of the town would be the best way to ensure early detection. On the whole, encouragement to desert was sufficiently successful that 210 soldiers left within 10 weeks. The value of watching troop movements was demonstrated a few months later, on 18 April 1775.[16]

Additionally, military stores "vanished" and were secretly conveyed out of town or destroyed. Stores for the troops, piled up on the wharves, "fell" into the muddy water. Even cannon belonging to the town were concealed and shipped off. After the siege began, all arms were collected and delivered to Gage, who in turn promised to let the inhabitants leave Boston with their effects. This agreement was viewed with distrust by some inhabitants, who suspected that the wealthy negotiators had staged "a Mere Farce . . . for which they recd. Favours from Gage."[17] At the end of September 1774, Boston and country towns joined to place an embargo on the troops.

RESISTANCE IN THE COUNTRY

The attention of the country focused on the militia. Many of the contingents marching in consequence of the powder alarm had been organized militia units. A British officer complained that every man "from sixteen to sixty, nay, to a hundred years old" was armed. "Who ever looks upon them as an irregular mob, will find himself much mistaken." The militia was reorganized, equipment was improved,

---

[16]For handbills and letters of military officers, see references in John Shy, *Toward Lexington: The Role of the British Army in the Coming of the American Revolution* (Princeton, N.J., 1965), pp. 413–414. Baker fined for encouraging desertion on the evidence of a soldier without a hearing by a Loyalist justice of the peace: Noyes to Henshaw [Aug. 1774], *NEHGR* 43:144–145; Samuel Dyer's deposition, 20 July 1774, Adm. Papers, Sec. Dept., 1.484:535–538, LC. Hutchinson and Boston newspapers considered Dyer "insane." Gage to Dartmouth, 30 Oct. 1774, State Papers, 13:102–103, Gay Transcripts, MHS; *BEP* and *BG*, 24 Oct. 1774, Shuttleworth to Spencer, 2 Nov. 1774, *Bostonian Soc. Proc.*, 1919, pp. 12–13. Dyer was later arrested on suspicion of spying for the British. *BG*, 22 July 1776; Stiles, *Diary*, 1:462–463, 482; Andrews, "Letters," 17–18 Oct. 1774, *MHSP* 8:377–378; Rowe, *Letters and Diary*, 18–19 Oct. 1774, p. 286.

[17]Boyle, "Journal," 22–23 April 1775, pp. 11–12; Rowe, *Letters and Diary*, 20–23 April 1775, pp. 292–293; Belcher Noyes, Diary, 4 March 1775, AAS; Andrews, "Letters," 20 Sept. 1774, p. 364, cf. pp. 361–362; Gage, General Orders, 16 Feb. 1775, MSS., BPL; Mackenzie, *Diary*, 1:7.

and moves of the troops were opposed. The higher militia officers had been appointed by the governor. They were forced to resign by crowds or county conventions, or, when inclining to the Whigs, they refused to serve under the Coercive Acts.[18]

The Worcester regiment, whose colonel, Artemas Ward, had been dismissed by the governor, assembled for reorganization upon the recommendation of the Worcester county convention. Solemnly and seriously, the men took into "consideration the present oppressed and distressed condition of this province in general," renounced their commissions, and chose new officers. Artemas Ward was again elected colonel. Colonel Saltonstall of Haverhill, who had attempted to raise an independent company for the protection of the stamps in 1765 and who had voted for rescinding the Massachusetts circular for united resistance in 1768, was visited by a crowd in July 1774. The men demanded his resignation. He parleyed with them at a tavern, gained time, and shortly afterward left for Boston.[19]

The colonials did not forget their military equipment either, as evidenced by a vote of Plymouth people: "That the divine direction may attend you [the representatives] and the Blessings of Heaven rest on our Country is the hearty and unremitted prayer of your constituents. Then voted to procure fifty guns and Bayonets. . . ." Other equipment was secured by taking guns, cannon, or powder belonging to the towns or to the province and putting it in places safe against Tories and British troops.[20] Marbleheaders boarded a vessel loaded with some arms that had been ordered to anchor under the guns of H.M.S. *Lively.* They carried off the arms before the mariners intervened.[21] Individuals bought arms from British soldiers who needed money. A countryman, Thomas Ditson of Billerica, was caught in the act

[18]Percy to Harvey, 20 April 1775, in *Letters of Hugh Earl Percy from Boston and New York, 1774–1776,* ed. Charles K. Bolton (Boston, 1902), pp. 52–53; Evelyn, *Memoir and Letters,* pp. 34–35; D'Bernicre, "Narrative of Occurrences, 1775," *MHSC* 2.4:209–210 (1816); Joseph S. Clark, *An Historical Sketch of Sturbridge, Mass., from Its Settlement to the Present Time* (Brookfield, Mass., 1838), pp. 16–18; Sheldon, *Deerfield,* 2:693–694; Henry Hulton to ———, Feb. 1775, Letterbooks, 1:111–122, HHL; Ballantine's Journal, Sept.–Oct. 1774, Judd MSS., Rev. Matters, p. 152, Forbes Library. Similar methods had been used in 1766, when a division of the Newbury militia regiment by the governor had caused complaints. Soldiers had refused to drill, and officers had resigned or been forced to do so by crowds. Joshua Coffin, *A Sketch of the History of Newbury, Newburyport, and West Newbury, from 1635 to 1845* (Boston, 1845), pp. 233–234.

[19]*Mass. Spy,* 20 Oct. 1774; Andrews, "Letters," 5 Oct. 1774, p. 373; Noyes to Henshaw, 13 July 1774, *NEHGR* 43:143–144; letter from Worcester, 27 Sept. 1774, in Force, ed., *Archives,* 4.1:806; "Sketch of Haverhill," *MHSC* 2.4:164 (1816); George W. Chase, *The History of Haverhill, Massachusetts, from Its First Settlement, in 1640, to the Year 1860* (Haverhill, Mass., 1861), pp. 376–377; Joseph B. Felt, *The Annals of Salem from Its First Settlement* (Salem, Mass., 1827), p. 490; Charles Martyn, *The Life of Artemas Ward, the First Commander-in-Chief of the American Revolution* (New York, 1921), Ch. 4.

[20]William T. Davis, ed., *Records of the Town of Plymouth, 1636–1783,* 3 vols. (Plymouth, Mass., 1903), 27 Jan. 1775, 3:297. Wrentham: *BG,* 5 Sept. 1774; William Lincoln, *History of Worcester, Massachusetts, from Its Earliest Settlement to 1836* (2d ed.; Worcester, Mass., 1862), pp. 87–88. Braintree: Abigail Adams to John Adams, 14 Sept. 1774, *Adams Family Correspondence,* 1:151–155. Providence, Rhode Island, and Newcastle, New Hampshire: *BEP,* 19 Dec. 1774; Gooch to Cumberland, 8 April 1774, *The Cumberland Letters, Being the Correspondence of Rich[ar]d Dennison Cumberland and George Cumberland between the Years 1771 and 1784,* ed. Clementina Black (London, 1912), pp. 57–58; *BTR* 23:219; William Tudor, *The Life of James Otis of Massachusetts: Containing Also Notices of Some Contemporary Characters and Events from the Year 1760 to 1775* (Boston, 1823), pp. 452–455; William Lincoln, ed., *The Journals of Each Provincial Congress of Massachusetts in 1774–1775 . . .* (Boston, 1858), pp. 85–87.

[21]Samuel Roads, *The History and Traditions of Marblehead* (Boston, 1880), p. 111; A. E. Brown, ed., *John Hancock*

and tarred and feathered by about 50 soldiers, who finally paraded him through town. The inhabitants were enraged about the "military" or "Royal mob" of "Officers, Negroes, Sailors." Officers knew about the preparations for the riot and tolerated it, probably even ordered it, to intimidate the country people and to discourage further arms trades.[22]

For several months after the powder alarm, the troops remained in Boston without attempting any expeditions into the country. The proportions of the crowd action at the end of August and the beginning of September 1774 also brought to a premature end all plans to send troops into the country for the protection of loyal officials. In January 1775 the troops began marches into the country, to familiarize the country people with the sight of troops or to achieve specific aims. The expeditions, however, did not result in the expected passive acceptance of the presence of soldiers, but in further resistance.

Several Loyalists of Marshfield, Plymouth, asked for troops for protection. Lieutenant Barker reported that 200 inhabitants had applied; the *Gazette* stated that it was some Tories, "idle young persons and some Negroes." Several other towns of the county soon told Gage that nobody had ever threatened the Marshfield Tories. Soon rumors circulated that "the Tories are almost Sick of the Regulars . . . but then they have got them and there they must keep them."[23]

Three hundred Loyalists in Freetown, Bristol, under Thomas Gilbert's lead formed a military association to keep "the Neighbourhood in Subjection to the King's Authority." In April 1775, just before Lexington, a crowd of 2500 assembled from the other towns of the county, apprehended and disarmed all Tories, ransacked Gilbert's house, and searched the woods for him.[24]

On 26 February an expedition was sent off by Gage to capture several cannons stored at Salem. But when the detachment arrived, Colonel Leslie found the drawbridge up and the Salemites busy scuttling all boats lying on his side of the river. Large crowds of men, women, and children assembled on both sides, some armed with guns. Under these circumstances Leslie negotiated, and finally both sides accepted a face-saving compromise: The bridge was lowered, and the troops crossed it, marched for 50 feet, and then turned back without a search. As in September 1774, when Gage attempted to arrest the Salem Committee of Corre-

---

His Book (Boston, 1898), p. 189.

[22]Rowe, *Letters and Diary*, 9 March 1775, p. 290; Noyes, Diary, 1775, AAS; Ditson's account, *BG* and BEP, 13 March 1775; Lincoln, ed., *Journals of Each Provincial Congress*, pp. 131–134, note 1 (reprinted from *Mass. Spy*, 17 March 1775); *BTR* 23:246; Samuel Adams to ———, 12 March 1775, *The Writings of Samuel Adams*, ed. Harry A. Cushing, 4 vols. (New York, 1904–1908), 3:198–200; letters and remonstrance of the selectmen of Billerica, in Force, ed., *Archives*, 4.2:120–121, 153; Mackenzie, *Diary*, 8 March 1775, 1:10–11; Gage to Dartmouth, 28 March 1775, *The Correspondence of General Thomas Gage*, ed. Clarence E. Carter, 2 vols. (New Haven, Conn., 1931, 1933), 1:394–395. The officers formed a "Military Congress" for determining a "summary mode of redress," to "ape" the Boston selectmen and to mock the Continental Congress. Andrews, "Letters," 11 April 1775, p. 403; report, 6 April 1775, in Force, ed., *Archives*, 4.2:284–286.

[23]Barker, "Diary," 23 Jan., 4 May 1775, pp. 396, 545; *BG*, 30 Jan. 1775; letters and remonstrances, in Force, ed., *Archives*, 4.1:1178, 1218–1219; *BTR* 23:247; Israel Litchfield, "Diary," 30 Jan. 1775, in W. J. Litchfield, ed., *The Litchfield Family in America, 1630–1900* (Boston, 1906), p. 325; Andrews, "Letters," 24 Jan. 1775, pp. 396–397.

[24]Memorial of Thomas Gilbert, B. F. Stevens, Transcripts of American Loyalist Claims, 13:394–403, NYPL, MF in MHS; memorial of Samuel Gilbert, *ibid.*, 14:31–32.

spondence, militia units in all neighboring towns got ready to march, but "Leslie's retreat" solved the affair, and no fighting ensued.[25]

The general impression left by these exercises was that the troops "marched over the people's lands—some where their grain was sown—and gardens; broke down their fences, walls, &c., and doing other injuries. It is thought such proceedings will bring on bad consequences, unless prevented." Watertown inhabitants posted two cannons alongside the road, to be prepared should troops be sent to town. Gage did order more such exercises, so that they might take place "without creating an alarm." This undertaking was doomed to failure. A single man, sent out as a spy, stumbled upon difficulties wherever he went. Teamsters spread news of his coming. He was told that a large tree growing at the roadside would be felled to block the advance of the soldiers if they dared come. Several times he was chased by crowds and search parties from different towns. Usually they were so close on his heels that he had to leave his lodgings by the back door before he could finish his meals. They also usually brought tar and feathers along, not only for him but also for his hosts. Thus, unable to stay with well-known Loyalists, he took rooms with free Negroes. There he had to keep quiet too, because they turned out to be staunch Sons of Liberty. Gage and his officers laughed when they heard his report. They were soon to discover he was correct.[26]

The contribution of Boston mechanics to the resistance in the country was the relaying of information. The troops were closely watched by a group of about 30 mechanics, who met secretly and informally to gather information, which they reported to selected leaders (Hancock, Adams, Warren, Church) or, if necessary, to the country and to other colonies. The vigilance of most of these men has gone unnoticed. Only Paul Revere, whose turn it was to stand on alert to warn the country on the night of 18 April 1775, has not been forgotten. But before that date, town and country had developed and enforced another method of resistance to the troops.[27]

THE EMBARGO

The quartering of troops in Boston and the fortification of the town against possible invasions from the country brought about an attempt by the colonists to combine noncooperation, strike, and embargo as methods to prevent the troops from

---

[25]*BNL*, 2 March 1775; Stiles, *Diary*, 1:522–523; William Wetmore, "Extracts from the Interleaved Almanacs of William Wetmore of Salem, 1774–1778," 26 Feb. 1775, *EIHC* 43:116 (1907); Joseph Seccombe, "Extracts from 'Text Books' of Deacon Joseph Seccombe, Salem 1756–1777," ed. P. Derby, *EIHC* 34:34, 26 Feb. 1775 (1898); Gage to Dartmouth, 4 March 1775, *Correspondence*, 1:393–394.

[26]Barker, "Diary," 30 March 1775, pp. 397–398; Mackenzie, *Diary*, March–April 1775, 1:14; Gage, General Orders, 7 April 1775, MSS., BPL; letter from Boston, 1 April 1775, in Force, ed., *Archives*, 4.2:253; extracts from the "Journal Kept by Mr. John Howe While He Was Employed as a British Spy during the Revolutionary War," in D. H. Hurd, *History of Middlesex*, 3 vols. (Philadelphia, 1890), 2:579–584. Note that this report has to be used very critically because it was written after Howe changed to the American side.

[27]Revere to MHS Secretary, 1 Jan. 1798, *MHSC* 1.5:106–112 (1798). The military expedition to Salem in February 1775 was reported to the New York Sons of Liberty by Joshua Brackett (innkeeper, Cromwell's Head), Paul Revere, Benjamin Edes, Joseph Ward, Thomas Crafts, and Thomas Chase, all of whom, except one, were members of the Northend Caucus or the Loyal Nine or both. Esther Forbes, *Paul Revere and the World He Lived In* (Boston, 1942), p. 237; Elbridge H. Goss, *The Life of Colonel Paul Revere*, 2 vols. (Boston, 1891), 1:234–235.

taking action or even to drive them off. Extralegal committees and regular magistrates met jointly, and Committees of Correspondence of different towns cooperated for this purpose. The countrymen, much more restless than Bostonians since the arrival of the troops, expressed their uneasiness about Boston workmen building barracks for the British army. A political stike was called. The first and most minimal act of resistance, the attitude of *bras croisés,* began.[28]

This attitude was reenforced when intelligence was received that the New Yorkers had decided not to let any ship carry troops to Boston or support the king's army. The ''Free Citizens'' of New York announced the refusal of the merchants to let their ships, asked pilots to boycott the navy, and warned artisans and contractors not to work for the British: ''should any sordid miscreant be found amongst us who will aid the enemies of this country to subvert her liberties, he must not be surprised if that vengeance overtakes him, which is the reward justly due to parricides.'' However, the merchants soon forgot their agreements and the ''Free Citizens'' and ''now go on compleating their orders without further Interruption.'' Under pressure from the Committee of Correspondence and in view of the general ''Dissatisfaction,'' they had to agree to a few minimal demands, aimed at preventing profiteering from the scarcity. Engrossers, defined as those attempting to create ''an artificial scarcity,'' were to be deemed responsible for ''all the disturbances that shall be consequent thereupon.''[29]

After the Boston carpenters had begun their strike, neither a call on the elected town authorities nor an informal conference between General Gage and John Hancock brought them back to work. But as in 1768, some town leaders and merchants seem to have been more moderate than other sections of the population. While carpenters struck, while other mechanics formed a committee for surveillance of the troops, while the Northend became the center of encouragement for desertion, Hancock told Gage that he had already done so much for the troops that he could not do anything more. He had been threatened with hanging. The Continental Congress in Philadelphia was informed of the strike. The messenger, Paul Revere, left the news at the towns along his route, and in New York a special broadside was printed.[30]

The strike had hardly begun when the next move was made. The troops were to be blockaded from supplies from the country. On 27 September Boston officials and committees from other towns in a joint conference resolved not to furnish any goods to the king's troops. This vote was passed in response to action taken by individuals

---

[28]Committee of Correspondence, Correspondence, 1774, NYPL; minutes of a joint meeting of 24 Sept. 1774, NYPL, printed in Force, ed., *Archives,* 4.1:802, *BTR* 23:229, *BEP,* 26 Sept. 1774.

[29]Andrews, ''Letters,'' 25 Sept. 1774, pp. 367–368; Gage to Dartmouth, 25 Sept. 1774, *Correspondence,* 1:376; Boston Committee to Continental Congress, 29 Sept. 1774, in Force, ed., *Archives,* 4.1:810, see also 4.2:283, 639; Brds., ''The Free Citizens,'' ''Humanus,'' ''A Card: New York, September 9th, 1774. The thanks of the public . . .'' [to those who refused to let their vessels to the British troops], reprinted in I. N. P. Stokes, *Iconography of Manhattan Island, 1498–1909,* 6 vols. (New York, 1915–1928), 4:866–867.

[30]*BTR* 23:229; Committee of Correspondence, Minute Books, 9:794, NYPL; Thomas Newell, ''Diary for 1773 to the End of 1774, of Mr. Thomas Newell, Boston,'' 26 Sept. 1774, *MHSP* 15:358 (1876–1877); Andrews, ''Letters,'' Sept.–Oct. 1774, *MHSP* 8:367–369 *passim;* Richard Frothingham, *History of the Siege of Boston, and of the Battles of Lexington, Concord, and Bunker Hill* (Boston, 1849), p. 26.

or single towns. The army, beginning to erect barracks, had contracted with a Mr. Thompson from Mistick (Medford) to supply bricks, necessary for building the chimneys in the barracks. He loaded a lighter, but "by some accident or other," the lighter sank. The British finally had to buy an old house, pull it down, and clean the bricks for reuse.[31] Thompson's fellow townsmen began to consider his business dealings, and a delegation from Woburn, several miles to the north, asked him to stop all further shipments till it could be determined whether the troops should be supplied and if so by what means and to what extent.

Several considerations lay behind this move. (1) As all suffered equally from the decline of trade, all should participate equally in any benefits (profits) arising from the presence of the troops. Contrary to the conduct of Boston merchants in 1768, this attitude was still rooted in the corporate economic concept of equitable benefits. (2) It was to be made as difficult as possible for the troops to remain. Since the Coercive Acts closed the port for civilian supplies and since land transport increased the cost of provisions considerably, sending privateers against military transport ships was suggested, so that the troops would have to rely on land transport too. (3) Finally, a general embargo on the troops was agreed upon. Merchants were forbidden to sell any kind of materials, blankets, or tools to the army. Daily provisions were excepted, but the threat that they would be cut off too was continually present. The embargo was vigorously enforced by direct action of crowds. When the less radical Boston Committee of Correspondence attempted to negotiate concessions from the governor for lifting the embargo, it met defeat in the town meeting and in joint conferences with country committees.[32]

Boston bakers refused to supply the troops with flour and bread. Crowds in Roxbury, the last town before Boston, burned several loads of straw destined for the troops. A Boston brazier who sold £500 worth of cannon and ammunition to the troops was visited by a crowd numbering several hundred. "Gentlemen" interposed to protect his person and property, but the crowd defaced the front of his shop and emptied several buckets of ordure into his chamber window. The technical term for such action was to give someone a "Hillsborough treat."[33]

The measures were effective. By 29 September, two days after the beginning of the embargo, Andrews noted that the soldiers were so enraged about the strike and the embargo "that I am in continual apprehension we shall soon experience another fifth of March, which God forbid!" He speculated on the possibility and expediency of removing all inhabitants to the country and then cutting off all provisions. By 3 October, again according to Andrews, the general faced the danger of mutiny. Gage assured the soldiers that they would be in the barracks soon. "But where he means to provide for 'em I don't know." Gage offered exorbitant wages for carpenters, but

[31]*BTR* 23:229; Boston to Charlestown Committee, 1 Nov. 1774, vol. 14, Misc. Bound Papers, MHS; Committee of Correspondence, Minute Books, 11:853–854, NYPL; minutes and letter of the joint committees, 27 Sept. 1774, in Force, ed., *Archives,* 4.1:807–808; Andrews, "Letters," 23 Sept., 16 Nov. 1774, pp. 366, 384–385.

[32]Andrews, "Letters," 23 Sept. 1774, p. 366; Evelyn, *Memoir and Letters,* 31 Oct. 1774, p. 39; Committee of Correspondence, Minute Books, Nov. 1774, 11:861–865, NYPL.

[33]Evidence for William Hill, B. F. Stevens, Transcripts of American Loyalist Claims, 13:243, NYPL; evidence for Archibald McNeill, *ibid.,* 14:431; Andrews, "Letters," 27 Sept., 29 Sept. 1774, pp. 368–371; letter from Boston, 27 Sept. 1774, in Force, ed., *Archives,* 4.1:806–807, 810; *BG,* 3 Oct. 1774.

the threat of incurring the townsmen's displeasure proved stronger, at least temporarily. Gage employed ship's carpenters from the navy, but the results were not altogether encouraging. The soldiers meanwhile did not even have straw to sleep on.[34]

While Revere spread the news of the strike, Bostonians debated whether the move was in the interest of the town or whether the building of barracks would be better. Would working for the troops be acquiescence? Or would it be preferable to a spreading of the troops all over town? Should Congress be asked for advice? Strikebreaking occurred, as did picketing and physical violence against those willing to work. One carpenter attempting to work was seized by a crowd and carried to the gallows but was then let off.

Finally the scale descended in favor of those who were for building the barracks. Constant disturbances, the general inconveniences, and large-scale strikebreaking contributed to this decision. On 10 October Bostonians received the news that New York carpenters would come. By the end of October, a group of carpenters from Cambridge was "cordially at work," though their colleagues in Salem had refused "so disgraceful a service" and had forced the recruiter to leave the town precipitately. He was "mobbed" later. A group of carpenters, probably sent from New Hampshire by Governor Wentworth, asked to be discharged from the work because they were pressured and threatened by the townsmen. They had hardly left when 15 Boston carpenters took their places. This led to distrust among Whig leaders and clamors among the country people. Local merchants began to let their stores to the troops. Captain Evelyn acidly noted that "money (for which these holy men would sell the Kingdom of Heaven) defeats their charitable intentions," and Gage offered extraordinarily high wages. Many, however, especially the poor, who were more dependent on town officials, did not dare work for the British and had to pay the high prices for fresh provisions occasioned by the demands of the troops and by the countrymen's reluctance to come to town. During the winter no further action was taken, although there was talk of starving the army.[35]

In February 1775 the movement began to gather momentum again. The committees of several towns applied to the Provincial Congress to prevent people from working for the army or from supplying it. It was resolved that committees and inhabitants in general should "by all reasonable means whatever" prevent any supplies, including straw, from reaching the troops. Daily provisions again remained excepted. A gunsmith from the Northend and the members of the committee

[34]Andrews, "Letters," 23 Sept., 29 Sept., 3 Oct., 16 Nov. 1774, 4 Jan. 1775, pp. 366, 371, 372, 384–385, 393.

[35]Swift to Cushing, 2 Oct. 1774, *MHSC* 6.4:54–56 (1891); Evelyn, *Memoir and Letters*, 31 Oct. 1774, pp. 34, 39; *BG*, 3 Oct. 1774; memorial of John Nutting, B. F. Stevens, Transcripts of American Loyalist Claims, 13:289–291, NYPL; extracts and remarks on the correspondence of J W [J. Wentworth?] and T W W [Thomas W. Waldron?], 1774 and 1775, Belknap Papers, vol. "Miscellaneous," no. 80, MHS; Alexander Fraser, *United Empire Loyalists: Enquiry into the Losses and Services in Consequence of Their Loyalty—Evidence in the Canadian Claims,* Second Report of the Bureau of Archives for the Province of Ontario, 1904 (Toronto, 1905), p. 58; proceedings of a New York committee and of the Committee of Correspondence of Rochester, New Hampshire [against a strikebreaker], 11 Nov. 1774, in Force, ed., *Archives,* 4.1:803–804, 974; Gage to Dartmouth, 24 Sept. 1774, *ibid.,* pp. 804–805; Revere's message to Congress, *ibid.,* pp. 820–821; Appleton to Quincy, 15 Nov. 1774, *ibid.,* p. 980; Wentworth to Dartmouth, 15 Nov. 1774, *ibid.,* pp. 981–982; see also *ibid.,* pp. 991–992, 4.4:159, 256–259, 883–884.

induced 11 Boston gunsmiths to stop working for the army. A twelfth, Mr. Whiston—active in several riots against the troops in 1768–1770—gave no definite answer, and a Mr. Seaward was marked "uncorrigible." Soon Gage reportedly gave orders for every soldier who could work to make cartridges. A circular letter advised Massachusetts people not to rent horses or cattle to the army, to prevent it from moving with cannon and wagons.[36]

On 14 April, five days before Lexington, the blockade tightened. The contractors refused to supply fresh meat. The soldiers had to live on salt provisions. One of them sourly noted that while they were successful in blockading the port, "the rebels certainly block up our town, and have cut off good beef and mutton, much to the discomfiture of our mess." Months later the troops were still on salt provisions, "without even vegetables. . . . Yes we get sometimes a piece of an old ox or cow, at the rate of fourteen times as much as we paid last summer. . . ."[37]

In most seaports along the coast, Committees of Inspection were appointed in 1775 to prevent ships from going to Boston with provisions for the army. Nantucket whaleboats cruised off Boston to stop fishermen from bringing their catches to town. The lighthouses at Boston and Cape Ann were destroyed to deceive military transports destined for Boston. The Loyalist refugees in Boston ran out of money to support themselves because the "rebels" prevented them from receiving the income of their estates. By common agreement, officers' bills were no longer accepted as payment, and the army ran out of cash. The situation became desperate. Customs Commissioner Hulton and others heard about a plan to seize all British officers after a public entertainment in April 1775.[38]

The Provincial Congress passed a resolve calling General Gage and Admiral Graves traitors. Graves wanted to burn down Boston in return. Instead he had to relax the blockade of the port because supplies for the troops had become extremely scarce. In other words, he evaded the Port Bill, which he had been sent to enforce. Subsequently, some merchants and ship masters were willing to sell or carry provisions for the military, as high prices meant high profits. But committees took precautionary measures. They seized ships carrying supplies, imprisoned the sailors, and caused all coasters that were not vital for their own provisions to be laid up. Sails and rudders had to be deposited with the committees. Ships running under contracts with the army and navy were burned, and in Portsmouth a crowd dragged the master of such a vessel through the town. With the exception of volunteer

---

[36]Lincoln, ed., *Journals of Each Provincial Congress,* 3 Feb., 7 Feb. 1775, pp. 85–87; Committee of Correspondence, Correspondence, 1775, NYPL; *BEP,* 27 Feb. 1775; Gage to Dartmouth, enclosure, 4 March 1775, State Papers, 13:110, Gay Transcripts, MHS; *Boston, February 25, 1775. Gentlemen, The Following Proceedings . . . , Mass. Brds.* 1794; Henry Hulton to ———, Oct.–Nov. 1775, Letterbooks, 1:156–166, HHL.

[37]Gage, General Orders, 14 April 1775, MSS., BPL; Lord Harris, *Life and Services,* 5 May, 24 July 1775, pp. 49–51, 57–59; Till to Spencer, 6 July, 5 Dec. 1775, *Bostonian Soc. Proc.,* 1919, pp. 13–15; Barker, "Diary," 1 May 1775, p. 545.

[38]Anne Hulton, *Letters of a Loyalist Lady* (Cambridge, Mass., 1927), April, 20 June 1775, 17 Jan. 1776, pp. 76–84, 97–100; Henry Hulton to ———, 7 May, 10 Aug. 1775, Letterbooks, 1:146–153, 153–356, HHL; Barker, "Diary," 4 May 1775, p. 545; Gage to Dartmouth, 24 July 1775, *Correspondence,* 1:409–411. Bostonians agreed to deliver up their arms for permission to leave town. Boyle, "Journal," pp. 11–13; Rowe, *Letters and Diary,* April–May 1775, pp. 292–295; Andrews, "Letters," 24 April 1775, p. 405; Andrew Eliot to his son, 23 April 1775, *MHSP* 16:182–183; Noyes, Diary, 1775, AAS.

companies in the garrisoned and besieged Boston, nobody dared work for the troops for fear of violence to their persons and property. When the news of the fight on 19 April reached New York, crowds unloaded transport ships destined for Boston. They seized arms and powder.[39]

After 19 April the resistance was led by the organized militia units of the country. In the preceding months, crowd action by militia units had happened but remained incidental and spontaneous. Crowds continued to act on their own behalf, without being organized or led by a superstructure of officials and institutions. Fishermen and lumberjacks captured a British tender and two sloops at Machias, Maine, in July 1775. A town meeting had reluctantly agreed to exchange wood for the troops at Boston for badly needed provisions. But inequitable distribution of the provisions, with preference given to pro-British inhabitants, provoked a group of men to seize the sloops and to capture the fleeing tender, using "guns, swords, axes, and pitchforks" for arms. Similar actions against "royal pirates" were reported from several other towns.[40] The best-known example of such self-organized action is the capture of Fort Ticonderoga by a private expedition of Connecticut and Massachusetts men before the colonial troops arrived. But this was only one instance of such crowd militia action. New Hampshire men had taken Fort William and Mary earlier.

In the period from the arrival of the British troops to the siege of Boston, town-meeting and crowd actions together with passive resistance were important factors in bringing about the final rupture with Great Britain. The crowd action was significantly different from that of previous years. Because of its target, large numbers of British troops, and because of its participants, militia-trained countrymen, its nature changed from limited affrays to mass action, "open-air town meetings," sometimes of a military character. The men acted spontaneously in ad hoc units. They were frequently armed with guns or sticks and elected temporary leaders. Once all officials appointed by the British governor, whether judicial, executive, legislators, or militia officers, had resigned (middle of September 1774), the embargo eclipsed the importance of crowd action, which, however, remained supplementary at least around Boston to enforce strikes, boycott, and embargo. A change from more or less isolated incidents to long-term action, which needed the support of a large section of the population, was necessary for a successful passive resistance. This was furthered by debates, votes, and resolves in town meetings throughout Massachusetts. A broader basis for the opposition and a more conscious attitude toward it were in part made possible by molding local grievances in the west

---

[39]Barker, "Diary," 8 Feb., 1 May 1775, pp. 396–397, 545; Henry Hulton to ———, 12 June 1775, Letterbooks, 1:130–133, HHL; Graves's reports, 24 Oct. 1774, 7 June 1775, Graves Papers, 1:23, 105, Gay Transcripts, MHS; Andrews, "Letters," 12 June, 20 Oct., 16 Nov. 1774, pp. 330, 378, 384–385; Justin Winsor, ed., *The Memorial History of Boston, Including Suffolk County, Massachusetts, 1630–1880*, 4 vols. (Boston, 1880–1881), 3:77; Gage to Dartmouth, 15 Nov. 1774, 24 July 1775, *Correspondence*, 1:384, 408–409; John Collins to commander at Roxbury, 26 April 1774, vol. 3, Ward Papers, 6 vols., MHS.

[40]James B. Connolly, *The Port of Gloucester* (New York, 1940), pp. 52–53; Committee of Machias to Provincial Congress, 14 July 1775, in Lincoln, ed., *Journals of Each Provincial Congress*, pp. 395, 396 note, 399; cf. *ibid.*, pp. 435–436; Enoch Freeman to Samuel Freeman, 10 May 1775, in Force, ed., *Archives*, 4.2:550, 585–586; Gerry to Provincial Congress, 1 May 1775, *ibid.*, p. 462; other incidents, *ibid.*, pp. 608, 1017, 1061; John White, "Extracts from the Interleaved Almanacs Kept by John White of Salem," 12 June 1775, *EIHC* 49:92 (1913).

to imperial issues, as had been done in Boston earlier. The town meeting, so far an institution used mainly to prevent violence, now became the institutional basis, supplemented by Committees of Correspondence or Inspection, for a large-scale resistance.

PART **IV**

Crowd Action and Whig Rule, 1774-1780

Whig rule had been challenged from below since the middle of 1774. The Tea Party success had given the Boston Committee of Correspondence somewhat too high a notion of its powers, influence, and position. As a result, it met with opposition in Boston as well as from country towns. The years from 1776 to 1780 saw a struggle between mainly rural and western forces fighting for local control and responsive government and eastern leadership trying to reassert its dominant position. The demand for local control was tied into a concept of government that no longer suited the Whig leaders, the compact theory of government. The dissolution of British government, according to many western farmers, meant a dissolution of society, which made a new compact necessary. At this point they also began to consider that instead of striving for a golden past the new compact might embody a few innovations, such as increased popular participation. At least, they were not content with simply resuming the charter of 1691 as the basis for government. The eastern leadership for a long time neither realized nor understood what was going on. They translated western demands for a constitution and, most important, a bill of rights into language suitable to their mentality and ideology: If proper officers would be appointed for the western counties, everything would be okay. Just as with the spontaneous social action of the Stamp Act crowds, they were disappointed with the reaction of the westerners to appointment of officers. Magnanimous as leaders are when their position is threatened, they pardoned the

311

people for demanding a constitution and finally came up with one. The crowd action necessary to bring about a constitution forms the concluding part of this study—but certainly not the conclusion of popular demands for participation in government and of crowd action.

Government and
People after Lexington

12

In April 1775 military action commenced; a year later British troops evacuated Boston. Did those who had rioted against arrogant British officials, who had protested against arbitrary taxation, now accept the American military discipline and submit to decisions of Whig leaders? Did American officers and magistrates develop attitudes similar to those of the British officials? Or did the lower sort, the middling interest, and the better sort separately or together strive to establish political institutions and a social framework that would guarantee relative social, economic, and political equality and participation for all groups of the society?

For a short time after Lexington and Concord, attention centered on the army. It was soon accepted as a matter of fact, and interest concentrated again on local and provincial political and judicial institutions. The court system, long unpopular, was to be reestablished, but people refused to accept the decision of the General Court, and crowds prevented the courts from being held. However, "anarchy and confusion," much feared by Whig leaders and by the silent majority of the middle class, did not reign. Instead a system of local government was developed. Numerous committees provided some influence for men from outside the old town hierarchies. The adherents of local rule favored a governmental system from the bottom—that is, the local level—up. They supported regional conventions in elections and by mass action. The opponents, among them, since 1775, the provincial Whig leadership, worked for the reestablishment of their stronghold, the provincial government in Boston.

The process of transition from colonial rule to independent government took place in the period from summer 1774 to 1780, from the time British troops and the Coercive Acts arrived to the ratification of the new Constitution. De facto independence was achieved in Massachusetts with the exception of Boston when the British administration and its soldiers were forced to restrict their activities to Boston in the period from September 1774 to April 1775. It was achieved in Boston with the evacuation by the British in early 1776. The formal resolution of the Continental Congress declaring independence came months later, in July 1776. This creates some chronological and conceptual difficulties unless the distinction made here between process and event is clearly kept in mind. The following five sections examine the processes leading to and following from independence, 1774 and later, rather than the event of July 1776. They deal, as the title of Part Four indicates, with de facto independent legislature, courts, military and interim committee, and convention government. The mass celebrations of the Declaration of 1776 are integrated into the analysis where they fit into the sociopolitical development.

"STANDING ARMIES" AND WHIG SOCIETY

For many years Americans had denounced "standing armies." After Lexington, when an American army had been established, the attitudes of Massachusetts leaders and people were ambiguous. Elbridge Gerry, Salem magistrate and Massachusetts delegate in Congress, hoped to contain aspirations of the military for political influence and power by legislation. Samuel Adams pleaded for a militia "of free Citizens"; severe discipline, separation from civilian life, obedience, and attachment to officers were opposed and dangerous to republican principles. The "Newburgh conspiracy" and the officers' Society of the Cincinnati later proved such fears to be well founded. But by 1776, Massachusetts leaders were convinced that a "Committee of War" with extensive powers was a necessity.[1]

Soldiers, used to the lax discipline and the participatory nature of the militia units, were now subjected to hard disciplinary action, ranging from severe corporal punishments to the death penalty for desertion. They were told by a member of the former Loyal Nine of the Stamp Act opposition that "by Voluntarily having entred the Army they give up their Right of Private Judgment, and are to look on themselves as Machines, to obey Orders implicitly." General Washington demanded "activity and zeal" from officers but "docility and obedience" from soldiers. A year earlier it had still been demanded that the rank and file clearly understand the reasons for their movements. Harsh punishments had so much civilian support that even a military commander and Boston Whig expressed surprise "how the peoples minds are altered about this matter from what it was when the British Troops were here—every man crying a deserter ought to die."[2] The Redcoats had been ridiculed for their submission to rules, arbitrary officers, and brutal corporal punishments. Their passive acceptance of these degrading regulations had induced the Bostonians to despise and harass them. Now American soldiers were expected to behave submissively. If they did, they were considered unfit to govern themselves, because they were too dependent; if they did not, they were considered "rascals."

[1]Letters from Samuel Adams, 2 Jan. 1774 [Peter Force, ed., *Americans Archives*, 9 vols. (Washington, D.C., 1837–1853), 4.4:541–542], 7 Jan. 1776 [*Warren–Adams Letters: Being Chiefly a Correspondence among John Adams, Samuel Adams, and James Warren*, 2 vols. (Boston, 1917, 1925), 1:197–198], 4 Dec. 1776 [*The Writings of Samuel Adams*, ed. Harry A. Cushing, 4 vols. (New York, 1904–1908), 3:322–325]; Elbridge Gerry to Samuel Adams, 13 Dec. 1775, in Force, ed., *Archives*, 4.4:255–256.

[2]A. C. Goodell *et al.*, eds., *Acts and Resolves, Public and Private, of the Province of the Massachusetts Bay*, 21 vols. (Boston, 1869–1922), 5:626–628, 1776–1777, Ch. 26; [Thomas Crafts], "Orderly Book of the Regiment of Artillery Raised for the Defense of the Town of Boston in 1776," ed. James Kimball, *EIHC* 13:115–134, 237–243 (1877), 14:60–76, 110–128, 188–211 (1878), 17 Aug. 1777, p. 240; Washington to Provincial Congress, 1 July 1775, in William Lincoln, ed., *The Journals of Each Provincial Congress of Massachusetts in 1774–1775 . . .* (Boston, 1858), pp. 439–440; Jackson to Knox, 15 Sept. 1777, Henry Knox Papers, 1770–1828, 55 vols., reel 4:55, MHS. But see Timothy Pickering, *An Easy Plan of Discipline for a Militia* (Salem, Mass., 1775), p. 10, main section.

American officers had high notions of their own rank and their superiority over the men, notions that increased with advancement in rank and from north to south. The Continental Congress and the colonial legislatures, many members of which came from the same socioeconomic section of the population as the officers, granted them special privileges. General Lee was to be indemnified for his loss of property while serving in the army; the son of the late General Warren was to be educated at public expense; John Adams imperiously named several persons of the better sort "whom I wish to hear provided for" by commissions in the army—for example, a governor's son who "has been so far carried away . . . with a Zeal" as to enlist as a private. About the same time General Washington demanded "vigorous measures" to ensure enlistment of soldiers without paying a bounty.[3]

In the Continental Congress John Adams declared about forming a constitution: "But we had a people of more intelligence, curiosity, and enterprise . . . to erect the whole building with their own hands, upon the broadest foundation." Two weeks after this people-rousing speech, he advised a friend how to receive General Washington and his staff in camp at Boston. The officers, whose "high importance" and "elevated" stations Congress wanted duly acknowledged, should be received with "the utmost politeness and respect." Popular participation? In this way: "The whole army, I think, should be drawn up upon the occasion, and all the pride, pomp, and circumstance of glorious war displayed."[4]

A pay raise for officers at the end of 1775 (and later measures about their pensions) met strong opposition among the population. The "large stipends," wrote Harvard inhabitants from Worcester county, "chilled the spirits of the Commonalty." They continued: "That the distresses of America should prove a harvest to some, and famine to others, this we deprecate." The raise endangered unanimity and the common exertions, because soldiers, comparing their pay to that of officers, refused to enlist. Many other towns held similar opinions.[5] The "more genteel" part of the population consciously cultivated admiration for rank and formal distinctions and was soon supported by the General Court. Opposition to such measures was difficult; it could be interpreted as disloyalty, Toryism. Deferential attitudes toward rank and the fear aroused by the presence of British troops also helped to smother criticism of hierarchical elements in the army structure.

[3]Worthington C. Ford *et al.*, eds., *Journals of the Continental Congress, 1774–1789*, 34 vols. (Washington, D.C., 1904–1937), 2:98–99, 7:243; MA 168:443; *Warren–Adams Letters*, 1:64, 87, 165, cf. *ibid.*, p. 51; Washington to Massachusetts General Court, 5 Dec. 1775, in Force, ed., *Archives*, 4.4:191.

[4]John Adams in Continental Congress, 2 June 1775, *The Works of John Adams*, ed. Charles F. Adams, 10 vols. (Boston, 1850–1856), 3:13–16; John Adams to Gerry, 18 June 1775, in Force, ed., *Archives*, 4.2:1019, and James T. Austin, *The Life of Elbridge Gerry, with Contemporary Letters, to the Close of the American Revolution*, 2 vols. (Boston, 1828, 1829), 1:87–90; *Warren–Adams Letters*, 1:57–58, 194–195. Oscar Handlin and Mary Handlin, eds., *The Popular Sources of Political Authority: Documents on the Massachusetts Constitution of 1780* (Cambridge, Mass., 1966), p. 14, note 35, for attitudes in the Continental Congress.

[5]Petitions of Harvard, Templeton, Worcester County Convention, 1775–1776, in Force, ed., *Archives*, 4.4:1245, 1354, 1399, 4.5:1258; action of the House thereon, *ibid.*, 4.4:1408; *Town Records of Dudley, Massachusetts*, 2 vols. (Pawtucket, R.I., 1893, 1894), 5 Dec. 1775, 2:166; James Warren to John Adams, 11 Dec. 1775, *Warren–Adams Letters*, 1:194; Lincoln, ed., *Journals of Each Provincial Congress*, 28 April 1775, p. 163; Lee Nathaniel Newcomer, *The Embattled Farmers: A Massachusetts Countryside in the American Revolution* (New York, 1953), p. 101; Robert J. Taylor, *Western Massachusetts in the Revolution* (Providence, R.I., 1954), pp. 113, 120, 122–123, 129, 137, 140, 143, 152, 165, 166.

The same goes for attitudes toward British prisoners of war. High-ranking officers were received politely, "the American gentlemen mixing with the British," and from the crowd "not a word or a gesture that was disrespectful." James Warren sourly noted that on the "Tyrants Birth day," 1778, "our General" dined with the captured General Burgoyne and presumably drank the king's (tyrant's) health. Lower-ranking prisoners were treated less respectfully. In return, they sometimes rioted or "frolicked" against their guards. Once they assaulted an American sentry who had shot at a *captured* British officer who, riding in a chaise between two women "of [easy] virtue," refused to stop.[6]

Thus, one pattern of social behavior, deference to rank, was maintained even against troops of the enemy. Another tradition, the hostility toward strangers, was maintained even against the allied French troops. French soldiers and sailors, including their officers, were repeatedly subjected to crowd action. Captain Decamps was insulted by American sailors, and Brigadier General Demauroy noticed "that Divers Despises me." The French were used as scapegoats when the Rhode Island expedition failed. Though only some troops from the French fleet were quartered in town, the inhabitants greatly resented the quartering. They were held responsible for the food shortage in Boston. On the evening of 8 September 1778, only 10 days after their arrival, a food riot against French bakers, sailors, and soldiers occurred.[7]

American troops in Boston and Massachusetts caused the same difficulties as had the British earlier. Although the commander instructed officers and soldiers to be as "Servicable to the Publick and agreable to Individuals" as possible, and although the inhabitants were persuaded that the presence of soldiers was necessary, grievances arose. Sentries hailed passers-by and once accidentally killed a man. Fishing boats and other vessels were stopped and searched. Disorders occurred because of the large liquor sales to the troops. Officers, requested to act "without any levity, or indecency of expression or behavior," nevertheless gave Boston wardens opportunity to complain. Soldiers, ordered to desist from "needlessly Crossing" private property, nevertheless did "Injury to Individuals." Inhabitants labored under arbitrary quarterings, undertaken without the presence of civil magistrates. Soldiers undertook rescue riots in obstruction of civil officers. One soldier, obviously familiar with the burdens of the farmers, noted, "A very disagreeable business—this foraging without money to pay." No large incidents were reported. Whether none in fact occurred or whether reporting of such disturbances was suppressed cannot be ascertained.

Militiamen and soldiers often acted according to their own judgment. Farmers went home without leave when the harvest season came. Whole units left when their

---

[6]William Heath, *Heath's Memoirs of the American War,* ed. Rufus R. Wilson (1798; reprint ed., New York, 1904), pp. 147–148; Charles Martyn, *The Life of Artemas Ward, the First Commander-in-Chief of the American Revolution* (New York, 1921), p. 226; Ezekiel Price, "Diary of Ezekiel Price, 1775–76," *MHSP* 7:258 (1863–1864); James Warren to Samuel Adams, 28 June 1778, *Warren–Adams Letters,* 2:28; Henley to Heath, 8 Jan. 1778, *Heath Papers, MHSC* 5.4, 7.4, 7.5 (1878, 1904, 1905), 7.4:201–202 (originals, 1774–1872, 26 vols., MHS); Scollay to Knox, 14 Jan. 1779, Knox Papers, reel 4:97, MHS; *BG,* 22 June 1778.

[7]*Heath Papers,* Sept. 1778, *MHSC* 7.4:267–272 *passim;* MA 200:69–70; *BG,* 7 Sept. 1778; Demauroy to Boston selectmen, 3 Sept. 1777, Misc. Unbound Papers, BCH; cf. Chapter 14, pp.363–364.

terms of enlistment expired. Inclination to serve in the army slumped further when the pay for officers was raised without a corresponding raise for privates and when soldiers' notes were accepted only at low rates or bought up wholesale.[8]

Impressment and drafting of Americans by Americans caused friction between draftees and officials, between those who served and those who got off. Impressments were conducted with the same ruthlessness the British had used. The numerous draft calls met resentment and were sometimes opposed. Inhabitants in western parts, fearful that the Tories would overpower those who stayed behind, refused to serve unless the Tories were disarmed or arrested. Ashfield men began a draft riot, refusing to serve until the economic situation was more stable.[9] At a military muster in Boston a few days after the Declaration of Independence had arrived and been celebrated, the authorities ordered the eligible men surrounded and guarded by the Independent Company, composed only of well-to-do men, who held pompous parades but paid for substitutes when actually drafted for service. The men on the common, who were treated more harshly than captured British officers, and most of whom could not afford to buy their freedom, rioted against their guards, and for several days the town was in great agitation.[10]

The situation of many soldiers—their political understanding, their regard for deference, as well as their shrewd emancipation from absolute submission—is evidenced in the following petition, quoted here at length because of its masterful phrasing:

> Jentlemen Representitives of this province.
>
> Know dout it is a truth acknowlidged among men that god his placd men in greater and Lower Stations in life, and that Inferiours are moraly Bound to obay their Superiors in all their lawful Commands, But altho our king is our Superiour, yet his Commands are unlawful. Therefore we are not bound to obay, but are in providence Cald to rise up against Such tiranical usurpations, and our province at this difficult Day is Necessiated to Chuse Representitives and officers to Rule as king over us. To which we Cheerfully Submit in all things lawful or just and Count it our hapiness, but if their laws are greavious to bare, then the agreaved is by the Same Rule authorized to Rise up in oppisition to Said laws, and their has been Some acts made for the Regulation of the armey, and his been So Short lifed and New acts in Stead thereof, that it his Constraind many to withdraw and others, viz.

[8]Heath, *Memoirs*, p. 239; Heath to Watson, 26 April 1777, William Heath Papers, 4:118, MHS; Heath's orders, 11 May 1777, *ibid.*, p. 213, 7:184; deposition of Justice Henshaw, Leicester, 21 May 1777, *ibid.*, 4:257; Crafts, "Orderly Book," pp. 117ff.; Moses Greenleaf, "Capt. Moses Greenleaf's Orderly Book, 1776–1777," in Papers, 1776–1780, MHS; Aaron Hall's Military Service, Judd MSS., Rev. Matters, p. 136, Forbes Library; Provincial Congress to Ward, 5 May 1775, in Lincoln, ed., *Journals of Each Provincial Congress*, p. 195; cf. *ibid.*, 8 July 1775, p. 475; Heath to council, 1 April 1777, MA 196:352–353; *Warren–Adams Letters*, 1:188, Hawley to Gerry, 18 Feb. 1776, in Austin, *Life of Gerry*, 1:162–163; *Acts and Resolves*, 5:600–603, 1776–1777, Ch. 22, note, pp. 687–691; *BTR* 18:292–293; Washington's orders, 21 March 1776, in Force, ed., *Archives*, 4.5:456; case of A. Brown, 1775, *ibid.*, 4.2:720–721.
[9]Petition of Ashfield to General Court, 26 May 1778, MA 184:130–131; George Sheldon, *A History of Deerfield*, 2 vols. (Deerfield, Mass., 1896), 2:722–723; John Rowe, *Letters and Diary of John Rowe, Boston Merchant, 1759–1762, 1764–1779*, ed. Anne Rowe Cunningham (Boston, 1903; reprint ed., 1969), 12 July 1779, pp. 329–330.
[10]John Boyle, "Boyle's Journal of Occurrences in Boston, 1759–1778," 9 Sept. 1776, *NEHGR* 85:124–125 (1931); William Pynchon, *The Diary of William Pynchon of Salem*, ed. F. E. Oliver (Boston, 1890), 22 July 1776, p. 13.

Companies and Ragements, Appearently broke or throne into Confusion, and by these that Remain Here are much Deuty Required, to which we, animated from a Spirit of Liberty, would Chearfully Submit, provided we had a Sufficient Support from day to day. we many times have drawn Such Roten Stinkin meat that the Smell is Sufficient to make us lothe the Same. . . . their is a large Number of men in verious Ragements that Rsents Their treatment with Regard to provision So fare that they have Sworn by the god that made them that, if the[y] Cannot have a Sufficient Support, they will Either Raise a mob and go to the general and Demand provision and obtain it that way, or they will Swing their packs Emediately and go home boldly throu all the Guards.

The eight signers wished the Congress "wisdom" to remove the "Defficultie" in order to prevent a "Rebelion." The Provincial Congress ordered General Thomas to inquire into the matter and to afford redress. Somebody privately called the paper "Pertition of 8 Scoundrels to the Honourable Provi Congress." In the public rhetoric of the General Court, however, soldiers were "our virtuous sons."[11]

Tensions arose between those who expected deference and those who might be willing to accept guidance but who refused submission and had become increasingly cognizant of their rights and interests. This was also evident in civil life and influenced the reestablishment of government. John Adams and Elbridge Gerry, both at first fearful of the political power an army might wield, soon considered the possibility of using the army to force the people into submission and to prevent the general discontent from turning into social action.[12]

PEOPLE VERSUS COURTS AND FEES

Since the Administration of Justice Act took effect on 1 September 1774, the courts in Massachusetts had been shut down. In many countries, especially in Hampshire and Berkshire, the courts were closed not merely for constitutional reasons. The complicated and costly lawsuits had long been a grievance of many inhabitants. Lawyers and judges, on the other hand, profited handsomely from their commissions. The opposition to British rule had taught the people that they could also oppose the "subordinate powers." Already in February 1774 Governor Hutchinson had heard "of town meetings held in the county of Berkshire . . . to form combinations against the payment of Lawyer's and Sheriff's fees" because the fees established by law were considered too high. But the opposition was not unanimous, particularly in its second phase, resistance to reestablishment of Whig authority, and in its third phase, when it was used to exert pressure on Whig leaders to stop

---

[11]*CSMP* 6:135–136 (1899–1900). The historian who published the document, F. L. Gay, showed an uncommonly clear bias in favor of rank. He conceded that there might have been some suffering "on the sudden massing of a horde of half-disciplined troops. . . . How to deal with such cases of rank insubordination at that juncture must have been a hard question. As an example of one of the many discouragements which beset those in authority at the beginning of the Revolution, the paper seems worth preserving." General Court to Washington, 29 March 1776, in Force, ed., *Archives,* 4.5:539–540.

[12]John Adams to James Sullivan, 1775, quoted in Richard B. Morris, "Insurrection in Massachusetts," *America in Crisis,* ed. Daniel Aaron (New York, 1952), p. 21; Austin, *Life of Gerry,* 1:78–79, and Force, ed., *Archives,* 4.2:905.

dragging their feet on the formation of a constitution (see Chapter 15). When a crowd stopped a court from sitting in March 1776, "The people in the *old* towns . . . [were] uneasy about the matter." In the long-settled "old" towns, the inhabitants were on the average more wealthy than those in recently founded plantations and districts. They probably wanted little change and thrived under the old system.[13]

A convention of Berkshire County Committees of Correspondence at Stockbridge in December 1775 made an attempt to establish judicial procedures according to the interests of the people. After voting their disapproval of the resumption of government under the old charter, granted by the crown after the "glorious Revolution" of 1688–1689 and more conservative than the original charter, the convention devised a system for the popular election of judges and demanded that all "civil officers" be nominated by the county. Again eight of the old towns protested, ostensibly because such innovations "tend to dissolve all Government, and introduce dissention, anarchy, and confusion, among the people; for when we deviate from the established rules, we are lost in the boundless field of uncertainty and disorder."[14]

While the arguments for and against courts raged, crowds prevented courts from opening, usually acting in conjunction with county conventions. The widespread discontent about the judicial system and the tenure and the conduct of the judges was explained to the provincial authorities in numerous memorials. In March 1776, committees of 28 Hampshire towns met to discuss the next session of one of the lower courts. The commissions of the judges dated from British rule; the new Whig authorities had not even considered new appointments necessary. Each delegate was asked to give "What he supposes is the sense of the Town he represents," and by a very close vote it was determined that it was necessary "for the Salvation of our Country" that the courts should not be opened. A committee informed the judges of this decision and they adjourned sine die.[15]

Discontent with the courts manifested itself in other counties too. A Worcester County Convention petitioned the General Court to adjust the fee tables downward before ordering the courts to be held, since the people were "grieved" to hear courts scheduled, "esteeming the late feetable too high and exorbitant." In Bristol County a crowd of 50 or more armed men prevented the holding of the Court of Sessions in March 1776. The inhabitants of Middleborough, Plymouth, instructed their representative to endeavor to obtain a resolve by the assembly to close the courts temporarily, criminal cases excepted, to reestablish "the Peace and harmony of the People." The House was conscious of the fact that the fees had been exorbitant in some cases, but it did not satisfy the expectations of the people.[16]

[13]Hutchinson to Dartmouth, Feb. 1774, *The Diary and Letters of His Excellency Thomas Hutchinson,* ed. Peter Orlando Hutchinson, 2 vols. (London, 1883, 1886), 1:115; Judd MSS., Rev. Matters, p. 166, Forbes Library.

[14]Protest against the convention, 15 Dec. 1775, in Force, ed., *Archives,* 4.5:807–808.

[15]Minutes of a meeting of committees, 11 March 1776, Military Papers, American Revolution, Forbes Library. Cf. Frank W. Grinnel, "The Influence of Thomas Allen and the 'Berkshire Constitutionalists' on the Constitutional History of the United States," *J. Am. Bar Assoc.* 22:168–174 (1936); Richard D. Birdsall, "The Reverend Thomas Allen: Jeffersonian Calvinist," *NEQ* 30:147–165 (1957); Theodore M. Hammett, ed., "Allen's Defense of the Berkshire Constitutionalists," *WMQ* 3.33:514–527 (1976).

[16]Force, ed., *Archives,* 4.4:1460, 4.5:1247–1248, 1258; Middleborough instructions, 7 Oct. 1776, MA 156:147–148.

While the people from Plymouth, Bristol, and Worcester Counties petitioned for redress of this particular grievance, the people in Hampshire and Berkshire demanded a general constitutional foundation for the courts. Meanwhile they kept them closed. Nevertheless, on 3 January 1777, the House of Representatives ordered the courts to be held, recommending "to the good people of these counties to consider how much the happiness and weal of society depends upon the orderly and regular execution of the laws, and to do all in their power to aid and support the civil magistrates in the execution of their office." Laws, the lawgivers explained, were made for "the encouragement of piety and virtue," to prevent profanity, Sabbath breaking, and "other immoralities" and "to detect and punish those persons who are trying to subvert the liberty of these free States." Laws had been passed by "our . . . venerable and virtuous" ancestors and by the will of the "Supreme Being." Economic tensions, social considerations, and east–west contentions were not mentioned. Neither did the representatives explain on what basis laws were to be made.[17]

A Hampshire convention, consisting of 92 delegates representing 38 of 49 towns, met on 5 February 1777 and voted, probably under the impression that a new constitution would be submitted to the people soon, that the courts should be held and that nothing be done "to discourage the same."[18] Berkshiremen did not submit, but held another convention at Pittsfield in 1778. The delegates resolved to lay before the towns the question of whether courts should be admitted. When they reconvened, 19 of a total of 28 towns reported the results of their deliberations. The sitting of the courts for criminal offenses was rejected by 545 nays to 329 yeas, that of the courts for civil actions by 660 nays to 161 yeas. These majorities suggest that debt collection was one factor in the decisions about the courts but that constitutional concepts were more important. Another petition for an immediate convening of a constitutional convention was sent to the General Court.[19]

Social tensions within a community were exacerbated by the opposition to the courts. Men from Lanesborough, Berkshire, stated that the townsmen—or rather a part of them—were willing to "support the just cause of America." They complained that another section, "from sinister designs of self-interest," refused to adhere to civil government without a constitutional basis. Their "considerable number of adherents" were "misled zealots," unwilling to pay "their just debts." They added that the better sort, "especially persons of understanding, interest and honesty," were for immediate resumption of government without waiting for a constitution. The matter was complicated by the conduct of Jonathan Smith, militia officer and Lanesborough's representative. He had been esteemed "a warm friend to liberty"—that is, an order-loving Whig. But then he opposed all appointments of judges and other officers, charging that they were of "arbitrary principles," had

[17]*Journals of the House of Representatives*, p. 244.

[18]Convention minutes, 5 Feb. 1777, Military Papers, American Revolution, Forbes Library.

[19]J. E. A. Smith, *The History of Pittsfield (Berkshire County), Massachusetts, from the Year 1734 to the Year 1876*, 2 vols. (Boston, 1869, 1876), 1:359–361; Charles J. Taylor, *History of Great Barrington (Berkshire County), Massachusetts* (Great Barrington, Mass., 1882), pp. 291–292; Elisha P. Douglass, *Rebels and Democrats: The Struggle for Equal Political Rights and Majority Rule during the American Revolution* (Chapel Hill, N.C., 1955), pp. 150–151.

Loyalist sentiments, and were "extortive in their practises." Large numbers of people in diverse towns agreed and supported Smith. However, when he also opposed the popular election of judges, the Lanesborough people began to suspect that he wanted the office for himself. The contentions ended a town meeting "in a passionate and tumultuous manner." Smith's opponents asked Timothy Edwards of Stockbridge whether "there is anything further we can, in justice, do" or whether "we must be passive with our superiors." Edwards advised against passive obedience. Smith, in turn, tried to raise a riot against Edwards, calling him a Tory.[20]

LOCAL GOVERNMENT AND OPPOSITION TO THE COMMITTEES

Necessity had contributed to the acceptance of military authority. The judicial authority, considered oppressive and as serving private interests, was rejected. As to political institutions, parallel to the decline of provincial government under crown authority, new institutions evolved on the local level. The resulting bodies were no revolutionary innovations; they were consciously developed and derived from traditional political structures and adapted to the present exigencies. Some, the Convention of 1768 and the Provincial Congresses, were intended to replace the legislative institutions of the province; others, the county conventions, to coordinate measures on a regional level. Long a feature of provincial political life, the committees administered local affairs. But under the new circumstances their nature and function changed from ad hoc to long-term, from advisory to executive. Often they, became increasingly independent from their parent body, the town meeting, first as Committees of Correspondence, later also as Committees of Safety, Inspection, and so on.[21]

In Massachusetts the most important Committee of Correspondence was not the one of the House of Representatives but that of Boston, first elected in November 1772. Its express function was the coordination of opposition with other towns and colonies. Tory Thomas Oliver believed that the people "were governed by no principles, but blindly led, or impelled by a set of wicked seditious Levellers, who in form of Committees of Correspondence, and under the name of Patriots, were propagating Treason and Rebellion, thro' the Country." Oliver erred: The Whig committeemen were not levelers, the people not blind. But he was correct in stressing the extensive influence of the committeemen, whose functions were deliberately extended by many towns and who often circumvented the established town elite.[22]

After the collapse of British rule in fall 1774, the committees called regional

[20]Letters to Edwards and to council, April 1776, in Force, ed., *Archives*, 4.5:806, 808–809.

[21]M. Chamberlain, ed., "Journal of the Massachusetts Committee of Correspondence, 28 May–21 Oct. 1773," *MHSP* 2.4:82–90 (1887–1889); Boston Committee of Correspondence, Papers, NYPL; Ben Cockram, "The Committees of Correspondence in the American Revolution" (Ph.D. diss., Univ. of Michigan, 1926); Richard D. Brown, *Revolutionary Politics in Massachusetts: The Boston Committee of Correspondence and the Towns, 1772–1774* (Cambridge, Mass., 1970).

[22]Oliver to Dartmouth, 9 Dec. 1774, *CSMP* 32:492 (1933–1937).

conventions and functioned as courts. Town-meeting votes regulated the takeover of judicial powers, mainly concerning criminal matters and due process for prisoners. The Granby committee held "regular trial[s]" and issued executions to the constable. Pittsfield decided to consider the "transactions and determinations" of its committeemen "as the actions and proceedings of an adjourned court." In a New Hampshire town, people considered the government dissolved, set up a code of laws for local use, and managed their town affairs without difficulties.[23]

Hutchinson, attacked for his extensive influence as governor, had said in 1767: "To suffer the Transactions and Opinions of the Executive Court to be illiberally animadverted upon is of the most dangerous Tendency to the Community." Now many committees took action against critics of their decisions and actions and demanded respect. A man calling the members of the Athol committee "a pack of *Low-life* half witted Devils" was told that by "reflecting on them he had reflected on the people that Constituted them." In Worcester, somebody was confined for insolent behavior toward the committeemen. The General Court, intent on inculcating due submission to the new powers, confirmed the decision. However, most of the population accepted the rule of the committees, even when their authority included search powers similar to those of customs officials.[24]

When the central government in Boston lamented disorders and impending anarchy, a Pittsfield town meeting described the situation in December 1775, 17 months after the last legal courts had been held there, as idyllic: "The people of the country, under the lenient and efficient rule of their several committees, and in the most vigorous and unintermitted exertions in the country's cause, had lived together in greatest love, peace, safety, liberty, happiness and good order, except the disorder and dissentions occasioned by the Tories." Many towns decided to extend and stabilize this form of local government by regional conventions. But middle-class discontent with self-government favored the resumption of the old institutions relying on established elites. Whig politicians in the seaboard towns, especially in Boston, pursued the same policy in order to strengthen their own authority.[25]

The imperious conduct of the Boston Committee of Correspondence brought forth an important challenge to committee rule. The lack of understanding for spontaneous mass action among Boston's committeemen had been evidenced by their reaction to the powder-alarm crowds. They came mainly from among those who had replaced the old merchant leadership in 1768, after the impressment and *Liberty* riot. The committee also served to unite the different echelons of the town's leadership. Top politicians (Otis, Adams, Warren) were members, as well as men

[23]Granby: Military Papers, American Revolution, Orders, 20 Oct. 1775, 15 March 1776, Forbes Library. Barnardston: Force, ed., *Archives*, 5.1:247. Pittsfield: *ibid.*, 4.5:806; Abner Sanger, "Ye Journal of Abner Sanger," [7 Dec. 1775], *Repertory* 1:241 (1924–1925).

[24]Samuel M. Quincy, ed., *Reports of Cases Argued and Adjudged in the Superior Court of Judicature of . . . Massachusetts Bay, 1761–1772, by Josiah Quincy, Junior* (Boston, 1865), pp. 242–243; Ichabod Dexter to Artemas Ward, 14 March 1775, Ward Papers, vol. 2, MHS; William Lincoln, *History of Worcester, Massachusetts, from Its Earliest Settlement to 1836* (2d ed.; Worcester, Mass., 1862), p. 101; Sheldon, *Deerfield*, 2:711–719; Thomas Hutchinson, *The History of the Colony and Province of Massachusetts Bay*, ed. Lawrence Shaw Mayo, 3 vols. (Cambridge, Mass., 1936), 3:187–188.

[25]Pittsfield to General Court, 26 Dec. 1775, in Smith, *Pittsfield*, 1:338.

close to the crowds (Molineux, Pierpoint, Young) or to the merchant–captains (Bradford, Mackay). But while in most towns the committeemen were elected annually, the Boston committee, elected in 1772, officiated till 1776 without electoral review. From the middle of 1774 onward, the deteriorating economic and political situation, combined with the growing arrogance of the committeemen, resulted first in an unsuccessful attempt to dissolve it and then in a successful move to limit the plural office holding of its members.

The question of a new nonimportation or nonconsumption agreement had been debated indecisively in summer 1774 among merchants and 800 tradesmen, meeting separately. Without consulting either of these groups, or the town in general, or the country towns, Boston's committee drafted a nonimportation agreement, the "Solemn League and Covenant." The committee, afraid of opposition in Boston, expected that nobody would dare counteract once the country towns had signed. The latter were usually more ready to exclude "foreign luxuries" and to place limitations on commerce. Therefore, the committee circulated the covenant in the country, explaining that nearly everybody in Boston had subscribed and demanding rather peremptorily that it should be accepted. First the country people complained about tone and timing, so that the committee had to placate the "respectable fellow countrymen." Then Bostonians mounted opposition because they felt imposed upon.[26]

On 27 June 1774 a town meeting attended by more than 1000 men voted that the whole correspondence of the committee be laid before them for scrutiny. Samuel Eliot gained wide applause for his masterly speech against the covenant: Nonintercourse meant that debts could not be remitted to Great Britain, which was dishonest. Small artisans would have a difficult time. One committee's having "such extensive Powers" was of "dangerous Tendency." The active men of the conservative branch of the Merchants' Society also spoke against the committee. For the committee spoke Adams, Quincy, Warren, Young, Molineux, and Kent. After two days of hot debates, a merchant moved to censure the committee, which might have gained a majority. But in the same motion he demanded "that the said Committee be annihilated." This motion lost by a four-to-one margin.[27]

The "Solemn League and Covenant" was soon superseded by the Association of the Continental Congress. Enforcement policies paralleled those of the earlier nonimportation agreements. In Boston 61 men, "principally young fellows," were

[26]A Solemn League and Covenant had been adopted in 1643 to reform the British nation and had been the title of the association of the Boston market rioters in 1737. Albert Matthews, "The Solemn League and Covenant, 1774," *CSMP* 18:103–122 (1915–1916); text, *MHSP* 12:45–48 (1871–1873), governor's proclamation, *ibid.*, 15:354 (1876–1877), protests, *ibid.*, 2.2:481–486 (1885–1886); *BTR* 18:177; Rowe, *Letters and Diary,* 27–28 June 1774, pp. 276–277; Thomas Newell, "Diary for 1773 to the End of 1774, of Mr. Thomas Newell, Boston," *MHSP* 15:352–354 (1876–1877); John Andrews, "Letters of John Andrews, Esq., Boston, 1772–1776," ed. Winthrop Sargent, *MHSP* 8:329–332 (1864–1865); Ebenezer Parkman, Diary, 10 vols., photostat, 13 June 1774, MHS; Ballantine's Journal, June 1774, Judd MSS., Rev. Matters, p. 160, Forbes Library; Thomas Young to John Lamb, 19 June 1774, in Isaac Q. Leake, *Memoir of the Life and Times of General Thomas Lamb* (Albany, N.Y., 1850), pp. 89–91.

[27]*BTR* 18:177–178; Henry Hulton to ———, 6 July 1774, Letterbooks, 1:96–99, HHL; *Mass. Spy,* 30 June 1774; *BNL,* 30 June 1774; *BEP,* 4 July 1774; cf. Lincoln, ed., *Journals of Each Provincial Congress,* 21 Oct. 1774, p.

chosen to enforce it. Other towns elected Committees of Inspection; in Scituate two shopkeepers who refused to adhere to it were ostracized.[28]

The second challenge to the Committee of Correspondence came in 1776. In May the town instructed its representatives to take measures against plural office holding. In August the townsmen began to consider the accumulation of offices of their own committee, whose functions were executive. Seven members were also legislators, and several more held military offices. Both, but particularly the mixing of "Military and Civil Authorities," were criticized during a debate lasting two days. James Otis and John Barrett argued for "one man—one office"; Colonel Crafts and Major Revere, committee members, argued for plural office holding. The committee lost. The town passed three sweeping votes: Members of the committee elected as representatives automatically lost their committee seats (according to a resolve of the General Court, passed 13 February 1776). It was, further, "the Sense of the Town" that no regular town official was eligible for the committee. Finally, any military commission in the Continental or Provincial Army was judged "incompatible with holding any Civil Trust."[29]

Among the committee members who lost their seats was the chairman, John Brown. The inhabitants were particularly enraged about his high-handed conduct. When the draft call for the expedition to Canada had come in July 1776, the committee commanded the draft-age inhabitants to assemble on the common. The Independent Company recruited from among those of the better sort displayed its expensive uniforms, ostentatiously mustered separately, and voted not to get into actual service but to pay the fines from a common fund. John Brown ordered the company to surround the other inhabitants and to place themselves "as sentriys round the square to prevent the people's going away"; those mustered were "kept in at the point of the Bayonet." William Cooper, town clerk, merchant factotum, and unable to understand crowd action, imperiously announced that either volunteers would step forward or every twenty-fifth man would be drafted. Seven men volunteered; the rest rioted against the sentries and the committee. Attempts were made to replace the committee's chairman, Brown, immediately. The people called him "Tyrant Nero" and decided that "Tyranny is Tyranny let it come from whom it may." Though he lost his committee seat, he was reelected representative in 1777 by a small margin as candidate of the Northend Caucus against the strong opposition of the Southenders.[30]

25; Force, ed., *Archives,* 4.1:490–491.

[28]Ford *et al.,* eds., *Journals of the Continental Congress,* 20 Oct. 1774, 1:75–81; *BTR* 18:205–207; Samuel Deane, *History of Scituate, Massachusetts, from Its First Settlement to 1831* (Boston, 1831), pp. 134–135; James Warren to John Adams, 5 Nov. 1775, *Warren–Adams Letters,* 1:176; *Mass. Gaz.,* 6 Feb. 1775; James Allen, "Diary," quoted in Herbert Aptheker, *The American Revolution, 1763–1783 . . . An Interpretation* (New York, 1960), p. 82, cf. 78–81; Force, ed., *Archives,* 4.1:1203, 1211.

[29]*BTR* 18:238, 240, 242, 243–244. When the choice of new members came up, the town did so "in the Room of those who have resigned, or looked upon by the Town, as ceasing to be Members." Then the 10 former members were named, so that none of them could slip by, and the new members were elected "by separate Votes" to prevent slates. William Knox to Henry Knox, 29 Aug. 1776, Knox Papers, reel 3:31, MHS. Cf. Ellen E. Brennan, *Plural Officeholding in Massachusetts, 1760–1780* (Chapel Hill, N.C., 1945), Ch. 4.

[30]William Knox to Henry Knox, 24 July 1776, Knox Papers, reel 2:173, MHS.

Committee rule was resented by many from the middle and upper sections of society, who were reluctant to defer to the new men, who often were less wealthy and had less social standing. They were angrily called "our Lords and Masters," "high and mighty Committee Men." The moderate John Eliot discontentedly noted about Boston: "It is a rare thing to meet with any body here without some lofty titles to declare their merit,—Colonel A., Major B., Captain C." Everybody was coveting some rank, if not military, then as a member of "some Committee of Correspondence, or Safety, or Supply, or else holds a seat under some gentlemen who fill these important places." To call someone a mechanic was an affront, according to Eliot. All new men "must be treated with such complaisance that we must learn all the twistings of the body which is necessary for a valet de chambre before we can receive a token of cognisance." James Otis, "Whig grandee," grumbled: "When the pot boils, the scum will arise." Whig James Warren wholeheartedly agreed. A Boston Tory added, "All is Tumult and Confusion here and the Mob seem to have taken the Reins of Government, a most miserable Chariotteer...."[31]

Several reasons can be assigned for this discontent of middle-class and upper-class people of all political persuasions. Some had just a few minor complaints, which they blamed on the new powers that be. Thus, John Eliot could not find a tailor or shoemaker who would work for him because they were busy working for the patriot cause. Others disagreed with specific political decisions, such as the nonimportation schemes. Then there was the aversion of the passive, the apolitical, to any change. Those who protested in Worcester against the town's approval of the tea riot were prototypes of a silent majority. For most of them, it was their first participation in town affairs in two decades.[32]

Most important were social causes. The large number of new committees and the ousting of Loyalist officials resulted naturally in the advance of new men into these positions. This preferment depended to a certain degree on their previous participation in the resistance against the British. Moderates and conservatives, not to mention many Whigs, who expected deference because of age, rank, or wealth suddenly found their "natural" position challenged and had to realize that this position was only "traditional." The new men, conscious of their achievements and proud of their station, demanded deference too. Concern about rank was universal among those who had any, had had any, or expected to get any.

The Whig James Lovell complained that the treatment of American prisoners by the British in Halifax was "Scandalous by neglecting all distinction of Rank." The Tory Benjamin Marston of Plymouth was piqued that one of the committeemen who questioned him was "a gentlemen with a ragged jacket and, I think, a leather apron." John White of Salem complained about the new "Taskmasters." He de-

---

[31]Andrews, "Letters," 1 Nov. 1774, p. 382; [Charles Startin] to Henry Pelham, 3 Dec. 1774, *MHSC* 71:276–277; Eliot to Belknap, 12 Jan. 1777, *MHSC* 6.4:99–104; James Warren to John Adams, 14 Nov. 1775, *Warren–Adams Letters,* 1:183; Gooch to Cumberland, 8 April 1774, *The Cumberland Letters: Being the Correspondence of Rich[ar]d Dennison Cumberland and George Cumberland between the Years 1771 and 1784,* ed. Clementina Black (London, 1912), p. 58.

[32]Dirk Hoerder, *Society and Government, 1760–1780: The Power Structure in Massachusetts Townships* (Berlin, 1972), p. 124.

scribed them as "Men, poor, without Moral Virtue, Blockheads, etc., in Government. The High Sheriff of this Country is a Tanner, two Magistrates one an Tanner, the other a Joiner." The ritualistic reversal of roles, practiced on Pope's Day and Plough Monday, had suddenly become the usual rather than the exceptional. However, most of the new men had achieved some status and prosperity before getting into office. They were master craftsmen, small employers, and entrepreneurs, but "poor" from the merchants' point of view. For John White and many other colonials, "poor" still meant lack of morals and intelligence as well as of leisure. Poor people could be bought by wealthy demagogues, the reasoning went, and it was preferable to exclude them from government rather than to punish the demagogues or to prevent the wealthy from buying. To many the main interest was the maintenance of the social and economic status quo. British impositions were disagreeable, but spontaneous popular action was worse.[33]

Such attitudes led to hostility toward the committees, which originally had opened channels of influence to persons of less standing, outside the town officialdom. At the end of the decade, most of the committees' functions returned to the regular town hierarchy, which had either adjusted to the new situation or had been replaced by Whigs. This was a return to normalcy not only politically but also in a socioeconomic sense: Town officials in the influential positions usually owned more property than committeemen.

REGIONAL CONVENTIONS: COOPERATION OF DELEGATES AND CROWDS

Conventions were ad hoc bodies to concert plans on a regional level, usually at the county level.[34] The delegates elected a clerk and a moderator or chairman, as in town meetings or the House of Representatives. They were convoked by town meetings, single committees, or groups acting together. The delegates were sometimes specially chosen by the town; sometimes they were members of the Committees of Correspondence. They debated measures about Tories, courts, the convening of a Provincial Congress, and riots.

This last topic of their deliberations was of great importance. All conventions that dealt with them condemned private violence, the "petty mobs" that used anti-Tory feelings to vent personal grievances.[35] But several of the conventions proceeded to public crowd action, mass meetings in the public interest. Cooperation between delegates and crowds was especially close in the two westernmost counties during the constitutionalist period.

The Worcester County convention "convoked" a mass meeting for the beginning

---

[33]James Lovell to Boston selectmen, n.d., *CSMP* 6:74–76 (1899–1900); Benjamin Marston, "Benjamin Marston of Marblehead, Loyalist . . ." [extracts of his diary], *New Brunswick Hist. Soc. Coll.* 3(7):84, 86 (1907); John White, "Extracts from the Interleaved Almanacs Kept by John White of Salem," *EIHC* 49:93–94 (1913).

[34]Handlin and Handlin, eds., *Popular Sources*, pp. 4–5, for earlier conventions; J. F. Jameson, "The Early Political Uses of the Word 'Convention,'" *AHR* 3:477–487 (1897–1898).

[35]Lincoln, ed., *Journals of Each Provincial Congress*, pp. 605 (Suffolk), 620 (Hampshire), 625 (Plymouth), 627 (Bristol), 633, 651 (Worcester), 653–654 (Berkshire), 659 (Cumberland).

of September 1774. It "recommended to the inhabitants of this county, to attend, in person, the next inferior court" session. Furthermore:

> *Resolved,* That it be recommended to the several towns, that they choose proper and suitable officers, and a sufficient number, to regulate the movements of each town, and prevent any disorder which might otherwise happen; and that it be enjoined on the inhabitants of each respective town, that they adhere strictly to the orders and directions of such officers.

After "some debate" a motion was withdrawn that, in case the governor should send troops to execute the Regulating Act, the inhabitants were "to attend, properly armed, in order to repel any hostile force." But an invasion of any town in the county was to be forcefully repelled. The convention then adjourned until 6 September.[36]

On that day, inhabitants of 37 towns (80 percent of all towns in the county) marched up to 45 miles to come to Worcester in companies ranging from 35 to 500 men, totaling 4722. The companies drew up next to one another in ranks six deep on both sides of the street. The line extended for a quarter of a mile. Each group or company elected a leader and a committee to confer with the other groups. The convention delegates met with the elected officers. Their first vote, somewhat more radical than a similar vote of the convention delegates at their 31 August meeting, was that the court should not act under any laws. "[I]f the people concur," each company was to elect one man "as a committee to wait on the judges to inform them of the resolution to stop the courts sitting." The convention delegates asked the people to assemble on the common, inquired how long the voting and electing would take, and then adjourned "to the green." This last vote shows that crowds, delegates, and committees were interdependent and understood this. The autocratic Boston committee always met separately and never mingled with crowds.

The crowd in Worcester concurred and informed the grand jurors of their decision. Then they stopped for a noon recess. After lunch three men were sent "to inquire the occasion of the delay of the judges in making their appearance afore the body of the people." The judges did not wait for further invitations and began their procession through the crowd. Their declarations were voted unsatisfactory. A second one, read—hats off—several times, so that all companies could hear it, was accepted. Then a number of officials and Loyalists had to recant. The county sheriff was so obnoxious that four men accompanied him to prevent disorders. Finally the delegates had "nothing further to lay before" the people and asked them "to march quietly home." The masses did so, after reorganizing the Worcester County militia and electing new officers.[37]

At the Worcester convention and mass meeting, the people and their delegates acted together, but the delegates voted before the companies did. Roles were re-

---

[36]Minutes of the Worcester County Convention, *ibid.,* pp. 632–633; Gage to Dartmouth, 2 Sept. 1774, *ibid.*

[37]*Ibid.,* pp. 635, 637; Parkman, Diary, 5–7 Sept. 1774, vol. 9, MHS; Samuel Paine to William Paine, 22 June 1775, *AASP* 19:435–438 (1908–1909); Paine's account, C.O. 5.160:37–39, PRO; *BG* and *BEP,* 12 Sept. 1774; Force, ed., *Archives,* 4.1:1261.

versed at a convention in Cumberland County. The delegates had hardly finished electing a clerk and a chairman when the clerk had to record:

> A committee from the body of the people, who were assembled at the entrance of the town, waited on this convention, to see if they would choose a committee of one member out of each town, to join them, to wait upon Mr. Sheriff Tyng, to see whether he would act in his office, under the late act of parliament for regulating the government.

The convention immediately sent for the sheriff, who, "after some interrogations," declared that he would not act under the new laws. The delegates then accompanied him to the people, who were satisfied, "and after refreshing themselves, returned peaceably to their several homes." The convention continued its deliberations in the afternoon in the town hall, where those interested could attend.[38]

The conventions set up interim systems of administration. When the courts in Worcester had been prevented from opening, a resolve "for administering justice, and to protect the justices in the execution of their offices," was passed. All justices of the peace of the county, excepting only three named Tories, should act "as single justices, except in judicial actions merely civil," such as collection of debts. Other officials were enjoined to execute their duties till the Provincial Congress could determine what should be done. They were to disregard any order to the contrary "that may be sent to them" by the remnants of the British colonial government. The delegates knew their and the justices' dependence and recommended to the people "that they consider and treat them as being in their said offices, and support and defend them in the execution thereof, according to the laws of this province."[39]

Most of the delegates regarded the cooperation of the people not only as necessary but also as a matter of course. Recommendations were thought sufficient to prevent riots against Tories, opposition to officials, even strife between creditors and debtors. Many conventions asked debtors to pay their "just" debts punctually, and some admonished the creditors to be lenient. Nearly all conventions supported the measures of the Provincial Congresses and advocated that taxes be paid not to the crown authorities but to the new treasurer appointed by the Provincial Congress.[40]

When independence was officially and formally declared, the interim administration of committees and conventions looked back on two years of smooth functioning. Crowds celebrated the event in many towns. Several thousand Bostonians heard the proclamation read in King Street. The Declaration of Independence was read by Thomas Crafts, member of the Loyal Nine, who had counteracted crowd action, been accused of Toryism, read material on class distinctions, supported

---

[38]Lincoln, ed., *Journals of Each Provincial Congress*, pp. 655–656; Force, ed., *Archives*, 4.1:798–799.

[39]*Ibid.*, pp. 638–639.

[40]Worcester County Convention, 31 Aug. 1774, *ibid.*, p. 633; Bristol County Convention, 28–29 Sept. 1774, *CSMP* 1:129 (1892–1894); cf. New Hampshire Provincial Congress, in Force, ed., *Archives*, 4.2:660. In subsequent years, conventions also dealt with the scarcity of provisions and the regulation of prices. Hampshire County Convention, minutes, 5 Feb. 1777, Military Papers, American Revolution, Forbes Library.

Figure 12. Destruction of all signs of royalty, here of the statue of George III in New York. Reproduction of William Walcutt's "Demolishing the Statue of George III," 1854. From the Frick Art Reference Library collection.

concessions to the military governor, and at this time supported plural office holding, including his own. As under British rule, well-to-do inhabitants assembled in the council chamber to celebrate and, as one of the participants wrote, "to drink the K I like to have wrote King damn him—to drink the States of America." The people outside made a bonfire "of all the Ensign's of Royalty that could be collected." Since then, not respect for the king but the "duty to the honour and dignity" of the country was the guideline for conduct, a less than revolutionary change. Whig politicians were now honored by "elegant entertainments," ringing of bells, and processions of inhabitants. Deferential patterns of conduct continued to exist, the spontaneous and participatory features of crowds, local committees, and regional conventions notwithstanding.[41]

CROWDS, PROVINCIAL CONGRESSES, AND NORMALCY

The institutional change on the provincial level took place when warrants were issued to elect representatives for the General Court in early fall 1774. The usual conflict between moderate and sharply anti-British politicians ensued: Should the representatives proceed to business or should a new body, a Provincial Congress, be established? Finally the representatives were instructed not to submit to the Coercive Acts and, in case the governor should react by dissolving the House of Representatives, to join the other delegates in a Provincial Congress. On 29 September Governor Gage issued a proclamation that because of the massive crowd action, the resolves of the county conventions, and the Boston instructions, "the representatives should not meet."[42]

Ninety representatives assembled nevertheless and organized themselves as the Provincial Congress, with Hancock as chairman (7 October). Thus, crowds, conventions, and town-meeting action created the conditions from which a new supreme legislative body was established. In it the delegates from Boston were "by far the most moderate" men present. The moderate, politically inactive John Andrews, who drank tea during the Tea Party, disconcertedly noted in October 1774 that the Provincial Congress was "principally composed of spirited, obstinate countrymen, who have *very* little patience to boast of. Am therefore much afraid they will adopt measures that may impede the adjustments of our differences."[43]

While committees and conventions cooperated with crowds, the Congress had no intention of causing, condoning, or submitting to mass action. Though socially and economically less distinguished than their predecessors, they viewed their electorate as a populace to be ruled. Many people accepted this view; some consciously

---

[41]*BG*, 14 Nov. 1774, 22 July 1776; "Records of the Committee of Safety," 25 April 1775, in Lincoln, ed., *Journals of Each Provincial Congress*, p. 522; Newell, "Diary," 10 Aug., 9 Nov. 1774, pp. 356, 361; Pynchon, *Diary*, 18 July 1776, pp. 11–12; David Cobb, Weekly Journal, 22 July 1776, R. T. Paine Papers, vol. 1766–1776, MHS; Rowe, *Letters and Diary*, 18 July 1776, p. 313; Abigail Adams to John Adams, 21 July 1776, *Adams Family Correspondence*, ed. L. H. Butterfield, 2 vols. (Cambridge, Mass., 1963), 2:55–57; Henry Jackson to Henry Knox, 18 July 1776, Knox Papers, reel 2:163 (MF), MHS; E. B. Robins, "Thomas Crafts, *Bostonian Soc. Proc.* (1914), pp. 31–38.
[42]*BTR* 18:190–192; *BPB*, 3 Oct. 1774.
[43]John Pitts, quoted in Martyn, *Artemas Ward*, p. 72; Andrews, "Letters," 29 Oct. 1774, p. 380.

furthered it. Honor guards of militia men were offered to the Congress. The delegates did not let criticism go by without asserting their dignity. "By God, if this province is to be governed in this manner, it is time for us to look out, and 'tis all owing to the [provincial] committee of safety, a pack of sappy-head-fellows. I know three of them myself." The author of this remark, an officer, had to appear before the Congress and was reprimanded by the president.[44]

But though the delegates were conscious of their station, they had no intention of perpetuating their office. When the time came for the election of the 1775–1776 General Court, they resolved, with certain reservations, that representatives should be sent. When the election warrants from the military governor came on 20 April, one day after Lexington, 94 of 107 delegates voted on 4 May, "after a long and serious debate," to reconsider the resolve. They annulled it and declared Gage an enemy of the country, to whom no obedience was due.[45]

Intent on getting back to the traditional institutions, "a very large majority" voted on 12 May to apply to the Continental Congress "for obtaining their recommendation for this colony to take up and exercise civil government." The letter was read, accepted, and sent on 16 May. It stressed the external threat to the colony and asked for resumption of the 1691 charter. Many westerners were striving for resumption of the first charter. When Congress did not reply by return mail, the delegates nervously sent a second letter, this time outlining internal dangers, which they felt were worse than the British army. "There are, in many parts of the Colony, alarming symptoms of the abatement of the sense in the minds of some people of the sacredness of private property, which is plainly assignable to the want of civil government." On 9 June the Continental Congress advised that "the inconveniences arising from the suspension of the powers of Government are intolerable" and made government according to the charter of 1691 necessary.[46]

The delegates called a new General Court on 19 July. The third and last Provincial Congress dissolved itself on the same day. Legalists always, the representatives passed an act "to confirm and establish the resolves of the several Provincial Congresses of this Colony." The "oppressed colony" had "been deprived of the free exercise of its usual powers of government," and the legality of the decisions made in the unusual Congresses might be questioned "and may occasion much litigation, unless confirmed and established in some known, constitutional manner." This implicitly denied constitutionality to the Congresses and the assumption that once a compact is broken by one side the other is dissolved from its obligations. At the same time the act declared as constitutional a General Court whose upper house could act legally only in the presence of a governor—there was none—and

[44]Lincoln, ed., *Journals of Each Provincial Congress,* pp. 280, note 1, 301.

[45]*Ibid.,* pp. 116–117, 163, 190, 192–193; John Adams to General Palmer, 26 Sept. 1774, *Works,* 1:154; H. A. Cushing, "Political Activity of the Massachusetts Towns during the Revolution," AHA, *Annual Report,* 1895, p. 109; H. A. Cushing, *History of the Transition from Provincial to Commonwealth Government in Massachusetts* (New York, 1896).

[46]Lincoln, ed., *Journals of Each Provincial Congress,* pp. 219–220, 224; Force, ed., *Archives,* 4.2:620–621; Provincial to Continental Congress, 11 June 1775, Continental to Provincial Congress, 10 June 1775, *ibid.,* 4.2:955, 959–960; Douglass, *Rebels and Democrats,* pp. 144–146, and Stephen E. Patterson, *Political Parties in Revolutionary Massachusetts* (Madison, Wis., 1973), pp. 118ff., explain the tactical reasons for the resumption of the Charter of 1691.

that derived its authority from the charter granted by the British. The leadership thus skirted the issue of making a new compact, which would occasion constitutional debates. They wanted order and continuity, and the council went so far as to assert "the supremacy of the Charter over natural rights." James Warren grumbled that the councillors "imagine themselves kings, and have assumed air and pomp of royalty but the crown and the scepter."[47]

This, however, was by no means what a large part of the electorate expected. Worcester inhabitants had given its representatives these ringing instructions:

> If all infractions of our rights, by acts of the British Parliament, be not redressed, and we restored to the full enjoyment of all our privileges, contained in the charter of this province . . . to a punctilio, before the day of your meeting, then, and in that case, you are to consider the people of this province as absolved, on their part, from the obligation therein contained, and to all intents and purposes reduced to a state of nature; and you are to exert yourself in devising ways and means to raise from the dissolution of the old constitution, as from the ashes of the Phenix a new form, wherein all officers shall be dependent on the suffrages of the people for their existance as such, whatever unfavorable constructions our enemies may put upon such procedure. The exigency of our public affairs leaves us no other alternative from a state of anarchy or slavery.

But this state-of-nature theory, frequently mentioned in contemporary writings, did not at all appeal to the more conservative Whig leadership, who wanted nothing new, especially no dependence on the people "for their existence as such." The mutuality of the compact had been claimed mainly by those governed; the ruling group had used it only as it suited their interests.[48]

As a result, some towns and counties denied the authority of the General Court. Especially Berkshire was cautious. The people had sent representatives to the 1775 session of the assembly; but when they returned, their constituents found that instead of agreeing on a new foundation for society and government, they had laid the basis for their own private emolument. Every single one of their members in the House had obtained a civil office from the House.[49]

While the people labored under the high taxes and the burdens of the war, their officials lived in high style. James Warren admonished John Adams:

> Give your self no trouble about the expences of your liveing. Your Constituents must be reconciled to it, without recalling you. For my own part I wish you to live genteely and in character, cost what it will. I am sure I would if I was in your place. Keep your servant and your horses. . . . We are not unacquainted with

[47]*Acts and Resolves*, 5:415–416, 1775–1776, Ch. 1. Cf. the confirmation of "Body" proceedings in Boston's town meetings. Similarly, the General Court confirmed the actions of the Committee of Safety. Douglass, *Rebels and Democrats*, p. 148; James Warren to John Adams, 14 Nov. 1775, *Warren–Adams Letters*, 1:183.

[48]Instructions, 4 Oct. 1774, in Franklin P. Rice, ed., "Worcester Town Records," *Worcester Soc. Antiq. Coll.* 4:241–245; cf. Otis's argument for the crown in *Surveyor General* v. *Logs:* "A great deal of Talk and Scribbling about mutual Compact," John Adams, *Legal Papers*, 2:267.

[49]Smith, *Pittsfield*, p. 334.

extravagancies here. We give five dollars for board, etc. which gives us feelings we are not used to.

Boston inhabitants, watching the representatives "live genteely" out of the public chest, demanded payment by the towns, where the taxpayers controlled the expenses. Several other towns complained about the "extraordinary pay" given to officers and other persons employed in the service of the province.[50]

Under the effect of criticism and spontaneous crowd action, the Whig leadership changed their attitude toward the people. The great principles of popular participation that had been advocated by John Adams and others in the exclusive atmosphere of the Continental Congress were now replaced by blunt demands for submission. When, in 1776, the Massachusetts towns demanded the right to reject or approve the constitution-to-be, Adams wrote to James Warren: "It is a Pity you should be obliged to lay it before them; it will divide and distract them." He dreaded the consequences of popular election of the governor. Whig ideology was replaced by or avowed to be the leaders' interest. As a high-ranking member of a stratified deferential society, he expressed mortification about demands for equality. Against this "levelling spirit," as he called it, it might even be necessary "to call in a military force to do that which our civil government was originally designed for." This was one of the most open avowals that government was designed to serve the interests of the ruling class.[51]

The people, in turn, were critical of the new set of officials. Within the social norms of provincial society, "extravagent" conduct and "extraordinary pay" justified extraordinary means of redress: riots. But, probably because of war efforts and the difficulties of obtaining provisions, the inhabitans merely acted in the town meeting against plural office holding and exorbitant pay. Whig Francis Dana publicly had to contradict rumors that he and other officials had been instrumental in drafting the Coercive Acts of the British Parliament. Ten years earlier Hutchinson had to disavow having participated in drawing up the Stamp Act. People distrusted leaders, whatever their political persuasion.[52] In 1778 "Bob Centinel" admonished the people: "Attention! my fellow citizens, to your *rulers* of every order; for if you do not attend to *them,* they will attend to *themselves,* and not to you. No free people ever long preserved their liberty and happiness without watching those who held the reigns of government." "Attention!—to the men that handle public money." Individuals frequently enriched themselves "to the impoverishment and ruin of the community." The draft constitution "designedly" did not mention rotation of offices: "Attention! to the form of government you may adopt." Plural office

[50]James Warren to John Adams, 10 July 1777, *Warren–Adams Letters,* 1:341–342; *BTR* 18:285; Force, ed., *Archives,* 4.4:1245, 1354, 1399, 1408, 4.5:1258.

[51]Letters from John Adams, 1775 and later, *Warren–Adams Letters,* 1:234, 243, 322, 2:36, *Adams Family Correspondence,* 1:420, to Sullivan, quoted in Morris, "Insurrection in Massachusetts," p. 21; John R. Howe, Jr., *The Changing Political Thought of John Adams* (Princeton, N.J., 1966). James Warren to John Adams, 31 April 1776, *Warren–Adams Letters,* 1:219: "I dread the consequences of the leveling spirit, encouraged and drove to sucn length as it is." Austin, *Life of Gerry,* 1:78–79.

[52]*BTR* 18:238, 287; *BG,* Sept. 1774.

holding was dangerous. "A few men, continued in the most important places for a succession of years, may so extend their connections and influence, as to become *really,* though not *openly,* masters of the State." Attention to "the army of your enemies," but also to "your own army." "Attention" that "the military [do not] encroach upon the civil power," that commissaries of prisoners act human, that "a British officer, tory merchant, or mercenary whig [!] and an American commissary" do not begin "clandestine trade" and "secret bargain." "Attention," finally, "to the freedom of the press: Some people, who have talked for it, who have wrote for it, may, upon a change of situation, be ready to wince at it."[53]

Aside from the tensions between rulers and ruled and the questions of courts or no courts, of constitution or no constitution, or charter or original liberties, innumerable other controversies developed. Whig politicians continued to be suspicious "of the avaritious spirit of merchants."[54] The plight of inland farmers and communities led to widespread rural discontent. Populous seaboard towns, led by the mercantile interest, clashed with inland communities over the question of representation. A Worcester County convention decided it would be "unsafe" to entrust the representatives with forming a constitution. Local communities looking to the provincial government, and the men in whose hands it was, expressed fear of "the undue influence of power of individuals," who kept "monopolizing incompatible offices."[55] Ambitious men of all political persuasions rocked the social system to get advancement for themselves. Tory "machinations" in the west added to the insecurity. In Boston another struggle began about the assessment of taxes. The poor distrusted the leadership, political as well as mercantile, and found their situation deteriorating. An almanac editor admitted that they suffered most and condescendingly added that though the poor were of low rank, they deserved notice and help.[56] Two issues, the presence of the Tories and the scarcity of provisions, grew to such dimensions that they will be treated separately in the next chapters.

[53]*Indep. Ledger,* 13 July 1778.
[54]*Warren–Adams Letters,* 1:185 (Nov. 1775), 223, and elsewhere.
[55]Ipswich Convention memorial, April 1776, *Acts and Resolves,* 5:542–543; act on representation, *ibid.,* pp. 502–503, 1775–1776, Ch. 26; Worcester County committees, memorial, Nov. 1776, in Force, ed., *Archives,* 5.3:866–867.
[56]Ephraim Dolittle to John Hancock, 21 March 1775, *ibid.,* 4.2:177; Ballantine's Journal, 7 Nov. 1774, Judd MSS., Rev. Matters, p. 153, Forbes Library; March meetings, 1779, *BTR* 26:53–54, 56, 60; Edward Bowen, "Almanacs," 23 Jan. 1779, *EIHC* 91:274 (1955); Nathaniel Low, "An Address to the People on the Subject of Monopoly and Extortions," *Almanack, 1778* (Boston, 1777).

Crowds against Tories 13

Depending on the nationality of the historian, the "king's friends" or "government men" are called "Loyalists" (British and recent American historians), "United Empire Loyalists" (Canadian), or "Tories" (American). The first two designations refer only to their political role. The last, used to describe political parties supporting crown prerogatives, for contemporaries also summarized a constellation of societally undesired traits. Therefore, the term "Tory" is used in the present study.[1]

It has been suggested that the expulsion of Tories and the confiscation of their estates should be dealt with in class terms. Many people besides top crown officials and large landowners left the new states. The confiscation of estates, at least in Massachusetts, did not result in any broadening of property holding, nor was it designed to do so. Economic tensions were an important aspect of the struggle. Small property holders, fearing the power of the wealthy, were quick to suspect them of Toryism. Wealthy and influential Tories and Whigs alike expressed fears that leveling principles motivated rioters and town meetings. Even the Loyalist Anne Hulton found that crown supporters acted "more from interest than principle . . . as there are few willg to acknowledge the Authority of Parliamt." Tories were set on "gain," "aggrandized [themselves] upon their Country's Ruin," "declare[d] War against the people" by accepting lucrative offices.[2]

---

[1]Editions of sources and secondary works on Loyalists are Lorenzo Sabine, *Biographical Sketches of Loyalists of the American Revolution*, 2 vols. (Boston, 1864; reprint ed., 1966); Alexander Fraser, *United Empire Loyalists: Enquiry into the Losses and Services in Consequence of Their Loyalty—Evidence in the Canadian Claims*, Second Report of the Bureau of Archives for the Province of Ontario, 1904 (Toronto, 1905); B. F. Stevens, Transcripts of American Loyalist Claims, vols. 13–14, Massachusetts Loyalist Claims, NYPL, MF in MHS; James H. Stark, *The Loyalists of Massachusetts and the Other Side of the American Revolution* (Boston, 1910); Edward A. Jones, *The Loyalists of Massachusetts, Their Memorials, Petitions, and Claims* (London, 1930); W. S. MacNutt, "New England's Tory Neighbors," *CSMP* 43:345–363 (1956–1963); L. F. S. Upton, ed., *Revolutionary versus Loyalist: The First American Civil War, 1774–1784* (Waltham, Mass., 1968). For a general historiographical note, see Bernard Bailyn, *The Ordeal of Thomas Hutchinson* (Cambridge, Mass., 1973), pp. 383–408.

[2]Jesse Lemisch, "The American Revolution from the Bottom Up," *Towards a New Past: Dissenting Essays in American History*, ed. Barton J. Bernstein (New York, 1968), pp. 4–5. Richard D. Brown, "The Confiscation and Disposition of Loyalists' Estates in Suffolk County, Massachusetts," *WMQ* 3.21:534–550 (1964). Similar studies for other states have yielded similar results. Anne Hulton, *Letters of a Loyalist Lady* (Cambridge, Mass., 1927), 8 July 1774, p. 74; *BG*, 10 Jan., 24 Oct. 1774; Bristol County Convention, Sept. 1774, *CSMP* 1:179. But see note 40. In

ATTITUDES TOWARD TORIES

"The present temper of the People throughout the Province is such, that they wont suffer a *tory* to remain any where among 'em without making an ample recantation of his principles," noted a moderate Whig. Those who refused to recant were the objects of frequent crowd action or, before the evacuation by the British troops, fled to Boston. Tories confirmed the statement: "Nothing but mobs and riots all this summer." Tories were suspected of doing mischief and of criminal conduct even by a man whom a crowd had arrested for Toryism.[3] In the rhetoric of the times, Tories were "secret Enemies . . . lurking among us . . . plotting our ruin," having "imbrued their hands in the Blood of their fellow Countrymen."[4] How did this unbridgeable gap between political opinions develop, leading to such extreme vilification of opponents?

One important factor was the political implications of the designations "Tory" or "Jacobite." According to an anonymous author, signing "Cato," a Tory "is a maintainer of the infernal doctrine of *arbitrary power,* and incontestable right on the part of the sovereign, and of *passive obedience* and non-resistance on the part of the subject." Massachusetts had been founded by dissenters attempting to remove themselves from arbitrary power. But their political institutions included few or no operational devices for a pluralism of political parties. The emergence of two active partisan groups would probably not have effected a breakdown of the political structure, since interest groups already existed. But as yet ideology had not adjusted to the new realities.

Cato's second important point was the absolute rejection of "passive obedience." Tories were wrong when they "maintained that the King held his crown of noe but God—that he could not by the most flagrant violation of the laws, and the most tyrannical exercise of his power, forfeit his right." The "people" were not made "entirely" for the king. In Cato's words, he had no "right to the use of their fortunes, lives, and liberties . . . and the eternal laws of realm without the subject having any right to demand redress of grievances." If a king became tyrannical, crowd action in defense of society—that is, for the common good—was justified and necessary.[5]

On the practical level this reasoning meant surveillance or expulsion of Tories but also rejection of Whig leaders' claims to power. The dangers of "passive obedi-

---

Philadelphia the "sober people who have property" wished for quiet and suppression of the "arbitrary rabble" by the British. Peter Force, ed., *American Archives,* 9 vols. (Washington, D.C., 1837–1853), 4.3:3.

[3] John Andrews, "Letters of John Andrews, Esq., Boston, 1772–1776," ed. Winthrop Sargent, 9 Sept. 1774, *MHSP* 8:357 (1864–1865); Thomas Hutchinson, *The Diary and Letters of His Excellency Thomas Hutchinson,* ed. Peter Orlando Hutchinson, 2 vols. (London, 1883–1886), 1:151, 397–398; Nathaniel Ames, "The Diary of Dr. Nathaniel Ames." ed. Sarah Breck Baker, 22 July 1778, *Dedham Hist. Reg.* 4:24 (1893); Abner Sanger, "Ye Journal of Abner Sanger," 18 April 1775, *Repertory* 1:114; *Warren–Adams Letters: Being Chiefly a Correspondence among John Adams, Samuel Adams, and James Warren,* 2 vols. (Boston, 1917, 1925), 1;50; *BEP* and *BG,* 24 Oct. 1774; James T. Austin, *The Life of Elbridge Gerry, with Contemporary Letters to the Close of the American Revolution,* 2 vols. (Boston, 1828, 1829), 1:270–272. *Description of the Pope, 1769* (Boston, 1769), *Mass. Brds.* 1502; Nathaniel Whitaker, *An Antidote against Toryism* (Newburyport, Mass., 1777).

[4] *BTR* 26:34, 66; George Sheldon, *A History of Deerfield,* 2 vols. (Deerfield, Mass., 1896), 2:675.

[5] *Mass. Spy,* 9 March 1775.

ence'' were repeatedly invoked against too much independence of rulers. Natural aristocrats of the type of John Adams turned the argument against the people: With the Declaration of Independence, the people were in power, and checks and balances had to be developed against them.

Samuel Adams argued that society set the norms by which individuals—including Tories—were ''bound to conduct'' themselves. ''Where did you learn that in a state or society you had a right to do as you please?'' The norms were usually set down in laws, but in emergencies, ''and the present case is without doubt one,'' direct and immediate action was required. As for those who preferred their own, separate interest, ''if you please, you may leave.'' Staunch defender of the corporate ideal, Adams himself was a few years later cast into the role of an opponent of Massachusetts federalist government, when changes in economic and social conditions were followed by changes, in the political systems and ideology. The corporate ideology won a battle against the Tories, but it lost a war against the changes in society.

Political and ideological contentions are in part a reflection of economic and social problems. Thus, it was natural that in the seventies the epithet ''Tory'' was used more generally against merchants for engrossing (that is, arbitrary exercise of their economic power); against lawyers, doctors, and ministers for acting in their own interest or against the majority; against Catholics or Episcopalians for submission to Pope or king; and against dissenting creeds for splitting the community.

Greater loyalty is always demanded of members of a community than of outsiders, and betrayal is accordingly punished more severely. The betrayal theme was one of the most important motives for crowd action against the local stamp masters. Tories were as ''lost to the feelings of Patriotism and the common Interest'' as the importers had been earlier. Significantly, the inhabitants of Boston had twice condemned those ''who not only deserted but opposed their country.'' The importers had been subject to more violence than the duty-collecting officials sent from Great Britain. Similarly, Americans professing loyalty to the British crown were subject to harsher treatment by the crowds than were members of the British army. The fears of Tory action and the consequent repression increased with the suspicion, often well founded, that Tories were assisting the British troops. From such apprehensions sprang crowd action.[6]

COMMUNITY ACTION AGAINST TORIES

Measures taken against Tories depended on the ''crimes'' of the Tories against the community, the local situation, the intensity of feeling, and the strength of Whig crowds and Tory groups or individuals. Sometimes private interests and incidental factors were also influential. Among the motivations for anti-Tory crowd action,

---

[6]*BG*, 8 Jan. 1770, reprinted in Samuel Adams, *The Writings of Samuel Adams*, ed. Harry A. Cushing, 4 vols. (New York, 1904–1908), 2:5; *BTR* 16:297–298, 18:16–17. On passive obedience, cf. Mayhew's sermon, Feb. 1750, *Discourse Concerning Unlimited Submission and Non Resistance to the Higher Powers* (Boston, 1750), Evans 6549. Cf. also the criticism in the town returns, Oscar Handlin and Mary F. Handlin, eds., *The Popular Sources of Political Authority: Documents on the Massachusetts Constitution of 1780* (Cambridge, Mass., 1966).

military considerations were foremost. Tories were disarmed to prevent resistance. Fears increased when Burgoyne's army advanced in 1777. In Montague, relief for the American troops assembled, but the men refused to march until all suspected Tories had delivered up their arms and had been put under "farm arrest."[7] Added to these military aspects were mercantile ones. Loyalist Thomas Robie of Marblehead charged an exorbitant price for gunpowder, urgently needed by the town. The town meeting did not interfere with his desire to sell at his price but voted to show no undue haste in paying him and to allow him no interest on the sum due. Other merchants were prevented from collecting their debts or forced to leave town.[8]

Underlying social tensions found expression in the frequency with which professional men, mostly belonging to the town elite, were suspected of Toryism. A precedent was the crowd action against ministers and merchants in 1765. At that time it was suggested that they coveted the office of stamp distributor. Doctors suspected of Tory sentiments were occasionally, especially during the 1775–1776 epidemic, accused of spreading smallpox or of inoculating contrary to the wishes of the inhabitants. Rumors prevailed in the provincial camp at Roxbury in 1775 that Loyalist inhabitants of Boston infected with smallpox were deliberately spreading it.[9] Lawyers were prevented from doing any business.[10] Officials and militia officers with Tory sentiments were forced to resign.[11]

Ministers, whose influential position could not be changed by elections, met with direct action by their parishioners. In Northfield the minister mentioned the king in his prayer and asked God's blessing for him. This was customary, but the particular Lord's Day was the first after Lexington. The ensuing conflict lasted for four years but was singularly free of repressive measures. The Tory-inclined Deerfield minister succeeded in one morning's sermon in offending his congregation so thoroughly that he found the door of the meeting house nailed shut when he returned for the afternoon lecture. Parson Forbes of North Brookfield "had given such evidence of Toryism" that his parishioners "determined to try him. They had him brought before them, finally decided that he must acknowledge he was wrong, make an apology." The Reverend Aaron Smith of Marlborough had shots fired through his windows. Other ministers were placed under arrest or humiliated. Some stopped preaching when rumors spread that they would be taken from their pulpits by force. "It is a very busy time with us, mobbing and dismissing ministers."[12]

[7]Sheldon, *Deerfield,* 2:722–723; Lee Nathaniel Newcomer, *The Embattled Farmers: A Massachusetts Countryside in the American Revolution* (New York, 1953), p. 69.

[8]Samuel Roads, *The History and Traditions of Marblehead* (Boston, 1880), pp. 125–126; *BNL,* 14 July 1774; *BG,* 5 Sept. 1774; Gage to Trumbull, 23 July 1774, in Force, ed., *Archives,* 4.1:629–633; Frank Moore, ed., *Diary of the American Revolution from Newspapers and Original Documents,* 2 vols. (New York, 1860; reprint ed., 1969), 1:40; Jolley Allen, "Jolley Allen's Account," ed. C. C. Smith, *MHSP* 16:69–99 (1878–1879).

[9]*BTR* 26:15; Newcomer, *Embattled Farmers,* p. 69; letters from Washington, 4 Dec., 11 Dec. 1775, in John C. Fitzpatrick, ed., *The Writings of George Washington from the Original Manuscript Sources, 1745–1799,* 39 vols. (Washington, D.C., 1931–1944), 4:141–145, 157.

[10]Peter Oliver, *Peter Oliver's Origin and Progress of the American Rebellion: A Tory View,* ed. Douglass Adair and John A. Schutz (Stanford, Calif., 1961), p. 154.

[11]B. F. Stevens, American Loyalist Claims, 13:231, NYPL (Court Clerk Samuel Paine, Worcester), 14:255 (Justice Fowler, Stockbridge), 14:289 (Selectman Jeremiah Pote, Falmouth).

[12]Northfield: Herbert C. Parsons, *A Puritan Outpost: A History of the Town and People of Northfield* (New York, 1937),

Episcopalian clergymen fared worse. Apprehensions about them and about their stand on authority had long persisted and were justified at least insofar as they frequently preached submission to the British government without acknowledging any right of resistance.[13]

In the persecution private motives sometimes mingled with others. Men who were interested in the crowd action bought drinks for the rioters. In the "Pelham movement," people from that town came to Northampton to join the crowd against Tory Stoddard. "The Pelhamites owed Mr. Stoddard, and part of their whiggism originated in a disposition not to pay their debts." In Springfield a tavern quarrel was turned against a "damned pack of Torys" who happened to arrive that moment.[14] When private motives mingled with others, support for the action was no longer unanimous. The private or "petty mobs" had little or no community support. They were disapproved of not only by officials, communities, committees, and regional conventions but also by counteracting crowds, almost spontaneous posses, and by public crowds. The mass movements often began or ended with a vote to oppose any petty mobs. When posses attempted to prevent petty mobs from acting, discussions often ensued about the reasonableness of grievances and crowd action. Sometimes both crowds peaceably returned home; sometimes one group was deterred; sometimes both joined forces and examined the target of the petty mob. As often as not, the target vindicated himself and was not molested further.[15]

The form of crowd or other action varied from peaceable meetings over crowd action to harsh violence. In town meetings Tories had to confess and recant. When they refused to appear, the participants in the meeting executed the resolves as a crowd. An Oakham man opposed a town vote, whereupon the selectmen noted that he was "an old insignifant Torey, and never ought to vote in any Case."[16] After trials by ad hoc bodies (crowds), Tories had to recant before committees, by published statements, or in front of crowds. The crowds often drew up in two files and ordered their victim to pass through the lane, hat off, proclaiming his errors and

pp. 184–187. Boston: John Rowe, *Letters and Diary of John Rowe, Boston Merchant, 1759–1762, 1764–1779*, ed. Anne Rowe Cunningham (Boston, 1903; reprint ed., 1969), 21 July 1776, pp. 19, 313. Deerfield: Sheldon, *Deerfield*, 2:694, 710–711 (attempt to dismiss minister, augmentation of salary reconsidered, vote not to supply firewood). North Brookfield: Judd MSS., Rev. Matters, pp. 143–144, Forbes Library. Salem: William Pynchon, *The Diary of William Pynchon of Salem*, ed. F. E. Oliver (Boston, 1890), 9 Feb. 1777, p. 24, cf. p. 42. Westford, Hebron, Groton, etc., in Force, ed., *Archives*, 4.1:715–716, 4.2:608–609, 4.6:712. Longmeadow: "Parson Williams' Diary," quoted in *Mag. of Hist.* 25:87 (1917). Shutesbury, Warwick: Josiah G. Holland, *History of Western Massachusetts . . .*, 2 vols. (Springfield, Mass., 1855), 2:434–436, 447–448. Falmouth: Jones, *Loyalists*, pp. 303–304. Summary: letter from Deerfield, 17 Jan. 1775, in Sheldon, *Deerfield*, 2:696.

[13]Oliver, *American Rebellion*, p. 154; Carl Bridenbaugh, *Mitre and Sceptre: Transatlantic Faiths, Ideas, Personalities, and Politics* (New York, 1962); letters from clergymen in Massachusetts, in William S. Perry, ed., *Historical Collections Relating to the American Colonial Church*, 5 vols. (Hartford, Conn., 1873), 3:521–581.

[14]John J. Sibley and Clifford K. Shipton, "Peter Oliver," in *Biographical Sketches of Those Who Attended Harvard College*, vol. 8 (Cambridge, Mass., 1951), pp. 737–763; Judd MSS., Rev. Matters, p. 169, Forbes Library; Pelham to Copley, 16 Feb., 3 April 1775, *MHSC* 71:291–293, 312 (1914).

[15]Cf. descriptions of antimandamus councillor actions and county convention procedures elsewhere in this study.

[16]Samuel Adams to John Pitts, 15 Feb. 1777, *Writings*, 3:359–360; W. Glanville Evelyn, *Memoir and Letters of Capt. W. Glanville Evelyn, of the 4th Regiment ("King's Own") from North America, 1774–1775*, ed. G. D. Scull (Oxford, 1879), pp. 35–36; "Plain English," *BNL*, 23 Feb. 1775; *BTR* 18:275–281, 26:27–28, 32–35. Amherst: Massachusetts Towns, Resolutions, 1773–1787, 6 vols., 2:59–60, LC; Handlin and Handlin, eds., *Popular Sources*, p. 398.

professing his allegiance and better conduct in the future. The victims had to stand at the pillory, were exhibited in carts, or hanged in effigy. They were jailed, placed under house arrest, or confined to the limits of their farm or town. On a single day a Tory saw and experienced the following: "I here a Mobb is in Town; I see the . . . Mobbers going home at Night . . . as soon as I get home El and I are Attacked with a Mobb; we fight till we are taken and carried before a Violent Committee."[17]

Whenever "a Government man" entered Newbury, a watchman with a drum proclaimed his arrival. Such men were hissed and sneered at; in winter they received "the discipline of snow balling." Crowds celebrating American victories often damaged or tarred the houses of Tories.[18] If Tories were unrepentant or even used offices to promulgate their views, they were tarred and feathered or covered with excrement. Edward Stow, a merchant–captain of Boston who needed a personal guard of soldiers for his safety, reported: "I have been mobbed and Libeled ever since the Stamp Act my House bedaubed with Excrement and Feathers . . . [or] with Blubber Oil and Feathers" three times in two months (1770). "A Mob of near 300 Men" damaged his house and severely injured him. "And on April 3rd 1775 bedaubed my House with Excrement and Feathers, the Occasion of it was because I seized for His Majesty two Gun Carriages, a pair of Swivels and a Cow Horn." Compared to other instances of violence, the persecution of Edward Stow was so unimportant that the papers did not even report it.[19]

Crowd action was supplemented by no less violent harassment from officials. Tories were bound out to hard labor, drafted repeatedly, trained hard, expelled from fire clubs, or told that they "would be put into the Front of the Battle" against the British.[20] Another method was to sever all business connections with them. They not only had to shut down their own shops but often nearly starved because nobody sold provisions to them. "The Mob Committee, of the County of York, where Sr. William Pepperells large Estate lay, ordered that no Person should hire any of his Estates of him, nor buy any Wood of him, nor pay any Debts to him that were due to him." Tory Reuben Tucker of Townsend had his license as innkeeper revoked. The Worcester County blacksmiths convened and resolved not to work for any Tories,

[17]John Trumbull, *M'Fingal: An Epic Poem in Four Cantos* (Philadelphia, 1791), p. 60; James R. Trumbull, *History of Northampton, Massachusetts*, 2 vols. (Northampton, Mass., 1902; 1st ed., 1898), 2:372–373; Jonathan Judd, Diary, 2 Feb. 1775, quoted *ibid.*, pp. 373–374; Sanger, "Journal," 18 Dec. 1775, 15–16 Jan. 1777, *Repertory* 1:246, 622, 2:38; Jabez Fitch, Jr., "A Journal, from August 5th to December 13th, 1775, Kept by Lieutenant Jabez Fitch, Jr., . . . at the Siege of Boston," 30 Oct. 1775, *MHSP* 2.9:74–75 (1894–1895). Judd MSS., Rev. Matters, p. 166, Forbes Library; Stevens, American Loyalist Claims, 13:597, 14:13–14, NYPL; Evelyn, *Memoir and Letters*, p. 49; convention of committees in Petersham, 12 July 1776, in Force, ed., *Archives*, 5.1:245–247; Fraser, *United Empire Loyalists*, p. 305; Charles T. Russell, *The History of Princeton Worcester County, Mass., from Its First Settlement* (Boston, 1838), p. 110; Oliver, *American Rebellion*, pp. 152–157.

[18]Andrews, "Letters," 5 Oct. 1774, p. 373; Thomas Hutchinson, "Hutchinson's Orderly Book," 27 March 1776, *MHSP* 16:339 (1878–1879); Pynchon, *Diary*, 19 Feb., 25 Feb., Oct.–Nov. 1777, pp. 25, 41–45; Joseph B. Felt, *The Annals of Salem from Its First Settlement* (Salem, Mass., 1827), p. 501; Oliver, *American Rebellion*, p. 156; D. G. Trayser, *Barnstable: Two Centuries of a Cape Cod Town* (Hyannis, Mass., 1939), p. 124; Fraser, *United Empire Loyalists*, p. 495; Stevens, American Loyalist Claims, 13:202, 336, 349, NYPL.

[19]Stow's memorial, *ibid.*, 14:209–210.

[20]Roads, *Marblehead*, p. 127; Jones, *Loyalists*, p. 76; Boyle, "Journal," 8 Sept. 1774, p. 379; Stevens, American Loyalist Claims, 14:25, NYPL.

their tenants or business partners, their hired laborers or artisans, or any person who did not conform to the nonconsumption agreement.[21]

Suffolk, Middlesex, and Essex town delegates voted that

> all such officers or private persons as have given sufficient proof of their enmity to the people and constitution of this country, should be held in contempt, and that those who are connected with them ought to separate from them: laborers to shun their vineyards; merchants, husbandmen, and others, to withhold their commerce and supplies.

Tories' property was destroyed and their enclosures laid waste to make it impossible for them to remain in their community.[22]

An analysis of the riots shows the following prominent patterns. In the treatment of Tories, vestiges of deferential attitudes could still be found, similar to those shown at the Harvard commencements, in the different treatment of high and low customs officials and in the attacks on symbols of wealth and power rather than on their owners. Now riding horses or special teams for coaches were mistreated instead of their Tory owners. Such cases were reported from Freetown, Dartmouth, Barnstable, and Hartwick.[23] Discrimination according to rank was also carefully upheld when the General Court passed the Exclusion Act against Tories. "Esquires" were separated from "gentlemen," and these from people without rank, as were merchants from traders, and these from shopkeepers. Omitted titles were inserted before final passage of the law.[24]

During the rioting against Tories, the customary forms of action were further developed. Crowds, even in small country towns, were watched by numerous spectators. This had been uncommon in earlier years, when the crowds did their work and then returned home. Now long political discussions, trials, and debates became an integral part of the action. Crowds did not act from passion but as political bodies. Sometimes they showed their "good" intentions by carrying white staves instead of their usual weapons. Crowds and leadership acted in much closer relationship than in earlier years. Spontaneous and directed actions became nearly indistinguishable. Long-term planning could come as well from the ranks as from the leaders. Town and committee meetings and conventions changed into crowd action. Crowds in turn acted as meetings, held trials, and sent committees.[25]

[21]Roads, *Marblehead*, pp. 126–127; Stevens, American Loyalist Claims, 13:513, 14:103 *passim*, 309, NYPL; Oliver, *American Rebellion*, p. 155; *BG*, 28 Nov. 1774; blacksmiths' agreement, MA 131:369, in William Lincoln, ed., *The Journals of Each Provincial Congress of Massachusetts in 1774–1775...* (Boston, 1858), pp. 639–640.

[22]*Ibid.* (note the biblical language, "vineyards"); Moore, ed., *Diary of the Revolution*, 1:38, 40; Oliver, *American Rebellion*, p. 157; Fraser, *United Empire Loyalists*, p. 273; William Clark to ———, Dedham, 5 Jan. 1778, in Perry, ed., *Historical Collections*, 3:593–594; Stevens, American Loyalist Claims, 13:394–403, 14:51–52, 289, NYPL; *BNL*, 14 July 1774; Noyes to Henshaw, 13 July 1774, *NEHGR* 43:143–144 (1889).

[23]*Gazetteer and New Daily Advertiser*, 11 Feb. 1775, quoted in John C. Miller, *Origins of the American Revolution* (Boston, 1943), p. 371; Moore, ed., *Diary of the Revolution*, 1:38; Oliver, *American Rebellion*, pp. 152–153.

[24]A. C. Goodell, *et al.*, eds., *Acts and Resolves, Public and Private, of the Province of the Massachusetts Bay*, 21 vols. (Boston, 1869–1922), 5:912–918, 1004–1009.

[25]Sanger, "Journal," 27 Dec. 1774, 9 March 1775, 5 Jan. 1777, pp. 33, 124, 622; Oliver, *American Rebellion*, p. 153;

The aims of crowd action were no longer as narrowly defined. Action originally directed against a single Tory was often followed by visits to a number of others. Men obnoxious to more than one community were visited by crowds assembling upon a preconcerted plan from the neighboring communities or—if caught in the act, so that the people lacked time to make regional plans—were carted to the town limits and there handed over to a crowd of the next town. Thus, Jesse Dunbar was taken by a Plymouth crowd. At the town limits the Kingston people waited, and they in turn conveyed him to Duxbury rioters. Some riots extended over several days, especially if the crowds met with opposition. Crowds rode or marched from town to town to force Tories to resign or to disarm them. In each town the groups were joined by local men. New Haven men rode through Berkshire into New York State. Committees or crowds of one town, discovering during their investigations hints or evidence of Tory connections to other towns, sent messengers to cause local crowds to take action there.[26]

The wider nature of the action plus the intensity of partisan feeling led to a reversal in the use of violence. Till 1773, Boston crowds could be very tough in dealing with low-ranking customs officials; country crowds, with the exception of moral norms enforcing riots, had usually confined their action to property. Now Bostonians concentrated more strongly on town-meeting action, while country crowds occasionally inflicted harsh punishments on persons whom they considered to be oppressing the people and/or to be Tories. The degree of violence applied also depended on the situation. Thus, William Jackson, a Tory merchant being conveyed to Boston, was forced by a first crowd to leave his carriage and walk. The next crowd ordered him to take his hat off and recant. A third crowd demanded that he kneel and beg for pardon.[27]

A good example of a combination of the diverse forms of town-meeting, committee, and crowd action was the proceedings against Israel Williams, a close friend of Governor Hutchinson and a mandamus councillor. His economic position in the Connecticut River Valley and his provincial offices made him one of the "River Gods."[28] At a meeting of about 150 men from several Berkshire towns (26 August 1774), he was accused of maintaining the right of the British government to tax the colonies, of countenancing the Regulating Acts, and of obstructing popular attempts "to obtain a Restoration of their constitutional Rights and Priviledges." These three errors were of especially "dangerous Tendency," coming "from a Man in your Place, and of your Ability and Influence." Williams had to promise better conduct for the future.[29] As judge he was met by a crowd action on 30 August; after the power alarm of 3 September, plans were made for a concerted action against him, but it did not materialize.

Force, ed., *Archives,* 4.2:215–218; Moore, ed., *Diary of the Revolution,* 1:23–24, 39; John Trumbull, *M'Fingal,* p. 61.

[26]Oliver, *American Rebellion,* pp. 154–155; Sheldon, *Deerfield,* 2:698; Ballantine's Journal, Judd MSS., Rev. Matters, p. 152, Forbes Library; Force, ed., *Archives,* 4.3:729. Cf. chapter on mandamus councillors.

[27]Peter Oliver to ———, 19 Aug. 1774, quoted in Miller, *Origins,* p. 371; Pynchon, *Diary,* 11 April 1776, pp. 7–8; Hutchinson, *Diary and Letters,* 2:61.

[28]Sibley and Shipton, "Israel Williams," *Harvard Graduates,* 8:301–333.

[29]Articles, 26 Aug. 1774, Israel Williams Papers, box 1758–1785, MHS.

At a militia muster one Hatfield man told those from other towns, "I wish in my Soul you would come in." Many others from Hatfield agreed, explaining that if they dealt with the Tories in their town themselves, "it would Brake Neighbourhood and therefore would Not Do so well as for . . . Stran[g]ers." While returning to their towns and farms, the men discussed the problem of Toryism further: Colonel Partridge had refused to deliver up his firearms, there had been opposition to the militia muster, Hatfield Tories had not kept a fast day for provincial liberties, "it would not be safe to go to battle and leave a Mess of Torymen behind to destroy the People at Home." Somebody proposed assembling at Hatfield, Williams's home town, on the following Tuesday.[30]

Consequently, a group from Williamsburgh rode into town on 6 September "to Gain Evidence." A Hatfield man queried "whather we were comeing to Rectifi privet Dameges Espicly to punish Coll Williams reletive to an old Dificalty Betwean him and us." But as soon as he was convinced that no private motives lay behind the coming, he joined and thundered against the "corupt vicious . . . crew" of Hatfield Tories, who "Deserved to be dealt with in Severity." Several were singled out for visits, the Hatfielders adding some other persons against whom they had private grievances. The men from Williamsburgh objected: "we was comeing in Regular order and that we did not Desire to Damage any person property with whom our Bussness might Lead us to have to Do." At this some Hatfielders lost interest. Nothing further came of the affair, probably because a countercrowd of Tories was coming to support Hatfield friends.[31]

A town meeting in Hatfield on 17 January 1775 was told that Williams had further offended: He had ostentatiously feasted, he had broken a fast, and he had sent intelligence reports to Boston. Crowds went in search of the messenger, and 150–200 men, half of them armed, surrounded Williams's house (2 February 1775). He was arrested and had to answer charges in a public hearing on the next day. His answers were voted unsatisfactory, "and to obtain his Liberty he was compelled to sign a covenant," which was published in the newspapers.[32]

Williams opposed execution of provincial resolves[33] and in December 1776 ordered a large quantity of goods from Loyalist merchants and wrote to former Governor Hutchinson that he hoped for and expected subjugation of America. The Hatfield committee explained that he not only opposed the steps taken by the people, but "he has been and still is a Man of Considerable Influence with the People, and consequently has perswaded a Considerable number of Persons not only in this Town but we apprehend more or less in every Town in the County to Adopt his Sentiments." The Hampshire County militia officers accused him of "one continued Series of Treason and Rebellion," of "constantly sowing the Seads of

---

[30]Joseph Clarke to ———, 30 Aug. 1774, in James R. Trumbull, *Northampton,* 2:346–348; *Conn. Courant,* 6 Sept. 1774; Williams to ———, Massachusetts Misc., LC: depositions of Seth Tubbs [?], William Read, Benjamin Read, and James Hunt, Israel Williams Papers, box 1758–1785, MHS.

[31]Deposition of Benjamin Read, *ibid.*

[32]Sheldon, *Deerfield,* 2:696–698; James R. Trumbull, *Northampton,* p. 373; Daniel W. Wells and Reuben F. Wells, *A History of Hatfield, Massachusetts, 1660–1910* (Springfield, Mass., 1910), p. 187; William Williams's petition and Israel Williams's account, Israel Williams Papers, box 1758–1785, MHS.

[33]John Dickinson, 23 May 1775, Elijah Morton, 12 June 1775, to Israel Williams, *ibid.*

Despotism, Tiranny and Slavery,'' of ''Shocking and glaring Falsehoods.'' Worse, he, with his ''little Banditti of Sons and Tools,'' had attempted to collect evidence against rioters and had promised offices to his ''Sons and Dependents'':

> Death [is] too mild a Punishment for you—and inadequate to your Crimes—you thirst for the Blood of your Country . . . and still you live and even Dwell among that People from whom you have received your all. . . . This is therefore to warn you immediately to depart and retire to Boston.[34]

The General Court ordered Williams and a relative confined and voted that both ''have by their Conduct rendered themselves unfit to hold any Office of place Under the Government of this State.'' From prison they sent rather strongly worded letters to officials and committees, terming them ''accessory'' to ''a Mobb'' and accusing the local minister of ''preaching Sedition.'' When the townsmen proposed a settlement of the difficulties and a lifting of the restrictions imposed on the two Williamses, provided they humbly petition the General Court and ''voluntarily'' take the oath of allegiance to the ''free Sovereign and Independent State'' of Massachusetts (1780), they refused.[35] In the case of Israel Williams, the Whig–Tory contentions were aggravated by his economic power, social position, and political influence. In other cases the designation ''Tory'' was applied to religious minorities or economic groups.

In the late seventies Shakers immigrated from Great Britain to the border regions of Massachusetts–New York. They were at once suspect because they came from Great Britain. Conversion to their faith broke up families, friendships, and sometimes whole congregations. They objected to oaths and were pacifists. This was bad enough in a war situation. But they also taught that ''sin and self produce *private* property, Innocence and self-denial produce *community* of property.'' Nothing could be worse for Calvinists, who saw private property as the basis of liberty (or profit). Shakers were termed ''Tories,'' and crowd action soon began. In July 1780 a crowd seized a Shaker, David Darrow, who was driving sheep to the market. They sent Darrow under guard to the authorities and divided the sheep among themselves. Shaker leaders traveling through western Massachusetts in May and June 1781 were repeatedly chased out of town by crowds. Many, among them women, were cruelly mistreated by crowds, often led by town officials and wealthy men.[36]

---

[34]Sheldon, *Deerfield*, 2:720; letter by John Dickinson on behalf of the Committees of Northampton, Hatfield, and Amherst to council, 7 March 1777, Committee of Safety of Hatfield to General Court, 29 March 1777, from James Easton on behalf of the militia officers, Israel Williams Papers, box 1758–1785, MHS.

[35]Proceedings of the House, 15 April 1777, and council, 26 April 1777, *ibid.;* MA 154:86–87, 104, 105–118; William Williams's petition to the General Court and instructions to the representatives, May 1780, Israel Williams Papers, box 1758–1785, MHS.

[36]F. W. Evans, *Shaker Communism* (London, 1871), p. 74; M. T. Melcher, *The Shaker Adventure* (Princeton, N.J., 1941), pp. 24–34; Henry S. Nourse, *History of the Town of Harvard, Massachusetts, 1732–1893* (Harvard, Mass., 1894), pp. 259–267; C. E. Robinson, *Concise History of the Shakers* (East Canterbury, N.H., 1893), pp. 20–24; Jacob C. Meyer, *Church and State in Massachusetts from 1740 to 1833; A Chapter in the Development of Individual Freedom* (Cleveland, 1930), p. 115.

Economic motives also mixed with political ones in the contentions between different groups of inhabitants in Hancock, Berkshire. Under the leadership of a justice of the peace, Asa Douglass, 68 men petitioned for the incorporation of the plantation. A messenger with a counterpetition was "ungenerously Stoped" on his way by a crowd. Douglass was active against any authority that seemed repressive or unresponsive to him. He accused General Schuyler of neglecting his men, who suffered badly, and of traitorous conduct in Canada. When the Continental Congress decided to abandon Fort Ticonderoga, which he had helped take, he found that the "land jobbers were the foundation or efficient cause" for the resolution. His followers belonged to the poorer sections of the community. Those 56 men who opposed Douglass's plea for incorporation pointed out that the town "has proved an Assalum for many Poor People, that had no whare Else to go, who have Settled upon the ungranted Lands, who greatly Swell our Numbers, but are not like to Increase our Abilities."[37]

Douglass arrested several of them for Toryism. He inquired of the provincial authorities when and where he could take the oath of allegiance, so that he could act in his capacity as justice of the peace against the prisoners. He added, "I am blamed by sum for not Prosecuteing," and he certainly did not like "to let them no how lame the Courts act." Of 35 arrested Tories, 23 had opposed the incorporation and had promised themselves redress by the British. Two-thirds had actively taken the British side during the Battle of Bennington.[38]

The assembly ordered the prisoners to remain in confinement and their estates to be run by the town. The Superior Court, however, freed several of them after they had posted bond for their future good behavior. These "imprudent Fellows," so conservative Whig Theodore Sedgewick said, returned to the town and found that their estates had been seized "for the Benifit of the State," as had the estates of many of "those whom they were disposed to call Tories." When these men demanded their possessions back, which were not the worst part of the town's lands, new contentions occurred.[39]

Sedgewick described the "state of Party among us" and "the Dangers to which the Friends of Order are exposed in this County." He realized that the opposition to Tories had at least partly become a class struggle and an attempt to increase popular participation in government. The reasons for crowd action were "the Fondness for Independence, the malice against those of difirent opinions, the Envy agt. those any way distinguished from the Commonalty, which are only smothered by a vigorous Government and which are apparent upon every return to a state of political Equali-

---

[37]*Acts and Resolves,* 5:550–551, 1776–1777, Ch. 3, notes pp. 656–660, cf. 1306–1307, 1388, 1462; MA 181:102, 198, 201, 205, 206, 209, 211. Douglass to Washington, 7 June 1776, and Douglass letter on behalf of a convention of Berkshire towns and King's District, New York, 7 June 1776, in Force, ed., *Archives,* 4.6:744–746. After incorporation Douglass had to petition for an abatement of taxes because the town had little usable land and "the rough remainder has ever since been the common resort of the poorest sort of people from different states, who could not get a living in the lower towns."

[38]Asa Douglass, 3 June 1777, *Acts and Resolves,* 5:850, 984–988

[39]Sedgewick to James Sullivan, 10 Jan. 1779, and to "the Honbl N. & B," 10 Jan. 1779, Sedgewick Papers, MHS.

ty.'' Sedgewick feared the opposition to the ''reistablishment of order,'' the ''sparks of sedition,'' the ''state of anarchical confusion.'' Demands for restoration of Tory property led to new clamors:

> the People were enraged, met in Town meeting and appointed a Mob Captain a man destitute of every valuable Qualification and recommended only by a blind and outrageous Zeal agt. Courts, Law and order, under his Command the most cruel and inhuman Punishments, even without the Formality of even a Mob Trial inflicted, not on those only who had been acquitted but on all those whose property they surreptitiously detained.

Crowds sent committees ''According to the usual and long approved Method.'' Men arrested for rioting were rescued. The rioters, whose leveling intentions Sedgewick condemned, ''said they now had full Evidence of what they always suspected *that all great men were Tories.*''[40]

OPPOSITION BY TORIES: INDIVIDUAL ACTION AND CROWD VIOLENCE

Tories by no means submitted quietly to community action and violence against them. Their sentiments were adequately expressed by Jonathan Stickney, Jr., of Rowley. He said that if he must fight he would chose the British side and that popery in Canada was a good institution; he called the Continental Congress ''a pack of rascally villains,'' the General Court a ''pack of ignorant souls'' who deceived the people, the local leaders ''creatures . . . vulgarly called Committees of Safety, . . . properly tyrants.'' His attitude toward Whig rioters was contained in his wish ''to see the blood streaming from the hearts of those that upheld the destruction of that tea.'' This, not surprisingly, was sufficient to jail him.[41]

In many instances Tories actively counteracted the Whigs, behaved arrogantly, and gave ample reason for apprehensions. Their conduct during the siege of Boston was described by the selectmen as ''most dreadful'': ''all the sufferings of the poor for the want of provisions and the necessaries of life, were not equal to the dreadful scorn, derision and contempt from them.'' Aside from the question of whether hunger or scorn is worse, the core of the statement was evidently correct. While Selectman Newell ''was invited by two Gentlemen to dine upon *rats,*'' Tory Isaac Winslow invited merchant leader John Rowe to dine on a fine ''Quarter of Veal.'' Militarily, Tories supported the British, harbored spies, and helped escaping British prisoners of war. In Boston three Loyalist Companies were formed after 19 April 1775, which did mainly police duty. In Bristol County 300 Loyalists armed themselves to support the British authorities. Others, ''owners of large Properties . . . and chiefly of a rank in Life, superior to the Class from which the common Seaman and Soldier are taken,'' were too arrogant (''averse'') to enter ''the Service as such.'' They aided British headquarters.[42]

---

[40]*Ibid.* (emphasis added).
[41]Rowley Committee to council, 15 April 1776, in Force, ed., *Archives,* 4.5:950–951, 1282.
[42]Anne Hulton, *Letters,* 8 July 1774, p. 74; Eldad Taylor to his wife, 18 March 1776, *NEHGR* 8:231–232 (1854); David

Berkshire Tories took £600 worth of powder and other goods from the towns, and a number took up arms on the British side with Burgoyne's army. They first opposed the settlement of two militia companies in Great Barrington, then took over, and "by a bare majority" made Tories captains and lieutenants. Among the rank and file, "the uneasiness in both companies has risen to that height, that they say they never will bear arms under these officers, so long as they are able to earn enough to pay their fines." Considering the usual lamentations about lawlessness in Berkshire by Whigs and Tories alike, this action reveals in what an orderly fashion these men proceeded. The companies were not broken up or the officers forced to resign, but the men were ready to pay the legal fines for their refusal to drill. The town consisted largely of dissenters and Anglicans, who, often taxed illegally, "have been very backward in all our late publick matters and amongst us are denominated Tories." While Whig men were off on military ("publick") service, the Tories remained behind and "thus, being all present, are able to outvote the Whigs."[43]

Military resistance was only a small area of Tory activity; their main opposition was exercised through town offices and in town meetings. The Deerfield town clerk did not record meetings or votes carried by the Whigs; elected Whig officials lost their offices; in 1781 they instructed the representative to endeavor to obtain a negotiated settlement with Great Britain.[44]

In Swanzey the selectmen opened the March 1776 meeting properly, but that was the last thing anybody succeeded in doing properly at that meeting. The choice of a moderator was interrupted when "a Large Number of Freeholders," Whigs, demanded "a Legal Meeting" in which the property qualifications for voters would be observed. Colonel Jerathmel Bowers, whose alleged purpose it was to get a slate of Loyalist selectmen elected, declared that all those paying a poll tax should vote, that there was no law prohibiting "any Person Voting for Moderator." Bowers and a large number of supporters opposed the "Freeholders." He was a very able manager of meetings and critic of Whig power. A year earlier he had prevented the raising of a company of minutemen by explaining in a town meeting that it would cost too much. The argument proved so persuasive that the inhabitants passed several votes against military units and committees. He judged that the Whigs "were very fond of offices, and would go to set up Government soon." In this he certainly was correct.[45]

Cobb, Weekly Journal, 29 July 1776, R. T. Paine Papers, 1766–1776, MHS; Belcher Noyes, Diary, 19 Oct. 1775, AAS. Timothy Newell, "A Journal Kept during the Time that Boston Was Shut up in 1775-6," *MHSC* 4.1:265 (1852); Sibley and Shipton, "Isaac Winslow," *Harvard Graduates,* 8:338; Samuel Paine to ———, 2 Oct. 1775, *NEHGR* 30:371–373 (1876), calling Boston the "Emporium of America for Plenty and Pleasure." Fraser, *United Empire Loyalists,* pp. 305, 495; "John Howe's Report," on D. H. Hurd, *History of Middlesex,* 3 vols. (Philadelphia, 1890), 2:581; Oliver, *American Rebellion,* pp. 152–156; Stevens, American Loyalist Claims, 13:243, 289–291, 394–396, 416, 459, 14:31–32, 117, 249, 413–414, 431, NYPL; Force, ed., *Archives,* 4.2:177, 255, 340, 1651, 4.6:998. The companies were the Loyal American Associators and two national groups, the Loyal Irish Volunteers and the Loyal North British [that is, Scottish] Volunteers. Jones, *Loyalists,* pp. 311–313.
[43]Petition from Stockbridge, 9 April 1778, *Acts and Resolves,* 5:986–987; Mark Hopkins to council, 30 March 1776, in Force, ed., *Archives,* 4.5:551–552.
[44]Sheldon, *Deerfield,* 2:681, 728–729, 739; Bruce G. Merritt, "Loyalism and Social Conflict in Revolutionary Deerfield, Massachusetts," *JAH* 57:277–289 (1970).
[45]Memorial from Swanzey, 27 May 1776, MA 181:23–24; Force, ed., *Archives,* 4.3:160–166, 1436.

Other towns had similar difficulties. Sometimes Tories even held regional meetings, analogous to the county conventions of the Whigs, to concert measures or to debate the situation.[46] As liberty trees and poles multiplied throughout Massachusetts, Loyalists took them as an easy target for their wrath and in turn became targets of crowd action. In Dedham a "Pillar of Liberty" was raised in 1765 and overturned at night in 1769. In Deerfield the Sons of Liberty, "upon Mature Deliberation, thought the Erection of a Liberty Pole would have ye most happy tendency of restoring and Establishing Peace and Harmony between ye Mother Country and ye Colonies." But it did not further harmony in town. On the same night, probably after equally mature deliberation, five Tories took a saw and soon "ye sd Pole was sawn in sunder." The Whigs erected another pole, and their opponents set up a "Tory Pole." The Tory to whom we are indebted for this account explained that the liberty pole was set up by a "pack of ignorant villains," while the Tory pole had been erected with "infinite wisdom."[47]

Colonel Williams considered such poles a "profanation," and parsons preached against them. The Montague minister devoted a whole sermon to "the sin of erecting such an Idol." But the townspeople only insulted him for his labors. Tories and Whigs nailed threatening letters to one another onto the poles. After Tories in Deerfield left several "such blackgard pesses [pieces]" that were "a disgras to the pool," a patriot answered: "O, you poor towryes! when shall i get some tar? i do command you to not defile the libertie poole with no more of your Dambd skrools." Unfortunately, a historian cannot accept this as the language of the common people, for the unknown author quaintly added, "this is tory grammar, faith it is." He was probably wrong. The Tory–Whig struggle in Deerfield pitted the well-established elite against newcomers and younger people. It was merely one more form of social conflict.[48]

Tories called new militia officers "sham officers" and refused to act under them. They obstructed the sale of confiscated lands and destroyed the chaises of Whigs or attacked them personally. To create disorder, and subsequently clamor for stronger government, they prevented courts from sitting by obstructing the return of jurors. In this they were so successful in Yarmouth and Barnstable that James Otis spoke about "this Tory County." After several Tories had been arrested in Berkshire, their political friends assembled and freed them. In the rescue riot, carried out by men who liked to style themselves adherents to law, order, and government, the guard was assaulted and "badly wounded." Tory students at Harvard publicly drank dutied tea. As with some Whigs, motives of private gain accompanied political and other motives when numerous attempts were made by Tories to hurt the economy of the province by forging provincial money.[49]

---

[46]Eastham: *ibid.*, 4.2:1050–1055. Falmouth: Stevens, American Loyalist Claims, 14:289, NYPL. Oakham: *ibid.*, 13:389. Barnstable: Andrews, "Letters," 29 Jan. 1775, p. 398; invitation of three committees for a county convention, 17 July 1776, Military Papers, American Revolution, Orders, Forbes Library; cf. Address of the Convention, March 1780 in Handlin and Handlin, eds., *Popular Sources*, p. 435.

[47]Dedham: Ames, "Diary," July 1766, 12 May 1769, pp. 96, 150. Deerfield: letter from an unknown author, in Sheldon, *Deerfield*, 2:677–678; Merritt, "Loyalism and Social Conflict," pp. 277–289.

[48]Sheldon, *Deerfield*, 2:678–679.

[49]*Ibid.*, pp. 693, 728–729; Isaac Foster, Jr., to ———, 25 Aug. 1776, Hancock Papers, HBS; Ezra Stiles, *The Literary*

It may not be the duty of a historian to write about "what would have happened," but Tory plans for victory illuminate colonial mentality. Simply enough: They would have treated Whigs as they themselves were being treated. No independent men were tolerated.[50] The "People in general" were in their opinion "perfect Machines," "blind," unable to reason or to feel.[51] John Mein, the Boston printer, painted a picture of Tory victory: "The deluded populace are already universally objects of Commiseration: and all the depredations committed on property must be raised from the Estates of the Opulent Rebels; for the poor, who are also the misguided, can make no pecuniary Compensation."[52] Peter Oliver, Jr., husband of Hutchinson's daughter Sally, harbored similar thoughts: "Hanging people won't pay me for what I have sufferd. Nothing short of forfeited estates will answer: and after damages are sufficiently compensated, then hang all the Massachusetts Rebells by dozens if you will."[53]

Even in rhetoric Whigs and Tories resembled one another. For Tories the rioters were "Sons of Anarchy," and they implored God to "turn the hearts of those deluded wretches from the power of sin and Satan." The *Censor* published a recipe for the making of "a modern Patriot." Ingredients were "imprudence, virulence, and groundless abuse." Take of "Conscience a quarter of a scruple; atheism, deism, and libertinism, ad libitum." Furthermore, false reports, plausible lies, groundless alarms, malignant abuse, fraud, imposition, hypocrisy. Considering this rhetoric, it is not surprising that the debates between Whigs and Tories often became so heated that the phrase "to get into a jaw" was coined.[54]

INSTITUTIONAL MEASURES VERSUS CROWD SPONTANEITY

Insecurity caused by violence and denunciations grew so much that "every person [is] in fear of what his Neighbour will do to him." A crowd in Braintree, merely taking action against the sheriff, caused the following side effects: "The church parson thought they were comeing after him, and run up garret they say, an other jumpt out of his window and hid among the corn whilst a third crept under his bord fence and told his Beads." Violence increased to such a degree that attempts were made to check it. Salem "leaders," in the words of a Tory, seemed to be "deter-

Diary, ed. F. B. Dexter, 3 vols. (New York, 1901), 1:465–466; Moore, ed., *Diary of the Revolution,* 1:138; James Otis to Benjamin Greenleaf, 18 March 1776, in Force, ed., *Archives,* 4.5:408; *Acts and Resolves,* 5:986–987; Josiah Quincy, *The History of Harvard University,* 2 vols. (Boston, 1860), 2:163–164; Fraser, *United Empire Loyalists,* p. 302.

[50]James Murray, a Tory, was chastized by his political friends for interceding with the British on behalf of "some of my Acquaintances and for several poor people" who were Whigs. James Murray, *Letters of James Murray, Loyalist,* ed. Nina M. Tiffany and Susan I. Leslay (Boston, 1901), pp. 202–205. Edward F. Coffin, "Some Historical Notes about 'Tory' John Murray and His Family," *Worcester Soc. Hist. Pub.,* n.s. 2:233–246 (Sept. 1940).

[51]Murray, *Letters,* p. 156; Oliver, *American Rebellion,* p. 65; cf. Governor Morris to Penn, 20 May 1774, in Force, ed., *Archives,* 4.1:342–343.

[52]John Mein to James Murray, 11 Jan. 1775, *Letters,* pp. 171–172.

[53]Peter Oliver, Jr., to ———, 7 Dec. 1775, in Hutchinson, *Diary and Letters,* 1:580–582.

[54]Peter Oliver to Elisha Hutchinson, 1 June 1775, to Polly Hutchinson, 26 May 1775, *ibid.,* pp. 457–460; *Censor,* 8 Feb. 1772.

mined and are really taking pains to prevent outrage,'' and a town meeting, condemn-ing the breaking of windows, ''recommend[ed] to the rioters to repair them and make satisfaction for the damage done on that day of rejoicing.'' A Marlborough town meeting offered a reward for information about those ''who wickedly dis-charged two loaded guns into the lodging room'' of a Tory minister.[55]

In consequence of several crowd actions against Hampshire Tories, Jonathan Judd remarked, ''People condemn the Mob very freely to-Day and I fancy that something will be done by the Committee about it.'' Five days later the North-ampton Committee sent out a circular stressing that a ''peaceable Course of Be-haviour'' had been recommended by the Continental and Provincial Congresses. They expected that the exertion of the committees and ''the Virtue of the People'' would be sufficient to effect conduct conforming to these resolves. At least some insults to Tories were ''repugnant to the Dictates of Humanity and the Precepts of Religion.'' Furthermore, ''such irregular Risings when unnecessary are dangerous, and as at the present Time they are in direct opposition to the Resolves of the Congresses they must tend to disunite the People and bring upon us the Distress and Ruin which we are all Solicitous to avoid.''[56]

In Boston, where the presence of British troops had reduced crowd action, it was said that ''since the Act for Tarring and Feathering has been repealed . . . [and] wiser Measures are adopted,'' more was effected than before. The backlash against violence was accompanied, however, by complaints about the slow and inefficient institutional action. Thus, ''Detector'' criticized that ''not a twentieth part'' of the absentees' estates had been advertised for sale or lease and threatened the responsi-ble agents.[57]

The first measures that the Provincial Congress took concerning Loyalists were, in fact, protective. It allowed all those who had fled to Boston to send out an unarmed person to carry their effects into the besieged town. That was much more than the British governor and military commander permitted Bostonians who had left the town to do. The army at Roxbury was even to provide an attendant for such persons. The next action concerned persons leaving the province to avoid military service or personal disadvantages. Though they ''desert the common interest, and basely refuse to contribute of their wealth, or assist, personally,'' in the common struggle, they should be allowed to leave the province. A curtailment of ''the natural right of an individual to remove his person and effects wherever he pleases, we apprehend, would ill become those who are contending for the *unalienable rights of every man to his own property,* and to dispose of it as he pleases.'' But 10 days later, as more disaffected persons began to move to Nova Scotia, the Congress

---

[55]Sheldon, *Deerfield*, 2:683; Abigail Adams to John Adams, 14 Sept. 1774, *Adams Family Correspondence*, ed. L. H. Butterfield, 2 vols. (Cambridge, Mass., 1963), 1:152; Samuel Curwen to ———, 18 Sept. 1774, Letterbooks, vol. 2. Essex Institute; Pynchon, *Diary*, pp. 41ff.; Charles Hudson, *History of the Town of Marlborough, Middlesex County, Massachusetts, from Its First Settlement in 1657 to 1861* (Boston, 1862), pp. 160–161.

[56]Judd, Diary, 4 Feb., 9 Feb. 1775, in James R. Trumbull, *Northampton*, 2:375; circular of the Northampton Commit-tee, 9 Feb. 1775, Forbes Library. In New York unlawful assemblies and assaults on Tories were prohibited because too many private quarrels were reportedly camouflaged as causes for liberty. Records of the New York Committee of Safety, Sept. 1775, in Force, ed., *Archives*, 4.3:894.

[57]*BEP,* 5 Sept. 1774; *BG,* 5 April 1779; cf. ''B. K.'' and ''A Card'' in *BG,* 8 March 1779.

reversed itself, ordering that nobody should be suffered to leave the province "to avoid their proportion of burdens necessarily incurred for our defense," except with special permission. As to "persons unfriendly to the country," the Congress also reversed its position without, however, advocating imprisonment or violence. Since such persons were acting "merely on principles of avarice," attempting to enslave America, and committing "atrocious and unnatural crimes against their country," it was resolved "that no person within this colony shall take any deed, lease, or conveyance whatever, of the lands, houses, or estates of such persons." This boycott was to be enforced by the Committees of Inspection.[58]

This last measure set the pace for the General Court, which during the next three years passed a series of acts directed mainly against Tories.[59] The first two acts were dictated by fear of military action by Tories, with British forces or separately. Their arms were to be confiscated, and active combatants were to be jailed without the right to post bail. Absentees were disenfranchised and lost their eligibility. Persons suspected of Toryism could be prosecuted, forced to take a test oath, and pay the cost of the inquisition. A third act provided that the towns should procure evidence against suspected Tories, exclude them from all business connections, and lay the material before the General Court. Convicted persons were to be exiled. A fourth act prohibited refugees from returning to the state, because they had betrayed the country, deprived it of their services, and aided the enemy.

At first only the loss and waste of Tories' estates were to be prevented, but by the end of the seventies the properties of the absentees and of "certain notorious conspirators against the government and liberties of the inhabitants" were confiscated to be used for the government and people. These laws only legalized what had long been common. Town meetings, committees, or selectmen had administered the farms of absentees since their departure.[60]

Even after exiling the Tories and confiscating their property, the General Court was flooded with petitions and memorials to take more decisive action. Sometimes town meetings and crowds took action themselves without waiting for the legislature. In Boston a crowd of 2000 threatened to prevent the landing of a transport loaded with Tories. In Marblehead a crowd prevented the return of the Robie family. Heated debates in town meetings were occasioned by the possible return of inhabitants who had sought the protection of the king.[61]

Berkshirites complained about the mildness toward Tories. Five active Loyalists

---

[58]Lincoln, ed., *Journals of Each Provincial Congress*, 2 May, 8 May, 15 May, 20 May 1775, pp. 184, 202–203 (emphasis added), 226–227, 249.

[59]Acts for disarming and restraining persons disaffected with the cause of America ("Test Act"), *Acts and Resolves*, 5:479–484, 1775–1776, Ch. 21; "for taking up and restraining persons dangerous to this state," *ibid.*, p. 641, 1776–1777, Ch. 45; to prevent danger from internal enemies, *ibid.*, pp. 648–650, 1776–1777, Ch. 48; to prevent the return of absentees (Exclusion Act), *ibid.*, pp. 912–918, 1778–1779, Ch. 24.

[60]*Ibid.*, pp. 966–967, 1778–1779, Ch. 48; *ibid.*, pp. 968–971, 1778–1779, Ch. 49. Dorothy Forbes to James Murray, 20 May 1775, and later, *Letters*, pp. 199ff. Dorothy Forbes administered the family's estates after the Loyalist-inclined men fled to Boston. Her letters and those of other women in similar situations would furnish ample material for a study of women in colonial/revolutionary society having a chance—and usually the capabilities—to act independently.

[61]*BG*, 5 Aug. 1776, 10 Aug. 1778; *Indep. Chron.* 13 Aug. 1778; *Essex Gaz.*, 6 Dec. 1774; David Cobb, Weekly Journal, 29 July 1776, R. T. Paine Papers, 1766–1776, MHS; petition to selectmen, Misc. Unbound Papers, 1778,

from the county had been convicted and sent to Boston to be deported. Instead, the Board of War set them free. They returned, forcefully rescued other Tories, and opposed the Whigs. One joined the enemy. Delegates of 15 towns assembled at Stockbridge to decide upon further measures. In a petition they called these Tories a "disgrace to Humane Nature" and "Cruel and Blood Thusty Tools of the Tyrant of Great Britain."

> [We] are constrained to observe that we the People of Berkshire, by some of our former Representatives have been stigmatized and branded as being a Lawless and disobedient part of this State, while we essert that the hand of Violence was never lifted so high in opposition to the Legislative and executive Authority of this State as by those Diebolical emisaries who were sent to the Board of War.[62]

When the council voted not to deport a Bostonian suspected of pro-British senti-ments, his fellow townsmen called a town meeting "to make enquirey why some obnoxious Persons" were permitted "to reside here." They were in prison. The council was charged with having violated the Exclusion Act, "well calculated" to preserve peace, safety, and order, provided it was "carried into execution." The inhabitants threateningly added that they would have to "exert themselves to the utmost in Supporting the civil Magistrate in the execution of this Law." The Tories were merely coveting "private advantages" while the patriots wanted to "enjoy in common, the fruits" of their struggles.[63] That many patriots did not share "in common" but looked for private profit was evidenced by opposition to "just prices." Food riots were the result.

BCH; *BTR* 26:27–28 (Aug. 1778); Abigail Adams to John Adams, 15 June 1777, *Adams Family Correspondence,* 2:265–266.

[62]Petition from Stockbridge Convention, 9 April 1778, *Acts and Resolves,* 5:986–987.

[63]*Ibid.,* pp. 1005–1006; *BTR* 26:32–35; MA 184:314–315; Rowe, *Letters and Diary,* 17 Nov. 1778, p. 324.

Scarcity of Provisions: Public Town Meetings and Riots versus Private Interest

14

When British troops evacuated Boston in 1776, adequate supplies of provisions became the most urgent problem for elected authorities and town meetings. Since the arrival of troops in summer 1774, food and firewood had been scarce and increasingly expensive. With the beginning of the inflation prices began to soar. Imported goods also became more costly because higher losses were sustained through privateering and because the Continental Association had reoriented trade toward new markets. Dairy products and other agricultural produce became more costly because the war further depleted the always low pool of agricultural labor. Boston's special situation made the food problem one of region, of city versus country, and of class.

The country surrounding Boston supplied the town with vegetables, dairy products, hay and firewood in winter. The British had easily been cut off from these supplies from 1774–1776, and Bostonians had suffered with them. Now Boston's need offered the farmers two alternatives. They could sell their products at a just price: production cost plus a reasonable profit. Or they could make a substantial profit by waiting for prices to rise even higher. The difference between just price and market price had severely strained the consciences of Massachusetts settlers since the founding of the colony.[1] In Boston and other coastal towns, rising food prices had received periodic attention when farmers and coasters did not come to town for fear of smallpox or impressment.[2] A clamor about extortion arose about those who sold their goods to the highest bidder. For imported goods the situation

---

[1] Bernard Bailyn, "The *Apologia* of Robert Keayne," *WMQ* 3.7:568–587 (1950), and *The New England Merchants in the Seventeenth Century* (Cambridge, Mass., 1955); John Dickinson, "Economic Regulations and Restrictions on Personal Liberty in Massachusetts," *Pocumtuck Valley Hist. Assoc.* 7:485–525 (1929); Joseph Dorfman, *The Economic Mind in American Civilization, 1606–1865* (New York, 1946); Edgar A. J. Johnson, "Economic Ideas of John Winthrop," *NEQ* 3:235–250 (1930), and *American Economic Thought in the Seventeenth Century* (London, 1932); Edmund S. Morgan, *The Puritan Dilemma: The Story of John Winthrop* (Boston, 1958), p. 67. R. H. Tawney, "Religious Thought on Social and Economic Questions in the Sixteenth and Seventeenth Centuries," *J. Pol. Econ.* 31:461–493, 637–674, 804–825 (1923), and *Religion and the Rise of Capitalism* (New York, 1926); Max Weber, *The Protestant Ethic and the Spirit of Capitalism,* trans. Talcott Parsons (New York, 1952).

[2] For impressment, see Chapter 1, pp. 61–62; on smallpox, see Chapter 1, pp. 52–54, and Chapter 9, pp. 250–251; on country reaction to nonimportation, see Chapter 6, pp. 197–199.

was the reverse. The Boston importers kept their prices up, and farmers and other people from the inland towns cried out against oppression. Many farmers also remembered that the merchants of Boston had broken the nonimportation agreements and demanded market prices for British goods rather than just prices, reaping enormous profits.

Second, the adoption of price controls was further complicated by Boston's social structure. Differences between rich and poor were more apparent than anywhere else in the province. The wealthy inhabitants were least interested in price controls. Those who were wholesale importers could gain from higher prices. By extending credit, they increased their income from interest. Those who owned farms worked by tenants could profit from inflated agricultural prices. The numerous small shop-keepers in town were hurt most by the rising prices for food and firewood and advocated price ceilings for these goods only. Artisans, sailors, and laborers, the only ones in favor of more general price controls, faced a community uniformly demanding wage controls. The situation was ripe for turmoil. The differences between the shopkeepers and mechanics prevented clear class alignments. Instead, a multitude of small skirmishes between groups ensued. The retailers voted with the artisans to obtain limitations on food and wood prices, then sided with the merchants against the artisans to keep wages down. No unity existed within the groups either, and different trades often voted against each other. The hatters petitioned to raise the price limits for their goods, but the other inhabitants turned the request down. One of the hatters, a member of the Committee of Correspondence, raised his prices nevertheless. The other hatters supported him, and the town could do nothing but publish his name. Butchers continued a private price war against the skin-processing tradesmen and vice versa.

In this situation of small interest groups, united action was difficult. Only once, in 1777, 129 Boston tradesmen agreed on a united petition to the General Court: They wanted to be protected against competition by strangers.[3]

TOWN MEETINGS ON PRICE CONTROLS

Town meetings began to deal with the question of prices and supplies late in 1776. A petition for a meeting in Boston gained an unusual 111 signatures and stated that the high prices for firewood were caused by the wharfingers, who were engrossing; the exorbitant prices for all other provisions, because every seller engrossed.[4] Discord arose at once. A bylaw to prevent forestalling was rejected. A second committee, to report other measures to be taken, could not reach agreement and, after more than three weeks, suggested enforcing existing laws and recom-

[3]Tanners versus butchers: *BTR* 20:108, 110–111, 149, 223, 279, 23:67–68, 75, 101, 105–106, 26:76. Hatters: *ibid.*, 26:87, 97; John Andrews, "Letters of John Andrews, Esq., Boston, 1772–1776," ed. Winthrop Sargent, 20 Aug. 1774, *MHSP* 8:344 (1864–1865); petition of the tanners, Dec. 1771, of the tradesmen, 1777, Misc. Unbound Papers, 1771, 1777, BCH.

[4]*BTR* 18:249, 250; petition in Misc. Unbound Papers, 1776, BCH; Oscar Handlin and Mary F. Handlin, *Commonwealth: A Study of the Role of Government in the American Economy—Massachusetts, 1774–1861* (New York, 1947), pp. 7–8; Robert A. East, *Business Enterprise in the American Revolutionary Era* (New York, 1938; reprint ed., 1964).

mended that "the Inhabitants be as sparing as possible in *purchasing.*" Nothing was done about selling.

The report was outspoken about the causes of the problems and was immediately attacked from the floor. The committee had said that some persons, "by engrossing and Forestalling, not only the Necessaries of Life, but many other Articles, are greatly injuring the Town." It was suggested that they might "expect to be held up as unworthy the Name of Friends to their Country." Such threats of public shame had been abandoned as ineffectual decades earlier, and during the nonimportation time had to be followed up by crowd action. Rival interests claimed to be *the* public. A large majority had stood up against a small minority of importers in 1768–1770; it is not surprising that the open expression of numerous competing economic interests rendered community sanctions ineffectual in 1776 and later.[5]

In December 1776, delegates from four New England states met to agree on a stable currency and prevent "Monopoly and high price of goods and the necessaries of Life." They reached an understanding about a regulation of prices and wages. Wages were set for farm laborers, who had the most difficulty in organizing. Wages for mechanics and tradesmen were "to be computed according to the usages and Customs." Maximum prices were listed mainly for a large number of New England products. Concerning imports, the committee only lamented the high charges (500–600 percent above the prime cost) and unreasonable profits (40–50 percent on cost and charges). It suggested an advance of 150 to 175 percent over prime cost as reasonable and sufficient for charges and profits in wholesale, plus an additional 20 percent for retail. To enforce these recommendations, each state was to appoint searchers with power to open stores and warehouses and to seize goods of "monopolizers and engrossers," paying nothing but the regulated prices for them.

The proposals became law in Massachusetts in January 1777. Its preamble states causes and intentions. In naming together "the avaritious conduct of many persons, by daily adding to the now exorbitant price of every necessary and convenient article of life and encreasing the price of labour in general," the law put product and labor under equal restraints, though only the price for labor was relatively easy to control. An attempt was made to decrease city–country tensions: The farmers had most of the necessities and had no reason to sell for just prices when merchants kept those for convenient articles high. The preamble then considered the social consequences of profiteering:

> it not only disheartens and disaffects the soldiers who have nobly entered into the service of their country for the support of the best of causes, and distresses the poorer part of the community by obliging them to give unreasonable prices for those things that are absolutely necessary to their very existence, but will be also very injurious to the state in general.

Penalties were enacted for violations of the law. Execution was delegated to the

[5]*BTR* 18:253–254; poem on extortion, *Mass. Brds.* 2114a; A. C. Goodell *et al.*, eds., *Acts and Resolves, Public and Private, of the Province of the Massachusetts Bay*, 21 vols. (Boston, 1869–1922), 5:669–673.

selectmen, who were empowered to fix prices for the enumerated goods (those in the law referring to Boston), as well as for commodities not mentioned. The provincial Board of War and the town selectmen, after obtaining a search warrant, could enter premises in which goods were suspected to be beyond those needed by the owner's family. Such stores were to be seized and sold. But the magistrates were cautioned to use their authority only when "the very existence of the community is depending" upon their exertions. Public exposure of offenders and special town meetings were expected to ensure adherence to the law.[6]

In many towns a fierce struggle over the enforcement of the regulations took place in town meetings and committees. Only 10 days after the Monopoly Act had been passed, a "very large and respectable" Boston meeting attempted to determine measures for enforcing compliance with the act, resented by some "as doing violence to liberty and property." A committee of three men, not connected with trade, was chosen for each of the 12 wards in Boston to give information to the legal authorities about breaches of the act.

One committee reported that "the great Scarcity of Provisions in the Town" was caused by "Engrossers, who have monopolized" numerous imported goods, which they refuse to sell "at the Prices affixt by" the Monopoly Act, so that "the People from the Country complain that they cannot get a necessary Supply of those Articles." It "earnestly recommended" to complying with the act and asked the Committee of Correspondence to contradict "false Reports by the Tory Party" about Boston's merchants or shopkeepers. Thus, the hostility between farmers and merchants was admitted only to be explained away, like the tradesmen's protests against the merchants during the tea crisis in 1773. Again Tories were artificially creating problems, a statement to which everybody could subscribe.[7]

Disagreement appeared immediately when actual measures had to be taken to obtain flour and grain. The "chearful Compliance" that had been expected gave way to "a sudden Stagnation of Business." In other words, the importers had closed up shop because they considered their profits too small. Reports about countermeasures to the town meeting were recommitted, referred, or rejected. Committees were elected, made inquiries, but frequently could not agree on remedies.

The town's supplies of grain and flour were meager. Imported grain could not be ground in Boston because the proprietors of the mills had found it more advantageous to let the Boston mills decay and to profit from the transport to neighboring towns. It was proposed "that Gentlemen may be found, who will undertake to import [flour and grain] for the Use of the Inhabitants . . . on being assured of a reasonable Profit on the same"; in other words, the grain importers wanted the backing of the town for disregarding the price ceilings. When a conference between

---

[6]An Act to Prevent Monopoly and Oppression, *ibid.*, pp. 583–589, 1776–1777, Ch. 14, addition, *ibid.*, pp. 642–647, 1776–1777, Ch. 46. Andrew M. Davis, "The Limitation of Prices in Massachusetts, 1776–1779," *CSMP* 10:119–134 (1904–1906). See also *Mass. Brds.*, 2050 (prices fixed), 2174–2176 (Concord Convention, 1779); Kenneth Scott, "Price Control in New England during the Revolution," *New Eng. Q.* 19:453–473 (1946).

[7]*Continental Journal* and *Independent Chron.* 13 Feb. 1777; S. A. Otis to Gerry, 17 March 1777, James T. Austin, *The Life of Elbridge Gerry, with Contemporary Letters, to the Close of the American Revolution*, 2 vols. (Boston, 1828, 1829), 1:263–265; *BTR* 18:259–263.

delegates of the town and the merchants brought no results, the inhabitants lost patience. Some merchants having flour in their stores were ordered to attend town meetings and explain their sales—among them were Lendall Pitts, an influential Whig, and Thomas Boylston. Others were visited by the committees. Those who agreed to sell at the prices fixed were listed in the newspapers to prove to the country that the townsmen were ready to abide by the regulations. But discontent remained high, and at the next March meeting two of the three regularly elected Purchasers of Grain who had been found guilty of mismanagement two years earlier were not reelected.[8]

Before dissolving the last of the enforcement meetings, the town voted a number of minor measures that constitute a sad commentary on their failure to agree on far-reaching solutions. Fishermen should be encouraged to land more fish, butchers to set up stalls, and those bringing provisions should have the use of the Faneuil Hall market stalls gratis. The inhabitants, if they wanted to "avoid the Displeasure of their Fellow Citizens," were not to go out of town to buy provisions. The reason was that persons who could afford to hire servants sent them out. This obstructed the inflow of adequate supplies for the town in general, raised prices, and—if the provisions were resold—added the profits of the middlemen to the final consumer prices.

The hectic activity of town meetings and committees could not prevent the Monopoly Act from becoming a dead letter.

> If tis not Toryism, tis a Spirit of avarice, a Contempt of Authority, an inordinate Love of Gain . . . in Town, . . . every where. . . . There is a general cry against the Merchants, against monopolizers etc. who tis said have created a partial Scarcity. That a Scarcity prevails of every article not only of Luxury, but even the necessaries of life is a certain fact. Every thing bears an exorbitant price.

In May 1777 Boston's representatives were instructed to achieve immediate and total repeal of the Price and Monopoly Act and two similar laws. The reasoning of the town went as follows. First, the failure of the regulations was blamed on the acts; "we have done our utmost to carry them into Execution, and find them so formed, that it is impossible to accomplish it." In fact, the town's attempts to execute them had been foiled by conflicting interests among the mercantile part of the community. Second, the acts were said to be the source of all ill-feeling between town and country.

Third, the acts were blamed for the rising prices, the scarcity of goods, and the depreciation of the currency. The acts ruined "the honest and fair Traders" (that is, the established merchants and shopkeepers) and encouraged "Mushroom Pedlars, who adulterate their Commodities, and take every Advantage." Thus, the acts brought disgrace and stagnation upon commerce, and without commerce the coun-

---

[8]Cotton Tufts to John Adams, 14 April 1777, *Adams Family Correspondence,* ed. L. H. Butterfield, 2 vols. (Cambridge, Mass., 1963), 2:210–211; *BTR* 16:282 (mills), 18:170 (mismanagement of purchasers of grain), 259–265 (Feb. 1777).

try would not be worth defending. The proposition that it was commerce that made a country worth defending would have been rejected by most of the farmers as well as by all those who adhered to the ideology of a corporate good. Obviously, the mercantile party was not at all easy with its arguments either, but for different reasons. The awareness that profits were higher in business than in artisanal production made people leave their "calling" to try making profits as "pedlars" and "knaves." This meant disorder in society—without artisans, farmers, and laborers, no commerce and no profits were to be had. The talk of unity, stemming on the one hand from the corporate ideology, on the other from the interest of the ruling merchant class, had to be changed. Everybody was told to get back to his job and with it to his place in a stratified society.

The fourth argument of the Boston town meeting addressed the heart of the matter. The acts were "directly opposite to the Idea of Liberty." Free enterprise would be the solution; the liberalist party had won over the defenders of corporate concepts and conduct.

> [We] are firmly of the Opinion, if the Acts are repealed, and our Trade freed from the cruel Shackles, with which it has lately been injudiciously bound, that a plentiful Import will, as assuredly lower the Prices, as a Scarcity has raised them: For it has been a known and acknowledged Truth, by all Nations, which were wise enough to encourage Commerce, that Trade must regulate itself; can never be clogged but to its ruin; and always flourishes when left alone; it is justly compared to a Coy Mistress, she must be courted with Delicacy, and is ruined by force.

But the Bostonians were not prepared to act with delicacy. The General Court and the town meeting had failed, but the latter had at least attempted to work off discontent and frustration. Angrily the inhabitants charged that strangers and "unfriendly" persons had moved into the town "who would sacrifice the public Interest to satisfy their Lust and Appetites." They "are daily using every Means in their Power" to subvert not only the acts "to prevent Monopoly and Oppression, but to lessen and depreciate the Value of the Money established by the Continental Congress."

Just as a few strangers and idle sailors had taken the blame for many riots and disturbances, private interests within the community were projected onto outsiders to keep the fiction of one public interest intact. Against these outsiders only force would do, a reasoning equally acceptable to those whose "Coy Mistress" was profit and to those whose sufferings under the existing scarcity built up hatred for the supposed culprits. The period of laws, debates, and committees was superseded by force and crowd action. In October 1777 the acts were repealed. The towns were advised to make provision for the families of the noncommissioned officers and soldiers, as the repeal deprived them of protection against high prices. The "poorer part of the community," named in the preamble to the first act as beneficiaries, was no longer mentioned.[9]

[9] Abigail Adams to John Adams, 20 April 1776, *Adams Family Correspondence*, 2:217–218; *BTR* 18:276, 284–285; *Acts and Resolves*, 5:733–734, 1777–1778, Ch. 6.

RIOTS AGAINST MONOPOLIZERS

In May 1777 a crowd of about 500 took five merchants from their homes, put them in a cart, and then paraded to the Neck. There the cart was tipped over and the men ordered not to return to town. Four of them—William Jackson, Nathaniel Cary, James Perkins, and Richard Green—were Bostonians and had been denounced in a town meeting. Green, business partner of Stephen Cleverly of the former Loyal Nine, and the others were crown supporters. The fifth, Epes Sergeant, was from Cape Ann. Two of his schooners had been seized for breach of the British trade laws in 1765. The five men were generally charged with "Tory principles." One Bostonian, disagreeing with the carting, complained that the fruit of liberty seemed to be chaos, but admitted that most of the persons carted were "justly obnoxious." Abigail Adams reported "that a week or two ago there was a publick auction at Salem when these 5 Tories went down and bid up the articles to an enormous price." A few days later she added, "It seems they have refused to take paper money and offerd their goods Lower for Silver than for paper. Bought up articles at a dear rate, and then would not part with them for paper."[10]

The action had been led by "Joyce, Jr.," who preceded the crowd on horseback, with a red coat, a white wig, and a drawn sword. The crowd marched to the tune of drum and fife and obeyed Joyce's orders. In the evening a poster appeared in town admonishing the merchants not to keep their goods unsold. Several weeks earlier Joyce had threatened Tories and then asked his followers to consult upon measures against Tories and for enforcing the Monopoly Act. The name presumably referred to Cornet George Joyce, leader of a troop of volunteers who captured King Charles I on 2 June 1647 and delivered him to the army, and who had also been one of the king's executioners.[11]

During the tea crisis, fall 1773 to the beginning of 1774, Joyce had threatened the Plymouth protesters and charged the tea consignees with acting for their "private interest" only and neglecting the public. But when John Malcom was tarred and feathered in 1774, he denied any responsibility, explaining that he reserved his activities for men of more importance. He continued to inform the public through the columns of the *Gazette,* threatening opponents and explaining that popular action was necessary because the General Court was too lax toward Tories. On 16 September 1777, six more men were carted out of town "for the Crimes of Monopolizing and Extortion." One of them, William Stackpole, had been told

---

[10]*BTR* 18:276–282; John Rowe, *Letters and Diary of John Rowe, Boston Merchant, 1759–1762, 1764–1779,* ed. Anne Rowe Cunningham (Boston, 1903; reprint ed., 1969), 24 July 1765, p. 87; William Pynchon, *The Diary of William Pynchon of Salem,* ed. F. E. Oliver (Boston, 1890), 19 April 1777, p. 28; Abigail Adams to John Adams, 20–21 April 1777, *Adams Family Correspondence,* 2:217–218, cf. 222–223; Eliot to Belknap, 9 May 1777, *MHSC* 6.4:108–113; John Boyle, "Boyle's Journal of Occurrences in Boston, 1759–1778," 19 April 1777, *NEHGR* 85:128 (1931); *BG,* 21 April 1777. Cf. *Continental Journal,* 9 Nov. 1780, "Benevolus" on behalf of the oppressed creditors who are forced to take paper money.

[11]Albert Matthews, "Joyce Junior," *CSMP* 8:89–104, 11:280–294 (1907); Alfred F. Young, "Pope's Day, Tar and Feathers, and 'Cornet Joyce, jun.': From Ritual to Rebellion in Boston, 1745–1775" (Paper prepared for the Anglo-American Labor Historians' Conference, Rutgers Univ., April 1973), Pt. VI. Esther Forbes, *Paul Revere and the World He Lived In* (Boston, 1942), pp. 328–329; *BG,* 17 March 1777; *BTR* 18:206–207; list of Sons of Liberty, 1775, *MHSP* 2.2:139–143 (1897–1898).

earlier to leave town within a week. At that, he petitioned the Committee of Correspondence for a "fair and impartial hearing."[12]

Joyce threatened several other merchants and asked "the good people of this State"—that is, the countrymen—that "when any traders appear among them belonging to this town, offering more than the regulated price for any article they have for sale," they should immediately inform him. He was a self-appointed servant of the public interest in the tradition of direct community action:

> I do hereby require, in Compliance with the good and wholesome Laws of this State for the Good of the Public, for whom I stand forth, That all who have left Butchering, Droving, Horse-jockeying, Shoemaking, Sand-driving, and assumed selling by Wholesale or Retail West India Goods, and all others in the same Business, and of Huxtering, that they forthwith open their Stores and Shops, and sell openly and publickly, Rum, Sugar, Molasses, Cotton-Wool, etc. etc. at the Prices stipulated by Law.

Joyce, Jr., was clearly one of those traditionalists who supported community interests over private profits, provided everyone remained in his calling. But people instead outbid one another. "Something must be done, to stop this growing evil," lamented Paul Revere, "or we shall eat one another."[13]

In July a surprised printer noted *"A Female Riot"* in Boston. The scarcity of sugar and coffee was surmised to be the result of hoarding. "Some Stores had been opened by a number of people and the Coffe and Sugar carried into the Market and dealt out by pounds." Among the accused was Thomas Boylston, the wealthy merchant who had been elected to enforce the Continental Association in December 1774, but was described as "one who loves his money better than his country, largely concerned in the slave trade." The women told him that they had heard that he had coffee to sell and that—for a reasonable price—they wanted to buy it, reportedly intending to resell it and other items to the poor. Boylston, who probably had different notions about reasonable prices and profits, bluntly answered that he would not sell. Upon this, about 100 women assembled and demanded coffee. When Boylston refused, they unceremoniously put him into a cart and drove off to the wharf, probably intending to give him a ducking. "A large concourse of Men stood amazd silent Spectators of the whole transaction." Boylston, realizing that he would get no assistance from them, and being roughed up, delivered the keys. The women tipped the cart over, turned around to get the coffee, and carried it off to the crowded and poor Northend.[14]

The following weeks were disrupted by "much rout and Noise" in other towns too. In Longmeadow, merchant Samuel Colton received an anonymous note fixing

---

[12]*BG*, 28 March 1774; *Brethren . . . the Modern Punishment Lately Inflicted on the Ignoble John Malcom* (Boston, 1774), *Mass. Brds.*, 1738. *BG*, 24 March, 21 April, 12 May 1777; Boyle, "Journal," 16 Sept. 1777, p. 130; Boston Committee of Correspondence, Correspondence 1777, NYPL.

[13]*Indep. Chron.* 24 April 1777; *BG*, 21 April 1777; Revere to Samuel Adams, 24 Aug. 1777, Samuel Adams Papers, NYPL.

[14]List of Sons of Liberty, 1775, *MHSP* 2.2:141 (1897–1898); Boyle, "Journal," 24 July 1777, pp. 129–130; Abigail Adams to John Adams, 30–31 July 1777, *Adams Family Correspondence*, 2:294–296; Scollay to Savage, *ibid.*, p. 296; Boylston's petition to leave for Great Britain, 1778, MA 184:152.

prices for his goods. When he did not comply, a crowd, among them several prominent townsmen, criticized the high prices for rum, molasses, and sugar and took some of his goods. In Beverly a number of women agreed in November 1777 to force the sale of sugar. Sixty of them seized some sugar, which induced other merchants in town to negotiate. Each of them agreed to sell a barrel of sugar to the women for paper money. This supply was carried to the shop of one of the women and sold in quantities and at prices previously fixed by general agreement. The money was then paid to the merchants who originally owned the sugar, including Stephen Cabot, whose sugar had been taken forcibly. In Salem the townsmen prohibited distilling of any grains into "spirits." In Marblehead, prices for firewood forced the poorer people to go begging for "every stick," and "many of the better sort" could not afford to have more than one fire in the house.[15]

People in the Massachusetts coastal towns were told that Rhode Island farmers blockaded Providence because of its merchants' "Extravagance and extortionate prices." Nathaniel Ames, almanac maker and physician in Dedham, noted that if the reports about their price demands were true, "they deserve to be blockaded longer than Boston was." John White, Salem merchant, faced with what he considered "mutinous" inhabitants in December 1776 because his salt was rather expensive, asked in his dairy, "May the Tumult of the People be stilled by Him who ruleth the Rageing of the Sea." The tumults were not stilled, and William Pynchon's diary gives a general impression of the continual strain on society and of the innumerable incidents.

31 January 1777: "The contest between farmers and Salem traders, etc., as to price of meal begins; the former threaten to starve the seaports." 28 April: "The Marblehead people and Salem people quarrel for bread at the bakers, and a scramble at the wharf in weighing out and selling Capt. Derby's coffee." 22 July: "Mob at Salem demand sugar, and the stores are opened." 24 July: "Ladies mob again on Copp's Hill." 26 July: " A countryman beat for not taking paper for his meat, which (he says) he had sold before." 2 January 1778: "Threats to set fire to the houses of those who were witnesses and prosecutors of the women's mob . . . some coals were placed at the front doors of several of the houses there." 18 March: "Tradesmen and salary-men grumble at the countrymen's extortion, and threaten to join the [British] Regulars against them." 24 March: "Grumbling at the extortion of the farmers, the blunders of politicians and legislators, the ambition and selfishness of the ministry and of the demagogues, badness of the times, etc., etc." 30 December: "It is continental Thanksgiving, but for want of provisions and the necessities of life [it] seems more like a Fast here."[16]

[15]Abigail Adams to John Adams, 30–31 July 1777, *Adams Family Correspondence*, 2:294–296. Longmeadow: " 'Fixing Prices' in 1775—The Story of Samuel Colton," *Mag. of Hist.* 25:81–87 (1917). Beverly: Edwin M. Stone, *History of Beverly, Civil and Ecclesiastical, from Its Settlement in 1630 to 1842* (Boston, 1843), pp. 83–85. Marblehead: Sewall to Jackson, 27 Jan. 1780, *EIHC* 7:195–197 (1865). Salem: Joseph B. Felt, *The Annals of Salem from Its First Settlement* (Salem, Mass., 1827), p. 501. For similar riots in other states, see Herbert Aptheker, *The American Revolution, 1763–1783 . . . An Interpretation* (New York, 1960), p. 245 (East Hartford, Connecticut), and Frank Moore, ed., *Diary of the American Revolution from Newspapers and Original Documents*, 2 vols. (New York, 1860, reprint ed., 1969), 1:287–288 (Fishkill, New York).

[16]Nathaniel Ames, "The Diary of Dr. Nathaniel Ames," ed. Sarah Breck Baker, 12 June 1776, *Dedham Hist. Reg.* 3:131–132 (1892); John White, "Extracts from the Interleaved Almanacs Kept by John White of Salem," 21 Dec. 1776, *EIHC* 49:93 (1913); Pynchon, *Diary,* pp. 24, 29, 34, 35, 46, 52, 61.

While the lower-income groups tried to get food for their families, officers of the army and other military units advertised for sashes, hangers, gorgettes, and genteel fuses—useless except for "idle" pomp and parade, as in the corrupt European states, according to Timothy Pickering. The officers were willing to pay a "generous price" and spent part of their time squabbling about who outranked whom.[17] No wonder William Pynchon registered general discontent with the authorities.

The food riots remained unconnected, ex tempore affairs. They were ineffective instruments for increasing supplies and lowering prices. The riots expressed consumer sentiments on local demands and wages. They were opposed by concepts of at least regional if not national or imperial markets. But the free trade demanded by Boston and practiced during this period after repeal of the Monopoly Act solved none of the problems either.

A THIRD MEASURE: RHETORIC AND SCAPEGOATS

The failure of the Monopoly Act had initiated a period of forcible distribution of goods combined with violence against scapegoats. When this remained unsuccessful too, a period of mere rhetoric followed.

In March 1778, 13 months after the Monopoly Act meetings and 10 months after its repeal had been urged in favor of free trade, a Boston town meeting was again occupied with how "to obtain Relief, in regard to the present extraordinary high Price of Provisions, and other necessary Articles of Life." The five men who reported on the articles were veterans in the service of the town or of the Merchants' Society. Their report outlined the situation in strong terms of individual versus community:

> One Great Reason of the present Excessive Price of Provisions in this Town arises from the Averice Injustice and Inhumanity of certain Persons within Twenty Miles of it, who purchase great Part of the same of Farmers living at a greater Distance, and put an exorbitant Advance upon it, which our Necessities oblige us to give; while they, having monopolized it, deal it out to us in such Quantities as they please. . . .

They recommended (1) a "decent, yet spirited" memorial to the General Court, proposing "as severe a Law . . . as can be framed" against monopolizing and forestalling; (2) that the "more opulent" relieve the "more indigent" by having no more than two dishes of meat per day, to lower demand and prices, and not consuming "Poultry, and every other Superfluity as much as possible"; and (3) that all inhabitants have two dinners per week of fish if available. The "decent" memorial blamed the town's distress on the farmers, the landowners, and

---

[17]*BG*, 19 May 1777; Jackson to Knox, 27 Aug. 1777, Knox Papers, reel 4:46, MHS; John Broome to William Palfrey, 28 July 1775, Palfrey Family Papers, vol. 3, no. 28, HHL; Timothy Pickering, *An Easy Plan of Discipline for a Militia* (Salem, Mass., 1775), pp. 11, 26 (main section).

the more than Brutish Conduct of those Wretches . . . known in the odious Character of Forestallers, who, lost to the Feelings of Humanity, purchase from those at a
Distance, and retail it out to these unhappy distressed Inhabitants, at a Price suited
to their unfeeling Hearts, and many of them add Insult to their Extortion.[18]

Posters appeared in the town again, threatening wholesale buyers of flour. The
Gazette printed the story of an engrosser who once upon a time had been seized by
the enraged people. He had been tied to a stake in the middle of his grain-filled
storehouse and left there to starve to death. "Quere [added the printer], Is it not now
necessary that one or more examples of the like nature should take place?"[19]

Since the repeal of the Monopoly Act, the distress of the poor had increased.
Boston had to borrow £8000 lawful money to supply the poor. Committeemen
purchased supplies and appointed retailers to sell for a price computed from cost,
charges, and allowances for waste and retail. These terms of the public report to the
town meeting were changed in private conversations of top town officials to "a
Moderate proffit" for those engaged in the transactions. The poor, from whose
pockets the profits would come, were admonished to observe the utmost frugality.
They should not "receive [that is, buy] a second Supply" until the first was
consumed. The poor, as always under strict control, could be ordered what to eat.
The same town meeting could not order traders and merchants to sell what they had.
Those who kept their stores closed waiting for further price increases were merely
"earnestly" admonished "immediately [to] open their stores, and sell indiscriminately to all that apply."[20]

At the same time, John Hancock gave elegant dinners for the officers of the
French fleet then in port, even inviting them to a "grand Ball." He thus violated the
town's demands for frugality and the eighth resolve of the Continental Association.[21] Bostonians did not riot against Hancock to enforce the regulation. They
turned against the traditional scapegoats, strangers, and attacked the bakers and
sailors of the French fleet to get bread. French officers interposed, but the rioters
dispersed only when American troops were ordered out to quell the riot. Though
James Warren blamed the affair on English sailors and Tories attempting to dis-
seminate misgivings "between us and our New Allies," the real cause was the
unalleviated scarcity of provisions and the continuing profiteering. Accordingly,
there were further riots, notwithstanding military patrols, armed intervention by
American soldiers, and council proclamations. Civil magistrates were "to use their

[18]*BTR* 26:8–10, 13.

[19]Rowe, *Letters and Diary,* 19 Dec. 1778, p. 322; *BG,* 5 Oct. 1778.

[20]*BTR* 18:289–290, and Boston petition to the General Court, fall 1777, stating that the increasing of prices "threatens
the poor with intolerable Distress." MA 183:93; Scollay to Savage, 26 July 1777, Savage Papers, MHS.

[21]Rowe, *Letters and Diary,* Sept.–Oct. 1778, pp. 322–323. In Philadelphia, threats of rioting in support of the eighth
resolve prevented a ball from being staged [Christopher Marshall, *Extracts from the Diary of Christopher Marshall,
Kept in Philadelphia and Lancaster, during the American Revolution, 1774–1781,* ed. William Duane (Albany,
N.Y., 1877; reprint ed., 1969), pp. 51–52]. Unemployed and poor people in New York had "mobbed" a theater a
decade earlier to express their resentment of the wealthy [Howard M. Jones, *O Strange New World* (1952: reprint ed.,
New York, 1974), p. 284].

utmost Endeavours'' to prosecute, and French officers were to apprehend rioters. But supplies did not increase.[22]

Aside from riots against scapegoats, no action was taken. A town meeting on supplying the poor was adjourned because of lack of attendance. The selectmen applied to the Board of War for its stores of grains and wood, but the board did not even supply the soldiers under its jurisdiction properly, though it had provisions. Then the inhabitants voted to obtain information about those who ''enrich their little Selves by Monopolizing.'' The committee, in bitter though unintended irony, took ''little'' to refer to social position and named no important men. It cited five strangers, one for monopolizing glass, the others for profiteering on small quantities of sugar, flour, and meat. Later two Boston bakers were reprimanded for buying flour and reselling it for profit instead of baking bread. About the same time, February 1779, fishermen from neighboring towns, who sold their fish at moderate rates, had their rigs and rudders destroyed and their fish thrown on the dock by Boston fishermen looking for higher profits. Prosecution for profiteering, forestalling, and monopolizing was nonexistent, a few unimportant cases excepted. Confession in the town meeting was the only punishment.[23]

Not being able to execute any constructive measures, the inhabitants rejoiced about makeshifts. Late in April 1779 a number of particularly valuable men-of-war and store ships were captured and brought into Boston harbor. This occasioned extensive celebrations and bonfires. But such temporary relief could not quiet people. The selectmen of Salem put it succinctly when they said that, ''Tho' some individuals may Acquire large fortunes, by fitting out private Vessels of war, it is a notorious truth that the people in general are not inriched by it.'' In Boston, only a few days after the celebrations, ''Mobility,'' in ''A Hint,'' squarely posed the problem to the obnoxious forestallers: In similar situations in Great Britain and France, the people

> broke open magazines—appropriated Stores to their own use without paying for
> them—and in some instances have hung up the Culprits who have created their
> distress, without judge or jury. Hear this and tremble ye enemies to the freedom

[22]The French officer Chevalier de St. Sauveur died from the wounds inflicted by the rioters. MA 169:152, 200, 200:73–74, 102–104; Council Records, 22:443–445, 489, MSA; *Acts and Resolves*, 20:508, 510, 515; *BG*, 14 Sept. 1778; Forbes, *Revere*, pp. 340–341; James Warren to John Adams, 7 Oct. 1778, *Warren–Adams Letters: Being Chiefly a Correspondence among John Adams, Samuel Adams, and James Warren*, 2 vols. (Boston, 1917, 1925), 2:51; Pynchon, *Diary*, 9 Sept. 1778, p. 57; William Heath, *Heath's Memoirs of the American War*, ed. Rufus R. Wilson (1798; reprint ed., New York, 1904), p. 206; *Papers*, MHSC 7.4:268–272; William Gordon, *The History of the Rise, Progress, and Establishment of the Independence of the United States of America*, 4 vols. (London, 1788), 3:197–198 (similar affray at Charlestown, South Carolina), 201; B. F. Stevens, ed., *Facsimiles of Manuscripts in European Archives Relating to America*, 25 vols. (London, 1889–1898), chronological list of principal events in Count D'Estaing's campaign, 23:2023; M. [Abbé Pierre Charpentier] de L[ongchamps], *Histoire impartiale des événements de la dernier guerre, dans les quatre parties du monde*, 3 vols. (Paris, 1785), 1:450–453; Henri Doniol, *Histoire de la participation de la France à l'etablissement des Etas-Unis d'Amerique*, 5 vols. (Paris, 1886–1892), 3:351–366.

[23]MA 169:378–379, 174:336, 175:270, 184:39–40; *BTR* 25:81, 26:36–47; Rowe, *Letters and Diary*, Jan. 1779, pp. 325–326; indictment against Thomas Leach, Superior Court of Judicature, Records, 1778–1780, f. 151, SCCH. Leach had been prosecuted earlier for selling bread ''at an extortionate rate'' (*BG*, 12 April 1779). The confession in the town meeting was made by a man who had brought unmerchantable meat to the town for sale (*BTR* 26:77).

and happiness of your country. Hunger will break through Stone-Walls, and the resentment exited by it may end in your destruction.

In Massachusetts, however, there was no violence. The threat of it remained empty rhetoric.[24]

AFTER THREE FAILURES: A POLICY OF SMALL STEPS, AN ATTITUDE OF RESIGNATION

The General Court in 1778 enacted a second Monopoly Act to eliminate the middlemen who had been squeezing the consumer, creating artificial shortages, and been a source of large profits for speculators, "lost to any sense of public virtue."[25] Bostonians turned to self-help in order to decrease dependence on farmers. They planted vegetables on empty town lands, raised livestock to supply the inhabitants and to employ butchers, soap boilers, and leather dressers. But the plan was ineffective because the butchers sold the hides out of town for higher profit, leaving the artisans of the leather trades in the lurch.

One last effort was made when news arrived that "redressers" had put pressure on Philadelphia merchants. Handbills appeared in June 1779.

> Sons of Boston! Sleep no longer! . . . rid the community of those Monopolizers and Extortioners, who, like cancer-worms, are gnawing upon your vitals. They are reducing the currency to waste-paper, by refusing to take it for many articles; The infection is dangerous. . . . Public examples, at this time, would be public benefits! . . . [signed] VENGEANCE.
>
> N.B. Lawyers, keep yourselves to yourselves! It is our determination to support the reputable merchant and fair Trader.

The merchants and selectmen, aware of the danger, met immediately. The inhabitants, under the allusive name of the "Body," ordered the merchants to appear. They came prepared with resolves, which were accepted, and "Vengeance" advertised popular enforcement of the resolves by "The Body set alive."[26]

In July 1779, delegates of 121 towns met at Concord to concert measures for lowering prices. While Bostonians had demanded exile for the "unworthy and dangerous members of the society," the convention decided that publishing the names of offenders would be sufficient. Other attempts to implement the Concord resolves also sounded like a replay of the procedures of 1776. The regulation of prices for European imports was first delayed and then confined to the demand that prices be lowered "from time to time." Fixed prices for imports were said to be

---

[24]Rowe, *Letters and Diary,* 16 April 1779, p. 328; *Indep. Ledger,* 26 April 1779; *BG,* 26 April 1779; Salem selectment to General Court, May 1778, MA 184:141–145.

[25]*Acts and Resolves,* 5:924–926, 1012–1020, 1778–1779, Ch. 31, continued, *ibid.,* p. 1118, supportive measures, *ibid.,* pp. 1073–1074 and 1114–1115 (paper money, export restrictions).

[26]*BTR* 26:58–60, 76; *Indep. Chron.* 17 June 1779; *Indep. Ledger* and *BG,* 21 June 1779; cf. "Harry Blunt," *BG,* 4 Jan. 1779.

''impracticable.'' It was practicable, however, to set maximum limits for the wages of artisans.[27]

All measures remained piecemeal and unsuccessful. Merchants continued to store imported provisions, waiting for further price increases. A member of the Whig Committee of Correspondence led the movement of the hatters to defy price regulations. In October the inhabitants plaintively voted to recommend to merchants, shopkeepers, and traders to supply inhabitants and ''our Brethren in the Country.'' In April 1780 the great distress of the people was on the agenda again but was listlessly deferred.[28]

Why this resignation? Why the failure of the representatives, of the inhabitants, in town meetings? Why the discarding of forceful distribution? The clue to the answer to these questions is the assumption for all these measures—that the public interest (adequate supplies at just prices) had to be defended against the profiteering of a small, though perhaps increasing, section of the community, and that statements of public virtue would be sufficient enforcement. The public interest was outlined in laws and reinforced by ostracism (publishing of names) or riots. But societal conditions had changed, and ideology lagged behind because the changes had never been accepted. The last effort to keep a closed corporation viable had been the expulsion of Tories and their forced recantations. The scarcity of provisions suddenly brought the differences among Whig groups to the surface. Four years passed before the inhabitants accepted this. Then they withdrew before the power of the great merchants. Whig ideology in the colonies had always been mainly concerned with political and constitutional issues. The corporate ideology had lost much of its viability. The rudimentary class consciousness of mechanics in coastal towns had been repressed. The participatory concepts of western farmers could not win against eastern mercantilism. In this stiuation the strongest asserted themselves. The next decades saw the further development of merchant capitalism, the rise of the ''American system'': mercantilism that included the manufacturing interest, and agrarian expansion by settler–speculators.

But this was in the future. The present held immediate problems. The first Monopoly Act had been enacted to protect those—soldiers and poor—who could not defend themselves against greed for high profits because they could not politically or economically protect their interests. The act presumed that the rest of the community would behave according to its stipulations without enforcement.[29] Failure was blamed on the regulations or outsiders. When free trade—that is, special preference for the merchants—also failed, town meetings accused ''Tories'' of preferring their private interest. Crowds acted as public redressers again, and ''Tory'' came very close to being a synonym for wealthy merchant or wealthy landowner. While these two powerful groups combined to restore government to institutions they considered ''orderly,'' crowds were not only used occasionally to

---

[27]*BTR* 26:76, 78–82, 100–101 (Aug. and Nov. 1779).

[28]*Ibid.*, pp. 84–85, 87, 88–89, 91–92, 93, 97, 99, 101–102.

[29]Nathaniel Low, ''An Address to the People, on the Subject of Monopoly and Extortion,'' in his *Almanack, 1778* (Boston, 1777).

further private interests but, as in the case of the Boston fishermen, spontaneously began to do so.

The failure of the concept of public interest was apparent, but as yet no forces were strong enough to develop new structures in society. Much attention was absorbed by the struggle with Great Britain. For many communities, redress of grievances and not conflict about and a change of social or political structures remained the aim of independence. Those aware of private interests, usually their own, did not wish to discuss the problem publicly. Those who felt that their interest might be a public interest—the western constitutionalists—did attempt to reach other sections of the public but were too weak financially and organizationally. It cost time and money to keep representatives in the legislature and in the constitutional conventions.

Crowds and People under Whig Rule: Submission or Participation?

15

CROWD ACTION, 1765–1780: A REVIEW

Throughout the colonial period, crowd action was one form of social and political action in Massachusetts. It was a legitimate and in some circumstances even a semilegal means of achieving redress of specific grievances. But it always remained an extraordinary means to be used only after all possible legal and regular institutional channels had been exhausted. Individuals, including rioters, were bound by social compact and tradition to observe the written and unwritten laws and codes of their society, which, however, in the course of time could become corrupt. A return to first principles would save society from further corruption.[1] Riots were intended to enforce such principles on those who broke them. They were not means to achieve social change; they could only reinforce patterns of the past. To strive for "innovations" was a social offense.[2] Thus, crowd action, the most intense form of social action, was basically conservative, used to maintain the status quo in a static society.

The paradox that action is necessary to prevent changes in a static social context is explained by the divergence between actual societal conditions and how members of society perceive them. Changes did indeed happen: The population increased, towns grew, the division of labor proceeded, and subsistence farming was partly replaced by cultivation of marketable crops. Land prices were comparatively high, unsettled lands became scarce, and the areas left were difficult to work and yielded meager crops. Opportunities lessened, and traditional ties loosened. Differentiation of jobs, tasks, and living conditions necessitated intermediaries: traders and merchants. Separate parishes and new settlements undermined the corporate cohesiveness of agricultural towns. In larger towns economic and social stratification and the resulting diversification of interests made the belief in one definable public interest

---

[1] Cf. Gerald Stourzh, "Resort to First Principles," in his *Alexander Hamilton and the Idea of Republican Government* (Stanford, Calif., 1970); H. T. Colbourn, *The Lamp of Experience: Whig History and the Intellectual Origins of the American Revolution* (Chapel Hill, N.C., 1965).

[2] The discussion about "arbitrary" innovations became particularly intense in the early seventies when governor and judges of the Superior Court were made independent of legislative appropriations for salaries by crown grants.

an anachronism, one public good unobtainable. Different interpretations of the common interest began to appear gradually, but the ideology of corporate society up to the sixties did not change correspondingly. When changes did become apparent, attempts were made to undo them. Such attempts were never directed against the social or economic system but against individuals who manifested changes or who profited from them at the expense of the rest of the community. In the thirties and increasingly thereafter, entire interest groups, not just individuals, challenged the system by subtly bending its principles to their advantage.

Open avowal or open defense of factional interests was still unthinkable to most. The partisan reality existed, but antipartisan theory prevailed. Organized opposition, anathema to corporate unity, was unacceptable.[3] Tensions between merchants and farmere were hushed up. Men acting from a notion of different interests among social groups were accused of preferring their private interest, if they came from higher echelons, or of "licentiousness" when belonging to the poorer part of the population. In Boston more than in any other colonial seaboard town, an elaborate system of political clubs and caucuses was designed to preserve the status quo by eliminating any open contests. Expression of demands and policies by the middling interest was smothered in the caucus system.

In the sixties economic changes were hastened by the postwar depression, the new colonial policy of the British government, and the increasing pressure from interest groups. Action against the British move was taken on a fairly large scale by various means—legal, extralegal, and illegal. For the first time in colonial history, the opposition was apparent everywhere, because the new policies of taxation hit all colonies equally. Its form, direct action, was influenced by the following factors.

First, since no colonials were left untouched by the tax, resistance was general. Sailors alone could not compel the British Empire to change impressment statutes; farmers could not shift mast-pine priorities from the British navy to suit their own interests; merchants acting alone were ineffective in opposing duties or trade regulations. Those discontented with the innercolonial fee tables could not change them because the General Court was the domain of beneficiaries of the system. But all these groups, indeed the whole society, was averse to paying taxes, and this issue became the unifying factor.[4]

Second, a few members of the community attempted to obtain lucrative appointments as stamp distributors (or later as commissioners, consignees, and British-paid officials). It was in the colonial tradition to act against ambitious outsiders. No disloyalty was intended. King and Parliament were far away, incapable of judging

---

[3]Cf. "Americanus" (*BNL*, 18 July 1771): "Although in all states, the interest both of the governors and the governed is naturally the same, viz. the peace, good order and prosperity of society; yet unhappily, from the imperfections of human nature, there are frequent instances of separate interests, which by clashing produce Injustice, Disorder, Tumult and Violence." This argument was difficult to accept for people brought up under the corporate ideology. A Springfield town meeting in July 1774 still hoped that those in power, instead of being biased by "personal Interest," would "gratefully" remember that they had been raised to their station by their constituents and would join with them in obtaining redress from the Coercive Acts. Mason A. Green, *Springfield, 1636–1886* (Boston, 1885), pp. 275–277, quoting town records.

[4]John Murrin, "Anglicizing an American Colony: The Transformation of Provincial Massachusetts" (Ph.D. diss., Yale Univ., 1966); Richard L. Merritt, *Symbols of American Community, 1735–1775* (London, 1966).

the colonial situation because their information came from a tiny fragment of provincial society, placemen who had a personal interest in the information they gave. Stamp distributors (and other agents of the British government) were attacked primarily because they turned against their own communities, thereby enhancing their private fortunes. The possibility that they acted from loyalty to Great Britain was of only marginal importance to the crowds, as well as perhaps to themselves. The presence of such targets for popular wrath made crowd action possible. Stamp, customs and tea agents were "outsiders" but at the same time scapegoats for specific laws of the Empire, merchants and fee-gobbling officials for societal changes. Scapegoats became targets to protest a wide range of interrelated grievances and to express conflicts.

Third, colonists felt that their liberty was endangered by the disregard with which British authorities had treated the legal means of redress. This was a touchy point because no enforcement agencies had been previously developed. No institution, in the eyes of the colonials, could enforce a decision or defend a right if voluntary submission or restriction was lacking. No army or navy existed against external enemies, no police force against internal discontent. Dangers to liberty were to be nipped in the bud by the pressure of public opinion and tradition. A rhetorical ritual had been developed to achieve this. Revolutionary rhetoric added little to the language of social control over those endangering the homogeneity and harmony of the community. Severe censure and the notorious jeremiads were turned against even minimal offenders, because small offenses, given human nature, would lead to bigger ones unless curbed. Punishment was the rule, not forgiveness. The only contemporary "due process" began after public confession of offenses, when the community would help the repentant sinner return to the fold.

But in 1765 the offender did not belong to the community and was not subject to its pressures. The offense alone, taxation without representation, was bad enough; but the great power of the offender compared to that of the colonies called for immediate countermeasures. The traditional means were exhausted: Petitions, colonial agents, bribery, and evasion either were not applicable or had been treated with neglect or contempt. Especially the contempt of British authorities fired apprehensions in the minds of colonists. Symbolic action of the population and actual violence were the last expedient.

Mass action and riots against the stamp distributors, or rather stamp *masters,* ensued. The particular scapegoat in Massachusetts was a wealthy individual. The close contact of crowd and wealth activated latent economic grievances. Oliver became a symbol of wealth, and soon the primary motive, Britain's attempt to collect revenues, was supplemented by secondary motives, and rioting was directed against wealth and arrogant officials. Influenced by the reports of these actions, border clashes flared up again, as did white-pine riots. Combinations of debtor, rescue, and leveling riots occurred. High officials were the target of crowd action because they were unresponsive to popular demands; lower officials, because they attempted to suppress the riots or because they had the power to arrest people for debt.

The grievances that caused these secondary riots were indeed basic conflicts, actions against the top sections of the colonial political, social, and economic hierarchies. But societal structures and practices made it difficult for the least organized and least influential part of society to articulate awareness of group interests. Class consciousness was rudimentary. The upper levels of society, however, sensed danger to their position and reacted with suppression.

The result of the anti-British action was an intense reexamination of the colonies' position in the empire, of the colonists' rights as Englishmen, and of the colonial society's foundation in natural law. The ideological sophistication and political skill of the leaders succeeded in focusing all opposition on the British. Given the colonials' fear of arbitrary power and abuse of authority, which had been individually internalized because society lacked adequate institutional defense mechanisms, it was logical and natural to interpret British policies as attempts to subvert American liberties. All British measures fitted into the same pattern. Writs of assistance made property subject to the powers of not easily controllable crown officers, who in addition gained personally one-third of every successful seizure. Taxation without representation endangered private property, and so did duties and quartering of troops. Duties on tea were only a continuation of the old taxation, but the monopoly on it granted to selected importing firms was a dangerous restriction of equal opportunities unacceptable to either corporate or Liberalist notions of economic life. Whether or how much trade regulations really hurt the colonies is relatively unimportant. One aspect, the constant drain of cash, was definitely perceived as detrimental. British mercantilism began to be opposed by colonial mercantilism.[5] Making governor, judges, or any other officials independent of the people gave the British government or its colonial placemen an undue influence over the community. While the ideological aspects of the opposition to Great Britain show a fairly consistent development from limited resistance to rebellion, this was not the case for direct action, official reaction, and the attitudes toward private property.

Property was the basis for liberty. According to contemporary ideology, it made men independent from the influence of others. Those with insufficient property could not vote. If sinking below subsistence level, they became a charge to the public, and had to be supported by tax money coming from the property of others. But wealthy people who "overcharged" the public were endangering private property too. Both encroachments on property were subversive of liberty. Furthermore, given the religious and worldly incentives to strive for property, British regulations and taxation impeded the economic advance of the colonial merchants, many of whom belonged to the political leadership. Merchant opposition was therefore not a disinterested fight for the good of the society but sprang from rather concrete private interests. This also explains the hostility of Whig politicians to merchants and the deep changes in political ideology after 1783. The currency

[5]Robert Thomas, "A Quantitative Approach to the Study of the Effects of British Imperial Policy upon Colonial Welfare: Some Preliminary Findings," *J. Econ. Hist.* 25:615–638 (1965); William A. Williams, *Contours of American History* (Cleveland, 1961); Robert A. East, *Business Enterprise in the American Revolutionary Era* (New York, 1938; reprint ed., 1964).

problems caused by British interventions hurt all colonists, thus welding together groups of very different economic interests.

Small and middling property owners spoke of fairly equally distributed property within a corporate social structure, while the richer members tended toward more liberalistic notions. In other words, they broke out of the corporate framework because it no longer fit their interests. This made them dangerously similar to crown officials, who—for the sake of private gain—disregarded the wishes of their fellow townsmen. The officials became representatives of a foreign power, and the wealthy became representatives of a foreign concept of socioeconomic organization. They began to act as members of a distinct social group (or class) instead of acting as members of the corporation. While private property as a basis of liberty was safe, the use of private property as a means for profit making was endangered. It had to be restrained because it undermined the economic wellbeing and thereby the liberty of all. Economic and political leaders looked upon the security of property as the opportunity to accumulate more capital and economic power. This kind of property and the power derived from it endangered the existence of widespread smaller property holding, the groundwork of society.[6]

To ensure the safety of *their* property, the leadership attempted to prevent any violent crowd action when the British government imposed the Townshend duties. This course, steered by the merchants and politicians, was doomed to failure from the outset. Pro-British merchants mounted determined internal opposition. Important segments of the population were adversely affected by nonimportation, the precarious balance between dependence on poverty-funds and liberty being tipped toward dependence. Shopkeepers were impoverished, artisans thrown out of work. These were a reservoir for social upheaval. But each time that tensions mounted, the British government conveniently furnished scapegoats, on which the Whig leadership eagerly seized rhetorically and ideologically, the crowds physically: stamp masters, commissioners, troops, tea chests, and, once again, troops.

The constant changes in the form of crowd action and in the attitudes toward it are due to its complex motives and consequences. Leadership-controlled symbolic action against the British tax measures was acceptable to those of the better sort. In the subsequent action, rioters destroyed property only after careful selection. The means to encroach on others' property became targets, the stamp office and the court clerk's office, as well as the unjustly obtained wealth itself, Hallowell's "extravagant" and "ostentatious" residence—built with the proceeds from exorbitant fees—, and Hutchinson's mansion, symbol of his arrogance. During nonimportation the political and economic elite soon had to rely on violent crowd action to support policies against dissenters of its own social rank (importers, loyal officials). The British countermeasure, the stationing of men-of-war in support of the customs establishment, touched a sore point with lower-class Bostonians from the waterfront. Spontaneous large-scale impressment riots could not be curbed in

[6]Cf. Crane Brinton, *The Anatomy of Revolution* (New York, 1938); Arthur M. Schlesinger, Sr., *Colonial Merchants and the American Revolution, 1763–1776* (New York, 1918); Marc Egnal and Joseph A. Ernst, "An Economic Interpretation of the American Revolution," *WMQ* 3.29:1–32 (1972).

town meetings. Instead, rioters and voters replaced the moderate merchant leadership with politicians, who were expected to be more responsive to the electorate's grievances.[7]

A different form of action was employed against the troops sent to suppress violence. Rioters used violence much more ruthlessly than the troops could use their power. Hierarchy-enforced and commonly accepted violence within the military—that is, the brutal corporal punishment of soldiers—contributed to this development. When, in 1774, the number of troops was too large for random violence or occasional great riots, the inhabitants used carefully planned and far-sighted nonviolent community action, strikes and boycotts, and encouragement of desertion.

At this point the resistance to Great Britain necessitated the obstruction of all political and legal institutions with the exception of town meetings. This implied a shift from central institutions, in which the wealthy and the officialdom had its stronghold, to local institutions, where popular participation was highest. The three problems—Tories, the scarcity of provisions, and foremost the British—evoked three different kinds of institutional, semiinstitutional, and crowd response. The British, first opposed by mass action, met with military resistance after April 1775. The Tories were ruthlessly suppressed. The emergence of a strong opposition (two-party system) was an "innovation" that endangered the whole social and political fabric, and rioters set out to defend the traditional system. Once the Tories had emigrated or humbly acknowledged their errors, the violence against them decreased. Furthermore, provincial authorities, eager to recapture their leading position, substituted legislative measures for spontaneous popular activity. By then more Tories had left than French fled from violence and persecution during the French Revolution.

The third problem, how to obtain provisions at a fair price, could be solved neither by debates and votes nor by riots. People became aware of the changes in the economic structures of society and of their own changed economic aims. This awareness was one prerequisite for changes in ideology. For many, production was no longer the "calling" and the only honorable means of gaining a livelihood. Numerous artisans, laborers, and especially farmers followed the lead of the merchants. Commerce (capital) yielded more profits than production (work),[8] and so many producers attempted to switch to trade, acting according to their economic interest as opposed to that of the whole community. This change in society was of more lasting importance than the Whig–Tory division.

A new form of mass action emerged during the universal political resistance to British authority in 1774. The crowds made it abundantly clear that they did not interpret their actions as rioting but rather as open-air town meetings and later county meetings, where debate and discussion, votes and resolves were more impor-

---

[7]For an early and interesting treatment of this question, see Friedrich Gentz [adviser to Count Metternich], "Der Ursprung der Amerikanischen Revoluzion, verglichen mit dem Ursprunge und den Grundsätzen der Französischen," *Historisches Journal,* May–June 1800, trans. John Quincy Adams (Philadelphia, 1800; reprint ed., R. Kirk, ed., 1955).
[8]Note that the colonial term "tradesmen" referred to artisans who had learned a "trade." Only after product and sale became separated, after middlemen intervened, did "trade" replace "commerce" or become almost synonymous.

tant than violent action and were sufficient to induce officials to resign or to submit. The masses continued to act defensively: Redress, restitution, and prevention were their essentials. Regulation followed hesitatingly, but some "innovative" elements were voiced, particularly concerning increased popular political participation. Gradually, there grew an awareness that present problems could be solved in new ways. But a conscious orientation toward the future and its possibilities, immense but different for each interest group, began only in the federalist era.[9]

The social composition of the revolutionary crowds changed according to the nature of the action. In the Stamp Act riots, the leveling movement was carried on by mechanics of little or no property and was limited to the tradition of stopping one or more members of the community from gaining an undue influence by economic power, by overcharging, and by exploiting. The customs riots, impressment riots, and the harassment of soldiers were carried out by the same people, plus local sailors and merchant–captains—the composition of the rioters depending on which group had the most serious grievance.

The assertions of well-placed contemporaries that "foreign sailors" or "boys and negroes" composed the rioting rabble were true only in part. Negroes participated in many riots but always remained a negligible minority. One ad hoc leader, Crispus Attucks, was black and Indian. Sailors participated often and had particular griev- ances. Boys were active in great numbers. But colonial society had proportionately more young people than present-day society. Second, the term "boys" referred to men up to their late twenties (when lower class). Finally, even schoolboys and apprentices had undergone a process of politicization. In 1765, schoolboys had paraded to Liberty Tree. The apprentices active in the King Street riot came from barbershops, which served as news agencies for the townsmen and saw daily politi- cal debate. By 1774, schoolboys on their own initiative elected a committee to remonstrate about a grievance to a British general.

In agricultural regions the vast majority of rioters were "yeomen"; in towns the majority were artisans, particularly journeymen. Most rioters had some profession or trade, and only a few were designated laborers. All, with rare exceptions, could at least sign their names. In numerous riots, "gentlemen" took part from private interest, as militia officers, or to restrain participants from the lower classes. To judge from the indictments, their share in the riotous activities was certainly larger than that of the blacks, society's scapegoats for all disorderly behavior. Gentlemen, if they had grievances on their own, also rioted on their own. Feeling insulted by one of Tory Mein's publications, they rioted against him, though disavowing lower- class riots at the same time.

The contemporary emphasis on strangers as the main agents in riots was a means to reachieve unity after riots. Their actual influence in riots was sometimes high, because crowds repeatedly selected strangers to act as ad hoc leaders for direct confrontations with other members or sectors of the community. This facilitated

[9]Cecilia M. Kenyon, "Republicanism and Radicalism in the American Revolution: An Old-Fashioned Interpretation," *WMQ* 3.19:153–182 (1962).

subsequent reunification of the community while making prosecution more difficult.

Means of forceful coercion varied. After 1774, participants in mass actions sometimes had firearms but to prevent bloodshed always left them at a distance. In the early years, rioters came in the evening with blackened faces; after 1774 several crowds in the country came openly with white cudgels or staves during the day. White was the color of innocence and purity; white were the staffs of wardens who watched that law and order were observed on Lord's Day.

In Great Britain the accounts of the violence retarded repeals and accelerated punitive measures. The latter in turn caused further rioting and growing unity among the colonies, which, feeling their united strength, proceeded more boldly. Riots made compromises and accommodations impossible.[10] Riots during the Stamp Act period intimidated crown officials and gave many of them a shock from which they never recovered. Numerous Whig officials were shocked too. Customs riots made a fresh set of officials realize their limits. Navy and army sent to protect them caused further riots and had to withdraw. Terror against loyal colonials took the last support from crown officials. Under the Coercive Acts, passed in response to the tea riot, crowd action made any military or political action impossible for the crown officials. They touched off a series of mass meetings that finally led to the hostilities at Lexington and Concord.

The political consciousness of crowds and voters was high and increased considerably from 1765 to 1780. The coarse and clear expressiveness of seamen and others was based on knowledge about rights as well as political and judicial procedures. Customs officials had to deal with well-reasoned arguments against their search procedures. Blackstone was quoted as authority for the legality of the tea meetings.[11] The popular leaders and crowds alluded to rebellions and revolutions throughout the history of the Western world. Depositions of rioters show assertiveness about their rights and awareness of the limitations of the power and authority of crown and later provincial officials.

Petitions of towns and individuals resounded with declarations that liberty and property were sacred, asserting that theirs had been imposed upon.[12] The Boston inhabitants watched the struggle between the Regulators and the government in North Carolina closely. One of them noted: "The Occasion of these People's rising in Opposition to Government was owing to exorbitant Taxes laid upon them, from

---

[10]Hutchinson to ———, 15 Jan. 1766, Cushing Papers, 1664–1780, MHS; John Wentworth to Thomas W. Waldron, 9 Dec. 1774, *MHSC* 6.4:69 (1899); Samuel Adams ["Shippen"], *BG,* 30 Jan. 1769, and *The Writings of Samuel Adams,* ed. Harry A. Cushing, 4 vols. (New York, 1904–1908), 1:297–306.

[11]L. F. S. Upton, ed., "Proceedings of Ye Body Respecting the Tea," *WMQ* 3.22:293 (1965); Gerald Stourzh, "William Blackstone: Teacher of Revolution," *Jahrbuch für Amerikastudien* 15:184–200 (1970).

[12]For example, the petition of Jacob Emmons (Misc. Unbound Papers, 1771, BCH) to a Boston town meeting demanding compensation for land confiscated legally and the parts of a building destroyed riotously to make room for a street: "Mr. Modert. Sir I am Sorrey I am Obliged to come at such a time as this when we are So Justly Contending for Liberty and property to set forth Before this town. that I Have ben Deprived of my Liberty and property by the justeses and the Selectmen of Boston.—and ben Harrest a bought from place to place to seek recompense and can get non." The town meeting merely referred him back to the courts.

which they could get no redress, Therefore, they thought it justifiable in redressing themselves by force of Arms. Their Conduct was in general approved of.''[13]

Conscious efforts for political education had been made too, as Thomas Young proudly wrote to a friend in New York. Of all Boston Whigs, Young was perhaps most willing to understand and to take seriously grievances as well as direct action of the ''common people,'' whether urban or rural.[14] But these efforts, at least partly, were intended to achieve support for a group of well-to-do officials and merchants, subsequently the Whig leadership. Contending groups of provincial leaders had to appeal to the people for support. Liberty poles were sometimes erected under the secret direction of conservative groups to divert the people from more substantial action.

In the seventies, politics was the universal topic of conversation of people of all ranks. Innkeepers kept a supply of political literature for their customers to read and discuss. Many had a good theoretical background for their arguments. The Bristol Convention in 1774 recognized George III as ''rightful Sovereign'' and added ''tho' not *jure divino* in the Sense of Laud or Sachererel,'' obviously expecting people to know what they were talking about. Terms like ''state of nature,'' ''natural rights,'' ''constitutional rights,'' ''birthrights of Englishmen,'' and ''duties'' of the king were part of everyday language. Merchants and others began to correspond regularly with their friends and business partners about political events. Diary entries about politics increased or for some persons began to appear for the first time. The one pamphlet even mentioned in diaries of backcountry farmers was Thomas Paine's *Common Sense*.[15]

Printed communications included an ever increasing number of political items. In almanacs, liberty songs and exhortatory prefaces to the readers were used to inculcate Whig principles. Political celebrations or memorial days of opposition to the British were listed in the calendar. Title pages carried the picture of John Wilkes or

[13]John Boyle, ''Boyle's Journal of Occurrences in Boston, 1759–1778,'' 17 June 1771, *NEHGR* 84:269–270 (1930). John Adams (''Novanglus V'') asserted that the Regulators ''were thought in Boston to be an injured people.'' *The Works of John Adams*, ed. Charles F. Adams, 10 vols. (Boston, 1850–1856), 4:75. Ezra Stiles noted, ''In truth all the Province except the Crown officers and Connexions are in heart Regulators.'' *The Literary Diary*, ed. F. B. Dexter, 3 vols. (New York, 1901), 1:149, cf. pp. 137ff; *BEP*, 10 June, 17 June 1771; *BNL*, 13 June, 25 July 1771. The severe riot law passed by the North Carolina Assembly against the Regulators was declared ''altogether unfit for any part of the British Empire'' by Richard Jackson, legal adviser to the British Board of Trade. Lawrence H. Gipson, *The Coming of the Revolution, 1763–1775* (New York, 1954), pp. 206–207. Only the *Journal of the Times*, reflecting Boston's merchant upper-class views, considered the Regulators ''alarming.'' Oliver Dickerson, ed., *Boston under Military Rule (1768–1769) as Revealed in a Journal of the Times* (Boston, 1936), p. 29.

[14]Thomas Young to Hugh Hughes, 21 Dec. 1772, Misc. Bound Papers, vol. 14, MHS; David F. Hawke, ''Dr. Thomas Young—'Eternal Fisher in Troubled Waters': Notes for a Biography,'' *N.Y. Hist. Soc. Q.* 54:6–29 (1970); Henry H. Edes, ''Memoir of Dr. Thomas Young, 1731–1777,'' *CSMP* 11:2–54 (1906–1907).

[15]John Adams, *Diary*, 1:263, 324, 2:97–116; *BEP*, 8 March 1773; Peter Oliver, *Peter Oliver's Origin and Progress of the American Rebellion: A Tory View*, ed. Douglass Adair and John A. Schutz (Stanford, Calif., 1961), p. 78; Abner Sanger, ''Ye Journal of Abner Sanger,'' 11 April 1771, 4 Sept. 1776, *Repertory* 1:341, 490. Letters: Hancock, Andrews, Lloyd, Curwen. Diaries: Holyoke, Chandler, Seccombe, Bowen, Green, etc. Bristol Convention, Minutes, *CSMP* 1:178. William Laud, 1573–1645; English archbishop whose policy was one of the main causes of the Puritan revolution in the seventeenth century. Henry Sacheverell, 1674–1724: English political preacher impeached by the Whig junto for his inflammatory sermons.

showed a personalized death, killing "The wicked Statesmen, or the Traitor to his Country." The output of broadsides increased considerably during these years. As for newspapers, not only crown officials regularly complained about the printers. John Adams, too, called them "hot, indiscreet Men."[16] Though circulation remained limited—the *Boston Gazette* probably never surpassed 2000 copies per issue—actual influence was larger because each copy was read by several persons.[17] The papers reported crowd actions in other countries and were an important means of making people realize that resistance was general.[18]

When the Whig leadership took office after 1775, it opposed the implementation of popular demands and attempted to suppress spontaneous action. Bostonians, more aware of differences in wealth, repeatedly tried to change this situation. When the town decided to light its streets, a town meeting voted that the charges should be defrayed by a tax on the owners of carriages and on innkeepers. Tenants on Hutchinson's farms refused to pay rent as long as the Regulating Acts were in effect. Western farmers demanded more rights and a better government.[19]

The knowledge that officials and the wealthy, whatever their political persuasion, could be opposed was an irrevocable gain for the people. So was the growth of political understanding and capabilities, acquired partly by political education, partly in the course of action. On this basis the British officials were ousted between 1774 and 1776. But internal grievances and conflicts remained. What different groups did about these grievances and about the new authorities, as well as official reactions, are the subject of the last part of this study. Samuel Adams, sympathizing with James Warren's complaints about dissenting opinions among the people, wrote, "I would they were all cut off (banished at least) who trouble you." This biblical phrase had been the text for the Jonathan Mayhew sermon that was instrumental in bringing about the Hutchinson riot on 26 August 1765.[20]

---

[16]For example, Benjamin West, *Bickerstaff's Boston Almanack,* 1769 (Boston, 1768); Ezra Gleason, *The Massachusetts Calendar . . . 1774* (Boston, 1773). *Mass. Brds.,* entries for 1765 to 1780, cf. also Evans, *American Bibliography.* John Adams to Abigail Adams, 3–5 July 1774, *Adams Family Correspondence,* ed. L. H. Butterfield, 2 vols. (Cambridge, Mass., 1963). 1:123.

[17]Cf. Thomas Randolph Adams, *American Independence: The Growth of an Idea—A Bibliographical Study* (Providence, R.I., 1965).

[18]*BNL,* 16 May 1765, Supp.; a similar increase in reports about crowd action has been traced by John Kern for the 1730s, the period of the market riots. Cf. Chapter 14 in this study.

[19]Pittsfield petitions, in Oscar Handlin and Mary F. Handlin, eds., *The Popular Sources of Political Authority: Documents on the Massachusetts Constitution of 1780* (Cambridge, Mass., 1966), pp. 63, 89 *passim.* John Adams (to Benjamin Hitchborn, 29 May 1776, *Works,* 9:379) dreaded "the spirit of innovation" that he expected to find among the new representatives but advocated innovations suiting his interests, such as "independent" judicial tenure and salaries. Cf. *ibid.,* p. 430, and his correspondence with John Winthrop, *MHSC* 5.4:308, 309–310. Political consciousness and deference met when towns were named after popular leaders. A Worcester County town named "Hutchinson" by Governor Gage debated in 1776 whether to change the name to "Barré" or to "Wilkes." Three towns in Berkshire and Vermont changed their names to "Hancock"—in one of them Hancock was among the proprietors. A. C. Goodell *et al.,* eds., *Acts and Resolves, Public and Private, of the Province of the Massachusetts Bay,* 21 vols. (Boston, 1869–1922), 5:592–593, 676–677; Stiles, *Diary,* 2:167; A. E. Brown, ed., *John Hancock His Book* (Boston, 1898), p. 174. *BTR* 18:116, 128 (1773).

[20]*Warren–Adams Letters: Being Chiefly a Correspondence among John Adams, Samuel Adams, and James Warren,* 2 vols. (Boston, 1917, 1925), 1:339, cf. 195, 219, 222, 234.

THE LEADERSHIP AND THE FORMING OF A
CONSTITUTION

While the people in crowds and in town meetings demanded a new foundation for society and its political structures, the leadership represented in the General Court wanted to preserve the old system and therefore resented constitutional debates. The elected representatives turned against their electors. They published a proclamation to the "good People of this Colony" congratulating them on the reestablishment of the customary governmental institutions and procedures. They brushed away any demands for increased participation of the people by declaring that the existing form of government was "more immediately in all its Branches, under the Influence and Controul of the People, and therefore more free and happy than was enjoyed by their Ancestors." Accordingly, it was the voters' duty again to support, assist, and obey the appointed magistrates. Disobedience and rioting, lumped together with debauchery and immorality, were to be punished. The General Court claimed to derive its authority from the advice of the Continental Congress but ended the proclamation with "God save the King."[21]

The constitutionalist movement in the west forced the representatives to face the basic issues. In the debates about a constiution, many people benefited not only from the political understanding gained in the course of anti-British direct action but also from an awareness that economic, social, and political structures were different from the ideals of corporate unity and individual equality. No longer were there merely demands for restoration but also cautious calls for innovation. Town meetings, conventions, and crowds compared constitutional principles and political practice, demanding popular participation and simplification of governmental structures and procedures. They had to be "the most Easy and plain to be understood by People of all denominations, whereby a Line may be drawn, that the Rulers and Ruled may know their duty."

Many opposed "the Least Apearance of them Old Tiranical Laws taking Place again." The revision of the laws would afford the opportunity to set up a code that was easily understandable. Whigs taking over Tory offices should be allowed to continue in them for only a limited number of years, as they had not obtained the offices with "the consent of the people."[22]

To get back to the head of the movement, the leadership decided to form the constitution themselves. Their attempts to do so were characterized by an obvious intent to concentrate power, especially the distribution of appointive offices, in their own hands. The consequent delays in the formation of a constitution resulted in increased distrust of the voters toward their representatives but also in increased participation.

[21]Proclamation, 23 Jan. 1776, in Handlin and Handlin, eds., *Popular Sources,* pp. 65–69.
[22]*Ibid.,* pp. 138 (Berwick), 111–112 (Ashfield), 506 (Berkshire), 747, 768, 800 (Suffolk), 285, 286, 598, 621 (Hampshire); limitation of offices, *ibid.,* p. 506. Elisha P. Douglass, *Rebels and Democrats: The Struggle for Equal Political Rights and Majority Rule during the American Revolution* (Chapel Hill, N.C., 1955), pp. 149, 151–152, 156–158, 168. Winthrop to Adams, 1 June 1776. *MHSC* 5.4:308. John Adams was so averse to simple and directly responsive forms of government as to charge that demands for localization of some administrative and judicial offices were inspired by Tories. *Ibid.,* pp. 309–310.

Four times the people were asked to voice their opinions: in 1776 whether they empowered the General Court to sit as a constitutional convention; in 1778, whether to call one; in 1778 and 1780, whether the draft constitutions were acceptable. Of 295 towns, 123 sent returns in 1776, 134 in 1779; 172 voted on the draft in 1778, 226 in 1780.[23]

In 1776 most towns demanded that they not only "inspect and peruse" the draft before its ratification, as the General Court had suggested, but "approve" it. After-the-fact criticism would not be a sufficient safeguard for "the Rights and Liberties of the People." County conventions should be part of the process of forming a constitution because their delegates could almost daily return to their respective constituents to debate the issues or resolves with them. Extended suffrage would be necessary; the constitution "effects every Individual, every Individual therefore ought to be consulting, aiding and assisting," and "the means or channels of information should all lay open to the People."[24]

The General Court's draft Constitution of 1778 was not the "self denying ordinance" that had been demanded. The representatives did not deny anything to themselves but many things to the constituents, who rejected the draft by a 4-to-1 margin. In an intensive examination of constitutional principles, rights, liberties, and privileges, the inhabitants scrutinized the draft and its premises. The "Essex Result" gave voice to the patriarchal point of view; the "Just Principle of Natural Freedom" was explained in a pamphlet entitled "The People the Best Governors." The inhabitants of Berkshire issued two more calls for a constitutional convention. They suspected that there were "Designing men in this state that Intends by Delaying the Forming a Bill of Rights and a free Constitution to Lull People to sleep" and obtain a constitution serving their private interests, "By which mean the People will Loose the Benefit of their Independance, and may Rather be said to have Changed Masters than Measures."[25]

The legislature decided that slaves, free blacks, and Indians of both sexes, white women, and everybody under 21 years of age, even tax-paying heads of families,

---

[23]In addition to the Handlins' publication, sources on the constitutional debates are Robert J. Taylor, ed., *Massachusetts, Colony to Commonwealth: Documents on the Formation of Its Constitution, 1775–1780* (Chapel Hill, N.C., 1961), and A. H. Everett *et al.*, eds., *Journal of the Convention for Framing a Constitution of Government for the State of Massachusetts Bay* (Boston, 1832).

[24]Returns of the towns, in Handlin and Handlin, eds., *Popular Sources*, pp. 101–166; on "encroachments," *ibid.*, pp. 114, 117, 163; on extension of suffrage, *ibid.*, pp. 106–107, 113, 124–125, 136, 144, 148; opposition to the exclusion of absent soldiers, *ibid.*, pp. 121, 130, 155, 163, 164; Robert J. Taylor, *Western Massachusetts in the Revolution* (Providence, R.I., 1954), p. 88; Douglass, *Rebels and Democrats*, pp. 163ff.

[25]*BTR* 18:284; returns, in Handlin and Handlin, eds., *Popular Sources*, pp. 202–365; Taylor, *Western Massachusetts*, p. 88; *Continental Journ.*, 8 Oct. 1778; William Pynchon, *The Diary of William Pynchon of Salem*, ed. F. E. Oliver (Boston, 1890), 4 April 1778, p. 53; John Adams to James Warren, 26 July 1778, *Warren–Adams Letters*, 2:36. "Essex Result": Handlin and Handlin, eds., *Popular Sources*, pp. 324–365; see also *Memoir of Theophilus Parsons*, by his son (Boston, 1859). *The People the Best Governors* (n.p., 1776), printed in Frederick Chase, *History of Dartmouth College*, 2 vols. (Cambridge, Mass., 1891), App. D, 1:654–663. Berkshire County remonstrance, 26 Aug. 1778, statement, 17 Nov. 1778, resolve of the House, 20 Feb. 1779, in Handlin and Handlin, eds., *Popular Sources*, pp. 366–368, 374–379, 383–384; opinions of Hampshire towns, *ibid.*, p. 386; H. A. Cushing, *History of the Transition from Provincial to Commonwealth Government in Massachusetts* (New York, 1896), pp. 245–246.

could not vote. The inhabitants of Hardwick countered, "All men, *whites and blacks,* are born free and equal." Abigail Adams, as extraordinary as her husband, John Adams, was ordinary, had demanded more rights for women in 1776. Blacks had petitioned for the abolition of slavery and for enfranchisement. But in 1777 the General Court had refused decisive action.[26]

The conservative position was voiced in 1778 by a convention of Essex towns. It was representative of the opinions and intentions of the property-owning middle class in the east and of the wealthy upper classes in the west. "The idea of liberty had been held up in so dazzling colours, that some of us may not be willing to submit to that subordination necessary in the freest states." In the bicameral legislature the House was to represent persons, the Senate property. Appointive power for executive officers was to be lodged in the hands of the governor. "Vox Populi, Vox Dei," the Boston slogan of the Stamp Act opposition in 1765, was now countered in the "Result": "The voice of the people is said to be the voice of God. No men will be so hardy and presumptuous, as to affirm the truth of that proposition to it's fullest extent." The delegates to the convention relied on the impartiality, wisdom, and benevolence of a wealthy and educated leisure class. Even if the people "have time to be informed, and the necessary means of information given them"—by whom?—"the bulk" of them "are so situated in life, and such are their laudable occupations, that they cannot have time for, nor the means of furnishing themselves with proper information." It was necessary "to look further than to the bulk of the people, for the greatest wisdom, firmness, consistency, and perseverance. These qualities will most probably be found amongst men of education and fortune."[27]

Such an opinion was much closer to John Adams's draft of the Constitution of 1780 than to the feelings of inhabitants of Westminster, Worcester, who explained the role of the people and the limitation of the power of the magistrates. Their opinion is representative of most critical comments on the Constitutions of 1778 and 1780. A government with centralized powers in the hands of a few was disagreeable "Because it Deprives the people att Large of appointing their own Rulers and officers and places the power where it may (and no Doubt) Will be greately abuised." To create an establishment of a selected few and to entrust them to appoint magistrates over whom the people "have no power: is a Daring Step to Despotism; . . . the oftener power Returns into the hands of the people the better." The delegation of powers had to be done by "the whole," or the result "Will Enevitabley prove fatal to the Liberties of Amarica." If, as the "Essex Result" had said, people were not capable of electing their own officers, "Why Doe we wast our blood and Treasure to obtaine that which When obtained We are not fitt to Enjoy—

---

[26]Handlin and Handlin, eds., *Popular Sources,* pp. 402–403, 830 (emphasis added). Blacks petitioned for freedom in this period, and whites supported them. See Lorenzo J. Greene, *The Negro in Colonial New England* (New York, 1968), pp. 216–217 *passim.* Abigail Adams demanded rights for women but got merely a "saucy" answer from John. Abigail Adams to John Adams, 31 March 1776, *Adams Family Correspondence,* 1:370, answer, *ibid.,* p. 382, Abigail's comments on the answer to Mercy Otis Warren, 27 April 1776, *ibid.,* pp. 397–398.

[27]Handlin and Handlin, eds., *Popular Sources,* p. 329; Douglass, *Rebels and Democrats,* pp. 180ff. Jack Pole, *Political Representation in England and the Origins of the American Republic* (London, 1966), pp. 182ff., gives a thorough analysis of the "Essex Result."

if but a Selected few only are fitt to appoint our Rulers—Why Ware we uneasie under George.'' As for appointment by representatives, having learned from experience, the people rhetorically asked, ''Will they not monopolise all places of Honour and prophit to themselves to the Exclusion of many others perhaps as capeable as themselves?'' Impeachment of ''Dissagreeable'' officials would be decided by ''those Verry beings Who gave them existance; Who always may, and We bleave will have to Greate a Degree of mercy on the works of their own hands.'' The people, certainly, would not consent to such ''heavie burthens.''[28]

Regarding the draft Constitution of 1780, the objections to the provisions for a legislature centered around (1) the role of property in representation and demanded (2) a limitation of legislative power and (3) a simplification of procedural matters. Property qualifications for voting or office holding were ''inconsistent with the Liberty we are contending for''; the inhabitants ''have a right to Such men, to represent them, whether rich or poor, as will feel the distresses of the poor.'' Estate was no sign of capabilities: ''Riches and Dignity Neither Makes the Head Wiser nor the Heart Better.'' This had been the argument many leading Whigs before 1775.[29] The Whig theory of government was applicable not only externally against a corrupt British government but also internally. People, whether western farmers or eastern mechanics, applied it against their own rulers—in the currency controversies of the first half of the eighteenth century, during the struggle against Great Britain, and under the new constitution. But in doing so the people also transcended the limits of Whig thought, welding to it popular notions of equality and moving toward participatory and responsive political structures.

Distrust of the elected representatives had increased because, after the expulsion of the British, they had been busy distributing honorary and lucrative posts among themselves. Again property was the underlying issue. High fees were a burden for most people; the provision that the representatives might increase the property qualification for state offices appeared ''pregnant with infinite mischief''—that is, exclusiveness.[30] Simplification of governmental procedures was proposed in innumerable instances to diminish expenses and to increase accountability.

Some towns feared that popular election of the governor would give ''Rich and Powerful Men'' coveting the office opportunity to divide and corrupt the people. This ''Naturally Flows from Bribery and undue Influence,'' the ''morals'' of the rich. But most towns wanted extension of voting rights and ''Quallifications preferable to that of Money.'' As for high salaries, one town acidly noted that ''a foundation Laid by Law for Extravagancy in Support of grandure and Dignity in

[28]John Adams to Benjamin Rush, 12 April 1809, *Works,* 9:618; Joseph Dorfman, ''The Regal Republic of John Adams,'' *Pol. Sci. Q.* 54:227–248 (1949); Handlin and Handlin, eds., *Popular Sources,* pp. 312–313.

[29]*Ibid.,* pp. 481, 567, 622–624, 810, 821–822, 860; *Indep. Chron.* 5 Sept. 1776; Douglass, *Rebels and Democrats,* pp. 152–161; Peter Force, ed., *American Archives,* 9 vols. (Washington, D.C., 1837–1853), 4.3:1248–1249, 4.4:255– 256, 541–542. The Whig argument, brought forward by the Adamses and Gerry as well as Warren, was still valid for them to a degree. Hancock, their new opponent, had the money but—in their opinion—insufficient brains.

[30]Berkshire memorials, cited in note 25. Ellen E. Brennan, *Plural Officeholding in Massachusetts, 1760–1780* (Chapel Hill, N.C., 1945), pp. 107–135. John Adams plainly stated that the patriots needed offices, *Works,* 4:75. Handlin and Handlin, eds., *Popular Sources,* pp. 411 (''a corrupt majority of the legislature''), 800.

office'' would be imprudent but would save the people "a great Deal of Time and trouble in Disposing" of their money in better ways. The appointive powers of the governor, opposed by about 25 percent of the towns, "will have a Tendancy to fill the State with the most Corrupt, Vitious, and Sodid Set of officers." Officials should be annually elected in the towns, should be accountable, and should be prevented from plural office holding and too long a continuance in their places.[31]

Strong criticism was directed against the provisions for the judicial branch. Annual election instead of service during good behavior with fixed salaries would prevent the judges from becoming "negligent" and "arbitrary" and from turning into "the most insolent haughty and imperious monsters that can be Ranked among the human Species." Frequent elections would motivate "a man" to "Look upon his opportunity of making his fortune in private Life Rather than in publick Life." This had been the argument of Whig leaders in the early seventies when the judges were offered grants from the crown.[32]

By 1780 many towns supported a constitution as the only possibility for uniting different interest groups or at least preventing the powerful ones from taking advantage of the situation. "[W]e do not consider ourselves united as brothers, with an united interest, but have fancied a clashing of interest amongst the various classes." Agrarian communities had interests different from those of the mercantile seaports and accused the latter that a new form of representation served "the Interest of perticuler parties under a pretence of Equal representation." Differences of interest between economic classes or groups were acknowledged by the Constitutional Convention when it suggested to young persons, disenfranchised because of lack of property, that their temporary status was "safer" than suffrage for the propertyless, "who will pay less regard to the Rights [interests] of Property." The inhabitants of the state reminded the convention: "Government is Instituted for the Common good; etc. and not for the Profit, Honour, or private Interest of any Man family or Class of Men etc."[33]

There were those who still believed in corporate unity.[34] But the riots caused by scarcity of provisions, if nothing else, had shown the impossibility of a common economic interest. The Constitution acknowledged this and explicitly outlawed riots against the House of Representatives or any of its members (Frame of Government I, iii, 10). The economic situation was more influential than the constitutional principles: By 1782, crowds again voiced economic discontent, and another rebellion followed by 1786. From 1774 to 1780, riots prevented the open emergence of organized opposition from the Tories. But less than a decade later, during the debates about the federal Constitution, alignments similar to those of political parties began to emerge.

---

[31]*Ibid.*, pp. 488–489, 505, 550–551, 616, 692, 696, 697, 850, 859. Some towns wanted more appointive powers for the governor in the military branch to prevent disorders within the communities over elections to honorary stations. *Ibid.*, pp. 730, 738–739, 740, 914–918.

[32]*Ibid.*, pp. 489, 536, 551 *passim*, 696 *passim*, 789; Gerry to Adams, 27 Oct. 1772, in James T. Austin, *The Life of Elbridge Gerry, with Contemporary Letters, to the Close of the American Revolution*, 2 vols. (Boston, 1828, 1829), 1:8; Samuel Adams, *Writings*, 3:85–89.

[33]Handlin and Handlin, eds., *Popular Sources*, pp. 154, 163, 329, 437, 571–572.

[34]*Ibid.*, pp. 735–738.

Intended by many of its framers to be a conclusion to spontaneous popular action and a return to law and order, the Constitution was for others a departure. It put an end to one kind of crowd action, rioting to enforce one public interest. Crowd actions continued to support economic interests of some groups, and were suppressed in the name of a political unity by representatives of different economic interests and social class. Rioting as a semi-institutional means of enforcing law lost its function when the changed political apparatus developed its own agents and means, but crowd action continued because neither political institutions nor social norms achieved the economic equality that would guarantee social and political equality.

Some towns perhaps foresaw these developments and attempted to keep the power to redress grievances and to solve social conflict in the hands of the people. Petersham inhabitants explained that the people "at all times have a Constitutional Power." Whenever a majority of the corporations think fit, they may call a constitutional convention "to propose Amendments," to try to punish any official guilty of maladministration, and "To Repeal and Remove Every Encroachment Made By the Legislature or otherwise on the Constitution or the Reasonable Liberties of the people."[35] But these demands of a minority, whose political and theoretical arguments were far advanced toward popular participation and equality and contrary to leadership interests, could not remedy the underlying socioeconomic causes of inequality.

POPULAR PARTICIPATION VERSUS THE ASSERTION OF POWER

From 1774 to 1780, the necessity for administration had been met by two seemingly complementary moves: increased activity of local institutions with extensive popular participation and the calling of the Provincial Congresses, later the General Court. But these two attempts at government competed: central authority with its socioeconomic implications versus local control. What Whig leaders had intended as a temporary diminution of deference and of submission to crown officials turned out to be a permanent change toward more critical supervision of authorities. But the General Court and the provincial executive, functioning on the basis of the Charter of 1691, challenged the legitimacy and legality of new institutions by limiting their influence and by attempting to restrict the extent of popular participation in government.

The influence of the Committees of Correspondence, not part of the charter government, declined. In response to a lawsuit against three members of the Plymouth committee whose position in the town hierarchy was not very strong, a law was drafted "to indemnify, and secure from prosecution in law, persons who, by their laudable exertions under the late government of the King of Great Britain, have exposed themselves to actions of damage, and other prosecutions, in certain cases." The House wanted the indemnification to cover actions between 1 January 1766 and 1 January 1780. But Samuel Adams, now councillor, persuaded the

[35]*Ibid.*, p. 861.

representatives to substitute as the terminal date 4 July 1776. After that date, according to the reasoning of the General Court, the necessity of opposition to tyranny had ended and any further opposition violated political and social unity and aided the enemy; in short, it violated the interests of the leadership, just established with the help of committees and crowds, and its demands for legitimizing tradition and a monopoly of power.[36]

Because the old government had taken "violent and destructive measures," the opposition had to be forceful. "That persons should be seized, and property taken, and, in some instances, destroyed" was an involuntary reaction to the violence from government.[37] But since 4 July 1776 these reasons ceased to exist. The people had become the new sovereign, and the people could—or should—not riot against themselves. The provincial leadership was certain that it was not oppressive but did only what was necessary to maintain law and order. Shortly after convening, the new government issued a proclamation for "inculcating a general obedience of the people to the several Magistrates."[38]

An important step toward the assertion of power was the attempt to subdue the western counties, where no courts had been held since August 1774. The measures taken by the legislators to achieve this end are an excellent illustration of their concern with order and the status quo and their absolute disdain for a constitutional foundation. The people of Berkshire were threatened with punitive legislation, including removal of their right to representation. County delegates retorted that the stopping of the courts had been a general demand in fall 1774 and that all other counties had followed the example set by the people in Berkshire. Had they, too, persisted in their opposition to the courts, they might by now have a Bill of Rights and a constitution, instead of having "Law dealt out by piece meal as it is this Day, without any Foundation to support it." Denial of representation had been specifically listed in the Declaration as a cause for independence. The Berkshire men now defiantly remarked that they could separate from the unconstitutional Massachusetts government. "There are other States, which have Constitutions who will We doubt not, as bad as we are, gladly receive us."[39] Among the leadership there was talk of sending an army to conquer Berkshire.[40] The council stated that "the Suspension of Civil Authority is pregnant with every political Evil." To restore "the Honor of Government, the Prosperity of this State, . . . the Peace of that County," as well as "good Order" and "Harmony," a committee should investigate the complaints of

---

[36]William Watson to James Warren, 29 March 1780, *Acts and Resolves,* 5:1319–1320; law, *ibid.,* 5:1169, 1779–1780, Ch. 32. An earlier attempt to pass a resolve to the same effect had been foiled by the council in 1779.

[37]*Ibid.,* 5:1169.

[38]*Journals of the House of Representatives,* 18 Dec. 1775, in Force, ed., *Archives,* 4.4:1345.

[39]The sitting of courts in the New Hampshire grants had been rendered possible only by the presence of New York troops in 1775. A county convention in Hampshire, Massachusetts, advised holding the courts in expectation that a constitution would soon be formed. Thus, only Berkshire remained adamant. Cf. Taylor, *Western Massachusetts,* and Lee Nathaniel Newcomer, *The Embattled Farmers: A Massachusetts Countryside in the American Revolution* (New York, 1953), pp. 12–13, 134–136. Berkshire statement, Handlin and Handlin, eds., *Popular Sources,* pp. 366–368, and response from Worcester, 8 Oct. 1778, *ibid.,* pp. 369–373.

[40]*Ibid.,* p. 90.

the Berkshire people. But an unbiased assessment of the grievances was prevented by severely limiting the scope of inquiry.[41]

At the hearing a number of delegates meticulously outlined the nature and sources of society and of political power as they and their constituents understood it. "In free States the people are to be considered as the fountain of power. And the social Tie as founded in Compact. The people at large are endowed with alienable and unalienable Rights." Unalienable was the right to be "governed by the Majority in the Institution or formation of Government."[42] The committee of the General Court showed a total lack of understanding for the fundamental principle of the opposition and reported on 14 January 1779 to the legislature "that if proper Civil Officers Should soon be Appointed in said County of Berksheir, that the Clamours about Executive Courts there, would very soon subside." The General Court discussed the report with its members from Berkshire and passed an act pardoning the Berkshire people and crowds for their activities and ordering court sessions for the county.

The enraged inhabitants of Pittsfield in response censured their two representatives and ordered them to get the law repealed in toto, "as it was undesired by the county, and is fraught with reproach, discrimination, and such severe reflections upon the county as they utterly disdain, and are not chargeable with; not to mention the manifest injustice contained in it." They icily continued that the holding of a Superior Court in Berkshire was "unnecessary and premature" and that its representatives, who had proposed this measure, "were not so instructed and directed."

The angry reproaches were certainly justified. The Berkshire people had demanded a constitution and not a pardon for demanding one. Furthermore, the law contained another insult and injustice by pardoning the crowd actions against the courts under the Administration of Justice Act, thereby implicitly declaring the resistance to Great Britain a punishable offense. In doing so, the General Court repudiated its own decisions of 1774, its indemnification law, as well as the general opinion of the inhabitants. Even John Adams and the Continental Congress had once declared that Massachusetts could live "wholly without a Legislature and Courts of Justice as long as will be necessary to obtain Relief."[43]

Berkshire constitutionalists combined political action of elected delegates with enforcement by crowds in a particularly successful form. A county convention was held on 3 May 1779, the day before the Superior Court was to sit at Great Barrington, according to the Pardon Act. The delegates were accompanied by a crowd

---

[41]*Acts and Resolves,* 5:1028–1029; Force, ed., *Archives,* 4.5:1281. A similar committee in 1776 had been unsuccessful too.

[42]Berkshire statement, 17 Nov. 1778, in Handlin and Handlin, eds., *Popular Sources,* pp. 374–379. Inhabitants of the town of Lee, Berkshire, voted in March 1779 (town records, quoted in Newcomer, *Embattled Farmers,* p. 98), when there was still no constitution: "We hold ourselves Bound to support the sivil Authority of this State for the time of one Year."

[43]*Acts and Resolves,* 5:932–933, 1778–1779, Ch. 38, notes pp. 1028–1033; J. E. A. Smith, *The History of Pittsfield (Berkshire County), Massachusetts, from the Year 1734 to the Year 1876,* 2 vols. (Boston, 1869, 1876), p. 363; Adams to Palmer, 26 Sept. 1774, in Edmund C. Burnett, ed., *Letters of Members of the Continental Congress,* 8 vols. (Washington, D.C., 1921), 1:48.

of 300 men, who took possession of the courthouse. The men chose a clerk, debated the convention's resolves, and agreed to them.

Upon their arrival, the judges of the highest court of the province were lectured by the rioters on the relationship of constitution and law. "It is creating a dangerous President to admit or consent to the operation of Law untill there is a Constitution or Form of Government with a Bill of Rights explicitly approved of and firmly established by a Majority of Freemen of this State." No just laws could originate from representatives who distributed offices among themselves "contrary to any Charter that we ever yet saw." Furthermore, all laws still stemmed from the period of the corrupt British domination.

The lack of understanding and the arrogance of legislature and judges strongly suggest that the apprehensions of the people were well founded. Even James Otis queried whether "too much attention has not been paid" to the question of order or disorder. The General Court should rather concentrate on constructive steps. Repression merely led "to this confusion through this part of the Government."[44]

The call was not heeded. Order remained the watchword. Any crowds and riots were suppressed by authorities of state and army. Pope's Day crowds, "destitute of Consideration" (council), were forbidden because they might offend Canadian Catholics or the allied French. Extralegal crowd action against Tories was discouraged and replaced by extraconstitutional laws. Mass movements for more responsive judicial and political authorities and for a constitution were suppressed. Traditionally, a riot was repudiated only after it had taken place, in a ritual to reunify the community. After the British had left, the new officialdom asserted its position by issuing proclamations and laws to prevent crowd action. Whig leaders could not understand popular discontent. They had identified themselves with the people and now fell first victim to their own ideology. But since they had the power, they asserted their position instead of reexamining the ideology. The people, who, according to Elbridge Gerry, were too conscious of their rights, had to be put back into their place, from that of sovereigns into that of subjects.[45]

The "age of the democratic revolution" (Palmer) was, at least for America, a period in which a new group of leaders seized political power after crowd and mass action had ousted the old set of crown officials. Shortly after the accomplishment of this aim, the new leaders denounced democracy—"democratic despotism," according to a former British governor—while favoring republicanism, which in their opinion was a safeguard for property. Protection of porperty from arbitrary taxation or seizure by the crown had been the original aim of the colonies' resistance. Protection of property concentration against claims for more equal distribution was the leadership's aim in the latter part of the revolutionary period. Popular participation was not a goal but a temporary means.[46]

---

[44]MA 201:5–10, reprinted in *Acts and Resolves*, 5:1275–1276; repeal act, *ibid.*, p. 1131, 1779–1780, Ch. 25; MA 158:144; James Otis to Benjamin Greenleaf, 18 March 1776, in Force, ed., *Archives*, 4.5:408.

[45]Washington, General Orders, 5 Nov. 1775, in John C. Fitzpatrick, ed., *The Writings of George Washington from the Original Manuscript Sources, 1745–1799*, 39 vols. (Washington, D.C., 1931–1944), 4:64–65; Council Records, MA 169:291; *BTR* 25:79 (1778); James Warren to *Boston Gazette*, 24 Sept. 1774, in Force, ed., *Archives*, 4.1:802.

[46]Major sources for such statements are Austin, *Life of Gerry*, and *Warren-Adams Letters*. For the mutual dependence

Submission and deference were expected but not always accorded. Tensions between low and hig still pervaded the society. In a "Political Catechism," to take one example, two men debated the problem of taxation. They agreed that taxation was necessary. Taxes were to be equal—that is, nonprogressive. Criticism was directed only at the methods in which the taxes were levied: "let the money and riches be taxed, and not the man [poll tax]." Privately owned woodlands should be taxed. Originally they were perhaps worth nothing to the owner, the argument continued, and only produced terror in those who had to pass through them.

> [But now] said land is far from being a terror to the owners thereof, . . . it is as profitable to them as money at interest.
> Q. Is wood land a terror to any body now a days?
> A. Yes, to a poor man, when he's passing by or through a tract of it especially in the month of November and December, it makes him cry out in the bitterness of soul, O! how shall I contrive to pay for some of this wood, and get it home to my house.

The wealthy Thomas Hutchinson had said in 1763 about one of his tenants, who was unwilling to pay the rent: "Sometimes such sort of Animals may be tamed gradually by gentle usage." Now Whig authorities expected the people to submit to high taxes, which paid for the genteel living style of the officials, among other things. In later years, people compared wealthy and influential Whig families who had accumulated offices to the Hutchinson clan. Town meetings realized the dangers accruing from those getting rich at public expense: "That would raise another set of tyrants such as we are fighting against."[47]

The objection that a legal system existed through which abuse of power could be prosecuted was rejected in "A Shorter Catechism" (1784): "What is law? . . . A servant to the rich and task master to the poor." The lawyers of Berkshire and Hampshire, as elsewhere perennial target of popular clamors about the costly court system, decided not to encourage unnecessary, long, and vexatious lawsuits, as they had sometimes done for the sake of their fees. But "Whereas Reason, Justice and the *Estimation in which we ought to be holden in the public Judgment* require that we should have an adequate recompense for our Labour," it was agreed not to give any advice "which requires Learning and Knowledge in Law *without an adequate and honorable recompense and reward first paid or secured to be paid.*" Having a monopoly ("common Principle") in the knowledge, they then combined and fixed

---

and influence of leadership and voters, see Ronald Hoffman's excellent study of Maryland, *A Spirit of Dissension: Economics, Politics, and the Revolution in Maryland* (Baltimore, 1973).

[47]*BG*, 16 Nov. 1778; *Mass. Spy*, 18 May 1776, 14 April 1784; *New Eng. Chron.* 20 June, 11 July, 29 Aug. 1776; *BTR* 18:238; William Lincoln, *History of Worcester, Massachusetts, from Its Earliest Settlement to 1836* (2d ed.; Worcester, Mass., 1862), pp. 111–113; Hutchinson to ———, 20 April 1763, Letterbooks, MA 26:55–56; *Warren–Adams Letters*, 1:341–342, 2:105; Handlin and Handlin, eds., *Popular Sources*, pp. 126–127. Worcester towns voted that nobody was "to have the Exclusive Power of Voting their own Salary or Voting money from the Comunity into their own Pockets." Cf. Robert A. Becker, "The Politics of Taxation in America, 1763–1783" (Ph.D. diss., Univ. of Wisconsin, 1971).

the price of their services. Newspaper articles and pamphlets about malpractices of the "gentlemen of the law" soon abounded.[48]

Laws were phrased so as to perpetuate social differentiation, measures taken for the "support of the poor" and the "advancing of the rich." But, argued Lenox, Berkshire, the poor had as much interest in government as the well-to-do, and there was no reason that "Honest Poverty" should be punished by exclusion from voting. Furthermore, the inhabitants of Beverly (Essex) added, once government was established, everybody parted with the same rights and therefore had an equal interest in government.[49]

Below the "rogues and the poor" ranged only slaves and Indians. Twisting liberty rhetoric to the demands of a slave-holding elite, the Massachusetts Committee of Safety resolved:

> That it is the opinion of this committee, as the contest now between Great Britain and the colonies respects the liberties and privileges of the latter, which the colonies are determined to maintain, that the admission of any person, as soldiers, into the army now raising, but only such as are freemen, will be inconsistent with the principles that are to be supported, and reflect dishonor on this colony, and that no slaves be admitted into this army upon any consideration whatever.[50]

In summary, it may be said that the attempts to maintain the social, political, and economic structure of the colonial society in the new state came from the provincial leadership supported by the many small property holders, especially in the coastal counties. Large capital needed to be freed from the limitations that British regulations imposed on it for the benefit of Britain, its owners from the competition with persons of their own economic group, who had a second, different set of ties of allegiance to the crown. Political leaders were content with changing "men," not "measures" or structures. But many agrarian communities and perhaps Boston's lower classes[51] were contending for property within the limitations and social responsibilities of a corporate society. That this was unsuccessful was noticeable during the struggle for adequate provisions but became clearer only in the national

---

[48]*Mass. Gaz.,* 17 Feb. 1784; cf. *Penn. Packet,* 16 June 1781, in Frank Moore, ed., *Diary of the American Revolution from Newspapers and Original Documents,* 2 vols. (New York, 1860; reprint ed., 1969), 2:408. A witness in the trial of William Prendergast (1766 New York tenant uprising and border riots) also declared, "There is no law for poor men." Staughton Lynd, *Anti-Federalism in Dutchess County, New York* (Chicago, 1962), p. 37. Hampshire and Berkshire lawyers' agreement, Springfield, 18 May 1781, Theodore Sedgewick Papers, vol. A, MHS (emphasis added). Lenox, Berkshire, inhabitants reported that lawyers used to toast "The Glorious uncertainty of Law." Handlin and Handlin, eds., *Popular Sources,* p. 254; cf. Pittsfield petititons, 29 May 1776, *ibid.,* p. 90. "Honestus" [Benjamin Austin], *Observations on the Pernicious Practice of the Law* (Boston, 1786).

[49]*Acts and Resolves,* 5:46, 1769–1770, Ch. 19, cf. 1699–1700, Ch. 8; Address of the Constitutional Convention, Handlin and Handlin, eds., *Popular Sources,* p. 437, see also pp. 254, 293.

[50]Committee of Safety, Journal, 20 May 1775, in William Lincoln, ed., *The Journals of Each Provincial Congress of Massachusetts in 1774–1775 . . .* (Boston, 1858), pp. 302, 553. During the constitutional debates a number of western communities demanded abolition of slavery. But the seaboard towns, in which slaves were concentrated, refused. Handlin and Handlin, eds., *Popular Sources,* pp. 216, 217, 231, 248–249, 263, 277, 282, 302, 312 (1778), 707, 769, 830, 859, 889 (1780). See also *Warren–Adams Letters,* 1:335.

[51]Alfred F. Young, "Pope's Day, Tar and Feathers, and 'Cornet Joyce, jun.': From Ritual to Rebellion in Boston, 1745–1775" (Paper prepared for the Anglo-American Labor Historians' Conference, Rutgers Univ., April 1973).

period. During the revolutionary period the top groups of society met with much opposition but succeeded in preserving considerable parts of the social status quo.

In 1780 the inhabitants of Sandisfield, Berkshire, realizing the dangers accruing from the normative powers of established political structures, phrased popular demands succinctly when they demanded that

> the System be so formed, that it shall be peculiarly out of the Power of Designing men to Encroach on the Inherent and Unalienable rights of the People, for the People as such, are less Disposed to incroach on their own Liberties than Individuals are, they are so far from it, that they are in one sense their only Guardians.[52]

This was also the basic principle on which crowd action against authorities rested in popular ideology.

---

[52]Handlin and Handlin, eds., *Popular Sources*, p. 418.

Subject Index

STUDIES IN SOCIAL DISCONTINUITY

Under the Consulting Editorship of:

CHARLES TILLY
University of Michigan

EDWARD SHORTER
University of Toronto

William A. Christian, Jr. Person and God in a Spanish Valley

Joel Samaha. Law and Order in Historical Perspective: The Case of Elizabethan Essex

John W. Cole and Eric R. Wolf. The Hidden Frontier: Ecology and Ethnicity in an Alpine Valley

Immanuel Wallerstein. The Modern World-System: Capitalist Agriculture and the Origins of the European World-Economy in the Sixteenth Century

John R. Gillis. Youth and History: Tradition and Change in European Age Relations 1770 – Present

D. E. H. Russell. Rebellion, Revolution, and Armed Force: A Comparative Study of Fifteen Countries with Special Emphasis on Cuba and South Africa

Kristian Hvidt. Flight to America: The Social Background of 300,000 Danish Emigrants

James Lang. Conquest and Commerce: Spain and England in the Americas

Stanley H. Brandes. Migration, Kinship, and Community: Tradition and Transition in a Spanish Village

Daniel Chirot. Social Change in a Peripheral Society: The Creation of a Balkan Colony

Jane Schneider and Peter Schneider. Culture and Political Economy in Western Sicily

Michael Schwartz. Radical Protest and Social Structure: The Southern Farmers' Alliance and Cotton Tenancy, 1880-1890

Ronald Demos Lee (Ed.). Population Patterns in the Past

David Levine. Family Formations in an Age of Nascent Capitalism

Dirk Hoerder. Crowd Action in Revolutionary Massachusetts, 1765-1780

Charles P. Cell. Revolution at Work: Mobilization Campaigns in China

In preparation

Harry W. Pearson. The Livelihood of Man by Karl Polanyi

Richard Maxwell Brown and Don E. Fehrenbacher (Eds.). Tradition, Conflict, and Modernization: Perspectives on the American Revolution

Juan Guillermo Espinosa and Andrew S. Zimbalist. Economic Democracy: Workers' Participation in Chilean Industry, 1970-1973

Frederic L. Pryor. The Origins of the Economy: A Comparative Study of Distribution in Primitive and Peasant Economies

Randolph Trumbach. The Rise of the Egalitarian Family: Aristocratic Kinship and Domestic Relations in Eighteenth-Century England